Andrew Johnson

ANDREW JOHNSON

A STUDY IN COURAGE

BY

LLOYD PAUL STRYKER

NEW YORK
THE MACMILLAN COMPANY
1929

SET UP BY BROWN BROTHERS LINOTYPERS
PRINTED IN THE UNITED STATES OF AMERICA
BY THE CORNWALL PRESS

TO

KATHARINE TRUAX STRYKER

INTRODUCTION

THE time has come when justice should be done to Andrew
Johnson. Abraham Lincoln, had he lived, would have been
crucified by the Radicals in Congress. Andrew Johnson suffered
that crucifixion for him.

Physical martyrdom is ofttimes an historical advantage to the
martyr. It is true, although a paradox, that the bloody hands of
Booth did much for Lincoln. Men are still living who saw Lincoln face to face and yet already he has become a legendary,
almost a mystic figure. And yet while he lived, Lincoln was
traduced and ridiculed as few men ever were. Now all the slander
of his enemies is forgotten, especially that surrounding his purpose
to achieve and his plan to accomplish a reconstruction of justice,
of mercy and of profound statesmanship. The Radicals of Congress opposed him at every step of the way; he stood between
them and their malignant hopes. They saw an opportunity to
treat the Southern states as conquered provinces and thereby to
exploit the South. They were dreaming of the carpet-bag régime.
Lincoln envisioned a Union reunited,—united not by force alone,
but by a reciprocity of justice and fair dealing. He had determined to "bind up the nation's wounds." The Radicals of Congress planned to keep them open.

The conflict between these divergent purposes was not foreshadowed only, but actually was raging long before Lee even
dreamed of Appomattox. When the larger flames of war were
quenched, the lesser fires of this controversy between Lincoln and
the Radicals burst forth into a veritable conflagration. Lincoln
was not seared because Booth's bullet found its mark. Andrew
Johnson took his place and became the seventeenth President of
the United States.

Johnson took not only Lincoln's place, but his plan of reconstruction also. Animated by a love of the Union as profound as

Lincoln's, Johnson put his back to the wall and fought Lincoln's fight. He, therefore, inherited Lincoln's enemies. There was no war now to distract them, and so they were able to employ, and with almost incredible malice used every weapon for the defeat of Lincoln's plan and for the destruction of Lincoln's successor who was following it. The story of his conflict with Lincoln's enemies is an epic of valor, and yet he is remembered not by what he said and did, but by what Lincoln's enemies said about him.

In our times we scarce can realize how much of slander Lincoln bore. History long since has done him justice. But in Andrew Johnson's case the historians have stirred the old embers of hate and in the form of "history" have given us little better than a digest of contemporary calumnies. The story of the reconstruction has never yet been told. The historians seem afraid to tell it. They know that its telling is to convict the authors of the Fourteenth Amendment and the architects of the Solid South of the meanest crimes and to portray Andrew Johnson as one of the most unjustly treated characters in America.

The words of so able an historian as Professor Burgess are typical. Speaking of the Southern states during the eight years following 1868 he writes: "A period of darkness now settled down upon these unhappy communities blacker and more hopeless than the worst experiences of the war. The conduct of the men who now appeared upon the scene as the creators of the new South was so tyrannic, corrupt, mean and vulgar as to repel the historian from attempting any detailed account of their doings, and incline him to the vaguest outline." [1]

Although he dedicated his whole soul to fight this tyranny and corruption, the writers of our history never speak of Andrew Johnson save with disrespect. "Of all the men in public life it is difficult to conceive one so ill-fitted for this delicate work," writes James Ford Rhodes of Johnson's accession to the Presidency. And then he adds this jibe at Johnson's origin: "Born in the midst of degrading influences (at Raleigh, N. C. 1808), brought up in the misery of the poor white class, he had no chance for breeding, none for book education, none for that half-conscious betterment which comes from association with cultivated and morally excellent people. It is said he never went to school for a day." [2]

It would require a strong palate for snobbery to enjoy that paragraph. What Johnson did and tried to do for his country will not suffer by a comparison with the "cultivated and morally excellent people" of his time. This narrative will compel that comparison.

CONTENTS

CONTENTS

ILLUSTRATIONS

ANDREW JOHNSON

ANDREW JOHNSON

I

UP FROM OBSCURITY AND POVERTY

IN the backwoods of Kentucky, twenty days before President Jefferson turned over the reins of office to his follower, James Madison, there took place an unheralded event,—the birth of Abraham Lincoln. Six weeks earlier and on the 8th day of December, 1808, at Raleigh, North Carolina, in a little one-story log house, humble and plain enough, there was an equally obscure occurrence. A good mother brought into this world of pain, travail and injustice,—a son, and called him Andrew Johnson.[1]

Jacob, his father, had been a captain in the militia of North Carolina.[2] Such livelihood as he was able to supply his family came from his joint earnings as city constable, sexton, and porter to the state bank. One day in 1811, he found sufficient leisure from these many duties to join a fishing party at Hunter's Mill Pond.[3] Young Col. Henderson, the editor of the Raleigh *Star*, and his friends, Pearce and Callum, were out fishing in a skiff. Whether the colonel's buoyant spirits arose from some fine catch or as a result of those artificial and now prohibited aids which fishermen from time immemorial have found stimulating, is an historical fact which must be left in doubt. Whatever was the cause of the editor's emotion, its manifestation was the rocking of the boat and its result that all three of its occupants were thrown into deep and treacherous water.[4] William Pearce, the second member of the party, was rescued from the shore with little difficulty and thus emerges from history. Callum, the third in that ill-fated boat, in a frenzy of fear seized Col. Henderson and dragged him to the bottom. Jacob Johnson was on the

1

shore; others were there with him, but he alone acted. He rushed to the water's edge and dove toward the place where the two had disappeared from view. With the dogged determination of the true Briton, he brought the practical joker and the Scotchman to the surface. Others helped to bring them to the land. This rescue, though of considerable benefit to those whose lives were saved, to the rescuer was no benefit at all. His health was permanently shattered.[5]

One of the solemn duties in Jacob Johnson's simple life appears to have been the tolling of funeral bells. While engaged one day in this sad office, nearly a year after his act of simple bravery, he fell from exhaustion and in a few days died. The boy Andrew, at the age of four, was thus left fatherless, penniless and friendless.[6]

Childhood, Andrew never knew, youth passed him by. At the age of ten necessity took him roughly by the hand and apprenticed him to one Selby, a tailor in his native town.[7] Poverty is a grim and cruel master, he teaches his lessons with long hours, sour looks and hard knocks. Andrew Johnson had a thorough knowledge of this tutor. Many years later he told his fellow Congressmen: "If being poor was a crime . . . I should have to plead that I was guilty; that I was a great criminal; that I had been born a criminal; and that I had lived a criminal a large portion of my life. Yes, I have wrestled with poverty, that gaunt and haggard monster. I have met it in the day and night. I have felt his withering approach and his blighting influence."[8]

An unschooled tailor's apprentice at ten,[9] where was there room for any hope with such a start? But in our favored land courage has unlocked the heaviest portals. Opportunity is there for those who seek her. There was in Raleigh during those first bitter years of apprenticeship a philanthropist whose benevolence consisted in reading good books aloud.[10] He would come to the tailor shop where Johnson worked and entertain him and his fellow apprentices with the orations of British statesmen. The style of the orators, it seems, was not impaired by the method of the reader,[11] and yet I can imagine a good many tailor shops where such reading would have fallen on deaf ears. To Johnson it was like a torch to tinder. It lighted in his soul the fire of high resolve.[12]

The title of this incendiary book was the "American Speaker." [13] The orations which struck home were those of the younger Pitt and of Charles James Fox. Johnson sought to borrow the book, but the owner gave it to him. Painfully and slowly from these classics of forensic art he learned to spell and to read.[14] A new and undiscovered country lay before him. Cross-legged, he plied with his fingers his busy tailor's needle, while his mind, white hot with a new hope, was far away within the English Parliament. And at night he found and pursued the company of books and stayed with them until, worn down from the long day's toil, he fell asleep.

At sixteen in 1824, his apprenticeship was over. He had no influential friends, he had never been to school, his mother was wholly dependent upon him for her support, but he had learned a trade and he was rich in courage and in hope.[15] In search of wider opportunities he went to Laurens Court House in South Carolina. He fell in love, but was repulsed. The lady, it seems, sneered quite openly at his poverty.[16] It was not the last sneer he was to suffer on that score. Though it wounded, it suffused him with new strength to battle with his obscure fate.

He returned to Raleigh in May, 1826, and in September of that year took his mother and went "west,"—to Greenville, Tennessee.[17] "An old wooden cart drawn by a worthless horse carried all their worldly goods." [18] Dust-laden, on a Saturday afternoon they arrived at their destination.[19] It could not have been a dramatic entrance and yet there was one who noted it with approval. Andrew, if he observed at all a little knot of giggling girls standing by the roadside, doubtless turned hastily away, recalling his travel-worn and unimpressive equipage. There was, however, in that feminine group seventeen-year-old Eliza McCardle; she had seen Andrew Johnson as he passed in his creaking cart, dust-laden and travel-worn as he was. She liked him and then and there to her friends confessed the fact. It was an un-Victorian method, but this was 1826. Eliza was seventeen and Johnson was less than two years older, but on the

17th of May, 1827, by Mordecai Lincoln, a magistrate of the town and a kinsman of Abraham Lincoln, they were married.[20]

Eliza was the only child of a Scotch shoemaker,[21] and her opportunities for education had been greater than those of her young husband. She took him mentally in hand. When he married he could read, but he knew nothing either of writing or arithmetic.[22] She taught him to write, she taught him to figure and she sat by him in the tailor shop and read to him as he worked.[23] And he had to work; now there were two to support, his wife and his mother, and the next year three, when the first child, Martha, was born.[24] Amid discouragements she cheered him on. Only such stark determination as he brought to this problem of self-improvement and only such assistance made it possible at all. Under her tutelage he grew. As a tailor he was debarred from equal association with the "aristocratic coterie" ruling the community,[25] so he spent his evenings and late nights in company with Eliza and his British statesmen.

As he grew in mental stature, his enlarging powers were noted by his fellown townsmen. He was liked and looked up to by the workmen of Greeneville, who soon began to make his tailor shop a kind of social meeting place.[26] In 1824, the hero of New Orleans and the political dictator of Tennessee, Andrew Jackson, had received the largest popular vote for President, but the election had been thrown into the House of Representatives and John Quincy Adams was made President. Jackson and his angered followers already were organizing for the election of 1828. The fires of disappointment were fusing the elements that were to form the Democratic party, of which Jackson was to become the inspiration and the iron leader. These things were discussed everywhere. No doubt they inspired the talks in Andrew Johnson's tailor shop.[27]

Johnson was learning to talk; his desire for knowledge was insatiable. At about this time a debating society was organized of which he became an enthusiastic member. It was in some way connected with Greeneville College, a little "fresh-water" institution near the banks of the Nolichucky River.[28] Once each week he walked four miles to and from the meetings. One of the debaters who was also fortunate enough to be an enrolled student at the college, writes that he remembers Johnson's "fascinating manners, his natural talent for oratory, his capacity to draw the students around him and make all of them his warm friends." [29] The students of the college, when in Greeneville, used Johnson's shop as a kind of rendezvous. This description comes down to us: "On approaching the village there stood on the hill by the highway a solitary little house, perhaps ten feet square. We invariably entered when passing. It contained a bed, two or three stools and a tailor's platform. Here we delighted to stop, because one lived here whom we knew outside of school, and made us welcome; one who would amuse us by his social good nature, one who took more than ordinary interest in catering to our pleasure." [30]

Here then was good soil in which political ambition might take root. To good advantage he had been strengthening his mind with the mastery of Burke and Chatham, Erskine, Fox and Sheridan. [31] From these masters and from his practice in debate, he was learning how to speak, and soon we find him seeking to put his dearly bought acquirements to some practical use.

The well-to-do of Greeneville owned slaves. They looked down on white men who sustained themselves through toil. The slave holders of the town were in the minority, but they were in power. Johnson determined to change this. It was not long before he was arousing his fellow laborers to assert their right to representation in town councils. In 1828 he himself was nominated and elected alderman. [32] He was twenty years of age. His contemporaries in the North were undergraduates. Charles Sumner was a junior at Harvard. [33] His opportunity for "book education" and that of his friends at Cambridge were, no doubt, superior to those of the Greeneville alderman and yet, I should like to have heard any of these young gentlemen try their fortunes in debate with this youthful stubborn follower of Charles James Fox.

When Johnson finished his first term as alderman, his constituents were satisfied with his work, and in 1829 gave him a second term. In the following year, at the age of twenty-two, he was elected mayor of Greeneville.[34]   His neighbors and his friends were coming to feel his power.   They trusted and believed in him, and in 1831 and again in 1832, they reëlected him as mayor.[35]   Eliza McCardle had found an apt and ready pupil. She had determined that her Andrew should do something worth while in this world.   But she had much besides ambition to occupy her time.   The birth of her first child Martha in 1828 was followed two years later by that of Charles, who received two years later a new sister, Mary, and again two years later on, a brother, Robert.[36]   There must have been plenty of hard work for the mother of that small home, nor could there have been much opportunity for idleness for the father, with his tailoring, his growing outside business interests, his British statesmen and his fellow statesmen of Greeneville.

In 1834 Johnson achieved prominence in the campaign to secure the adoption of a new fundamental law for Tennessee.[37] In 1835 he became a candidate for the House of Representatives, —the lower house of the state legislature.   The contest for representative from Washington and Greene counties lay between Matthew Stevenson, Whig, and Andrew Johnson, Democrat.[38] Stevenson had been a member of the Constitutional Convention of the previous year and was known as an able man and an effective advocate.   Pitted against the "mechanic" of Greeneville, he was thought to await an easy victory.[39]   Johnson's fellow Democrats of Greeneville and his former allies of the debating society were trembling for their champion.   The first meeting of the campaign was held at Boon's Creek in Washington County. Johnson came from Greene; this was Stevenson's home ground. Johnson was to be weighed in a hostile balance; he did not intend to be found wanting.   He had busied himself with Major Stevenson's political record and he exposed it in such a way as to cause "consternation" in the ranks of his opponent.[40]

A little later Johnson was elected.   He now assumed the responsibilities of membership in the lower House of Tennessee. He lacked three years of being thirty, yet it was the seventh time he had been chosen for public office by the suffrages of the

people. Eliza McCardle's confidence in him was apparently infectious. Her pupil was coming on.

§

The state of Tennessee measures four hundred and thirty-two
miles from east to west.[41] The Unaka Ridges of the older Apal-
lachian Mountains form a natural boundary separating North
Carolina on the east, extending as far to the west as the Tennessee
River. Thus, approximately one-fifth of the entire state is mountainous while the remainder lies in broad and fertile valleys.
Greeneville, where Johnson had made his home and whose
spokesman he was now becoming, rests in the foothills of the
Great Smoky Mountains at the extreme east of the state, about ten
miles distant from the western border of North Carolina. Virginians from the north and North Carolinians from the east,
Scotch Irish stock, had largely peopled this region, becoming the
Tennessee mountaineers, famed in story and in history. However they may lag behind the advanced skirmishers of intellectual
warfare, or may straggle after the forward banners of science,
whenever in our history there has been real fighting to do with
fists or with rifles, these mountaineers were ready. They were
sinewy, self-reliant men. They knew how to love, to hate, and to
fight. Men who can do their own fighting usually do their own
thinking also; they can do either alone and single-handed.
Johnson belonged to these people, he understood them and they
him. Their kind of willingness to fight for convictions, regardless of the odds or the weapons, was his kind. But what with
his own ambition and the secret promptings of his Eliza, he had
become their intellectual superior. They recognized the fact and
were proud to push him forward as their spokesman and their
representative.

The narrow valleys nestling in among the mountains of Eastern
Tennessee were sown with grain or used as pasturage for live
stock. The farms were small, men of wealth were rare,—here
was everything to stimulate robust democracy. It was a region
requiring the industry and the providence of white inhabitants.
Its agriculture was of a kind unsuited to slave labor.[42] Of its

population, but one in twelve were slaves,[43] whereas in the middle and western parts of the state the broad and fertile valleys were more propitious for slave labor, and there the blacks were nearly as numerous as white men.

The love for the Union, inherited by the mountaineers from their ancestors of King's Mountain days, was confused neither then nor later by the question of slavery; the residents of this region were indifferent, if not hostile, to the "institution." [44] It is not, therefore, so surprising that Benjamin Lundy, one of the first abolitionists,—to whom Garrison acknowledged that he owed "everything," [45]—should have hailed from Eastern Tennessee.[46] From Johnson's later strictures upon the abolitionists, I would not surmise that there was any great sympathy between Lundy and himself. But he was not indifferent to the plight of the hapless African or unwilling (as we shall later see) to strike from the negro's arms the shackles of bondage.

Since Johnson's unimpressive entry into Greeneville, he had been prospering. With thrift, hard work and the loving help of his Eliza, his interests had outgrown the tailor shop. In 1831 he purchased a dignified and substantial home. He had amassed other property as well. For his mother he procured a farm not far from town and settled her there in comfort.[47] There was little paid labor at that time even in Eastern Tennessee. It was natural enough, therefore, for him now to purchase a few slaves as personal servants; he never sold one. As late as 1901 Sam, the old colored sexton of the Methodist church of Greeneville, was still living. It was his proud boast that he was "President Johnson's fust servant." [48] Concerning this boast, Johnson's daughter Martha laughingly used to say: "The fact is my father was Sam's servant."

At about the time of his first election to the legislature, Johnson sold his tailoring establishment.[49] He was now turning his eyes definitely toward a political career. He was in every way a growing and a coming man. Much the same might then be spoken of him as was written by Lincoln in 1863: "When I speak of your position I mean that of an eminent citizen of a slave state and himself a slave holder." [50]

Johnson had known "the slings and arrows of outrageous fortune." He had suffered under class distinction. Having been one himself, he had a fiery sympathy for the underdog. He became a champion of measures designed to broaden opportunity. The hopes, the fears, and the discouragements of the laboring classes he understood with his heart as well as with his mind. He became now their defender.

§

The Tennessee legislature of 1835 assembled in October, and Johnson promptly took his seat, and for some days sat still, listening hard, studying the rules and participating not at all in the debates.[51] "Though plainly clad and not so robust in figure as in later life," an eye-witness has written, "his marked and expressive features presented him well and engaged attention when he rose to speak. He made more than the ordinary impression of a new member. He was punctual, laborious, but not unduly forward."[52] He was about five feet, ten inches in height, with a sturdy, well-knit frame; he dressed always in sober black. His dark complexion and smooth face enhanced his great determination of appearance.[53]

We have not even a daguerreotype portraying him at this period, but as we examine later portraits, we find his features of deep interest. First of all there is the high, broad forehead, with large facilities for brains. The bushy brows overhanging two piercing eyes with shrewd lines on either side. The nose is large and well made; the mouth wide and firm; the chin is strong. Noticeable above everything else are the eyes. Posterity needs no better index of his character than the study of his face. We should have to examine the portraits of Cromwell's Roundheads to find its prototype. Every line serves to emphasize a dauntless quality, arresting and compelling. It is the countenance of the Tennessee mountaineer,—with all of his self-reliance, contempt for danger and quiet self-esteem, animated by a controlled and quick intelligence. Such features would add to the power of any orator. It was an age of oratory and he possessed forensic gifts unusual and brilliant. His manner was direct and his natural charm was aided by the "modulation of a clear and mellow voice."[54]

A bill for internal improvements absorbed the legislature's attention during his first year.[55] The measure contemplated what for those times was the vast state indebtedness of four million dollars. It was popular, but Johnson thought the outlay onerous, despite the need for better roads.

The law passed, but Johnson continued to denounce it as a "system of wholesale fraud." [56] And now the election of 1837 was upon him. His opponent this time was one Campbell, who had been a strong advocate of the liberal expenditure of public money. At the end of a hard contest Johnson was defeated by a small majority. In the meanwhile, Johnson's erstwhile constituents were forced to witness all that he predicted. The state was defrauded, public works were begun only to be abandoned. With dismay they watched the mounting of the public debt, and in contrition reëlected Johnson in 1839.[57]

The year 1840 will be remembered for the campaign of "Tippecanoe and Tyler too." General Harrison had lived in a log cabin and had drunk hard cider. It helped him. Whigs of the North and of the South had combined to nominate him. He was opposed by Martin Van Buren, then President, and seeking reelection as the Democratic nominee. His shortcomings weighed heavily against him. Unforgivable sin,—he hailed from New York City! Furthermore, it was whispered that he was the owner of a silver tea service.[58]

It was a picturesque campaign. There was humor as well as intensity in the Tennessee politics of those days. It was during this canvass that "old Father Aiken," a Methodist preacher of great force and a Democrat, met William Brownlow, known as the "fighting parson," and an ardent Whig, at a camp meeting on a Sunday morning. It was agreed that Aiken should pray and that Brownlow should do the preaching. There was just a touch of the temporal in the Democrat's divine invocation when he cried: "O Lord, deliver us from Whiggery!" "God forbid," cried Parson Brownlow. Turning toward him and departing somewhat from the literal text of his bucolic orison, Father Aiken shouted: "Billy, keep still when I am praying." [59]

Johnson was a Democrat and he put his whole heart into the

campaign in Van Buren's support. The fact that the New Yorker was the friend and favorite of Andrew Jackson added impetus to Johnson's efforts in Eastern Tennessee. Here Johnson matched his wits and his oratory with the leading Whigs of the day. Among the Democrats of his own state who joined him in the canvass was James K. Polk.[60]

Van Buren was defeated, but Johnson's reputation as a capable political combatant was now statewide.[61] Such was his growing fame that in 1841, from his old district of Greene and Washington counties he was nominated for the State Senate and was elected by a majority of two thousand.[62]

At the next session he proposed that the basis of representation in Tennessee should rest upon the census of white voters only, thereby cutting down the political power of the large slave holder.[63] His proposal met with wide approval in the mountainous district of the state, and in 1843 the mountaineers of the first Congressional district nominated him for the National House of Representatives. He defeated John A. Asken, a United States Bank Democrat who was supported by the Whigs.

The bank issue had been created by Andrew Jackson, who hated the bank as ardently as secession. Civilians and politicians, as well as soldiers, had followed the victor of New Orleans. He had become the idol of his state and of all Democrats throughout the Union. He was the kind of man men follow. He lived in Nashville, Tennessee, and long had been dictator in her politics.[64] From 1829 to 1837 he was President of the United States. His administration has been termed,—the "Reign of Andrew Jackson." His hostility to the United States Bank involved fallacies enough, but when it came to a question of the Union, hickory was not more sound nor the flag itself more true. His toast on April 13, 1830, at the Jefferson dinner: "Our Federal Union, it must be preserved," made an impression on South Carolina. John Calhoun and Senator Hayne decided that on the whole the time for secession was not yet. When Jackson sent Lieutenant David Farragut to Charleston Harbor and assured the nullifiers that there would be an army too, Clay came forward with his compromise tariff and nullification was postponed for the next generation.

It is not strange, therefore, that Andrew Johnson very early should have accepted Andrew Jackson as his leader. There was between them a strong similarity of temperament and character. They came from the same stock; they had both hewed their fortunes from the rough rock of adversity; both were of the people and knew their hopes and fears; both were men of physical as well as intellectual courage; both hated sham and both were passionate lovers of the Union. Johnson put his whole heart, therefore, in the congressional contest of 1843, into the defense of Jackson's policies.

There were no railroads in Tennessee in those days, but Johnson was a fine horseman.[65] The mount he rode that Fall was said by his old servant Sam to have been one of the "finest" in the country.[66] We catch a note of good nature and of good sportsmanship as we follow him over mountain trails. The rival candidates had for each other that respect which leads to mutual understanding. However ardent on the stump, when the speaking was over, they mounted their horses and rode away in friendly converse, boot to boot and cracked their jokes.[67]

Johnson laughed and joked and fought his way through that campaign and was elected to Congress. He was thirty-five. He had come a long way since Eliza, through the dust, had first espied him in his crazy cart.

II

FOUR CONTEMPORARIES

BRIEFLY, let us here note what during this time one of Johnson's friends and three of his enemies had been doing. Lincoln had had his hard childhood in Kentucky and his gaunt youth in Illinois. In 1831, when Johnson had been twice elected alderman and twice mayor of Greeneville, Lincoln had just returned from his flatboat voyage to New Orleans and was settling down as a clerk in Denton Offutt's New Salem store.[1] During the young Greeneville mayor's tenure of office, Lincoln had announced his candidacy for the Illinois State Legislature, had been defeated, had been a captain in the bloodless Black Hawk war, had been surveyor and local postmaster, and having finally abandoned his fleeting ambition to become a blacksmith, was studying law. He was finally elected to the Legislature of Illinois during the last year of Johnson's term as mayor. He continued there until 1842.[2]

Lincoln from his twelfth to his twenty-fifth year, brooding in that melancholy which followed him throughout his life, seems to have been conscious of intellectual power that would render him capable of carrying heavier burdens. But there was no one at this period or perhaps at any other who thoroughly understood him.[3] He did not, like Johnson at eighteen, have the stimulus, the comfort and the inspiration of an Eliza's comprehension.

While these two youths in their obscure surroundings were struggling with their hard fate, there was in Boston a young gentleman who would have considered them, if he had been willing to consider them at all, as quite unworthy of his notice. The name of this Bostonian was Charles Sumner. He was fitted out with everything to make life decorous, even to a proper ancestor who settled in Dorchester in 1635. He was three years Johnson's junior. Everything about his life was easy and serene.

13

An independent fortune enabled him to pursue a leisurely course through the Boston Latin School and Harvard College, from which he graduated with the class of 1830. Neither of these institutions appeared to have quickened in him any understanding of the problems of the common man,—at least the white man. His passion for the negro was yet to develop into its full flower. He, of course, graduated from the Harvard Law School and with great dignity embarked upon the practice of the law in Boston. From 1833 to 1837 he essayed it. He had everything to make a lawyer eminent,—except clients. These somehow did not come then or for that matter later on, or at all. He decided after four years, as one biographer has put it, that "his chief laurels were to be won in other fields."

From December 1837 to May 1840, he pursued his studies in France, England, Italy and Germany. With all of his credentials it did not appear difficult for him to meet "almost every person of note." [4] He had no inclination for meeting others. He achieved the companionship of great lords and great ladies, earls, and duchesses with whom he established a lifelong correspondence.[5] But he met one Englishman who appraised him. "Oh yes," wrote Thomas Carlyle, "Mr. Sumner was a vera dull man, but he did not offend people and he got on in society here." [6]

At this time Benjamin Franklin Wade was a young lawyer in the West. Born in Massachusetts in 1800, he moved to Ohio in 1820, migrating thence three years later to Albany, New York, where he studied medicine, taught school and worked as a day laborer on the Erie Canal. He returned to Ohio, studied law, was admitted to the bar, and in 1827 began at Jefferson to practice. Four years later he formed a partnership with Joshua R. Giddings, one of the ablest and most original political leaders of that state. Wade identified himself with the Whig party, and was sent to the State Senate, where he remained until 1843. His strong anti-slavery opinions seemed to have originated in 1839, when commissioners from the southern states endeavored to procure state fugitive state laws from the legislatures of Ohio as well as other northern commonwealths. In 1847 he became presiding judge of the Third Judicial District, and four years later was elected to the United States Senate. Salmon P. Chase was the Senior Senator from his state.[7]

Up in Danville, Vermont, in 1792 a man was born whom his biographers have called a statesman. His name was Thaddeus Stevens, he had a club foot. While attending the University of Vermont, he witnessed the battle of Plattsburg from the roof of one of the college buildings.[8] Perhaps the conflict was too close, for presently we find him enrolled at Dartmouth. He graduated there in the class of 1815, finding at York, Pennsylvania, employment as a teacher.[9] He studied law, but his admission to the bar was resisted by the lawyers of his county, upon the ground that he had followed another vocation while studying law.[10] Since teaching school while preparing for the bar is a course thousands of the leading lawyers of America have trod, it would seem that the attitude of the legal brotherhood of Lancaster was based on other grounds than those assigned. Stevens now moved to Gettysburg where again the legal profession ostentatiously refused to welcome him with open arms.[11] It seems he was not liked. In 1831 there came a movement to which his character was well attuned, since it involved destructive opposition,—it was the campaign against the Masons. He was an active delegate to the Anti-Masonic Convention which met at Baltimore on September 11th of that year. The ensuing campaign enlisted all the enthusiasm of his acrid nature. He had never been received into the councils either of the Democrats or Whigs, and here now upon a platform of attack against Freemasonry he found at thirty-nine his first opportunity to enter politics.

That he had genuine interest in what he espoused, there is no evidence to suggest, but he had found an opportunity through the stirring up of hate, to further his own purposes. Two years later he was elected as an anti-Mason to the Pennsylvania legislature.[12] It was his first public office. Early in the session he introduced a resolution aimed at Masonry. It failed. He later launched an attack upon the House itself.[13] His vitriolic tongue served him as a well-stored quiver of malice.[14]

In 1842 he moved to Lancaster. The excitement over anti-Masonry was dying out, and the following year he attempted

to revive the issue. His scheme was to divert enough Whig votes
to throw the election to the Democrats of his county and thereby
prove the importance of his support to the Whigs whose friendship he had in vain sought to curry. His plan miscarried, and
further separated him from the party whose patronage he desired.
Not only did the Whigs fail to consult him in any way, "but
his opposition became a passport to party favor." [15] Nevertheless, in 1848, by dint of shrewd maneuvering, he was nominated
by the Whigs for Congress and was elected.

In the meantime, there had been developing an agitation into
which he could pour all the malice of his soul,—the anti-slavery
movement. His hatred for the slaveholder became, now that
anti-Masonry was dead, the passion of his life. On February
29th, 1850, in the lower House at Washington he declared: "The
South has always furnished officers for our armies; Presidents for
the republic; most of our foreign ambassadors. . . . But whence
are drawn the common soldiery, the men who peril their lives and
win victories for your glory? Almost entirely from the Free
States. . . . The South has lent us the gentlemen to wear the
epaulettes and the swords; . . . Virginia is now only fit to be the
breeder not the employer of slaves. . . . She is reduced to the
condition that her proud chivalry are compelled to turn slave-
traders for a livelihood!" [16]

The Representatives of the South, as well they might be, were
stung to anger by this reptile speech. "If," said one, "the gentleman with his disposition to vilify and slander persons of whom he
knows nothing should come among us there is not a respectable
negro who would deem him a fit associate." [17] Stevens enjoyed
making himself offensive. "His policy," admits his own biographer, "was to bring not peace but the sword." [18]

III

CONGRESSMAN AND GOVERNOR

NOT long after December 4th, 1843, when Johnson took his seat as a member of the twenty-eighth Congress,[1] he made his maiden speech. He argued for the restitution of the fine imposed on General Jackson in 1814 for placing New Orleans under martial law.[2] Old John Quincy Adams, the Nestor of the House, watched with approval the new Representative from Tennessee.

During his first term, Johnson took at least two strong positions: the championship of religious liberty through a defense of the Roman Catholic faith, of which of course he was anything but a communicant, and opposition to the high protection tariff of 1842.[3] The latter, at least, was not calculated to endear him to the gentlemen of New England who were the chief protagonists and beneficiaries of the economic theories he assailed.

In the debates upon the Texas question, Mr. Clingman of North Carolina added to the excitement by the assertion that British gold had elected James K. Polk as President, and further charged that "had the foreign Catholics been divided in the late election, as other sects and classes generally were, Mr. Clay would have carried by a large majority the state of New York, as also the states of Pennsylvania, Louisiana and probably some others in the northwest."[4]

Second in intensity only to his love for Eliza McCardle and his children, was Johnson's passion for the Constitution of his country. Along with his British statesmen he had conned and pondered its pages. He had studied the writings of Madison, of Hamilton and the other founders of the Republic.[5] Webster himself was not more attached to this great charter of our rights. Johnson knew its sacred guarantees among which is that bulwark of civil and religious liberty,—the first amendment: "Congress

17

shall make no law respecting an establishment of religion, or prohibiting the free exercise thereof." [6]

In the face of Mr. Clingman's charge it would have been good politics for Johnson to sit silent. Politicians are not prone to look for trouble. Congressmen seldom espouse measures not popular "back home." But Johnson was no truckler to the prejudices of constituents. And now at the age of thirty-seven, filled with as strong a personal ambition as ever stirred young man whom poverty had tried to thwart,—in his first term, and with a desire that it should not be his last, he stood up to champion a principle unpopular in Tennessee, opposed to his personal interest, but founded on eternal justice.

"I am," he said, "a member of a Protestant church and a citizen of Greeneville where there are few Catholics, and where the citizens are somewhat prejudiced against them. . . ." [7] "The Catholics of this country," he continued, "had the right secured to them by the Constitution of worshipping the God of their fathers in the manner dictated by their own consciences. . . . Is the guillotine to be erected in this Republican form of government and all who differ with the Whig party brought to the block? Is then a crusade to be commenced against the Church to satiate disappointed party vengeance? . . . From whence or how obtained the idea that Catholicism is hostile to liberty political or religious? During the Reformation did not the demon of persecution rage as fiercely among Protestants? Did not the Calvinists, Lutherans, Arminians oft array themselves against each other? . . . During our colonial state when Protestants, Puritans and Quakers were disfranchising and waging a relentless war of persecution against each other through Pennsylvania and the New England colonies, did not Catholic Maryland open her free bosom to all, and declare in her domain that no man should be persecuted for opinion's sake? And was she not from this fact the sanctuary of the oppressed and persecuted not only of America, but of Europe? . . . And is Catholicism a foe to liberty? Is Ireland's Catholic isle the nursery of slaves, though her evergreen shamrock no longer wreathed the brows of her warriors, though her palaces are in ruins, her cities in tears, her people in chains?" [8]

It seems that Eliza and he, in addition to their British states-
men and the Constitution, had been reading a good deal of history, English, European and American. He continued to inquire:
"Was Catholic Poland the birthplace of slaves? Go ask Cracow
and Warsaw when they last beheld against combined Russia,
Austria and Prussia, in death arrayed, their patriot bands,—few
but undismayed; Freedom too . . . did she not shriek when
Poland under Madalinski and Kosciusko fell? Were Lafayette,
Pulaski, McNeill, DeKalb and O'Brien foes to liberty? Was
Charles Carroll of Carrollton, the last survivor of the signers of
the Declaration of Independence, a friend of despotism?" [9]

It is the fashion now to sneer at oratory, but so long as the
human heart is capable of emotion, it will be stirred by fact and
argument, marshalled like the soldiers of some dauntless military
leader, and animated with the impulse of a flaming personality.
Where you find this, even in our own supercilious and sophisticated day, the soul, the heart and the mind, will move together
as under the influence of some Olympian force. If you had heard
this Protestant's oration in behalf of Catholic tolerance, you
would have been profoundly stirred, no matter what church you
attend, or whether you attend any. Johnson's speech, coming as
it did in the middle forties from a Protestant church member
whose constituents were Tennessee mountaineers, should help us
to discern that it was no ordinary Representative whom they had
sent to Washington.

§

A Connecticut Yankee in 1820 obtained a grant of land in one
of the provinces of Mexico. Texas was the name of the province
and Moses Austin the Yankee who went to settle there. Some
twenty thousand citizens of the United States soon followed him.
Inoculated with the virus of independence, they were able to
tolerate for just sixteen years what they considered the oppressive
rule of Mexico. In 1836 under the leadership of Sam Houston
they defeated the Mexicans commanded by Santa Anna at the
battle of San Jacinto. Texas became the "Lone Star State,"—an
independent country. It was not long before she was knocking
at the gates of the Union for admission. [10] Her petition, favored

by the Southern slavery men, was resisted by the Northern Whigs who were not slow to discern what the Southerners had so clearly seen, that here was a large area favorable to the growth of their "peculiar institution."

The question was heatedly discussed in Congress. By this time the abolitionists had begun their work. Both Lundy, whom we have met, and James Birney, whose wealthy slave-holding family were planters of the type of Washington and Jefferson,[11] unearthed as they thought a Southern conspiracy aimed at the acquisition of territory from Mexico for the extension of slavery.[12]

There is nothing more timid in this country than the established political parties unless it is the politicians who compose them. Both the Whigs and the Democrats in 1840 evaded the issue of Texan annexation. Four years later the contribution made by the Whig platform to this question of the day was a complete and profound silence.[13] The Democrats did little better. But Johnson met this, as all his issues, squarely, without a quiver or equivocation.

On the 21st day of January, 1845, he delivered on the floor of Congress, with that strong advocacy of which he had long since become consummate master, an address in favor of Texan annexation.[14] "The admission of Texas," he told his colleagues, "would give this government the command of the Gulf Stream, extending protection and security to the great valley of the Mississippi."[15] Texas he said would "prove to be the gateway out of which the sable sons of Africa are to pass from bondage to freedom; where they can become merged in a population congenial with themselves, who know and feel no distinction in consequence of the various hues of skin or courses of blood."[16]

Ideas of this kind sprang naturally from his section of the country. Tennessee and Kentucky were border states. Lying midway between the North and the South, their people shared the institutions and were, therefore, able to comprehend the fears and aspirations of both, better than could the citizens of Boston or of Charleston understand each other. It is not surprising, therefore, that that most sensible and practical instrument of abolition,—the colonization society—should have come from the border states.[17] Its program was that slavery should cease, but that justice should be done to the South in doing away with it. It was approved by Lincoln, who was thoroughly opposed to the agitation of Northern abolitionists seeking to abolish bondage without compensation. Their measures, he felt, "tended to increase rather than abate the evils of slavery," and thus expressed himself in 1837.[18] Johnson was in accord with Lincoln in searching for conservative and rational measures of emancipation, consonant with the colonization plan originating in his section of the country.

§

No one can read the history of Tennessee in this period without coming many times upon the trail of an interesting and eccentric Methodist minister, William Brownlow, whom friends and enemies alike delighted to call the "Fighting Parson." He was a Whig. He was indeed a Whig! "When," he was once asked, "will you join the Democrats?" "Never," he replied, "so long as there are sects in churches, weeds in gardens, fleas in hog pens, dirt in victuals, disputes in families, wars with nations, water in the ocean, bad men in America, or bad women in France! . . . When I join Democracy the Pope of Rome will join the Methodist Church."[19]

We have already encountered him in an emphatic refusal to unite in Father Aiken's divine petition to "deliver us from Whiggery." He published for a time what he called a newspaper; it was known as the "Jonesboro Whig,"[20] but it was known as a good many other things besides, especially by those who had felt its cutting edge. It was a kind of combination of buzz saw, a surgeon's knife, a steam hammer and a rasp. In approach and touch it was as subtle as an adze. Its perusal was like the study of anatomy, the reading of its political columns an excursion into the amphitheatre of an operating room where major surgery is performed with a hatchet and no anæsthetic.

In discovering motives and treading the tortuous trails of private life, Brownlow had the gifts of a clairvoyant and the capacity of a sleuth of fiction. These latter powers, however, proved of no avail when in 1845 he decided to contest Andrew

Johnson's seat in Congress. There were no dark avenues in that career to ferret out, but Brownlow employed every other weapon in his well-stored, if prehistoric arsenal. That must have been a campaign worth both hearing and seeing. The followers of Andrew Johnson delighted in nothing so much as in taking hard blows and returning them with interest. When, therefore, the fighting was over and the smoke had cleared away, it was found that with all his implements of un-Christian warfare the "Fighting Parson" had fought in vain. Johnson was reëlected.[21]

That he was liked and trusted in the first Congressional district of Tennessee, despite his independent espousal of measures which the mountaineers did not approve, is sufficiently attested by the fact that after this signal victory over Brownlow, two years later in 1847 he was again reëlected,[22] and in 1849 was once more returned; this time with a majority of 1008,[23] and finally in 1851 his constituents sent him back to Washington with 1696 votes to spare.[24] He served, therefore, in the lower House in the 28th, 29th, 30th, 31st and 32nd Congress from December 4th, 1843 to March 3rd, 1853, or ten years altogether.

Here was an experience which would have been enlarging to the dullest mind. To Johnson it was a decade of incalculable mental growth. He had a quenchless thirst for the reading of good books which, despite his manifold employments, he had found time to satisfy. He steeped himself in history, the writings of Jefferson, Hamilton and Washington, but especially in the English Bible, the British poets and the Constitution. His mind was burning with desire to make up for that lack of "book education" whose absence he deplored as keenly as Mr. Rhodes was later to deplore it for him. This, together with his contact with the important and the coming men of the country,— Lincoln, Seward, Douglas, Webster, Polk, Van Buren, Clement C. Clay, Judah Benjamin, Jefferson Davis, Alexander H. Stephens, Henry Clay, John C. Calhoun and many others—the occasion and the need for the study of the pressing problems of the day, and the public opportunity to make use of his knowledge dearly bought and, therefore, valued, furnished the ingredients of an education which it would have been difficult to surpass at Harvard.

Abraham Lincoln was a member of the 30th Congress (1847-1849). During this time many of the members lived in boarding houses or clubs over which the owner was the presiding deity. Mrs. Spriggs' in Duff Green's Road was the one where Lincoln lived. Nearby on Capitol Hill dwelt Johnson.[25] They belonged to different political parties but they had many things in common. Both had weathered a hard struggle with adversity. Both had known poverty. Both were without formal education. Lincoln was born in, and Johnson came from a border state, and they could, therefore, grasp the point of view of both sections of the country. While Johnson was the owner of a few slaves whom he used as personal servants,[26] Lincoln owned none, and was against any extension of the institution. But both men were opposed to the agitation of the Northern abolitionists. Both were seeking a reasonable method for the final elimination of slavery. Johnson, as we have already observed, considered Texas as a gateway through which the negro might pass to freedom.[27] Lincoln while in Congress introduced a bill "for the gradual and compensated extinction of slavery in the District of Columbia."[28]

Johnson, for his resolution of 1842 looking to the elimination of the negro population as a basis for representation in Tennessee as well as his later advocacy of the Homestead Law, was strongly criticized by the radicals of the South. Lincoln, who hated slavery, was the subject of frequent abuse on the part of Northern abolitionists. Both men were lovers of the Union. Johnson in 1850 said: "The preservation of the Union is paramount to all other considerations."[29] While Lincoln as late as August 22, 1862, wrote Horace Greeley: "If I could save the Union without freeing any slaves, I would do it. If I could save it by freeing all the slaves I would do it. If I could do it by freeing some and leaving others alone I would also do that. What I do about slavery and the colored race, I do because I believe it helps to save the Union, and when I forbear, I forbear because I do not believe it would help to save the Union."[30] On the Mexican war Johnson and Lincoln held strongly opposite opinions, Lincoln opposed[31] and Johnson supported[32] its prosecution.

Lincoln served but two years in Washington. "There was,"

says Charnwood, "no movement to reëlect him." [33] But two of Johnson's ten years in Congress, therefore, were spent in company with the tall representative from Illinois. It was long enough, however, for them to become acquainted.

Before leaving his Congressional career, we should at least glance at Johnson's fine speech on the subject of the Veto Power.[34] Its eleven pages constitute as capable a discussion of a constitutional provision as will be found within the Federalist itself. "I do not look upon the veto power," he said, "as a 'snag' on the Mississippi to obstruct the navigation of our commerce, but as a breakwater, . . . to arrest the mighty current of Federal power setting in. . . . The veto . . . is conservative and enables the people through their tribunitian officer to arrest or suspend for the time being hasty and improvident legislation until the people, the sovereigns in this country, have time and opportunity to consider of its propriety." [35]

It was well that Johnson should be making this personal inspection of that well-made ordnance, that he was examining the sights and the bores and studying the range tables of that mighty weapon of the Constitution. For there was to come a time when he would stand alone upon the ramparts and, with his gun crews shot to pieces, single-handed load, aim and fire that piece at more dangerous enemies of America than ever threatened from within or without her borders.

Johnson's unusual personality and extraordinary strength explain how, despite his advocacy of measures calculated to find disfavor among the mountaineers of Tennessee, he held for ten consecutive years his seat in Congress. His speech for Catholic tolerance sounded with peculiar dissonance among the supplications of the followers of John Knox, Charles Wesley and John Calvin. Nor did his long advocacy of the Homestead bill, beginning in 1846,[36] endear him to the Whigs of the western and middle sections of the state. This measure was designed to grant to any citizen, the head of a family, a homestead of one hundred and sixty acres of public land upon condition of occupancy and cultivation for a period of five years.[37] Its purpose was to "place every man in the possession of a home and an interest in the country." [38]   Its natural tendency would be the rapid settling by non-slave holders of that part of the new territory that was closed to slavery, and it, therefore, met the prompt and persistent opposition of the South. [39]

The advocacy of these measures, which politicians would call "dangerous," bore fruit in 1852 in a Whig scheme to eliminate Johnson from public life.   They had found that trying to defeat him at the polls was hopeless, and they, therefore, brought to bear the device of gerrymandering.   Controlling the legislature of Tennessee, they changed the boundaries of his district so as to include large numbers of Whigs and to exclude many of his old Democratic followers. [40]   But Johnson had not had for nothing a lifetime of struggle.   He taught his enemies that he had learned something about the game of politics by securing the Democratic nomination for Governor.   His Whig opponent was Gustavus A. Henry, a leading lawyer of Tennessee, and known there as the "Eagle Orator." [41]   He was a descendant of Patrick Henry and inherited his fire and brilliance. [42]

Here was a campaign indeed.   While in Congress, Johnson had voted against an appropriation for famine-stricken Ireland, believing it wrong to divert from the public treasury funds collected for other purposes.   Here was a fine implement to use against him with the Irish vote.   With fiery rhetoric Henry plied him with this on the stump.   This was Johnson's answer: "I proposed to the members that we give our salaries for a certain length of time and when they would not agree to this I put my hand in my pocket and gave $50 to the cause."   Turning sharply to Henry he inquired: "How much did you give?"   Amid the jeers of the crowd the "Eagle Orator" admitted that he had given nothing. [43]   Henry's friend Judge Gaut toward the end of the campaign asked him why Johnson seemed to be making such great headway, and the descendant of the great Virginian replied: "You have underestimated my opponent.   I have never met so powerful a speaker as Andrew Johnson." [44]

Neither the oratory of the "Eagle Orator" alone nor in combination with the glamor of his descent, proved adequate to withstand the body blows of Johnson who was elected by a large majority.[45] That his old neighbors of Greene County had once more rallied to his aid, his surplus there of one thousand and thirteen votes, is ample testimony.[46]

In the new state capitol, then as yet unfinished, on October 3rd, 1853, Johnson took his oath of office as Governor of the state of Tennessee. During his first term he strove for the improvement of the schools. "All who entertain any personal and state pride," he said, "must feel deeply wounded . . . that Tennessee, though the fifth state in the Union, stands lowest in the list of education, save one. . . . While millions are being appropriated to aid in the various works of internal improvements, can there be nothing done for education?"[47]

In his message to the legislature he found occasion to strike another blow for his favorite project,—the Homestead Law, and argued that the Senators and Representatives from Tennessee be instructed to give it their support in Congress.[48] He sponsored also an amendment to the Federal Constitution providing for the election of the President and Vice-President by popular vote.[49]

At the conclusion of his first term as Governor he was renominated.[50] His opponent this time was Meredith P. Gentry[51] whom John Quincy Adams had called the "greatest natural orator in Congress."[52]

§

The year 1846 had added famine to the manifold miseries of unhappy Ireland. It was not long after this that the Irish began in dead earnest their emigration to America. So large before long had the influx grown, that the 100% Americans of that day began entertaining serious fears lest so many "foreigners" could not be assimilated, and presently were forming a secret society with lodges and other paraphernalia of mystery, to oppose the easy naturalization of newcomers. The members soon were making political nominations in secret conventions. The mysteries of this occult political faith were whispered among those who had penetrated the higher degrees of its clandestine rites. The neophytes knew nothing of them,—hence the name "Know-Nothing." This brotherhood became the "American Party,"[53] deriving its name from one of the celebrated orders of General Washington: "Put none but Americans on duty tonight." [54] It rallied to its standards large numbers of the Whigs, and mustered in 1855 sufficient strength to carry the elections in nine states. [55]

One of the by-laws of this order required that a member "must be a native born citizen of the United States, a Protestant either born of Protestant parents or reared under Protestant influences and not united in marriage with a Roman Catholic." [56] This bilious bigotry was the animating spirit of the "American,"— that most un-American of all our parties.

When Johnson finished with the Whigs in his first gubernatorial campaign of 1853, their defeat was of that decisive kind from which there is no recovery. [57] But the American party found in Tennessee a fertile and luxuriant soil, the study of whose political chemistry would form a diverting and perhaps not an irrelevant inquiry. The Whigs, still battered from their encounter of two years before, already entertaining the religious bias of the "Know-Nothings," embraced with eager promptitude their political principles, boasting that they could muster in Tennessee one hundred thousand votes.

It was these apostles of prejudice who in 1855 nominated against Governor Johnson their spokesman and their partisan, Mr. Gentry. [58] From the Unaka mountains of Johnson's county to the Chickasaw Bluffs in Shelby the battle raged. [59] At this time a similar campaign was raging in Virginia where Henry A. Wise, with all the ardor of his fiery nature, likewise entered the lists against the party of prejudice. With all the force and strength by which he had vanquished the "Fighting Parson," and later the lineal and vocal descendant of Patrick Henry, Johnson went into this struggle against the "greatest orator in Congress." "When I feel that I have got truth on my side," he told his colleagues of the United States Senate five years later, "when I know that I have got facts and arguments that cannot be answered, I never inquire as to the difference of ability or experience between myself and those with whom I have to contend." [60] Acting upon this principle he now took up again the cudgels against Catholic persecution. If objection to tolerating the Catholic religion be because it and its followers are foreign, "Who was John Wesley," he asked, "and where did the Methodist religion have its origin? If John Wesley were alive today and here, . . . Know-Nothingism would drive him and his religion back to England whence they came, because they were foreign. . . . And so with Martin Luther, the great Reformer; he would have been subjected to the same proscriptive test." [61]

In 1854 Stephen A. Douglas had secured the passage of his Kansas-Nebraska Bill, repealing the Missouri Compromise and leaving the question of slavery in the territories for the settlers there to decide.[62] His action was approved, of course, by the South. In the North its effect was to unite the Free Soilers with the anti-slavery Democrats and Whigs in what, in 1856, became the Republican party.[63] Johnson was a follower of Douglas. That he was a "Democrat east, west, north or south or anywhere else" [64] and "as good a Southern man as anyone who lives within the borders of the South," [65] was ever his proud boast. He espoused, therefore, in this gubernatorial campaign the Kansas-Nebraska Bill. He always had and expressed a sincere and "an abiding confidence in the intelligence, the patriotism and the integrity of the people." [66]

What Johnson thought was right, he declared in plain words; there was no doubt where he stood on Kansas and Nebraska.[67] Mr. Gentry, it seems, preferred the discussion of religious questions, and throughout the canvass took a non-committal course upon the topic of the hour. Finally in his desire to win, Gentry came down to personalities. Martha, Johnson's eldest daughter, was then a pupil in a Protestant "seminary for young ladies." As the campaign waxed warm so did Mr. Gentry; they waxed warm together. At last he leveled at Johnson's head the devastating accusation that Martha Johnson had been educated in a convent! [68]

The passions aroused in those early Tennessee campaigns were hot, and where argument failed there were plenty of ruffians "to threaten the pistol and the bowie." No one lacking either in physical or moral bravery could have been Governor of Tennessee in those days. When Johnson was on the stump "he saw more men with than without pistols in their breast pockets, and knives in their boots or parallel to their backbones." [69] At one time "anecdotes of the coolness and courage of Governor Johnson were among the current coin of conversation," in his state. One of his political opponents and an eye-witness of the occurrence, has told how "a placard was posted in the town one morning announcing in the well-known language of Tennessee, that "Andie Johnson" was to be shot on sight. Friends of the Governor assembled at his house desirous of forming a bodyguard to escort him to the State House. "No," said he, "gentlemen, if I am to be shot at, I want no man to be in the way of the bullet.' He walked alone with his usual deliberation through the streets to his official apartments on Capitol Hill." [70]

Another first-hand witness has told us how threats were uttered that if Johnson dared to appear at a certain meeting he would not leave the hall alive. At the appointed hour he ascended the platform, walked to the front, laid down his pistol on the desk and began his speech, which was: "Fellow citizens: It is proper when free men assemble for the discussion of important public interests, that everything should be done decently and in order. I have been informed that part of the business to be transacted is the assassination of the individual who now has the honor of addressing you. I beg respectfully to propose that this be the first business in order. Therefore, if any man has come here tonight for the purpose indicated, I do not say to him, let him speak, but, let him shoot." No one appeared to have attended for that purpose so Johnson continued: "It appears that I have been misinformed. I will now proceed to address you on the subject which has called us together." [71]

Johnson in 1855 was elected Governor a second time. Neither Mr. Gentry's pussyfooting on the Kansas-Nebraska Bill, nor his slavish following of "Know-Nothingism," nor his actual knowing nothing of how Martha Johnson received her education, seemed to help him.

During his second term Governor Johnson continued his advocacy of a better educational system. Through state fairs he stimulated the interests of the farm. He sought to limit the state banks in their issuance of paper money, but what interested him most perhaps, was his ability to report Tennessee's purchase of the "Hermitage,"—the residence and the tomb of Andrew Jackson."

Better evidence of the esteem in which he was now held could not be found than that shown him on October 8th, 1857, when the legislature of his state met and on the first ballot elected him a United States Senator from Tennessee." The following year he told his fellow Senators at Washington: "I have reached the summit of my ambition. The acme of all my hopes has been attained, and I would not give the position I occupy today for any other in the United States." " He could not know what lay in store for him.

IV

UNITED STATES SENATOR

IN great cities such, for example, as New York, one encounters large numbers of well-known, if not of famous men, celebrities whose names form the steady staple of the daily press and whose reputations reach as though by the magic of the radio to the remotest corners of the land. New York thinks she knows these men and yet she does not know them. She only reads about them. For a long time now New Yorkers have ceased walking to the post office for their mail and it is some while back since they stopped meeting in their strolls upon the Battery, or congregating of an evening in "the Bowling Green." There is no common meeting place, no corner store where they can be natural and get acquainted. No one knows anyone in the cities any more except through the pages of the morning paper. How often, therefore, is the actual encountering of "great men" the source of wondering surprise. On close inspection the astonishing discovery is made that many of them after all are things of lath and plaster thinly cloaked beneath good coats of paint, or sometimes of shellac and varnish. The evidence of their greatness has been hearsay,— autobiography the record of their accomplishments.

Such things are impossible in the villages and small towns. Your country lawyer who has traveled the circuit, has gained by sturdy character the confidence of judges and stormed the affections of his juries and, through years of honorable and fair dealing with his neighbors, has gradually enlarged the circle of his friends,—if he has won a reputation for ability and strength, you can be sure it is deserved. He is known,—his friends know him, if there is anything they have concealed, his enemies who know him also will reveal it. Even more true is this of those who have borne the heat of the day in public life.

31

When, therefore, after thirty-one years of residence in Greeneville and twenty-nine of almost constant struggle in Tennessee's political arena, Johnson found himself a Senator of the United States, it was no mere accident. His fellow artisans had known him, the debating society had found his forensic gifts a contribution. Alderman and mayor of his town, state representative and Senator, Representative in Congress, governor of his state and now its ambassador to the National Senate, tempered in the fiery crucible of politics, no base alloy had been detected, and if he was not assayed, then no one ever was! Now in this larger trutination we shall find that he was not found wanting.

§

The Senate of the United States was once the meeting place for statesman, the goal of the greatest of our countrymen, the highest reward for preëminent attainment. On its floor were fought the great battles of the Constitution. Clay and Calhoun were dead, so was Webster, but the echoes of his apostrophe to Liberty and Union in his reply to Senator Hayne, were still reverberating when, on the 7th day of December, 1857,[1] Andrew Johnson took his seat there. And he encountered not memories alone, but the mighty champions of the public questions of the hour that rocked and terrified the country.

There he came in close contact with Stephen Douglas, the "little giant" of Illinois, William Seward of New York, Crittenden of Kentucky, Mason of Virginia, Toombs and Iverson of Georgia, Slidell and Benjamin of Louisiana, Charles Sumner of Massachusetts, Fessenden and Hamlin of Maine, Bell of Tennessee (his senior Senator), Bayard of Delaware, Doolittle of Wisconsin, Clement C. Clay of Alabama, Foster of Connecticut, Stuart of Michigan, Clingman of North Carolina, Simon B. Cameron and Bigler of Pennsylvania, Sam Houston of Texas, Shields of Minnesota, Lane of Oregon and Jefferson Davis of Mississippi.[2] Here were the men Johnson was now called upon to meet. The names of many of them are now all but symbols for the causes they espoused. Proud landed families, brilliant products of the colleges, wealth and the haughty position of privilege were here represented. Self-made men were less highly thought of in those days than now. It was for Andrew Johnson, therefore, an ordeal indeed to take his seat in that imperious chamber.

He had not been there long before he made his membership in this great Council of the States an opportunity to advocate again one of the favored projects of his life,—the Homestead Bill. It was a well-considered program for the "winning of the west." His previous sponsorship of it in the House, despite Webster's aid, had not accomplished its enactment. Undaunted, Johnson now pressed on. "I can go back to that period in my history," he said, "when I could not say that I had a home. This being so, when I cast my eyes over one extreme of the United States to the other, and behold the great numbers that are homeless, I feel for them. . . . Transfer the man from the point where he is producing nothing. . . . In a short time he has a crop. . . . He becomes a better man for all governmental purposes, because he is interested in the country in which he lives." [3]

He held no brief for city life. "I do not look," he said, "upon the growth of cities and the accumulation of population about cities as being the most desirable objects in this country." [4] What would he have thought of the "accumulation" of today? With telling effect he quoted from Vattel: "The inhabitants of cities, even the most servile artist and the most lazy citizen, consider him who cultivates the soil with a disdainful eye; they humble and discourage him, they dare to despise a profession that feeds the human race—the natural employment of man. A stay-maker places far beneath him the beloved employment of the first consuls of Rome." [5] And Johnson continued: "Then let us go on . . . interesting men in becoming connected with the soil; . . . prevent their accumulation in the streets of your cities; and in doing this you will dispense with the necessity for all your pauper system . . . and break down the great propensity that exists with men to hang and loiter and perish about the cities of the Union as is done now in the older countries." [6]

With cold disapprobation the statesmen from the slave states listened.[7] Among them there was no prouder product of the South than Senator Clement Clay of Alabama. "I regret," a little earlier he had said, "to see the growing spirit in Congress and throughout the country to democratize our government; to submit every question whether pertaining to organic or municipal laws to the vote of the people. This is sheer radicalism; it is the Red Republicanism of Revolutionary France. . . . Property is the foundation of every social fabric. To preserve, protect and perpetuate rights of property society is formed, and government is framed." [8]

"These," answered Johnson, "are not notions entertained by me; . . . I favor the policy of popularizing all our free institutions. We are Democrats occupying a position here from the South; we start together but we turn our backs on each other very soon. His policy would take the government further from the people. I go . . . to . . . bring it nearer to the people . . . and then you will . . . have a purer and better government. I hold to the doctrine . . . that man can be elevated; that man can be exalted. . . . We are told on high authority that he is made in the image of God. . . . Let us go on elevating our people. . . ." [9] And Johnson continued: "Mr. Jefferson laid it down in the Declaration of Independence that it was a self-evident truth that government was instituted,—for what? To protect men in life, liberty and the pursuit of happiness. . . . When the declaration came forth from the old Congress Hall, it came forth as a column of fire and light. . . ." [10]

But Johnson was a good deal more than merely eloquent, he had not had for nothing thirty years of Tennessee polemics,—he was a debater! "If, however," he continued, "the Senator from Alabama holds that property is the main object and basis of society, he, above all other men, ought to go for this bill so as to place every man in the possession of a home and an interest in his country." [11]

Clement Clay had said: "Your whole hireling class of manual laborers and 'operatives' as you call them, are essentially slaves. The difference between us is that our slaves are hired for life and well compensated; there is no starvation, no begging, no want of employment among our people; and not too much employment either. Yours are hired by the day, not cared for, and scantily compensated, which may be proved at any hour, in any street, in any of your large towns. Why, you would meet more beggars in one day in any single street of the City of New York than you would meet in a lifetime in the whole South. We do not think that whites should be slaves either by law or necessity." [12]

This was Johnson's answer: "I do not think whites should be slaves; and if slavery is to exist in this country I prefer black slavery to white slavery. . . . In one sense of the term we are all slaves. A man . . . is a slave to his necessities . . . but . . . it will not do to assume that every man who toils for his living is a slave. . . . If this were true it would be very unfortunate for a good many of us, and especially so for me. I am a laborer with my hands, and I never considered myself a slave. . . . I do own some; I acquired them by my industry, by the labor of my hands. In that sense I should have been a slave while I was earning them. . . ."[13] Socrates, who first conceived the idea of the immortality of the soul, Pagan as he was, labored with his own hands,— yes, wielded the chisel and the mallet, giving polish and finish to the stone; he afterwards turned to be a fashioner and constructor of the mind. Paul, the great expounder, himself was a tent maker, and worked with his hands; was he a slave?" [14]

The true criterion of statesmanship is the capacity to look into the future and to prepare for it. Johnson had this power. As we read that speech we seem to hear the heavy rumble of the covered wagons and to catch a vision of the dauntless pioneer, taking wife and children, his few possession, his Bible and his long rifle, facing a thousand deaths and pushing towards the setting sun. The march of Empire! Westward Ho! The quest of land, of opportunity, of larger life, all that has made America the hope of the world.

These things Johnson saw, but he saw more than these. In his vision there lay a vast expanse where slavery could not flourish, with new settlers there carrying neither slaves nor slavery with them,—new territories that if permitted at the polls the choice, would vote against the institution.

At the close of that speech there are two sentences of simple, but of moving eloquence: "The people need friends. They have a great deal to bear." [15]

V

SLAVERY AND THE ABOLITIONISTS

QUESTIONS arising from the importation of African negroes long antedated the Constitution. The Declaration of Independence as Johnson so eloquently declared "came forth as a column of fire and light," [1] but it came forth unfortunately with one of Mr. Jefferson's best paragraphs omitted. One of the most resonant of all the charges in the original of that long indictment of King George was this: "He has waged cruel war against human nature itself, violating its most sacred rights of life and liberty in the persons of distant people who never offended him, captivating and carrying them into slavery in another hemisphere or to incur miserable death in their transportation thither. This piratical warfare, the opprobrium of infidel powers, is the warfare of the Christian King of Great Britain. Determined to keep open a market where men should be bought and sold, he has prostituted his negative for suppressing every legislative attempt to prohibit or restrain this execrable commerce." [2]

The lovers of mankind may well regret that the growers of rice and indigo in Georgia and the Carolinas, and their friends and sympathizers, were powerful enough to exclude this Virginian's arraignment of slavery and the slave trade from the Declaration of Independence. Had this not been done historians might have found the decades from the Missouri Compromise to the presidency of Hayes a less fertile field for their inquiries—cynics will add for their romances. Military strategists might have been deprived of the measureless material found in the swift advances and retreats, the strokes and counterstrokes of Lee and Stonewall Jackson, or the campaigns of dogged determination in the wilderness with which Ulysses Grant contributed so much to save the Union. Artists would have been stripped of all the flaming colors of the war between the States.

Long before Jamestown was founded by the English, Vasquez d'Ayllon in 1556 pushed up from Hayti and not far from the spot where John Smith in 1607 founded the first British colony in America, began the building of a town. The hands that built it were those of negro slaves.[3] The institution grew and spread. By the time the embattled farmers fired their far heard shot, there were negro slaves in every colony,[4]—New England through her Yankee clippers was the backbone of the slave trade.[5]

When the delegates assembled in 1787 at Philadelphia in the Constitutional Convention, the main point of controversy was the representation of the large and of the small states,—not slavery.[6] George Washington, who presided, was a large slave holder and so were many of the other delegates.[7] The writings of Rousseau, the torch that Thomas Paine kept lighted in his Pennsylvania magazine, the novel doctrine expressed so unequivocally in the great Declaration that "All men are created free and equal,"— all these stimulated a desire among some of the delegates to prohibit slavery in the Constitution.[8] The same forces, however, that had compelled Jefferson to omit this subject from his celebrated strictures on King George, wrote the constitutional provisions whereby, without mentioning slavery by name, its existence was both recognized and protected. A slave counted as three-fifths of a man for the purposes of representation. The slave trade was protected until 1808, and slave owners were guaranteed the return of slaves who fled to other states, irrespective of the laws there prevailing.[9]

In February 1790, the Pennsylvania Abolition Society presented a petition to the first Congress of the United States; it bore the signature of its president, Benjamin Franklin, and called "attention to the subject of slavery," praying Congress "to countenance the restoration of liberty to those unhappy men who alone in this land of freemen are growing in servile subjection." [10] Profound respect was accorded the petition and those who came presenting it. Generous support was given by the representatives of Virginia and other states where slavery was flourishing, but Georgia and South Carolina voiced their opposition and prevented action.[11]

§

Intelligent reading of the history of races and of nations demonstrates that that which we call progress is a flower of slow and anxious growth. Especially is this true of man's institutions and of his conceptions of his place, his rights and above all of his duties on this revolving sphere in its measureless whirl through time and space. England's literature and her poetry, her common law and especially her sagacious time-worn constitution, her venerated customs having more of sanction than many of our laws, all these were not made in one day, but are the product of the centuries.

The statesman has patience, the reformer never. The statesman sees and recognizes evil; he desires its correction, but in correcting it he is unwilling to destroy all that is good. With as much, perhaps with more of clarity than the reformer he sees wrong, with as much perhaps more of sympathy he observes injustice, with as much perhaps more sincerity he desires the remedy, but he is unwilling to kill when his purpose is to heal. You have in Robespierre your typical reformer, in Washington the statesman. The men of the Mountain chose as the instrument of progress the guillotine and sought in one red summer to correct the evils of the centuries. It was not long before their changed calendar was marking them for the tumbrils and their work for the ash heaps of history. The British Constitution was not the work of red-handed fanatics, but of the slow accumulation of centuries of light.

In 1787 the statesmen at Philadelphia knew history,—especially English history. They had read the annals of the Republics and the Democracies of all times, and understood their failures and successes. With this knowledge and the desire to apply it, yet with statesmanlike willingness if they could not at once procure exactly what they wanted, then to take the best that they could get, working with as pure a patriotism as ever stirred the breast of man, they wrote the greatest document of the human race. Had the reformers had the work to do they could never have agreed. Each would have been willing that all should go rather than that his special plan should be altered or omitted. After it was written, your typical reformer would have sulked in his tent unless it expressed exactly his conception. Statesmen act as Hamilton acted. In the Constitution that finally emerged from Philadelphia the plan that he had drawn and in which, with all of his passionate nature he believed, was scarcely recognizable. Yet he accepted this work of other minds feeling that on the whole it was the best that could be gotten.

Lincoln was no "reformer." No one of his generation hated slavery more than he, but he did not confuse his detestation of the institution with malice towards those who were its beneficiaries. Above the hatreds and the reckless passions engendered by the abolitionists,—as a kind of obligato to their notes of bitterness, I hear Lincoln's solemn words written eighteen months after Sumter: "If I could save the Union without freeing any slave, I would do it; if I could save it by freeing all the slaves, I would do it. And if I could do it by freeing some and leaving others alone I would also do that. What I do about slavery and the colored race I do because I believe it helps to save the Union, and what I forbear, I forbear because I do not believe it would help to save the Union." [12] No Wendell Phillips, no John Brown, no Thaddeus Stevens, no Charles Sumner could either understand or do what was both understood and done by Hamilton and Lincoln.

In the character of the reformer, the central element is egotism. "My way and not thine," sums up both him and his philosophy. Whatever he believes should be done must be done, and done his way and done at once. Either that or count him out or count him against any other's plan. Single-minded men, they see often with sincerity a single end, and will justify any means in order to attain it. The abolitionist John Brown, for instance, whose passion against slavery and slaveholders was little more intense than that of his fellow agitators, though its immediate manifestation differed from that of many of them, three years before his raid at Harper's Ferry decided that he would strike a blow for negro liberty. In May of 1856 he struck one; he struck several. Five of his Pattawatomie neighbors were pro-slavery men and so he and a party of his followers went over one night and murdered them, "literally hacked them to pieces with cutlasses." [13] It was cold-blooded, deliberate murder; there was no heat of passion, no self-defense, nothing to extenuate this cowardly act of premeditated barbarism. Yet his partisans proclaimed that this clandestine butchery had kept Kansas with the cause of freedom! [14]

The abolition movement was a typical "reform." All shades of character were found beneath its motley colors, from first degree murderers like Brown, to spotless graduates of Harvard College like Wendell Phillips and Charles Sumner.

To me, Sumner perhaps more than any of the rest personifies the cause of abolition. Tall and well formed, there was about him the air of authority, his singularly handsome face made him a striking figure. But he possessed withal a coldness and detachment that made all of his philanthropy seem studied, his love for negroes was in the abstract, his concern for them a kind of "book philanthropy." [15]

One night Julia Ward Howe set this down in her diary: "Sumner to tea. Made a rude speech on being asked to meet Edwin Booth. Said: 'I don't know that I care to meet him. I have outlived my interest in individuals.'" "Fortunately," continues this girl (whose eyes perhaps had already seen "the glory of the coming of the Lord"), "God Almighty had not by last accounts got so far." [16]

Sumner had an interest in individuals only if they were black. Senator Bradbury of Maine chanced one day to look up into the gallery and saw a woman faint. It was after the rejection of a private claim. She lived in eastern Massachusetts. "But why don't you go to Mr. Sumner and ask him to take charge of your case?" asked Bradbury, who had sought her out. "Oh, sir, I did," she answered, "but really, sir, Mr. Sumner takes no interest in claims unless they be from black people." [17] It was the Senator from Maine and not from Massachusetts who finally secured for her that to which she was entitled. [18]

"Toward the slave holders," wrote one of Lincoln's Cabinet, "he is implacable, and is ready to go to extremes to break up

not only the system of bondage, but the political, industrial and social system in all the rebellious states. . . . He would not only free the slaves, but elevate them above their former masters, yet with all his studied philanthropy and love for the negroes in the abstract, is unwilling to fellowship with them, though he thinks he is." [19]

Another member of Lincoln's Cabinet has written of Charles Sumner: "His friendship was confined to the very few whom he acknowledged to be his equals, or to the many who looked up to him as a superior. His sympathies were for races,—too lofty to descend to persons. For the freedom of the slaves he was an earnest worker; of their claims to all the privileges of freedom, after their emancipation, he was an able and an eloquent advocate and defender; but to appeals by needy colored people to his charity . . . he was seemingly indifferent." [20]

Sumner thought himself a scholar, in fact he was a pedant. Take down the index (I ask no more) of the fifteen volumes of his published addresses and orations. [21] He himself supervised the beginning of their publication. All that he ever said about anything he felt posterity should have. Until I made myself read some of these diffuse, labored and ornate effusions, I had never had a clear conception of what dullness was.

He was vain, arrogant, egotistical, opinionated. "His prejudices," says Hugh McCulloch, "were hastily formed and violent. His self-esteem was limitless. Impatient of contradiction, his manner to those who differed with him was arrogant and offensive. His ears were ever open to flattery of which he was omnivorous." [22] Francis Lieber, long his friend and admirer, has written: "Sumner requires adulation and I am no flatterer." [23] Grant's brief comment when told that Sumner had no faith in the Bible was: "No, he didn't write it." [24] And Lord Morley's that he was "too often the slave of words when he thought he was their master." [25] And Carlyle's: "The most completely nothin' of a mon that ever crossed my threshold,—naught whatsoever in him or of him but wind and vanity." [26]

Sumner was not only pedant, he was a prig. He was totally devoid of humor and, therefore, of capacity to grasp another's point of view. We are furnished this picture of his youth. One morning when his mother reproved him for being late at breakfast, he gravely reproached her: "Call me Mr. Sumner, mother, if you please." [27] And we have this too: "He once told me," says Noah Brooks, "that he never allowed himself even in the privacy of his own chamber, to fall into a position which he would not take in his chair in the Senate." [28]

Like his fellow New England abolitionists, he had neither knowledge nor familiarity with the South. He neither comprehended nor sought to grasp the enormous complexities of the race problem. [29] In 1850 he attacked the fugitive slave law. This was neither dangerous nor unpopular at that time,—in Boston. And it was helpful to him; it was the cause of his election to the Senate the next year. [30]

§

An English gentleman and his wife, whether through neglect to make sufficiently prompt reservations, or for some other reason, failed to secure passage for America, on a well-known ship, so they took the next boat. The vessel which they missed was the *Mayflower*, the accommodations they secured were on the *Arabella*, and the couple in question were the ancestors of Wendell Phillips. [31] No account of the abolition movement could be given without mention of his name. He was born on November 29th, 1811; his birthplace, of course, was Boston. He seems to have had the proper background. Like Sumner he entered the Boston Latin School from which he graduated in 1822, and in 1831 received from Harvard his diploma. He came through college with the reputation of having defeated the first attempt to organize a temperance society there. Evil-disposed persons might consider this a hopeful sign. But for the benefit of the pure, let me quickly add that after the negroes had been not only freed, but with the aid of Northern bayonets placed in political control of Southern white men, Phillips embraced (chastely let us hope) the temperance movement.

Such spare time as he could find, he devoted to the cause of woman suffrage, Irish Home Rule and the furthering of the

Greenback Theory.[32]   He seems to have had no regular employment of his own, but throughout his seventy-two years of talk and agitation, he kept himself reasonably employed with the business of others.   James Russell Lowell liked him and wrote a poem about him,—something about standing upon "the world's broad threshold," where the "din of battle and slaughter rose," and seeing "God stand upon the weaker side."[33]   I find no suggestion in these verses that the person praised did anything but see, or was it hear, "the din of battle and of slaughter."   Also when Mr. Lowell was speaking of the divine alliance with the "weaker side," he did not mention (perhaps they did not have those figures up in Boston) that the Confederates were outnumbered three to one, and the disparity between their economic resources and those of their opponents was even greater.   Such things do not matter much when you are writing poetry.

In October 1835, there were a good many persons in Boston who did not seem to like William Lloyd Garrison.   In fact their distaste for him was so marked not to say pointed, that some, afterwards described by the friendly Press as "gentlemen of property and standing," secured a rope, tied it snugly about his waist, dragged him through the streets and were about to hang him when he was rescued through the efforts of the mayor.[34]   They desired, it seems, to make their position plain and unequivocal. Their dissent from Garrison's contention that the Constitution of the United States was "a covenant with death and an agreement with Hell," was equally as strong as that of John Marshall of Virginia, though it found a somewhat different medium of expression.[35]

Wendell Phillips liked Garrison and his doctrine and from this moment began espousing both of them.[36]   Not long after the rescue of the liberator, Phillips "as beautiful as a young Apollo" made a speech at Faneuil Hall.   "He ascended the platform," one of his eulogists has said, "a young gentleman of one of the first families of Boston; he descended it one of the foremost orators of the world."[37]   Which, we wonder, was it that has so stimulated this biographer, membership "in one of the first families of Boston," or the oratory?   A true reformer, he advocated the immediate and above all the unconditional liberation of negroes. To the impartial consideration of the problem he contributed nothing.

In the origin of slavery Massachusetts was guilty equally with South Carolina and with Georgia. Of any plan of compensated emancipation, or consideration of what was to be done with the slaves when freed, we find nothing in Wendell Phillips' speeches. Reformers do not concern themselves with such problems. It is not necessary, because it is always the property or the errors of others, not their own, which engages their attention and their enthusiasm.

Phillips continued friendly with Mr. Garrison, although there was not always perfect unanimity between them. In 1864 for example, Garrison felt that Lincoln had done reasonably well and should be reëlected. Mr. Phillips did not think so.[38] Again, in 1865 Garrison favored the dissolution of the Anti-Slavery Society through which he had organized and led the abolitionists, though Phillips had become recognized as "its chief apostle." [39] "The young Apollo," though he was now not quite so young, contended that the work of the Society was not complete until the ex-slaves were presented with the vote. In a speech delivered in 1861 he placed above the names of Cromwell and of Washington, Toussaint L'Ouverture, the negro liberator of Hayti.[40]

Aside from speechmaking he took no actual part in government at any time. Though he devoted his entire life to telling others how to vote and to act, he never himself cast a single ballot at the polls.[41] Reformers quite frequently consider this a superfluous detail of citizenship. They prefer to instruct others how to use their franchise to the actual, perhaps fatiguing, exertion of doing so themselves.

On October 21st, 1865, Gideon Welles summed up his opinion of Wendell Phillips thus: "Censorious and unpractical, the man, though possessed of extraordinary gifts, is a useless member of society and deservedly without influence." [42] Take a composite picture of Charles Sumner, Thaddeus Stevens, John Brown and Wendell Phillips and you will have the perfect portrait of an abolitionist.

§

The abolition movement dates its real beginning from the year 1831. It was then that William Lloyd Garrison at Boston shouted in the first number of his *Liberator:* "I shall contend for the immediate enfranchisement of our slave population,—I will be as harsh as truth and as uncompromising as justice on this subject,—I do not wish to think or speak or write with moderation . . . I will be heard." [43]   Garrison was against every form of colonization; every program of gradual emancipation and demanded immediate and unconditional liberation of the slaves. [44]

In August, following the first publication of this sheet, Nat Turner, a negro, led at Southampton, Virginia, an insurrection of the blacks. Sixty-one white persons were murdered. [45]   The House of Burgesses convened three months later, and although the memory of Nat Turner's butchery was still fresh, there had been by no means destroyed a strong anti-slavery sentiment traditional in Virginia since its representatives in 1790 had looked favorably upon the petition of the Abolition Society of Pennsylvania. [46]

No fiercer denunciation of slavery can be found than that uttered in the Virginia House of Burgesses that year. The "institution" was charged with blighting every industry except agriculture, and with driving free laborers from the state. Slavery was depicted as a "curse." [47]   No one of the debaters was more eloquent than McDowell, later the Governor of his state, who said: "You may place the slave where you please—you may put him under any process which, without destroying his value as a slave, will debase and crush him as a rational being—you may do all this and the idea that he was born to be free will survive it all. It is allied to his hope of immortality—it is the ethereal part of his nature which oppression cannot reach—it is a torch lit up in his soul by the hand of the Deity, and never meant to be extinguished by the hand of man." [48]   The newspapers of Virginia entered the discussion. The Richmond *Inquirer* urged that slavery be abolished. Harriet Martineau in her travels through the South in 1835 found few slave holders who would call the institution just.[49]

Here then was the material with which to work. All that was required was patience, intelligence, tact and fairness. There was room for such men as James Birney of Kentucky, whom we have met before. He was an advocate of gradual emancipation.[50] His family had long been slave holders, but in 1834 he freed his slaves. He understood slave holders; he had a tactful and a civil tongue. He "was and continued to be a typical slave-holding abolitionist of the earlier period."[51] His early efforts "were those of a slaveholder seeking to induce his own class to support the policy of emancipation."[52] With such a man and such a method a reasonable program might have been worked out. Why not? Other countries were able to effect emancipation without civil war or even bloodshed. Denmark peacefully freed her slaves at the end of 1802.[53] In England Lord Mansfield decided in 1782 that as soon as a slave set foot on British soil, he became a free man, and finally in 1833 Parliament by purchase abolished slavery throughout Great Britain.[54]

In 1840 Wendell Phillips represented the Massachusetts abolitionists in the Anti-Slavery Convention held at London.[55] Perhaps if he alone, surely if in company with Sumner, John Brown and Garrison, could have been transported to England before the institution was peacefully abolished there, they might have been able to engender enough of bitterness and misunderstanding so that England too could have had a bloody struggle over slavery.

In 1836 Benjamin Lundy began an anti-slavery paper and called it the "National Inquirer," with which another medium of propaganda the "Genius of Universal Emancipation" was soon merged.[56] In his younger years Lundy had found, south of the Mason-Dixon line, the largest measure of support; indeed, the majority of the abolition societies of which he was the originator, began in that section of the country.[57] But the writings and the speeches of the Northern reformers began now to take a harsher tone. With ignorance or neglect of the history of the institution, they began attacking slaveholders more bitterly than slavery itself. They saw that negro bondage was confined almost entirely to the South and ignored the fact that it had once flourished in the North, and had been abandoned there on economic, not on moral grounds. There was north of Virginia little that the slaves could do that could not be better done by white men, while in the South cotton made slave labor valuable if not indispensable, and everybody "took it for granted that negroes would not work except as slaves." [58] Down to the eighteen-thirties the evil of slavery had been recognized both North and South, and the hope and purpose to eliminate it had been by no means sectional. In moral perception there was no difference between Massachusetts and Virginia. On February 3rd, 1865, Lincoln told the Confederate Commissioners at Hampton Roads that he "believed the people of the North were as responsible for slavery as the people of the South." [59]

After 1831 there came into the language of the abolitionists an exasperating note of approval for Northern virtue and horror at the depravity of the South. This was something less than pleasing to a race as proud and as jealous of its good name as the heroes of Scott's romances, whose chivalric life formed a standard of conduct below the Mason-Dixon line. [60]

Before the war, Robert E. Lee had said: "In this enlightened age there are few, I believe, but that will acknowledge that slavery as an institution is a moral and political evil in any country." [61] Is there any doubt that fair dealing and the muzzling of the trouble-makers might have brought a settlement of the question without war or disunion? But the abolitionists wanted both. In his *Liberator* of 1835 Garrison had sworn that he was "not hostile to the Constitution of the United States," but in 1843 at the head of his paper he wrote these words: "The compact which exists between the North and the South is a covenant with death and an agreement with hell—involving both parties in atrocious criminality and should be immediately annulled." [62] In 1854 he publicly burned a copy of the United States Constitution in the streets crying out: "So perish all compromisers with tyranny." [63] This was the co-worker and friend of Wendell Phillips!

In 1830 Garrison was convicted of a libel on one Francis Todd, the owner of a slave trade vessel. It might be not without interest for the "cultivated and morally excellent people" of Boston to note that this slaveholder was a resident of Massachusetts and plied his calling from the New England coasts.[64]

There was, of course, among these Northern zealots a total inability or unwillingness to comprehend the problem. They ignored the fact that about one-third of the entire population of the South were slaves.[65] At the commencement of the Civil War "the ownership of slaves greatly exceeded the value of all railroads as well as all manufacturing interests of the country."[66] In a speech that has been little quoted, Abraham Lincoln, six days after his great Cooper Union address, told his audience at Hartford, Connecticut, that "a little more than one-sixth of the population of the United States are slaves looked upon as property, as nothing but property. The cash value of these slaves at a moderate estimate is two billion dollars. This amount of property value has a vast influence on the minds of these owners, very naturally. The same amount of property would have an equal influence upon us if owned in the North. Human nature is the same in the South as in the North, barring the difference in circumstances. Public opinion is founded to a great extent on a property basis. What lessens the value of property is opposed, what enhances its value is favored."[67]

No one hated slavery more than the speaker of those words, but he could envision facts and handle them honestly. As late as December 1st, 1863, he proposed a constitutional amendment providing for compensated emancipation through the issuance of government bonds,[68] and thus urged its adoption: "Some would perpetuate slavery; some would abolish it suddenly and without compensation; some would abolish it gradually with compensation; some would remove the freed people from us and some would retain them with us; and there are yet other diversities. Because of these diversities we waste much strength in struggles among ourselves. By mutual concession we should harmonize and act together. This would be compromise, but it would be compromise among the friends and not with the enemies of the Union. These articles are intended to embody a plan of such mutual concessions."[69]

Measures such as this touched the highest pinnacle of statesmanship; they comprehended both sides of the controversy, and
with a large understanding of the claims of each, proposed justice
for both. Is it any wonder that Lincoln dissented from the
expressed purpose of Garrison and Phillips not "to speak or write
with a moderation"; or their assertion that the United States
Constitution was a "covenant with death and an agreement with
hell," or their treasonable utterances while burning that instrument in the streets of Boston "so perish all compromises with
tyranny?"

"I am accused," said Garrison, "of using hard language. I
admit the charge." [70] How successful he was in using the language of his choice may be fully comprehended from one sentence of a speech made by him in 1835: "Southern slaves ought,
or at least had a right, to cut the throats of their masters." [71] At
about this time the negroes of Santa Domingo took up a little
abolition on their own account and when they were through, had
butchered all the white residents of the island. These same
negroes incited the blacks of South Carolina to insurrection.[72]
Then, too, in Virginia Nat Turner, the black man who had spe-
cialized in the butchery of white women and children, had by no
means been forgotten. "It was," says Woodrow Wilson, "the most
formidable and terrible of the outbreaks among the Southern
negroes . . . and . . . seemed to the startled Southerners to
have some connection with the anti-slavery movement." [73]

It is not surprising, therefore, that there was something less
than a cordial reception in the Southern states for Mr. Garrison's
Liberator, promulgating sentiments such as these: "Whenever
commenced, I cannot but wish success to all slave insurrections.
. . . Rather than see men wearing their chains in a cowardly and
servile spirit, I would as an advocate of peace, much rather see
them breaking the heads of the tyrant with their chains." [74]

These incitements to violence were interpreted by the South
as the unanimous conception of the North. So loud, so raucous
and so minatory was the voice of Garrison, it was believed by
Southern men to represent his section. They could not know for
how small a minority he was speaking.[75] It should not occasion

surprise, therefore, that after the launching of the abolitionist
movement, and as its result, the South which theretofore had
shared the Northern view that slavery should somehow be abolished, now, in the face of this hostility was finding apologists for
slavery itself. And so in 1835 we find Professor Thomas Dew,
the holder of the chair of history at William and Mary College,
publishing an argument that any program of emancipation for
Virginia was impossible.[76] And in the same year the Governor of
South Carolina said to his legislature: "Domestic slavery is the
cornerstone of our republican edifice." [77]

The "irrepressible conflict" was begun,—begun by reformers.
A conflict whose pain and bitterness was carried down to the
third and to the fourth generations.

§

Assault should never be condoned; it is immoral; it is wrong.
And yet if there was ever one that could enlist sympathy with
the perpetrator rather than the victim of the blows, it is the one
we are about to witness.

The more one studies the character of Sumner, the easier it
becomes to picture him in his celebrated speech in the Senate on
the Kansas question, delivered in May, 1856. Tall, well-groomed,
serene, bland, cold, can't you see him? Comparing Senators Butler
and Douglas to Don Quixote and Sancho Panza he said: "The
Senator from South Carolina has read many books of chivalry and
believes himself a chivalrous knight, with sentiments of honor and
courage. Of course, he has chosen a mistress to whom he has
made his vows, and who, though ugly to others, is always lovely to
him; though polluted in the sight of the world, is chaste in his
sight. I mean the harlot Slavery. Let her be impeached in character, or any proposition be made to shut her out from the extension of her wantonness, and no extravagance of manner or hardi-
hood of assertion is then too great for the Senator." [78]

Perhaps among Mr. Sumner's "cultivated and morally excellent" friends of Boston this may have seemed a model of diplomacy animated by the bright if somewhat heavy sparks of Back Bay
humor. Here is the way Stephen A. Douglas regarded it: "Is it

Wendell Phillips

his object to provoke some of us to kick him as we would a dog in the street?" [79]

Two days later Preston Brooks, a member of the lower House and a nephew of Senator Butler, met Sumner and after charging him with the libel of his kinsman struck the Massachusetts reformer on the head with his cane, raining so many blows that he broke the implement with which he inflicted them.[80]

It was a dastardly assault, though it was provoked if any ever was. It was resented and condemned in the North and highly praised below the Mason-Dixon line. In Massachusetts, Sumner was a martyr, while the South hailed Preston Brooks as its hero. Here was the "irrepressible conflict"; here in miniature was the Civil War of which it was one, although a relatively unimportant, provocation. Is there not here a lesson for the advocates of peace and the enemies of war? Whenever in any country a leader takes up a cause provocative of hatred and recrimination in another, let him in person fight it out with a representative of the injured country. Such a plan would have many strong advantages. It would save vast expense, enormous bloodshed, untold misery and an aftermath of hatred. Charles Sumner of Massachusetts, bland, intolerant, self-opinionated, of course sincere, challenged an institution and sneered at those who harbored it! Preston Brooks, the fiery representative of the South, quick, far too quick to resent insult, in person visited punishment upon the slanderer! Why not in all future controversies pit the Brookses and the Sumners against each other and let them fight it out? This plan would doubtless thoroughly have appealed to Brooks, I think Sumner would have taken less kindly to it. Your Sumners are the kind who start wars knowing that others will have to fight them.

With a stroke of that genius which renders him one of the most brilliant portrayers of Americans, Gamaliel Bradford has made a comment on the Brooks affray worth quoting: "Sumner, we can well understand, was a husband, always gentle, always considerate, and always exasperating. I imagine that after six months of marriage Mrs. Sumner came to have a certain tenderness for the memory of Preston Brooks." [81]

§

Why have we made this long detour among the abolitionists?
It is not a detour; it is the main road. It was these agitators and
their friends and sympathizers who gained control of the legislative branch of the government in 1866, and as the "Radicals of
Congress" visited upon the vanquished South as mean and cowardly injustice as was ever done a beaten foe. Between them and
Andrew Johnson seeking the consummation of Lincoln's just plan
of reconstruction, there was waged one of the fiercest combats in
Anglo-Saxon constitutional history.

Sumner in person after recovering from the punishment of
Preston Brooks became a leader of the Radicals in the Senate.
Garrison and Phillips were not there, nor was the Pottawotomie
homicidal maniac, but behind the cruel eyes and in the misshapen
body of Thaddeus Stevens, John Brown's gnarled soul went
marching on. Sumner in the Senate abetted by Wade and other
lesser lights, Stevens in the House seconded by Benjamin Butler
of Massachusetts,—they and their followers and dupes became
the implacable foes of Andrew Johnson and enemies of the United
States.

We shall leave the abolitionists here to meet them again as
the "Radicals of Congress." Before doing so, however, let us
see how Johnson, long before these men had marked him as
a target for their hate, considered them and what they called
their services to their country. Here is what he said in the United
States Senate on February 6th, 1861: "There are two parties in
this country that want to break up the government. . . . The
nullifiers of the South, the secessionists, or disunionists. . . .
Who else is for breaking up this government? I refer to some
bad men in the North. There is a set of men who are called
abolitionists and they want to break up the government. They
are disunionists; they are secessionists; they are nullifiers. Sir,
the abolitionists and the distinguished Senator from Mississippi,
and his party, both stand in the same attitude, to attain the
same end, a dissolution of this Union; the one party believing
that it will result in their aggrandizement South, and the other

believing that it will result in the overthrow of the institution of slavery." [82]

Johnson then quoted from a resolution of the Massachusetts Anti-Slavery Convention, "that the one great issue before the country is the dissolution of the Union, in comparison with which all other issues with the slave power are dust in the balance; therefore, we give ourselves to the work of annulling this covenant with death. . . ." [83] He drove home the fact that Wendell Phillips had expressed approval of these sentiments. [84] And he called attention to this language of the *Liberator:* "We demand nothing short of a dissolution absolute and immediate. The Union which was founded by our fathers was cemented by the blood of the slave, and effected through his immolation." [85]

Then, from a Fourth of July oration delivered by William Lloyd Garrison at Framingham, Massachusetts, he revealed to the Senate this treason: "Let us then today . . . register our pledge anew before Heaven that we will do what in us lies to effect the eternal overthrow of this bloodstained Union"; [86] and these traitorous counsels uttered by Wendell Phillips at Boston on the twentieth of the previous month: "Sacrifice everything for the Union? God forbid! Sacrifice everything to keep South Carolina in it? Rather build a bridge of gold and pay her toll over it. Let her march off with banners and trumpets, and we will speed the parting guests. Let her not stand upon the order of her going, but go at once. Give her the forts and arsenals and sub-treasuries and lend her jewels of silver and gold, and Egypt will rejoice that she has departed." [87]

Johnson concluded his arraignment of the abolitionists with these words: "Whose allies are the abolitionists of the North if they are not the allies of the secessionists and disunionists of the South? . . . Their object is the same. They are both employing to some extent the same means. Here is Wendell Phillips; here is Garrison; here is the Anti-Slavery Society of Massachusetts, . . . the allies of the distinguished Senator from Mississippi. . . . Allies laboring to destroy the Government! . . . Here they stand presenting an unbroken front, to destroy this glorious Union which was made by our fathers." [88]

Their bigotry, their determination to bend all things to their purpose, their treasonable designs, their provocative publications and their threatening speeches arousing passion and engendering recrimination and retaliation,—all of those things Johnson knew. But that when they as Radicals would gain control of Congress, and conspire by cowardly and dishonorable means to wreak their vengeance on the bleeding and exhausted South, and that when he sought to thwart them in their purpose, they would turn from their blows upon a prostrate foe, and attempt to destroy him and his good name, and scatter his reputation down the avenues of history; these things he was yet to learn!

DRUMS

THERE is a novel charm in viewing a familiar scene from some new point of vantage. This is one reason why Lord Charnwood's "Life of Lincoln" is so valuable to us. Viewing him and his times through friendly yet discriminating British eyes, we seem to catch a new vision of the great American. Especially of interest is the English biographer's description of the Republican Convention of May 16th, 1860: "It met at Chicago in circumstances of far less dignity than the Democratic Convention at Charleston. Processions and brass bands, rough fellows collected by Lincoln's managers, rowdies imported from New York by Seward's, filled the streets with noise and the saloon keepers did good business. Yet the actual convention consisted of grave men in an earnest mood." [1]

Lincoln, although the most obscure of any of the candidates, was nominated on the third ballot. Seward, Chase or almost any of the prominent contenders were thought at first to have a better chance. For the vice-presidential nominee Hannibal Hamlin of Maine was chosen.[2] There was a premonition of success among the delegates as they reflected upon the dissension dismaying and dividing the councils of their opponents. The Democratic Convention had met at Charleston, South Carolina, on the twenty-third of the previous month. Its Southern and its Northern delegates were in disagreement as to the platform,—the Dred Scott case, the acquisition of Cuba and the attitude towards Northern legislation (no doubt unconstitutional) intended to nullify the operation of the Federal fugitive slave law in Vermont and other Northern states.[3] The Southern delegates were outvoted and most of them withdrew from the convention which thereupon adjourned to meet at Baltimore on June 18th. Before making any nomination at this adjourned convention, all the remaining Southern delegates left the hall and at Charleston ten days later nominated John C. Breckenridge of Kentucky.[4]

The Tennessee delegates thirty-six successive times gave their twelve ballots for their favorite son—Andrew Johnson.[5] In a letter of great dignity he withdrew his name.[6] Finally on June 23rd, Douglas received the necessary two-thirds' vote giving him the nomination.[7]

Feeling that Breckenridge of all the candidates was the one most favorable to the Union, Johnson gave him his support.[8] Entertaining this opinion, mistakenly as he afterwards admitted, it was but natural that he should wish to go along with what he considered the better sentiment of his state.[9] There were four candidates in the field: Lincoln, Douglas, Breckenridge and Bell. In the campaign, Johnson as the supporter of Breckenridge was, of course, opposed to Lincoln. "I voted against him; I spoke against him; I spent my money to defeat him, . . ." [10] he afterwards told the Senate. It was a strange fate that was to lead him into the very center of Lincoln's confidence, and to an unswerving support of Lincoln's policies. And yet when we reflect that with both of these men preservation of the Union was the strongest impulse of their lives, the fate was not so strange that brought them to work together for that end.

No graver error was ever made than that of the South, that Lincoln was an abolitionist. They had smarted under the strictures of Garrison and Phillips. They had been held up by such fanatics as the perpetrators of iniquity and had been castigated as a society built on wilful sin, although they knew "that their lives were honorable, their relations with their slaves humane, their responsibility for the existence of slavery among them remote." [11] In the heat of their resentment at these things, they mistakenly associated Lincoln with them. They remembered Nat Turner's rebellion and John Brown's raid at Harper's Ferry designed as a beginning of a general slave uprising throughout the South. South Carolina and her neighbors had not failed to note that John Brown had obtained arms and money in the North.[12]

The South forgot, however, or ignored Lincoln's Cooper Union speech wherein he said: "John Brown's effort was peculiar. It was not a slave insurrection. It was an attempt by white men to get up a revolt among slaves in which the slaves refused to participate. In fact, it was so absurd that the slaves with all their ignorance saw plainly enough it could not succeed. That affair in its philosophy corresponds with the many attempts related in history of the assassination of kings and emperors. An enthusiast broods over the oppression of the people until he feels himself commissioned by Heaven to liberate them. He ventures the attempt which ends in little else than in his own execution." [13]

The South knew that Northerners such as Emerson had described Brown as "the new saint" who was to "make the gallows glorious like the cross," [14] but they overlooked that the Convention which nominated Lincoln had denounced Brown's conspiracy as "among the gravest of crimes." [15]

It was, of course, impossible for the South during the campaign to know that on March 4th, 1861, Lincoln would say to them: "Apprehension seems to exist among the people of the southern states that by the accession of a Republican administration their property and their peace and personal security are to be endangered. There has never been any reasonable cause for such apprehension." [16]

But even if they had foreknown this language of conciliation it would not have changed their feeling; to such excitement had they come through thirty years of threat and insult,— thirty years of Phillips, Garrison and their fellow trouble-makers.

And so we find South Carolina's legislature in November, 1860, remaining in session to learn how the entire country had spoken at the polls. She had already heard from other Southern states that encouragement might be found in her secession plans if Lincoln were elected. When word of his victory was flashed, she purchased arms! She did more than that; she called a convention to meet at Charleston on the 20th of December. On the day appointed the convention met, repealed the action of its state convention of 1788 that had ratified the Federal Constitution, and formally decreed the dissolution of the Union "subsisting between South Carolina and other states under the name of the United

States of America." She declared herself a separate sovereignty and prepared for defense in case of war.[17]

George Pickett was a Virginian, a singularly gallant figure. It was he who later led the Confederate charge at Gettysburg. He had been the first to scale the parapets of Chapultepec in 1847 and it was he who unfurled the stars and stripes over the castle of the enemy.[18]   In 1861 he was stationed at Fort Bellington in the northwest and so could not reach Richmond until the 13th of September.   From there he wrote his sweetheart: "I at once enlisted in the army and on the following day was commissioned Captain.   But so bitter is the feeling here that my being unavoidably delayed so long in avowing my allegiance to my state has been most cruelly and severely criticized by friends—yes, and by relatives too."[19]   And again: "I of course, have always strenuously opposed disunion, not as doubting the right of secession, which was taught in our text book at West Point, but as gravely questioning its expediency.   I believed that the revolutionary spirit which infected both North and South was but a passing phase of fanaticism which would perish under the rebuke of all good citizens who would surely unite in upholding the Constitution; but when that great assembly composed of ministers, lawyers, judges, chancellors, statesmen, mostly white-haired men of thought met in South Carolina, and when their districts were called, crept noiselessly to the table in the centre of the room and affixed their signatures to the parchment on which the ordinance of secession was inscribed, and when in deathly silence, in spite of the gathered multitude, General Jamison arose and without preamble read: 'The ordinance of secession has been signed; I proclaim the state of South Carolina an independent sovereignty,' and lastly when my old boyhood's friend called for an invasion, it was evident that both the advocates and opponents of secession had read the portents aright."[20]

§

On the day before South Carolina's attempted withdrawal from the Union, but with knowledge, of course, that it was in the air, Andrew Johnson delivered in the United States Senate, "On the

Constitutionality and Rightfulness of Secession," as cogent an argument against it as was ever heard, there or elsewhere. It was the only voice in the Senate from below the Mason-Dixon line speaking the language of the Union: "I believe it is the imperative duty of Congress to make some effort to save the country from impending dissolution; and he that is unwilling to make an effort . . . is unworthy of public confidence . . . I am opposed to secession. I am unwilling voluntarily to walk out of the Union . . ., the result of the Constitution made by the patriots of the Revolution." [21]

Johnson proceeded then with an argument displaying as profound a patriotism and understanding of the nature of our government as was possessed by Jefferson, Hamilton or Marshall, from all of whom he quoted. "In July, 1788," he said, "when the Constitution of the United States was before the convention for ratification . . . Mr. Hamilton wrote a letter to Mr. Madison to know if New York could be admitted into the Union with . . . the privilege of receding within five or seven years if certain alterations and amendments were not made to the Constitution. . . . Mr. Madison in reply to that letter . . . says . . . that . . . New York could not be received on that plan. . . . The Constitution requires an adoption *in toto* and forever. It has been so adopted by the other states . . . The idea of reserving a right to withdraw was started at Richmond and considered as a conditional ratification which was itself abandoned as worse than a rejection." [22]

Johnson then read from a letter written by Jefferson to Col. Monroe from Paris on August 11th, 1786: "The states must see the rod, perhaps it must be felt by some one of them. . . ." And from another by the same pen: "When two parties make a compact there results to each a power of compelling the other to execute it." [23] And then from John Marshall's opinion in Cohens vs. Virginia: "But this supreme and irresistible power to make and unmake resides only in the whole body of the people, not in any subdivision of them. The attempt of any of the parts to exercise it is usurpation and ought to be repelled by those to whom the people have delegated their power of repelling it." [24]

He quoted from Madison's letter of December 23rd, 1832: "It is high time that the claim to secede at will should be put down by the public opinion, and I am glad to see the task commenced by one who understands the subject." [25]   Thus spoke Madison of Andrew Jackson!

Johnson's study of the Constitution was profound. Using the term "consolidation of government" to which he expressed himself as heartily opposed, by a strange prescience he seemed almost to foresee the dangerous Constitutional tendencies which have unhappily overtaken our own generation. "I am opposed to the consolidation of government," he said, "and I am as much for the reserved rights of states as any one; but rather than see this Union divided into thirty-three petty governments, with a little prince in one, a little potentate in another, a little aristocracy in a third, a little democracy in a fourth, and a republic somewhere else, . . . with quarreling and warring amongst the little petty powers which would result in anarchy; I would rather see this government today . . . converted into a consolidated government; it would be better for the American people; it would be better for humanity; better for Christianity, than breaking up this splendid . . . fabric . . . which has succeeded thus far without a parallel in the history of the world." [26]

And there was conciliation too in Johnson's speech. As a Senator from a border state he addressed both North and South, with a note of warning for each. To the North he said: "We in the South have complained of and condemned the position assumed by the Abolitionists." [27]   For the South he quoted from the speech of a South Carolinian: "South Carolina single-handed and alone was bound to go out of this accursed Union. . . . But if she could not, she could at least throw her arms around the pillars of the Constitution and involve all the states in a common ruin." [28] "Will the border states," Johnson cried, "submit to such a threat? . . . We say to you of the South we are not to be frightened and coerced. . . . When you come to break up and turn loose the different elements, there is no telling what combinations may take place in the future. It may occur for instance to the Middle States that they will not get so good a government by

going a little farther south as by remaining where we are; . . .
that by erecting themselves into a central independent republic,
disconnected either with the North or South, they could act as
a peacemaker, . . . as a great breakwater resisting the heated
and surging waves of the South, and the fanatical abolitionism
of the North." [29]

And then there is this fine sympathetic appeal: "When we
look around in the four states of Tennessee, Kentucky, Virginia
and Maryland, there are things about which our memories, . . .
linger with pride and pleasure. Go down into the old Dominion,
. . . where in 1781 Cornwallis surrendered his sword to the
immortal Washington. In the bosom of her soil are deposited
her greatest and her best sons. Move along in that trail and there
we find Jefferson, Madison and Monroe, and a long list of
worthies. We come next to North Carolina, God bless her! . . .
Go to King's Mountain, on her borders, and there you will find
the place on which the battle was fought that turned the tide of
the Revolution." [30]

To his adopted state he said: "In Tennessee we have our own
illustrious Jackson. . . . We have our Polk and our Grundy, and
a long list of others who are worthy of remembrance. . . . And
you are talking about breaking up this Republic with this cluster
of associations, these ties of affection around you. . . . We will
cherish these. . . . Angry waves may be lashed into fury . . .
blustering winds may rage; but we stand immovable upon our
basis, as on our own native mountains—presenting their craggy
brows, their unexplored caverns, their summits 'rock ribbed and
ancient as the Sun'—we stand speaking peace, association and
concert to a distracted Republic." [31] Nowhere in the North was
there a stronger voice speaking for the Union. In the South,
Johnson stood single-handed as its champion.

At the time of the delivery of Johnson's speech, both the House
and Senate were filled with those plotting destruction of the
Republic. Johnson's seat was not far from that of Senator Jefferson Davis, it was directly behind that of Judah P. Benjamin,[32]
the former about to become the President of the Confederacy and
the latter its Secretary of War and then of State. How John-

son's speech was received by Southern men let his own later words describe: "When I stood on this floor and fought the battle for the supremacy of the Constitution, and the enforcement of the laws, has the Senate forgotten that a bevy of conspirators gathered in from the other House and that those who were here crowded around, with frowns and scowls, and expressions of indignation and contempt toward me because I dared to raise my feeble voice in vindication of the Constitution, and the enforcement of the laws of the Union? Have you forgotten the taunts, the jeers, the derisive remarks, the contemptuous expressions that were indulged in? If you have, I have not." [33]

VII

BUCHANAN AND HIS CABINET

WHENEVER there shall be written a complete and authoritative anatomy of ineptitude, its central chapter will concern itself with the life and public services of James Buchanan. He was President from March 4th, 1857 to March 4th, 1861. His portrait affords the reader of character a study in kindly weakness and of vague vacillation. His administration was the greatest failure of any before or since his time, and we have had several both before and since whose blunders were impressive. What South Carolina needed on December 20th, 1860, was the kind of advice she received from the President of the United States on the 11th of December, 1832! But Buchanan was constitutionally weak. In the greatest crisis of America he quavered and failed!

In the whole history of impotence there is nothing more relaxed than his message to Congress on December 4th, 1860, denying the right of secession, but fearing to oppose it. The best picture of that low-water mark of statesmanship was drawn by Seward when he said it showed "conclusively that it is the duty of the President to execute the laws—unless somebody opposes him; and that no state has a right to go out of the Union—unless it wants to." [1]

Eight days after Andrew Johnson made his great speech against secession, commissioners from South Carolina held two conferences with Buchanan. They were angered because Major Anderson had dismantled Moultrie and had removed his garrison to the more defensible position of Fort Sumter. They said they thought that the President had given a pledge against that course, and told Buchanan bluntly to his face that he had broken his word. Here was Buchanan's answer: "You are pressing me too importunately; you don't give me time to consider; you don't give me time to say my prayers; I always say my prayers when required

63

to act upon any great state affair." [2]   If he had read Johnson's speech delivered eight days before, he could have known how to answer them, with or without his prayers!

In all the history of deliberative assemblies there was never uttered greater truth than that spoken by Andrew Johnson on the 6th of February, 1861, in the Senate while Buchanan was still President: "If such a man as Andrew Jackson were President of the United States at the present time, before this moment, steps would have been taken which would have preserved us as a united people without the shedding of blood, without making war." [3]

§

Out in Steubenville, Ohio, on the 18th of December, 1814,[4] there was born one whose character we must understand. Benjamin Lundy, the abolitionist whom we have met, was a frequent visitor at his father's home and held the lad upon his knee while he discoursed on abolition. Despite this early training, in 1836 it seems, no conscientious scruple prevented the young man from securing a nomination from the Democrats, and with their aid the election to the office of prosecuting attorney of Harrison County, nor six years later from obtaining "by a strict party vote" an election by a Democratic legislature to the post of law reporter. On the eve of his election he accosted Salmon P. Chase on the streets of Columbus and told him of his "entire accord" with the latter's anti-slavery opinions, and that he "hoped he should soon be able to take his place by his side." [5]   He never did so, but these inconsistencies will surprise us less as we pursue the story of this man, for his name was Edwin M. Stanton.

There is not a little difficulty in studying this character; it is always a problem to know just where to find him; he was so nimble and so versatile. That breadth of view which enabled him to be on both sides of the same question at the same time and to maintain such intimate relations with the protagonists of each as to render the other confident that he was acting as a spy within the hostile camp, reveals a pinnacle of ambidexterity which few attain. It was in keeping with his life's program when at an early

Edwin M. Stanton

day he found himself seeking and accepting Democratic prefer-
ment while secretly espousing ideas hostile to the party yielding
him support.

In 1849 he removed to Pittsburgh and at this time frequently
appeared in the United States Supreme Court. He was a good
lawyer. He achieved at this period an acquaintance with Judge
Jeremiah S. Black which helped him much.[6] From this friend
we learn that Stanton's "condemnation of the abolitionists was
unsparing for their hypocrisy, their corruption, their enmity to the
Constitution, and their lawless disregard for the rights of states
and individuals. Thus he won the confidence of the Democrats.
On the faith of such professions we promoted him in his business
and gave him office, honor and fortune." [7] In 1851 he met
Charles Sumner, who tells us that "whenever they met it was as
friends." [8]

One might suppose that this versatility in achieving association
with men and measures in such deadly conflict with each other
as to make each of the warring camps consider him its partisan,
would develop social gifts. But not so. His earliest expressed
opinion of Abraham Lincoln, for instance,—an opinion which in
various forms he afterwards voiced many times—lacks something
of that grace usually accompanying so valuable a capacity to
mingle with men who, under no circumstances, would mingle
with each other. In 1856 Stanton was a lawyer much better
known than Lincoln, and the latter felt not a little pleased to
find himself associated with him in a case. Lincoln could not,
however, have derived real pleasure from overhearing Stanton say
that "he would not associate with such a damned, gawky, long-
armed ape as that." [9] It would be unjust, however, to assume
from this that Stanton was always rude. To understand that
story it must be recalled that there seemed then no likelihood that
the obscure Lincoln could advance Stanton's strong ambitions. In
dealing with those from whom he expected benefit, the Pittsburgh
advocate could be polite indeed,—perhaps something more than
that. "It cannot be forgotten," says John T. Morse, Jr., one of
the ablest American biographers, "that he had the odious faults
of a bully; he was violent and insolent, but only when violence

and insolence were safe; he was supposed to be personally timid; he could be mean and unjust." [10]

These things help to a better grasp of his activities from December 20th, 1860, to March 4th, 1861, during which time he was the Attorney General of James Buchanan. By a strange circumstance he was appointed on the very day South Carolina seceded from the Union.[11] Judge Black, Buchanan's Secretary of State, who secured him the appointment, has told us that "though he was not in my debt, the apparent warmth of his nature impelled him to express his gratitude in most exaggerated language. . . . He sometimes overwhelmed me with hyperbolical demonstrations of thankfulness and friendship." [12] Buchanan afterwards thus wrote of him: "I appointed him Attorney General when Judge Black was raised to the State Department. . . . He was always on my side, and flattered me *ad nauseam*." [13]

Stanton was for seventy-two days a member of Buchanan's Cabinet. They were fateful days for the United States. Following South Carolina other states were prompt to join her in secession. By February 1st, 1861, Georgia, Florida, Alabama, Mississippi, Louisiana and Texas had followed her. On February 4th, 1861, delegates from the seceding states came together in Montgomery, Alabama, adopted a provisional Constitution for the "Confederate States of America" and elected as provisional President Jefferson Davis of Mississippi, and Alexander Stephens of Georgia as provisional Vice-President.[14]

On December 26th, 1860, Major Anderson abandoned Moultrie to take a stronger position at Fort Sumter. Three days later South Carolina took possession of the former fort and of the United States Arsenal at Charleston. On January 9th, 1861, secessionists attempted the seizure of the fort at Pensacola, and on the following day the *Star of the West* came bringing supplies and reinforcements to Fort Sumter, but was fired on by the Southerners and turned back. On January 11th, Commander Armstrong of the United States Navy was forced to surrender the Navy Yard at Pensacola. Of the arsenal at Baton Rouge, the loyal Major Haskins was in command. He was given neither guidance, orders, nor support from Washington, he had less than forty men, and when he was surrounded by five hundred of the militia of Louisiana, he surrendered.[15] During all this time Stanton sat quietly in the Cabinet of a President whose supine character encouraged Southerners in these aggressions.

How quietly Stanton sat within that Cabinet has been recorded for us by Judge Black, his sponsor and his fellow Cabinet member. "Mr. Stanton," he says, "was in perfect accord with the Administration before and after he became a part of it, on every question of fundamental principle. He had unlimited confidence in the men with whom he was acting and they confided in him. For his chief and some of his colleagues he professed an attachment literally boundless. . . . Stanton was no stormer in the presence of such men as he then had to deal with. His language was habitually deferential, . . . and his behavior . . . free from insolence. . . . He maintained unbroken his fraternal relations with his colleagues. . . . His language glowed with gratitude, his words spoke all the fervor of personal devotion to his chief and his colleagues; he gave his thorough approval to the measures they thought necessary to preserve the unity of the nation in the bonds of peace. To Mr. Toucey's face Mr. Stanton breathed no syllable of censure upon his conduct as head of the Navy Department. To the President or Cabinet he expressed no doubt of his wisdom, much less of his honesty. He met him every day with a face of smiling friendship."[16]

Who were those colleagues on whom Stanton beamed? Among them was Toucey of Connecticut, the Secretary of the Navy with strong Southern sympathies.[17] The head of the Interior Department was Thomson, a Mississippi states-rights man. During Stanton's first nine days of office, James Buchanan Floyd was Secretary of War.[18] He later became a brigadier-general in the Confederate service.[19] The quality of loyalty animating Buchanan's Cabinet was not improved by its inclusion of Howell Cobb of Georgia, the Secretary of the Treasury.[20] He became president of the Convention which drafted the provisional Constitution for the Confederacy, later a colonel, and finally a brigadier-general in the Confederate Army.[21] Four years later when Sherman was marching through Georgia, he discovered one night that the plantation at which he had been stopping was that of Howell Cobb. To his corps commander he issued this brief order: "Spare nothing." [22]

While Stanton thus sat smiling with his colleagues in that Cabinet, he was having dealings with men of other views. By Seward we are told: "Immediately after Mr. Stanton took office he put himself into direct communication with me at my house, employing Mr. Watson for that purpose. . . . Mr. Watson often brought with him suggestions in writing from Mr. Stanton and returned to Mr. Stanton with mine." [23]

The Attorney-General of James Buchanan was also at this time consorting with Charles Sumner, who has told us how in January 1861, he called upon him at his office and how Stanton, looking about and seeing someone in the room "whispered that we must be alone." He then sought various inner offices, but finding them all locked took Sumner into the corridor "where he began an earnest conversation saying that he must see me alone, that this was impossible at his office, that he was watched by the traitors of the South, that my visit would be known to them at once." That night at one o'clock he came to Sumner's house and there described to him a plan of the Southern leaders to gain possession of the National Capital. [24]

Let us leave Stanton here, "deferential" at Buchanan's council board, maintaining "unbroken his relations with his colleagues," [25] and return to Andrew Johnson of Tennessee standing alone among the Senators and Representatives of the South in his outspoken denunciation of secession.

VIII

JOHNSON AND LINCOLN

THE Confederate States of America were organized on the 4th
of February, 1861. On the following day Senator Johnson
addressed the Senate from which the "Ambassadors" of those
states had taken their departure. He reminded his remaining colleagues that on the previous December 19th he had denounced
secession as a "great political heresy. . . . Since I made that
speech . . . I have been the peculiar object of attack. I have
been denounced because I happen to be the first man south of
Mason and Dixon's line who entered a protest. . . ." [1]

After reviewing the condition of the country, he thus paid his
compliments to Buchanan: "It seems the inability of the United
States to defend and take care of its own property has been an
invitation to them to take possession of it. . . ." [2]   Has it come to
this that . . . your vessels must be fired upon, that your flag must
be struck, and still you are alarmed at coercion; and because a gallant officer has taken possession of a fort where he cannot very
well be coerced, a terrible cry is raised. . . ." [3]

Not many arguments are as telling as that which Johnson based
on the Richmond *Inquirer* of November 1st, 1814. This authority
from Virginia,—what could be more perfect!   In 1814 a convention had met at Hartford animated by New England's opposition
to the War of 1812 and threatened to withdraw from the Union.
Here is what Virginia thought about it: "Turn to the convention
at Hartford and learn to tremble at the madness of its authors.
How far will those madmen advance? . . . No man, no association of men, no set of states has a right to withdraw itself from
this Union of its own accord. The same power which knit us
together can only unknit. . . . Countrymen of the East! We call
upon you to keep a vigilant eye upon those wretched men who

would plunge us into Civil War and irretrievable disgrace. Whatever be the temporary calamities which may assail us, let us swear upon the altar of our country to save the Union." [4]   Here was a precedent if there was ever one!   "It was all right," said Johnson, "to talk about treason then; it was all right to punish traitors in that direction.   For myself I care not whether treason be committed North or South; he that is guilty of treason deserves a traitor's fate." [5]

"Go to Massachusetts during the War of 1812 and the Hartford Convention," he continued, "and there you will find men engaged in this treasonable and unhallowed work.   Even in 1845 Massachusetts in manifesting her great opposition to the annexation of Texas to the United States, passed a resolution resolving herself out of the Union. . . . Thus we find South Carolina and Massachusetts taking the lead in this secession movement." [6]

Was it not in reality Charles Sumner whom Johnson had in mind when he made this suggestion which, despite the tensity of the troubled hour brought down the laughter of the Senate: "I have sometimes thought it would be a comfort if Massachusetts and South Carolina could be chained together as the Siamese twins, separated from the continent, taken out to some remote and secluded part of the ocean, and there fast anchored to be washed by the waves and to be cooled by the winds; and after they had been kept there a sufficient length of time, the people of the United States might entertain a proposition of taking them back." [7]

Knowing that in the absent states the question of secession had not been submitted to the people, but had been decided entirely by convention,[8] Johnson said: "If the question could be taken away from politicians; if it could be taken away from the Congress of the United States, and referred to . . . the intelligent voting population, . . . they would settle it without the slightest difficulty and bid defiance to secessionists and disunionists." [9] The galleries applauded.[10]

After his speech of December 19th, 1860, the Southerners in the Senate began leveling against him attacks unprecedented in expressions of contempt and scorn.   Jefferson Davis had charged him with being the ally of Ben Wade. Here was Johnson's answer: "If Senator Wade or Senator anybody else is willing to . . . perpetuate . . . this great Union . . . I am his ally and he is mine; and I say to every Senator . . ., to every man that loves his country . . ., if you are for preserving this Union in its great and fundamental principles, I am your ally, without reference to your antecedents or what may take place hereafter." [11]

Between the making of that jibe by Davis and Johnson's reply to it, the Mississippian had become President of the Confederacy. "When I look at his gallant services," said Johnson, "finding him first in the military school of the United States, educated . . . at the expense of his country,—taught to love the principles of the Constitution; afterwards entering its service fighting beneath the Stars and Stripes, . . . I cannot understand how he can be willing to hail another banner, and turn from that of his country; . . . if I could not unsheathe my sword in vindication of the flag of my country . . . I would return the sword to its scabbard; I would never sheathe it in the bosom of my mother; never! never! never!" [12]

§

When Johnson made his speech of February 6th, North Carolina, Arkansas, Virginia and Tennessee had not yet seceded. While Buchanan faltered, the flames of disunion spread down the Atlantic coast and around the Gulf of Mexico. It was all but spontaneous combustion in the gulf states and in Georgia. The eyes of the country were turned upon the commonwealths to the north of these. There was the old Dominion, the mother of Presidents, whose inspiration had lit the troublous way to the Federal Constitution, whose sons in 1814 had turned with horror from the secession advocates of New England,—where would she take her stand? Where would stand North Carolina and Arkansas? And where the state whose Senator was sounding the tocsin against "treason"? When Johnson spoke, therefore, it was not the Senate alone, but the whole country that was listening, —the South with execration and the North with tumultuous approval.[13]

On February 9th Tennessee held an election to determine whether or not to assemble a convention "for vindicating the sovereignty of the state and the protection of its institutions." [14] In his speech three days earlier Johnson asked: "Whom are we going to fight? Who is invading Tennessee? Conventions are got up; a reign of terror is inaugurated, and if by the influence of a subsidized and mendacious press, an ordinance taking the state out of the Confederacy can be extorted, those who make such propositions expect to have an army ready; . . . then they will tell the people . . . that they must join a Southern Confederacy whether they will or not; they shall be lashed on to the car of South Carolina who entertains no respect for them, but threatens their institution of slavery unless they comply with her terms. Will Tennessee take such a position as that? I never will believe it!" [15] He was destined to disappointment.

Before the legislature of Tennessee adjourned on January 19th, it adopted resolutions asking the President of the United States and the Southern commonwealths each to communicate assurances of peaceable designs, deploring New York State's tender of men and money to the Federal government, and warning New York that if ever she sent armed forces south for the purpose of coercion, that Tennessee uniting with their Southern brethren would resist such an invasion to the last extremity.[16]

On February 9th, there was still in Tennessee sufficient loyalty to defeat even the calling of a convention to determine the question of secession. This victory for the Union, however, could not have been achieved but for the overwhelming majority of 24,749 votes rolled up in Eastern Tennessee for Federal allegiance.[17] Eight days before, Lincoln stood on the back platform of his train at Springfield and bade good-bye to old friends. "I now leave," he said, "not knowing when or whether ever I may return, with a task before me greater than that which rested upon Washington. Without the assistance of that Divine Being who ever attended him I cannot succeed. With that assistance I cannot fail." [18] On the very day of his departure the House of Representatives passed a resolution "that neither Congress, nor the people, or the government of the non-slave holding states have the right to legislate or interfere with slavery in any of the slave-holding states in the Union." [19]

Lincoln journeyed through New York, Philadelphia and other cities, arriving by a circuitous route finally on February 23rd in Washington. He had passed through Baltimore secretly and at night because of the warnings of Seward and of General Scott that there was a plot afoot to murder him. [20]

The nine days between his arrival in Washington and his taking of the oath on March 4th, were for Lincoln, as well as for the country, anxious days. Some of the time was spent with Seward who gave valuable advice as to the inaugural address. Seward's suggestion and Lincoln's recasting of it into the "Mystic Chords of Memory" paragraph [21] should present a joyous study to the anatomists of style. But literary labor could have had a more congenial atmosphere than that of Washington during the last days of February and the first days of March, 1861. Who were the Union's friends and who its foes? Everywhere the ferment could be felt.

It must have been a source of encouragement to Lincoln that there was at least one Southern voice shouting in this wilderness, proclaiming the integrity of the Union. Of course, Lincoln had read Johnson's February 6th oration; everyone had read it, North and South. And now while Lincoln waited for his inaugural and but ten days before the 4th of March, Johnson made his great reply to Senator Lane. Lane had indulged in abuse of the Tennessean and here was Johnson's answer: "It must be apparent not only to the Senate, but to the whole country that either by accident or design, there has been an arrangement that anyone who appeared . . . to vindicate the Union of the states should be attacked. . . ." [22] "In some of the states," he continued, "even the flag of our country has been changed. One state has a palmetto, another has a pelican, and another has the rattle-snake run up instead of the Stars and Stripes. . . . The people ought to be aroused to the condition of things; they ought to buckle on their armour. . . . I trust in God that the old flag of the Union will never be struck." [23]

The speech was interrupted frequently by applause from the

galleries; four times the presiding officer threatened to clear them. When Johnson finished there was a great outburst of excitement. Somewhere in the southeast corner of the ladies' gallery there was at first the clapping of a single pair of hands. This was hesitatingly imitated by a few spectators in the southern range of the same balcony,—and now there was cheering too. The galleries were packed, the applause grew and swept them back and forth like leaping flames. At first the powerful blows of the speaker's hammer could be heard above the tumult, but now they were lost in the growing cheers,—three cheers and three cheers more for the Union and for Andrew Johnson of Tennessee! "The exhibition," says the *Reporter*, "was the most vociferous and unprecedented that ever took place in either House of Congress."

Lincoln in his tragic isolation perhaps found solace in those cheers. Cheers for the Union! There were none too many in Washington that month!

§

Complete understanding of the causes of dissension, precise statement of the issue, definite announcement of a course of action, firmness and yet gentleness, all of these things contributed to make Lincoln's first inaugural address a masterpiece of conciliation. Having all these merits it possesses still one other; it is a nearly perfect model of English prose.

For our purpose its chief interest lies in the similarity of its views with those Johnson had been proclaiming in the Senate. In his speech of December 19th, 1860, Johnson said: "I am for abiding by the Constitution and according to law; and in abiding by it I want to retain my place here and put down Mr. Lincoln, and drive back his advances upon Southern institutions *if he designs to make any*." [24]

The third paragraph of the Inaugural came as his reassurance. "Apprehension," said Lincoln, "seems to exist among the people of the Southern states that by the accession of a Republican administration their property, their peace and personal security are to be endangered. There has never been any reasonable cause for such apprehension. . . . I have no purpose directly or indirectly to interfere with the institution of slavery. I believe I have no lawful right to do so and I have no inclination to do so." [25] The new President went even further. A proposed amendment to the Constitution that the Federal government should never interfere with slavery had passed Congress when he took his oath. Lincoln in his Inaugural told the country that "holding such a provision to be now implied in constitutional law I have no objection to its being made express and irrevocable." [26]

In his Inaugural Lincoln said: "I hold that in contemplation of universal law and of the Constitution the Union of these states is perpetual." [27] In his December speech, Johnson declared: "The Constitution was formed for perpetuity; . . . it never was intended to be broken up. It was commenced, it is true, as an experiment, but the founders . . . provided that this instrument could be amended and improved, . . . but they made no provision whatever for its destruction. . . ." [28] In Lincoln's Inaugural these words are found: "Perpetuity is implied, if not expressed, in the fundamental law of all national governments. . . . We find the proposition that in legal contemplation the Union is perpetual confirmed by the history of the Union itself." [29]

In December, Johnson, calling the silent graves of Washington, Madison and Jackson to bear mute testimony in support of his appeal to save the Union, exclaimed to the Senate: "And you are talking about breaking up this Republic with this cluster of associations, these ties of affection around you. May we not expect that some means may be devised by which it can be held together?" [30] Like some majestic organ tone, the perfect closing sentences of Lincoln's Inaugural reëchoed this appeal: "We are not enemies, but friends. We must not be enemies. Though passion may have strained it must not break our bonds of affection. The mystic chords of memory stretching from every battlefield and patriot grave to every living heart and hearthstone all over this broad land will yet swell the chorus of the Union when again touched, as surely they will be, by the better angels of our nature." [31]

The minds of Johnson and of Lincoln were moving in the same direction!

§

Had the South accepted Lincoln's constitutional amendment, they would have gained all they sought, save independence. "In your hands, my dissatisfied fellow citizens," Lincoln said, "is the momentous issue of Civil War." [32]   But the hotheads of South Carolina and her friends could not see it. They staked everything on the issue of war and lost,—everything.

We left Major Anderson at Fort Sumter. At the north side of the mouth of Charleston Harbor stood Fort Moultrie, which Anderson on December 26th had abandoned to the secessionists. At the south of the harbor lay the batteries on Cummings Point; to the west of Sumter stood Fort Johnson. The Union vessels bearing supplies and reinforcements were turned back. On April 11th, Anderson knew that four days more would starve him out. Nevertheless, when General Beauregard, acting for the Confederate government on that day demanded his surrender, he refused.

The next morning Southern pilots sighted a Federal vessel making for the harbor. Beauregard renewed his summons at 12.45 A. M. that morning. Anderson again refused, and was told that at 3.20 A. M. fire would be opened on his fort.

The South Carolinians were a little late in keeping their appointment, but at 4.30 A. M. a sudden flash lit the morning sky and with a dull roar a mortar projectile gracefully rising, its burning fuse marking its elliptical trajectory, buried its nose deep into the center of Fort Sumter. [33]   It was a clean hit. Any artillerymen, save those inside the fort, might have congratulated the executive officer at Fort Johnson on his accurate calculation of the firing data.

It was the first shot of the war! In Charleston there was at the harbor's edge a flagstone promenade. With the firing of that mortar the residents of the town came flocking here to see the show. The target lay but three miles out. At daybreak the guns of Robert Anderson opened up on Moultrie and the flashing batteries nearby. All day the firing continued. As the sun dropped behind the horizon Sumter ceased fire, but the Confederate guns kept on through the night at long intervals. In the morning the Confederates pushed their gun crews harder. The flagstaff went down and Anderson ran his colors up again. But the flames were creeping toward the powder magazine. Nevertheless, his guns continued speaking. It was game! Appreciating full well the situation, the watchers on the shore cheered the Yankee gallantry. But there were no reinforcements; there was no help to come from any quarter, and in the afternoon Anderson surrendered. Beauregard's terms were generous. The little garrison saluted Old Glory with fifty guns and with colors flying and their fifes screaming "Yankee Doodle" they marched down to the transport. Charleston went mad with frantic joy.[54]

"It seems that at this time," Johnson afterwards told the Senate, "Mr. Pryor from Virginia was in Charleston. The Convention was sitting and it was important that the cannon's roar should be heard in the land. Virginia was to be taken out of the Union, although a majority of the delegates in the Convention were elected against secession, and in favor of the Union. We find that after being in possession of the fact by the fifteenth of the month the garrison would be starved out and compelled to surrender. On the morning of the twelfth, they commenced the bombardment, fired upon your fort and upon your men. They knew that in three days the troops in Fort Sumter would be compelled to surrender; but they wanted war. It was indispensable to produce an excitement in order to hurry Virginia out of the Union, and they commenced the war." [55]

It was war now! On the day after Anderson's surrender, Lincoln called for "the militia of the several states of the Union to the aggregate number of 75,000." [56]

Governor Isham G. Harris of Tennessee belonged to the pro-slavery faction of his state. To Lincoln's call he answered: "Tennessee will not furnish a single man for coercion, but fifty thousand if necessary, for the defense of our rights and those of our Southern brothers." [57] The tide in favor of secession was sweeping in in Tennessee. John Bell declared for the Confederacy;

his friends followed him. Everywhere, except among her Eastern mountains, the lovers of the Union through fear adopted silence.[38]

On April 24th, Gideon Pillow wrote from Nashville to the Confederate Secretary of War: "We are now united in Middle and West Tennessee, and we think East Tennessee will soon be so, or nearly so. Etheridge attempted to make a speech at Paris yesterday, but was prevented by the people after a short conflict with pistols, in which four were wounded and one killed. Johnson has at last returned to East Tennessee and had his nose pulled on the way; was hissed and hooted at all along on his route. . . . His power is gone and henceforth there will be nothing left but the stench of the traitor." [39]

It was only a mob that would dare attempt indignities such as these upon this man. On his return from Washington after Lincoln's Inaugural, while passing through Virginia his train stopped at Lynchburg. It was Sunday; a large crowd was loitering about the station. They learned that Johnson was in the train. They dragged him from his car by the nose, they spat in his face, they kicked him and knocked him down, they procured a halter and were leading him toward a tree, when an old man in the crowd raised his voice above the ribald cheers of the lynching party and cried: "His neighbors at Greeneville have made arrangements to hang their Senator on his arrival. Virginians have no right to deprive them of that privilege." The mob acquiesced and Johnson's life was spared.[40] Tennessee was in an uproar over his bold stand for the Union. At Knoxville, at Memphis, at Nashville and elsewhere throughout the South he was hung and shot in effigy, his name became a thing to madden secessionists everywhere into a tumultuous frenzy of execration.[41]

On the 25th of April the Tennessee legislature reconvened and Governor Harris urged the passage of an ordinance of secession.[42] Hilliard, a Confederate agent, was on the ground and wrote to Secretary Toombs of the Confederacy: "A great change has taken place in public sentiment here within a few days, and the feeling in favor of our government rises into enthusiasm. . . . Governor Harris is now sending troops into Virginia." [43] The news of Sumter had given Harris and his fellow disunionists increased prestige in Tennessee. On May 6th the legislature placed in his hands unprecedented military power. It empowered him to raise and equip 55,000 volunteers, placed him in charge of the troops and of the direction of the state's defense.[44] On May 1st it authorized him to enter into a military league with the Confederacy. It was done. Jefferson Davis was given control of the state militia, and the Confederate government was invited to make its capital at Nashville. Five days later an election was decreed for June 8th to determine the question of secession; [45] but Harris had already irrevocably committed his state to the Confederacy before the people had a chance to vote upon it.

Throughout the month of May, utterly oblivious to the death threats of men not unaccustomed to the use of arms, Johnson canvassed Eastern Tennessee speaking for the Union.[40] The known loyalty of this region was a thorn in the flesh of the disunionists of the west and middle sections of the state. They knew they could carry their constituencies for rebellion, but how about the mountaineers where Johnson lived? The most persuasive speakers among the Confederate sympathizers were hurried into Eastern Tennessee. One of these was our old friend, Gustavus A. Henry, "the eagle orator" whom Johnson had defeated for the governorship in 1853.[47] Eastern Tennessee became in every sense a battle ground on which this issue was fought out. While the contest was waging on the stump, soldiers were recruiting both for the Union and the Confederacy. Here indeed, were the materials for a campaign unprecedented for heat and fire.[48] The loyal men were described by the "Memphis Appeal" and other disloyal organs as "the little batch of disaffected traitors who hover around the noxious atmosphere of Andrew Johnson's home." [49]

Before great crowds the debates continued under circumstances of unparalleled excitement. Conflicts between soldiers and civilians were of everyday occurrence. As he rode the mountain passes, journeying from town to town, there was not an hour when Johnson's life was not in danger. He laughed at warnings and continued on his way, pressing home his arguments for the Union. In the meantime Governor Harris was raising troops,

and had filled the state with soldiers. An overwhelming sentiment in favor of the Confederacy was growing. It was a brave
man who dared to speak his mind in favor of the Union.[50]

At last on the 8th of June the people came down to the polls
to vote upon secession. The Union cause was defeated by a great
majority. But in Eastern Tennessee neither soldiers, nor threats,
nor imported orators could turn the tide of loyalty, and the Union
cause rolled up a majority there, albeit an ineffective one, of more
than 33,000 votes. On the 24th of June, Harris proclaimed his
state a member of the Confederacy.[51] She was the last to join;
Arkansas on May 6th, North Carolina on May 20th and Virginia
on May 23rd had previously given their allegiance to the Davis
government.[52]

Eleven states had now declared their independence. Of their
twenty-two Senators there was one alone who stood by the government, whose Constitution they had all sworn to support and to
uphold. The Old Dominion might secede, North Carolina might
secede, their confederated neighbors might secede, his own state
might secede, but Andrew Johnson would not secede!

§

Congress was not in session when Lincoln called for volunteers.
For four months Lincoln ruled alone, straining to the uttermost
the war powers granted him by the Constitution. It was not
until July 4th that Congress met in extra session.

Johnson now made his way back to Washington. His journey
carried him through Cincinnati. As he came into the station there
was a great gathering of loyal men to express appreciation of his
conduct. Overwhelmed by the enthusiasm of the demonstration,
at first he scarce could speak, but finally he began: "I am a citizen
of the South and of the state of Tennessee . . . I am also a
citizen of the United States!"[53] Amid torrents of applause he
denounced the doctrine of secession as "hell-born and hell-
bound."[54]

While Johnson was yet speaking a train filled with Confederate
soldiers drew into the station. They learned that he was there
and threatened to kill him. Warning of this reached Johnson

while he spoke; he did not pause, but continued with renewed vigor his denunciation of secession. As the Confederates were making for the speaker's stand, the engine whistle blew calling them back to their train.[55] At this point the speaker launched into a description of what the loyal men in Tennessee had just been through. The secessionists had declared, he said, "that our fate was to be the fate of traitors, and that hemp was growing, and that the day of our execution was approaching. . . . We have met all these things. . . . We have met them face to face, . . . at least in one portion of the state. . . ."[56]

"I know," he continued, "that in reference to myself and others, rewards have been offered, and it has been said warrants have been issued for our arrest. Let me say to you here today that I am no fugitive, especially no fugitive from justice." There was laughter at this sally, and Johnson went on: "If I were a fugitive, I would be a fugitive from tyranny,—a fugitive from the reign of terror. . . . We, the people of Tennessee have been handed over to this Confederacy, I say, like sheep in the shambles to be disposed of as Jefferson Davis and his cohorts may think proper."[57]

It was small wonder that he should have been serenaded in Cincinnati by the Union men. It is even less surprising that Confederate soldiers should have sought to kill him. His appeals in the Senate, his struggles to keep his own state loyal, the persecution and abuse that he had suffered had made his name known and admired wherever the lovers of the Union lived,—known and execrated wherever disloyalty reared its head. As though by some seismic shock the whole structure of the Constitution was shaking with titanic tremors. They who loved the old temple and did not wish to see it fall, watched with frightened applause while Andrew Johnson, as with some steel stanchion, put his mighty shoulders underneath the very keystone of the central arch.

§

On July 4th, 1861, Abraham Lincoln sent a message to the Congress reciting what had taken place since his Inaugural. He spoke of his call for volunteers, his suspension of the *habeas corpus*, and renewed his argument against secession. He questioned whether there was a majority of the legally qualified voters in any state, except perhaps South Carolina, in favor of disunion. "There is much reason to believe," he wrote, "that the Union men are in the majority in many, if not in every one, of the so-called seceded states. The contrary has not been demonstrated in any one of them. It is ventured to affirm this even of Virginia and Tennessee; for the result of an election held in military camps, where the bayonets are all on one side of the question voted upon, can scarcely be considered as demonstrating popular sentiment. At such an election all that large class who are at once for the Union and against coercion would be coerced to vote against the Union." [58] Lincoln had not been unobserving of what had taken place in Tennessee nor could he have failed to note what Andrew Johnson had been doing there.

The President then defined the nature of his country's struggle: "This is essentially a people's contest," he told them. "On the side of the Union it is a struggle for maintaining in the world that form and substance of government whose leading object is to elevate the condition of men; to lift artificial weights from all shoulders; to clear the paths of laudable pursuit for all; to afford all an unfettered start and a fair chance in the race of life." And he continued: "I am most happy to believe that the plain people understand and appreciate this. It is worthy of note that while in this the Government's hour of trial large numbers in the Army and Navy who have been favored with the offices have resigned and proved false to the hand which had pampered them, not one common soldier or common sailor is known to have deserted his flag. . . ." [59] To the last man, so far as known, they have successfully resisted the traitorous efforts of those whose commands but an hour before they obeyed as absolute law. This is the patriotic instinct of plain people. They understand without an argument that destroying the Government which was made by Washington means no good to them." [60]

Lincoln asked that he be given "the legal means for making this contest a short and decisive one." "The people," he said, "will save their Government if the Government itself will do its part only indifferently well." [61]

For many days in that July, Lincoln's message was debated in the Senate and the House. There were many who deplored his acts as those of a "dictatorship," and were hesitant to grant coöperation. There were many who supported him; there was not one who accorded him more powerful aid than Andrew Johnson.

There were many who advised immediate action, ignoring the fact that an army, especially the intricate machinery of supply, could not be improvised. The public voice demanded instant action. "On to Richmond!" was the cry.[62] The agitation was stimulated by the press. General McDowell and his 36,000 troops, with bands blaring and colors flying, were reviewed by the President. Beauregard and his 22,000 at Bull Run were to be annihilated,—the South in one encounter was to be humbled.

The agitation among civilians was intense. "The various regiments," wrote one of General McDowell's staff, "were brilliantly uniformed according to the aesthetic taste of peace and, during the nineteenth and twentieth, the bivouacs at Centreville almost within cannon range of the enemy were thronged with visitors, official and unofficial, who came in carriages from Washington, were under no military restraint, and passed to and fro among the troops as they pleased, giving the scene the appearance of a monster military picnic."[63]

On the first day of this "military picnic" General McDowell at Blackburn's Ford began the Battle of Bull Run. His difficulties were enormous. He had no reliable surveys, no adequate maps, no proper guides, no trained staff; his supply wagons were driven by undisciplined civilian drivers. He was commanding an armed mob.

The climax of the battle came on Sunday, July 21st, a glorious midsummer day,—glorious overhead, not so glorious unfortunately, for the Union arms. There was a great desire on the part of Congressmen to see the "boys in blue" at work. Printed passes had been issued. Senator Benjamin F. Wade, whom we have met before and will meet often again, was one of the pass-holders; with other legislative friends he went over into Virginia to see the battle.[64] It was very hot; a little past noon the trouble began. As the Union soldiers were ascending Henry Hill, two of their batteries galloped forward, coming within five hundred yards of the Confederates. The batteries were supported by two battalions of gaudy Zouaves with their white turbans and red trousers, but there was a Confederate there who saw his opportunity. He had with him one hundred and fifty horsemen, but that much cavalry with "Jeb" Stuart in command was an army in itself. He charged the Zouaves. In a moment he had cut them to pieces; those who were not sabred, ran. The Thirty-Third Virginians were waiting, and at this moment charged the guns. The gun crews were slain; the horses went down; all the Zouaves who were alive were running. It was the beginning of the rout. Other Federals, however, pressed forward and plunged up Henry Hill; on its reverse slope Stonewall Jackson was waiting for them. As the Federals appeared Jackson gave this final order: "Reserve your fire until they come within fifty yards, then fire and give them the bayonet; and yell like furies when you charge." [65]

As the Union soldiers reached the crest, the long gray lines rose, and screaming the high Rebel yell, charged home! At this moment Kirby Smith's brigade arrived and bore down upon the Union flank. The Federal advance melted; by companies, platoons and squads they turned and fled. Their panic was infectious. There was no discipline, there had been little drill. They were civilians after all, scarcely accustomed to their uniforms. In a moment the army became a mob in disorderly retreat. Horses and soldiers and sightseeing Congressmen and civilians milling and churning in one disordered mass, were running for their lives. [66] Somewhere in this torrent of retreat Benjamin F. Wade was running with his fellow legislators.

Washington was waiting for the news. It came soon enough. Before long Ben Wade and his friends arrived [67] with the whole story of the rout.

Five days later Edwin M. Stanton, who sat watching events at the capital, wrote Buchanan: "The dreadful disaster of Sunday can scarcely be mentioned. The imbecility of the administration culminated in that catastrophe; an irretrievable misfortune and national disgrace never to be forgotten are to be added to the ruin of all peaceful pursuits, and national bankruptcy is the result of Lincoln's running the machine for five months." [68]

Stanton was not the only one to prophesy the irretrievability of this defeat, nor was his the only Northern voice denouncing Lincoln for the battle. In the South there was corresponding jubilation.

§

The day after Stanton wrote his denunciation of the President, Andrew Johnson delivered an impassioned defense of Lincoln in the Senate.

This was the way he handled the Bull Run disaster: "Although the Government has met with a little reverse within a short distance of this city, no one should be discouraged and no heart should be dismayed. It ought only to prove the necessity of . . . exerting still more vigorously the power of the Government. . . . Let the energies of the government be redoubled, and let it go on with this war. . . . Let the Constitution be inscribed on its banners, and the enforcement of the laws be its watchword." [69] After quoting from Lincoln's message, "This is essentially a people's contest," Johnson continued: "I think the question is fairly and properly stated by the President, that it is a struggle whether the people shall rule; . . ." [70]

There had been many days of angry debate before Johnson rose to make this speech, scathing criticism of Lincoln was heard everywhere. Senator Breckenridge of Kentucky (the same whom Johnson had supported against Lincoln) argued that the passage of a joint resolution approving Lincoln's action would make him "feel himself warranted . . . to subordinate the civil to the military power; . . . if we pass it we are upon the eve of putting . . . in the hands of the President . . . the power of a dictator." [71]

Johnson now took up the cudgels for the badgered President, with both hands. Referring to Lincoln's suspension of the *habeas corpus* act, he said: "The power which has been exercised in this instance is no new thing. In great emergencies, when the

life of a nation is in peril, . . . to scan too critically its acts
. . . is to . . . paralyze its energies. . . . If those who seem to
violate the laws . . . in their efforts to preserve the Government
are to be called to account, wait until the country passes out of
its peril . . . and ascertain to what extent the law has been
violated, if indeed it has been violated at all." [72]

He sustained Lincoln's call for volunteers, quoting from an
opinion written by Judge Story: "One of the best means to repel
invasion is to provide the requisite force for action before the
invader himself has reached the soil; . . . the authority to decide
whether the exigency has arisen belongs exclusively to the President and . . . his decision is conclusive upon all other persons.
. . ." [73] Johnson was not a lawyer, but he had made himself a
statesman. With the great decisions of the Supreme Court he
was as familiar as with the history of his country. There was
no one in the Senate of his time who could draw from those
arsenals more powerful weapons or use them more effectively.

He continued: "Traitors and rebels are standing with arms in
their hands, and it is said that we must go forward and compromise with them. . . . I say to them: . . . 'Ground your arms;
obey the laws; acknowledge the supremacy of the Constitution;
when you do that, I will talk to you about compromises. All the
compromise that I have to make is the compromise of the Constitution of the United States. It is one of the best compromises that
can be made. We lived under it from 1789 down to the 20th
day of December, 1860, when South Carolina undertook to go out
of the union.' " [74]

He quoted exhaustively from Southern newspapers and the
words of Southern men. From the speech of a Louisiana delegate to the Constitutional Convention of the Confederacy, he cited
this: "The contest is not between North and South as geographical sections; . . . the real contest is between the two forms of
society which have become established, the one at the North and
the other at the South." [75] From the Richmond *Whig* he quoted:
"Rather than submit to the administration now in power in the
city of Washington . . . we would prefer passing under the constitutional reign of the amiable Queen of Great Britain." [76] "They

have," said Johnson, "lost confidence in the integrity, in the capability, in the virtue and intelligence of the great mass of the people to govern; . . ." [77]

It is a strong man and an honest one who dares to admit his own mistake. He had supported Breckenridge for President, he said, because he had believed him "a better Union man than any in the field." [78] Manfully he acknowledged now his error.

Of the President's proclamation blockading Southern ports, Johnson declared: "I think he did precisely what was right. He would have been derelict in his duty, and to the high behest of the American people, if he had . . . failed to exert every power within his reach. . . ." [79] "I am a Democrat," he said, "believing the principles of this Government are Democratic. . . . I believe Democracy can stand notwithstanding all the taunts and jeers that are thrown at it throughout the Southern Confederacy." [80]

Nohing could be more telling than his account of what loyal Tennesseeans had suffered for the Union. He told how laws had been enacted "declaring it treason to say or do anything in favor of the government of the United States." "Since I left my home," he said, "having only one way to leave the state through two or three passes coming out through the Cumberland Gap, I have been advised that they had even sent their armies to blockade these passes in the mountains, as they say, to prevent Johnson from returning with arms and munitions to place in the hands of the people to vindicate their rights, repel invasion and put down domestic insurrection and rebellion." [81]

His appeal for Union support in his own state struck a note of such lofty exhortation as could only have been voiced by one who had read and reread the King James version of the old Testament: "We want the passes in our mountains opened, we want deliverance and protection for a downtrodden and oppressed people who are struggling for their independence without arms. . . . You may be too late in coming to our relief; or you may not come at all, though I do not doubt that you will come; they may trample us under foot; they may convert our plains into graveyards, and the caves of our mountains into sepulchres; but they will never take us out of the Union or make us a land of slaves;—no, never! We intend to stand as firm as . . . our own majestic mountains that surround us." [82]

Perhaps the finest character among the leaders of the Confederacy was Alexander H. Stephens, its diminutive vice-president,—diminutive in physical stature, not in courage, physical or moral, in intellectual attainment or wise comprehension of his times. [83] The effect of Johnson's words was not lost upon this former Senator from Georgia. Writing after the war was over and with a detached capacity to see both sides, he tells us that Johnson's speech "was one of the most notable . . . ever delivered by any man on any occasion. I know of no instance in history when one speech effected such results, immediate and remote, as this one did. . . . This speech throughout was characterized by extraordinary fervor and eloquence, and in my judgment, did more to strengthen and arouse the war passions of the people at the North than everything else combined." It "had a special . . . influence springing from the very source from which it emanated. The author stood solitary and alone,—isolated from every public man throughout the Southern states, and from nearly every public man throughout the Northern states attached to the same political party to which he belonged, upon the questions involved." [84]

Is it any wonder that Andrew Johnson's winged words sped their way down Pennsylvania Avenue straight to the heart of the greatest Democrat of time, or that when the occasion came Lincoln chose that voice and right arm to sustain the Union cause in Tennessee, and later as his second in command, in the whole nation?

§

Let us leave Johnson in his valiant support of the administration and turn for a moment to two men, one of whom was then Lincoln's Secretary of War, and the other about to hold that office.

Simon Cameron was one of the ablest political bosses of his time in Pennsylvania. In 1860 he was a competitor of Lincoln for the Presidential nomination. [85] Despite the general belief that Cameron was a shady politician, Lincoln as a result of a

political deal made for him without his knowledge, appointed
Cameron his first Secretary of War. His management of the War
Department from the beginning was a failure; it was scandalously
corrupt.[86]   An able historian has catalogued him as one of the
"astute grafters." [87]   Congress finally passed a vote censuring him
and his administration.   Lincoln sterilized this infection point by
kicking Cameron upstairs and making him his minister to
Russia.[88]

After the retirement of Buchanan, Stanton had stayed on in
Washington watching the new administration and reporting to
his former chief.   Stanton's letters are unpleasantly suggestive of
the reports made by an operative to the head of a detective agency.
On March 14th, he wrote Buchanan: "There is no doubt of Sumter being evacuated.   Report says the order has gone, but that, I
think, is doubtful." [89]   He was watching closely, and two days
later again reported to the former President: "During the last
week the order for the removal of troops has not as . . . yet
been given.   Yesterday it was still under debate.   Every day
affords proof of the absence of any settled policy or harmonious
concert of action in the administration. . . . There has been
agreement in nothing.   Lincoln, it is complained in the streets,
has undertaken to distribute the whole patronage small and great,
leaving nothing to the chiefs of departments; . . . it is certain
that Anderson will be withdrawn.   I do not believe there will be
much further effort to assail you. . . ." [90]

On April 3rd Stanton again poured out his accumulated information: "The policy in respect to seceding states remains in
obscurity.   There has been a rumor in the last two or three days
that notwithstanding all that has been said, there will be an
effort to reinforce Fort Sumter; but I do not believe a word of
it. . . . The first month of the administration seems to have furnished an ample vindication of your policy, and to have rendered
all occasion of others' defense needless.   The rumors from Richmond are very threatening; secession is rapidly gaining strength
there. . . ." [91]

Why was Stanton reporting so assiduously about the progress of
secession to a former President whose Cabinet had been a hotbed

of secessionists? On April 10th, Stanton again wrote to Lincoln's predecessor: "I saw Mr. Holt on Sunday. I had supposed he might have some knowledge of the designs of the administration and the purpose of the recent military and naval movements; but he said he had none. . . . Quinn has just returned from Mississippi. He speaks with confidence of the stability and power of the Confederacy and evidently sympathizes strongly with them. . . ." [92]

There was a strange pertinacity in this correspondence. At twelve midnight Stanton added this postscript to his letter of April 10th: "It is certain the administration is panic-stricken for some cause. They commenced this morning an active enrollment of the militia. I have just been told . . . that the administration designed to succor Major Anderson. . . . It is now reported . . . that the batteries have opened on Sumter." [93] Stanton's midnight report of April 10th was a little premature. The firing did not begin until 4.20 A. M. on April 12th.[94] His postscript, however, would indicate how closely he was advised of Confederate intentions.

The day before South Carolina's guns awoke, he renewed with James Buchanan the correspondence he had broken off twelve hours before. "There is great soldiering in the town the last two days. . . . The feeling of loyalty to the government has greatly diminished in this city. Many persons who would have supported the government under your administration refuse to be enrolled. Many who were enrolled have withdrawn and refuse to take the oath. The administration has not acquired the confidence and the respect of the people here. Not one of the cabinet has taken a house or brought his family here. . . . They all act as though they meant to cut and run at a moment's notice. . . . This is secretly felt and talked about by the people of the city, and they feel no confidence in the administration that betrays so much insincerity. And besides a strong feeling of distrust in the candor and sincerity of Mr. Lincoln personally and of his cabinet has sprung up. If they had been merely silent and secret there might have been no ground of complaint. But assurances are said to have been given and declarations made in conflict with the facts

now transpiring in respect to the South, so that no one speaks of Lincoln or any member of his cabinet with respect or regard. . . ." [95]

No rumor about Lincoln was too circuitous, or adverse report of him too mean, for Stanton gleefully to hurry off to old Buchanan. On May 16th he wrote: "No description could convey to you the panic that prevailed here for several days after the Baltimore riot, and before communication was reopened. This was increased by the reports of the trepidation of Lincoln that were circulated through the streets." [96]

Thus wrote Stanton before he entered Lincoln's Cabinet. When the war portfolio was offered him he found no difficulty in accepting the trust from one whom he had secretly condemned. The quality of his loyalty is illuminated by his comment in 1862 made three months after he took his seat at Lincoln's council board. It became current gossip that Stanton and Black had both threatened to resign from the Buchanan Cabinet because the latter in February, 1861, was about to order Anderson back from Sumter to Fort Moultrie. [97] Judge Black when confronted with this made a direct answer: "The story . . . is wholly fiction, . . ." [98] But Stanton pronounced the story merely as "exaggerated," and added: "I have no time now to be watching and correcting what may be told of last winter's troubles in Mr. Buchanan's cabinet in which I was an unwilling member. . . ." [99] Of all the giant qualities of Lincoln's soul, there is none more impressive than his forbearance with his second Minister of War and his willingness to tolerate that harsh and unlovely personality in the very center of his councils. Lincoln would tolerate anything, even one who had considered him an ape, if he thought that it would help to save the Union.

Gideon Welles pronounced Stanton as "more violent than vigorous, . . . more vain than wise; . . . rude, arrogant and domineering toward those in subordinate positions if they will submit to his rudeness, but . . . a sycophant and dissembler in deportment with those whom he fears." [100]

"Undoubtedly," says Mr. Morse in one of the ablest biographies of the war President, "Mr. Lincoln was the only ruler known to history who could have coöperated for years with such a minister." [101]   And yet Stanton, adds this same writer, "had virtues, devotion to the cause,—a very greed for hard work, financial integrity and merciless energy against the rascal contractors. But it cannot be forgotten that he had the odious faults of a bully; he was violent and insolent, but only when violence and insolence were safe; he was supposed to be personally timid; he could be mean and unjust; above all he repeatedly outraged the magnanimous forbearance of Mr. Lincoln in a way which no American can forgive." [102]

IX

MILITARY GOVERNOR

WITH the exception of Virginia alone, Tennessee was the chief battle ground of the Civil War. Four hundred and fifty-four battles and engagements were fought out within her borders.[1] Much of the fighting took place in Eastern Tennessee. The armies of the Union and of the Confederacy marched and countermarched through her mountain passes and availed themselves of her principal railroad as a medium of communication and supply.

The mountaineers suffered much for their loyalty to the Union cause, yet they never faltered in their steadfast courage. In August, 1861, Confederate soldiers overran this region. Loyal men were impressed into the Southern ranks, the Confederate conscription law was executed, so as surely to include those of known loyalty to the Lincoln government. Any who offered resistance were certain to await the fate of traitors. Crops were confiscated and sent South while uncontrolled groups of mounted men burned barns and houses and drove off the cattle before them. Special objects of plunder were Johnson's old supporters.[2] "Parson Brownlow's book" is a Jeremiad of these sufferings.

It was with no docility that the hardy mountaineers submitted when they had to, to these indignities, and always they saw the vision of a Union army coming to their aid. "They look for the reëstablishment of the Federal authority," wrote a Southern sympathizer to Jefferson Davis on November 12th, 1861, "with as much confidence as the Jews look for the coming of the Messiah, and I feel quite sure when I assert that no event or circumstance can change or modify their hope."[3] But these Unionists had a spokesman within the Senate of the United States in Andrew Johnson. On January 31st, 1862, he again laid before the country

93

how dear a price loyalty was forced to pay in Tennessee: "The people of my state, downtrodden and oppressed by the iron heel of Southern despotism, appeal to you for protection. . . . The only response to their murmur is the rattling and clanking of chains that bind their limbs. . . . Our people are oppressed and downtrodden and you give them no remedy. . . . They are hunted and pursued like the beasts of the forest by the secession and disunion hordes. . . . They are shot or hung for no crime save a desire to stand by the Constitution of the United States. Helpless children and innocent females are murdered in cold blood. Our men are hung and their bodies left upon the gibbet." [4]

From this speech too we catch another glimpse of Eliza McCardle and the children, and what it meant in Tennessee in 1862 to belong to the family of a loyal Senator. Poor Eliza, the years had dealt none too kindly with her. Toil and worry had not tamed her spirit, but they had broken her strength. She was now an invalid. Let her husband's words to the Senate and the listening country tell her story: "My wife and children have been turned into the street, and my house has been turned into a barrack, and for what? Because I stand by the Constitution. . . . This is my offense. . . . My sons have been imprisoned; my son-in-law has had to run to the mountains." [5]

Lincoln was quick to sympathize, nor was he slow to appreciate the strategic political importance of Eastern Tennessee. In October, 1861, he was pressing upon the War Department the advantage of holding an outlet from the Cumberland Water Gap into Virginia and Kentucky. In November General Buell was urged to make a prompt advance into Eastern Tennessee. Johnson's prayer had not fallen on deaf ears. But Buell was slow to move. in January, 1862, he confessed that his opportunity had been lost. [6] In the following month, however, Ulysses Grant on the northern borders of the state struck one of his hammer blows for the Union. He captured Fort Henry and Fort Donnelson and took 9,000 prisoners, and forced the virtual Confederate evacuation of west and central Tennessee. [7] On February 22nd he placed western Tennessee under martial law. [8] On the following day the Confederate state government evacuated Nashville and moved to Memphis.[9]

Lincoln at this time saw an opportunity to take the first step in his reconstruction program. He determined to permit its loyal inhabitants as speedily as possible to restore their commonwealth to its proper relation with the Union. Rather than continue the rule of a Northern general, he decided to place the state government in the hands of one of its own inhabitants. Accordingly, on March 4th, 1862, he appointed Andrew Johnson military governor of Tennessee with the rank of brigadier-general of volunteers.[10]

It was a dangerous and thankless post, but Johnson accepted promptly. When he opened his commission he read: "You are . . . appointed . . . with authority to exercise . . . within the limits of that state, all . . . the powers . . . pertaining to the office . . . (including the power to establish all necessary offices and tribunals and suspend the writ of habeas corpus) during the pleasure of the President or until the loyal inhabitants of that state shall organize a civil government in conformity with the Constitution of the United States." [11] This enormous grant of power is proof enough of Lincoln's confidence in Johnson.

"It is obvious to you," Johnson's instructions from the War Department said, "that the great purpose of your appointment is to reëstablish the authority of the Federal government in the state of Tennessee, and to provide the means of maintaining peace and security to the loyal inhabitants of that state until they shall be able to establish a civil government. Upon your wisdom and energetic action much will depend in accomplishing the result. It is not deemed necessary to give any specific instructions but rather confide in your sound discretion to adopt such measures as circumstances may demand. Specific instructions will be given when requested. You may rely upon the perfect confidence and full support of the department in the performance of your duties." [12]

The appointment was submitted to the Senate and was made by and with its consent,[13] although the President's constitutional power to create a military governorship was questioned in both houses of Congress. It furnished Thaddeus Stevens an opportunity to begin developing his doctrine that the seceded states were out of the Union and that the Constitution did not extend to them.[14] But in the Constitution, Lincoln found plenty of authority for the powers which he assumed. It was no James Buchanan who was then sitting in the White House!

Andrew Johnson knew what he would find on his return. There could have been little information, therefore, in General Buell's letter reaching him on his way south, and containing this sage advice: "You must not expect to be received with enthusiasm, but rather the reverse."[15] On his trip from Washington he again experienced what it was to be a loyal man in Tennessee. Hostile crowds gathered at the stations and he missed again by a narrow margin being mobbed.[16]

On the 14th of March he arrived at Nashville. That evening a vast throng assembled in front of his hotel demanding from him a speech. Stepping out on the balcony he addressed them in brief words of simple dignity. He pictured the desolation, the families torn apart, the burnt bridges, crops and dwellings. He closed his short address with an appeal to loyal men to "show their hands, speak their minds and fear not."[17] The next morning he went over to the empty and deserted state house with General Buell and Horace Maynard, and took possession. All the public records had been removed to Memphis by Governor Harris.[18]

Four days later he issued an "Appeal to the People of Tennessee."[19] He recalled the prosperous and contented condition of the people under the government of the United States. He told of Lincoln's efforts to discharge his "momentous and responsible trust." He explained the Congressional resolution (modestly suppressing that he had been its proposer in the Senate) defining the objects of the war and declaring that it was not waged for conquest or oppression or for overthrowing "the established institutions of the state," but to defend and maintain the Constitution and further, that when "these objects are accomplished the war ought to cease."[20] "In this spirit," he said, "the President . . . has caused the national flag again to float undisputed over the capital of our State. Meanwhile the State govern-

ment has disappeared. . . . The great ship of state . . . has
been suddenly abandoned by its officers and mutinous crew . . .
to be plundered by every rover upon the deep. . . ." [21]

He explained how the national government was endeavoring to
give Tennessee, along with other states, the constitutionally guaranteed republican form of government, and continued: "I have
been appointed in the absence of the regular and established state
authorities as Military Governor for the time being, to preserve
the public property of the State, to give the protection of law
actively enforced to her citizens and as speedily as may be to
restore her government to the same condition as before the existing rebellion." [22]   The temporary officers whom he was about
to appoint would, he said, hold office only "until their places can
be filled by the action of the people." [23] "To the people themselves," he continued, "the protection of the government is
extended.   All their rights will be duly respected, and their
wrongs redressed when made known. Those who through the
dark and weary night of the rebellion have maintained their allegiance will be honored. The erring and misguided will be welcomed on their return." [24]

"While it may become necessary," he said, "in vindicating the
violated majesty of the law, . . . to punish intelligent and conscious treason in high places, no merely retaliatory or vindictive
policy will be adopted. To those especially who in a private unofficial capacity have assumed an attitude of hostility to the Government, a full and complete amnesty . . . is offered, upon the one
condition of their again yielding themselves peaceful citizens to
the just supremacy of the laws. This I advise them to do for their
own good, and for the peace and welfare of our beloved
State. . . ." [25]

There was a moving quality in that whole address, especially in
its closing sentence: "And appealing to my fellow citizens of
Tennessee, I point you to my long life as a pledge for the sincerity of my motives, and an earnest for the performance of my
present and future duties." [26]

Parson Brownlow, after his release from Confederate incarceration in a Knoxville jail, by slow and painful stages made his way

to Philadelphia. On March 20th he passed through Nashville and made this record in his diary: "Governor Johnson is here as military Governor, and is now organizing a State Government. . . . The Governor issued a proclamation yesterday which is an able and well-timed document and meets the case as it exists here." [27]

On the fourth of the following month, Brownlow arrived at Cincinnati where a large audience gathered at "Pike's Opera House" to do him honor. [28] "I have battled against Andrew Johnson," he said, "perseveringly, systematically and terribly, for a quarter of a century. He has basted me on every stump in Tennessee. We have each given the other as good as he sent. Honors are easy with us now, and we are hand-in-hand fighting the same battle for the preservation of the Union. We will fight for each other against the common foe. He is now at the head of our new State Government; and I take pleasure in saying that he is the right man in the right place. If Mr. Lincoln had asked the Union men of Tennessee whom they wanted for a military governor, the answer would have been Andrew Johnson!" [29]

Johnson took prompt hold of the duties that Lincoln had assigned to him. His first task was the appointment of temporary state officers, and these accordingly he promptly chose. [30]

In his "Appeal to the People" he had announced his intention to have the state and local offices occupied by men "bearing true allegiance to the Constitution." [31] Nine days after his assumption of his duties the city government of Nashville found out that he meant exactly what he said. On March 25th the oath of allegiance was tendered to Mayor Cheatham and the city council. They refused. Johnson immediately filled their places with loyal men. Having briefly dispatched this first business, the military governor now gave his attention to the press. In April he suppressed the "Daily Times" and "Banner" and placed the "Banner's" editor in jail. He found two religious publications, one Methodist and the other Baptist, preaching disloyalty; he closed their plants. [32]

On June 17th six ministers were charged with preaching treason. He requested them to take the oath. All six refused. He promptly arrested five of these, paroling the sixth because of feeble health. He passed them all a little later through the Federal lines into the Confederacy whose cause instead of Christ's they had been espousing from their pulpits.[33] "These assumed ministers of Christ," wrote Johnson, "have done more to poison and corrupt the female mind of this community than all others, in fact changing their entire character from that of women and ladies to that of fanatics and fiends. One of those very ministers in leaving here for Louisville told those who were collected to see him off: 'Don't forget your God, Jeff Davis and the Confederacy.' This is a specimen of the 'blameless course' pursued by these traitors and hypocrites, who, in the language of Pollock, are 'wearing the livery of heaven to serve the devil in.'"[34]

Johnson's authority embraced all of Tennessee, but throughout 1862 the state was the scene of war, and the actual exercise of his prerogative, therefore, was limited to Nashville and a little of the surrounding country.[35] General Buell with his army was there, but at the beginning of April he marched out to join Grant at Pittsburg Landing.

Albert Sidney Johnston and Beauregard, however, had in the meantime engaged Grant in the great battle of Shiloh.[36] The complete Union victory here achieved was a large aid to the Union cause, but the withdrawal of Buell's army from Nashville was a serious handicap to the administration of Governor Johnson. Immediately upon Buell's departure, Confederate horsemen,— Forrest's hard-riding men and Morgan's troopers, scoured the countryside.[37] Only the strong points could be held by the Unionists. Nashville itself was thinly garrisoned.

Johnson appreciated the importance of holding the Capital. He realized that its capture would ruin Union prestige in Tennessee. At all hazards he determined that Nashville should not fall. This city, as well as the neighboring towns of Lebanon and Murfreesboro after Buell's departure had been stripped of troops and lay open to attack.[38] Buell assured Washington that the regiments withdrawn would be replaced, but this was not done.[39] On July 5th, having taken the outlying towns, Morgan's raiders surrounded Nashville itself.

Before the beginning of August, the capital was cut off from all communication with the North. Supplies could not be secured, the price of necessaries rose, the streets were barricaded, there was consternation in the city. Johnson now put his whole soul into the capital's defense. With feverish energy the work of fortification was pushed forward. A thousand slaves of the secessionists were set to work.[40] He stiffened the whole defense with his resolve that come what might Nashville should not be surrendered. "I am no military man," he said, "but anyone who talks of surrendering I will shoot." [41]

The best story of Johnson's defense of Nashville is the one which Lincoln loved to tell. This is the way he told it. "I had a visit last night from Colonel Moody, the fighting Methodist parson, as he is called in Tennessee. . . . He told me this story of Andy Johnson and General Buell which interested me intensely. Colonel Moody was in Nashville the day it was reported that Buell had decided to evacuate the city. The Rebels strongly reinforced were said to be within two days' march of the capital. Of course, the city was greatly excited. Said Moody: 'I went in search of Johnson at the close of the evening and found him at his office closeted with two gentlemen who were walking the floor with him, one on each side. As I entered they retired leaving me alone with Johnson, who came up to me manifesting intense feeling and said: "Buell is a traitor. He is going to evacuate the city, and in forty-eight hours we shall all be in the hands of the rebels." . . . Suddenly he turned and said: "Moody, can you pray?" "That is my business, sir, as a minister of the Gospel," returned the Colonel. "Well, Moody, I wish you would pray," said Johnson; and instantly both went down upon their knees at opposite sides of the room. . . . Closing the prayer with a hearty "Amen!" from each, they arose. Johnson took a long breath, and said, with emphasis: "Moody, I feel better." . . . He then commenced pacing the floor again. Suddenly he wheeled, . . . and said, "Oh, Moody, I don't want you to think I have become a religious man because I asked you to pray. I am sorry to say it, but I am not, and have never pretended to be religious. No one knows this better than you; but, Moody, there is one thing about it,—I do believe in Almighty God! And I believe also in the Bible and I say I'll be damned if Nashville shall be surrendered," and Nashville was not surrendered.' " [42] It is not surprising that Lincoln wrote to General Halleck: "The governor is a true and a valuable man,—indispensable to us in Tennessee." [43]

On August 31st Johnson wrote to Lincoln about Buell and ended his letter with this sentence: "May God save my country from some of the generals that have been conducting this war." [44] Buell's failure to defend Nashville was reviewed by a military court of inquiry in the latter part of 1862. The court reached the conclusion that he had been hesitating, half-hearted and inefficient, that he had failed to close the road by which Nashville could be attacked, and gave entire credit for the saving of the capital to Johnson. [45] On October 24th Buell was relieved and his command was given to General Rosecrans. [46]

§

It was not strange that such a vigorous upholder of the Union cause, one whom Lincoln had declared "indispensable to us in Tennessee" should have been the object of secession wrath, or that we should find a Confederate court solemnly adjudging that "Andrew Johnson is an alien enemy, and all the property, rights and credits belonging to him . . . are sequestrated, . . . and the receiver for this district is directed to proceed to dispose of the same as provided by law." [47] But he had no time to worry over such pronouncements.

General Buell had found to his sorrow how great was Lincoln's confidence in Andrew Johnson. Rosecrans, who succeeded Buell, was presently to learn the same lesson. There was at Nashville at this time both civil and military authority. The former was represented by the courts, the city marshals and municipal police, the latter by the military tribunals and the provost-guards. Differences after a time arose between Rosecrans and Johnson over their conflicting jurisdictions. [48] On hearing this the War Department, through General Halleck, told Rosecrans to keep his hands off the civil authority, and suggested that Johnson as brigadier-general be put in command of the troops at Nashville. [49]

Rosecrans replied that Nashville was too important for the trust suggested, but that if Johnson would "report" to him, he would "place him in command at Gallatin." [50] Halleck's reply brought Rosecrans up with a short turn; he was told that Johnson was no ordinary brigadier-general, but the governor of a state with the full powers of that office, and that Rosecrans' suggestion that Johnson should report to him "was in direct opposition to the wishes of the government" and "was received by the War Department with marked dissatisfaction." [51]

Rosecrans now came down from his high horse. "No one appreciates the sacrifice, and the delicate and trying position of Governor Johnson more than I do," he wrote, and further, that his intention was "not to treat the suggestion about putting the governor in military command with disrespect. . . ." [52] Harmony was restored.

Throughout 1862 Johnson was eagerly awaiting opportunity to effect a reëstablishment of civil government throughout Tennessee, but military operations rendered this impossible. On September 22nd of that year Lincoln issued his preliminary Emancipation Proclamation, beginning with the declaration "that hereafter as heretofore the war will be prosecuted for the object of practically restoring the constitutional relation between the United States and each of the states . . . in which . . . the relation is . . . suspended or disturbed." [53]

Thus again was defined the object of the war. Lincoln further proclaimed that at the next Congress he would again recommend "pecuniary aid" to the free acceptance or rejection of all slave states not then in rebellion which would "voluntarily adopt immediate or gradual abolishment of slavery within their respective limits, and that the effort to colonize persons of African descent with their consent upon this continent or elsewhere . . . will be continued." [54] Thus, after eighteen months of civil war, Lincoln was still ready to do justice to the white as well as to the black men of the South.

The proclamation then declared that on January 1st, 1863, "all persons held as slaves" within any state then in rebellion, "shall be thence, thereafter and forever free. . . ." [55] The proclamation expressly excluded from its terms certain parishes in Louisiana and the counties in Virginia that were considered loyal;[56] but of all those that had seceded Tennessee was the only entire state omitted from the proclamation. This was done upon the advice of Johnson,[57] who later assured the President that this step had worked great benefit for the Union cause within his state.[58]

How thoroughly Johnson's mind had been moving along with the President's, appears from his 4th of July speech delivered at Nashville two and a half months before Lincoln issued his great proclamation. Johnson there said: "I am for this Government above all earthly possessions, and if it perish, I do not want to survive it. I am for it, though slavery should be struck from existence and Africa swept from the balance of the world. I believe, indeed, that the Union is the only protection of slavery—its sole guarantee; but if you persist in forcing this issue of slavery against the Government, I say in the face of Heaven, give me my Government and let the negro go!"[59] Both Lincoln and Johnson placed the saving of the Union first; both contemplated negro emancipation as an incident to the attainment of that end.

In October of the same year, Lincoln sent commissioners into Tennessee to stimulate sentiment for holding Congressional and state elections. Their instructions told them: "In all available ways give the people a chance to express their wishes at these elections. Follow forms of law as far as convenient; but at all events get the expression of the largest number of the people possible. All see how such action will connect with and affect the proclamation of September 22. Of course the men elected should be gentlemen of character, willing to swear to support the Constitution, as of old, and known to be above reasonable suspicion of duplicity."[60]

On December 8th Johnson issued a proclamation for a Congressional election in the 9th and 10th districts to be held twenty days later. He was prompt to further Lincoln's plan. It was felt that there was sufficient Union sentiment in those districts to justify the experiment.[61] The public's response to this proposal was not encouraging; but what would have happened at the polls cannot be known as they were not opened; a Confederate raid by

General Forrest on election day prevented this; a discouragingly small vote, or the election of anti-Lincoln congressmen was, however, thus forestalled.[62]

In February, 1863, Johnson made a speaking tour through Ohio, Pennsylvania, New Jersey and New York. His close coöperation with Lincoln was here again apparent. He left Nashville on the 26th, delivering there an address, the substance of which he gave to every audience on his tour. "The time has come," he said, "to teach the South and North that institutions are not to exist here that are more powerful than the government itself. . . . Has slavery a right to agitate the government and shake it to its center, and then deny to the government the privilege to agitate slavery?"[63]

Johnson's conciliatory advice, followed by Lincoln in his omission of Tennessee from the Emancipation Proclamation, had helped the Union cause within that state.[64] But what helped it even more were increasingly frequent successes of the Union arms. Federal hold upon the western area of the commonwealth was growing more secure and hope for the recapture of Eastern Tennessee had brightened. Confederate sympathizers in the state were beginning to know discouragement. Their slaves had escaped or had been carried off. The poorer citizens had been conscripted into the Confederate armies. They began to see that they were suffering for a cause foredoomed to failure, and they began to think in terms of peace.[65]

June, 1863, was the time and the little town of Winchester, about ten miles north of the state's southern boundary, the place in which was enacted the last political act of the Confederate drama in Tennessee. Governor Harris had called a convention for June 1st to select Confederate candidates for Congress and for governor. The convention met and made nominations, but what had been intended as a serious political move the Union armies turned into an impotent and empty gesture.[66]

The loyal leaders also understood the importance of political action. A Unionists' convention called at Nashville on July 1st passed a resolution approving Lincoln's appointment of Johnson and the latter's administration as military governor. All laws enacted by the Confederate legislature of Tennessee were declared void. Johnson was requested to issue writs of election for the first week in August, but declined, believing that this was inexpedient until the driving of Confederate guerillas from Eastern Tennessee had rendered that section capable of participating in the councils of the state.[67]

§

Johnson had carried on much correspondence with Lincoln as to the time and method of restoring Tennessee to its proper relation with the Union. In the spring of 1863 he journeyed to Washington and there held an extended conference with the President. Both desired the prompt restoration of the state government, but both understood that this must wait upon the success of Union arms.[68]

Six months later Burnside, with the aid of Rosecrans, pushed over from Kentucky into the mountains of Eastern Tennessee and drove the Confederates before him. At last the day of liberation for the loyal mountaineers had come! It was more than eighteen months since Johnson's voice had rung out in the Senate demanding arms and soldiers for his people. They were slow in coming; but they had come![69] The Union troops were received by the mountaineers with frantic joy.[70]

Lincoln telegraphed to Johnson: "All Tennessee is now clear of armed insurrectionists. You need not be reminded that it is the nick of time for reinaugurating a loyal state government. Not a moment should be lost. You and the coöperating friends there can better judge of the way and means than can be judged by any here. . . . The whole struggle for Tennessee will have been profitless to both state and nation if it so ends that Governor Johnson is put down and Governor Harris is put up. It must not be so. You must have it otherwise. Let the reconstruction be the work of such men only as can be trusted for the Union . . . It cannot be known who is next to occupy the position I now hold nor what he will do. I see that you have declared in favor of emancipation in Tennessee, for which may God bless you.

Get emancipation into your new state . . . constitution and there will be no such word as fail for your case." [71]

Johnson again set to work. All over Tennessee mass meetings were organized, and he addressed them in these words: "The rebel army is driven back. Here lies your state, a sick man. . . . The physician comes. . . . The United States sends . . . a military governor . . . to aid you in restoring your government. Whenever you desire in good faith to restore civil authority, you can do so, and a proclamation for an election will be issued as speedily as it is practicable to hold one. One by one all the agencies of your state government will be set in motion." [72]

Once again, however, hopes of prompt reconstruction were deferred by military failure. Bragg, whom Rosecrans had been driving through the mountains, turned suddenly upon the Union general and drove him back to Chickamauga Creek, and finally to Chattanooga. The brave stand of General Thomas,—from thence on known as "the Rock of Chickamauga"—brought him Rosecrans' command. On October 23rd, Grant arrived, Sherman was also ordered up from Vicksburg. Twenty-four hours later came the decisive Union victories of Lookout Mountain, Hooker's "Battle above the Clouds," and on the following day "Missionary Ridge." [73]

In the meanwhile Longstreet began attacking Burnside who lay in desperate straits at Knoxville. Longstreet made no headway; he learned to his sorrow and at first-hand how the mountaineers were cherishing their loyalty to the Union. After Chattanooga he returned to Virginia. The old flag was waving over all of Tennessee.[74] The path was now open to Lincoln and to Johnson to renew their thwarted work of reconstruction.

X

LINCOLN'S PLAN OF RECONSTRUCTION

WHILE with Johnson's aid Lincoln was endeavoring to reconstruct Tennessee, he was making similar attempts in other Southern states wherein the Union arms had gained a foothold.

On July 28th, 1862, he wrote to Reverdy Johnson: "The people of Louisiana—all intelligent people everywhere—know full well that I never had a wish to touch the foundation of their society, or any rights of theirs. With perfect knowledge of this, they forced a necessity upon me to send armies among them. . . . They very well know that the way to avert all this is simply to take their place in the Union upon the old terms." [1]

Two days later he wrote Cuthbert Bullett: "The people of Louisiana who wish protection to person and property have but to reach forth their hands and take it. Let them in good faith reinaugurate the national authority and set up a state government conforming thereto under the Constitution. They know how to do it, and can have the protection of the army while doing it. The army will be withdrawn as soon as such State government can dispense with its presence, and the people of the State can then upon the old constitutional terms govern themselves to their own liking." [2]

In August of the same year Lincoln appointed General George F. Shepley military governor of Louisiana, [3] and an election was decreed for December. [4] Two months earlier Lincoln had written Shepley: "We do not particularly need members of Congress to enable us to get along with legislation here. What we do want is the conclusive evidence that respectable citizens of Louisiana are willing to be members of Congress and to swear support to the Constitution, and that other respectable citizens there are willing to vote for them. To send a parcel of Northern men here as representatives, elected as would be understood (and perhaps really so) at the point of the bayonet, would be disgusting and outrageous; and were I a member of Congress here I would vote against admitting any such man to a seat." [5] Had he a vision of the carpet-bag régime?

Benjamin F. Flanders and Michael Hahn were elected to Congress from Louisiana in December, 1862.[6] They appeared in Washington and were seated two months later.[7] Here was a precedent. Louisiana was still in the Union! In the middle of the war this state was not treated as a conquered province! The infection of Thaddeus Stevens had not yet produced the political necrosis of 1867!

Arkansas, like Virginia, North Carolina and Tennessee, was late in joining the Confederacy.[8] In its northern section, as in the eastern part of Tennessee, there was always a strong Union sentiment.[9] The Confederate government had been unable to assist the state of Arkansas and she was forced, therefore, to rely upon her own resources and what could be obtained from Texas, Missouri and the Indian territory.[10]

Smarting with the feeling of neglect, Governor Rector, who in April, 1861, had shown himself an ardent disciple of disunion,[11] in May of the following year gave utterance to these words of secession from secession: "Arkansas lost, abandoned, subjugated is not Arkansas as she entered the Confederate Government. Nor will she remain Arkansas a Confederate state, desolated as a wilderness." [12]

On May 1st, the Union General Curtis occupied Batesville, where he observed many demonstrations of attachment to the Union.[13] It was not long after this that Lincoln appointed John S. Phelps of Missouri as military governor of Arkansas.[14] He had, however, little opportunity to exercise his prerogative until after the fall of Vicksburg in July, 1863.[15] Union sympathizers now became more active. A loyal newspaper was established at the Capital. Loyal meetings were held, resolutions in support of the Union were adopted. By December, 1863, eight Arkansas regiments had enlisted in the Union army.[16]

§

Separated by the Appalachian Mountains, there was no homogeneity and never much of understanding between the two sections of the original old Dominion now known as Virginia and West Virginia.[17]   In the Convention of 1861, wherein Virginia adopted her ordinance of secession, but nine of the forty-seven delegates from what is now West Virginia voted to secede.[18] They represented a people whose history and pursuits had rendered them more sympathetic with Ohio and Pennsylvania than with the state of which they were an unwilling part.[19]

At a mass meeting called on May 13th, 1861, therefore, we find 425 delegates from twenty-five counties of southwest Virginia assembling at Wheeling to decide upon a course of action. Before forming a new state,—a project warmly advocated—it was decided to await the vote of all the people of Virginia upon the ordinance of secession.   On May 23rd, by a large majority, that ordinance was sustained, although 40,000 of the 44,000 votes of the western counties were cast against it.[20]

On June 11th, a second Wheeling convention repudiated secession and resolved to maintain the rights of Virginia in the Union, and commanded all in arms against the Federal government to disband.[21]   On June 19th an act purporting to reorganize the government of the entire state was passed and on the following day Francis H. Pierpont was chosen "Governor of Virginia."[22]

On the first of the following month a further act of alleged state-wide sovereignty was performed when the members of the legislature elected from the western counties met at Wheeling and elected Wiley and Carlisle as United States Senators from "Virginia," to fill the seats of Mason and Hunter, who had abdicated.   The certificates of election were presented four days later by Senator Andrew Johnson, and though there was a protest these Senators were seated.[23]

There were now, therefore, two governments of the old Dominion, one loyal to the United States, the other to the Confederacy, the former exercising, however, jurisdiction only in the west, the latter in the east.   "It was not the object of the Wheeling convention," Governor Pierpont said, "to set up any new government in the state. . . ." Nevertheless, on August 6th, the convention reconvened and provided for a popular vote on the question of forming a new state to be called "Kanawha." [24] By an overwhelming vote it was decided to set up a new commonwealth. On the thirteenth of the following month the "Legislature of Virginia,"—the Pierpont legislature—consented to this excision from the old state.[25] This "Legislature of Virginia," though claiming to legislate for the entire state, in fact exercised jurisdiction only in West Virginia and a few other counties.

The consent of Congress was then asked. The debates in the lower House gave Thaddeus Stevens opportunity to exploit his theories. "I hold," he said, "that none of the states now in rebellion are entitled to the protection of the Constitution. . . ." [26] He continued: "I see the Executive one day saying 'You shall not take the property of rebels to pay the debts which the rebels have brought upon the Northern states.' Why? Because the Constitution is in the way. And the next day I see him appointing a military governor of Virginia, a military governor of Tennessee, and some other place. Where does he find anything in the Constitution to warrant that? If he must look there alone for authority, then all those acts are flagrant usurpations, deserving the condemnation of the community. He must agree with me or else his acts are as absurd as they are unlawful; for I see him here and there ordering elections for members of Congress whenever he finds a little collection of three or four consecutive plantations in the rebel states, in order that men may be sent in here to control the proceedings of this Congress. . . ." [27] Congress nevertheless approved the creation of West Virginia, the Senate in July, 1862,[28] and the House on the tenth of the following December.[29]

Lincoln signed the bill. "We can," he said, "scarcely dispense with the aid of West Virginia in this struggle; much less can we afford to have her against us in Congress and in the field. Her brave and good men regard her admission into the Union as a matter of life and death. They have been true to the Union under very severe trials. We have so acted as to justify their hopes, and we cannot fully retain their confidence and coöperation if we seem to break faith with them; . . . the admission of the new state turns that much slave soil to free, and this is a certain and irrevocable encroachment upon the cause of rebellion. . . . It is said that the admission of West Virginia is secession and tolerated only because it is our secession. Well, if we call it by that name, there is still difference enough between secession against the Constitution and secession in favor of the Constitution. I believe the admission of West Virginia is expedient." [30]

Arthur I. Boreman as governor and other officers of the new state were chosen, and upon their inauguration on June 20th at Wheeling, Governor Pierpont turned over this fledgling commonwealth to its new custodians, and retired to Alexandria, chosen by him as the "capital of Virginia," where he exercised jurisdiction only in that part of the old state which was embraced within the Union lines. How tenuous was his hold was revealed when his constitutional convention, called to abolish slavery, could muster only sixteen members. [31]

There were now three governments in what had been Virginia; West Virginia, the Confederate state of Virginia, and Pierpont's "Restored Virginia" embracing Alexandria and a little of the surrounding territory. Of the latter Lincoln later wrote: "Governor Pierpont . . . at first as the loyal governor of all Virginia, including that which is now West Virginia, . . . was as earnest, honest and efficient to the extent of his means as any other loyal governor. The inauguration of West Virginia as a new state left to him, as he assumed, the remainder of the old state; and the insignificance of the parts which are outside of the Rebel lines, and consequently within his reach certainly gives a somewhat farcical air to his dominion, and I suppose he, as well as I, has considered that it can be useful for little else than as a nucleus to add to." [32]

"A nucleus to add to"—Lincoln was constantly on the alert for that. These five words might serve as a key to his whole reconstruction plan.

§

With the experience gained from his experiments in Louisiana, Arkansas, Virginia and Tennessee, with the conviction expressed in his first Inaugural still firm, that "no state upon its own mere motion can lawfully get out of the Union," [33] on December 8th, 1863, Lincoln issued a proclamation setting forth his reconstruction plan.

He recited his constitutional power to grant "reprieves and pardons," that "loyal state governments of several states have for a long time been subverted," that Congress had given the President the power "by proclamation to extend to persons who may have participated in the existing rebellion in any state or part thereof, pardon and amnesty, . . ." and that "it is now desired by some persons heretofore engaged in said rebellion to resume their allegiance to the United States and to reinaugurate loyal state governments within and for their respective states." [34]

The proclamation with certain exceptions granted to all who had in any way participated in the rebellion a full pardon "with restoration of all rights of property except as to slaves, . . ." but required of these an oath not only to "support, protect and defend the Constitution," but also to abide by and support "all acts of Congress passed during the existing rebellion with reference to slaves" so long as not repealed or judicially declared void, and to support "all proclamations of the President . . . having reference to slaves" [35] until similarly modified.

The proclamation then continued: "Whenever in any of the states of Arkansas, Texas, Louisiana, Mississippi, Tennessee, Alabama, Georgia, Florida, South Carolina and North Carolina a number of persons not less than one-tenth in number of the votes cast in such state at the Presidential election of the year A. D. 1860, each having taken the oath aforesaid, and not having since violated it, and being a qualified voter by the election law of the state existing immediately before the so-called act of secession, and excluding all others, shall reëstablish a state government which shall be republican and in no wise contravening said oath, such shall be recognized as the true government of the state and the states shall receive thereunder the benefits of the constitutional provision which declares that 'the United States shall guarantee to every state in this Union a republican form of government and shall protect each of them against invasion, and . . . domestic violence. . . .' " [36]

Virginia, it will be noted, is not among the states enumerated in the proclamation. Weak as it was Lincoln always recognized Pierpont's as the government of Virginia,—a "loyal government." [37]

Lincoln was proclaiming that the Southern states should continue to be treated as members of the Union with all their old laws and institutions, except slavery, intact, but only those persons who recognized the Emancipation Proclamation were to be pardoned and thereby to become qualified "to establish a state government." [38]

In his last paragraph he made it clear that "whether members sent to Congress from any state shall be admitted to seats constitutionally rests exclusively with the respective Houses and not to any extent with the Executive." [39] There is no malice here, no meanness, no bitterness, no negro suffrage, no confiscation, no chicane, no plunder, no subjugation. This was no shoddy politician's concept.

His message accompanying the proclamation thus amplified his purpose: "The suggestion in the proclamation as to maintaining the political framework of the states on what is called reconstruction is made in the hope that it may do good without danger or harm. It will save labor and avoid great confusion." [40] "In some states," he continued, "the elements for resumption seem ready for action, but remain inactive apparently for want of a rallying point—a plan of action. . . . By the proclamation a plan is presented which may be accepted by them as a rallying point, and which they are assured in advance will not be rejected here. This may bring them to act sooner than they otherwise would." [41] It was a practical scheme for taking advantage of such loyalty as might be found within the Southern states. One-tenth of the entire electorate in each state—this indeed was a modest beginning, "a nucleus to add to." To this nucleus he knew, when at

last the war was over, there would be added the entire white population of each Southern state.   It was a plan whereby the secessionists could renew their fealty to the Federal government like
honest litigants who had lost their case.   There were no pains
or penalties attached.

From the very beginning of the war Lincoln had proclaimed
that "no state upon its own mere motion can lawfully get out of
the Union," [42] and that all the states had "their status in the
Union" and could "have no other legal status." [43]   He had no
intention to repudiate these indisputably correct Constitutional
opinions, he intended rather to follow and enforce them. Through
the exigencies of war slavery was to go, but except for this and
the men and money expended in the struggle, there was to be no
punishment for the South because of her unsuccessful effort to
secede.

Born in Kentucky, Lincoln understood the Southern mind.
He understood that the North originally was as responsible for
slavery as the South.   He understood how the abolitionists had
provoked the South to take up arms.   He knew that the Constitution, except by inference, did not declare which of the opposing
litigants, in the bloody trial of war, was right.   Sumner and
Stevens might sneer at Southern chivalry, but Lincoln knew that
the South Carolinians and their allies were men of honor, that
they could be trusted, and that if defeated they would accept the
decision like gentlemen and sportsmen.

Lincoln worked for the restoration of national unity,—a reunion
of feeling as well as fact.   To the South, even in the matter of
slavery, he had been seeking to do justice.   He understood the
negro problem and the complications that would follow the
liberation of the slaves.   Six months before the issuance of his
first Emancipation Proclamation, he secured from Congress a
resolution in favor of gradual compensated emancipation.   "In
my judgment," he wrote, "gradual and not sudden emancipation
is better for all." [44]   He urged the South to adopt it.   "This proposal," he said, "makes common cause for a common object, casting no reproaches on any.   It acts not the Pharisee.   The
change it contemplates would come gently as the dews of

Heaven, not rending or wrecking anything. Will you not embrace it?" [45]

Nine months later he advocated a constitutional amendment for the accomplishment of this purpose. Its adoption would require the vote of at least some of the Southern states in order to secure the necessary three-fourths of all. Lincoln implored the South's support. "In giving freedom to the slave," he said, "we assure freedom to the free,—honorable alike in what we give and what we preserve." [46]

But the refusal of the South to listen did not deflect the great President from his purpose with gentle hand to lead her back before the hearthstone of the Union, and except that she might never bring slavery into the home again, to treat her as if she had not strayed away. Hence his plan of reconstruction.

But other voices were resounding in the North. Charles Sumner and Thaddeus Stevens were beginning their pandemonium of hate, their hue and cry in which the Radicals of their party were presently to join. A year and ten months before the announcement of Lincoln's plan, Sumner declared that "any vote of secession becomes a practical abdication of all rights under the Constitution, . . . so that from that time forward the territory falls under the exclusive jurisdiction of Congress . . . and the state . . . ceases to exist." [47]

Thaddeus Stevens took up the refrain a little later. "I would lay a tax whenever I can, upon the conquered provinces," he said, "just as all nations levy them upon provinces and nations they conquer." [48] He told Congress that it "must treat those states now outside of the Union as conquered provinces, and settle them with new men, and drive the present rebels as exiles from this country. . . ." [49]

Lincoln brought forth his plan in answer to this program of vengeance. When it came, Stevens was beside himself. "If ten men fit to save Sodom," he shouted to the House, "can elect a governor and other state officers for and against Sodomites in Virginia, then the democratic doctrine that the majority shall rule is discarded. . . ." [50]

"Conquered provinces!"   "Confiscation!"   "Drive the present rebels from the country!"—there you have the statesmanship of Thaddeus Stevens and Charles Sumner. The difference between their vindictive purpose and Lincoln's effort "with malice toward none and charity for all" to bind up the nation's wounds, was to grow and widen during Lincoln's life. After his death it was to form the issue that will presently become the main theme of this book.

§

We left Andrew Johnson amid the turmoils of Tennessee. He had been living in the very furnace of the war. His duties, in the midst of a state overrun by hostile armies, ran the whole gamut of civil and military responsibility. Military and civil administration, however, by no means defined the range of his endeavors. He became a railroad builder! From the beginning of the war he had urged the necessity of constructing the Nashville and Northwestern road and had repeatedly urged it upon the War Department. In the summer of 1863 he was given entire responsibility for its construction. Even the guarding of the road fell upon the military governor.[51] The work was energetically pushed to a conclusion. In May, 1864, trains ran. But for Johnson's work the Union generals might have been unable to subsist their men in Tennessee.[52]

Of all the duties assigned him, perhaps the most trying were the harassing details of his office. He had to listen to the grievances of officers and soldiers. He had somehow to supply the Union armies with reinforcements, horses and arms. Soldiers with back pay expected help. There was the problem of the destitute wives of absent warriors. There was the "army paper work," for he was a brigadier-general, required to make returns and to account for equipment and supplies.[53]

Only a man of unflinching patriotism could have withstood all the demands upon his time, his strength, his courage and his patience.

His real opportunity to further reconstruction did not come, however, until after the military success of Grant and Sherman had driven the Confederate soldiers from the state. The approach to order thus obtained now augured hope for the success of Lincoln's plans in Tennessee. Eighteen days after the President's Reconstruction Proclamation, a mass meeting on December 26th, 1863, assembled at Memphis and petitioned for a reëstablishment of civil government in accordance with its terms.[54]

During the middle of January, 1864, Lincoln began to enroll those who would take the oath formulated in his proclamation. He sent an agent to Tennessee with blanks for this purpose.[55] At the election, held on March 5th, between forty and fifty thousand votes were cast and officers for about two-thirds of the counties of the state were chosen.

LINCOLN AND JOHNSON—THE UNIONIST TICKET

DURING the spring of 1864 the Unionists of Tennessee discerned, in the coming National Convention at Baltimore, a new opportunity through which to bring their state more rapidly into alignment with the Union. On May 30th a convention met at Nashville and, after recommending Lincoln's renomination, resolved that Johnson should be the vice-presidential nominee. It spoke of his "unflinching courage and patriotism," it praised his administration as military governor and declared that he had "endeared himself to all American patriots," and had "gained the entire confidence of all the loyal people of Tennessee."[1] Their delegates now repaired to Baltimore—of course, Parson Brownlow was one of them.[2]

Before the convention met on June 7th, there had been much doubt as to Lincoln's renomination. The failure of the Union arms in the summer of 1862, the tragedy of Fredericksburg in December, the calamity of Chancellorsville in 1863 were all laid at his door. His availability as a candidate had become a matter of grave doubt among the leaders of his party.[3]

During this period the Presidential cravings of Chase had become so acute as to disturb even Lincoln's large magnanimity.[4] In August, 1863, Chase wrote: "I think a man of different qualities from those the President has will be needed for the next four years. I am not anxious to be regarded as that man; and I am quite willing to leave that question to the decision of those who agree in thinking that some such man should be chosen."[5]

Nothing is more revealing of Lincoln's patience than his remark to John Hay two months later: "Mr. Chase makes a good secretary and I shall keep him where he is. If he becomes President, all right. I hope we may never have a worse man. I have observed with regret his plan of strengthening himself. Whenever he sees that an important matter is troubling me, if I am compelled to decide in a way to give offense to a man of some influence, he always ranges himself in opposition to me, and persuades the victim that he has been hardly dealt with and that he would have arranged it very differently. It was so with General Fremont, with General Hunter when I annulled his hasty proclamation, with General Butler when he was recalled from New Orleans. . . . I am entirely indifferent as to his success or failure in those schemes so long as he does his duty at the head of the Treasury Department." [6]

Charnwood says of Chase: "This dignified and righteous person was unhappily a sneak." [7] Lincoln's characterization is more just and probably more accurate: "Mr. Chase is a very able man. He is a very ambitious man, and I think on the subject of the presidency a little insane." [8]

A newspaper editor from Pennsylvania and a supporter of the President, in the winter of 1864 came to Washington and asked Thaddeus Stevens to introduce him to "some member of Congress friendly to Mr. Lincoln's renomination." "Come with me," was the reply, and limping over to the seat of Representative Arnold of Chicago, Stevens exclaimed: "Here is a man who wants to find a Lincoln member of Congress. You are the only one I know and I have come over to introduce my friend to you." [9]

One of the more subtle means of opposing Lincoln's renomination was the suggested postponement of the convention until September. William Cullen Bryant, with his *Evening Post*, was the leader in this movement. [10] But if Lincoln had been blamed for the Union disasters, he received some of the credit for Gettysburg and Vicksburg. Grant's tragic failure at Gold Harbor, four days before the convention met, had not yet been well enough comprehended to have altered the convention's choice. [11] And so the movement for postponement failed, [12] and on June 7th the Republican Convention met at Baltimore.

Among the delegates were the outstanding upholders of the Union cause. Five of the leading war governors were there. Massachusetts sent her eloquent Governor John A. Andrew, New

York named Henry J. Raymond and Daniel S. Dickinson, and Lyman Tremain. New Jersey and Ohio each sent two of their ex-governors. Simon Cameron and ex-Speaker Grow were there from Pennsylvania, Thaddeus Stevens also came.[13]

A serious question arose almost at once: Should the roll of the Southern states be called? To reject those from Tennessee, Parson Brownlow said would be acknowledgment that his state was no longer in the Union. "I hope you will pause, gentlemen," he declared, "before you commit so rash an act as that, and thereby recognize secession. We don't recognize it in Tennessee. We deny that we are out. We deny that we ever have been out." [14] The delegates from Tennessee, Arkansas and Louisiana, over the objection of Thaddeus Stevens, were thereupon admitted. Those from Virginia were likewise seated, but without the right to vote.[15]

The twenty-two delegates from Missouri voted at first for Grant, all the rest of the four hundred and ninety-seven ballots were recorded for the great war President. The gentlemen from Missouri had been shown, and so "amid great enthusiasm" Lincoln's nomination was declared unanimous.[16]

The contest for the vice-presidency was a spirited one. Hannibal Hamlin of Maine had been elected with Lincoln four years before and was then Vice-President. He had served three terms in Congress and had twice been elected a United States Senator and governor, and during his vice-presidency had been a trusted adviser of the President.[17] Hamlin was warmly supported for renomination. The Republicans, however, had smarted under the taunt that theirs was a sectional party, since both the candidates four years before were Northern men. The nomination of a Southerner, but one who had done valiant service for the Union would silence that reproach.[18]

There was no one in the country so exactly fitting this requirement as Andrew Johnson of Tennessee, and accordingly he was placed in nomination. Allen of Indiana presented his name to the convention and Horace Maynard of Tennessee then said: "From the time he arose in the Senate of the United States . . . on the 17th of December, 1860, and met the leaders of treason face to face and denounced them there, . . . for which he was hanged in effigy in the city of Memphis, in his own state, by the hands of a negro slave, and burned in effigy I know not in how many more places throughout that portion of the country; from that time . . . until he returned to Tennessee, after the firing upon Fort Sumter when he was mobbed in the city of Lynchburg in Virginia, on through the memorable canvass that followed in Tennessee, till he passed through the Cumberland Gap on his way to the North to invoke the aid of the Government for his people, his position of determined and undying hostility to this rebellion . . . has been so well known that it is a part of the household knowledge of every loyal family in the country." [19]

Johnson received on the first ballot 200 votes, Dickinson 113, Hamlin 145, the rest were scattered. Before it was over there were many changes; the final ballot stood 492 for Johnson, 17 for Dickinson, and 9 for Hamlin. [20]

Did Lincoln have a hand in Johnson's nomination? It is incredible that he did not. Lincoln was not only a profound statesman, —he was one of the shrewdest politicians of all time. He had the human desire to be himself renominated and reëlected. [22] He was not unacquainted with the ways of delegates and of conventions, and despite the opposition which he had encountered before the convention met he had a powerful influence with both. It is impossible that his running mate could have been chosen without his approval.

"The President's advice," says Mr. Morse, "was eagerly and persistently sought. Messrs. Nicolay and Hay allege that he not only ostensibly refused any response, but that he would give no private hint; and they say, therefore, that it was 'with minds absolutely untrammelled by even any knowledge of the President's wishes, that the Convention went about its work of selecting his associate on the ticket'; others assert, and, as it seems to me, strongly sustain their assertion that the President had a distinct and strong purpose in favor of Andrew Johnson . . . and that it was due to his skillful but occult interference that the choice ultimately fell upon the energetic and aggressive war Democrat of Tennessee." [23]

In 1899 Hamlin's biography was written by his grandson. Twenty-nine of its pages seek to prove that Lincoln did not favor Johnson's nomination, but that of his old running mate of 1860.[24] He quotes the statements of delegates written out more than thirty years after the convention had adjourned, but none of these directly assert that Lincoln did not wish Johnson's nomination. Throughout Hamlin's work there are many things that suggest the direct opposite of what he was endeavoring to establish. On the back of a letter seeking "a confidential intimation" as to where he stood, Lincoln wrote: "Wish not to interfere about V. P."[25] This does not prove that Lincoln wished to "interfere" in Hamlin's favor, although the latter's grandson thought it did. And here is another one: "Thad Stevens and Simon Cameron were talking to the President about Johnson and he asked 'Why would not Johnson be a good man to nominate?' Stevens replied in his vigorous blunt way: 'Mr. President, Andrew Johnson is a rash demagogue and I suspect at heart a damned scoundrel.'"[26] As though to indicate Lincoln's concurrence, Charles Hamlin adds: "Mr. Lincoln made no reply!"[27] But if Lincoln had agreed with Stevens, would he have done nothing to prevent the choice of a "damned scoundrel"? When Johnson's nomination was announced, Lincoln quietly observed: "I thought possibly he might be the man."[28]

Chauncey M. Depew, who was present at that convention, has left this record: "Mr. Seward took Judge Robertson and me into his confidence . . . and said the situation demanded the nomination for vice-president of a representative from the border states, whose loyalty had been demonstrated during the war. He eulogized Andrew Johnson of Tennessee, and gave a glowing description of the courage and patriotism with which Johnson at the risk of his life had advocated the cause of the Union and kept his state partially loyal. 'You can quote me to the delegates,' he said, 'and they will believe I express the opinion of the President. While the President wishes to take no part in the nomination for vice-president, yet he favors Mr. Johnson!'"[29]

The day after the nomination Gideon Welles confided to his diary: "It was the wish of Seward that Hamlin should again be

Andrew Johnson

the Vice, and the President was inclined to this policy, though personally his choice is Johnson." [30]

When the subject of Johnson's nomination was before the convention Thaddeus Stevens asked: "Can't you find a candidate for Vice-President in the United States without going down to one of those damned rebel provinces to pick one up?" [31]

The nomination of Andrew Johnson was a shrewd political move. Lincoln's unpopularity at the time of the convention and for more than two months afterwards was such as to make his reëlection all but a hopeless undertaking. Eight days before the Baltimore nominations, Lincoln's radical opponents, under the leadership of Wendell Phillips [32] and other fanatics, met at Cleveland and nominated General John C. Fremont for President. [33] Wendell Phillips denounced Lincoln and pledged his support to Fremont because of the latter's "clearsighted statesmanship and rare military ability." [34] The twelfth plank of the platform adopted by Phillips' friends declared "that the question of the reconstruction of the rebellious states belongs to the people through their representatives in Congress and not to the executive." [35] From this tinder, ere the campaign ended, a smudge arose designed to suffocate Lincoln's chances of election; it was two years later to provide the fagots with which Wendell Phillips, Thaddeus Stevens and their dupes would seek to burn Andrew Johnson at the stake of their conspiracy.

Johnson's name was a strong addition to the Lincoln ticket. "His record and character," says James G. Blaine, "had much to attract the patriotic respect of the country. The vigor and boldness with which, though a Southern Senator, he had denounced secession at the beginning of the outbreak, had taken hold of the popular heart, the firmness and unyielding loyalty he had displayed as military governor of Tennessee greatly deepened the favorable impression. The delegates from his own, and other Southern states had been admitted as an evidence that the Republican party honored the tried and faithful loyalists of the South, and many felt that the nomination of Mr. Johnson would emphasize this sentiment, and free the party from the imputation of sec tional passion and prejudice." [36]

XII

"CULTIVATED AND MORALLY EXCELLENT PEOPLE"

ON the morning following the Baltimore nominations, when the good citizens of Washington Square and Gramercy Park sat breakfasting in the midst of their black walnut and their Victorian draperies and turned to the editorial page of the New York World, this is what they read: "The age of statesmen is gone; the age of rail splitters and tailors, of buffoons, boors and fanatics has succeeded. . . . In a crisis of the most appalling magnitude requiring statesmanship of the highest order, the country is asked to consider the claims of two ignorant, boorish, third-rate backwoods lawyers for the highest stations in the Government. Such nominations, in such a conjuncture, are an insult to the common sense of the people. God save the Republic!" [1]

This was read, no doubt, with much complacency by those whose offspring were improving at home the many fine business opportunities created by the war, while displaying a vicarious patriotism through hired substitutes. It may have met with somewhat less approval from those whose sons had been fighting six days before with General Grant at Cold Harbor. Perhaps they were more in sympathy with the *Tribune's* milder views. Mr. Greeley on that morning said: "We cannot but feel that it might have been wiser to spike the most serviceable guns of our adversaries by nominating another for President. . . . The will of the majority of Unionists has been heard. . . . We bow to the decision."

But in that same editorial Mr. Greeley added: "As to the selection of Andrew Johnson for vice-president, it is in many respects a happy one. There are various kinds of war Democrats, from those fighting under Lee and Beauregard for the Rebel cause, to those who have from the outbreak of the struggle, done their

124

very utmost by word and blow, for the maintenance of the Union, and Johnson's war democracy is of the very best sort. He was always a Democrat; he was a senator from a slave state; he supported Breckenridge for President; but he never wavered or faltered in his devotion to the national cause; and he has carried his life in his hands from the outset. Were the rebels to recover Tennessee and capture him tomorrow they would probably hang him as a traitor before noon of the next day. They have no more original, consistent, implacable foe, and not many more effective. His nomination is a pledge to the Unionists of the seceded states that they at least are not deemed outcasts from the pale of our nationality, that, though they, from peculiar circumstances, were enabled to cast but few votes in our national convention, yet their only candidate was readily accepted and nominated. We hail this nomination as an assurance to Southern Unionists that their long-suffering devotion to the national cause is appreciated, and will not be forgotten." [2]

There was in the North a general feeling of despondency, if not despair. They had found three years of war a tiring experience. General Grant that summer was struggling in the Wilderness before Richmond and it looked as if his offer "to fight it out on these lines if it takes all summer" would be cordially accepted by General Lee.

Take it all in all, the newspaper readers of New York had been having some pretty hard reading since 1861. They had not forgotten their gooseflesh (even if it was the 3rd of July), when the year before Longstreet and his great commanding officer pushed up through Maryland as far as Pennsylvania and it seemed, until General Meade took charge at Gettysburg, as though they might have an opportunity to hear the rebel cheer in the streets of New York. That would have been very bad for business! And then there had been that long succession of unsuccessful Union generals. George B. McClellan had not proved very satisfactory—north of the Mason-Dixon line. Then Pope had taken charge in Virginia in 1862. He fought the second battle of Bull Run that August against Lee and Stonewall Jackson, and was given about the same treatment which General Beauregard had accorded to McDowell at the first battle of that name. Then in November of that year Burnside replaced McClellan and the next month lost the battle of Fredericksburg. He was relieved the following January by General Hooker, who promptly lost the battle of Chancellorsville. The bloody struggle of the Wilderness had now somewhat dimmed all of the Union's successes in the West. It was all rather confusing and tiring to men who had their own affairs to attend to. It seemed, therefore, not unnatural that the Democrats should be proposing to make their campaign upon the platform "The War is a Failure!" choosing with all but a poetic sense of the fitness of things, General McClellan as their standard bearer. There were few men who had had his wide experience in failure. He, if any one, could understand that issue.

In addition to all this hard reading, the city had had several not altogether pleasant personal contacts with the war and with the issues causing it. In January, 1861, Mayor Fernando Wood proposed to the Common Council that Long Island, Staten Island and Manhattan should secede from the Union and constitute a free city to be named "Tri-Insula." The Council approved this program and it was not until April of that year, when the guns of South Carolina, vomiting disunion into the bastions of Fort Sumter, awoke something of the city's heart and soul, that a majority of the Democrats joined with their political opponents to discard this Northern effort at secession.[3]

Then, too, the 13th of July, 1863, had not been by any means forgotten. On that day the opposition to the Draft Law had found its voice and its right hand. The act of Congress had exempted from its operation all who would make a money payment of Three Hundred Dollars. The measure was not entirely popular in New York. The politicians, with vulgar championship of the poor (so it seemed to the indignant residents of the better quarters) were contending that the law was not altogether a perfect thing and that it would work out just a bit inequitably for those utterly negligible but quite numerous persons who could not pay others to fight for them. In fact, finally on that Monday morning, the poor people of the city took arms against their "sea of troubles," and used them somewhat effectively throughout five days and nights. When they had finished their work the limp forms of nearly one thousand negroes were found hanging to the lamp posts or were left crumpled in beaten heaps upon the sidewalks. More than fifty buildings were burned and sacked. The police, as always, battled bravely, but they were too few, and it was not until ten thousand troops marched into town that order was restored.[4]

On July 14th Joseph H. Choate wrote to his mother: "Yesterday morning when the riot commenced in the 22d Ward it was headed by the Alderman of that Ward. There was not a military company in town—all having been sent to Pennsylvania. All night the sky was red with whole blocks burning—and today the violence of the mob increases. Many have been shot, but as yet the effect is hardly perceptible. . . . In our immediate neighborhood in 21st Street there has been no outbreak, but, in addition to our two servants, last night we had four helpless negroes under our roof for shelter—they were being murdered in all parts of the city and no negro out of doors was safe. . . . I have no fears but that this mob will soon be quelled, though only by slaying them. Have no fears for us. We are in no possible danger."[5]

It seemed that not all the fighting in that July had been at Gettysburg. The North, in the abundance of its superfluous numbers, had time and strength for such digressions. The whole country's population in 1860 was less than thirty-one and one-half million souls. Of this number less than one-third dwelt in the states which were next year to eschew the Union. The Confederacy had less than nine million two hundred thousand in its population, and of this more than three and one-half millions were slaves. Reckoning the whites alone, the Southerners were outnumbered more than three to one.[6] These figures may somewhat explain, if they do not justify, the rather detached interest in the conflict on the part of many Northerners. Joseph H. Choate, for example, was busily engaged in building up his law practice during those eventful years. With youthful energy he was laying the foundation of his future leadership in his profession.

In April, 1861, Choate was vigorous and strong, was unmarried,[7] and was twenty-nine years old.[8] His letters to his mother, and afterwards to his wife, are always bright and filled with keen and witty observation of all that was taking place about him. Almost all of them make some reference to the war. His office, it seems, took quite an interest in the struggle. Ten days after the bombardment of Fort Sumter he writes his mother: "One of our clerks has got a commission as First Lieutenant of Zouaves and we are fitting him out with sword, uniform and equipments. Another young man who has been a student with us for a year or two had gone as a Lieutenant of Infantry, so that we are not without our representatives at least, in the field." [9] To his wife, on August 8th, 1862, when he was thirty years of age, he writes: "As to the drafting . . . the Government is certainly entitled to our services and to our lives if need be and I know that you and I would bear it with brave hearts, if duty should require me to go in person. But I have no idea that that will happen, unless our late disasters are repeated a great many times." [10] He wrote that letter twenty-one days before the second battle of Bull Run—a Northern disaster comparable only with the first tragic debâcle by that name.

Choate was a busy young man. It seems that he was "dragged" into making speeches to the soldiers on their way to the front. On September 5th, 1861, he writes his fiancée: "I was in hopes that you wouldn't see that I had been dining and speech-making again to a Massachusetts regiment, for the fact was that I was dragged into it." [11] Many of the young lawyers in blue uniforms who heard that speech were soon to sleep within Virginia's bleeding soil; brilliant careers at the bar did not await them.

Choate's interest for these pages, of course, lies solely in the fact that he was representative of the "best and most cultivated" society of which he was always a part and a leader. His personal abstention from the conflict was shared by what, in our times, seems an amazingly large number of ambitious young business and professional men. Even in this study, which deals with one whose fate did not lie in this favored circle, we cannot ignore what those who belonged to it are pleased to call "the better class of people," or in the words of Mr. Rhodes, the "cultivated and morally excellent."

Choate's brethren of the bar in Georgia, North Carolina and their Confederate States during those years, for the time being, had forgotten their judges and their juries, and were testing out their sacred rights as they understood them, through a trial by combat. That summer their only oratory emerged through the mouths of cannon. They made their legal points with bayonets, and carried on their arguments with clubbed rifles. Perhaps this is why, outnumbered as they were, that for three years they had waged successful battles, and that McClellan's followers in 1864 proclaimed the war a failure.

"The age of rail splitters and tailors!" "Two ignorant, boorish, third-rate, backwoods lawyers for the highest station in the Government!" "An insult to the commonsense of the people. God save the Republic!"

XIII

JOHNSON NOTIFIED OF HIS NOMINATION

As soon as Andrew Johnson's nomination became known in Tennessee, a mass meeting of the Unionists was called at Nashville. He spoke to this gathering and was "hailed with great acclamation." [1] "I accept the nomination on principle," he said, "be the consequences what they may. I will do what I believe to be my duty."

"I know there are those who profess to feel a contempt for me," he continued, "and I . . . feel my superiority to them. I have always understood that there is a sort of exclusive aristocracy about Nashville which affects to condemn all who are not within its little circle. . . . This aristocracy has been the bane of the slave states; nor has the North been wholly free from its curse. It is a class which I have always forced to respect me, for I have ever set it at defiance. The respect of the honest, intelligent and industrious class I have endeavored to win by my conduct as a man. One of the chief elements of this rebellion is the opposition of the slave aristocracy to being ruled by men who have arisen from the ranks of the people. This aristocracy hated Mr. Lincoln because he was of humble origin, a railsplitter in early life. One of them . . . said to me one day: 'We people of the South will not submit to be governed by a man who has come up from the ranks of the common people as Abe Lincoln has.' He uttered the essential feeling and spirit of the Southern rebellion. Now it has just occurred to me, if this aristocracy is so violently opposed to being governed by Mr. Lincoln, what in the name of conscience will it do with Lincoln and Johnson?" [2] Wendell Phillips' operations at that time would have furnished a complete answer to his question.

Johnson continued: "I believe that man is capable of self-gov-

130

ernment, . . . whether he be a laborer, a shoemaker, a tailor or a grocer. . . . I hold with Jefferson that government was made for the convenience of man, and not man for the government; . . .[3] Now if any of you secessionists have lost faith in man's capability of self-government, and feel unfit for the exercise of this great right, go straight to rebeldom, take Jeff Davis, Beauregard and Bragg for your masters, and put their collars on your necks." [4]

The meeting Johnson addressed was called as soon as his nomination became known.[5] At that time he had not seen the platform which the Republican Convention had adopted. Its third plank declared "in favor of such amendment to the Constitution . . . as shall terminate and forever prohibit the existence of slavery within the limits of the jurisdiction of the United States." [6]

Johnson did not derive his opinions from the platform makers, but how fortunate were the carpenters of that plank in selecting one who could squarely stand upon it, is apparent from these further words of his: "Let us fix the foundation of the government on principles of eternal justice which will endure for all time. Let me say to you Tennesseans and men from the Northern states that slavery is dead. It was not murdered by me. I told you long ago what the result would be if you endeavored to go out of the Union to save slavery, and that the result would be bloodshed. . . . Slavery is dead and you must pardon me if I do not mourn over its dead body. . . . In restoring the state leave out that disturbing and dangerous element. . . . I want to say to the blacks that liberty means liberty to work and enjoy the fruits of your labor. Idleness is not freedom. I desire that all men shall have a fair start and equal chance in the race of life, and let him succeed who has the most merit. . . . I am for emancipation . . . because it is right . . . and because in the emancipation of the slaves we break down an odious and dangerous aristocracy. I think that we are freeing more whites than blacks in Tennessee." [7]

To the pessimists both civilian and military, Johnson had this to say: "We can destroy this rebellion. With Grant thundering on the Potomac before Richmond, and Sherman and Thomas on their march toward Atlanta, the day will ere long be ours." [5]

That his long advocacy of the Homestead policy was not unrelated to his hope for the destruction of slavery appears from these words: "I want to see slavery broken up, and when its barriers are thrown down I want to see industrious thrifty immigrants pouring in from all parts of the country." [9] There was now reasonable ground to hope for this, as the Homestead bill had on January 1st, 1863, become a law. [10]

The eleventh plank in the Republican platform declared that our people "can never regard with indifference the attempt of any European power to overthrow . . . any Republican government on the western continent." [11] Without knowledge of this and but little dreaming that during his administration the ill-starred dreams of "Napoleon the Little" would be shattered, Johnson said to his Nashville audience: "The nations of Europe are anxious for our overthrow. France takes advantage of our internal difficulties and sends Maximilian off to Mexico to set up a monarchy on our borders. The day of reckoning is approaching. The time is not far distant when the Rebellion will be put down and then we will attend to this Mexican affair and say to Louis Napoleon, 'You can get up no monarchy on this continent.' An expedition into Mexico would be a sort of recreation to the brave soldiers of the Union, and the French concern would quickly be wiped out." [12] I wonder if poor Maximilian and his ambitious young Carlotta read these words.

Toward the close of that speech occurs a sentence strongly prophetic of those hurled fifty-four years later at the German empire. Woodrow Wilson might have been inspired by these words of Andrew Johnson: "I am for putting down this Rebellion because it is a war against democracy." [13]

Johnson did not receive official notice of his nomination until the 25th of June. [14] His letter of acceptance immediately followed. It was a model of clear statement, and in perfect harmony with the party platform. "It is vain," he said, "to attempt to reconstruct the Union with the distracting element of slavery in it. . . . While it remained subordinate to the Constitution and laws of the United States I yielded to it my support; but when it became rebellious and attempted to rise above the government and control its action I threw my humble influence against it. . . ." [15]

It had been the part of wisdom for the Union party to seek democratic support by the nomination of Andrew Johnson. But it was no mere campaign strategy when Johnson wrote: "In accepting the nomination . . . I cannot forego the opportunity of saying to my old friends of the Democratic party proper, with whom I have so long and pleasantly been associated, that the hour has now come when that great party can justly vindicate its devotion to true democratic policy. . . . Minor questions of . . . policy should give way to the higher duty of first preserving the government. . . . This is not the hour for strife and division among ourselves. . . ." [16]

XIV

LINCOLN AND THE RADICALS

To Herndon in 1866 John Hay wrote: "Lincoln with all his foibles is the greatest character since Christ." [1] It was a valuation of Lincoln dead. There is not more difference between death and life than between Hay's estimate of 1866 and that of many of his countrymen in 1864. In the latter year Congress began the struggle over reconstruction that was not to end until the blackest chapter in our history had been written.

The ink on Lincoln's reconstruction proclamation of December 8th, 1863, had not had seven days to dry when Thaddeus Stevens reported to the House a resolution to refer the proclamation to a special committee of which Henry Winter Davis of Maryland became chairman.[2] Davis had been elected a representative from his state in 1855 as a "Know-Nothing," and had served continuously until 1861. In the election of 1860 he was defeated. He thereupon became a Republican and as such was reëlected in 1862.[3] In 1864 he was 47. Whatever else was wanting this young man did not lack self-confidence. He strongly preferred his own statesmanship to that of Abraham Lincoln and loudly proclaimed the superiority of his opinions to those of the chief executive of the nation. He was cocky, intolerant, egotistical, self-opinionated, unyielding. In short, he was splendid material for the Radicals. He was a man after their own heart. On January 18th, 1864, he presented a bill embodying the Congressional scheme of reconstruction.[4] The differences between this and Lincoln's plan were fundamental.

The theory of the Radicals was that the eleven states adopting ordinances of secession were no longer "states"; that they had become mere territories and as such were under the direct control of Congress. In the last analysis, it was the recognition of the

134

rightfulness of the Southern claim. If the Radicals were correct then all the blood and treasure which had been expended by the North were spent in an unlawful cause.

The Congressional plan repudiated Lincoln's oft-repeated declaration that the Southern states, despite their efforts to withdraw, were still states in the Union and that they could have "no other legal status." The Davis bill required the Southern states to amend their constitutions in accordance with certain Congressional requirements, and that then and not till then they could resume their status in the Union and be represented in the Senate and the House. Among these Congressional requirements was that directing each state to abolish slavery.[5] No one desired to do away with slavery more than Lincoln, but he recognized that its permanent abolition could lawfully be secured only through an amendment to the Federal Constitution. His emancipation proclamations were based upon a temporary and extreme exercise of his war power. His reconstruction plan was founded on his power to grant reprieves and pardons. The real issue then was whether Congress or the President could carry out the reconstruction.

The Southern states were either in the Union or they were not. If they were in the Union, Congress had no power to provide what constitutions or laws they should adopt; if they were out of the Union, then they had succeeded in their war and Congress had no greater right to interfere with them than with Canada or Mexico. But the difference between Lincoln and his Congress lay far deeper than a mere dispute as to their constitutional prerogatives. Lincoln divined the inner purpose of the Radicals and he had set his will to thwart their hidden schemes to spoliate and trample down the South when her armies were defeated. If Congress could abolish slavery it could disfranchise Southern white men and give the vote to the illiterate ex-slaves. Lincoln determined to prevent these things.

Thaddeus Stevens and his friends were dreaming of the "conquered provinces," where they might work their unscrupulous, untrammelled will. A bright vision of the "carpet-bag" régime loomed up before them. Let us look in for a moment on the

Congressional debates over the Winter Davis bill. Davis on March 18th, 1864, addressed Congress in furtherance of his plan and in criticism of Lincoln's program.[6] But even the Davis measure was not radical enough for Stevens. "I have offered a substitute to the bill of the Committee," he said, "because that does not, in my judgment, meet the evil. It partially acknowledges the rebel states to have rights under the Constitution which I deny, as war has abrogated them all. I do not inquire what rights we have under it, but they have none. The bill takes for granted that the President may partially interfere in the civil administration not as a conqueror but as President of the United States. It seems to me to take away the chance of the confiscation of property of the rebels. . . ."[7] Stevens continued: "When we come to enforce the rights of conquest we should be justified in insisting upon the extreme rights of war. . . ."[8] The abuse of Lincoln throughout the debates was flagrant and offensive. Representative Dennison, for instance, declared: "There does not exist on the earth a more despotic government than that of Abraham Lincoln. He is a despot in fact if not in name."[9]

The Davis bill was intended as a rebuke to the President.[10] There were men in that Congress, however, who appraised it clearly, its supporters and their motives; one of these was Representative Pendleton of Ohio. Boutwell had just declared that he would not have South Carolina and Georgia appear again within the Union,[11] when Pendleton arose and said: "The veil is drawn aside. We see clearly. The party in possession of the powers of the government is revolutionary. It seeks to use those powers to destroy the government, to change its form, to change its spirit. . . . It is in rebellion against the Constitution; it is in treasonable conspiracy against the government. It differs in nothing from the armed enemies except in the weapons of its warfare."

"Call things by their true names," shouted Pendleton. "Admit you are in revolution; admit you are revolutionists; . . . admit that you do not fight to restore the Union. . . . Avow that you exercise the powers of the government because you control them; that you are not bound by the Constitution, but by your own sense of right."

"The acts of secession," continued Pendleton, "are either valid or they are invalid. If they are valid they separated the states from the Union. If they are invalid . . . the state officers who act upon them are rebels to the Federal government. The states are not destroyed; their constitutions are not abrogated; their officers are committing illegal acts for which they are liable to punishment; the states have never left the Union. . . ."

"The duty imposed on Congress is doubtless important," he continued, "but Congress has no right to use a means of performing it forbidden by the Constitution, no matter how necessary or proper it might be thought to be. But sir, this doctrine is monstrous. It has no foundation in the Constitution. It subjects all states to the will of Congress; it places their institutions at the feet of Congress. It creates in Congress an absolute unqualified despotism; . . . my own state of Ohio is liable at any moment to be called in question for her constitution. She does not permit negroes to vote. . . . From that decision of the Congress there is no appeal to the people of Ohio, but only to the people of Massachusetts, and New York, and Wisconsin at the election of Representatives, and if a majority cannot be elected to reverse the decision the people of Ohio must submit. Woe be the day when that doctrine shall be established, for from its centralized despotism we will appeal to the sword." The bill nevertheless passed the House on May 4th, 1864.[12] It went over to the Senate where with certain amendments it was reported by Benjamin F. Wade twenty-three days later. Between then and the last of June, when it came up for consideration, the convention at Baltimore renominated Lincoln. Both Wade and Davis had done all they could to render this impossible.[13] With peculiar relish, therefore, on June 30th, Wade rose in the Senate to sponsor this measure so opposed to Lincoln's views. "The executive," he declared, "ought not to be permitted to handle this great question to his own liking." [14] The next day it was passed in the upper chamber and two days later was sent to the President.[15]

Congress was to adjourn on July 4th. When the bill was placed before Lincoln, "he laid it aside and went on with the other work of the moment. Several prominent members entered in a state of intense anxiety over the fate of the bill. Mr. Sumner and Mr. Boutwell, while their nervousness was evident, refrained from comment. Zachariah Chandler . . . asked the President if he intended to sign the bill. The President replied: 'This bill has been placed before me a few moments before Congress adjourns. It is a matter of too much importance to be swallowed in that way.' 'If it is vetoed,' cried Mr. Chandler, 'it will damage us fearfully in the northwest. The important point is that one prohibiting slavery in the reconstructed states.' Mr. Lincoln said: 'That is the point on which I doubt the authority of Congress to act.' 'It is no more than you have done yourself,' said the Senator. The President answered: 'I conceive that I may in an emergency do things on military grounds which cannot be done constitutionally by Congress.' Mr. Chandler, expressing deep chagrin, went out, and the President, addressing the members of the Cabinet who were seated with him, said: 'I do not see how any of us now can deny what we have always said, that Congress has no constitutional power over slavery in the states.' " [16]

The President continued: "This bill and the position of the gentlemen seem to me, in asserting that the insurrectionary states are no longer in the Union, to make the fatal admission that states, whenever they please, may of their own motion dissolve their connection with the Union. Now we cannot survive that admission, I am convinced. If that be true, I am not President; these gentlemen are not Congress. I have laboriously endeavored to avoid that question ever since it first began to be mooted, and thus to avoid confusion and disturbance in our own councils. It was to obviate this question that I earnestly favored this movement for an amendment to the Constitution abolishing slavery, which passed the Senate and failed in the House. I thought it much better, if it were possible to restore the Union without the necessity of a violent quarrel among its friends as to whether certain states have been in or out of the Union during the war—a merely metaphysical question, and one unnecessary to be forced into discussion." [17]

That quarrel was now inevitable. But it was Lincoln's successor and not Lincoln who was to bear the brunt.

§

How clearly Lincoln comprehended the Radical opposition was revealed on the very day the Davis bill was sent to him by Congress. "Although every member of the cabinet agreed with the President," John Hay tells us that "when a few minutes later, he entered his carriage to go home, he foresaw the importance of the step he had resolved to take and its possibly disastrous consequences to himself. When some one said to him that the threats made by the extreme radicals had no foundation, and that people would not bolt their ticket on a question of metaphysics, he answered: 'If they choose to make a point upon this, I do not doubt that they can do harm. They have never been friendly to me. At all events I must keep some consciousness of being somewhere near right. I must keep some standard or principle fixed with myself.' " [18]

That they would indeed "choose to make a point upon this" he was presently to discover. That they could "do harm" he was in part to learn, though full knowledge of this was to be reserved for Andrew Johnson.

On July 8th, 1864, Lincoln issued a proclamation setting forth the reasons for his failure to approve the Davis bill. He was unwilling that the "free state constitutions and governments adopted . . . in Arkansas and Louisiana" should be "set aside . . , thereby repelling the loyal men who have set up the same, . . . or to declare a constitutional competency in Congress to abolish slavery in states. . . ." He was "expecting" that an amendment to the United States Constitution for that purpose might be adopted. That the adoption of state constitutions was a matter for the states themselves and not for Congress to decide he thus tactfully made plain: "I am fully satisfied with the system for restoration contained in the bill as one very proper plan for the loyal people of any state choosing to adopt it. . . ." [19]

When Ben Wade and Winter Davis read this proclamation they saw the frustration of their hopes. The vision of the carpetbag régime was fading. These things, together with their hatred for Lincoln himself,[20] prompted them to action. They considered long, and finally in cold blood published in the New York *Tribune* of August 5th, the "Wade-Davis Manifesto." It was a thoroughly unbridled and dishonorable composition. Its language was personally insulting. "We have read," it began, "without surprise, but not without indignation the Proclamation of the President of the 8th of July, 1864. The supporters of the Administration are responsible to the country for its conduct; and it is their duty and right to check the encroachments of the Executive on the authority of Congress, and to require it to confine itself to its proper sphere. . . . The proclamation is neither an approval nor a veto of the bill; it is therefore a document unknown to the laws and Constitution of the United States."

"Supporters of the administration!"—on what did they base their title to that claim? "So far as it proposes to execute the bill which is not law" these righteous critics continued, "it is a grave executive usurpation. . . . The reasons now assigned for not approving the bill are full of ominous significance." And further: "The President by preventing this bill from becoming a law holds the electoral votes of the Rebel states at the dictation of his personal ambition. . . . The President has greatly presumed on the forbearance which the supporters of his administration have so long practiced. . . ." These stern patriots warned Lincoln that to secure Congressional support he must "confine himself to his executive duties,—to obey and execute, not make the laws; to suppress by arms the rebellion, and leave political reorganization to Congress." [21]

In this paper we begin to see the Radicals in action. In the middle of the most serious political campaign in American history and of the most crucial military campaign of the war these "supporters of the administration" were capable of this attack. "If they really meant what they said, or any considerable part of it," says Mr. Morse, "they would have been obliged to vote 'guilty' had the House of Representatives seen fit to put these newspaper charges of theirs into the formal shape of articles of impeachment against the President." [22] That is true,—but the Radicals were not yet ready; the war was on. So dastardly a move would not then have been entirely safe! The Radicals were sharpening their knives, but they were waiting until the Southerners should be disarmed.

The spleen of these men did not in the least deter Lincoln from his course, his only comment was: "Well, let them wriggle." [23] Welles understood their motives when he wrote: "The President . . . is denounced with malignity for . . . the prudent and wise omission to sign a law prescribing how and in what way the Union shall be reconstructed. . . . In getting up this law it was as much an object of Mr. Winter Davis and some others to pull down the Administration as to reconstruct the Union. I think they had the former more directly in view than the latter. Davis's conduct is not surprising, but I should not have expected that Wade, who has a good deal of patriotic feeling, common sense, and a strong though coarse and vulgar mind, would have lent himself to such a despicable assault on the President." "There is, however," continued Welles, "an infinity of party and personal intrigue just at this time. A Presidential election is approaching and there are many aspirants not only for Presidential but other honors or positions. H. Winter Davis has a good deal of talent but is rash and uncertain. There is scarcely a more ambitious man, and no one that cannot be more safely trusted. He is impulsive and mad and has been acute and contriving in this whole measure and has drawn Wade, who is ardent, and others into it. Sumner, I perceived, was bitten before he left Washington."

"The assaults of these men on the administration may break it down," our diarist continues. "They are, in their earnest zeal on the part of some, and ambition and malignity on the part of others, doing an injury that they cannot repair." [24]

With unerring vision the Secretary of the Navy thus discerned the secret hopes coiled at the bottom of Ben Wade's heart. "The conduct of Wade for some time past, commencing with the organization of the present Congress in December last, has, after the amnesty proclamation and conciliatory policy of reconstruction, been in some respects strange and difficult to be accounted for, except as an aspiring factionist. I am inclined to believe that he has been bitten with the Presidential fever, is disappointed, and

in his disappointment with a vague, indefinite hope that he may
be successful, prompted and stimulated not only by Davis but
Colfax, he has been flattered to do a foolish act." [25]

We shall have further occasion to study Wade's "vague and
indefinite hope." We shall have opportunity to see Colfax in his
artful stimulation of that "Presidential fever," and finally we shall
witness Ben Wade playing the master hypocrite of American history, and all but attaining the ambition he was nursing when he
confederated with Winter Davis to libel Abraham Lincoln. But
the Wade-Davis Manifesto had at least one good effect: "It
probably defeated the renomination of Mr. Davis for Congress." [26]

SNIPING FROM THE REAR

HORACE GREELEY was an eccentric, such only as our America of the nineteenth century's middle decades could produce. His early experiments with the *Northern Spectator*, the *New Yorker*, the *Log Cabin*, and finally the *Tribune*, his interests extending from the Fourierite associations to the Phalanx Colony of Red Bank, New Jersey, Brook Farm, the Spiritualism of the Fox Sisters, the Protective Tariff, opposition to Woman Suffrage, Prohibition, the Crystal Palace Exhibition, experimental agriculture and the Universalist Church, present a range perhaps never equalled except by the journeyman printer of Philadelphia.[1] Whittier once called him "our later Franklin." [2]

Greeley's peace efforts of July, 1864, form one of the most fantastic chapters in the history of diplomacy. His ludicrous and grotesque failure was such as Cervantes might have written into Don Quixote. So impressively abortive a foray into diplomacy might for some time have silenced a less blatant egotist, but not Greeley. Four days after his *Tribune* had published the Wade-Davis Manifesto, we find him writing Lincoln: "Nine-tenths of the whole American people are anxious for peace—peace on almost any terms." [3]

Greeley's chagrin over the poor figure he had made, his constitutional incapacity to appreciate Lincoln, and his opposition to the latter's renomination which he had expressed as early as four months before the convention,[4] led him now fully to cast his lot with Wade, Davis and other enemies and traducers of the President.

Twelve days after his publication of the Manifesto, Greeley wrote: "Mr. Lincoln is already beaten. . . . He cannot be elected.

143

And we must have another ticket to save us from utter over-throw." [5]   There was momentum behind this movement for "another ticket."   Chase wrote expressing sympathy with the idea. Winter Davis voiced his enthusiastic approval and promised the support of Wade. Governor Andrew of Massachusetts gave his backing also. [6]

On August 18th, the very day Greeley wrote demanding "another ticket," a committee met in New York City and decided to send out a circular letter enclosing a petition for a new convention to be held at Cincinnati on September 28th. [7] The expressed object of the proposed convention was to "concentrate the Union strength on some one candidate who commands the confidence of the country, even by a new nomination if necessary." [8]

The circular was dispatched to "Union men of every sort in the North." [9] It was signed by John Austin Stevens alone,—"not to involve people unnecessarily." [10]   Arrangements were made for an adjourned meeting to be held at the home of David Dudley Field on Tuesday evening, August 30th. In the meantime the responses from newspapers and public men voiced the feeling that "the only hope was in a new candidate." [11]   Henry Winter Davis promised to be present at this meeting. It was arranged that Chase and Butler as "possible candidates to supplant Lincoln" were to be present "only by proxy." Sumner declined to come for the same reason, but put himself "in Andrew's charge." In the meantime in a letter marked "private and confidential," Sumner wrote: "I see no way of meeting the difficulties from the candidacy of Mr. Lincoln unless he withdraws patriotically and kindly, so as to leave no breach in the party. Will he do this? · . . . You know well that I have always regretted that the Republican Convention was called at so early a day. Its action seemed to me ill-considered and unreasonable. If it were regarded as merely temporary then its errors might be corrected by another convention, which with the concurrence of Mr. Lincoln might nominate a candidate who would surely be elected. Let me know by telegraph if I can be of service and I will try to meet you." [12]

§

The Democratic Convention met at Chicago on the 29th of August and nominated McClellan and Pendleton. The platform declared: "that after four years of failure to restore the Union by the experiment of war . . . justice, humanity, liberty and the public welfare demand that immediate efforts be made for a cessation of hostilities. . . ."[13]

The last two weeks of August, 1864, contained perhaps the blackest hours of the republic. On the 20th of that month an address was sent from Boston to General Frémont asking him if "in case Mr. Lincoln will withdraw, you will do so," and "unite the thorough and earnest friends of a vigorous prosecution of the war in a new convention."[14] "The withdrawal of Lincoln and Frémont," urged the Cincinnati *Gazette*, "and the nomination of a man that would inspire confidence and infuse a life into our ranks would be hailed with general delight."[15] On August 22nd, Henry J. Raymond, chairman of the Republican National Executive Committee and the editor of the New York *Times*, reported to the President: "The tide is setting strongly against us."[16]

Winter Davis, smarting from the defeat of his reconstruction measure, watched with keen delight Lincoln's expected humiliation. Two or three days after McClellan's nomination he wrote: "The Chicago men seem to take well and I hear daily of defections to them in quarters least expected from us."[17]

With the unswerving determination of true zealots, the Radicals were seeking Lincoln's ruin. They had said and done more than enough, if sincere, to have required the filing of articles of impeachment against him. But impeachment was not necessary then, there were subtler methods of attaining the same end. "Grave executive usurpations"—"The President by preventing the bill from becoming a law holds the electoral votes of the Rebel states at the dictation of his personal ambition"—"The encroachments of the executive,"—these words of the Wade-Davis Manifesto were the rallying cry and the inspiration of those who sought to discredit and destroy Abraham Lincoln. Even above this Babel, we seem to catch the shrill notes of Sumner's voice like the high staccato of a riveting machine: "Let me know by telegraph if I can be of service and I will try to meet you." [18]

The Radicals, however, had not counted upon one obstacle: the war! On the 5th of August, Farragut mastered Mobile Bay; [19] the news was suggestive to the Radicals, as well as to the South, of what was soon to follow. At the adjourned meeting called at the home of Davis Dudley Field for August 30th, the replies to the circular letters were read and every possibility of furthering their purpose was considered. After much discussion, however, they concluded to abandon the plan of forcing Lincoln to withdraw. [20]

Four days later the North was thrilled with this dispatch: "General Sherman has taken Atlanta." A storm of patriotism revived the Union heart. [21] "Sherman and Farragut have knocked the bottom out of the Chicago nominations," Seward said. [22] During the same month the brilliant campaigns of Sheridan in the Shenandoah Valley electrified the followers of Lincoln. On September 15th Winchester, and five days later Fisher's Hill! [23] Is it strange that at about this time the efforts of Sumner, of Winter Davis and their friends began to pale, or that on September 21st Frémont and Pendleton, despite the sponsorship of Wendell Phillips decided to abandon Presidential aspirations? [24]

The Lincoln tide was rising, nor was it stemmed by charges of ignorance, incompetency and corruption hurled at him by the New York *World*. "Mr. Lincoln, has he or has he not an interest in the profits of public contracts?" it asked and again: "Is Mr. Lincoln honest?" The *World* thus answered its own questions: "That Lincoln has succumbed to the opportunities and temptations of his present place is capable of the easiest proof," and further: "This claim of honesty will not bear examination. . . . Honest old Abe has few honest men to defend his honesty." [25] Certainly he did not find Charles Sumner, until Sherman and Farragut and Sheridan began issuing their most effective of all campaign documents.

On October 19th the Battle of Cedar Creek [26] was added to the Lincoln arguments. The political campaign took on a brighter hue. During July and August Chase had been not only "sulky and wavering," but, on one occasion at least, at a dinner in Boston had spoken "with no attempt at concealment in offensively contemptuous terms of Lincoln." [27] He now made speeches for the Union candidate.[28] The "Radicals," said Whitelaw Reid, "had returned to their old allegiance and would fight in the van." [29] Governor Andrew at about this time wrote "that the plain duty for them as practical men was to give Lincoln their energetic support." [30]

On November 8th, Abraham Lincoln was elected President and Andrew Johnson Vice-President of the United States. Their plurality was less than 6,000 short of half a million votes.[31] Sumner's bland and pious prayer "for a candidate who would surely be elected" had been answered, though not quite as he had planned. The time for the Radicals to depose a President had not yet come.

XVI

SALMON P. CHASE BECOMES CHIEF JUSTICE

THE death of Chief Justice Roger Taney on October 12th,[1] 1864, marks the closing of an era illuminated and explained by his opinion in the Dred Scott case.

As usual the aspirants for this high judicial post were many. Among those considered was William M. Evarts, whom we shall later meet.[2] Other claimants were pushed forward, but for no one was there greater pressure than for Chase.[3] Less than a year before he had contemptuously sneered at the President whose favor he was now importunately seeking. It seems that as Secretary of the Treasury he was concerned over governmental expenditures, for on the 24th of the previous January he wrote: "The spigot in Uncle Abe's barrel is made twice as big as the bung hole. He may have been a good flat-boatman, and rail-splitter, but he certainly never learned the science of coopering." [4]

How little jibes or sneers affected Lincoln in his official conduct appears from his conversation about Chase held in November with Judge Hoar and Richard Dana. Lincoln said: "He has not always behaved very well lately and people say to me—'Now is the time to crush him out.' Well I'm not in favor of crushing anybody out! If there is anything a man can do, and do it well, I say let him do it. Give him a chance." [5]

On December 6th Lincoln nominated Chase; the Senate immediately confirmed the nomination.[6] That night the new Chief Justice wrote to Lincoln thanking him "for this mark of your confidence and especially for the manner in which the nomination was made. I will never forget either and trust you will never regret either." [7] While he was closing this note with the effusive assurance that he prized Lincoln's "confidence and good will more than nomination to office," [8] Gideon Welles sat making this record in his diary: "I hope the selection may prove a good one.   I would not have advised it, because I have apprehensions on that subject.   Chase has mental power and resources, but he is politically ambitious and restless, prone to, but not very skillful in, intrigue and subtle management.   If he applies himself strictly and faithfully to his duties, he may succeed on the bench, although his mind, I fear, is not so much judicial as ministerial.   He will be likely to use the place for political advancement and thereby endanger confidence in the court.   He, though selfishly stubborn, sometimes wants moral courage and frankness, is fond of adulation, and, with official superiors, is a sycophant.   I hope the President may have no occasion to regret his selection." [9]

Here was the judge who was later to preside at the greatest trial in American history.

XVII

LINCOLN AND THE RADICALS AGAIN

ON the evening of November 10th, 1864, two days after Lincoln's reëlection, he was serenaded and thus responded to those who came to honor him: "Now that the election is over, may not all having a common interest reunite in a common effort to save our common country. For my own part I have striven and shall strive to avoid placing any obstacle in the way. So long as I have been here, I have not willingly planted a thorn in any man's bosom." [1]

On the same day Lincoln nominated Chase for Chief Justice, he sent his fourth and last annual message to the Congress. The Union arms were triumphing, his own cause had triumphed at the polls, upon the issue between Congressional Reconstruction and his own,—an issue joined between the Wade-Davis Manifesto and the Republican platform demanding a constitutional amendment for the abolition of slavery, he had been triumphant, but there was no note of triumph in his message.

The proposed thirteenth amendment having been one of the issues in the campaign, Lincoln recommended the immediate reconsideration and passage of the amendment. [2] On the 14th of the previous March, Arkansas, [3] and on the 5th of September, Louisiana, [4] had each adopted constitutions abolishing slavery in those states. [5] "Important movements," the President continued, "have also occurred during the year to the effect of molding society for durability in the Union. Although short of complete success, it is much in the right direction that 12,000 citizens in each of the states of Arkansas and Louisiana have organized loyal state governments, with free constitutions and are earnestly struggling to maintain and administer them. The movements in the same direction, more extensive though less definite in Missouri, Kentucky and Tennessee should not be overlooked." [6]

150

On January 31st, 1865, the House acted favorably on Lincoln's plea, by its approval of the thirteenth amendment. That it acted less from a desire to follow Lincoln than from the recognition that, as his message declared "the voice of the people" had been "heard upon the question," would appear from the struggle which was now renewed with Lincoln over reconstruction. On January 12th, Mr. Ashley presented a substitute for the Wade-Davis measure.[7]   Once again the motives of the Radicals were exposed and their vision of the carpet-bag régime laid bare,—this time by Mr. Dawes of Massachusetts: "My friend (Mr. Ashley) has reported here a bill," said Dawes, "which authorizes an army of thousands of these office holders to go into those states with commission from this Capital in their pockets, to lord it over the poor miserable inhabitants left behind the army there. These rebel states may be thus converted into asylums for broken-down politicians." [8]

Joseph Edgerton of Indiana declared that the purpose of the Ashley measure was "to enfranchise and elevate negroes and to disfranchise and degrade white men; a bill to change the social and industrial systems and internal policy of eleven states; a bill to take from those states their inherent reserved constitutional rights to regulate in their own way their internal policy, not inconsistent with the Constitution of the United States. It is a bill to punish treason without a trial or conviction; in short a bill to reconstruct states and make state constitutions, when in truth no states or their constitutions have been destroyed or need reconstruction unless by the voluntary action of their own people." [9]

How clearly this representative understood the accumulating malice of the Radicals was more fully revealed when he declared that the proposed measure "embodies a spirit and purpose toward the Southern people which if impolitic and vindictive a year ago when the bill first came before the House, and when our enemy was far stronger and more defiant than now, is still more impolitic and vindictive at this time when the minds of all good men are searching diligently for ways of reconciliation and peace." [10] And further: "The Congress . . . is asked by this bill to be the minister and executioner of the great revenge of section upon section,

states North upon states South.   For one, Sir, I want to wash my
hands of the deed." [11]   There were many who were eager to be
the executioners "of the great revenge." The debate afforded Winter Davis another opportunity publicly to insult Lincoln.   "When
I came into Congress ten years ago," said Davis, "this was a
government of law.   I have lived to see it a government of personal will.   Congress has dwindled from a power to dictate law
and the policy of the government to a commission to audit
accounts and to appropriate moneys to enable the Executive to
execute his will and not ours." [12]

Winter Davis had become the friend and the ally of Thaddeus
Stevens.   It was a fitting friendship.   With such a mentor it should
not surprise us to find him berating Lincoln outside as well as
within the halls of Congress.   In the first days of February,
General Cox was passing through Washington.   This was about
the time of the Hampton Roads Conference which we shall later
notice.   Cox has thus recorded what he heard: "Garfield invited
me to meet Schenck and Winter Davis at dinner at Weleker's
restaurant.   The berating of Lincoln by the two last named was
something to take one's breath away. . . . Mr. Lincoln . . . was
charged with all the folly, stupidity and semi-treason that could
be imagined. . . ." [13]

But Davis was not speaking for himself alone when he told
Congress that after Lincoln had "destroyed the armies in the field
he should go further and do as I think he ought to do, what the
judgment of this country dictates, treat those who hold power in
the South as rebels and not as governors or legislators; disperse
them from the halls of legislation; expel them from executive
mansions, strip them of the emblems of authority." [14]

The Ashley bill was laid on the table on February 22nd, 1865, [15]
—it was a good day on which to discard such a measure!   Before
the vote was taken Ashley laid bare his own as well as the purposes of his fellow Radicals.   "I do not expect," he said, "to pass
this bill now.   At the next session when a new Congress, fresh
from the people, shall have assembled, with the nation and its
Representatives far in advance of the present Congress, I hope
to pass even a better bill."   He knew, he said that "our loyal

HENRY WINTER DAVIS.

people" would never "deny those loyal blacks political rights while consenting that pardoned but unrepentant white rebels shall again be clothed with the entire political power of these states." [16]

Here it was, the carpet-bag régime! "Even a better bill!" The promise of the Reconstruction Acts of 1867! Davis later publicly advocated the extension of suffrage to the negroes.[17] His death on the 30th of the following December prevented him from viewing the consummation of his dreams. He did not live to see "those who hold power in the South" humbled by the Northern bayonets long after they had peacefully laid down their own. He did not live to see those same Northern bayonets place the negro in control of Southern white men. Death prevented him from witnessing the followers of Lee and Stonewall Jackson dispersed "from the halls of legislation" and stripped of "the emblems of authority." Death enjoined his participation in the further struggles with the President over reconstruction. He could not see those things, but to his friend Thaddeus Stevens this joyous treat in all its fullness was accorded. Presently we shall observe him gorging at the feast, gloating, as the Aborigines were wont to do, while they watched their victims harnessed to a flaming stake and writhing amid slow-burning fagots.

XVIII

THE CONFERENCE AT HAMPTON ROADS

LINCOLN did not need Greeley's abortive peace efforts to convince him that in 1864 the time for peace had not arrived. "It seems to me," he wrote in December of that year, "that no attempt at negotiation with the insurgent leader could result in any good. He would accept nothing short of severance of the Union, precisely what we will not and cannot give. . . . He cannot voluntarily reaccept the Union; we cannot voluntarily yield it." [1]

Nevertheless at Hampton Roads on February 3rd of the following year, Lincoln and Seward met three Commissioners of the Confederacy to explore the possibilities of peace. Their conference was one of the dramatic episodes of the war. The Confederate Commissioners were Alexander H. Stephens, R. T. M. Hunter and Judge Campbell. For four hours Lincoln and his Secretary of State conferred with the Vice-President of the Confederacy and his two associates on board the *River Queen*. "Mr. President, is there no way of putting down an end to the present trouble?" Stephens asked. "There is but one way," Lincoln answered, "and that is for those who are resisting the laws of the Union to cease that resistance. . . . The restoration of the Union is a *sine qua non* with me." [2] Judge Campbell inquired on what terms the Southerners could have peace. "By disbanding their armies and permitting the national authorities to resume their functions," Lincoln answered. [3]

In the discussion of slavery Lincoln declared that "he never would change or modify the terms of the proclamation in the slightest particular," and Seward called attention to the thirteenth amendment abolishing slavery just passed by Congress and awaiting action by the states. [4]

Would the Southern states if they abandoned war "be admitted to representation in Congress?" Stephens asked. The President said that he thought "they ought to be but he could not enter into any stipulation on the subject." [5]   After some further discussion Lincoln exclaimed: "Stephens, if I were in Georgia, and entertained the sentiments I do—though I suppose I should not be permitted to stay there long with them . . ., if I were in your place: I would go home and get the Governor of the state to call the legislature together, and get them to recall all the state troops from the war; elect senators and members to Congress and ratify this constitutional amendment (the thirteenth) prospectively, so as to take effect—say in five years. . . . Whatever may have been the views of your people before the war, they must be convinced now that slavery is doomed. It cannot last long in any event, and the best course it seems to me for your public men to pursue, would be to adopt such a policy as will avoid, as far as possible, the evils of immediate emancipation." [6]

At the end of the interview Hunter complained that no terms were offered them "but unconditional submission to the mercy of conquerors." [7]   Seward assured them that this was not so and Lincoln added that so far as the Confiscation Acts were concerned, he would "exercise the powers of the Executive with the utmost liberality." He declared that even at this late date he "would be willing to be taxed to remunerate the Southern people for their slaves," believing as he did that "the people of the North were as responsible for slavery as the people of the South," and that "if the war should then cease, with the voluntary abolition of slavery," he personally would be in favor "of the government paying a fair indemnity for the loss to the owners." [8]

Two days later Lincoln submitted to his Cabinet a proposal for a government bond issue of $400,000,000 to provide compensation for the Southern slaves. Not a single member of his Cabinet supported him in this. Nothing ever came of it. [9]

Thaddeus Stevens could not wait a week before demanding that Lincoln inform Congress of the results, if any, of his conference. [10] In one sentence of five words the substance of the President's report was thus summed up: "The conference ended without result." [11]

A few days later General Pickett wrote his wife: "On every side gloom, dissatisfaction and disappointment seem to have settled over all, men and officers alike, because of the unsuccessful termination of the Peace Conference on board the *River Queen* on the fatal third. The anxious despairing faces I see everywhere bespeak heavy hearts. Our commissioners knew that we were gasping our last gasp and that the Peace Conference was a forlorn hope. Because of the informality of the conference and my knowledge of Mr. Lincoln, his humanity, his broad nature, his warm heart, I did believe he would take advantage of this very informality and spring some wise superhuman surprise which would somehow restore peace and in time insure unity. Now, heaven help us, it will be war to the knife, with a knife no longer keen, the thrust of an arm no longer strong, the certainty that when peace comes it will follow the tread of a conqueror." [12]

When on February 6th, Jefferson Davis received the report of his commissioners,[13] he determined once more to rally the Confederacy, and accordingly at Richmond on that day delivered "the master oration of his life." [14] One eulogist compared his efforts with the forensics of Demosthenes and Rienzi.[15] "My life is bound up with the Confederacy," Davis declared. "With the Confederacy I will live or die." [16] The enthusiasm aroused by this and like efforts of Hunter and Benjamin three days later, was necessarily shortlived. "There is great enthusiasm at the meetings but not a man is put in the army. When will these farces cease?" the Raleigh *Progress* asked.[17]

Two days after Jefferson Davis had dramatically declared that "with the Confederacy I will live or die," [18] a report from General Lee made the latter alternative the more probable one. "Some of the men had been without meat for three days," ran this discouraging dispatch, "and all were suffering from reduced rations and scant clothing, exposed to battle, cold, hail, and sleet. . . . If some change is not made and the commissary department reorganized, I apprehend dire results." [19] With tragic legibility the writing on the wall appeared.

"In the same hour came forth fingers of a man's hand, and wrote over against the candlestick upon the plaster of the wall of the king's palace, and the king saw the part of the hand that wrote." [20]   Neither Belshazzar, the King, nor his wise men nor astrologers could decipher the words, but Daniel translated them: "God hath numbered thy kingdom and finished it." [21]   That Jefferson Davis did not need a Daniel to decipher Lee's report would appear from his message to the Confederate Congress twelve days later: "Very few weeks remain for preparation, and we are threatened by a concentration of forces around us, which cannot be successfully resisted without the aid of large reinforcements to our armies." [22]

The final days of the Confederacy were approaching.   And yet with a courageous determination, to which the whole world now pays its tribute of respect, the Southern people struggled on. To John Slidell in Paris, still dreaming of Napoleonic intervention, with perfect truth Judah Benjamin had written six weeks earlier: "No people have ever poured out their blood more freely in defense of their liberties and independence, nor have endured sacrifices with greater cheerfulness than have the men and women of these Confederate states. . . . They have asked for nothing, fought for nothing, but for the right of self-government, for independence." [23]

Outnumbered three to one, worn down from four years of bleeding sacrifice, in the last month of that unequal conflict, the Southern people still stood steadfast.   Who is there that has read the awful story of the decade after Appomattox, the shameful history of the carpet-bag régime, that cannot sympathize with the appeal of the Confederate Congress in March 1865, [24] before its last adjournment?   How clearly was discerned and how justly apprehended the malice of the Northern Radicals: "The Southern people would be held as conquered provinces by the despotic government at Washington," this document proclaimed.

That the Southern statesmen had divined the purpose of Thaddeus Stevens and his fellow Radicals was evident, for they declared: "Not only would we be deprived of every political franchise dear to freemen, but socially we would be degraded to the level of slaves. . . . Not only would the property and estates of vanquished rebels be confiscated, but they would be divided and distributed among our African bondsmen. . . . Our enemies, with a boastful insolence unparalleled in the history of modern civilization, have threatened not only our subjugation, but some of them have announced their determination, if successful in this struggle, to deport our entire white population and supplant it with a new population drawn from their own territory and from European countries. . . . Think of it! That we the descendants of a brave ancestry who wrested from a powerful nation by force of arms the country which we inhabit—bequeathed to us by them, and upon which we have been born and reared; that we should be uprooted from it and an alien population planted in our stead is a thought that should inspire us with an undying hostility to an enemy base enough to have conceived it." [25]

With such a prospect do you blame the Southerners for fighting on? Were their fears far-fetched? Thaddeus Stevens had announced that the Republican party would have to "treat those states now outside of the Union as conquered provinces and settle them with new men, and drive the present rebels as exiles from this country. . . ." [26] And Winter Davis had exhorted: "Treat those who hold power in the South as rebels and not as governors or legislators; disperse them from the halls of legislation; expel them from executive mansions, strip them of the emblems of authority." [27]

The last words of the Confederate appeal with dramatic clarity revealed how perfectly the Southern men had understood their Northern enemies: "Failure will compel us to drink the cup of humiliation even to the bitter dregs of having the history of our struggle written by New England historians." [28]

For twelve years they bore the misery of the carpet-bag régime; for more than three decades they suffered under the results of negro domination. For sixty years have they tasted "the bitter dregs"; by "New England historians" indeed has their history been written!

LINCOLN AND THE RADICALS FOR THE LAST TIME

THE final struggle over reconstruction between Lincoln and his Congress arose in 1865 over the recognition of Louisiana as a state and the counting of her electoral ballots, as well as those of Tennessee. Benjamin F. Flanders and Michael Hahn in the middle of the war had been elected Representatives in Congress and had both been seated.[1] How could this have been done if Louisiana was not still within the Union? But this was 1863 when the full opposition to Lincoln's plan had not yet developed. In 1864 there was an election of state officers.[2] Nearly twelve thousand white votes were polled,[3]—more than one-fifth of those cast in 1860.[4] Michael Hahn was elected governor. Delegates to a Constitutional Convention were chosen and in April met at New Orleans.[5]

Twenty-four days earlier Lincoln wrote to Hahn: "Now you are about to have a convention which among other things will probably define the electoral franchise. I barely suggest for your private consideration whether some of the colored people may not be let in—as for instance, the very intelligent and especially those who have fought gallantly in our ranks. They would probably help, in some trying times to come, to keep the jewel of liberty within the family of freedom. But this is only a suggestion, not to the public, but to you alone." [6]

The Constitution, adopted five months later, abolished slavery within the state, and though restricting suffrage to white males, empowered the legislature to confer it on colored men in accordance with the suggestion Lincoln made.[7]

To General Hulbert, then in command at New Orleans, on November 14th, 1864, Lincoln wrote: "A very fair proportion of the people of Louisiana have inaugurated a new state govern-

159

ment making an excellent new constitution—better for the poor black men than we have in Illinois. This was done under military protection, directed by me, in the belief still sincerely entertained, that with such a nucleus around which to build we could get the state into position again sooner than otherwise.   In this belief a general promise of protection and support, applicable alike to Louisiana and other states, was given in the last annual message. During the formation of the new government and constitution they were supported by nearly every loyal person and opposed by every secessionist. And this support and this opposition from the respective standpoints of the parties was perfectly consistent and logical. Every Unionist ought to wish the new government to succeed; and every disunionist must desire it to fail. Its failure would gladden the heart of Slidell in Europe, and of every enemy of the old flag in the world." [8]

How implacable a foe of Lincoln's purposes Charles Sumner was, became apparent more than ever when the joint resolution recognizing this government of Louisiana in February, 1865, was debated in the Senate.[9] "The pretended state government of Louisiana," he said, "is utterly indefensible whether you look at its origin or its character. To describe it I must use plain language. It is a mere seven months' abortion, begotten by the bayonet in criminal conjunction with the spirit of caste, and born before its time, rickety, unformed, unfinished—whose continued existence will be a burden, a reproach and a wrong." [10]

To Charles Francis Adams on March 3rd, Richard Dana wrote: "Sumner has been acting like a madman in the Louisiana question . . . in the positions he took, the arguments he advanced, and the language used. . . ." [11]

To Ben Wade also these debates gave further opportunity to abuse the President. "When the foundation of this government is sought to be swept away by executive usurpation," he shouted, "it will not do to . . . say that this came from a President whom I helped to elect. . . . If the President . . . can initiate a state government and bring it here and force us, compel us to receive as associates on this floor these mere mockeries, these men of straw who represent nobody, your republic is at an end. . . . Talk not to me of your ten per cent principle. A more absurd monarchical and anti-American principle was never announced on God's earth." [12]

The complots of Sumner and Ben Wade proved successful. The passage of the resolution recognizing Louisiana was prevented. [13] The Radicals were gaining ground! Sumner, Wade and Stevens,—Lincoln's words fitted them exactly; they had arrayed themselves with "Slidell in Europe" and with "every enemy of the old flag in the world!"

There was good reason not to count the electoral votes of Virginia, Georgia, Florida, Alabama, Mississippi, Arkansas, Texas, and the Carolinas, for in 1864 no Presidential elections had been held there. [14] Arkansas, although having previously organized a loyal state government, [15] did not participate in that election, feeling that its electoral vote "would not be received even if offered." [16] But both Tennessee and Louisiana had held elections and presented their electoral votes to Congress. [17] Should they be counted? If Louisiana and Tennessee were still states, having presented their electoral votes, the Constitution required them to be counted. [18] But on February 6th, 1865, Congress resolved that the electoral votes of all the states that had "rebelled" should not be counted! [19]

How sharp was the issue between Lincoln and the Radicals appeared clearly when Mr. Cowan in the House of Representatives declared: "This involves a direct conflict between the legislature and the Executive bodies of this government, and at this time I am of opinion that we can't afford to enter into that conflict." [20] A large majority, however, felt that they were entirely ready for it, when on February 8th, Vice-President Hamlin announced to the House and Senate in joint session assembled that the returns from Louisiana and Tennessee were in his possession, but that it was his "duty" not to present them. [21] And they were not presented!

Once more the Radicals had triumphed! "Conquered provinces" have no vote! Conquered provinces? But was not Andrew Johnson a resident of one of them? Welcome enough was the support which his fighting name had given to the ticket!

Andrew Johnson of Tennessee!   How could he have been elected Vice-President if he was not a resident of a *state* within the Union?   The Constitution requires that the President and Vice-President must each be an inhabitant of a "*state*."   "It is difficult," quietly remarks Professor Burgess, "to see how the Republicans could have consistently rejected the vote of Tennessee after they nominated and elected a citizen of Tennessee as Vice-President of the United States."[22]

Why was it difficult?   There was only the Constitution in the way, and what was that?

XX

JOHNSON COMPLETES HIS WORK IN TENNESSEE

LET us turn back to Tennessee and observe Andrew Johnson in his final healing work of reconstruction. Four days after the Presidential election, a call was issued for a state convention to be held on December 19th, at Nashville.[1] A good many events were to occur between those dates,—events of vital moment, not to Tennessee alone, but to the United States as well.

The unhappy residents of his state had no reason to doubt that a war was going on throughout 1864. When in November, Hood led the remnant of his Confederate army westward to Decatur, Alabama, he hoped to frighten Sherman back to Nashville.[2] Something must be done—there was to be no repetition of 1862, when Buell left Andrew Johnson to defend the capital almost with his bare hands! General George Henry Thomas was a Virginian who remained loyal to the United States. He was a gallant Union officer.[3] As Hood approached, Sherman detached Thomas with 60,000 veterans and sent him to defend the capital.[4] He was a good man to send! Johnson was glad to have him come! They had much in common, these two Southerners who had remained loyal to the Union!

On December 15th, Thomas destroyed Hood's army.[5] At last in Tennessee the work of reconstruction could proceed. The Convention called for December 19th had been postponed until January 9th, 1865, because of Hood's invasion. It met at Nashville on that day,[6] and three days later Andrew Johnson appeared before the delegates.[7] The stage was set for him, and without difficulty he filled the leading rôle.[8] Under his leadership, amendments to the state constitution abolishing slavery were submitted to the people, and the ordinance of secession was repealed.[9]

163

The closing act of that drama witnessed the realization of a life-long hope,—the hope of Parson Brownlow. He was nominated for governor and later elected.

On January 13th, 1865, Johnson wrote to Lincoln: "All is now working well, and if Tennessee is now left alone (she) will soon resume all the functions of a state according to the genius and theory of the government." [10] To which Lincoln answered: "Thanks to the Convention and to you. When do you expect to be here?" [11]

The proposed constitutional amendments were now submitted to the people. On February 22nd they were approved by a vote of 25,293 to 48. Thus Lincoln's ten per cent requirement was fully met; the state was now reconstructed in accordance with his plan.[12] It had been a long pull! To Johnson it must have seemed a lifetime since the 14th of March, 1862, when he assumed the Herculean tasks of military governor. Only a man of his iron purpose could have carried through the burdens he so cheerfully assumed and bore with uncomplaining fortitude.

The election for governor was scheduled for the 4th of March. Johnson wished to remain in Tennessee until the election of his successor.[13] But Lincoln wanted him in Washington, and on January 24th, 1865, thus telegraphed: "Several members of the Cabinet with myself, considered the question today as to the time of your coming on here. While we fully appreciate your wish to remain in Tennessee until her state government shall be completely reinaugurated, it was our unanimous conclusion that it is unsafe for you to not be here on the 4th of March. Be sure to reach here by that time." [14]

Three days after the people of Tennessee ratified the work of the Convention, Johnson issued his last proclamation as military governor.[15] His resignation was accepted by Secretary Stanton in these words: "Permit me on this occasion to render to you the thanks of this department for your patriotic and able services during the eventful period through which you have exercised the high trusts committed to your charge."

"In one of the darkest hours of the great struggle for national existence against rebellious foes," continued Stanton, in words which it will be well for us later to recall, "the government called you from the Senate and from the comparatively safe and easy duties of civil life to place you in the front of the enemy and in a position of personal toil and danger, perhaps more hazardous than was encountered by any other citizen or military officer of the United States. With patriotic promptness you assumed the post, and maintained it under circumstances of unparalleled trials, until recent events have brought safety and deliverance to your state, and to the integrity of that constiutional Union for which you so long and so gallantly periled all that is dear to man on earth. That you may be spared to enjoy the new honors and perform the high duties to which you have been called by the people of the United States is the sincere wish of one who in every official and personal relation has found you worthy of the confidence of the government and the honor and esteem of your fellow-citizens." [16]

JOHNSON MAKES A BAD SLIP

WITH the progress of the Union arms as he himself described it, "reasonably satisfactory and encouraging to all," [1] on the 4th of March, 1865, Abraham Lincoln delivered his second Inaugural address. One perfect sentence is its final paragraph. As long as English literature endures these words will live: "With malice toward none, with charity for all, with firmness in the right as God gives us to see the right, let us strive on to finish the work we are in, to bind up the nation's wounds, to care for him who shall have borne the battle and for his widow and his orphan, to do all which may achieve and cherish a just and lasting peace among ourselves and with all nations." [2] Unless it is the Sermon on the Mount, there is nothing that excels the simple majesty of that paragraph.

Andrew Johnson was inaugurated at noon on the same day. The scene in the Senate was a brilliant one. All the seats within the spacious galleries were occupied and every spot where men could stand was filled. The galleries were set apart exclusively for ladies. In lovely crinolines they made a striking and a brilliant scene. [3] The retiring Vice-President occupied the chair, and the officers of the Senate were in their places. Seated at the clerk's desk in front of Mr. Hamlin was the Vice-President elect. The Judges of the Supreme Court were there, the Cabinet, the Diplomatic Corps and the attachés of foreign nations. The high officers of the Army and the Navy were arranged behind the diplomats, while back of the Cabinet sat the Senators and Senators-elect. [4]

At 12 o'clock Johnson was introduced by the outgoing Vice-President and the oath was then administered. Then for fifteen minutes he addressed the audience. It was not up to his high

H. Hamlin.

standard; it was far below it! He was worn down with his work in Tennessee, and had been ill for some days before his departure. On his way to Washington he had taken brandy as an astringent.[5] On his arrival at the Capital, Hamlin had given him a little whiskey.[6] When he stood up to address the Senate he showed the influence of liquor.[7] It was unfortunate. Welles was in doubt whether alcohol or sickness was responsible for his appearance; both were.

While Johnson was speaking Charles Sumner "covered his face with his hands and bowed his head down on his desk." [8] He must have been delighted when the *World* recorded that the Vice-President had "not proceeded far when Senators on the Republican side began to hide their heads." [9] Sumner promptly moved a resolution calling upon Johnson to resign.[10]

Hamlin never forgave Johnson for defeating him for the vice-presidential nomination. His attitude has been faithfully preserved by his grandson,[11] who describes the scene immediately preceding the Inaugural address and pictures Johnson as taking a first, a second and then a "third tumblerful" of whiskey, "without any water." [12] I leave to those more competent to judge, the probability of this story. In this same account, however, there is corroboration of the fact that Johnson was a sick man, for it records him as saying to the retiring Vice-President: "Mr. Hamlin, I am not well and need a stimulant, have you any whiskey?" "No," replied Mr. Hamlin, "when I became Vice President I gave an order prohibiting the sale of liquor in the Senate restaurant; but if you desire I will send across the street for some whiskey." [13]

That Johnson was not a total abstainer there is no doubt; neither was General Grant, but the assertion that he was unduly addicted to the use of alcohol is but one of the baseless slanders by which the Radicals of his time and historians since have endeavored to becloud his name. Lincoln's reputation for credibility will not be impaired on account of his famous inquiry as to what kind of whiskey General Grant was accustomed to employ because he desired to procure some for his other generals. A day or two after Johnson's Inaugural, Lincoln said to his Secretary of the Treasury: "I have known Andy Johnson for many years; he made a bad slip the other day, but you need not be scared; Andy ain't a drunkard." [14]

Albert Brown, Jr., was in Washington shortly after the Inaugural and wrote to Governor Andrew on March 21st: "I met Mr. Blair yesterday on the portico of the White House and . . . I remarked that you are glad that the Blairs have taken Andrew Johnson in charge. To which he replied that A. Johnson is 'all right'; that 'he didn't say anything that was bad sense, only bad taste'; and that 'it is not true that he is a drunkard or was drunk then'; but he had been sick with typhoid for six months and had taken a little whiskey that day, and was a little disordered by the situation and all other things. Mr. Blair further remarked . . . that it wouldn't have been 'nearly so much of a thing if Sumner hadn't been so exquisite about it.' " [15]

XXII

"ENEMIES! WE MUST NEVER SPEAK OF THAT"

"OUR country is now environed with perils which it is our duty calmly to contemplate." [1] Thus wrote Jefferson Davis to the Confederate Congress on March 13th, 1865. "Recent military operations of the enemy," he continued, "have been successful in the capture of some of our sea ports, in interrupting some of our lines of communication and in devastating large districts of our country. These events have had the natural effect of encouraging our foes and dispiriting many of our people. The Capital of the Confederate States is now threatened, and is in greater danger than it has heretofore been during the war." [2]

The end was approaching and yet "the more profound the study of the last days of the Confederacy, the firmer will be the conviction that the best management was required of the North to assure the end of the war in the spring of 1865." [3] The Southerners were fighting with the fierce courage of desperation. They knew what Thaddeus Stevens and his followers had in store for them; they anticipated the carpet-bag régime in the "conquered provinces,"—negro domination over white men. "There remains then, for us no choice but to continue the contest to a final issue," wrote Jefferson Davis on March 13th, "for the people of the Confederacy can be but little known to him who supposes it possible that they would ever consent to purchase at the cost of degradation and slavery, permission to live in a country garrisoned by their own negroes and governed by officers sent by the conquerors to work over them." [4]

Lincoln had at last found his generals, Sherman, Sheridan and Grant, but he wanted to be personally present at the finish. His reasons for this were thus recorded by Welles on March 23rd: "The President has gone to the front. . . . There is no doubt he is much worn down; besides he wishes the war terminated, and to this end, that severe terms shall not be exacted of the Rebels." [5]   Three days later Welles recorded: "The President still remains with the army. . . . Stanton remarked that it was quite as pleasant to have the President away, that he (Stanton) was much less annoyed. . . ." [6]

On April 1st, Sheridan disastrously defeated the Confederates at the Battle of Five Forks.[7] "Charge after charge was made and repulsed," wrote General Pickett on April 2nd to his wife, "and division after division of the enemy advanced upon us. Our left was turned; we were completely entrapped. . . . 'Take this, Marse George,' said one of my boys earlier in the action, hastily thrusting a battle flag into my hand. I took the flag stained with his blood, sacred to the cause for which he fell, and cheering as I waved it called on my men to get into line to meet the next charge. Seeing this, a part of the famous old glee club . . . began singing 'Rally round the flag boys; rally once again,' I rode straight up to where they were and joined in singing, 'Rally once again,' as I waved the blood-stained flag. And, my darling, overpowered, defeated, cut to pieces, starving, captured as we were, those that were left of us formed front and north and south, and met with sullen desperation their double onset. . . . The sorrow and song of my glory-crowned division nears its doxology. May God pity those who wait at home for the soldier who has reported to the Great Commander! God pity them as the days go by and the sad nights follow." [8]

The next morning was Sunday, and at 10:40 this dispatch from Lee reached Richmond: "I see no prospect of doing more than holding our position here till night. I am not certain that I can do that. . . ." [9] Jefferson Davis sat quietly at St. Paul's Episcopal Church, the clergyman was reading the prayer for the President of the Confederate states. Here Davis received Lee's dispatch and then silently he left the church.[10] The congregation was dismissed with the notice that there would be no evening service. At 2:00 that afternoon the Confederate government retired from Richmond.[11]

The candle of the Confederacy was flickering out. The glorious courage of her lovely womanhood and the stark valor of her sons are imperishable memories for the South; memories that will for all time excite the silent reverence of all Americans, North and South. Whether mistaken or not in their interpretation of their rights, the devotion of the Virginians, the South Carolinians and their Confederated neighbors to what they conceived to be the cause of independence, was not excelled by Washington and his tattered Continental army. The exploits of the first Virginian and of Lee have their high abiding place upon the holy altars of Anglo-Saxon liberty!

On the morning following the announcement in St. Paul's Church, General Weitzel, in command of the Wisconsin troops, entered Richmond and at a quarter past eight at the city hall received the surrender of the city.[12] The next day Lincoln himself entered the fallen capital of the Confederacy. Andrew Johnson was with him.[13] It was a dramatic entry, but it was not the entry of a conqueror. There was no pomp, no blare of martial music, no shining columns of triumphant soldiers. Abraham Lincoln, accompanied only by Andrew Johnson, Admiral Porter, three other officers and ten common sailors, walked a mile and a half through the streets of the abandoned capital.[14] "With malice toward none, with charity for all," he had come bringing peace.

§

Back in the old days, in Illinois, Lincoln was at one time associated in the practice of law with a certain Andrew Johnston, who despite the similarity of the name, was in no wise connected with the subject of these pages. Johnston had a nephew for whom he desired the study and career of law. But it was the young man's ambition to become a soldier. Lincoln knew him from his early boyhood, was fond of him, and finally was the means of securing his appointment to West Point. The young man was George Pickett.[15] As long as courage is revered, Pickett's charge at Gettysburg will excite admiration.

Abraham Lincoln understood the Southern people. He would have read with sympathetic understanding George Pickett's letter written in May, 1862: "The enemy is our enemy because he neither knows nor understands us, and yet will not let us part in peace and be neighbors, but insists on fighting us to make us one with him, forgetting that both slavery and secession were his own institutions. The North is fighting for the Union, and we— for home and fireside. All the men I know and love in the world are exposed to hardship and dangers, and are fighting on one side or the other, and each for that which he thinks to be right." [16]

Neither Gettysburg nor four years of war could change Lincoln's feeling of affection for the young Virginian whose admission to West Point he had secured. It would have been difficult even for a harder heart than Lincoln's to harbor hatred for this Confederate soldier who could write from Cold Harbor in 1864: ". . . thousands of Grant's soldiers have gone to reinforce the army of the dead. Oh, this is all a weary, long mistake. May the merciful and true God wield power to end it ere another day passes!" [17] Nor did George Pickett forget his affection for his old friend. After recounting an amusing anecdote in one of his letters to his wife, he continued: "Now, my darling, forgive this foolish story. I learned to like story-telling, listening as a boy to the best story-teller in the world, Mr. Lincoln." [18]

Understanding the aims of Thaddeus Stevens and his fellow Radicals, General Pickett in February, 1865, had written home: ". . . when peace comes it will follow the tread of a conqueror." [19] But two months later, though the capital of the Confederacy had fallen, it seemed no conqueror who came there to call on Mrs. Pickett. "I was in Richmond," she later wrote, "when my soldier fought the awful battle of Five Forks, Richmond surrendered, and the surging sea of fire swept the city. News of the fate of Five Forks had reached us, and the city was full of rumors that General Pickett was killed. I did not believe them. I knew he would come back, he had told me so. But they were very anxious hours. The day after the fire, there was a sharp rap at the door. The servants had all run away. The city was full of Northern troops, and my environment had not taught me to love them. The fate of other cities had awakened my fears for Richmond. With my baby on my arm, I answered the knock, opened the door and looked up at a tall, gaunt sad-faced man in ill-fitting clothes, who with the accent of the North, asked: 'Is this George Pickett's place?' 'Yes, sir,' I answered, 'but he is not here.' 'I know that, ma'am,' he replied, 'but I just wanted to see the place. I am Abraham Lincoln.' 'The President,' I gasped. The stranger shook his head and said: 'No ma'am; no, ma'am, just Abraham Lincoln, George's old friend.' 'I am George Pickett's wife and this is his baby,' was all I could say. I had never seen Mr. Lincoln, but remembered the intense love and reverence with which my soldier always spoke of him. My baby pushed away from me and reached out his hands to Mr. Lincoln, who took him in his arms. As he did so an expression of rapt almost divine tenderness and love lighted up the sad face. My baby opened his mouth wide and insisted upon giving his father's friend a dewy infantile kiss. As Mr. Lincoln gave the little one back to me, shaking his finger at him playfully he said: 'Tell your father, the rascal, that I forgive him for the sake of that kiss and those bright eyes.' He turned and went down the steps talking to himself, and passed out of my sight forever, but in my memory those intensely human eyes, that strong, sad face,—that face which puzzled all artists but revealed itself to the intuition of a little child, causing it to hold out its hands to be taken and its lips to be kissed." [20]

§

On his return to City Point on April 6th, Lincoln wrote Weitzel that he might permit "the gentlemen who have acted as the legis-lature of Virginia . . . to assemble at Richmond and take meas-ures to withdraw the Virginia troops and other support from resistance to the general government." [21] When he arrived at Washington, however, he found his suggestion meeting with the strongest opposition. Stanton and Wade stood solidly against him. [22] Even Welles did not agree with him, expressing anxiety lest the legislature thus convened would "be inclined perhaps to conspire against us." But the President said he "had no fear of that. They were too badly beaten, too much exhausted." His idea was that "the members of the legislature comprising the prominent and influential men of their respective counties had better come together and undo their own work." He felt assured that they would do this and the movement he believed a good one. "Civil government must be reëstablished," he said, "as soon as possible; there must be courts and law and order, or society would be broken up and the disbanded armies would turn into robber bands and guerillas, which we must strive to prevent." These were the reasons why he wished "prominent Virginians who had the confidence of the people to come together and turn themselves and their neighbors into good Union men." [23]

Lincoln's plan for the Virginians was not followed, but his attitude was strikingly revealed on April 9th, when coming up the Potomac from City Point. As the boat was nearing Washington Mrs. Lincoln stood gazing toward the national Capital. "That city," she said, "is filled with our enemies." But Lincoln answered: "Enemies! We must never speak of that!" [24]

§

On April 3rd Lee began his last retreat. What happened four days later at McLeans' house at Appomattox is fit material for the dramatist. Drinkwater has used it with fine skill. But let Grant's blunt soldier words unfold the story.

"What General Lee's feelings were," Grant wrote, "I do not know. As he was a man of much dignity with an impassive face, it was impossible to say whether he felt inwardly glad that the end had finally come, or felt sad over the result and was too manly to show it. Whatever his feelings, they were entirely concealed from my observation; but my own feelings, which had been quite jubilant on the receipt of his letter, were sad and depressed. I felt like anything rather than rejoicing at the downfall of a foe who had fought so long and valiantly. . . ." [25]

"General Lee," Grant continues, "was dressed in a full uniform which was entirely new, and was wearing a sword of considerable value, very likely the sword which had been presented by the State of Virginia; . . . In my rough traveling suit, the uniform

HON. GIDEON WELLES.

of a private with the straps of a lieutenant-general, I must have contrasted very strangely with a man so handsomely dressed, six feet high and of faultless form. But this was not a matter that I thought of until afterwards." [26]

"We soon fell into a conversation about old army times. He remarked that he remembered me very well in the old army; and I told him that as a matter of course I remembered him perfectly. . . . Our conversation grew so pleasant that I almost forgot the object of our meeting. After the conversation had run on . . . for some time, General Lee called my attention to the object of our meeting and said that he had asked for this interview for the purpose of getting from me the terms I proposed to give his army." [27]

Grant then wrote out the formal terms of the surrender: "The officers to give their individual paroles not to take up arms against the government of the United States until properly exchanged, and each company or regimental commander sign a like parole for the men of their commands. The arms, artillery and public property to be parked and stacked and turned over to the officers appointed by me to receive them. This will not embrace the side-arms of the officers, nor their private horses or baggage. This done, each officer and man will be allowed to return to their homes, not to be disturbed by United States authority so long as they observe their paroles and the laws in force where they may reside." [28]

"Not to be disturbed by United States authority!" Little did they dream how Thaddeus Stevens and his followers would later flaunt those terms! When General Lee read over the terms about side-arms, horses and private property, he remarked with some feeling that this "would have a happy effect" upon his army. [29]

General Grant was then told that in the Confederate army "the cavalrymen and artillerists owned their own horses," [30] to which he replied that he "took it that most of the men in the ranks were small farmers. The whole country had been so raided by the two armies that it was doubtful whether they would be able to put in a

crop to carry themselves and their families through the next winter without the aid of the horses they were then riding. The
United States did not want them and I would therefore instruct
the officers I left behind, to receive the paroles of his troops, to let
every man of the Confederate army who claimed to own a horse
or mule take the animal to his home. Lee remarked again that
this would have a happy effect." [31]

Grant had evidently not yet become infected by the ideas of
Thaddeus Stevens!

"When the news of the surrender first reached our lines," Grant
continues, "our men commenced firing a salute of a hundred guns
in honor of the victory. I at once sent word to have it stopped.
The Confederates were now our prisoners, and we did not want
to exult over their downfall." [32] "The war is over," Grant said,
"the Rebels are our countrymen again; and the best sign of
rejoicing after the victory will be to abstain from all demonstrations in the field." [33] From Appomattox, General Pickett wrote
his wife: "It is finished! Ah, my beloved division! Thousands
of them have gone to their eternal home, having given up their
lives for the cause they knew to be just. The others, alas, heart-
broken, crushed in spirit, are left to mourn its loss. Well, it is
practically all over now. We have poured out our blood and suffered untold hardship all in vain. And now, well, I must not
forget, either, that God reigns. . . . It is finished—the suffering
the horrors, the anguish of these last hours of struggle. . . .
Peace is born." [34]

That afternoon several of Grant's staff, with the permission of
General Lee, went over into the Confederate lines and "had a very
pleasant time with their old friends, and brought some of them
back with them when they returned." [35] To the house of Mr.
McLean, where the surrender had been signed, "the officers of
both armies came in great numbers, and seemed to enjoy the
meeting as much as though they had been friends separated for a
long time while fighting battles under the same flag. For the
time being it looked very much as if all thought of the war
had escaped their minds." Such was the spirit of the fighting
men! [36]

"Duncan is in his grave,
    After life's fitfull fever he sleeps well,
    Treason has done his worst; nor steel nor poison,
    Malice domestic, foreign levy, nothing
    Can touch him further."

Twice on Sunday, April 9th, Lincoln read aloud these lines from Macbeth to the little group returning with him to Washington.[37] "Do not allow Jefferson Davis to escape the law; he must be hanged," some one said to him. "Judge not that ye be not judged," Lincoln answered.[38]

"At day-dawn," wrote Welles on the following day, "a salute of several guns was fired. The first discharge proclaimed as well as words could have done the capture of Lee and his army. The morning papers detailed the particulars. . . . The tidings were spread over the country during the night, and the nation seems delirious with joy. Guns are firing, bells ringing, flags flying, men laughing, children cheering; all, all are jubilant. This surrender of the great Rebel captain, and the most formidable and reliable army of the Secessionists, virtually terminates the Rebellion."[39]

That evening a rejoicing throng came to the White House and Lincoln, reading from his notes by the light of a candle which he held,[40] addressed his serenaders. "By these recent successes," he began, "the reinauguration of the national authority—reconstruction—which has had a large share of thought from the first, is pressed much more closely upon our attention. . . . I am much censured for some supposed agency in setting up and seeking to sustain the new state government of Louisiana."[41]

"The amount of constituency, so to speak, on which the new Louisiana government rests," continued Mr. Lincoln, "would be more satisfactory to all if it contained 50,000, or 30,000, or even 20,000 instead of only 12,000 as it does. It is also unsatisfactory to some that the elective franchise is not given to the colored man. I would myself prefer that it were now conferred on the very intelligent and on those who serve our cause as soldiers."[42]

"The question is," he went on, "not whether the Louisiana

government, as it stands, is quite all that is desirable. The question is will it be wiser to take it as it is and help improve it, or to reject and disperse it? Can Louisiana be brought into proper practical relation with the Union sooner by sustaining or discarding her new state government? Some twelve thousand voters in the heretofore slave state of Louisiana have sworn allegiance to the Union, assumed to be the rightful political power of the state, held elections, organized a state government, adopted a free state constitution, giving the benefit of public schools equally to black and white, and empowering the Legislature to confer the elective franchise upon the colored man. Their Legislature has already voted to ratify the constitutional amendment recently passed by Congress abolishing slavery throughout the nation. These twelve thousand persons are thus fully committed to the Union and to perpetual freedom in the state—committed to the very things, and nearly all the things the nation wants—and they ask the nation's recognition and its assistance to make good their committal."

"Now," proceeded Lincoln, "if we reject and spurn them, we do our utmost to disorganize and disperse them. We, in effect, say to the white man: You are worthless or worse; we will neither help you nor be helped by you. To the blacks we say: This cup of liberty which these your old masters hold to your lips we will dash from you, and leave you to the chances of gathering the spilled and scattered contents in some vague and undefined when, where and how. If this course, disorganizing and paralyzing both white and black, has any tendency to bring Louisiana into proper practical relation with the Union, I have been so far unable to perceive it. If on the contrary we recognize and sustain the new government of Louisiana, the converse of all this is made true. We encourage the hearts and nerve the arms of the twelve thousand to adhere to their work and argue for it, and proselyte for it, and fight for it, and feed it, and grow it, and ripen it to a complete success. The colored man too in seeing all united for him, is inspired with vigilance and energy and daring to the same end. Grant that he deserves the elective franchise, will he not attain it sooner by saving the already advanced steps towards it than by running backward over them. Concede that the new government of Louisiana is only to what it should be as the egg is to the fowl, we shall sooner have the fowl by hatching the egg than by smashing it." That he was arguing his reconstruction program in behalf of all the Southern states was clear, for he continued: "What has been said of Louisiana will apply generally to other states." [43]

Finally looking out upon the throng that had come with drums and shouts to rejoice at Lee's surrender, Lincoln added these three sentences: "Now I am about to call upon the band for a tune that our adversaries over the way have endeavored to appropriate. But we fairly captured it yesterday, and the Attorney-General gave me his legal opinion that it is now our property. So I ask the band to play 'Dixie!' " [44]

A few days later Charles Sumner wrote to his friend Lieber: "The President's speech and other things augur confusion and uncertainty in the future, with hot controversy. Alas! Alas!" [45]

§

Friday, the 14th of April, was the fourth anniversary of Fort Sumter's fall. There was a celebration there, the flag was raised, there were speeches which posterity will never notice and much "fuss and parade." [46]

While all this was going on, Lincoln held the last meeting of his Cabinet. We have Stanton's word that the "President was very cheerful and hopeful; spoke very kindly of General Lee and others of the Confederacy and the establishment of government in Virginia," and further that he "rejoiced at the near prospect of firm and durable peace at home and abroad, manifested in marked degree the kindness and humanity of his disposition and the tender and forgiving spirit that so eminently distinguished him." [47]

The Cabinet was eager for news of General Sherman. Grant who was present said that hourly he was expecting word. The President remarked that news would soon come and that it would be favorable, for he had had the night before a dream which had presaged every important event of the war. In his dream he "seemed to be in some singular indescribable vessel . . . moving with great rapidity toward an indefinite shore." [48]   He was indeed upon the eve of a great victory and that indefinite shore was drawing near!

The discussion of the Cabinet centered around reconstruction. "We must," said Lincoln, "extinguish our resentments if we expect harmony and union. There is too much of a desire on the part of some of our very good friends to be masters, to interfere with and dictate to those states, to treat the people not as fellow citizens; there is too little respect for their rights. I do not sympathize in these feelings." [49]   Reconstruction, he said, "is the great question pending and we must now begin to act in the interest of peace." [50]

XXIII

LINCOLN'S CABINET,—AND JOHNSON'S

LET us look in upon that Cabinet, meeting as it was with Abraham Lincoln for the last time. The chair of the Secretary of State was empty, for William Seward nine days before had been thrown from his carriage and had been badly injured,[1]—an injury which by a strange irony of fate was presently to preserve his life.

Seward was then sixty-four. He had graduated from Union College in 1820 and was admitted to the bar two years later.[2] Carriage accidents, it seems, came to him as blessings in disguise. In 1824 he journeyed to Niagara and while driving through Rochester a wheel came off his coach and most of the passengers were thrown out. One of the passersby who noted the traveler's plight was the editor of an obscure newspaper. He was one of the worst-dressed and poorest men in the town, but already a force in Western New York politics. His name was Thurlow Weed. The acquaintance thus achieved proved one of the most important influences in Seward's life. It ripened as Weed later wrote, "into a very close friendship. . . . Our views in relation to public affairs and our estimate of public men rarely differed. I saw in him in a remarkable degree rapidly developing elements of character which could not fail to render him eminently useful in public life. I discerned also unmistakable evidences of stern integrity, earnest patriotism and unswerving fidelity." [3]

With such a mentor, and a natural predilection for politics, the young graduate early manifested for this field of endeavor, a preference over his chosen profession of the law. His public career was notable. He was elected to the New York Senate at 29,[4] governor at 37, and United States Senator at 48.[5] In his first prepared speech delivered in the National Senate on March 11th, 1850, concerning the compromise measures then pending, he

181

aroused the whole country with the assertion that for the regulation of the territories, "there is a higher law than the Constitution." [6]

During four of the eleven years of his Senatorship, Andrew Johnson was his fellow Senator, and it was at this time that he advocated with enthusiasm the passage of Johnson's Homestead Bill. [7] In the early part of 1861, in avowing his adherence to the integrity of the Union, he declared that he would follow "the example of the capable Senator from Tennessee." [8] Perhaps Seward's most famous speech was that delivered at Rochester in 1858 when he proclaimed that there was "an irrepressible conflict between opposing and enduring forces, and it means that the United States must, and will sooner or later, become either entirely a slave holding nation or entirely a free labor nation." [9] The day before the Chicago Convention, of 1860, Lincoln wrote: "I agree with Seward in his 'irrepressible conflict,' but I do not endorse his 'higher-law doctrine.' " [10]

As early as 1856, Seward was harboring Presidential aspirations. During the two previous years it had become evident that the Whig party had outlived its usefulness and Seward had been active in leading its scattered forces into the ranks of the Republicans then forming. [11] The first convention of the new party was held in Philadelphia in 1856. The Auburn statesman entrusted his aspirations to his old friend Thurlow Weed; but if he had found in Weed a sincere friend he had secured in Horace Greeley, his former political ally, an even sincerer enemy.

The year before Seward's reëlection to the Senate had seen the ripening of Greeley's hope to become the Whig candidate for governor of New York. Because of his "advocacy of various hobbies and crotchets," he was destined to disappointment. He held Seward responsible for his defeat and wrote him on March 11th, 1858, a letter which as it later proved, was a declaration of permanent hostility. [12] It announced "the dissolution of the political firm of Seward, Weed & Greeley by the withdrawal of the junior partner." [13]

In the Philadelphia convention of 1856, Greeley struck hands with Seward's enemies in a movement resulting in the nominating

HON. WILLIAM H. SEWARD.

of Frémont.[14] After Frémont was defeated by Buchanan, Seward became the outstanding figure among the Republicans. He had opposed Douglas on the Kansas question,[15] he had charged the Supreme Court in the Dred Scott case "with forgetting its own dignity," and had accused Buchanan and the court of failing to remember that "judicial usurpation" was more odious than any other form of tyranny,[16] and had publicly proclaimed that the President and the Chief Justice were combining to undermine the liberties of the people.[17] Judge Taney retorted that if Seward were elected President, he would decline to administer him the oath of office.[18]

Throughout Buchanan's administration Seward's prestige grew.[19] The South recognized this when one of her newspapers declared: "Mr. Seward is a great political leader. . . . We concede to him honesty of purpose and the highest order of talent; . . . he has stood forth in the Senate of the United States the great champion of freedom and the stern opposer of slavery." [20]

There seemed to be no doubt that Seward would receive the Republican nomination in 1860, but after the Lincoln-Douglas debates, Lincoln himself was urged to seek it. Lincoln replied that Seward and Chase were more entitled to it, and that he foresaw no such "good luck" for himself. It was not until May of 1859 that he allowed his friends to work for him.[21]

When on May 16th the Republican Convention convened in the great "Wigwam" at Chicago, Seward was regarded as the choice both of the delegates and of the people. At the close of the first day so confident were the Seward managers that, with real sincerity, they went about inquiring of the opposition whom it might desire for second place.[22] But there were factors working against Seward that were soon to tell. There was his "irrepressible conflict" speech, there was his "higher-law" doctrine and especially there was Horace Greeley.[23] The rôle played by the *Tribune's* editor was one of underhand revenge. He had succeeded in 1859 in convincing Weed that he was "seeking to be useful" in California, and as though to give his treachery a double mask, had on the very eve of his departure dined with Seward himself. What must have been then the surprise of the two remaining members of the firm of "Seward, Weed & Greeley" when they found Greeley at Chicago coming as an alternate delegate from Oregon! Nominally he was there to advocate the cause of Bates, but in reality he had come to ruin Seward's hopes.[24]

On the third ballot Lincoln was nominated.[25] Seward's supporters were cast down. Thurlow Weed shed tears.[26] The convention, on the low ground of mere "availability," had made the most fortunate choice since the selection of Washington to lead the Continental army.[27] "Yet," writes Lincoln's most capable American biographer, "the Convention deserved no credit for its action. It did not know the true ratio between Seward and Lincoln, which only the future was to make plain. By all that it did know, it ought to have given the honor to Seward. . . ." [28]

During the Convention, Seward sat waiting at his home in Auburn confidently expecting news of his nomination. When the result of that third ballot became known, none of his friends possessed the heart to compose for the *Daily Republican* the usual endorsement of the ticket. So Seward himself sat down and wrote for it: "No truer or firmer defenders of the Republican faith could have been found . . . than the distinguished . . . citizens on whom the honors of the nomination have fallen," [29] nor did he later sulk in his tent, but throughout five weeks of that critical campaign, spoke throughout New York, the northwest and the states whose delegates had supported him in the convention.[30] It was fine sportsmanship!

In December, 1860, Lincoln invited Seward to become his Secretary of State, and Seward accepted. Mistrusting somewhat perhaps the "Democratic complexion" of the Cabinet and fearing also that his own influence would be inferior to that of Chase, ten days before Lincoln's Inaugural, Seward withdrew his previous acceptance. But Lincoln persuaded him to reconsider,[31] and on March 5th he was appointed.[32]

In the light of these things it was generally expected that Seward would prove "the master spirit of the administration," [33] nor in view of his outstanding political career is it altogether surprising that he should have considered himself somewhat in that light. This may explain his act of all but inexplicable folly when on April 1st he wrote out his "thoughts for the President's consideration," [34]—a proposal for a general war with Spain, France, Great Britain and Russia. His program closed with the suggestion that either the President must operate it himself or "devolve it upon some member of the cabinet. . . . It is not in my special province. But I neither seek to evade nor assume responsibility." [35]

Lincoln kept this fantastic suggestion secret,[36] but rejected it briefly, decisively and without thanks.[37] Who was to be President and who Secretary of State was thus quietly but once and for all time decided. There was never any question of Seward's loyalty or devotion to his chief.[38] "The President," he wrote his wife three months later, "is the best of us all. . . . There is but one vote in the cabinet and that is cast by the President." [39] Seward's culture, his amiability and his gentle manners made him "a most agreeable man in council." [40] He became the most trusted and the most acceptable of all the President's advisers.

His handling of our foreign affairs is a credit to American statesmanship. When on that dark October night of 1861, Captain Charles Wilkes of the United States frigate *San Jacinto* boarded the British mail steamer *Trent* and removed Mason and Slidell, the Confederate commissioners bound for England, all the materials were furnished for a disastrous foreign war. As soon as Great Britain heard of it a transport of British troops left Mersey en route for Canada with their regimental band thundering out: "I wish I was in Dixie." [41] The credit for the final solution of that difficult problem accomplished on Christmas Day by Seward's answer to Lord Russell, whereby the Confederate commissioners were released, belongs more to Seward than to Lincoln.[42]

Lincoln's "council of state" was a heterogeneous if not quite an ill-assorted assemblage.[43] From the discords of that body historians and novelists have fashioned a background against which the magnaminity of the great President stands out in colors that can never fade.

The division between the Radicals and the Conservatives was

early felt,—a division which was to widen. Seward was soon
known as the chief Conservative, while of the Radicals, Chase and
Stanton were recognized as the moving spirits.[44] The first concerted effort of the Radicals to dictate to a President as to the
membership of his Cabinet occurred after Burnside's loss of Fredericksburg in December, 1862.[45] With a subsequent and not dis-
similar though vastly more poisonous attempt, these pages ere
long will principally concern themselves. The Radical Senators
were now determined to drive Seward out. Those behind the
scenes saw Stanton's fine Italian hand.[46]

With the tact of genius Lincoln foiled his enemies and Seward
stayed.[47] "If I had yielded to that storm and dismissed Seward,"
Lincoln later said, "the thing would have slumped over one way,
and we should have been left to a scanty handful of supporters." [48]

Historians have expressed difficulty in appraising Seward.[49]
That he possessed intellectual greatness the study of his state
papers will abundantly establish, although his power perhaps was
"inadequately expressed by his wizened face and ordinary
form." [50] He had amiable and genial manners; [51] these may have
aided, but they did not alone make him Lincoln's "favorite coun-
sellor." [52]

He was not always right. His first week of office was especially replete with error. His suggestion for a general European
war has been already noted. During March, 1861, he was assuring
the Confederate commissioners that there was "no design to reinforce" Fort Sumter.[53] Folly as that now seems, many able Northern minds then agreed with him. Lincoln himself from the day
of his Inaugural to March 29th, examined both sides of the question and hesitated.[54] It is, however, a big man who could say as
Seward said to Welles after his view had been rejected, that "old
as he was, he had learned a lesson from this affair and that was,
he had better attend to his own business, and confine his labors
to his own Department." [55]

Seward was a scholar and a gentleman in politics with the
merits and some of the defects that are usually written into the
lines of that dual rôle. Much of the difficulty experienced by
historians in appraising him may be due to the task of piercing

through the dark clouds of prejudice surrounding the decade following Appomattox,—a period as we shall presently discern, in which he played a brave part, daring to number himself among that pitiful minority remaining true to Lincoln's hopes.

Seward had something of the artist's temperament.[56] He enjoyed words and knew how to use them. He had eloquence,[57] he had personal charm,[58] he had the art of influencing men.[59] Lincoln recognized these things and was drawn toward them. Once when Seward and he were traveling together, at a way-station where they stopped a speech was demanded by the crowd. Lincoln refused, but, turning in his berth, called out: "Seward, you go out and repeat some of your poetry to the people." [60]

Shortly after his return from Richmond on April 9th, 1865, Lincoln called on Seward at his home, where he lay in great pain from his accident. Entering with kindly expressions of sympathy the President sat down at the bedside of the invalid. "You are back from Richmond?" whispered Seward, who was barely able to speak. "Yes," said Lincoln, "and I think we are near the end at last." For an hour or more the President regaled him with his experiences at the front. The door then softly opened and Lincoln came out, indicating by his gesture and his silent look that Seward was asleep and must not be disturbed.[61] On this earth they never met again.

§:

Stanton was present at that last Cabinet meeting. He had held his portfolio since January, 1862.[62] Under Seward's wing he had become Secretary of War three years earlier; "but," wrote Welles at that time, "Stanton is by nature an intriguer, courts favor, is not faithful in his friendships, is given to secret underhand combinations. His obligations to Seward are great but would not deter him from raising a breeze against Seward to favor himself," [63] and again at a later date: "Stanton has a cabinet and is a power in his Department. He deceives the President and Seward, makes confidants of certain leading men, and is content to have matters move on without being compelled to show his exact position." [64] We have already become acquainted with this man; later we shall know him better.

§

Present also at that last meeting of Lincoln's Cabinet was Gideon Welles, the Secretary of the Navy. Born at Glastenbury, Connecticut, in 1802, he received his education at Norwich University, Vermont. Beginning at twenty-four, for eleven years he was the editor of the Hartford *Times*. In southern New England his paper became the official mouthpiece of Jacksonian democracy. For six years he served in the State House of Representatives, three years as State Comptroller and seven years as the Hartford postmaster. From 1846 to 1849 he was chief of the Bureau of Provisions and Clothing in the Navy Department at Washington. The Kansas-Nebraska struggle aroused him and he left the Democratic ranks to assist in organizing the Republican party in Connecticut. He was its unsuccessful candidate for governor in 1856. In the same year and four years later he was a delegate to the Republican National Convention. At the beginning of his administration Lincoln made him Secretary of the Navy.[65]

Despite his hirsutic ambuscade so characteristic of the period, Welles was a handsome man, with broad and high forehead, large nose, firm and powerful mouth (powerful chin too, no doubt, if we could but see it), and piercing clear, yet kindly eyes. We find him none the less attractive because "he was complacently aware of the advantages of features, form and manner, and did not neglect their due cultivation." [66]

But if Gideon Welles was a handsome gentleman, he was far more than that. When he became Secretary he was confronted with an initial difficulty, namely, the embarrassment of being Secretary of a navy which did not exist. In all the Northern ports there was one vessel only fit for engagement in aggressive operations,—and this too in a war whose central program involved the blockade of Southern ports. He was called upon to create an effective blockade from Cape Henry to the Rio Grande, and for the accomplishment of this task he was given but one ship.[67]

Welles acted. By the end of 1863 his Department commanded

six hundred vessels of war and seven hundred before Lincoln's last Cabinet meeting. Seventy-five of these were iron-clad. The challenge hurled in the United States Senate on the 4th of March, 1858, by Senator Hammond of South Carolina: "No, you dare not make war on cotton. No power on earth dares to make war on cotton. Cotton is King!" [68] was accepted by the Hartford postmaster. Within one year after the first battle practically all legitimate commerce with the Southern states had been cut off. [69]

Historians have dwelt all too little on the fact "that it was because the blockade strangled the Confederacy that the armies were able to slay it." [70] A large measure of credit for this feat justly belongs to the Secretary of the Navy. [71]

Welles, writes Mr. Morse, "had singular sagacity in judging men; for he was observant, and could see the moral, mental and temperamental material which lay stored away in one man or another. He had a like shrewdness in estimating situations and in sifting the news and rumors of events; so that his forecasts were singularly accurate. For these reasons it was natural that while the War Department was painfully learning, on many a lost and bloody battlefield, who could not command victory, the Navy Department sent well-chosen captains from one success to another." [72]

Possessing these traits together with unquestioned trustworthiness and absolute loyalty it was but natural that he should receive the affection and support of Lincoln, who "upheld him in times of need or controversy; notably when Mr. Stanton arrogantly claimed the right to dominate the Navy Department and insisted that commanders of vessels on the rivers should take orders from commanders of the army on land. Mr. Lincoln made short work of this theory." [73]

The diary of Gideon Welles is an invaluable record of the Civil War and of the Reconstruction, not only because of its author's opportunity to observe the men and the events of which he wrote, his ability to describe them vividly and clearly, but because he was "a man of integrity," [74] was possessed of "an accurate memory" [75] and was "a very shrewd and a very fair judge of men." [76] Naïvely complacent with his own work his pages sometimes are,—"Pepysian," Gamaliel Bradford calls them,[77] perhaps not unjustly,—they are nevertheless the product of a clear, fair-minded thinker who "took pains not to permit either passion or prejudice to divert the movement of his reasoning." [78] Presently we shall be studying his full-length portraits of Andrew Johnson.

§

The newest member of the Cabinet was Hugh McCulloch, the Secretary of the Treasury. Born in Maine in 1808, his single year of higher education had been spent at Bowdoin College. He became a lawyer and at the age of twenty-five, in search of wider opportunities, migrated to Fort Wayne. His association with the State Bank of Indiana led him permanently into the financial field, in which his reputation had become so high in 1863 that Chase made him Comptroller of the Currency. In March, 1865, Lincoln promoted McCulloch to the Secretaryship of the Treasury, and thus made at least one appointment for which sheer merit rather than political considerations was responsible.[79] He was a man of great ability, he had the banker's instinct for the proper management of obligations.[80] "Though not trained in public office or an experienced politician," Welles regarded him "as the most reliable and sensible man in the Cabinet." [81]

James Harlan of Illinois was Secretary of the Interior. He was forty-five years old and the youngest man in that Cabinet. Before his appointment he already had had a brilliant career. He was President of Ohio Wesleyan University at thirty-three, and a member of the United States Senate at thirty-five.[82] He was confirmed as Secretary of the Interior five days after Lincoln took his second oath of office.[83]

The Postmaster General was William Dennison, a former governor of Ohio. The circumstances surrounding his appointment presaged his adherence to the Radicals. In the summer of 1864, one of the obstacles that obstructed Lincoln's election was General Frémont. His nomination for the Presidency, it is true, had not excited much enthusiasm, his withdrawal from the race was nevertheless a desirable objective. The price the Radicals demanded for his retirement was the dismissal of Montgomery Blair as Postmaster. During Blair's tenure of that office many improvements in the service had been brought about, nevertheless Frémont's withdrawal on September 22nd was followed the next day by Lincoln's demand for Blair's resignation, which was immediately forthcoming.[84] "To seal such a bargain," writes Mr. Rhodes, "was not a dignified proceeding on the part of the President of the United States, but it was a politic move." [85] Dennison, whose sympathies and associates were with the Radicals, was then appointed in Blair's stead.[86]

Lincoln's Attorney General, James Speed, was a Clay Whig and a Kentuckian. His brother Joshua was the first to lend Lincoln a helping hand when the melancholy young lawyer with his pair of saddle bags, a few pieces of clothing and three law books in 1837 came none too hopefully to Springfield.[87] It was Joshua Speed who introduced Lincoln to Mary Todd [88] and who brought him to his parents' home near Louisville to recover from that fateful New Year's day of 1841, when Lincoln failed to appear at his own marriage ceremony.[89] These two men were life-long friends, and it was with kindling eye that Lincoln always spoke of "Josh Speed," and told as only Lincoln could, the stories of their early friendship.[90] It was with keen pleasure, therefore, that he had appointed Joshua Speed's brother as his Attorney General.[91]

§

There was one other present at the last meeting of the Cabinet, —Ulysses Grant. The laurels of Appomattox were but five days old; his generosity to Lee had thrilled the Northern heart. He had been the right arm with which Lincoln saved the Union, his dogged determination, a sword and a shield to the Republic. With the antidote of his blunt will the North recovered from McClellan. In three years and ten months this clerk in a Galena leather store had sprung from poverty and obscurity to the dizzy pinnacle of fame. His name was now a talisman to conjure with, his influence a power which no partisan could ignore. Where would that influence be placed?

The Radicals, now that peace was coming, were preparing in

dead earnest for war on Lincoln's plan. What a valuable ally
Grant could make for them! Giving back to the surrendered
Confederates their horses for spring plowing was not a good
omen to those who were plotting vengeance for the conquered.
His whole course at Appomattox seemed to offer little hope that
the Radicals might appropriate this popular hero to their own uses.
But then as they reflected Grant was a simple man unversed in
the wiles of politicians. In his whole life he had shown capacity
for nothing else save war. In 1854 he had resigned from the
army, and at the age of thirty-two began a new struggle for his
family's support,—a struggle which he essayed with only indifferent success. He tried to run his wife's farm near St. Louis,—
it did not pay. He became a real estate agent in St. Louis,—success did not attend him. Finally at thirty-eight he sought the
assistance of his father who enjoyed the affluence of a hardware
and leather store in Galena, Illinois. As a last resort he received
at this not too youthful age a clerkship in that store with eight
hundred dollars a year for his remuneration. He was in debt, he
was impecunious, he was shiftless and he was intemperate. Those
who knew him both in Galena and St. Louis were accustomed to
avoid meeting him on the street lest he solicit them for a small
loan of money.[92]

These things the Radicals were pondering. Could not a man
with such a simple inability to comprehend the ways of men
(when they were not in arms) be fooled, or flattered or deceived
into joining forces with them? The employment of his great
prestige was a goal worth striving for.

Such was Lincoln's Cabinet as it sat with him on April 14th,
1865. The problems of the war were lifting, the greater tasks
of peace would be presently upon them. They had sat with
Abraham Lincoln, they had heard his voice and knew well his
beneficent program of reconstruction. How many of them would
prove loyal? It would be fortunate indeed if there were but one
Judas among them!

XXIV

ANDREW JOHNSON BECOMES PRESIDENT OF THE UNITED STATES

AFTER the Cabinet meeting was over, in the afternoon Mr. and Mrs. Lincoln went for a drive. A load seemed to have lifted from the President, peace was at hand. He talked hopefully of their future. "Mary," he said, "we have had a hard time of it since we came to Washington; and with God's blessing we may hope for four years of peace and happiness and then we will go back to Illinois and pass the rest of our lives in quiet." [1]

For the evening Mrs. Lincoln had arranged a theatre party to see Laura Keene in "Our American Cousin" at Ford's Theatre. Lincoln was not eager to go but yielded to the wishes of his wife. [2] General and Mrs. Grant were to have been in the party, but the General excused himself because of his desire to see his children in New Jersey. [3]

The Presidential party was late in arriving, but when they appeared the orchestra broke into "Hail the Chief," and the audience rose in their seats, and waving hats and handkerchiefs cheered and cheered again. The actors stood still on the stage. When the outburst of enthusiasm had subsided the play went on.

A little after ten John Wilkes Booth, himself an actor, although not in the play, having first fortified his courage with strong drink, sneaked stealthily into the Presidential box, lifted his Derringer pistol, aimed carefully at the head of the smiling President and fired. The murderer then shook himself from the grasp of Major Rathborne and leaped to the stage. There for one brief moment he stood facing the audience, and brandishing a dagger shouted, "Sic semper tyrannis,"—alas, it was the motto of Virginia! [4]

The ball had entered Lincoln's brain rendering him at once

unconscious. They bore him across the street to the house of Mr. Petersen, opposite the theatre. At 7:22 the next morning, the 15th of April, the great and good man died.[5] With bowed heads and streaming eyes America was pondering the ways of an all-knowing God.

§

Lincoln was murdered as the result of conspiracy between Booth, Louis Payne, George Atzerodt and seven others.[6] Their purpose was not only the murder of the President, but also of Johnson, Grant and Seward.[7] During the very hour of the assault on Lincoln, Payne gained admission to Seward's house and having first felled Frederick Seward with the butt of his revolver, pushed his way into the room where the Secretary of State lay ill. This dastard then attacked the sick man with a bowie knife, slashed his right cheek and stabbed him twice in the neck.[8]

In his carriage accident Seward's jaw had been fractured, and in order to hold the bones in apposition an elastic wire bandage had been adjusted upon one side of his face. This contrivance now acted as a shield against his assailant's blows, and prevented one directly aimed at his throat from being fatal.[9]

To Atzerodt the murder of Andrew Johnson had been assigned. With homicidal intent he lay in wait for the Vice-President, but finally his courage failed him; he seemed to find no relish for a personal encounter with the Tennessean,[10]—perhaps he used good judgment.

Immediately after Lincoln breathed his last, the Cabinet, with the exception of Stanton, Seward and McCulloch, assembled in the back parlor of the Petersen home and there composed a letter to Johnson officially advising him of Lincoln's death. "The emergency," they wrote, "demands that you should immediately qualify according to the requirements of the Constitution and enter upon the duties of the President of the United States."[11]

Johnson replied that he would take the oath at 10 o'clock that morning, and accordingly at the appointed hour at Kirkwood House, where he then lived, he was attended by Chief Justice Chase, the members of the Cabinet and several of the Senators.[12]

ANDREW JOHNSON TAKING THE OATH OF OFFICE IN THE SMALL PARLOR OF THE
KIRKWOOD HOUSE, WASHINGTON.

"Soon after leaving Mr. Seward," Chase later wrote, "I went to see the Vice-President and found him at his hotel; calm apparently but very grave." [13] In the parlor of that simple inn, Andrew Johnson, upon the holy Bible, as the seventeenth President, took this oath: "I do solemnly swear that I will faithfully execute the office of President of the United States, and will to the best of my ability preserve, protect and defend the Constitution of the United States." [14] With great earnestness the Chief Justice said: "May God guide, support and bless you in your arduous labors!" [15]

From tailor shop to the chief magistracy of the United States,— once more democracy was vindicated! Into the hands of this plain toiler from the mountains of Tennessee the reins of government were thrust. Perhaps the most exacting task which ever fell to the lot of an American confronted him. A proven patriot, he stood there impressing his witnesses, no doubt, as he had impressed Charles Francis Adams in 1861. Adams, who met him then for the first time, thus described him: "Mr. Johnson's manners were quiet, gentle, though slightly formal. He has a deep black eye and with his somewhat neat black clothes and clean shaven face looks physically and intellectually like a strong man." [16] A few days later Adams again recorded his impressions: "The evening of the 28th (February, 1861) I passed with Andrew Johnson, whose acquaintance I had made in the Senate writing room a few days before. Johnson was then at the highest point of his reputation. A Southern Unionist, a 'poor white' of Eastern Tennessee, who by native energy had elevated himself to the Senate, he was holding his own then against Davis and all the representatives of 'Slaveocracy,' who were trying in vain to dragoon him. . . . The great thing about the man is evidently his nerve—his apparent force and coolness in a position of danger." [17]

It was thirty-nine years since Johnson, in his creaking cart, had entered Greeneville, and fifty-seven since he was born. Like seasoned oak he had weathered all the storms and was strong. The love and encouragement of his Eliza had comforted and inspired him, but the battle with adversity had shattered her health. What must have been her feelings on that gloomy April morning? She could have had but confidence as she reflected upon his life. Tailor and then alderman, mayor twice, representative in the State Legislature, member of the State Senate, at thirty-five a Representative in the National House, five terms there and then twice governor of his state, United States Senator, military governor and brigadier-general, Vice-President and now President of the United States!

What President has ever had a wider training for the office? His life had been a vindication of democracy, no less than Lincoln's struggle from flat-boatman to the White House. Hardship and poverty had given him the common touch. Like the rail-splitter of Illinois, this Tennessee mechanic had learned to sympathize with suffering. Alongside all the strictures upon his poverty and humble origin, I shall place from Abraham Lincoln's first annual message these sixteen words: "No men living are more worthy to be trusted than those who toil up from poverty. . . ." [18]

As soon as he had taken the oath, President Johnson said to those who had acted as his witnesses: "Gentlemen . . . I have been almost overwhelmed by the announcement of the sad event which has so recently occurred." Concerning his future policy he told them, that "that must be left for development as the administration progresses. . . . The only assurance that I can now give of the future is reference to the past. The course which I have taken in the past in connection with this rebellion must be regarded as a guaranty of the future. . . . I believe that the government in passing through its present perils will settle down upon principles consonant with popular rights more permanent and enduring than heretofore. . . . I want your encouragement and countenance. I shall ask and rely upon you and others in carrying the Government through its present perils." [19]

The impression made by the new President was a favorable one. "He was grief stricken like the rest," wrote Hugh McCulloch, "and he seemed to be oppressed by the suddenness of the call upon him to become President . . ., but he was nevertheless calm and self-possessed. He requested the members of the Cabinet to remain with him after the Chief Justice and the other witnesses to the ceremony had retired, and he expressed to each and all of us his desire that we should stand by him in his difficult and responsible position." [20]

At noon a Cabinet meeting was held at the office of the Secretary of the Treasury. Johnson deported himself with dignity. His policy, he said, in all essentials would be "the same as that of the late President." [21] How many in those crowded hours gave thought, I wonder, to the words of that solemn oath which Andrew Johnson had that morning called upon Almighty God to witness: "To preserve, protect and defend the Constitution!"

§

"There was a cheerless cold rain, and everything seemed gloomy," on the morning Lincoln died. [22] "The joy," wrote Grant, who returned to the Capital that day, "that I had witnessed among the people in the street and in public places in Washington when I left there had been turned to grief; the city was in reality a city in mourning." [23]

Gideon Welles and Attorney General Speed went over to the White House soon after breakfast. "As we were descending the stairs," wrote Welles, "Tad, who was looking from the window at the foot, turned and seeing us, cried aloud in his tears, 'Oh, Mr. Welles, who killed my father?' Neither Speed nor myself could restrain our tears nor give the poor boy any satisfactory answer." [24] Gloom was everywhere. To the accompaniment of heavy rain the bells were tolling. The rejoicing over Lee's surrender had been turned to ashes. [25]

There was no Atlantic cable, and so the news was not received in England until twelve days later when the English people joined Americans in their mourning. "For fifty years," John Bright wrote to Sumner, "I think no other event has created such a sensation as the great crime which has robbed you of your President. The whole people positively mourn, and it would seem as if again we were one nation with you, so universal is the grief and the horror of the deed of which Washington has been the scene." [26]

After funeral services were held in the east room of the White

House on the 19th of April, the body of the murdered President was taken to the rotunda of the Capitol.[27] Two days later it was started on its way to Springfield,—the route selected being that which Lincoln four years before had traveled, when he left home for the last time. At Independence Hall in Philadelphia, at the City Hall of New York, and in Chicago his body lay in state.[28] All along the route and at every opportunity great throngs came to pay their tribute of respect. *Harper's Weekly* of the Period in all too minute detail has recorded this last mournful journey. Finally, on May 4th, all that was mortal of Abraham Lincoln was committed to the earth.

> Duncan is in his grave;
> After life's fitful fever he sleeps well;
> Treason has done his worst; nor steel nor poison,
> Malice domestic, foreign levy, nothing
> Can touch him further.

§

The plain people of the North,—Lincoln's people, mourned their fallen leader. With Walt Whitman they cried:

> My captain does not answer, his lips are pale and still,
> My father does not feel my arm, he has no pulse nor will,
> The ship is anchored safe and sound, its voyage closed and done.
> From fearful trip the victor's ship comes in with object won.

"With object won?" Perhaps for those who recognized the purpose of the war as the saving of the Union and the suppression of slavery. But there were others whose object by no means had been won, for whom Lincoln had stood as an obstacle, and whose death seemed to offer opportunities for the accomplishment of aims against which the rail-splitter had stood as he stood against Lee and Stonewall Jackson.

To the Radicals the name of Andrew Johnson seemed an augury of hope. Here indeed would be a force to assist them in working their will upon the "conquered provinces." Here was one of the "poor whites" who would joyously join their plans of confiscation and their schemes of placing the slave holders under the subjugation of their former slaves! The poor mechanic who had been shunned by the great of Greeneville, who had every reason to hate the landed gentry, flourishing as they had under a system which he had done so much to destroy! Surely in this man they would find none of the compunctions which had made Lincoln the hated target of Winter Davis and Ben Wade! Then in the Senate they remembered how in 1861 he had declared: "He that is guilty of treason deserves a traitor's fate." [29] And again in the same speech as to those in arms against the government: "Were I the President of the United States, I would do as Thomas Jefferson did in 1806 with Aaron Burr, who was charged with treason; I would have them arrested and tried for treason, and if convicted by the Eternal God they should suffer the penalty of the law at the hands of the executioner. Sir, treason must be punished." [30]

The Radicals now fondly recalled these fiery sentiments, forgetting that they were uttered when there was still real fighting to be done,—fighting in which none of them participated. The Conservatives recalled how when he took charge as military governor he had announced that "while it may become necessary . . . to punish . . . conscious treason in high places, no merely retaliatory or vindictive policy will be adopted." [31]

The lovers of fair play were hoping,—so also were those who characterized the exhausted followers of Lee as the "Sodomites in Virginia." Almost immediately after he had taken the presidential oath, Johnson "was at once surrendered by radical and conservative politicians" so Julian tells us, "who were alike anxious about the situation." [32]

Julian tells us further that on the very day Johnson became President: "I spent most of the afternoon in a political caucus held for the purpose of considering the necessity for a new Cabinet and a line of policy less conciliatory than that of Lincoln; and while everybody was shocked at his murder, the feeling was nearly universal that the accession of Johnson to the presidency would prove a godsend to the country. Aside from Mr. Lincoln's known policy of tenderness to the Rebels, which now so jarred upon the feelings of the hour, his well-known views upon the subject of reconstruction were as distasteful as possible to Radical Republicans." [33]

The Radical position was promptly echoed from the pulpit. Of the twenty-one sermons preached in New York and Brooklyn on the following Sunday, nearly all in unmeasured terms demanded the severest punishment of the Confederates. Stephen H. Tyng, a low-church Episcopalian, declared that Good "had introduced a ruler whose stern experience of Southern wickedness will cut off all pleas of leniency to the base destroyers of this country." [34] The Rev. J. E. Rockwell thus addressed his flock of Presbyterians: "May it not be that God has permitted this great crime . . . to awaken us to a sense of justice and to a full exaction of the penalty of God's law upon those who have planned and accomplished the horrible scenes of the past four years." [35] During the same hour Albert S. Hunt was preaching to his Methodist congregation: "Wherever Lincoln has erred it has been on the side of mercy. . . . And there are those who listen to me today who think that Providence has permitted this calamity to befall us that a sterner hand might rule in our national affairs." [36]

The press too took a hand to urge on Andrew Johnson by flattery and by threat the doctrine of vengeance for the beaten South. Horace Greeley's followers, for example, on Monday morning, April 17th, in the treasured *Tribune* read: "We know nothing, say nothing of President Johnson's purposes; but in the present state of public feeling, he could not do with safety what President Lincoln might easily have done a little week ago. And though the military power of the Rebellion is broken, its spirit is untamed; and that spirit still burning in many bosoms will have been intensified and embittered by the tragedy of Friday night and the consuming wrath which that tragedy has excited throughout the loyal states. Andrew Johnson is emphatically a self-made man, with the energy, self-reliance and courage befitting that character. He believes in the Republic, venerates the Union and has learned to hate Slavery and Rebellion with his whole soul. As the director of a great war, we believe he has qualities superior to that of our late President; if he desires a general to move, who nevertheless stands obstinately still, he will give the order again but to another man." [37]

For twenty days after the tragedy at Ford's Theatre "the uppermost thought in men's minds was Lincoln, and it was kept vivid by the press, by speeches and by sermons from the pulpit. And always the desire for vengeance alternated with grief." [38] It was urged that the leaders of the Confederacy were the instigators of the murder. While these accusations were being circulated and believed in the North, one of the greatest of the Southern military leaders, General Joe Johnston (and there has long since ceased to be any doubt that he voiced the sentiments of his people) declared: "The loss was most serious to the people of the South, who had begun to realize that Mr. Lincoln was the best friend the South had." [39]

To the Radicals, Lincoln's death spelled opportunity,—opportunity to arouse the passions of their followers to thoughts of vengeance upon the "conquered provinces," under the leadership of a new Executive who would exercise "a sterner hand." At no time did Winter Davis and Ben Wade or their followers express regret for their treatment of the martyred President. There was heard from them no manly contrition for their "manifesto." The downright character of the Britishers' atonement forms a refreshing contrast. On May 6th, these lines were printed in the London *Punch:*

> You lay a wreath on murdered Lincoln's bier
> You who with mocking pencil wont to trace,
> Broad for the self-complacent British sneer
> His length of shambling limb, his furrowed face.
>
> You whose smart pen backed up the pencil's laugh
> Judging each step as though the way were plain,
> Reckless so it could point a paragraph
> Of chief's perplexity or people's pain.
>
> Beside his corpse that bears for winding sheet,
> The stars and stripes he lived to rear anew,
> Between the mourners at his head and feet,
> Say, scurril-jester, is there room for you?

XXV

ABRAHAM LINCOLN OR THADDEUS STEVENS?

To no Chief Executive of the United States before or since have there befallen problems more perplexing than those now confronting Johnson. For four years the states had been tearing at each other's throats, and now that the Union soldiers had done their work, the stay-at-homes who had sat safely in the uninvaded North, were crying out for vengeance on the gallant vanquished. They longed to administer the Southern states as "conquered provinces."

"There should now," wrote Senator Sherman, "be literally no terms granted. We should not only brand the leading rebels with infamy, but the whole rebellion should wear the badge of the penitentiary, so that for this generation at least no man who has taken part in it would dare to justify or palliate it." [1] These were the words of a "statesman!" Now listen to the language of a soldier,—the brother of the statesman. "The mass of the people south," wrote General Sherman, "will never trouble us again. They have suffered terrifically, and I now feel disposed to befriend them,—of course not the leaders and lawyers, but the armies who have fought and manifested their sincerity, though misled, by risking their persons. . . . It will be difficult for anyone to tread a straight path amid these new complications, but I will do my best. I perceive the politicians are determined to drive the Confederates into guerilla bands, a thing more to be feared than open organized war. They may fight it out, I won't. We could settle the war in three weeks by giving shape to the present disordered elements, but they may play out their game." [2]

On another occasion General Sherman wrote: "The South is broken and ruined and appeals to our pity. To ride the people

202

down with persecutions and military exactions would be like slashing away at the crew of a sinking ship. I will fight as long as the enemy shows fight, but when he gives up and asks for quarter I cannot go further. This state of things appeals to our better nature." [3]   And then this letter to his wife: "Now that the war is over, how brave and fierce have become the men that thousand-dollar bounties, patriotism, the appeal of generals and others would not bring out. . . . Washington is as corrupt as Hell, made so by the looseness and extravagance of war. I will avoid it as a pest house." [4]

The negroes were an even greater problem in 1865 than throughout the troublous years that led up to the war. The freed men in that year "were an element in the South utterly unlike anything previously dealt with by the country. Entirely ignorant, untrained as a rule, except for servile occupations, lacking any civilized customs or domestic or public morality, and devoid of economic instincts, the former slaves formed an alien race fitted in no single respect for citizenship." [5]   Despite this should these people who had just emerged from barbarism be allowed to vote? General Sherman held clear views on this subject as on many others. "I do not favor the scheme," he wrote, "of declaring' the negroes of the South now free, to be loyal voters, whereby politicians may manufacture just so much more pliable electioneering material. The negroes don't want to vote. They want to work and enjoy property, and they are no friends of the negro who seek to complicate him with new prejudices." [6]

The state of our foreign affairs was enormously complex and threatening. Relations with Great Britain had been strained to the breaking point. The *Trent* had not been forgotten, and the *Alabama* claims awaited settlement. With France, however, far more than with England, the situation was fraught with danger. The very presence of Maximilian in Mexico was a constant threat.

Both at home and abroad, the problems were of a magnitude unparalleled in American history. How could all the losses and economic wreckage be repaired? Of the Northern soldiers

359,528 had been killed in action or by disease, while the South had lost approximately 258,000 through the same causes.[7] More than half a million of the finest American young manhood,—it was a loss that could never be replaced. Volunteers for the most part,—they represented all that was glorious in youth, their potentialities for leadership and as the progenitors of a better race had been consumed within the flaming holocaust of civil strife. In money alone the war had cost the Union three and one-quarter billions of dollars and the Confederacy nearly half that sum.[8] "What of the war!" wrote Phillips Brooks in May, 1861. "Isn't it grand!" [9]

To Andrew Johnson's lot these problems fell,—the backwash of the greatest of all civil wars. The cry of the Radicals echoed in the newspapers and reverberating from the pulpits was that a sterner hand might rule in our national affairs." [10] Four days after Lincoln's death Emerson wrote: "And what if it should turn out in the unfolding of the web, that he had reached the term; that the heroic deliverer could no longer serve us; that the rebellion had touched its natural conclusion, and what remained to be done required new and uncommitted hands. . . ." [11]

"New and uncommitted hands!"—the hands of Andrew Johnson. Was it a good description of them? What policy would he pursue? This was the question upon every tongue. "Mr. Lincoln's latest utterances," wrote Julian, "had been far from assuring or satisfactory. The question of reconstruction had found no logical solution, and all was confusion respecting it. The question of negro suffrage was slowly coming to the front, and could not be much longer evaded. The adequate punishment of the Rebel leaders was the demand of the hour. What would the new President do? He had suddenly become the central figure of American politics, and both Radicals and Conservatives were as curious to know what line of policy he would follow as they were anxious to point the way." [12]

On Sunday, April 16th, the Congressional Committee on the "Conduct of the War," by appointment called upon President Johnson, who received them with "decided cordiality." [13] Ben Wade who was one of the Committee and its spokesman then stepping forward said: "Johnson, we have faith in you. By the Gods, there will be no trouble now in running the government." [14] Johnson's reply unfortunately was such as to have encouraged hope among Wade's followers. "I hold that robbery is a crime"; he said, "rape is a crime; murder is a crime; treason is a crime and must be punished. Treason must be made infamous, and traitors must be impoverished." This pleased the Radicals. "We were all cheered and encouraged by this brave talk," wrote Julian, "and while we were rejoiced that the leading conservatives of the country were not in Washington, we felt that the pressure and influence of the Committee of which Johnson had been a member, would aid the Administration in getting on the right track. We met him again the next day and found the symptoms of a vigorous policy still favorable, and although I had some misgivings, the general feeling was one of unbounded confidence in his sincerity and firmness, and that he would act upon the advice of General Butler by inaugurating a policy of his own, instead of administering on the political estate of his predecessor." [15]

The Radicals were wasting no time, they were well organized, they were hopeful and they were determined. They had been in part successful in thwarting Lincoln's reconstruction plans, now they hoped to be wholly so by annexing the new President to their Juggernaut. Stanton lost no time to demonstrate how cordially he would support the schemes of those who had opposed his former chief. On the evening of the same Sunday when Wade expressed his confidence in Johnson, Stanton held a private meeting at the War Department to which Sumner and his friends had been invited. [16] At this meeting the subject of negro suffrage was discussed. Lincoln had been dead forty-eight hours, but Sumner could wait no longer to begin anew his advocacy of measures the late President had opposed.

Such were the questions and some of those who agitated them. Every problem in the last analysis could be reduced to one question: "Would Johnson prove loyal or disloyal to the plans and principles of Lincoln?" The Radicals hoped that he would prove disloyal!

§

Three days after Lincoln's death, Governor Oglesby with a group of citizens from Illinois, called on the new President and said to him: "We may safely trust our destinies in your hands." To which Johnson answered: "I shall enter upon the discharge of my great duty firmly, steadfastly, if not with the signal ability exhibited by my predecessor, which is still fresh in our sorrowing minds. Need I repeat that no heart feels more sensibly than mine this great affliction? . . . Our Chief Magistrate, the beloved of all our hearts, has been assassinated. . . . No one can say that if the perpetrator of this fiendish deed be arrested he should not undergo the extremest penalty the law knows for crime; none will say that mercy should interpose." [17]

Here was hope for the Radicals, and as he continued they might have gathered even more encouragement. For, referring to Lincoln's assassin, Johnson asked: "Is he alone guilty? The American people must be taught—if they do not already feel—that treason is a crime and must be punished; that the Government will not always bear with its enemies; that it is strong not only to protect but to punish." [18]

So stimulated were the Radicals by these sentiments that they failed to note other sentences of that speech among which were these: "When the question of exercising mercy comes before me it will be considered calmly, judicially, remembering that I am the Executive of the nation. . . . I shall not anticipate the future." [19]

The importance of restoring concord between his own and foreign nations was forcibly displayed when two days later Sir Frederick Buell, Envoy Extraordinary of her Britannic Majesty, presented his credentials to the President together with a message of condolence and sympathy from Queen Victoria. "It is with pleasure," said Sir Frederick, "that I convey the assurances of regard and good will which her Majesty entertains towards you, sir, as President of the United States." [20] Did Johnson's mind travel back to those days in the tailor shop when crosslegged on his bench his dreams were fired by Pitt and Fox, and he had dreamed of the great scenes within the English Parliament, little thinking that to him would one day come a message from the English Queen?

Whatever may have flashed across his memory Johnson's reply was a model of diplomacy. Each of the countries, he said, "is charged with the development of the progress of the human race, and each in its sphere is subject to difficulties and trials not participated in by the other. The interests of civilization and of humanity require that the two should be friends. I have always known and accounted as a fact honorable to both countries, that the Queen of England is a sincere and honest well-wisher to the United States." [21] Johnson knew of what import had been Victoria's friendship for the Union.

During the latter part of April, a deputation of loyal men from various Southern states called upon the President. There was in his response a further clue of how he intended to administer his trust: "Mercy and clemency have been pretty large ingredients in my composition, having been the Executive of a state, and thereby placed in a position in which it was necessary to exercise clemency and mercy. I have been charged with going too far, being too lenient," [22] he told them. The likelihood of a repetition of these charges were he again to be guilty of mercy, was apparent to him.

Treason and what should be done with it were uppermost in his mind. Lincoln's assassination was ever before him. "This man we have seen revered and loved," he said, "one who if he erred at all erred ever on the side of clemency and mercy—that man we have seen Treason strike. . . ." [23] That the assassin "should pay the forfeit with his life" was plain enough. But "what should be done with him or them who have raised impious hands to take away the life of a nation composed of thirty millions of people? What should be the reply to that question?" [24]

What indeed? The Radicals' reply was known, what Johnson's would be the country was eagerly awaiting. He was not yet ready to reveal it, yet it is not hard to see whither his thought was tending. While for "the leaders" he was proposing stern justice, he continued: "I also say amnesty, conciliation, clemency and mercy to the thousands of our countrymen whom you and I know have been deceived or driven into this infernal rebellion. . . ." [25]

I intend to . . . bring back peace to our distracted country." [26]

At the very close of the month, to a delegation from Indiana, President Johnson again gave utterance to his views: "Upon this idea of destroying states," he said, "my position has been heretofore well known, and I see no cause to change it now. . . . Some are satisfied with the idea that the states are to be lost in territorial and other divisions; are to lose their character as states. But their life-breath has only been suspended, and it is a high constitutional obligation we have to secure each of these states in the possession and enjoyment of a republican form of government."

Here was fair notice served upon Sumner, Stevens and Ben Wade. He was speaking directly for their benefit when he continued: "In . . . putting the government on its legs again, I think the progress of this work must pass into the hands of its friends. If a state is to be nursed until it again gets strength, it must be nursed by its friends, not smothered by its enemies." [27] This was the fundamental principle of Lincoln's reconstruction plan.

§

Andrew Johnson was taking a firm hold. The great questions of the hour were crowding fast upon him, but he was moving carefully. Always the pressure upon a new President is all but insupportable, but upon no occupant of that office before or since has it been more so. All of his great strength was dedicated to his task.

As soon as he had taken his oath of office, he sent courteous word to Mrs. Lincoln inviting her to occupy the White House as long as she might wish. [28] In the meantime he accepted the hospitality of Mr. Sam Hooper, a member of the House of Representatives, who placed his comfortable home at the corner of Fourteenth and H Streets at the President's disposal. [29] For his office he occupied a room in the Treasury Department adjoining and communicating with that of Secretary Hugh McCulloch. [30] Because of this we are fortunately furnished with a witness of unimpeachable veracity, whose word once and for all time should set at rest the charge then and since hurled most frequently at Johnson that he was intemperate.

Like all truly temperate men he was abstemious in food as well as drink. He arrived at his office, says McCulloch, "every morning before nine o'clock and he rarely left before five. There was no liquor in his room. It was open to everybody. His luncheon, when he had one, was like mine: a cup of tea and a cracker. . . . For nearly four years I had daily intercourse with him frequently at night, and I never saw him when under the influence of liquor. I have no hesitation in saying that whatever may have been his faults, intemperance was not among them." [31]

Early in May, the number of deputations calling upon him became less frequent. They had been a drain upon his strength, although, in the absence of an Inaugural address, they had given him an opportunity to enunciate his views. "But," wrote Gideon Welles, "they have been annoying at times, obstructions to business, and were becoming irksome. The President was not displeased with these manifestations and has borne himself well through a period which has been trying and arduous, and is gathering to himself the good wishes of the country." [32]

Of all the reconstruction problems there was none more permanently important than the highly controversial one of negro suffrage. The war had been fought to give the negroes freedom, it was not waged to give them votes. "As he died to make men holy, let us die to make men free," sang Julia Ward Howard in words deservedly immortal. "To make men free,"—not to equip incompetent illiterates with the ballot!

Sumner perhaps, with his bigot mind, saw the question as one of principle, but the politicians saw it solely as one of votes. What a boon to the Republican party would be the addition of 672,000 colored votes in the "rebel states,"—more than two-thirds of the 923,000 white votes in that area! [33] The schemers well knew that the Southern states would not at once grant the franchise to the negroes. But suppose the Federal government forced them to do so! What mattered it that the North itself had not yet adopted this radical departure. Of what concern to

Stevens and to Wade was it that, of the Northern states, all save six then denied their blacks the right to vote, and that of these six, New York required a property qualification for the negro which it did not exact of white men? [34]

These questions were pondered everywhere, sometimes honestly and with intelligence. On May 6th, General Sherman wrote to Chase: "To give all loyal negroes the same political status as white voters will revive the war," and four days later Schofield in a letter to Grant asserted "the absolute unfitness of the negroes as a class" to exercise the right of franchise. "They can neither read nor write," he continued, "they have no knowledge whatever of law or government; they do not even know the meaning of the freedom that has been given them, and are much astonished when informed that it does not mean that they are to live in idleness and be fed by the Government." [35]

On May 9th, Welles wrote in his diary: "The question of negro suffrage is beset with the difficulties growing out of the conflict through which we have passed, and the current of sympathy for the colored race. The demagogues will make use of it regardless of what is best for the country, and without regard for the organic law, the rights of the states or the troubles of our government. There is a fanaticism on the subject with some who persuade themselves that the cause of liberty and the Union is with the negro, and not the white man. White men and especially Southern white men are tyrants. Senator Sumner is riding this one idea at top speed. There are others less sincere who are pressing the question for party purposes. On the other hand, there may be unjust prejudice against permitting colored persons to enjoy the elective franchise under any circumstances; but this is not, and should not be, a Federal question. No one can claim that the blacks, in the slave states especially, can exercise the elective franchise intelligently. In most of the free states they are not permitted to vote. Is it politic and wise or right even, when trying to restore peace and reconcile differences to make so radical a change—provided we have authority which I deny—to elevate the ignorant negro who has been enslaved mentally as well as physically, to the discharge of the highest duties of citizenship, especially when our free states will not permit the few negroes to vote?" [36]

"It was never intended by the founders of the Union," Welles continued, "that the Federal government should prescribe suffrage to the states. We shall get rid of slavery by constitutional means. By conferring on the black civil rights is another matter. I know not the authority. The President in the exercise of the pardoning power may limit or make conditions, and, while granting life and liberty to traitors, deny them the right of holding office or of voting. While, however, he can exclude traitors, can he legitimately confer on the blacks of North Carolina the right to vote? I do not see how this can be done by him or by Congress." [37]

That these were the views of Abraham Lincoln gave them no added sanction with the Radicals. They were the views of Lincoln, would Andrew Johnson follow them? All that lay within their power the Radicals had done to thwart and to discredit Lincoln while he lived, a champion of his views was certain to invite the same vituperation. A mere politician would never dare to court it.

What the politicians were about to do was plain enough to Welles when he continued: "Stanton has changed his position, has been converted, is now for negro suffrage. These were not his views a short time since. But aspiring politicians will as the current now sets generally take that road." [38]

§

On the 22nd of May, President Johnson reviewed Sherman's army. In front of the White House a reviewing stand had been erected; it was adorned with flags and ornamented with the names of victories. There in company with General Grant, surrounded by his Cabinet, the Diplomatic Corps and other dignitaries, the new President stood to pay the nation's tribute to the 65,000 bronzed and hardened veterans. [39]

The newspapers had proclaimed the great event, and all the railroads were sorely taxed to accommodate the multitudes that had come to honor the defenders of the Union. [40] Overhead the day was glorious, it was a glorious day for the Republic. The people came with flowers for their favorite regiments,—the wives, the mothers, the sweethearts and the fathers to weep their tears of joyous welcome. The war was over! The shouts of joy were mingled with the thunder of the drums, the bugles' high fanfare and the thrilling marching melodies in a golden stream flooding from a thousand throats of brass. It was a day for martial music! Bright sabres flashed and burnished bayonets were gleaming.[41] But let the General who led the march describe it. "Punctually at 9 A. M.," Sherman wrote, "the signal gun was fired, when in person, attended by General Howard and all my staff, I rode slowly down Pennsylvania Avenue, the crowds of men, women and children, densely lining the sidewalks and almost obstructing the way. . . . When I reached the Treasury Building and looked back the sight was simply magnificent. The column was compact and the glittering muskets looked like a solid mass of steel moving with the regularity of a pendulum. . . . It was in my judgment the most magnificent army in existence—sixty-five thousand men in splendid physique, who had just completed a march of nearly two thousand miles in a hostile country, in good drill, and who realized that they were being closely scrutinized by thousands of their fellow countrymen and by foreigners."[42]

They were indeed scrutinized by foreigners. It was such a sight as when reported by the French Ambassador to his Emperor might well have induced Louis Napoleon to pause and to reflect upon his trans-Atlantic dreams, and the probable future in Mexico of his poor dupe Maximilian. The Monroe Doctrine! Perhaps there was something in it after all.

What were the thoughts that moved in Andrew Johnson's mind as Sherman's soldiers swept before him? From Atlanta to the sea and north through the Carolinas like the followers of Attila, these men had swept the southland, breaking the back of the Confederacy as with some giant butcher's cleaver. Burned houses, ruined granaries, and despoiled plantations marked the dreadful march like the guide posts of death. They had confirmed the definition of their own commander: "War is Hell." The story of that march and the burning and sack of Columbia, South Carolina, in Southern literature are drawn in colors as vivid as any that portrayed Lisle and Louvain forty-nine years later.[43] Desolation, poverty and desperation lay in the wake of the advancing hosts, and there were other concomitants of war. But two cases of rape had come to Sherman's personal attention.[44] Perhaps there was less of that than usually attends invasion. Most of the meanest crimes, no doubt, had been committed by nondescript camp followers,—but they were committed. "The authority of the government is weakened and brought into contempt," General Joseph Hawley in April, from Wilmington, had written, "by the impunity with which stragglers, deserters from either army, marauders, bummers and strolling vagabonds, negroes and whites commit outrages upon the inhabitants." [45]

That march, justifiable perhaps, though far more horrible than all the fighting, at last was over, but the march of the political marauders had just begun. Encouraged by Stevens and his followers, the bummers and the strolling vagabonds of politics were ready for their ravages upon the South. Lincoln had set his face like flint against them. For Johnson the great decision was at hand. Which should it be, Abraham Lincoln or Thaddeus Stevens?

XXVI

JOHNSON TAKES UP LINCOLN'S CAUSE

On the 29th of May, forty-four days after he had become President of the United States, Andrew Johnson cast the die. It was one of the great decisions in the history of the Republic! He had counted all the cost, he had considered the consequences, he had weighed the opposition that would arise to thwart and to destroy him as it had sought to thwart and to destroy his predecessor; he knew that the popular road lay on the side of vengeance for a beaten foe, yet knowing these things, he chose the course he thought was right,—for the sole reason that it was right. On that day, selecting Abraham Lincoln as his mentor and his guide, he issued his reconstruction proclamation. It related to North Carolina, but as we shall see, he by no means intended to stop there.

"To the end . . . that the authority of the government of the United States may be restored and that peace, order and freedom be established, I, Andrew Johnson, President of the United States, do . . . hereby grant to all persons who have . . . participated in the existing rebellion, amnesty and pardon with restoration of all rights of property except as to slaves. . . ." [1]

From the benefits of this amnesty and pardon, fourteen classes were excepted. The thirteenth excluded those who had "voluntarily participated in said rebellion and the estimated value of whose taxable property is over $20,000." [2] With this exception Johnson's proclamation in every essential and in much of its actual language was the same as that which Abraham Lincoln had issued on December 8th, 1863. [3] For those thus excluded, however, he declared "that special application may be made to the President for pardon by any person belonging to the excepted classes, and such clemency will be liberally extended as may be

214

consistent with the facts of the case and the peace and dignity of the United States," [4] a promise that was afterwards fulfilled, sincerely, fully and wisely. [5] Johnson found full authority for his proclamation within his constitutional power to grant "reprieves and pardons" [6] and in acts of Congress previously passed, but the star that led him was the lamp of justice lit by Lincoln's hand.

In the vast literature of detraction which has surrounded Andrew Johnson's name, one formula invariably followed has been this: Whenever his action must be praised, the charge is made that he merely followed the advice of some one else. A few days before the 29th of May, Secretary Seward had been sufficiently restored to health to resume some of his duties at the State Department. Because of this, Blaine asserts that the proclamation was not the result of Johnson's thought, but of Seward's persuasion, [7]—and adds: "Mr. Seward's influence was supplemented and enhanced by the timely and artful interposition of clever men from the South. A large class in that section quickly perceived the amelioration of the President's feelings and they used every judicious effort to forward and develop it. . . . He was not especially open to flattery, but it was noticed that words of commendation from his native section seemed peculiarly pleasing to him." [8]

Even Rhodes dissents from Blaine's assertions. [9] Andrew Johnson placed a high value upon the counsel of able men. He admired Seward, and no doubt talked with him before issuing his proclamation; but the charge that Seward persuaded Johnson to "modify" his original purpose, is not true. "The persons who charge the President with reversing his entire policy towards the South," says Seward's own biographer, "have confounded two things which Johnson himself kept quite distinct, the proper treatment of individual wrongdoers, the leaders in rebellion, for whom he thought no punishment too severe, and the leniency to be shown to the communities who had followed their guidance, whom he was always disposed to treat with the utmost consideration. His opinions upon constitutional questions were those he had maintained before his election as Vice-President." [10]

Yet it must not be assumed that Seward's advice was not welcome to the new President. One of Johnson's finest qualities was his ability to recognize and his willingness to accept the counsel of able men. Throughout his whole career his associates and his friends were chosen for their character and independent judgment. Seward's wise counsel and his bright urbanity were welcome to the new Executive. Lincoln's Secretary of State, according to Blaine, now set before Andrew Johnson "the glory of an Administration which should completely reëstablish the Union of the states, and reunite the hearts of the people. . . . He impressed him with the danger of delay to the Republic and with the discredit which would attach to himself if he should leave to another President the grateful task of reconciliation." [11] Probably some such advice was offered, if so it was welcome, but whether given or not, Johnson had been making up his own mind.

On the same day on which he took his stand for Lincoln's reconstruction plan, he issued a second proclamation evidencing more clearly still his determination to carry on the healing work just where it had been left off when Booth's bullet found its mark. He declared that for the purpose of enabling the loyal people of North Carolina "to organize a state government whereby justice may be established, domestic tranquillity insured and loyal citizens protected in all their rights of life, liberty and property," William W. Holden was appointed Provisional Governor of the state.[12]

Under this proclamation the Federal government was intervening not to overthrow but to assist in the restoration of the state. It expressly declared that a person "qualified as a voter" for choosing delegates to the state convention, or "eligible as a member of such convention" must be "a voter qualified as prescribed by the Constitution, and laws of the state of North Carolina in force immediately before the 20th day of May, A. D. 1861, the date of the so-called ordinance of secession." There was this additional proviso that such electors or members of the convention "shall have previously taken and subscribed the oath of amnesty as set forth in the President's proclamation" of the same day.[13]

Though only the subscribers to the oath were authorized to participate in the initial work of reconstruction, how completely the principle of local self-government was preserved appears from these further words: "The said convention when convened, or the legislature that may be thereafter assembled will prescribe the qualification of electors and the eligibility of persons to hold office under the constitution and laws of the state—a power the people of the several states composing the Federal Union have rightfully exercised from the origin of the government to the present time." [14]

Thus if North Carolina desired, she had the right to grant the franchise to her freed slaves, but only if she desired. She was to decide, not the Federal Congress. This was sound, it was just, it was constitutional,—it was Lincoln's plan.

The proclamation directed that "all officers and persons in the military and naval service aid and assist the said provisional governor in carrying into effect this proclamation," and expressly enjoined them "to abstain from in any way hindering, impeding or discouraging the loyal people from the organization of a state government as herein authorized." [15]

Every word of the proclamation recognized North Carolina as a state within the Union subject not only to the duties, but entitled to the rights and privileges of a state. To Johnson it must have been a peculiar satisfaction that he could thus begin his work of restoration in the state where he was born. How little in his dreams could he have foreseen his destined part, when he sat there forty years before plying his tailor's needle and dreaming of the statesmanship of Pitt and Fox!

§

Johnson's invitation to Mrs. Lincoln to occupy the White House as long as it might be agreeable for her to do so, was indeed accepted; she remained eight weeks. [16] It was not until the 9th of June, therefore, that the new President was able to move in. [17]

His health had been impaired by all that he had undergone in Tennessee, nor was there in what was yet to come anything conducive to a serene life. It must, therefore, have been some alleviation for the worries under which even his sturdy shoulders bent, that Eliza presently could join him. Her presence was a solace, but there was little she could do in the discharge of the exacting duties of her position. She had suffered with her husband for the Union, and the years with all their pain had taken toll.[18]

Martha, the President's eldest daughter, whose husband David T. Patterson had just been elected a United States Senator from Tennessee, presided at the White House for her father. The visits she had paid there during the administration of President Polk, her acquaintance with the Blairs, the Lees and other old families of Washington, together with her own charm and grace, were all of inestimable value. She filled her position with dignity, good sense and clear judgment and brought to bear upon varied and exacting tasks an unusual executive ability.[19] She was a young woman of rare tact. "We are plain people from the mountains of Tennessee," she announced, "called here for a short time by a national calamity. I trust too much will not be expected of us."[20]

Johnson himself had little time save for the performance of his official duties. His life while President was a simple one. Each morning at six o'clock he began his work.[21] He realized that the sole opportunity of consummating Lincoln's plan lay in pushing forward to a practical conclusion the healing work before Congress should reconvene. While Thaddeus Stevens and his followers were not there, perhaps it could be done. It was a dangerous task, but it was worth attempting. He realized that his opportunity was now. "I think it providential," said Lincoln on the day before he died, "that this great rebellion is crushed out just as Congress has adjourned and there are none of the disturbing elements of that body to embarrass us. If we are wise and discreet we shall reanimate the states and get their governments in successful operation, with order prevailing and the Union reëstablished before Congress comes together in December."[22]

Lincoln himself could not have begun the work more promptly or pursued the task with more persistence and determination.

§

How easy would it have been for Johnson to cast his fortunes with the Radicals,—to join with them in the hue and cry against the South! This would have meant the approval of the Repub-

(Sketched by Albert Berghaus.)

THE FIRST RECEPTION OF AMBASSADORS BY ANDREW JOHNSON, AT HIS ROOMS IN THE TREASURY BUILDING, APRIL 20, 1865.

lican leaders, the acclaim of their followers and the praise of their historical apologists. There was nothing against such a course except justice and honor. Knowing that to follow Lincoln instead of Stevens would turn the fires of hatred against himself, and would lead to attempts similar to those by which Sumner, Ben Wade and Winter Davis had sought to thrust Lincoln from the White House, Andrew Johnson pressed forward with his work,— Lincoln's work!

The Radicals had been strengthened a thousand times by the hysteria resulting from the Presidential murder, they were organized as they had never been throughout the war, they were hindered by no obstacles such as the victories in the field that had saved Lincoln from Sumner's grasp, and they were determined like the cowards they were to kick the foe now that they had him down. There was but one way in which they might be thwarted, and that was speed! If the South could be restored before Congress could convene, if peace were under way, perhaps even Thaddeus Stevens would not then dare to wither it with his hot breath of hate.

"If we are wise . . . we shall reanimate the state . . . before Congress comes together in December," [23]—with these words of Lincoln ringing in his ears, with all the energy of his soul, Johnson proceeded with his task. Fifteen days after his North Carolina proclamation he issued an identical one for Mississippi,[24] two days later for Texas and for Georgia,[25] on the 21st of June for Alabama,[26] for South Carolina nine days later,[27] and on the 13th of July for Florida.[28]

Full twenty days before his proclamation for North Carolina he had issued a similar one for Virginia, but instead of appointing a provisional governor, he recognized Francis H. Pierpont and directed that he be aided by the Federal government in the "extension and administration of the State Government throughout the geographical limits" of the state.[29] Such was the paucity of the archives of Pierpont's government, that it was Thaddeus Stevens' sneer that they had been removed from Alexandria to Richmond in an ambulance.[30] On the same day he issued his proclamation for Mississippi, Johnson likewise proclaimed that the "insurrec-

tion so far as it relates to . . . Tennessee . . . is suppressed,"
recognizing the reorganization of the state under the new Constitution adopted a few days after he left there to take his oath
as Vice-President.[31]

Lincoln's reconstructed governments in Arkansas and Louisiana
were likewise recognized by Johnson.[32] Thus long before the
summer waned he carried to a conclusion the work his predecessor
had begun. That he followed Lincoln's plan even the historians
admit.[33] "In confronting the problems of restoring civil government in the South," Professor Dunning writes, "President Johnson was under no necessity of devising a solution. That already
applied by Lincoln in three of the states was ready to the hand of
his successor. . . . Accordingly Johnson took up the work at the
precise point where Lincoln had left it."[34] But none of the historians had expressed himself so clearly or so forcibly as Professor
Burgess when he wrote: "In a word Johnson's policy and acts in
reconstructing the 'states' in which secession ordinances had been
passed, and rebellion committed, were but a continuation of those
of Mr. Lincoln. If Lincoln was right so was Johnson, and vice
versa."[35]

The primary object of the war was to restore the Union.
Throughout the conflict Lincoln was developing and, where he
could, applying his plan for doing this. For his services Lincoln's
name has been lifted to the sun-lit pinnacles of honor. Johnson,
who pledged his life and character to the fulfillment of his predecessor's aims, has been the target of the abuse which Lincoln
would have suffered had he lived. No word of praise for Lincoln
is too much, but those who praise him and denounce Johnson
are either ignorant or insincere or both. "If Lincoln was right
so was Johnson!"

§

Johnson gave the Southerners a generous opportunity. They
embraced it promptly and in the same spirit in which it had been
offered. They had been gallant foes; they were not unaccustomed
to victory on their own account. Such men make good losers.
They had fought to secure their independence from the Union,—

to save the Union Lincoln called his volunteers. The contest had broadened into a struggle over slavery. The South had lost. She was prepared to abide by the result, just as the followers of Washington would have been, had their struggle for independence eighty years before resulted in an Appomattox instead of Yorktown. Men who had won as gloriously as they had often done, could bear defeat with equal equanimity.

As the tattered Confederates made their way back to their ruined farms and desolate plantations, and sat down amid the ashes of their hopes, they read Andrew Johnson's proclamations and resolved with all sincerity to lend their coöperation for the restoration of the Union as it was, except with slavery omitted.

The provisional governors whom Johnson chose set speedily to work to carry out the purpose of his proclamations. Conventions met within the various states; in Mississippi on August 14th, in Alabama on September 12th, in South Carolina the following day, in North Carolina on October 2nd, and in Georgia and Florida on October 24th. The convention in Texas did not convene until March of the following year.[36]

"I am gratified that you have organized your convention without difficulty," wrote President Johnson to Governor Sharkey of Mississippi on August 15th. "I hope that without delay your convention will amend your state constitution abolishing slavery and denying to all future legislatures the power to legislate that there is property in man; also that they will adopt the amendment to the Constitution of the United States abolishing slavery."[37]

Lincoln's letter to Governor Hahn of March 13th of the year before "barely suggesting" that the franchise might be extended to the "very intelligent" colored people, should be recalled when we read this next sentence of Johnson's letter: "If you could extend the elective franchise to all persons of color who can read the Constitution of the United States in English and write their names, and to all persons of color who own real estate valued at not less than two hundred and fifty dollars, and pay taxes thereon, you would completely disarm the adversary and set an example the other states will follow. This you can do with perfect safety, and you thus place the Southern states in reference to free persons of color upon the same basis with the free states. I hope and trust your convention will do this, and, as a consequence the Radicals who are wild upon negro franchise will be completely foiled in their attempt to keep the Southern states from renewing their relations to the Union by not accepting their senators and representatives." [38]

Three days after the Georgia convention came together, President Johnson wrote to her provisional governor: "The people of Georgia should not hesitate one single moment in repudiating every single dollar of debt created for the purpose of aiding the rebellion against the government of the United States. It will not do to levy and collect taxes from states that are loyal and are in the Union, to pay a debt that was created in an effort to take them out, and thereby subvert the Constitution of the United States." [39]

"I do not believe," the President continued, "the great mass of the people of the state of Georgia when left uninfluenced will ever submit to the payment of a debt which was the main cause of bringing on their past and present suffering, the result of the rebellion. Those who vested their capital in the creation of this debt must meet their fate and take it as one of the inevitable results of the rebellion, though it may seem hard to them. It should at once be made known at home and abroad, that no debt contracted for the purpose of dissolving the Union of the States can or ever will be paid by taxes levied on the people for such purpose." [40]

Here was kindly common sense advice,—advice that squared with every Union object of the war; restoration of the Union, abolition of slavery, repudiation of debts incurred in furtherance of the rebellion. Negro suffrage was treated exactly as Lincoln himself had treated it. It was the recognition of a fundamental truth,—the ignoring of which may some day prove fatal to our Republic—that the franchise is a privilege and not a right.

The South now followed this advice. By November 8th every Southern state, except South Carolina and Mississippi, had repudiated debts incurred in furtherance of the Rebellion. By the 5th of December all the Southern states save Florida, Texas and Mississippi had ratified the Thirteenth Amendment to the Federal Constitution abolishing slavery, and Florida three days before the closing of the year joined her ratification with the rest.[41]

The results of the war had been accepted by the South. In the arbitrament of arms, the decision had gone against them, and like an honest litigant they had accepted the award and were prepared to abide by it in good faith. The work of reconstruction was indeed proceeding. The leading Southerners came forward promptly to seek the personal pardon of the President,—within nine months after his proclamation nearly fourteen thousand of them came to Andrew Johnson asking amnesty and "recognizing the fact that the Rebellion had failed, turned as the only alternative to the Government which had conquered, and which was now ready to extend a magnanimous forgiveness." [42]

More rapidly than anyone had dared to hope, Lincoln's dream of restoration was coming to fulfillment. Johnson himself on October 13th declared: "We are making very rapid progress—so rapid I sometimes cannot realize it. It appears like a dream!" [43]

§

Throughout the summer of 1865 the North was looking on,—for the most part with approval, while Johnson bent his shoulders to the task. "We can assure him," wrote the New York *Herald* on May 10th, "that he is universally regarded from his trenchant loyalty, his antecedents, his energy and decision of character as the proper man for the crisis. . . ." [44] Three days later it spoke of him as "an experienced statesman who in working out his program of reconstruction will be strengthened by the cordial support of the whole country." [45]

On May 31st this paper declared that Johnson's two proclamations of May 29th "bring out his policy into clear and bold relief. . . . First shaking off the dust and ashes of the Rebellion, President Johnson plants himself upon the laws of Congress and the Proclamations of President Lincoln. . . . In the meantime we may expect from the Republican Radicals of the Sumner school and of the Chief Justice Chase school, too, as well as from Wendell

Phillips and his school a lively movement and a stirring agitation of negro suffrage, henceforward if necessary to the next Presidential election. . . . We are content with the reconstruction policy proclaimed by President Johnson. It is a practical program . . . it will be supported by the country." [46]

Johnson's proclamations were approved by every member of the Cabinet, even Stanton. [47] "I had myself," Stanton later testified, "had no doubt of the authority of the President to take measures for the organization of the Rebel states on the plan proposed during the vacation of Congress and agreed in the plan specified in the proclamation in the case of North Carolina." [48]

On August 22nd McCulloch wrote to Sumner: "The policy which is now being tried is, I believe, approved by a large majority of the Union men at the North." [49] Party conventions, both Democratic and Republican, convening during the summer cordially endorsed Johnson's policy. [50] Governor Morton of Indiana heartily applauded the measures of the President and declared that he was faithfully trying to carry out the policy of amnesty and reconstruction which Lincoln had bequeathed to him. [51] In Maine, Massachusetts and Pennsylvania only was there dissent. [52] In Pennsylvania, Thaddeus Stevens was at work and in Massachusetts, Sumner. The Republican conventions of those states, while expressing confidence in Johnson, condemned his policy. [53] Save these small clouds, the horizon seemed serene. Johnson expressed confidence that the people of the North would give him their support. [54] "In truth, it seemed for the moment," admits Rhodes, "as if another 'era of good feeling' had arrived." [55]

But the Radicals had not lost heart. On August 19th, Welles wrote: "The proceedings of the political conventions in Maine and Pennsylvania leave no doubt in my mind that extensive operations are on foot for an organization hostile to the Administration in the Republican or Union party. . . . It is the old radical anti-Lincoln movement of Wade and Winter Davis with recruits." [56] Sumner bewails the unanimity of the Cabinet; says there is unexpected unanimity in New England against the policy of the Administration; thinks I ought to resign; says Wade and

Fessenden are intending to make vigorous opposition against it. . . ." [57]

Although he did not know it, there was a member of Johnson's Cabinet who from day to day was sitting for his portrait. In the somber hues of yellow and burnt umber that Rembrandt might have envied, stroke by stroke the masterpiece was being executed. The subject of these unfading colors was Edwin Stanton, and Gideon Welles the artist. We shall watch the painter at his easel, realizing that his deft brushes are creating for us accurate as well as brilliant portraiture.

On August 8th, at a Cabinet meeting, Postmaster Dennison asked Stanton about a recent general order dividing the country into eighteen military departments and assigning a multitude of generals to them. The question was polite, but in answering it, says Welles, "Stanton evinced intense feeling and acrimony." He referred his fellow Cabinet member to Grant, declaring that he had no doubt the latter "would have been glad to have had Dennison's advice and direction on the subject. . . . There was a sneer and insolence in the manner more offensive even than the words. . . ." [58] I fell in with Dennison . . . when taking my usual walk, and we at once got on the subject of Stanton's insolent replies today. . . . He says he has known Stanton well for twenty-five years; that he is a charlatan and that he wanted D. to make a sharp reply on Grant in order that he might report it to that officer and thus create a difference." [59]

Eleven days later Welles wrote: "That Stanton has a full understanding with these men styling themselves Radicals I have no doubt. It is understood that the Cabinet unanimously support the policy of the President. No opposition has manifested itself that I am aware. At the beginning Stanton declared himself in favor of negro suffrage or rather in favor of allowing by Federal authority, the negroes to vote in reorganizing the Rebel states. This was a reversal of his opinion of 1863 under Mr. Lincoln. I have no recollection of any disavowal of the position he took last spring, although he has acquiesced in the President's policy apparently,—has certainly submitted to it without objection or remonstrance."

"The Radicals in the Pennsylvania Convention," Welles continued, "have passed a special resolution indorsing Mr. Stanton by name but no other member of the Cabinet. Were there no understanding on a point made so prominent by the Radicals, such a resolution would scarcely have been adopted or drafted." [60] On Monday, August 21st, the Secretary of the Navy thus recorded an interview with the elder Blair: "I found his views in most respects correspond with my own as to demonstrations now being made by ultra-partisans. He attributes much to Stanton. . . ." [61]

Eight days later our diarist wrote: "There is an apparent determination among those who are ingrained Abolitionists to compel the government to impose conditions on the Rebel states that are wholly unwarranted." [62] And at the close of September, he again noted the progress of events: "The rebellious states are reorganizing their governments and institutions,—submitting to results they could not arrest or avert. In the free states, political conventions have been held and movements made to revivify old parties, and, on the part of the extremists, or Radicals, an exhibition of intense hate towards the Rebels which bodes mischief, has manifested itself." [63]

The time was ripe for Wendell Phillips. There had not been, since the old abolition days, so good an opportunity to stir up strife as during the critical summer of 1865. Agitators of the Phillips' school do not want peace. Their mission in life is discord, destruction of what other men have sought to build, their joyous avocation. On June 2nd the New York *Herald* truthfully declared: "Wendell Phillips is a man whose mission is to oppose everything. He first opposed slavery, then the Union, then the rebellion, and now he opposes President Johnson. Among other things he occasionally opposes himself. . . . He (said) that President Johnson's plan of reconstruction was a practical fraud upon the North. He denounced the President as a robber and a 'Jeff Davis' sycophant." [64]

On October 17th Wendell Phillips, from the platform of the Boston Music Hall, poured out his spleen upon the President: "He ranges himself," this agitator said, "with the Southern half-converted rebel. He makes himself ex-rebel in order that they

may be one-fourth Union. . . . I do not believe that Abraham
Lincoln could balk the country nor Andrew Johnson betray as
much as the anti-slavery purpose of the North has achieved since
1861. . . . The President has put a rebel in every spot, he has
put a bayonet in front of every Southern claim, he has spiked
every Northern cannon. . . . Andy Johnson may not be a traitor
but he is an enemy. . . . You cannot trust Andy Johnson." [65]

This was the same Wendell Phillips who in 1860 had called
Lincoln the "slave-hound of Illinois." [66] The same Phillips who
declared: "The Union then is a failure. . . . Disunion is abolition! That is all the value disunion has for me. . . . All hail,
then disunion." [67] . . . Disunion is gain. . . . Disunion is
honor!" [68] It was the same Phillips who in August, 1862, had
said: "I believe Mr. Lincoln is conducting this war at the present
with the purpose of saving slavery; . . . if he had been a traitor
he could not have worked better to strengthen one side, and
hazard the success of the other. . . . The President . . . may be
honest,—nobody cares whether the tortoise is honest or not; he
has neither insight, nor prevision, nor decision. . . . I never did
believe in the capacity of Abraham Lincoln. . . . With chronic
Whig distrust and ignorance of the people, Lincoln halts and fears.
. . . I will tell you what he is. He is a first-rate second-rate
man." [69] Phillips was now warming to his work, before long he
began to speak of Andrew Johnson "as an obstacle to be
removed." [70]

Although Sumner had prevailed upon the convention of Massa-
chusetts to condemn Johnson's policy, he by no means had suc-
ceeded in inducing everyone to follow him; Representative Henry
L. Dawes, of that state, for one, continued to sustain the President.
And so on July 26th we find Winter Davis writing Sumner: "Will
Massachusetts tolerate Dawes? His speech is very discouraging."
And one month later Thaddeus Stevens wrote: "I fear Dawes.
Can he be brought right?" [71]

The Radicals were worried, they knew that the great majority
of the Northerners approved of Johnson's work. "If something
is not done," wrote Thaddeus Stevens to Sumner on June 14th,
"the President will be crowned king before Congress meets." And

again on August 17th: "The danger is that so much success will reconcile the people to almost everything." While on July 29th, Ben Wade wrote to the same correspondent: "To me all appears gloomy. The President is pursuing and resolved to pursue a course in regard to reconstruction that can result in nothing but consigning the great Union or Republican party, bound hand and foot to the tender mercies of the rebels we have so lately conquered in the field and their copperhead allies of the North." [72]

In the early part of August, Sumner wrote John Bright: "Some of our friends are in great despair; I am not," although he admitted disappointment that the Radicals in the Cabinet had abandoned the "good cause." In Speed, however, he found encouragement, calling him the "best of the Cabinet." "But," he continued, "they are all courtiers unhappily, as if they were counsellors of a king." [73]

The Sherman brothers, too, the general and the Senior Senator from Ohio, were not unobserving of what was taking place about them. On November 10th the Senator wrote his soldier brother: "I have seen Johnson several times. He seems kind and patient with all his terrible responsibility." [74] But the Radicals resented Johnson's popularity, they resented his progress, they resented his advocacy of Lincoln's measures and they were laying quietly their plans to thwart him.

XXVII

THE RADICALS DECLARE WAR ON ANDREW JOHNSON

WHILE Congress was not in session "to hinder and embarrass," Johnson had reanimated the Southern states and had put their "governments into successful operation with order prevailing and the Union reëstablished." And now December was at hand and the "disturbing elements" were trooping into Washington, determined if they could to upset all that he had done, as they had sought to hinder and dismay his predecessor while engaged in the same work.

Among the Senators whom we shall later meet, there came William Pitt Fessenden and Lott M. Morrill from Maine, Luke P. Poland from Vermont, Charles Sumner and Henry Wilson from Massachusetts, Henry B. Anthony and William Sprague from Rhode Island, James Dixon and Lafayette S. Foster from Connecticut, the latter the President of the Senate and since Andrew Johnson's elevation, the acting Vice-President of the United States. From New York came Ira Harris and Edwin P. Morgan, from New Jersey Willaim Wright and John P. Stockton, from Maryland Reverdy Johnson, from Ohio John Sherman and Benjamin Wade, from Iowa James W. Grimes and from Illinois Lyman Trumbull.[1]

Among the members of the lower House were these: James G. Blaine from Maine, who was later to aspire, always unsuccessfully, to the Presidency. From Massachusetts, George S. Boutwell, Henry L. Dawes and Oakes Ames, whose name shortly was to become infamous because of "Credit Mobilier"; from New York Henry J. Raymond and Roscoe Conkling, from Pennsylvania Thaddeus Stevens; from Ohio James M. Ashley, and two subsequent Presidents, Rutherford B. Hayes and James A. Garfield; from Indiana George W. Julian and Schuyler Colfax, the Speaker of the House, and presently to become Ames' partner in the "Credit Mobilier." [2]

But in addition to these Senators and Representatives from the non-seceding states, there were others knocking at the doors of Congress. All of the Southern states excepting Texas had chosen Senators and Representatives. If Lincoln's theory of the war was right, they were as much entitled to occupy the seats to which they had been legally elected, as the Senators and Representatives of Illinois and Massachusetts. And what could be more natural than that the South having accepted the results of the war, should employ their accepted leaders as their spokesmen? The leaders of the Confederacy had brought their followers back into a practical relation with the Union. Among those who now repaired to Washington as Senators could therefore be found Alexander H. Stephens, the former Vice-President of the Confederacy, H. V. Johnson, a former Senator in the Confederate Senate, both of Georgia, and with him W. A. Graham of North Carolina, likewise formerly a member of the Confederate Senate, from South Carolina B. F. Perry, a former Confederate state Judge and J. L. Manning, volunteer aid to General Beauregard at Fort Sumter and Manassas. [3]

To the lower House these among other Southern Representatives had come: from Alabama Cullen A. Battle, a former Confederate general and T. J. Foster, a former Representative in the Confederate Congress; from Georgia Phillip Cook and W. T. Woffard, former Confederate generals also; from Mississippi A. E. Reynolds and R. A. Pinson, former Confederate colonels, and J. T. Harrison a former Confederate Congressman, and from the Carolinas other civil and military leaders. [4]

Suppose at Yorktown Washington had been the giver instead of the recipient of the surrender, and that war for independence had been lost, upon whom would the thirteen colonies have called to lead them back into a practical relation with the mother country? Suppose Virginia's effort to secede from England had miscarried, would she not have called upon her Washingtons, her Madisons, her Lees, her Jeffersons and her Monroes to lead her back? Would not Massachusetts naturally have turned to Adams,

Pennsylvania to Robert Morris and to Franklin, and New York to Hamilton, John Jay and Livingston? Or would the rebellious colonies have selected the Tories and the Indians or Benedict Arnold as their spokesmen? And England of course would have preferred the trusted leaders for carrying out a surrender made in good faith,—perhaps not if she had then numbered among her spokesmen a Thaddeus Stevens or a Charles Sumner.

Now that Congress was convening in December, 1865, what would be done with Andrew Johnson's consummated work of reconstruction? Should the former leaders of the Confederacy, now pardoned, and who had come on in good faith with their credentials of election, be allowed their seats? There were at least a few fair-minded men there from the North, but in the Senate Ben Wade and Charles Sumner were the leaders and in the House Thaddeus Stevens the unquestioned dictator. Could these bitter advocates succeed in forcing their fellow legislators to adopt the way of malice for the South? It was certain that they would try.

"Members of Congress are coming in fast, though not early," Welles noted on December 1st, "Speaker Colfax came several days since. His coming was heralded with a flourish. He was serenaded and delivered a prepared speech which was telegraphed over the country and published the next morning. It is the offspring of an intrigue, and one that is pretty extensive. The whole proceeding was premeditated." [5]

The Radicals were prepared for their work. The day before Congress convened there was a preliminary organization of the House whose policy Thaddeus Stevens of course dictated.[6] On December 3rd Welles wrote: "Told the President I disliked the proceedings of the Congressional caucus on Saturday evening. The resolution for a joint committee of fifteen to whom the whole subject of admission of Representatives from states which had been in rebellion (should be referred) was in conflict with the spirit and letter of the Constitution, which gives to each house the decision of election of its own members. . . . Then in appointing Stevens an opponent of state rights, to present it, there was something bad. The whole was in fact revolutionary, a blow to our governmental system, and there had been preconcert to bring it about. The President agreed with me but said they would be knocked in the head at the start. There would be a Representative from Tennessee who had been a loyal member of the House since the war . . . who would so state the case that he could not be controverted. I expressed my gratification if this could be accomplished,—knowing he alluded to Maynard—but suggested a doubt whether the intrigue which was manifest by the resolution, the designation of Stevens, and Colfax's speech had not gone too far." [7]

Edward McPherson of Pennsylvania was clerk of the House of Representatives.[8] He was as completely under Stevens' domination as the Republican caucus of the day before had been. And so when the House on December 4th convened, acting as the tool of the Congressional dictator, McPherson when he called the roll omitted the names of all the Southern Representatives.[9] The law required the clerk to read the entire roll, but what was the law to Stevens and his dupes! There was violent protest from Maynard of Tennessee.[10] Niblack of Indiana offered a resolution that these elected representatives be entitled to the privileges of the floor pending a decision as to their admission.[11] But by a motion to adjourn, Stevens prevented even the courtesy of a vote upon the resolution.[12] "No action of a more decisive character," says Blaine, "could have been taken to indicate on the threshold of Congressional proceedings the hostility of the Republican party, not merely to the President's plan of reconstruction, but to the men who under its operation in the South had been chosen to represent their districts in Congress." [13]

Before the adjournment Schuyler Colfax was reëlected Speaker and Thaddeus Stevens succeeded in performing a further overt act in furtherance of his conspiracy. From time immemorial it has been the courteous custom of Congress to refrain, until the President's message has been received, from all consideration of important public questions.[14] Courtesy to the President! To a degree only equalled by his malicious hatred of all Southerners, in Thaddeus Stevens the common instincts of a gentleman were lacking. It was therefore with keen joy that he awaited an oppor-

tunity to let fly his poison-barbs. In the debate over seating
Maynard as the Representative from Tennessee, James Brooks of
New York with great force argued: "If Tennessee is not in the
Union, the President of the United States must be a foreigner and
a usurper." [15] And further referring to the resolution adopted
by the Stevens caucus of the day before he asked him when he
intended to present it.[16]

Stevens had a large reputation among his followers as a wit.
"I have no objection to answer the gentleman," he said in a tone
of mock seriousness. "I propose to press it at the proper time." [17]
Stevens' biographer records with pride that this astonishingly
brilliant sally made Brooks "the victim of a general laugh." [18]
The same biographer is so fascinated with what he has called
Stevens' "sense of humor" that he has devoted a whole chapter
to his "wit." [19] If elsewhere in my reading I have encountered fourteen drearier pages I do not at this moment recall
where.

Representative Brooks was not required to wait for long.
Stevens sat watching with his resolution in his pocket and in a
few minutes introduced it. It was a declaration of war against
Andrew Johnson.[20] It provided for a joint committee on reconstruction of nine Representatives and six Senators who were
directed to inquire into the condition of the Southern states and
"report whether they or any of them are entitled to be represented
in either House of Congress," and the resolution provided further
that until the report was acted on, no member would "be received
in either House from any of the so-called Confederate States." [21]
Stevens lashed the resolution through.[22]

With a naïveté amazing in one who was endeavoring to praise
his hero, Stevens' biographer declares "that as a piece of political
strategy this move was admirable. In all probability the House
would not at that time have voted to condemn the President. It
was regarded as the policy not only of Johnson but also of Lincoln,
and the influence of Lincoln had never been so potent as during
the years which followed his assassination." [23]

Stevens was made chairman of the committee on reconstruction
and secured among his associates such bitter opponents of Presi-

dent Johnson as James A. Bingham of Ohio, George Boutwell of Massachusetts, Lott M. Morrill of Maine and Roscoe Conkling of New York.[24]

§

In the Senate, on the same day, the proceedings were conducted, says Blaine "with even more disregard of the President than had been manifested in the House. An entire policy was outlined by Mr. Sumner without the slightest reference to what the President might communicate 'on the state of the Union' and a system of reconstruction proposed which was in absolute hostility to the one that Mr. Johnson had devised. Mr. Sumner submitted resolutions defining the duty of Congress in respect to guarantees of the national security and national faith in the Rebel states. While the conditions were not put forth as a finality, they were significant, if not conclusive, of the demands which would be made first by the more advanced Republicans and ultimately by the entire party." [25]

Throughout the summer Sumner had been waiting and preparing for this opportunity. Before the Massachusetts convention in September, he declared for negro suffrage and said: "I am for a velvet glove; but for a while I wish the hand of iron." [26] His speech there had evoked this letter from Thaddeus Stevens: "I am glad you are laboring to avert the President's fatal policy. I wish the prospect of success were better. I have twice written him to stay his hand till Congress meets. Of course he pays no attention to it. Our editors are cowardly sycophants. I would make a speech as you suggest, if a fair occasion offered. Our views (reconstruction and confiscation) were embodied in our resolutions (in the Republican State Convention, recently held) at Harrisburg, amidst much chaff. Negro suffrage was passed over as heavy and premature. Get the rebel states into territorial condition, and it can be easily dealt with. That I think should be our great aim. Then Congress can manage it." [27]

There had been concert between these fellow Radicals in September, as there was on December 4th when Sumner introduced his resolutions designed to subvert the policy of Lincoln and of Johnson. Sumner's resolutions demanded "the complete suppression of all oligarchical pretensions" and the immediate enfranchisement of negroes.[28] Ignoring the fact that Johnson had already done ten times as much as he for the repudiation of the Confederate financial obligations, he demanded "the rejection of the rebel debt."[29] His resolution required that Congress should take care that no one of the seceding states should be allowed to resume its relations to the Union until after the satisfactory performance of the conditions which he laid down.[30]

All within his power Sumner was doing in coöperation with Thaddeus Stevens to "get the rebel states into a territorial condition,"—a condition where Congress could "manage it!" That the Southerners were honorable men, that they could accept defeat bravely and abide loyally by the decision of the sword Sumner's puritanical and narrow mind was incapable of grasping. He ignored all the evidence, such for example as the reports of the mass meeting at Richmond on August 29th, 1865.

To the public square on that day the Virginians had come, their bands were playing "Yankee Doodle" and the "Star Spangled Banner."[31] Leaders of the Confederacy addressed the meeting and these resolutions were adopted: "Resolved, That we have witnessed with just indignation the persistent and wicked efforts of a portion of the press and Northern states to brand the people of the South with perfidy and insincerity, in the honest attempts they have made and are making to resume their former relations with the Union, by questioning their fidelity and truth in the oath of allegiance which they have taken, and by vague and unsupportable charges that they desire, if they do not contemplate, further resistance to its authority." And further: "That, the general temper and disposition of the Southern people, including our own, is to accept and acquiesce in the results of the late sanguinary struggle, and to resume the duties of citizenship in the Union. That the men of character and ability who have hitherto influenced public sentiment, neither advise nor intend anything different from the discharge of their duties as citizens of the

United States, and are setting an example of full and ready submission to the authority of the Government, and counsel a full recognition of the facts of the actual situation, including the acceptable and irreversible abolition of slavery." [32]

Sentiments such as these Charles Sumner was incapable of understanding. He knew that he would have been incapable of similar generosity and he was judging others by himself. "For a while I wish the hand of iron!" The blows of Preston Brooks' retaliatory cane were ringing in his ears.

To the honor of Massachusetts during the same month when Sumner was preparing to strike down a beaten foe, John A. Andrew, the governor of the state, in the State House at Boston declared: "We ought to demand and to secure the coöperation of the strongest and ablest minds and the natural leaders of opinion in the South. If we cannot gain their support of the just measures needful for the work of safe reorganization, reorganization will be delusive and full of danger. Why not try them? They are most hopeful subjects to deal with in the very nature of the case. They have the brain and the experience and the education to enable them to understand the exigencies of the present situation. They have the courage as well as the skill to lead the people in the direction their judgments point, in spite of their own and the popular prejudice. Weaker men, those of less experience, who have less hold on the public confidence, are comparatively powerless. Is it consistent with reason . . . to believe the masses of the Southern men able . . . to turn their backs on those they have trusted and followed, and to adopt the lead of those who have no magnetic hold on their hearts and minds?" [33]

And further the Governor of Massachusetts said: "There ought now to be a vigorous prosecution of the Peace,—just as vigorous as our recent prosecution of the war. We ought to extend our hands with cordial good-will to meet the proffered hands of the South; demanding no attitude of humiliation from any; respecting the feelings of the conquered—notwithstanding the question of right and wrong, between the parties belligerent. . . ." [34] What a God-send to our country it would have been had Andrew and not Sumner represented Massachusetts in the Senate!

§

Having planned, corresponded and prepared throughout the summer, the Radicals had come together in December to prejudice the constructive efforts of the Chief Executive, and to poison the country against the Lincoln policies that now had been carried so successfully to a conclusion. It was under these circumstances that Andrew Johnson on Tuesday, December 5th, sent to the Congress his first annual message as President of the United States. Couched in energetic English, it was nevertheless a thoroughly calm, conservative and statesmanlike report of all that he had been endeavoring to accomplish since the day of Lincoln's death.

He thanked God for "the preservation of the United States," and referring to Lincoln's death, "by an act of parricidal treason," he declared: "The grief of the nation is still fresh. It finds solace that he lived to enjoy the highest proof of its confidence . . ., that his loss was deplored in all parts of the Union, and that foreign nations have rendered justice to his memory. His removal cast upon me a heavier weight of cares than ever devolved upon any one of his predecessors. . . ."[35] I need the support and confidence of all who are associated with me in the various departments of Government and the support and confidence of the people. There is but one way in which I can hope to gain their necessary aid. It is to state with frankness the principles which guide my conduct . . . well aware that the efficiency of my labors will in a great measure depend on your and their undivided approbation."[36]

Then, after expounding the doctrine so eloquently set forth in the first annual message of his predecessor, and now confirmed by four years of fratricidal strife,—the doctrine that the Union is perpetual—the President went on to a discussion of the states. Even in the opinions of John Marshall, there is no finer statement of their relation to the national establishment,—"states with proper limitations of power," he said, "are essential to the existence of the Constitution of the United States. . . . The perpetuity of the Constitution brings with it the perpetuity of the states;

their mutual relation makes us what we are, and in our political system their connection is indissoluble. The whole cannot exist without the parts, nor the parts without the whole. So long as the Constitution of the United States endures, the States will endure. The destruction of the one is the destruction of the other; the preservation of the one is the preservation of the other. . . . It has been my steadfast object to escape from the sway of momentary passions and to derive a healing policy from the fundamental and unchanging principles of the Constitution." [37]

"I found the states," the President went on, "suffering from the effects of a civil war. Resistance to the general government appeared to have exhausted itself. . . . Whether the territory within the limits of those states should be held as conquered territory, under military authority . . . was the first question that presented itself for decision." [38] It was indeed a question,—it was a question upon which Thaddeus Stevens and his co-conspirators had made up their minds; but if they had, so had Johnson, for he continued: "Now military governments, established for an indefinite period, would have offered no security for the early suppression of discontent, would have divided the people into the vanquishers and the vanquished, and would have envenomed hatred rather than have restored affection. Once established, no precise limit to their continuance was conceivable. They would have occasioned an incalculable and exhausting expense." [39]

Perhaps when he was reviewing Sherman's army six months before, Johnson had indeed been thinking of the bummers, the camp followers and the strolling vagabonds that skulked behind it, for he continued: "The chief persons who would have followed in the train of the army would have been dependents on the general government or men who expected profit from the miseries of their erring fellow-citizens. The powers of patronage and rule which would have been exercised under the President over a vast and populous and naturally wealthy region are greater than, unless under extreme necessity, I should be willing to intrust to any one man. They are such, as for myself, I could never, unless on occasion of great emergency, consent to exercise. The wilful use of such powers, if continued through a period of years, would have endangered the purity of the general administration and the liberties of the states which remained loyal." [40] This from a man who Thaddeus Stevens professed to fear would be "crowned king" before Congress met! In Stevens' dream of the carpet-bag domination, the President foresaw the nightmare from which the South is only now recovering.

"Besides," Johnson continued, "the policy of military rule over a conquered territory would have implied that the states whose inhabitants may have taken part in the rebellion had by the act of those inhabitants ceased to exist. But the true theory is that all pretended acts of secession were from the beginning null and void." [41]

The President then spoke of his reopening of the Southern ports, the removal of the blockade, the reëstablishment of the custom houses, the post-office and the Federal Courts, and asked: "And is it not happy for us all that the restoration of each one of these functions of the general government brings with it a blessing to the states over which they are extended?" [42] And he continued: "I know very well that this policy is attended with some risk; that for its success it requires at least the acquiescence of the states which it concerns. . . . But it is a risk that must be taken. In the choice of difficulties it is the smallest risk; and to diminish and if possible to remove all danger, I have felt it incumbent on me to assert one other power of the general government—the power of pardon." [43]

Referring to the Thirteenth Amendment, Johnson continued: "Every patriot must wish for a general amnesty at the earliest epoch consistent with public safety. For this great end there is need of . . . the spirit of mutual conciliation. All parties in the late terrible conflict must work together in harmony. . . . The adoption of the amendment reunites us beyond all power of disruption; it heals the wound that is still imperfectly closed; it removes slavery . . . which has so long perplexed and divided the country; it makes of us once more a united people, renewed and strengthened, bound more than ever to mutual affection and support." [44]

"The amendment to the Constitution being adopted," the President went on, "it would remain for the states whose powers have been so long in abeyance to resume their places in the two branches of the National Legislature, and thereby complete the work of restoration. Here it is, fellow-citizens of the Senate, and for you fellow-citizens of the House of Representatives to judge, each of you for yourselves, of the elections, returns and qualifications of your own members." [45]

On the very day of the reading of this message, the legislature of Georgia was ratifying the anti-slavery amendment. [46] Twenty-three days before South Carolina ratified it; during December Alabama, Georgia, North Carolina and Florida also ratified. [47] Before the year was out all the Southern states but Texas and Mississippi had done so.

"On the propriety of attempting to make the freedmen electors by the proclamation of the Executive," continued Johnson, "I took for my counsel the Constitution itself. . . . When at the first movement towards independence, the Congress of the United States instructed the several states to institute governments of their own, they left each state to decide for itself the conditions for the enjoyment of the elective franchise." [48]

"Moreover," he continued,—and here was something for the statesmen of Ohio, Massachusetts and Pennsylvania to think about —"a concession of the elective franchise to the freedmen by act of the President of the United States, must have been extended to all colored men wherever found, and so must have established a change of suffrage in the northern, middle and western states, not less than in the southern and southwestern. Such an act would have created a new class of voters, and would have been an assumption of power by the President which nothing in the Constitution or laws of the United States would have warranted." [49]

"On the other hand," he proceeded, "every danger of conflict is avoided when the settlement of the question is referred to the several states. . . . In my judgment the freedmen, if they show patience and manly virtues, will sooner obtain a participation in the elective franchise through the states than through the General Government, even if it had power to intervene. When the tumult of emotions that have been raised by the suddenness of the social change shall have subsided, it may prove that they will receive the kindest usage from some of those on whom they have heretofore most closely depended." [50]

Five months before, Mallory, who had been the Confederate Secretary of the Navy, had written Senator Chandler of Michigan: "I know many negroes whom I would trust with the ballot and the number will steadily increase and they must at no distant day become voters under certain qualifications." [51]   While a little later Lee testified that if it should be plain to the state of Virginia that the negroes would vote "properly and understandingly she might admit them to vote." [52]

"But while I have no doubt that now after the close of the war," continued Johnson, "it is not competent for the General Government to extend the elective franchise in the several states, it is equally clear that good faith requires the security of the freedmen in their liberty and their property; their right to labor and their right to claim the just return of their labor. I cannot too strongly urge a dispassionate treatment of this subject, which should be carefully kept aloof from all party strife. We must equally avoid hasty assumptions of any natural impossibility for the two races to live side by side in a state of mutual benefit and good will. The experiment involves us in no inconsistency; let us go on then and make that experiment in good faith and not be too easily disheartened." [53]

§

The Radicals listened with dismay to the reading of the message.[54] With consternation the newspapers the next day were read by the enemies of Lincoln who had now transferred their enmities to his successor. They saw the declaration in the New York *Times* that Johnson's views were "full of wisdom" and were expressed "with great force and dignity," and the New York *Tribune's* editorial doubting "whether any former message has contained so much that will be generally and justly approved and so little that will or should provoke dissent." [55] The *Evening Post* declared that it had found the message "frank, dignified, direct and manly," and without a single sentence that was ambiguous. The New York *Herald* endorsed it also, while the *Nation* declared that any American might read it with pride and find solid hope for democracy in the fact that such a document had been produced by "this Tennessee tailor who was toiling for his daily bread in the humblest of employments when the chiefs of all other countries were reaping every advantage which school, college or social position could furnish." [56]

What was to be done with this message? The Radicals must find a way to ruin its effect. They were alert, determined and unscrupulous. Lincoln's successor, like Lincoln himself, had made it harder for them to strike with the "hand of iron" a prostrate foe. But they were equal to the task and if necessary they would strike Andrew Johnson also.

To the historians Johnson's first annual message has been a problem. They know, as Rhodes admits, that it was "in the spirit of Lincoln's second Inaugural," [57] but if they praise Andrew Johnson then they must condemn ten years of American history following 1866 and repudiate the men and measures who were responsible for the "Solid South," and historians have not yet dared to tell the whole truth about the Reconstruction.

It is interesting to watch Rhodes' struggle with the message. He has to admit that its words "are those of a statesman." [58] He is forced to concede the "excellent tenor and style of this paper," though of course he couples this with the jibe that it "is in striking contrast with the tiresome redundancy and offensive egotism of his speeches." [59] He admits that "the message was very well received by every one except the extreme Radicals," and that "if his plan had been sanctioned by the Republican majority in Congress it would undoubtedly have worked out pretty well the problem of the reconstruction," [60]—high praise for Lincoln's program that Johnson had adopted! And our historian adds patronizingly that "Johnson had almost atoned for his mistake in not convening Congress in the early autumn." [61] Rhodes and Abraham Lincoln did not agree upon that subject. Well, then, what is to be done with this message? Somehow Andrew Johnson must be deprived of credit. Rhodes adopts the formula with which the readers of these pages are now familiar. He declares that the message was "written by George Bancroft." [62]

As his authority, Rhodes cites Professor Dunning's monograph. In one letter Bancroft wrote to Johnson: " . . . I must ask a day or two more for a careful revision. . . ." [63] Dunning then asserts: "That Mr. Johnson himself did not write the final *draft* of his message is thus conclusively established." How far is this from a charge that the *message* "was written by George Bancroft" appears from Dunning's next sentence: "To what degree the actual writer was dependent upon the direction of the President,— whether he was draftsman with full discretion or merely a literary reviser of Johnson's own draft—does not appear from the evidence at hand." [64] To conclude that Bancroft acted in any capacity other than as adviser in the same way as Seward had assisted Lincoln with his first Inaugural, would be impossible for one familiar with Johnson's many speeches.

But suppose Bancroft had written the message and Johnson had adopted it as his own? This would merely prove that he employed competent advisers. Blaine, like Rhodes, has sought to deprive Johnson of the credit for his message, only he attributes it to another pen,—any pen will do so long as it is not Johnson's. "The moderation in language and the general conservatism which distinguished the message," says Blaine, "were perhaps justly attributed to Mr. Seward. . . ." [65]

But Gideon Welles knew what he was talking about when on December 5th he wrote: "I think the message which went in this P. M. will prove an acceptable document. The views, sentiments and doctrines are the President's, not Seward's. He may have suggested verbal emendations,—nothing except what related to foreign affairs. But the President himself has vigorous common sense and on more than one occasion I have seen him correct Seward's dispatches." [66]

THADDEUS STEVENS,—A CLOSER VIEW

FROM Mechanicsville Turnpike on June 1st, 1862, General Pickett wrote to his fiancée: "I have heard that my dear old friend McClellan is lying ill about ten miles from here. May some loving soothing hand minister to him. He was, he is and he will always be, even were his pistol pointed at my heart, my dear loved friend. May God bless him and spare his life." [1] And one year later: "No, my dear, there is something radically wrong about my Hurrahism. I can fight for a cause I know to be just, can risk my own life and the lives of those in my keeping without a thought of the consequences; but when we've conquered, when we've downed the enemy and won the victory I don't want to hurrah. I want to go off all by myself and be sorry for them. . . ." [2]

When Lee's advancing hosts were surging up through Pennsylvania, Pickett again wrote: "Yesterday my men were marching victoriously through the little town of Greencastle, the bands all playing our glorious soul-inspiring Southern airs. . . . As Floweree's band playing 'Dixie' was passing a vine-bowered home, a young girl rushed out on the porch and waved a United States flag. Then, either fearing that it might be taken from her, or finding it too large and unwieldly, she fastened it around her as an apron, and taking hold of it on each side and waving it in defiance, called out with all the strength of her girlish voice and all the courage of her brave young heart:

" 'Traitors—traitors—traitors, come and take this flag, the man of you who dares!'

"Knowing that many of my men were from a section of the country which had been within the enemy's lines, and fearing lest some might forget their manhood, I took off my hat and bowed to her, saluted her flag and then turned, facing the men who felt and saw my unspoken order.   And don't you know that they were all Virginians and didn't forget it, and that almost every man lifted his cap and cheered the little maiden who, though she kept on waving her flag, ceased calling us traitors, till letting it drop in front of her she cried out:

" 'Oh I wish—I wish I had a rebel flag; I'd wave that, too.' " [3]

On July 17th, 1864, a son was born in the Pickett family.   "My men," he wrote to the young mother, "had all heard of the 'Little General,' as they call him, and when I was riding out of camp last night to surrender to him, I noticed the bonfires which were being kindled all along my lines, and knew that my loyal loving men were lighting them in honor of my baby.   But I did not know until this morning that dear old Ingalls, at Grant's suggestion, had kindled a light on the other side of the lines, too, and I was overcome with emotion when I learned of it.   Today their note, marked unofficial, came to me through the lines." [4]   This was the note:

"To George Pickett: We are sending congratulations to you, to the young mother and the young recruit.
July 18, 1864.   Grant, Ingalls, Sucklay." [5]

A few days later there was carried through the Confederate lines a baby's silver service engraved: "To George E. Pickett, Jr. from his father's friends, U. S. Grant, Rufus Ingalls, George Sucklay." [6]

Andrew Johnson understood the chivalric spirit of the soldiers. A thorough comprehension of it had brought him to a vigorous espousal of Lincoln's plan of restoration.   Lincoln, who had said to Pickett's baby: "Tell your father, the rascal, that I forgive him." [7]   Lincoln was dead, but his vision of a lasting peace had been bequeathed to his successor.   Thaddeus Stevens could not comprehend these things.   He had no understanding of justice, no conception of generous treatment for a fallen foe.   What he could understand however and what he could not forget was that during the Confederate invasion of Pennsylvania in 1863 his iron works near Chambersburg were burned. [8]   It was therefore with peculiar zest and with flaming personal malevolence toward Southerners that he demanded the confiscation of their estates. "To get rich" had been one of the objects of his life,[9] and now he was afforded a golden opportunity for usurious retribution.

His hatred and jealousy of the slave owner were only matched by his professed affection for the negro race,—some said a very personal affection for some members of it. He was a bachelor. "He had," wrote Blaine, "the reputation of being somewhat unscrupulous as to his political methods, somewhat careless in his personal conduct, somewhat lax in personal morals." [10] His most recent biographer admits that "it will not be claimed that his life was above reproach." [11] Jonathan Blanchard summed up Stevens' reputation when he wrote him: "In every part of the United States people believe that your personal life has been one prolonged sin; that your lips have been defiled with blasphemy; your body with women! A man at Newburyport . . . told me three weeks since that he had at the card table heard from your mouth language fit only for an ordinary brothel, and such is the general belief." [12] To that charge Stevens wrote this pious answer, and it will not require a legal mind to note that it contains no denial of any of the accusations made: "This is the first line or word I have ever penned in explanation of my conduct as assailed by my enemies. Probably as between us and our Creator all of us are somewhat deficient. I know I am deplorably so. But as to my fellow men, I hope so to live that no one shall ever be wronged or suffer on my account," [13]—this from one who was gathering all his strength to wrong the Southern states and to cause suffering to their white inhabitants that would linger down through the third and fourth generations!

In December, 1865, Thaddeus Stevens was in his seventy-fourth year. His countenance was cadaverous, while from under shaggy brows flashed eyes whose fire the flight of years seemed to have kindled to a fiercer flame.[14] "I once heard him make a stump speech," wrote Carl Schurz, "which was evidently inspired by intense hatred of slavery, and remarkable for argumentative pith and sarcastic wit. But the impression his personality made on me was not sympathetic; his face, long and pallid, topped with an

ample dark brown wig which was at the first glance recognized as such; beetling brows overwhelming keen eyes of uncertain color which sometimes seemed to scintillate with a sudden gleam, the underlip defiantly protruding; the whole expression unusually stern; his figure would have looked stalwart but for a deformed foot which made him bend and limp. His conversation carried on with a hollow voice devoid of music, easily disclosed a well-informed mind, but also a certain absolutism of opinion with contemptuous scorn for adverse argument. . . . What he himself seemed to enjoy most in his talk was his sardonic humor, which he made play on men and things like lurid freaks of lightning. He shot out such sallies with a perfectly serious mien, or at best he accompanied them with a grim smile which was not at all like Abraham Lincoln's laugh at his own jests." [15]

On one occasion General Taylor, late of the Confederate army, while endeavoring to gain permission to visit Jefferson Davis at Fortress Monroe, called on this apostle of hate in Washington. "Thaddeus Stevens," he wrote, "received me with as much civility as he was capable of. Deformed in body and temper like Caliban, this was the Lord Hategood of the Fair; but he was frankness itself. He wanted no restoration of the Union under the Constitution, which he called a worthless bit of old parchment. The white people ought never again to be trusted with power, for they would inevitably unite with the Northern 'Copperheads' and control the government. The only sound policy was to confiscate the lands and divide them among the negroes, to whom sooner or later suffrage must be given. . . . Had the leading traitors been promptly strung up, well; but the time for that had passed. (Here I thought he looked lovingly at my neck, as Petit André was wont to do at those of his merry-go-rounds.)" [16]

Thaddeus Stevens was not responsible for his club foot, but for his face he was responsible. "Every man," Stanton once well said, "is responsible for his face at fifty,' [17] and Stevens was seventy-three. His sardonic bitter soul had recorded itself in hard and cruel lines. His countenance was an impressive one, high and massive forehead, deep-set eyes that flashed like livid coals of fire, a large and bony nose, but most of all the mouth engages and rivets the attention. The heavy underlip protruding with the corners depressed. It is a mouth of unexampled cruelty. Even in repose the marks of malice indelibly have left their stamp. There is a fascination about that countenance,—the horrid fascination that comes from gazing into the cold visage of a snake. It is such a face as one might have seen among the crowds of Paris in 1793, smiling as the tumbrils rumbled by, or watching with malevolent and cruel pleasure the guillotine at work. And now in December, 1865, weaving his way among the men and measures of his time like some malignant cancer, this horrible old man was craftily preparing to strangle the bleeding, broken body of the South, and to strike down, if he could, the advocates of justice.

SUMNER BEGINS TALKING OF IMPEACHMENT

ABOVE the arid wastes of talk, the tiring tumult of Congressional debate, there shines the glorious light of Lincoln's hope like a golden lamp hung high aloft in some black sky,—and Andrew Johnson was following the gleam. With the pertinacity of crusaders of old times, he had dedicated his heart, his soul and his great courage to the consummation of the work his predecessor had begun.

When the reading of Johnson's message had been completed, and the country had received and heartily applauded it, it seemed as though the opponents of Lincoln and of Johnson would be baffled in their work of opposition. But they were ingenious, they were prepared, they were determined, and there were circumstances ready at hand to aid them. One of these was the legislation being then enacted by the Southern states for the control of their freed slaves,—legislation designed and executed in perfect good faith and based upon a sound appraisal of the actualities of the situation, but offering golden opportunities to Stevens and his friends to distort the motives and purposes of those enacting it.

In the very center of Lincoln's reconstruction proclamation there was this sentence: "And I do further proclaim . . . that any provision which may be adopted by such state government in relation to the freed people of such state which shall recognize and declare their permanent freedom, provide for their education, and which yet may be consistent as a temporary arrangement, with their present condition as a laboring, landless and homeless class, will not be objected to by the National Executive." [1] Lincoln knew the Southern white men could be trusted. The former slaveholders harbored no hatred for the negro. While the white men were away fighting, the negroes remained, caring for the plantations and protecting their white mistresses with true devotion,—a devotion for which Southern white men were not slow to feel or to express their gratitude.[2]

After the war the Southern legislatures went about their work with full understanding of the colored race, and the necessity of regulating its members in their unaccustomed liberty. One of the last acts approved by Lincoln was the law signed on March 3rd, 1865, for the relief of freedmen and refugees.[3] It furnished temporary relief, but one of its sections was the occasion of much harm, for it created in the ignorant minds of the ex-slaves the expectation that without labor each of them was to receive from the Federal government forty acres and a mule.[4] Before the close of 1865 there was among the negroes an impression generally prevailing that between Christmas and New Year's Day their masters' land would be divided up among them. This dream of what "seemed to them a fortune, fostered the native laziness and improvidence of the race; they became unwilling to work and wished to wander about—a life which of necessity was partly supported by theft. To many of the negroes freedom meant idleness."[5]

To the white men, especially those in South Carolina and Mississippi, where they were outnumbered by the negroes, and in Louisiana where the two races were nearly equal in number, viewing these tendencies, and remembering perhaps Nat Turner, there arose a fear of a general uprising—"the black terror."[6] It was under these circumstances that South Carolina in October, 1865, enacted laws for the government of their emancipated slaves, and Mississippi between November and December of the same year passed statutes "to regulate the relation of master and apprentice relative to Freedmen, Freed Negroes and Mulattoes," and other laws for their control.[7]

In all the states the power to sue and be sued, and to testify in court was fully given, the marriage relation was fully recognized, as well as the right to acquire and dispose of property, to make contracts and to enjoy the fruits of their labor. Trespass, carrying fire arms, malicious mischief, assault and other crimes were strongly dealt with. For rape of a white woman by a negro the penalty was death. The Mississippi Act provided that negro children under the age of eighteen who were orphans or children of parents who would not support them should be apprenticed by the clerk of the Probate Court to some suitable person "provided that the former owner of said minor shall have the preference when in the opinion of the court he or she shall be a suitable person for that," in which case the males were to be bound until the age of twenty-one and the females until eighteen." [8]

As to the control of the apprentices the master or mistress was given power to "inflict such moderate corporal chastisement as a father or guardian is allowed to inflict on his or her child or ward at common law," but it was expressly provided that "in no case shall cruel or inhuman punishment be inflicted." [9] Other provisions required that negroes who would not work at the current rate of wages were to be considered vagrants and subject to penalties. Of course the privilege of serving on juries or in the militia, or of holding office was not accorded, [10] nor is it surprising that the Southerners should not at once have given the franchise to the negroes, when at that time all but six of the Northern states denied that right even to the comparatively few blacks within their borders. [11]

"As a matter of fact," says William Dunning, "this legislation, far from embodying any spirit of defiance towards the North or any purpose to evade the conditions which the victors imposed, was in the main a conscientious and straightforward attempt to bring some sort of order out of the social and economic chaos which a full acceptance of the results of war and emancipation involved. In its general principle it corresponded very closely to the actual facts of the situation. The freedmen were not and, in the nature of the case, could not for generations be, on the same social, moral and intellectual plane with the whites; and this fact was recognized by constituting them a separate class in the civil order. As in general principles, so in details, the legislation was faithful on the whole to the actual conditions with which it had to deal." [12] But these "black codes," as the Radicals began to call them, were to furnish Stevens and his friends an opportunity to thwart Johnson's reconstruction plan by raising a false hue and cry that the South was reënslaving negroes,—suppressing of course the fact that those Southern measures could be duplicated by similar enactments then in force in Connecticut, Rhode Island and other Northern states, not only as to content and effect, but even to the use of the much criticized words of master, mistress and servant.[13]

Then too, in collecting the means with which to arouse Northern suspicions and Northern fear, the Radicals with well-feigned concern were pointing to the presence in Washington of the former civil and military leaders of the Confederacy. This, President Johnson had foreseen before Congress sat, when on November 27th he wrote to Provisional Governor Perry suggesting that it would be wiser for these men not to present their certificates of election until both Houses had been organized.[14]   In the same letter Johnson said: "I hope that your legislature will adopt a code in reference to free persons of color that will be acceptable to the country, at the same time doing justice to the white and colored population." [15]

Party feeling at this time was attaining a white heat of partisanship. The Republican party, though not originally having sought or desired Abraham Lincoln,—and its leaders in 1864 having done all within their power to eliminate him from public life—posed now as the savior of the Union. The Republican faith they set up almost as a religion, and persistently asserted and pretended to believe that those only who subscribed to it were worthy of the public confidence. They were aided in this by the position of doubtful loyalty which the Democrats had assumed throughout the war when the highly suggestive name of "Copperhead" was applied to them.[16]

The Republicans were assisted in their propaganda by the fact that the stronghold of the Democratic party had been below the Mason-Dixon line. The name "Republican" was therefore held up as a symbol of patriotism while the word "Democrat" was presented as a synonym for treason. Behind these things there lurked, as there always lurk in the minds of professional partisans, plans and hopes for office and pecuniary aggrandizement.   The Democrats of the South were the leaders of the Confederacy,—if they could be disfranchised, the negroes given the vote and drilled and marshalled in the ranks of the Republicans, "the Grand Old Party" might indefinitely be kept in office.   The holy object of making South Carolina, Florida, Mississippi and their neighbor states as Republican as Maine, was presented as a lofty aspiration.   Every broken-down Republican politician of the North could then migrate to warmer climes and protected by the soldiery could pillage the treasuries of the Southern states.   Anyone whose possessions could be contained within a single carpet-bag might go there "to lift the negro from his plight" and incidentally alleviate all financial embarrassments of his own.

The rôle of the reformer is often a suspicious, usually an unattractive one.   The conduct of the Republicans in the late sixties did little indeed to render this unpleasant fact less true.   Is there anything more odious than the grafter posing as an instrument of virtue?   While they were talking of reform and the poor negro, many of them, were engaged in the Credit Mobilier,—a scheme of grafting more comprehensive and more flagrant than anything this continent before or since has witnessed.

One of the many things considered by the Republican caucus presided over by Thaddeus Stevens the day before Congress convened in December, 1865, was the fact that the Southern Senators and Representatives who had come to Washington were Democrats.   From the twenty-five non-seceding states but ten of their fifty Senators and forty-four of their one hundred and eighty-four Representatives were Democrats.   The accession to the Democratic ranks of twenty-two Senators and fifty-eight Representatives entailed, therefore, consequences not lightly to be disregarded.[17]   To accord these the rights to which they were entitled, would cut down the Republican majority in the Senate from twenty-eight to six and in the House from ninety-eight to forty.   Such a contingency was not one to be ignored by Thaddeus Stevens and his allies.   Suppose enough of the Republicans refused to obey his long and ugly lash?   What then might become of all his contemplated legislation for the "conquered provinces?"   These Southerners were daring and courageous men, it would be difficult while they were present to legislate for their dishonor. To deny them their constitutional rights might "purge" one branch of the government, but there was another,—the Executive. Andrew Johnson was a Democrat!

This was to the Radicals a source of perplexity and alarm. Nor were their anxieties relieved by reflecting on the course which he had followed before they came together in December, and that that course had received the approbation of Northern and Southern Democrats as well. Herein lay a fruitful opportunity for spreading the fear that the President had gone over to his old Democratic allegiance, that he was betraying the Republican party and that he had joined and would further coöperate with the hated Copperheads and other enemies of the Union to nullify the results of the Civil War. Charles Sumner took peculiar delight in voicing this accusation. He declared that Johnson's "heart was with the ex-rebels. For the Unionist, white or black, who had borne the burden of the day he had little feeling. He would not see the bad spirit of the rebel states, and insisted that the outrages there were insufficient to justify exclusion from Congress. . . . I left the President . . . with the painful conviction that his whole soul was set as flint against the good cause, and that by the assassination of Abraham Lincoln the rebels had vaulted into the Presidential chair. Jefferson Davis was then in the casemates at Fortress Monroe, but Andrew Johnson was doing his work." [18] It was a dastard and false charge and known to be such by the person making it.

§

On December 8th Sumner sought out the Secretary of the Navy. "We had quite a talk on the policy of the government and his own views," wrote Welles. "Sumner's vanity and egotism are great. He assumes that the Administration is wholly wrong, and that he is beyond peradventure right; that Congress has plenary powers, the Executive none, on reëstablishing the Union. He denounced the policy of the President on the question of organizing the Rebel states as the greatest and most criminal error ever committed by any government. . . . He is confident that he shall carry Stevens' resolution through the Senate and be able to defeat the President in his policy." [19]

Already the Radicals were beginning to count noses in the Cabinet; their search for allies in that quarter had begun. In this same conversation Sumner declared that Seward, McCulloch and Welles had "involved the President in this transcendent error," that Welles had "misrepresented New England's sentiment," that McCulloch "was imbued with the pernicious folly of Indiana." [20] But it was not alone their enemies, but their friends within the Cabinet that the Radicals were counting. When Welles insisted that the President's policy was correct "and that the country aside from heated politics approved it," and asked if it numbered any opponents in the Cabinet, Sumner replied that "he knew Stanton was opposed to it," when Welles told him he was not aware of it, Sumner seemed surprised. [21]

Forty-eight hours later, wrote Welles: "I gave the President a full relation of my interview with Sumner. He was much interested and maintains well his position. I think they will not shake him." [22] On that very day Sumner sent Welles through the mails a communication that was designed to "shake him,"—it was a deliberate threat that any blackmailer might have looked at with approval,—its purpose was by fear to dissuade Johnson from carrying into effect the restoration policies of Lincoln. The communication Sumner sent was "a newspaper containing a memorial for the impeachment of the President." [23] It was an unworthy and thoroughly coarse attack upon Andrew Johnson; certain of its passages were underscored by Sumner. [24] Here then was a full revelation of what the Radicals intended, a full disclosure of their hand,—the blackhand.

Welles showed Johnson a copy of the memorial for his impeachment. Without comment Johnson asked permission to retain it and Welles gave it to him. [25] Impeachment! This weapon had never before been taken from the arsenal of the Constitution for use against a President. The Radicals were examining its cutting edge. Could it be that they would dare to use it? Johnson was watching.

On the following day the Senate concurred in the House resolutions demanding the appointment of a joint committee on reconstruction.[26] There was little debate in the upper Chamber, but there was enough to disclose that Senator Cowan of Pennsylvania, Senator Dixon of Connecticut and Senator Doolittle of Wisconsin would not join forces with the Radicals. Presently the meager ranks of the independents were augmented by Senator Norton of Minnesota.[27] For the Radicals here was food for thought! The loss of these four would cut down their majority from twenty-eight to twenty-four, and if the Southerners were seated it would be cut from six to two!

The Senate members of the committee as well as those of the House were carefully selected. "It was foreseen," says Blaine, "that in especial degree the fortunes of the Republican party would be in the keeping of the fifteen men who might be chosen. The contest predestined and already manifest, between the President and Congress might, unless conducted with great wisdom, so seriously divide the party as to compass its ruin."[28] In the hope that they would faithfully reflect the purpose of the Radicals, William Pitt Fessenden of Maine, Grimes of Iowa, Harris of New York, Howard of Michigan, Williams of Oregon and Reverdy Johnson of Maryland were placed on that committee.[29]

"The Radicals," wrote Welles on December 12th, "have been busy. They are feeling their way now. The President has been deceived I think in some persons in whom he has confided, and the patronage of the government without his being aware of it has been turned against the Administration."[30] And three days later: "Senator Sumner called again this evening. He is almost beside himself on the policy of the Administration which he denounces with great bitterness. . . . I said to him there are two lines of policy before us. One is harsh, cold, distant, defiant; the other kind, conciliatory and inviting. 'Which,' said I, 'will soonest make us a united people?' He hesitated and gave me no direct answer, but said the President's policy was putting everything back. This I told him was a general assertion; that conciliation, not persecution was our policy, and therein we totally disagreed with him."[31]

On the 15th of December General Grant returned to Washington from an inspection tour of the South. He reported to the President that the people there were more loyal and better disposed than he had expected and that every consideration called for the early reëstablishment of the Union.[32] During the previous month Carl Schurz, who also had made a Southern tour, reported his conclusions.[33] It was with knowledge of the latter that the Senate on December 12th had called upon the President for information as to the "condition" of the Southern states, and at the instance of Charles Sumner demanded copies of any reports that might have been received from Schurz.[34]

President Johnson on December 18th forwarded the report of Schurz together with a brief message of his own informing the Senate "that the rebellion . . . has been suppressed; that the United States are in possession of every state in which the insurrection existed. . . ."[35] The aspect of affairs is more promising than, in view of all the circumstances, could well have been expected. The people throughout the entire South evince a laudable desire to renew their allegiance to the Government and to repair the devastations of war by a prompt and peaceful return to peaceful pursuits, and abiding faith is entertained that their actions will conform to their professions, and that . . . their loyalty will be unreservedly given to the Government whose leniency they cannot fail to appreciate. . . . It is true that in some of the states the demoralizing effects of the war are to be seen in occasional disorders; but these are local in character, not frequent in occurrence, and are rapidly disappearing as the authority of civil law is extended and sustained. Perplexing questions are naturally to be expected from the great and sudden change in the relations between the two races, but systems are gradually developing themselves under which the freedman will receive the protection to which he is justly entitled and by means of his labor make himself a useful and independent member in the community in which he has a home."[36]

These words of sanity were distasteful to the Radicals, but Grant's report, which Johnson forwarded, they liked even less. Grant held the confidence of the country. To him no political views were attributed save those of loyalty to the nation.[37] The Schurz report was a Radical document; that is why the Radicals had sent for it. But Grant's contained the findings of a man whose prestige would becloud all that Schurz might say. Johnson had outwitted them, and the Radicals were angry.

"I am satisfied," declared Grant, "that the mass of thinking men of the South accept the present situation of affairs in good faith. The questions which have heretofore divided the sentiments of the people of the two sections, . . . they regard as having been settled forever by the highest tribunal—arms—that man can resort to. I was pleased to learn from the leading men whom I met, that they not only accepted the situation arrived at as final, but now that the smoke of battle has cleared away and time has been given for reflection, that this decision has been a fortunate one for the whole country, they receiving like benefits from it with those who opposed them in the field and in council. . . . My observations lead me to the conclusion . . . that they are in earnest in wishing to do what they think is required by the Government, not humiliating to them as citizens, and that if such a course was pointed out they would pursue it in good faith. It is to be regretted that there cannot be a commingling at this time between the citizens of the two sections, and particularly of those entrusted with the law-making power." [38]

These findings were distasteful to the Radicals, but they enjoyed the words of Schurz. While he admitted that the generosity shown had "led many of those who had been active in the Rebellion to take part in the act of bringing back the states to their constitutional relations," [39] he quickly added: "Treason does under existing circumstances not appear odious in the South . . . the people are not impressed with any sense of its criminality";— that their submission had sprung from "necessity and calculation"; that "while accepting the abolition of slavery, they think that some species of serfdom . . . may be introduced without a violation of their pledge." Schurz argued for the immediate enfranchisement of negroes, and that no state should be "readmitted" until her negroes were allowed to vote.[40] This was what the

Radicals desired to hear! But something must be done to bolster up these accusations against Southern white men. Denunciation of the President and his policies might help!

Sumner began it. After characterizing the Schurz report as "a very important document," he proceeded: "We have a message from the President which is like the whitewashing message of Franklin Pierce with regard to the enormities of Kansas." [41] And the next day: "When I think of what occurred yesterday in this chamber . . ., the attempt to whitewash the unhappy condition of the rebel states, and to throw the matter of official oblivion over sickening and heart-rending outrages . . . I feel that I ought to speak of nothing else," [42]—he kept his word.

One of the many devices the Radicals began now vigorously to employ was the reading and publishing of letters penned by Northern sojourners in the South, portraying, sometimes truthfully perhaps, isolated disorders of which they had been told. By such a method it would not be difficult at any time to establish that New York City is in a hopeless state of anarchy. Sumner enjoyed this method, and he now read to the Senate copious extracts from such missives. These excerpts are typical: "The former masters exhibit a most cruel, remorseless and vindictive spirit toward the colored people. In parts where there are no Union soldiers I saw colored women treated in the most outrageous manner. They have no rights that are respected. They are killed and their bodies thrown into ponds or mud holes. They are mutilated by having ears and noses cut off." [43] "An avenging God cannot sleep," said Sumner, "while such things find countenance." The same insomnia, he hoped his hearers would believe affected him. [44]

This method of arousing Northern opinion against the South appealed to Sumner, although its unfairness had been pointed out to him two weeks before by none other than Andrew Johnson. On the Saturday before Congress convened, they had held this conversation:

The President: Are there no murders in Massachusetts?

Mr. Sumner: Unhappily yes—sometimes.

The President: Are there no assaults in Boston? Do not men there sometimes knock each other down, so that the police is obliged to interfere?

Mr. Sumner: Unhappily yes.

The President: Would you consent that Massachusetts on this account should be excluded from Congress?

Mr. Sumner: No, Mr. President, I would not.[45]

On the very day that Grant's report was forwarded to the Senate, Thaddeus Stevens in the House took up once more the sharp weapons of hate. "As there are no symptoms," he declared, "that the people of these provinces will be prepared for constitutional government for some time I know of no arrangement so proper for them as territorial governments. There they can learn the principles of freedom and eat the fruit of foul rebellion. Under such governments, while electing members to the territorial legislatures, they will mingle with those to whom Congress shall extend the right of suffrage." [46] None of the "rebel states" should be consulted as to constitutional amendments.[47]

Thaddeus Stevens was warming to his work of vengeance,— it was genial work for him. He was the kind of fighter who enjoyed striking hard blows below the belt, and kicking an opponent who has fallen. Every word was designed to arouse the hatred of all Southern white men. He was inviting them to his feast where they might gorge upon the "fruit of foul rebellion," and was preparing for the political domination of the negroes. To the legislators of the reconstructed states he pleasingly referred as that "aggregation of whitewashed rebels, who without any legal authority have assembled in the capitols of the late rebel states and simulate legislative bodies. . . ."[48] The future condition of the conquered power depends on the will of the conqueror." [49]

On the very day when Stevens and Sumner were uttering their catcalls against the restoration plan that Lincoln had devised and Johnson carried through, William Seward as Secretary of State certified that the Thirteenth Amendment abolishing slavery had become "a part of the Constitution of the United States." [50] His official certificate revealed that the legislatures of all the Southern states, except Texas, Florida and Mississippi had ratified it. And there was this recital: "Whereas *the whole number of states in the United States* is thirty-six" and that the twenty-seven states enumerated "constitute three-fourths of the whole number of *states in the United States,*" therefore the amendment was declared in force.[51]

The thirty-six, of course, included those where secession ordinances had been adopted. Here was the lie direct to the contentions of Thaddeus Stevens and Charles Sumner! Upon this subject the Radicals maintained a discreet and a profound silence. The total absence of sincerity in their assertions that the Southern states were now mere territories was thus exposed in all its naked shame.

§

One of the reasons that had made Andrew Johnson's Congressional career notable had been his ability to see beyond the interests of his own state and district. As a Representative and a Senator he believed that his obligation was to contribute to the best interests of the whole nation. This unhappily is a point of view to which few Congressmen attain. They talk occasionally of larger aims, but what excites their real enthusiasm is a River and Harbor bill, or other local measure advantageously affecting their own constituents. To secure the passage of such laws they will often barter votes on national measures which interest them but faintly. For these reasons it usually happens that two or three strong men are enabled to dictate the vital policies of Congress. Such at all events was the case during Andrew Johnson's Presidency. During those years Wade, Sumner and Stevens, aided by a few trusted lieutenants, exercised a kind of dictatorship over the lawmaking branch of the government. That there was no one in the House or Senate courageous enough to meet them on their own ground, or strong enough to arouse the country against their vindictive and pernicious aims, was a misfortune from which America is only now recovering,—from which perhaps she never will get well.

There were some of the Republicans who, had they possessed the independence and the courage, would have preferred to sustain the President, but they were soon frightened. One of the things that frightened them was the increasing evidence that the Democrats were preparing to sustain him,[52] and it is the first principle of the partisan that that which is espoused by his opponent, regardless of its merits, must be opposed by him.

Daniel Voorhees, a Democratic Representative of Indiana, spoke in support of resolutions declaring that "the President's message is regarded by the House as an able, judicious and patriotic state paper."[53] This would never do, and John A. Bingham, a Radical Republican from Ohio, therefore promptly moved a resolution which was an adroitly worded threat that Johnson would fail to coöperate with Congress at his peril.[54]

On January 8th, 1866, Welles wrote: "The President and the Radical leaders are not yet in direct conflict, but I see not how it is to be avoided. . . . The President will sooner or later have to meet this question squarely . . . and have a square and probably a fierce fight with these men."[55]

XXX

JOHNSON VETOES THE FREEDMAN'S BUREAU BILL

THE Radicals were warming to their work and they were growing bolder. They were in search for means with which to subvert the governments of the Southern states, and to humble and humiliate the Southern white men. The more they reflected upon their aims and planned the accomplishment of their purpose, the more apparent it was becoming that Andrew Johnson was standing in their way.

The Freedman's Bureau had been created on March 3rd, 1865; it was to terminate one year after the suppression of the Rebellion.[1] The purpose of the original measure was humane, it furnished some needy relief to the freed slaves, but it furnished, as bureaus usually do, an even greater measure of relief to the numerous commissioners, bureaucrats and agents who controlled it. Its power to lease to each freedman forty acres of the "abandoned lands" of Southern white men, had succeeded in inculcating among the negroes the belief that the "new Jerusalem" had come, and that they need never work again. Large numbers of the negroes quit work altogether and congregated in the cities.[2]

One of the matters to which Grant, during his Southern tour had directed his attention, was the operation of this new experiment. It was his opinion that its affairs had "not been conducted with good judgment or economy, and that the belief widely spread among the freedmen of the Southern states that the lands of their former owners will at least in part be divided among them has come from the agents of this bureau." This belief, he thought, was seriously interfering with the willingness of the freedmen to make contracts for the coming year.[3] But the Radicals were now plotting for a Freedman's Bureau of even greater power. They

263

dreamed of legislation that would assist them to subvert the Southern governments, and to an unprecedented patronage for their followers. On January 9th a bill was introduced vastly to enlarge the Freedman's Bureau jurisdiction. It divided the South into "districts," each containing one or more states, and into sub-districts each to comprise a county or parish, each district to be presided over by an assistant commissioner, and each sub-district by one "agent either a citizen, officer of the army or an enlisted man." The commissioner in charge of the whole bureau could assign "to each assistant commissioner not exceeding three clerks and to each of said agents one clerk." [4] The original act entailed a personnel of but one commissioner and ten assistants. Here then was a vast increase of patronage.

"Whenever," this bill declared, "any person who under color of any state or local law . . . shall cause to be subjected any negro . . . to any other or different punishment than white persons are subject to for the commission of like acts . . . shall be deemed guilty of a misdemeanor and be punished by fine not exceeding one thousand dollars or imprisonment not exceeding one year or both. . . ." [5] Thus in one stroke all the Southern laws were to be abrogated by Congress, not by the Supreme Court of the United States! "It shall be the duty of the officers and agents of this bureau," the bill declared, "to . . . hear and determine all offenses committed against the provisions of this section . . . also of all cases affecting negroes. . . ." [6]

The bill provided "a sort of palatine jurisdiction over the freedmen in the section lately the scene of the rebellion. It was a stiff measure even for the transition period from war to peace." [7] It was more than "a stiff measure,"—it was an overt act on the part of the Radicals in furtherance of their conspiracy to set aside the state governments whose reconstruction Lincoln planned and Johnson carried out; it was a definite committal to the doctrine that the Southern states were now mere "conquered territories."

On the day following the introduction of the bill, Gideon Welles held a conversation with Judge Blair, in which the latter told him that Stanton was "intriguing," and expressed the opinion that already there was a "cloud" between the War Secretary and the President. "It would be well," our diarist recorded, "if there was a wall between them." [8]

Two days later Charles Sumner again called upon the Secretary of the Navy, and again condemned unqualifiedly the policy of the President, proclaiming it "the greatest mistake which history has ever recorded," and declaring that Johnson was "the greatest enemy of the South that she had ever had, more than Jeff. Davis, and the evil which he had inflicted upon the country was incalculable. All was to be done over again and done right. Congress . . . is becoming more firm and united every day . . . and while they would commence no war upon the President, he must change his course, abandon his policy." [9]

Had Johnson been willing to follow this advice, had he been satisfied to stand to heel at the Radicals' command, had he faltered in his courage as he heard their long lash hissing through the air, had he been willing to "abandon" the policy of Lincoln, he would have had Sumner, Wade and Stevens fawning upon him, and he would have received the plaudits of historians who praise them.

In the same conversation with Welles, Sumner referred to the Southern states as "conquered people subject to terms which it is our duty to impose." Welles replied that "were his assumption true, and they a foreign conquered people, instead of our own countrymen, still they had their rights, were amenable to our laws and entitled to their protection. . . ." [10] But it was idle to argue with Charles Sumner. He only said: "The President in his atrocious wrong is sustained by three of his Cabinet. Seward is as thick and thin a supporter of the whole monstrous error as you or McCulloch." [11]

The Radicals were satisfied with their progress in the Congress, —they had reason to be! But how persistently they were reaching into the very center of Johnson's council appeared from the same conversation between these two New England men. Welles asked Sumner "if he supposed that the Cabinet was not a unit for the President's policy," and the latter replied that "he knew it was not." Three of the members concurred with him (Sumner) fully, entirely. When Welles expressed doubt, Sumner said: "Why, one of them has advised and urged me to prepare and bring in a bill which should control the action of the President and wipe out his policy." [12] Was there a Judas in that Cabinet?

§

In the White House Johnson sat quietly observing all that was taking place about him. He held his peace as he watched the Radicals at work, but his black eyes snapped as he divined their inner aims and foresaw their ultimate objectives. If they were bringing up their heavy guns, they might find that he too was not unacquainted with the science of ballistics; if it was war they wanted they might soon enough discover that he too could fight with heavy guns, or for that matter close up with the bayonet. But for the time he wished to wait, to play out the conciliatory hand as long as there were any cards.

Welles was growing restless. Those endless conversations with Charles Sumner! On January 11th he recorded: "Blair believes a rupture inevitable, and thinks the President is wise in delaying the conflict. Therein I think he is mistaken." [13]

On January 25th the Senate passed the Freedman's Bureau bill,[14] and five days later Sumner again sought out the Secretary of the Navy. His was a strange persistence even for a man who had but one idea. Sumner well knew what an aid would be the counsel and coöperation of this Cabinet member possessing as he did the confidence of the President. But he was yet to learn that Gideon Welles was no Edwin Stanton! "There are four members of the Cabinet who are with us and against the President," [15] he now told Welles,—in his last conversation it had been three.

On the very day of Sumner's call, Welles talked with Johnson also. "The President," he recorded, "is satisfied that his policy is correct, and is, I think, very firm in his convictions and intentions to maintain it. The Radicals who are active and violent are just as determined to resent it. I took occasion to repeat what I have several times urged, the public enunciation of his purpose, and at the proper time, and as early as convenient or as there was an opportunity to show by some distinct and emphatic act his intention to maintain and carry into effect his administrative policy." [16]

How subtly the Radicals were working to create prejudice against the President among Northerners appears from Welles' record on the last day of January: "The new shape of affairs," he wrote, "shows itself in the social gatherings. At Mrs. Welles' reception to-day a large number of the denizens of Washington, who have not heretofore been visitors and whose sympathies and former associations were with the Rebels, called. So many who have been distant and reserved were present as to excite her suspicions, and lead her to ask if I were not conceding too much. These new social friends are evidently aware of existing differences in the Administration. I noticed at the reception at the Executive Mansion last evening the fact that there was a number in attendance as if by preconcert. This I attribute more to the insane folly of the Radicals who under Thad Stevens are making assaults on the President than to any encouragement which the President has given to Rebel sympathizers. If professed friends prove false and attack him, he will not be likely to repel such friends as sustain him. I certainly will not." [17]

Our diarist was watching everything, especially he watched his fellow Cabinet members. On February 2nd he wrote: "There can be no doubt that Stanton has given certain of the leading Radicals to understand that his views correspond with theirs, but I do not know that the President is fully aware of that fact." [18] There was no doubt that Seward was with the President; Harlan,—well, possibly. But there was that dreaded support of Democrats,— perhaps that would affect Postmaster Dennison. "The truth is," Welles wrote, "the Radical leaders in Congress openly and secretly have labored to defeat the President, and their hostility has engendered a distrust in their own minds and caused fairer men like Dennison to have fears that the President might identify himself with the Democrats. This subject gives me no uneasiness whatever. . . . He will naturally feel kindly disposed toward those who sustain him and his measures, and will not be likely to give his confidence to those who oppose both." [19]

Having passed the House four days before, the Freedman's Bureau bill was sent to the President on February 10th.[20] "Sumner," Welles that evening wrote, "made me his usual visit this P. M. He is as earnest and confident as ever, probably not without reason. Says they are solidifying in Congress and will set aside the President's policy. I inquired if he really thought Massachusetts could govern Georgia better than Georgia could govern herself,—for that is the kernel of the question: Can the people govern themselves?" [21] Sumner's answer was Sumnerian: "Massachusetts could do better for them than they had done for themselves!" [22]

When Welles told him that "every state and people must form its own laws and government . . . that the elements there must work out their own condition, and that Massachusetts could not do this for them," Sumner could only answer: "We can instruct them and ought to do it. . . ." [23] Here it was, that attitude of complacency of the New England Puritans who had been virtuous on the subject of slavery after it had ceased longer to be profitable to them.

Sumner was delighted with his collection of the sufferings of the emancipated slaves, and told Welles as he had told the Senate, "that he had letters showing a dreadful state of things South, that the colored people were suffering beyond anything they had endured in the days of slavery." [24] What a calamity for our country that Welles' answer could not have been heeded by this enemy of the South and those who followed him. "I told him," said Welles, "that I had little doubt of it; I had expected this as the first result of emancipation. Both whites and blacks in the slave states were to pass through a terrible ordeal, and it was a most grievous and melancholy thing to me to witness the spirit manifested toward the whites of the South who were thus afflicted. Left to themselves they have great suffering and hardship without having their troubles increased by any oppressive acts from abroad." [25]

On the following day General Sherman wrote to his brother: "We cannot shove the South back as territories, and all steps to that end must fail for many reasons, if for no other than that it compels the people already there to assume a hostile attitude. The well-disposed of the South must again be trusted—we cannot help it. You are classed universally as one of the rising statesmen, above mere party rules. And whilst you should not separate from your party, you can moderate the severity of their counsels. . . ." [26] Thus wrote the soldier to the statesman.

Twenty-four hours later at a Cabinet meeting, Andrew Johnson referred to "some extraordinary features" of the Freedman's Bureau bill. Warming to the discussion, he alluded with some feeling "to the extraordinary intrigue which he understood was going on in Congress having nothing short of a subversion or change in the structure of government in view." And he continued: "The unmistakable design of Thad Stevens and his associates was to take the government into their own hands . . . and to get rid of him by declaring Tennessee out of the Union," and that "a sort of French Directory was to be established by these spirits in Congress, the Constitution was to be remodeled by them." [27]

The next evening Welles soliloquized: "Have examined the bill for the Freedman's Bureau, which is a terrific engine and reads more like a decree emanating from despotic power than a legislative enactment by Republican representatives. I do not see how the President can sign it. Certainly I shall not advise it. . . . I am apprehensive that the efforts of our Northern philanthropists to govern the Southern states will be productive of evil, that they will generate hatred rather than love between the races. The Freedman's Bureau scheme is a governmental enormity. There is a despotic tendency in the legislation of the Congress. . . ." [28]

Two days later Johnson indicated to his Cabinet that he intended vetoing the bill.[29] He was still hopeful that he might thwart the Radicals by the telling of the naked truth. Furthermore, there were not lacking signs of discord among his enemies. "They wish to make terms," that evening Welles recorded. "Will admit the representation from Tennessee if the President will yield. But the President cannot yield and sacrifice his honest convictions by way of compromise." [30]

When the Cabinet met on February 11th the President had his veto message ready and read it to his advisers. There was a full discussion. Seward, McCulloch and Dennison pronounced their agreement with the message. Stanton, Harlan and Speed "evidently regretted that the President had not signed the bill. Stanton was disappointed. Speed was disturbed. Harlan was apprehensive." [31] Johnson eloquently reviewed the intrigues of the Radical leaders and the proposed dictatorship of Stevens' council of fifteen.[32]

"The effect of this veto," recorded Welles, "will probably be an open rupture between the President and a portion of the Republican members of Congress. How many will go with him and how many with the Radical leaders will soon be known. Until a vote is taken, the master spirits will have time to intrigue with the members and get them committed. They will be active as well as cunning." [33]

§

Andrew Johnson was becoming gradually aroused to the sinister motives and secret aims by which the old enemies of Lincoln had prepared and were now executing their design to thwart and ruin Lincoln's hopes. But there was no trace of feeling in the veto message which he sent the Senate on the same day on which he read it to his Cabinet. With the sure precision of a great surgeon he exposed the gangrenous organs of the Freedman's Bureau bill, when he declared: "I share with Congress the strongest desire to secure to the freedmen the full enjoyment of their freedom and property and their entire independence and equality in making contracts for their labor, but the bill before me contains provisions which . . . are not warranted by the Constitution and are not well suited to accomplish the end in view." [34]

"There is," he continued, "no immediate necessity for the proposed measure. The act to establish a bureau . . . which was approved in the month of March last has not expired. It was thought stringent and extensive enough for the purpose in view in time of war. Before it ceases to have effect further experience may assist to guide us to a wise conclusion as to the policy to be adopted in time of peace." [35]

Through the provisions granting to the Bureau agents military jurisdiction Johnson's logic penetrated. "In those eleven states," he said, "the bill subjects any white person who may be charged with depriving a freedman of 'any civil rights or immunities belonging to white persons' to imprisonment or fine or both, without, however, defining the 'civil rights and immunities' which are thus to be secured to the freedmen by military law. This military jurisdiction also extends to all questions that may arise respecting contracts. The agent who is thus to exercise the office of a military judge may be a stranger entirely ignorant of the laws of the place, and exposed to the errors of judgment to which all men are liable. The exercise of power over which there is no legal supervision by so vast a number of agents as is contemplated by the bill must, by the very nature of man, be attended by acts of caprice, injustice and passion." [86]

Johnson had seen through the plan the Radicals had concocted. Whether or not he then surmised all that their schemes ultimately contemplated,—negro rule through Northern white men abetted by bayonets—he pierced to the very heart of their program when he said: "The trials having their origin under this bill are to take place without the intervention of a jury and without any fixed rules of law or evidence. The rules on which offenses are to be 'heard and determined' by the numerous agents are such . . . as the President through the War Department shall prescribe. No previous presentment is required nor any indictment charging the commission of a crime against the laws. . . . The punishment will be not what the law declares, but such as a court-martial may think proper; and from these arbitrary tribunals there lies no appeal. . . ." [87]

With what a wanton disregard of every constitutional restraint the Radicals had gone about their work Johnson thus exposed: "I cannot reconcile a system of military jurisdiction of this kind with the words of the Constitution which declare that 'no person shall be held to answer for a capital or otherwise infamous crime unless on a presentment or indictment of a grand jury, except in cases arising in the land or naval forces or in the militia when in actual service in time of war or public danger,' and that 'in all criminal prosecutions the accused shall enjoy the right to a speedy and public trial by an impartial jury of the state and district wherein the crime shall have been committed.' " [38]

Johnson had not forgotten that day at Kirkwood House when he had called upon Almighty God to witness that he would "preserve, protect and defend the Constitution." With thrusts as keen as surgery he continued: "The safeguards which the experience . . . of ages taught our fathers to establish as securities for the protection of the innocent . . . are to be set aside, and . . . we are to take the risk of the many acts of injustice that would necessarily follow from an almost countless number of agents established in every parish or county in nearly a third of the states of the Union, over whose decisions there is no supervision or control by the Federal Courts." [39] Was it Johnson's ambition that dictated his dissent? To those who have made that charge in good faith or in bad, I would commend this sentence: "The power that would be thus placed in the hands of the President is such as in time of peace certainly ought never to be intrusted to any one man." [40]

Was the creation of these military courts justifiable as a war measure? Johnson eliminated that contention. "If it be asked," he said, "whether the creation of such a tribunal within a state is warranted as a measure of war, the question immediately presents itself whether we are still engaged in war. . . . At present there is no part of our country in which the authority of the United States is disputed. Offenses which are committed by individuals should not work a forfeiture of the rights of whole communities." [41]

And Thaddeus Stevens' favorite scheme of confiscation! Here was Johnson's answer: "The bill proposes to take away land from its former owners without any legal proceedings being first had, contrary to that provision of the Constitution which declares that no person shall 'be deprived of life, liberty or property without due process of law.' " And then echoing the sentiments contained in Grant's report he continued: "The bill will tend to keep the freedmen in a state of uncertain expectation and restlessness, while to those among whom he lives it will be a source of constant and vague apprehension." [42]

Johnson as well as Sumner recognized that the negro should be protected, but that "he should be protected by the civil authorities, especially by the exercise of all the constitutional powers of the courts of the United States and of the states. His condition is not so exposed as may at first be imagined. He is in a portion of the country where his labor cannot well be spared. Competition for his services from planters . . . will enable him to command almost his own terms. . . . Neither is sufficient consideration given to the ability of the freedmen to protect . . ., themselves. It is no more than justice to them to believe that . . . they will distinguish themselves by their industry and thrift and soon show the world that in a condition of freedom they are self-sustaining, capable of selecting their own employment and their own places of abode, of insisting for themselves on a proper remuneration, and of maintaining their own asylums and schools. It is earnestly hoped that instead of wasting away, they will by their efforts establish for themselves a condition of respectability and prosperity. It is certain that they can attain to that condition only through their own merits and exertions." [43]

Johnson saved his most fundamental argument for the last. The Southern states had had no opportunity to be heard! "The Constitution," he said, "imperatively declares . . . that each state shall have at least one Representative. . . . It also provides that the Senate . . . shall be composed of two senators from each state and adds with peculiar force 'that no state without its consent shall be deprived of its equal suffrage in the Senate.' The original act was necessarily passed in the absence of the states chiefly to be affected, because their people were then contumaciously engaged in the Rebellion. Now the case is changed, and some, at least, of those states are attending Congress by loyal representatives, soliciting the allowance of the constitutional right for representation. At the time, however, of the consideration and the passing of this bill there was no Senator or Representative in Congress from the eleven states which are to be mainly affected by its provisions." [44]

Having in mind Charles Sumner's epistolary propaganda, Johnson continued: "The very fact that reports were and are made against the good disposition of the people of that portion of the country is an additional reason why they need and should have representatives of their own in Congress to explain their condition, reply to accusations, and assist by their local knowledge in the perfecting of measures immediately affecting themselves. While the liberty of deliberation would then be free and Congress would have full power to decide according to its judgment, there could then be no objection that the states most interested had not been permitted to be heard. . . . I would not interfere with the unquestionable right of Congress to judge each House for itself, 'or the elections, returns and qualifications of its own members,' but that authority cannot be construed as including the right to shut out in time of peace any state from the representation to which it is entitled by the Constitution." [45]

Referring to the fact that Tennessee, although not included in the emancipation proclamation, had adopted a free constitution, he continued: "I know no reason why Tennessee should not enjoy all her constitutional relations to the United States." [46]   And as to the other states which the bill declared had not been "fully restored to their constitutional relations to the United States," Johnson said: "If they have not, let us at once act together to secure that desirable end at the earliest possible moment. It is hardly necessary for me to inform Congress that in my own judgment most of those states, so far at least as depends upon their own action, have already been fully restored and are to be deemed as entitled to their constitutional rights as members of the Union." [47]

Finally Johnson declared: "The President of the United States stands toward the country in a somewhat different attitude from that of any member of Congress. Each member of Congress is chosen from a single district or state; the President is chosen by the people of all the states. As eleven states are not at this time represented in either branch of Congress, it would seem to be his duty to present their just claims to Congress." [48]

For a wise comprehension of the negro problem, for a sound knowledge of the relative positions of our states and of our national government, this message is without a peer. It was, says Rhodes, "a dignified paper calculated to win support in the country as well as in Congress. It is unusual for an executive to refuse power and patronage, and his act of putting them by must have confirmed the universal belief in his patriotism and good intentions." [49] Our historian omits this time any charge that Johnson was not the author of his own message.

The country was to wait for sixty years before another Republican President was to proclaim the true doctrine of state rights. Referring to the Virginia Resolutions of 1776, Calvin Coolidge on May 15th, a century and a half later, told his audience at William and Mary College [50] "that the states are the sheet anchors of our institutions. If the Federal government should go out of existence the common run of people would not detect the difference in the affairs of their daily life for a considerable length of time. But if the authority of the states were struck down disorder approaching chaos would be upon us within twenty-four hours. No method of procedure has ever been devised by which liberty could be divorced from local self-government. No plan of centralization has ever been adopted which did not result in bureaucracy, tyranny, inflexibility, reaction and decline."

Mr. Coolidge's utterances were universally applauded. Americans have learned something in the last sixty years. When Andrew Johnson's message was read, though there was applause there were hisses too. In fact, the demonstration in the galleries was such that they were ordered cleared. In their anger the Radicals at first demanded an immediate vote, but concluded to wait until the following day. [51] On February 20th in the Senate, effort to pass the bill over Johnson's veto was made and failed. There were two votes short of the required two-thirds. [52] That there were vestiges of independence appeared when six Republican Senators,—Dixon of Connecticut, Morgan of New York, Doolittle of Wisconsin, Norton of Minnesota and VanWinkle and Willey of West Virginia voted to sustain the President. [53] In the first battle between Johnson and the Senate, Johnson had come off victorious.

The Radicals were excited; if they could not secure the necessary two-thirds they would be thwarted in all their future efforts to dominate the "conquered provinces" by martial law, and to govern white Americans in time of peace through military rule. Redoubled efforts were required! If their waves of malice were to inundate the South, they must needs overleap the breakwater of Andrew Johnson's vetoes!

That evening Welles recorded in his diary: "The Cabinet was pleasant and harmonious on the matters before it to-day, though outside rumors make them divided. Much excitement exists in Congress and out of it on the subject of the veto. The dark, revolutionary, reckless intrigues of Stevens manifest themselves. In the House the bigoted partisans are ready to follow him in his vindicative passionate schemes for Radical supremacy. Radicalism having been prevalent during the war, they think it still popular. . . . Violent and factious speeches were made in the Senate and also in the House. Stevens, as I expected he would, presented his schemes to oppress the South and exclude the states from their constitutional right of representation. Such men would plunge the country into a more wicked rebellion, one more destructive of our system of government, a more dangerous condition than that from which we have emerged, could they prevail." [54]

"As an exhibition," he continued, "of the enlightened legislation of the House, Stevens the Radical leader, Chairman of the Reconstruction Committee—the committee which shapes and directs the action of Congress, and assumes executive as well as legislative control—announced that the committee, or directory it may be called, was about to report in favor of admitting the Tennessee Members, but the President having put his veto on the Freedman's bill, they would not now consent, and he introduced his resolution declaring virtually that the Union is divided, that the states which were in rebellion should not have their constitutional right of representation." [55]

§

Andrew Johnson had been President for ten months. With full knowledge that he would achieve the hatred of those who had done all within their power to thwart his predecessor, he had adopted and put through Lincoln's plan. Wendell Phillips spoke of him as "an obstacle to be removed," [56] and placing him with Benedict Arnold and Aaron Burr, declared that he had taken Jeff Davis' place as a leader of the Confederacy. Not satisfied with this he was threatening impeachment! [57]

Sumner had spoken of Andrew Johnson's "whitewashing message," and had declared that "by the assassination of Abraham Lincoln the Rebellion had vaulted into the presidential chair." [58] Thaddeus Stevens had referred to Johnson as an "alien enemy, a citizen of a foreign state . . . and therefore not now legally President." [59]

When after the adoption of the Thirteenth Amendment, early in the year, Johnson expressed a doubt as to "the propriety at this time of making *further amendments* to the Constitution," [60] Stevens declared of that statement that "centuries ago, had it been made to Parliament by a British king it would have cost him his head." [61]

All this because Johnson had dared to follow Lincoln! Wendell Phillips' venomous assaults had not deterred him! Sumner's underscored impeachment memorial had not seemed to frighten him! Thaddeus Stevens had not swerved him from his plan of just conciliation. Was there not some unequivocal and dramatic way in which these Radicals, in the presence of the entire country, could issue Andrew Johnson this direct challenge: "We hated Lincoln and opposed him, when he refused to yield, we libeled him and then sought to destroy him. Continue to follow him and we will ruin and destroy you as we attempted to destroy him."

Winter Davis, the friend of Thaddeus Stevens, who had joined Wade in libeling Lincoln, was now dead. He had been dead for nearly sixty days. [62] February 12th, the anniversary of Lincoln's birth, had been celebrated by a memorial service in the capitol, [63] but February 22nd was the day the Radicals selected on which to exhibit their true feelings for the dead President. It was suggested that an elaborate tribute should be paid to the memory of one of Lincoln's most relentless enemies. It was a plan to engage their enthusiasm, and it was adopted.

And so on Washington's birthday, both Houses of Congress

adjourned to hold at the capitol a memorial service to the memory
of Winter Davis, the libeler of Lincoln. The program was copied
almost literally from that of February 12th. It was a sinister and
minutely planned burlesque designed to belittle Lincoln's
memory. "I could not go," wrote Welles, "without a feeling of
degradation. . . . Stevens and his secret joint committee or directory have taken into their hands the government and the administration of affairs. It is an incipient conspiracy . . . the majority
of Congress are but puppets in the hands of the Directory and do
little but sanction and obey the orders of that committee." [84]

If the issue between Andrew Johnson and the Radicals had not
been drawn before, it was drawn now! It was the issue between
Abraham Lincoln and Thaddeus Stevens, between charity and
malice, statesmanship and chicane, justice and oppression, constitutional government and unlawful military domination, sportsmanship and foul play, sound understanding of the negro problem
and spurious philanthropy, between binding up the nation's
wounds and throwing salt into them, between justly achieving a
lasting peace, and the stirring up of hatreds that would endure
for fifty years!

XXXI

JOHNSON NAMES THE TRAITORS

ON the evening of the day the Radicals had selected to burlesque Lincoln's memory, a large popular meeting assembled in Washington to express its appreciation of Johnson's veto of the Freedman's Bureau bill.[1] After the adoption of suitable resolutions the meeting adjourned and its members marched in one enthusiastic body to the White House. On the same portico where Lincoln had last addressed an audience before he died, Andrew Johnson spoke to those who had come to pay him their just tribute.

Thanking his fellow citizens for their endorsement, he reminded them that it was the "day that gave birth to him who stood at the portal when all these states entered into this glorious Confederacy. . . . Washington whose name this city bears, is embalmed in the hearts of all who love their government. [A voice, 'So is Andy Johnson.']"[2]

Referring to a call from the association that was laboring to complete the Washington monument, and the pledges for its completion placed within it, Johnson continued: "Let me refer to one from my own state—God bless her—which has struggled for the preservation of this Union in the field and in the councils of the nation. . . . The sentiment which that state inscribed upon her stone . . . deposited within the monument . . . she is struggling to stand by . . . and she is now willing to maintain. . . . It is the sentiment enunciated by the immortal and illustrious Jackson—'The Federal Union, it must be preserved.'"[3]

His massive head thrown back, erect, strong, his black eyes flashing fire, he continued with sonorous and compelling voice: "I stand before you as I did in the Senate of the United States in 1860. I denounced there those who wanted to disrupt the gov-

279

ernment, and I portrayed their true character. I told them that those who were engaged in the effort to break up the government were traitors. . . . There were two parties. One would destroy the government to preserve slavery; the other would break up the government to destroy slavery. . . . I stand now where I did then vindicating the Union of these states and the Constitution of our country." [4]

He was warming to his work as he recalled his old enemies, the Abolitionists. His words were now on fire. Referring to the Southern states he continued: "Their armies have been disbanded. They come now to meet us in a spirit of magnanimity and say: 'We were mistaken . . ., we now acknowledge the flag of our country, and promise obedience to the Constitution and the supremacy of the law.' . . . I say let the door of the Union be opened and the relation be restored to those that had erred and strayed from the fold of our fathers." [5]

No one had endured more for the Union. It was not unfitting therefore, that he should remind Sumner, Phillips, Stevens and their friends,—who had suffered nothing—of this fact. "Who has suffered more than I have?" he asked. "I shall not recount the wrongs and sufferings inflicted upon me. It is not the course to deal with a whole people in a spirit of revenge. . . . But while conscious and intelligent traitors are to be punished, should whole communities and states be made to submit to the penalty of death? I have quite as much asperity, and perhaps as much resentment as a man ought to have, but we must . . . conform our actions . . . to the example of Him who founded our holy religion. . . . He went forth on the cross and testified with His wounds that He would die and let the world live."

Sweeping his audience with eyes of deep magnetic fire he continued: "The rebellion is put down by the strong arm of the government in the field. But is this the only way in which we can have rebellions? . . . I am opposed to the Davises, the Toombses, the Slidells and the long list of such. But when I perceive on the other hand, men—[A voice: 'Call them off.'] I care not by what name you call them—still opposed to the Union. . . . I am still for the preservation of these states. . . ." [6]

He had scarcely proceeded when louder and more insistent came the calls: "Call them traitors—give us their names." Well, should he do it? Why not take the problems to the country and let the people know who were these new enemies of the Union? He had tried conciliation and the answer was base insult,—insult to him and insult to Lincoln. Why not seek for his measures the support of the whole people?—the people whom he trusted.

His own words, the magic impulse of his audience, the character of the struggle in which the Radicals were engaging him, had stirred him to a white heat. "The gentleman calls for three names," he said. He hesitated, he was deliberating,—his decision came—he would throw down the challenge, the country should hear it, and he shouted: "Suppose I should name to you those whom I look upon as being opposed to the fundamental principles of this government, and as now laboring to destroy them. I say Thaddeus Stevens of Pennsylvania; I say Charles Sumner of Massachusetts; I say Wendell Phillips of Massachusetts." [7]

Referring to Stevens' declaration that had an English king been guilty of Johnson's "usurpation," he would have lost his head, the President asked: "Are those who want to destroy our institutions and change the character of the government not satisfied . . . with one martyr? Does not the blood of Lincoln appease the vengeance and wrath of the opponents of this government? [8] Have they not honor and courage enough to effect the removal of the presidential obstacle otherwise than through the hands of the assassin? I am not afraid of assassins; but if it must be, I would wish to be encountered where one brave man can oppose another. I hold him in dread only who strikes cowardly. But if . . . my blood is to be shed because I vindicate the Union . . . let an altar of the Union be erected, and then if necessary lay me upon it, and the blood that now warms and animates my frame shall be poured out in a last libation as a tribute to the Union; and let the opponents of this government remember that when it is poured out the blood of the martyr will be the seed of the church." [9]

"I say," he continued, "that in all the positions in which I have been placed—many of them as trying as any in which mortal

man could be put—so far, thank God, I have not deserted the
people, nor do I believe they will desert me. What sentiment
have I swerved from? Can my calumniators put their finger on
it? . . . Have you heard them at any time quote my predecessor,
who fell a martyr to his course, as coming in controversy with
anything I advocated? . . . Where is there one principle in reference to this restoration that I have departed from? Then the
war is not simply upon me but it is upon my predecessor. I have
tried to do my duty." [10]

And then, his great sonorous voice with thrilling cadence boom-
ing in the fresh night air, he closed: "Let us stand by the principles of our fathers though the heavens fall; . . . I intend to
stand by the Constitution as the chief ark of our safety, as the
palladium of our civil and religious liberty. Yes, let us cling to
it as the mariner clings to the last plank, when the night and the
tempest close around him." [11]

It was time that Johnson should thus throw down the gauntlet
to Lincoln's enemies. To these disunionists it was plain at last
they could not work their will with the Executive. With the
lash of truth and righteous anger he had flayed the bare backs of
the Radicals, and he had drawn blood.

§

"The political aspect now is interesting to a looker-on," wrote
General Sherman to his brother the next day. "Sumner and
Stevens would have made another civil war inevitably—the
President's antagonistic position saves us war save of words, and
as I am a peace man I go for Johnson and the veto. I recollect
that Congress is but one of three coördinate branches of the government. I want to hear the Supreme Court manifest itself. . . .
Let Johnson fight it out with Sumner, who, though sincere, represents an antagonism as ultra as Davis itself." [12]

"The Republican party," he continued, "has lost forever the
best chance they can ever expect of gaining recruits from the
great middle class who want peace and industry. The white men
of this country will control it, and the negro in mass will occupy a
subordinate place as a race. We can secure them the liberty now

gained, but we cannot in one day raise them to a full equality, even if at all. Had the Republicans graciously admitted the great principle of representation, leaving members to take the iron-clad oath, you would have secured the active coöperation of such men as Sharkey, Parsons, William A. Graham, Johnston and others of the South, and it would not be many years before some of those states would have grown as rabid as Missouri, Maryland and Arkansas are now disposed to be. The foolish querulousness of the secessionists untamed would soon make a snarlish minority in their own states. Now, however, by the extreme measures begun and urged with so much vindictiveness, Sumner has turned all the Union people south as well as west against the party." [13]

This letter, written not by a politician but a soldier, expressed the honest views of a highly intelligent observer, and more of statesmanship unfortunately than was displayed by the brother addressed, whose business it was to be a statesman. "It is surely unfortunate," the General went on, "that the President is thus thrown seemingly on the old anti-war Democrats, but from his standpoint he had no alternative. To outsiders it looks as if he was purposely forced into that category." [14]

Two days later Governor Cox of Ohio had an interview with the President. "If you could meet his straightforward honest look," he wrote, "and hear the hearty tone of his voice, as I did, I am well assured you would believe with me, that although he may not receive personal assaults with the equanimity and forbearance Mr. Lincoln used to show, there is no need to fear that Andrew Johnson is not hearty and sincere in his adhesion to the principles upon which he was elected." [15]

Three days after General Sherman's letter, the brother to whom he wrote thus addressed the Senate of the United States: "I do most deeply regret his (Johnson's) speech of the 22nd of February. I think there is no true friend of Andrew Johnson who would not be willing to wipe out that speech from the pages of history. It is impossible to conceive a more humiliating spectacle than the President of the United States invoking the wild passions of a mob around him with the utterance of such sentiments as he uttered on that day." [16]

Senator Sherman's words were reminiscent of Sumner's "Alas, Alas" uttered after Lincoln's speech to a similar crowd the year before, but they have furnished a text for the historians who, like Rhodes, have declared that Johnson's address filled "almost the whole North with dismay." [17] How false this is, let the Washington dispatch, published in the New York *Herald* two days after Johnson's speech proclaim. "A desperate effort was made here last night by the Radicals to create the impression that the President had made an outrageous speech. Dispatches were sent all over the country to this effect for the purpose of prejudicing the minds of the party leaders in advance against it. . . . Numerous dispatches of approval received from leading Republicans from all directions this morning prove that the false stories sent from here have accomplished nothing against the speech." [18]

On the same day the New York *Times* declared that Johnson's speech would "arrest the attention and command the assent of the great body of the American people," and pronounced its language "strong, direct, manly." [19] There was only one way in which the "Northern rebellion" could be put down, the Chicago *Times* asserted, and that was by arresting Stevens, Sumner and Phillips for the "crime of treason." The President like Cromwell, should dissolve the "Rump Congress" at Washington. [20] A mass meeting was held at Cooper Union in New York City to endorse the policy of the President. Seward addressed the gathering. [21] Later he telegraphed from New York: "The Union is restored and the country saved. The President's speech is triumphant." [22]

"The extremists," wrote Welles that night, "are angry and violent because the President follows his own convictions and their operations through the press are prolific in manufacturing scandal against him. . . . The President says there has been a design to attempt impeachment if he did not yield to them." [23]

As we read Sherman's speech to the Senate, it is pleasant to note that his brother's letter had not been wholly disregarded. The conciliation of the soldier had somewhat tempered the hardness of the politician. They had no right, he told the Senate, to arraign Andrew Johnson for following in the footsteps of his predecessor. He reminded his fellow Senators of all that Johnson

had endured at the hands of Phillips and Charles Sumner.   The
President, declared Sherman "has been fighting all the days of
his life; the very courage with which he resists opponents whenever they present themselves, we commended five years ago as the
highest virtue of Andrew Johnson's life.[24]   Regarding the President as he is, a man who never turned his back upon a foe,
personal or political, a man whose great virtue has been his
combative propensity; as a man who repelled insults here on the
very spot where I now stand, when they came from traitors arm-
ing themselves for the fight; can you ask him, because he is
President, to submit to insult?" [25]

Sherman expressed the strongest sympathy with Johnson's feelings over the delayed admission of his own state, and declared
that Tennessee had been reconstructed "before the death of
President Lincoln, under his guiding hand, with Andrew Johnson
as his main agent. . . . Its government was reorganized before
President Johnson came here. . . . The men who are sent here to
represent Tennessee are as true and loyal as any of your Senators
without exception." [26]

It was a day for the partisan.   Adherence to the Republican
party in the opinion of its followers involved a kind of super-
patriotism.   It embraced "in its ranks" declared Senator Wilson,
"more of moral and intellectual worth than was ever embodied in
any political organization in any age or in any land."   It was,
declared Sumner's colleague, "created by no man or set of men,
but brought into being by Almighty God himself!" [27]   Johnson it
seems had not sufficiently appreciated this divine origin.   Lincoln
too, we suspect, must at times have doubted it, especially when its
leaders were engaged in libeling him in Greeley's columns.

JOHNSON UNLIMBERS WITH HIS VETOES

How keenly the Radicals were determined to destroy local self-government in the South had been strongly revealed on the 5th of January, when, having brought forth their Freedman's Bureau measure, there was on the same day introduced in Congress a bill "to protect all persons in their civil rights and furnish the means of their vindication." [1] It was the first of the "force bills." [2] Its progress through the Congress was less rapid than the companion Freedman's Bureau bill; it did not pass the Senate until February 2nd and the House until the 15th of March. [3] Having been thwarted in their Freedman's Bureau scheme, the Radicals did not intend that the President should again stay their hand.

The scene in Congress on March 10th possessed the distinction that might have been discovered in a longshoremen's saloon where some great bully bleary-eyed held the floor evoking the ribald guffaws of his submissive listeners. Thaddeus Stevens, in the opinion of the little men who permitted him to rule them, was an incomparable wit. They considered irresistible his mock eulogy of Andrew Johnson. When he had finished, he sent to the clerk's desk an excerpt from the New York *World* of March 7th, 1865, wherein Johnson was described as "an insolent drunken brute in comparison with whom Caligula's horse was respectable." [4]

Gideon Welles that night painted this defamer in his true colors. "Thad Stevens," he wrote, "has to-day made a blackguard and disreputable speech in the House. . . . This wretched old man displayed . . . those bad traits of dissimulation, insincerity, falsehood, scandal-loving and defamation that have characterized his long life. The Radical managers and leaders were cognizant of his speech, and had generally encouraged it, but I shall be disappointed if they do not wish the vain old man had been silent before many months. Such disgraceful exhibitions can do the author and his associates no good, nor those whom he assails enduring harm. The people may not in the first excitement and under the discipline of party be enabled to judge of the conspirators correctly who are striving to divide the Union, not by secession but by exclusion. It is clearly a conspiracy though not avowed." [5]

Having passed both Houses the Civil Rights bill reached the President on March 18th. [6] Some hoped that the abuse which had been spewed upon him might stay his hand from vetoing it. But the wiser heads knew his veto was inevitable. Slander of a President was a pleasing pastime for the Radicals, but would this suffice to override the veto when it came? More practical and efficient means must be sought out! They had failed in the Senate to overcome his last veto by two votes. Could they but unseat one or more of their opponents, perhaps this time they could succeed in thwarting him. It was a bold plan.

One of the Democratic Senators who had voted to uphold the President was John P. Stockton of New Jersey. [7] He had taken his seat on December 4th, 1865, and had been regularly sworn in. A protest against his election had been filed, but on January 30th, after a two weeks' investigation, he was declared elected. On March 22nd, however, four days after the Civil Rights bill was forwarded to the President, the subject of Stockton's election was reopened. On the following day a vote was taken and by 21 to 20 his title was again sustained. [8]

Stockton's colleague, William Wright, was sick and Lott M. Morrill of Maine had been paired with him. His obligation not to vote until Wright returned rested upon the most solemn compact known to honorable men,—a gentleman's agreement. Charles Sumner now advised him to break his word, and so when the roll had been completed Morrill arose in his place and asked to have his vote recorded against Stockton. It caused a tie, 20 for and 20 against expulsion. Stockton then demanded, in view of Morrill's breach of faith, that to him also the privilege of voting be accorded. It was done. By one vote his tenure was made safe. Three days later Sumner moved to strike out

Stockton's vote, his motion was carried and Stockton was expelled! [9]

It was in the nick of time for this was March 26th and on the following day Johnson's veto of the Civil Rights bill reached the Senate. He exposed the objects of the Radicals and pilloried their aims. "The grave question presents itself," he declared, "whether when eleven of the thirty-six states are unrepresented in Congress . . . it is sound policy to make our entire colored population and all other excepted classes citizens of the United States. . . . Have the people of the several states expressed such a conviction?" [10]

"The bill in effect proposes a discrimination against large numbers of intelligent . . . foreigners, and in favor of the negro to whom, after long years of bondage, the avenues to freedom and intelligence have just now been suddenly opened. . . . Yet it is now proposed . . . to confer the rights of citizens upon all persons of African descent born within the extended limits of the United States, while persons of foreign birth who make our land their home must undergo a probation of five years, and can only then become citizens upon proof that they are 'of good moral character attached to the principles of the Constitution of the United States and well disposed to the good order and happiness of the same.' " [11]

The bill declared that "any person who under color of any law . . . shall subject . . . any inhabitant of any state or territory to the deprivation of any right secured . . . by this act or to different punishment . . . on account of . . . having at any time been held in . . . slavery . . . than is prescribed for the punishment of white persons shall be deemed guilty of a misdemeanor. . . ." [12] Under this provision, declared the President, "members of the state legislature who should vote for laws conflicting with the provisions of the bill . . ., judges of the state courts who should . . . render judgments in antagonism with its terms . . . could be brought before other tribunals and there subjected to fine and imprisonment for the performance of the duties such state laws might impose." [13]

"The fourth section," Johnson went on, "provides that officers and agents of the Freedman's Bureau shall be empowered to make when eleven of the thirty-six states are unrepresented in Congress and the superior courts of the territories to appoint, without limitation, commissioners who are to be charged with the performance of quasi-judicial duties. The fifth section empowers the commissioners . . . to appoint . . . one or more suitable persons from time to time to execute warrants and other processes described by the bill.[14] These numerous official agents . . . are authorized . . . even to call to their aid such portion of the land and naval forces of the United States or of the militia 'as may be necessary to the performance of the duty with which they are charged.' This extraordinary power is to be conferred upon agents irresponsible to the government and to the people . . . and in whose hands such authority might be made a terrible engine of wrong, oppression and fraud."[15]

These are a few of the objections which Andrew Johnson pointed out, but what a veritable Pandora's box the bill concealed, the final paragraph of his message made fully manifest. "The white race and the black race of the South," he said, "have hitherto lived together under the relation of master and slave,—capital owning labor. Now suddenly, that relation is changed. . . . In this new relation . . . there will be a new adjustment, which both are deeply interested in making harmonious. Each has equal power in settling the terms, and if left to the laws that regulate capital and labor it is confidently believed that they will satisfactorily work out the problem. . . . This bill frustrates this adjustment. It . . . attempts to settle questions of political economy through the agency of numerous officials whose interest it will be to foment discord between the two races, for as the breach widens their employment will continue, and when it is closed their occupation will terminate."[16]

"In all our history," he continued, "no such system as that contemplated by . . . this bill has ever been proposed or adopted. They establish for the security of the colored race safeguards which go infinitely beyond any that the general government has ever provided for the white race. In fact the distinction of race and color is by the bill made to operate in favor of the colored and against the white race. . . . It is another step or rather stride toward centralization and the concentration of all legislative powers in the National government. The tendency of the bill must be to resuscitate the spirit of rebellion and to arrest the progress of those influences which are more closely drawing around the states the bonds of union and peace." [17]

He declared however, his willingness to coöperate with Congress in any constitutional measure "necessary for the protection of the civil rights of the freedmen, as well as those of all other classes of persons throughout the United States. . . ." [18] Of what avail, however, was it to talk of reason or constitutionality to men determined to achieve their aims regardless of the means employed!

When, on March 27th, Johnson's veto reached the Senate, the Radicals were imbued with one single purpose: to corral and hold the votes to override it. Haste they knew would aid them. Wright of New Jersey was still away. His absence, combined with Morrill's breach of faith, had enabled them to unseat Stockton. Dixon of Connecticut was seriously ill. Both these votes if cast would be against the Radicals. Time might enable these absentees to come,—therefore no delay! Haste! Haste! [19]

On April 5th the vote was about to be recorded when Cowan of Pennsylvania, because of the absent Senators, requested a postponement. But Ben Wade was on his feet. "If the President of the United States," with great excitement he declared, "can . . . by a veto compel Congress to submit to his dictation he is an emperor and a despot. Because I believe the great question of Congressional power and authority is at stake here I yield to no importunities on the other side. . . . I will not yield to these appeals of comity . . . but I will tell the President and everybody else that if God Almighty has stricken a member of this body so that he cannot be here to uphold the dictation of a despot, I thank him for it and I will take every advantage of it I can." [20]

An adjournment was nevertheless taken, but only until the next day. When the roll was called, it would be close, but the Radicals knew what they were about. Morgan of New York had given Welles to understand that he would sustain the President, [21] but when his name was called, he recorded it against the veto. [22] What had happened? Nobody knew.

Wright of New Jersey at the peril of his life was brought into the Senate chamber [23] and voted to sustain the President.[24] But his vote without that of his colleague Stockton was without avail. The balloting showed 15 in favor of and 33 against the President. The Radicals had two more than the required two-thirds!

Three days later by a vote of 122 to 41 the House of Representatives followed the example of the Senate. With great unction Speaker Colfax directed that his name be called in order that he might record himself with the majority.[25] It is pleasant to be with the majority, especially such a large one! He then announced that the Civil Rights Bill had become a law; the President's objections to the contrary notwithstanding.[26]

The two-thirds were now in working order in both Houses. What mattered it that this had been accomplished in the Senate by a breach of faith. Stockton's vacant chair was eloquent of dishonor!

§

When in 1858 near Denver, on the tributaries of the South Platte, gold was found, Colorado was practically an unknown country. Three years later it achieved a temporary fame when its frontiersmen defeated a few Texans who came there to win the territory for the Confederacy. For six years following 1864 her venturous inhabitants were busily engaged in fighting Arapohoe and Cheyenne Indians.[27] On May 3rd, 1866 [28] her population numbered thirty thousand souls. There was therefore, no urgent need then,—at least not in Colorado—for the passage by Congress of a bill admitting her to statehood. But the Radicals had not been slow to heed the narrow margin of two votes by which twenty-four days before they overrode the veto of the Civil Rights Bill. It had been accomplished by their ejection of Stockton from the Senate, but it would be well to make their two-thirds doubly safe,—and Colorado if admitted as a state would give the Senate two more votes.

They were thinking of the measures they had yet in store with which to strike the bleeding South with Sumner's "hand of iron." But they were thinking more and more of the man standing in their path. Something must be done with Andrew Johnson!

A hundred and forty-three days had passed since Sumner had underscored and sent to Welles the memorial for the impeachment of the President.[29] The Radicals had had abundant time to take down and study the Constitution of the United States. Despite their willingness to flaunt it, there were two sentences of that document that interested them greatly. These were: "The Senate shall have the sole power to try impeachment. . . . And no person shall be convicted without the concurrence of two-thirds of the members present."[30] Yes, it was important by whatever means to make sure, especially in the Senate, that a serviceable two-thirds was at their disposal!

On May 15th President Johnson sent his veto of the Colorado bill.[31] He made no reference to the motives of those seeking its enactment. He was content to demolish the alleged reasons for its passage. He exposed the paucity of the population, "some estimating so low as 25,000, while advocates of the bill reckon the number at from 35,000 to 40,000 souls."[32] He demonstrated that since 1861 the population had been declining.[33] He showed that at the only lawful election on the question of statehood "a majority of 3,152 was given against the proposed change."[34] There was not much of the bill left when he reached the final paragraph of his message. "Eleven of the old states," he said, "have been for some time and still remain unrepresented in Congress. It is a common interest of all the states . . . that all those who are expected to bear the burdens of the Federal government shall be consulted concerning the admission of new states; and that in the meantime no new state should be prematurely and unnecessarily admitted. . . ."[35]

This time the Radicals were foiled. They failed to muster enough votes to override the veto and it was not until ten years later that Colorado was admitted as a state.[36]

XXXIII

THE NEGRO PROBLEM AND THE FOURTEENTH AMENDMENT

THE problem of the negro has perplexed America since three centuries or more ago when the savages from Senegambia and the dark jungles of Central Africa were captured and brought here as slaves. It disturbed the counsels of the Constitutional Convention and was evaded; it was fumbled in the Compromise of 1820, and again three decades later. Through its agitation the Abolitionists brought on the War between the States, but never was it the cause of direr or more durable discord than in the dozen years that followed the collapse of the Confederacy.

Like any other question it was capable of analysis, it was susceptible of light as well as heat. Without passion it was open to an accurate appraisal, and such appraisals had been made before the Radicals began to act. But they were made by scientists, not by politicians purporting to be statesmen. Among Sumner's nearly limitless acquaintances was Louis Agassiz, distinguished in the field of science. "We should beware," in August, 1863, Agassiz had written, "how we give to the blacks rights, by virtue of which they may endanger the progress of the whites before their temper has been tested by prolonged experience. Social equality I deem at all times impracticable,—a natural impossibility from the very character of the negro race. . . . No man has a right to what he is unfit to use. Our own best rights have been acquired successively. I cannot, therefore, think it just or safe to grant at once to the negro all the privileges which we ourselves have acquired by long struggles. History teaches us what terrible reactions have followed too rapid and too extensive changes. Let us beware of granting too much to the negro race in the beginning lest it become necessary hereafter to deprive them of some of the privileges which they may use to their own and our detriment." [1]

Lincoln, whether or not he was acquainted with the findings of the scientist, expressed substantially the same opinion when he said: "There is a natural disgust in the minds of nearly all white people at the idea of an indiscriminate amalgamation of the white and black men." [2] His letter of March, 1864, to the governor of Louisiana on the subject of the franchise should never be forgotten. What a problem the mere presence of the colored race presented, appeared from what he told a committee of negroes in the second year of the war. "White men are cutting each others' throats about you," he said. "But for your race among us there would be no war, although many men on either side do not care for you one way or the other. . . . Your race suffers from living among us, ours from your presence." [3]

Andrew Johnson understood the question also. To a colored delegation who called upon him on February 7th, 1866, requesting negro suffrage throughout the Union, he said that it was for the people of the various states to determine. Negro suffrage, with true prophetic vision, he declared, if forced upon the states would be "resisted." "I would it were so that all you advocate could be done in the twinkling of an eye," he said, "but it is not in the nature of things, and I do not assume or pretend to be wiser than Providence or stronger than the laws of nature." [4]

The Radicals ignored the fact that the white race is "three or four thousand years in advance in mental capacity and moral force," and that the great mass of the ex-slaves had remained "in their notions and their habits much what their ancestors were in the forests of the Niger and the Congo." [5] Into such hands they were about to thrust the vote, proposing at the same time to wrest the franchise from the descendants of the Revolutionary patriots and the founders of the Constitution.

The Radicals cared nothing for the negro, except as the wielder of a vote that would maintain them and their friends in office. Everyone knew that "in the North before the war there was a marked aversion to the negro and a complete absence of social intercourse with him." [6] In the South, however, "the whites had before the war no sense of personal repulsion from the negro. The domestic slave was in the closest relation with his master's family. Sometimes he was his master's trusted friend. The white child grew up with the black child as its playmate. The legal inequality was so immense that familiarity was not felt to involve any disturbance of the attitude of command." [7]

With a reckless disregard of every fact of race, with the low desire to trample down a gallant but defeated foe, and the unworthy aim to maintain the Radical party permanently in power,[8] the followers of Stevens were about to embark upon what Elihu Root has called "the grave error of reconstruction legislation which went upon the theory that by merely giving a vote to the negro he would be made competent to govern." [9]

With these motives and with this indifference to the real welfare of the negro and the future of their country, in the early months of 1866 the Fourteenth Amendment to the Constitution of the United States was conceived. Of all the contrasts history affords, none is more depressing than that between the statesmen who convened in Philadelphia in 1787, through conciliation and wise counsel to form a more perfect Union, and the men who sat in Washington in 1866 plotting to change the Constitution of the founders.

Roger Sherman, Alexander Hamilton, James Madison, John Rutledge, Benjamin Franklin and George Washington,—these and their thirty-one associates, on September 17th, 1787, presented to the disunited colonies a plan of union, little dreaming how greatly they had wrought.[10]

Thirteen sparsely settled colonies occupying but a little fringe of the Atlantic slope of North America, numbering inhabitants scarcely more than half the population of our present New York City, believing in their inalienable English rights and inspired by the consciousness of the rectitude of their purpose, had vindicated their liberty against the strongest power on earth, and when this was done had sat down to give the world a lesson in political philosophy that no nation since the dawn of history has equaled. As architects delight in the plans of a cathedral, every student of government must find joy in the great and calm debates over which George Washington presided.

They had their problems, the delegates to that Philadelphia Convention. There was the vital decision: Should the new government be strongly national or a loose Confederacy? There was the question of the relative powers of the large and of the small states, the intricate problems of taxation, the already mooted matter of the slave trade, the basis of representation, and whether slaves in whole or in part should be calculated for that purpose. But finally the great compromise was effected. Had the founders been obsessed by party or by faction, had they been unwilling to conciliate, to judge only after thorough study, and finally to give as well as take, there never would have been a Union.

How dreary is the contrast between these far-sighted statesmen, and the politicians who dominated Congress when Andrew Johnson was President of the United States! Their motives were dishonorable, their aims unworthy, their manners offensive and provocative, and their malicious purpose was covered with a cloak of sickening hypocrisy. They neither liked nor understood the negro,—their real interest was his vote. Their aim was to becloud the issue. Of course, slavery was wrong, so wrong that even war, perhaps, was not too great a price to pay for its extinction. Of course, the Union should be preserved, no bloodshed was too much to ask for that. But both of these objects had been achieved beyond the possibility of a doubt. Negro suffrage was not an issue of the war, for it not a single rifle had been fired. That the emancipated slave was then ready for the grave responsibilities of citizenship became the lying slogan of the patriots who had not fought.

Where was the Hamilton, the Madison or the Franklin in 1866? Where was the statesman to recognize that a prompt reconciliation with the Southern white men must be effected, and that Virginians and their neighbors would be prompt to accept the olive branch of reasonable conciliation? Where was the statesman to recognize that oppression always breeds revolt and when employed against men whose sires had loved and fought for liberty, oppression will never permanently succeed? Where was the statesman to comprehend that the love of local self-government,—the very basis of liberty—could not be suppressed by leg-

islative fiat or be stifled out by constitutional enactment? Where
was the statesman to divine that the only sure way to secure the
negro his ultimate right of franchise in the South was by winning
the coöperation of Southern white men to the gradual accomplishment of that aim? Was there no one who could see that the only
practicable way of effecting a reconciliation with Southerners was
by giving their Senators and Representatives a voice in legislation?
There was just one such man and he was standing practically
alone. His name was Andrew Johnson.

The Radicals by progressive steps were seeking the humiliation
of the South. No sooner was one measure of oppression planned
than another and a harsher one was joyously brought forward.
The spirit of the Founders was not in them. The thought that
animated the discussions leading to the Fourteenth Amendment
was a change in the basis of representation that would permanently curtail the power of Southern states in Congress.[11] Blaine
proposed that representation should be "determined by taking
the whole number of persons, except those whose political rights
or privileges are denied or abridged by the Constitution of any
state on *account of race or color.*"[12]

The mere denial of the right to vote, unless based on *race or
color,* would not under this plan diminish the number of representatives from the North. For the North, having few negroes
but large numbers of foreigners to contend with, might limit the
right of suffrage as sharply as she chose, but the South whose
political incompetents were almost entirely black, could restrict
their right to vote only on the pain of losing representatives. It
was the kind of justice the Radicals approved.

When, in substantially this form, the amendment reached the
Senate, Sumner took the floor to denounce it. It did not go far
enough for him! He demanded immediate and unconditional
enfranchisement of the negro.[13] While the proposed amendment
was debated in both Houses, Stevens' Joint Committee on Reconstruction stealthily was preparing to strengthen its dictatorship.
They were seeking to create a new Union, the terms of which the
North should dictate to the South.

On April 30th they reported favorably on Blaine's apportionment provision and other proposals which were finally to become the Fourteenth Amendment. The plan was to secure its adoption by duress! The report contained a proposed bill providing that not until the Fourteenth Amendment should be ratified by the Southern states would their Senators and Representatives be admitted! [14]

"The Central Directory or Stevens' Reconstruction Committee have submitted their plan of Reconstruction which means division for four years longer at least," wrote Welles that evening. "No one can read the propositions submitted without seeing that the whole scheme is one for party ascendancy. The result will be after a struggle perhaps of years, the ultimate overwhelming and disgraceful defeat of the authors and their party." [15]

§

There is in this Constitution-tinkering of the Radicals and Johnson's opposition to it a study of amazing interest to our own times. [16]

It was not that the achievements of the Founders had been perfect beyond the possibility of improvement, but that the instrument they wrought had been conceived without passion and fashioned without haste by statesmen and philosophers, that now caused Andrew Johnson to caution against the ill-considered altering of their work. "Propositions to amend the Constitution," he declared, "were becoming as numerous as preambles and resolutions at town meetings called to consider the most ordinary questions connected with the administration of local affairs. [17] All this . . . had a tendency to diminish the dignity and prestige attached to the Constitution of the country, and to lessen the respect and confidence of the people in their great charter of freedom." [18]

On the 8th of May the amendment in nearly completed form was again debated in the House. Stevens wanted it as harsh as possible. He deplored the existence of "a morbid sensibility sometimes called mercy," and piously declared that "the *punishment* now prescribed is the mildest ever inflicted upon traitors." [19]

The third section as finally drawn disqualified any Southerner who participated in the rebellion from holding office or from becoming Presidential elector. Thus all the leading men of the South were to be stripped of power, and they were required to give their ex-slaves the vote or suffer a proportionate loss in representation! The last sentence of the section seemingly intended to ameliorate those which preceded it, was in fact aimed at Andrew Johnson himself. "But *Congress* may," it declared, "by a vote of two-thirds of each House remove such disability."[20] It was a direct blow at one of his great constitutional prerogatives,—the pardoning power. It set aside his pardons.[21]

All the ex-slaves were made citizens.[22] A thousand times less fit than were the hardy immigrants from Germany, from Ireland, from England and from Scotland, who were required to serve out their period of probation before becoming citizens, the illiterate descendants of savages, as little versed in the problems of government as were their jungle-dwelling ancestors, by one stroke of the pen were given rights and privileges that the graduates of Oxford or of Dublin must wait five years to acquire.

The Fourteenth Amendment contained a conglomeration of ideas, some of which would not have excited opposition, especially if the Southern Senators and Representatives had been given, as they should have been, an opportunity to be heard. It was intended to deal a blow at local self-government in the South, and to prevent the two races from working out their own destinies by themselves.

Before it reached its final form, the Amendment was debated many weeks. The reading of the speeches in the Senate and in the House is a dreary undertaking. Whether their course was right or wrong went practically unnoticed. But there was one at least who had the courage to ask the question, although it was unheeded. "I know," Senator Doolittle of Wisconsin declared, "that by an amendment to the Constitution . . . you can annul all existing rights. You could perhaps by an amendment . . . deprive individual citizens of their property. . . . You might perhaps by a constitutional amendment pass a bill of attainder by which certain men would be sentenced to death and to corruption of blood. But sir, would it be right? That is the question."[23]

On June 13th the amendment passed both Houses. Voicing the opinions of large numbers among the thinking persons of the North, the Springfield *Republican* characterized it as "a shabby piece of joiner-work." [24]

§

When Stevens' "Directory" reported the Fourteenth Amendment, it reported also a bill declaring that whenever "any state lately in insurrection" ratified the amendment, representation in the Senate and in the House would be again accorded.[25] In other words, until the South surrendered its constitutional right to reject a proposed constitutional amendment,—one especially designed to humiliate, injure and degrade her—her states would be denied all rights of statehood. The Radicals knew full well that they had no constitutional right to inflict pains and penalties upon a state not desiring to concur in an amendment. The measure failed of passage at this session,[26] but this was not the last that we shall hear of it.

Five days after the amendment had passed both Houses, Stevens' "Directory" submitted a majority report reasserting this philosophy of force as offensively as possible. One of the "legislative consequences" of the war they said, "was that within the limits prescribed by humanity, the conquered rebels were at the mercy of the conquerors!" [27] Therefore, they concluded, "the so-called Confederate states are not at present entitled to representation in the Congress of the United States," [28] and that this right should not be accorded until they accepted the Fourteenth Amendment that had been concocted for them.[29] In her exhausted state they anticipated small difficulty in forcing this bitter medicine down their patient's throat. "The testimony," they declared, "is conclusive that after the collapse of the Confederacy the feeling of the people of the rebellious states was that of abject submission." [30]

Throughout the report no words are so prominent as "conquered," "conqueror," and "conquered territory." Joyously it was proclaimed that the territory of the Southern states had been "overrun and occupied by the Federal armies and their people

reduced to the condition of enemies conquered in war, entitled
only by public law to such rights, privileges and conditions as
might be vouchsafed by the conqueror." [31]   They were pressing
a sponge with vinegar to the famished and parched lips of the
exhausted South.

All that Johnson had attempted of course, was wrong! The
plan that he had followed, if permitted to succeed, would constitute a precedent, they said, "fraught with danger to the Republic." [32]   They sought to vindicate "the exclusive right of Congress
in the work of reconstruction." [33]   The powers of a "conqueror"
they said, were not "vested in the President." [34]

Upon the great question: were the Southern states still "states,"
the report hedged and trimmed. Declaring that the Constitution
acts not on states but on the people and that "while therefore the
people cannot escape its authority the states may through the acts
of their people cease to exist in an *organized* form, and thus dissolve their political relations with the United States." [35] "In an
organized form!" The omission of these words would have been
a plain admission of the right to secede, a declaration that might
and not right had finally triumphed. To leave these four words
in was a confession that whether "organized" or not the Southern
states were still "states."

Twelve signed the majority report, and but three that of the
minority. Reverdy Johnson was the author of the latter. "States
unequal," it declared, "are not known to the Constitution." [36]
To submit the amendment to the Southern states was an admission that they "are and never ceased to be states of the Union." [37]
How then could they be coerced? The effect of the amendment
would be either to deny representation to the Southern states
"forever," or if they accepted it, to weaken their representation
and thereby "secure a continuance" of the Republican party in
power. The purpose of the amendment was "to degrade the
Southern states. To consent to it will be to consent to their own
dishonor." [38]

They declared that if President Johnson's measures for the
restoration of the states "were not justified by the Constitution
the same at least may be said of his predecessor. . . . The sole

object of each was to effect a complete and early union of all
the states, to make the General Government embrace all, and to
extend its authority and to secure its privileges and blessings to
all alike." [39]

It was high time that someone should take up the cudgels for
Johnson's defense of the Union, as valorous and as true as that
of Lincoln! "He sins against light and closes his eyes to the
course of the President during the rebellion, from its inception
to its close who ventures to impeach his patriotism," the minority
declared. "Surrounded by insurrectionists, he stood firm. His
life was almost constantly in peril, and he clung to the Union,
and discharged all the obligations it imposed upon him, even the
closer because of the peril. And now that he has escaped
unharmed, and by the confidence of the people has had devolved
upon him the executive functions of the Government, to charge
him with disloyalty is either a folly, or a slander; folly in the
fool who believes it; slander in the man of sense, if any such
there be, who utters it." [40]

§

Seward, as he was obliged to do, on June 16th transmitted
the Fourteenth Amendment to the governors of the various states
for the decision of their legislatures. [41] He submitted it to all the
states, [42]—South Carolina, Virginia, and the other "conquered
provinces" with the rest! If the Radicals were honest in their
assertion that these commonwealths were no longer states, why
did they permit them to share in one of the most solemn prerogatives of statehood? They hoped that these exhausted regions
would, in the impotence of their prostration, accept humiliation
tamely!

The President of the United States has no function to perform
in connection with constitutional amendments. [43] Johnson nevertheless determined to record himself. On June 22nd, therefore,
the same day on which the minority had filed its report, he sent
Congress a message deploring any further efforts to amend the
Constitution while the South was not represented. [44] To emphasize the formal character of Seward's act, he declared that it was

"to be considered as purely ministerial and in no sense whatever committing the Executive to an approval or a recommendation of the amendment to the state legislatures or to the people." [45]

Johnson, however, was by no means the only one at that time to deplore this ill-considered Constitution-tinkering. Referring to the provisions disfranchising the late participants in the rebellion, Chief Justice Chase wrote one of his associates: "Will not these propositions be received with some alarm by those who, though opponents of secession or nullification, yet regard the real rights of the states as essential to the proper working of our complex system? . . . I fear the undertaking of too much . . .; it seems to me that nothing is gained sufficiently important, and unattainable by legislation, to warrant our friends in overloading the ship with amendment freight." [46]

Even Stanton, while the amendment was still in Congress, regarded the proposed change as deplorable.[47] But Sumner, whose only criticism was that it did not go far enough, was writing to John Bright: "I can see nothing but 'agitate and convert' until the franchise is extended . . . our deadlock continues with no chance of relief. The people sustain Congress which stands firm. But there is no hint that the President will give way; he is indocile, obstinate, perverse, impenetrable and hates the education and civilization of New England. Seward encourages him; McCulloch is bitterly with him; Dennison sometimes with him and sometimes against him; Welles is with him; Stanton, Harlan and Speed are against his policy,—so that his Cabinet is nearly equally divided. When I speak of the opinions of these men, I speak according to my personal knowledge, from conversations with each of them. I do not think they are always frank with the President. Seward is rash and visionary with a most wonderful want of common sense. . . . I read the *Times* constantly. The perversions of its correspondent about our affairs is almost as great now as during the war, only in a different way; nothing he says is true. I never see my own name without saying, 'What falsehood!' The correspondent writes like a Presidential hireling." [48]

§

It was only fourteen days after Seward had transmitted the proposed Fourteenth Amendment to the states that Connecticut gave her assent; New Hampshire followed her example on the 7th of July.[49] The circumstances leading to the ratification by the third state have an interesting relation to this narrative.

We left Parson Brownlow—Governor Brownlow—in Tennessee some fifteen months before. His predilection for the Radicals had been growing as he watched their growing power. Like all aspiring politicians of his time who called themselves Republicans, he had cocked both ears to catch the piercing dissonance of Stevens' voice, and had schooled himself to sing a part in the raucous and discordant chorus.

In his first message as governor of Tennessee in 1865, Brownlow had opposed in no uncertain terms the granting of suffrage to the negro. He had even advocated the removal of colored men from the United States, and colonization of them elsewhere.[50] But he had not then begun to hearken to the siren calls of Charles Sumner and Thaddeus Stevens. Like all successful politicians, he was reasonably nimble, nor was his agility diminished by the Tennessee Congressional elections of August, 1865. These had resulted in the defeat of half the Radicals within his state.[51] New and stronger measures were, therefore, demanded to keep the Radicals in power. Accordingly, on May 3rd, 1866, further strides were taken towards the disfranchisement of white citizens who had championed the South. A law was enacted that no one who had participated in the lost cause could vote unless he subscribed to an oath that he "rejoiced" at the defeat of the Confederacy.[52]

Lest this measure would not suffice to convince the Radicals at Washington of their pupil's aptitude in Tennessee, Brownlow pushed through both Houses of the state legislature a resolution that Jefferson Davis, Judah Benjamin, Slidell, Robert E. Lee and other leaders of the Confederacy "had justly forfeited their lives; and that in expiation of their great crime, and as an example for all time they deserve and ought to suffer the extreme penalty of the law, and be held as infamous forever." [53]

How closely and with what approval the Radicals at Washington were watching those at Nashville, appeared when Thaddeus Stevens wrote into the report of his "Directory," that it had no satisfactory proof that any of the late insurrectionary states *"except perhaps the state of Tennessee* has placed itself in a condition to resume its political relations to the Union." [54]

Not until the 19th of June, 1866, however, did Brownlow secure his perfect opportunity to show how gladly he was wearing the collar of the National Dictators. On that day, but seventy-two hours after its receipt from Washington, he issued a proclamation to convene the state legislature in extra session for July 4th to consider the adoption of the Fourteenth Amendment. On the appointed day the members were dilatory in assembling. Ill-concealing his vexation, Brownlow waited until the 14th, when he appealed to force. On that day he called on General Thomas for military aid to compel the obdurate legislators to attend. Loath to use his soldiers for the work of politics, Thomas by telegraph promptly sought the advice of Secretary Stanton. [55]

This was July 14th. For reasons of his own (and of his Radical Confederates) Stanton delayed for three days any action on the Thomas telegram, and it was not until the 17th that he laid it before the President and the Cabinet. Unaware that the telegram had originated from the request of Brownlow, the President declared that "if General Thomas had nothing else to do but to intermeddle in local controversies he had better be detached and ordered elsewhere." [56] Stanton, who knew of the President's warm friendship for the General, replied that he had intended to order Thomas to "avoid mixing up in this question." "But," he said looking at the President, "shall I add your remark?" "My wish is," responded Johnson, "that the answer should be emphatic and decisive not to meddle with local parties and politics. The military are not superior masters." [57]

Before the day was over Stanton wired Thomas not to interfere, [58] but in the meantime Brownlow had had an opportunity to act independently, and he had acted. The state Senate had ratified the amendment on the 11th. For the lower House, how-

ever, fifty-six were necessary for a quorum, and Brownlow had
secured but fifty-four.[59] He decided to arrest and then by force
secure the attendance of the two unwilling members.[60]

The recalcitrants were Pleasant Williams and A. J. Martin.
They had refused to attend on the ground that the proposed question had not been before the voters at the time of their election,
and hence they were unable to represent the will of their constituents.[61] On the 16th Williams, and on the next day Martin,
was arrested and brought to the bar of the House. The former
promptly obtained a writ of habeas corpus returnable before
Judge Thomas Frazier, a competent and conscientious judge,—
the appointee of Military Governor Andrew Johnson.[62]

On the 19th, before the hearing on the writ, there occurred
in the lower House of the legislature of Tennessee a dishonorable
proceeding. The two members were restrained by force in one of
the committee rooms and the sergeant-at-arms reported this fact
to the House. The roll was then called; there were two short of
a legal quorum. They proceeded nevertheless. Forty-three voted
for, and eleven against the proposed amendment. The Speaker
promptly ruled that there had been no quorum, but on an appeal
to the House, his decision was overruled. It was in this way, as
lawless as any proceeding in the most volatile of the Central
American Republics, that the Radicals of Tennessee secured her
adoption of the Fourteenth Amendment to the Constitution of the
United States.[63] That evening Brownlow telegraphed to the
Secretary of the United States Senate: "We have fought the battle
and won it. We have ratified the constitutional amendment in
the House—forty-three voting for it and eleven against it, two of
Andrew Johnson's tools not voting. Give my respects to the dead
dog of the White House." [64]

Upon the return of the writ, Judge Frazier discharged the two
members from custody and declared that their arrest had been
illegal.[65] For this upright and courageous decision, articles of
impeachment "for high crimes and misdemeanors" were later preferred before the Tennessee Senate and he was convicted and
deposed from office! [66]

§

The action of Tennessee was jubilantly applauded by the Radicals at Washington. They gloated in the fact that the Fourteenth Amendment had there been "ratified." The lawless methods Brownlow's legislature had adopted were strongly to their liking. The fact that Tennessee adopted the amendment by force and fraud caused the Radicals to exult.[67]

So great was the rejoicing that Stevens' servile followers determined to proclaim their triumph in some lasting form. They decided to serve new notice on the President, the country and especially on the South that a condition precedent to regained statehood was the ratification of their dear-prized Fourteenth Amendment. Three days after the receipt of Brownlow's telegram, both Houses adopted a joint resolution declaring that "Whereas" Tennessee's "state government can only be restored to its former political relations to the Union by the consent of the lawmaking power of the United States," and her government had ratified both the Thirteenth and Fourteenth Amendments to the Constitution, and had done other acts "denoting loyalty," therefore, "the state of Tennessee is hereby restored to her former practical relation to the Union, and is again entitled to be represented by Senators and Representatives in Congress."[68] Welles characterized the resolution as "a burlesque on republican government and our whole system of popular rights, opinion, state action, and constitutional obligation."[69]

That Brownlow's death certificate was premature must have appeared evident to the Fighting Parson, as well as to his fellow morticians in Washington, when on the day following the receipt of the Congressional resolution Andrew Johnson sent another message to Congress, in which he rent asunder the lawless doctrine of the Radicals.

"If," he wrote, "state government can only be restored to its former political relations in the Union by the consent of the lawmaking power of the United States, it would really seem to follow that the joint resolution which at this late day has received the sanction of Congress should have been . . . approved . . .

before any amendment to the Constitution was submitted to the legislature of Tennessee for ratification. Otherwise, the inference is plainly deducible that while the people of a state may be too strongly disloyal to be entitled to representation, they may nevertheless during the suspension of their 'former proper practical relations to the Union' have an equally potent voice with other and loyal states in propositions to amend the Constitution, upon which so essentially depend the stability, prosperity and very existence of the nation." [70]

Neither in the contemporary literature nor among the long pages of the historians is this logic answered. Blaine's comment is illustrative of the best that Johnson's critics can achieve. "The argument in the message," he said, "was regarded as an ingenious censure of Congress, and was loudly applauded on the Democratic side of the House." [71] From the other side, however, there came ironic laughter. [72]

"Earnestly desiring to remove every . . . delay," Johnson's message concluded, "to the admission to seats of loyal Senators and Representatives from the state of Tennessee, I have notwithstanding the anomalous character of this proceeding affixed my signature to the resolution. My approval, however, is not to be construed as an acknowledgment of the right of Congress to pass laws preliminary to the admission of duly qualified Representatives from any of the states." [73]

Then, expressly disclaiming any commitment to the assertion that Tennessee lawfully had ratified the Fourteenth Amendment, Johnson continued: "No official notice of such ratification has been filed in the Department of State; on the contrary unofficial information from most reliable sources induces the belief that the amendment has not yet been constitutionally sanctioned by the Legislature of Tennessee." [74] This surely was a statement to evoke laughter from the Radicals! What cared they how the work had been accomplished!

Johnson's final words contained a calm and reasonable appeal "for the admission of Tennessee and *all other states* to a fair and equal participation in national legislation when they present themselves in the persons of loyal Senators and Representatives who can comply with the requirements of the Constitution. By this means harmony and reconciliation will be effected, . . . and the work of restoration inaugurated upon the termination of the war successfully completed." [75]

From Tennessee thus "readmitted," there came eight Representatives, four of whom were supporters of the President and four were Radicals. Her Senators were likewise equally divided, or so the enemies of Johnson thought, and believing Joseph F. Fowler to be in sympathy with them, they promptly accorded him his seat.[76] They were to have cause later to regret this act. In the seating of David T. Patterson, the other Senator, there was long delay,—he was the son-in-law of the President;[77] Martha, his gracious wife, was the accomplished mistress of the White House. It was with peculiar joy, therefore, that the Radicals sought to becloud Senator Patterson's good name with charges of disloyalty. That the accusation was as false as it was wanton, was finally admitted by one of their own number who declared that there was not a "shadow of doubt" that the President's son-in-law had been "not only a Union man but such a Union man as would put some of us to shame." [78] The committee appointed to investigate his case having finally no other course, grudgingly on July 25th, granted him his seat.[79]

XXXIV

THE RADICALS LAY PLANS TO MAKE WADE PRESIDENT BY IMPEACHING JOHNSON

BEFORE Congress adjourned on July 28th,[1] the Radicals put forth two further efforts to strengthen their position: a second Freedman's Bureau Act and a bill to erect the territory of Nebraska into a state.

This Freedman's Bureau bill, like its predecessor, was a vicious measure. All of the objections marshaled by Johnson in his veto of the first were applicable to the second. Large numbers of commissioners and other bureaucrats, confiscation of Southern lands, judicial powers in the hands of irresponsible bureau agents; these and other enormities, all were there. Equally noticeable again was the large grant of power to the Secretary of War.[2]

Quick and straight Andrew Johnson's veto came. He once again laid bare the Radicals' proposal. How ill-founded was the contention of Sumner and his friends that the "Southern outrages" were a justification for martial law, the President exposed anew. "I believe," he said, "that public sentiment will sustain me in the assertion that such deeds of wrong are not confined to any particular state or section, but are manifested over the entire country, demonstrating that the cause that produced them does not depend upon any particular locality, but is the result of the agitation and derangement incident to a long and bloody civil war. While the prevalence of such disorders must be greatly deplored, their occasional and temporary occurrence would seem to furnish no necessity for the extension of the Bureau beyond the period fixed in the original act." [3]

The veto reached the House of Representatives on the 16th of July. It took the harsh goads of party discipline to hold all

310

Eng. by W. G. Jackman

of the Radicals in line, for those whose consciences were still alive knew the nature of their handiwork.[4]   But discipline prevailed. On the very day the veto reached the House, the bill was repassed there by a vote of more than three to one, and in the Senate on the same day by a bare two-thirds.[5]   Once more the veto of the President had been overridden.

Here was the real beginning of a series of laws so base that no American can read them even now without a sense of shame. Here was a measure that would give to Edwin Stanton hitherto undreamed-of authority.   That he would so manage it "as to cause the greatest possible friction between the Government and the whites of the South," [6] was plain enough to those who had devised the unprecedented requirement that "military protection" should be carried on "under such rules and regulations as the President *through* the Secretary of War shall prescribe." [7]

"There is no doubt," with the sober vision of the true historian, Professor Burgess has declared, "that the Freedmen's Bureau with its powers, jurisdiction and charities was a far greater source of irritation in the South than was the presence of the United States army.   While its superior officers were generally men of ability and character, a large number of the subalterns were canting hypocrites and outright thieves.   They kept the negroes in a state of idleness, beggary and unrest and made them a constant danger to the life and property of the whites; and their inevitable tyranny over the white population did more to destroy Union sentiment among the whites and make them regard the United States Government in a hostile light, than anything which had happened during the whole course of the rebellion." [8]

A two-thirds majority had been secured to pass the Freedman's Bureau measure over Johnson's veto, but in the Senate at least, there were no votes to spare.   The expedient of admitting Colorado as a state had failed two months before, but Ben Wade was resourceful, and now toward the closing hours of the session he called up a bill for the admission of Nebraska introduced by him a few days earlier.[9]   It was a plain and exceedingly unvarnished scheme to strengthen the Radicals' majority in the Senate.[10]

With this much of the plan Charles Sumner was perfectly in

accord, but so great was his devotion to the cause of negro suf-frage that he balked at Nebraska's constitution confining the vote to "white male citizens." [11]   Of Sumner, Senator Nye declared that his "conscientious friend mistook twinges of dyspepsia for constitutional scruples."   More revealing than whole dreary volumes of his speeches was Sumner's priceless answer: "I have never had dyspepsia in my life." [12]

The Nebraska bill passed both Houses on Friday, July 27th, the day before adjournment.   But President Johnson did not sign it, and it failed, therefore, at that session to become a law.[13]   That Ben Wade would not be deterred from furthering this scheme at some later day was evident enough to those who knew him. "Congress," wrote Welles, "has agreed to adjourn on Saturday. God speed them hence." [14]

§

It was not in Congress alone that the Radicals were working; their machinations long since had penetrated into the Cabinet itself.   Sumner's prophecies of six months before were receiving their fulfillment.   It had long been evident to those who knew, that Speed, Harlan and Dennison were not in sympathy with the Administration.   Stanton's defection was even more apparent.   In the middle of July the three first named, acting from a sense of decent self-respect, resigned.[15]

"Whether," wrote Welles, "Stanton will go with them is doubt-ful.   Although he has been fully with the Radicals in all their extreme measures from the beginning, he has professed to abandon them when the President made a distinct stand on any subject. I am therefore, uncertain what course he will take; but if he leaves he will be likely to be malevolent.   He is selfish, insincere, a dissembler and treacherous. . . . Blair says the Radical pro-gram is to make Wade President of the Senate, then to impeach the President.   Having done this the Radicals will be prepared to exclude the Southern members from the next Congress and the Southern states from the next Presidential election." [16]

Ben Wade President of the Senate!   Andrew Johnson to be impeached!   If this were done under the law as it then was, Wade would become President of the United States! [17] What could be more fitting than that the chief libeler of Lincoln should be chosen by Lincoln's enemies to lead in thwarting Lincoln's plans! Here was indeed a program! No wonder that this Presidential aspirant so feverishly should be working to pack the court to be convened for the removal of "the Presidential obstacle!" Colorado and Nebraska,—their four senatorial votes would indeed be welcome!

For sixteen months, with a patience as long-suffering as Lincoln's own, Johnson had borne with Lincoln's Cabinet. Seward, Welles and McCulloch had loyally supported him. Harlan, Dennison and Speed under the proddings of the Radicals had grown steadily away from him, but now they had the decency to retire. But if Johnson exercised patience with these three, his long-suffering with Stanton amounted to a fault. From the very start, Stanton's arrogance, his bad manners and his obvious lack of sympathy with Johnson's course, had made him an objectionable and unreliable adviser.

The Cabinet which Johnson had inherited for better or for worse was Lincoln's Cabinet. By letting Stanton stay, he felt that he might win the aid or at least diminish the hostility of Stanton's friends. And Johnson was willing to suffer anything to achieve the consummation of Lincoln's hopes,—even Stanton. Moreover, Johnson hoped that his War Minister might follow of his own accord where his three associates had led. But Stanton was too thick-skinned ever to resign himself; moreover the Radicals had need of him and he of them! His failure to retire at this time "may," declares Professor Burgess, "be looked upon as a conspiracy with the Republican majority in Congress to rob the President of his constitutional prerogatives, to change the form of government from the presidential system to the parliamentary system of administration. It is difficult to find any sufficient defence for Mr. Stanton's course." [18]

Johnson acted promptly in filling the three vacant Cabinet positions. "I learn," wrote Welles on July 20th, "that the President today sent in the nomination of Mr. Stanbery for Attorney-General. He made no mention of it in the Cabinet. There is a reticence on the part of the President—an apparent want of confidence in his friends—which is unfortunate, and prevents him from having intimate and warm personal friends who would relieve him in a measure. . . . It is a mistake, an infirmity, a habit fixed before he was President, to keep his own counsel." [19]

Johnson was not loquacious; while Stanton was in that Cabinet the President's ability "to keep his own counsel" was evidence of wisdom. For a long time he had had reason to suspect that Stanton was a sneak. He had been almost from the beginning of his administration surrounded by Stanton's spies. Many of the things he had said in friendly confidence were taken directly to the Secretary of War, who kept a constant espionage on all that transpired within the White House. Stanton, in constant contact as he was with the Radical conspirators, was enabled to betray the measures and purposes of his chief. Thus he and his confederates in Congress were constantly prepared with schemes for the defeat of Johnson's policy. The President either knew or suspected these things before the close of 1865.[20] Undoubtedly he erred in not having ejected Stanton at that time.

Henry Stanbery, whom Johnson selected to fill Speed's place, was sixty-three years old. Born in New York City, at the age of eleven he had removed with his father to Zanesville, Ohio. At the youthful age of sixteen he had graduated from Washington College, Pennsylvania. He became a lawyer, and ultimately the law partner of Thomas Ewing, who had adopted at about this time a rather promising young man whom he sent later to West Point. The young man's name was James Tecumseh Sherman. When he was forty-three, Stanbery became the first Attorney-General of Ohio, and four years later was a member of the Constitutional Convention of that state.[21] He was, wrote Blaine, "a lawyer of high reputation and a gentleman of unsullied character." [22] For his new Postmaster General, Johnson chose Alexander Randall of Wisconsin. Born forty-seven years before in New York State, like Stanbery, early in life he had heard the call of the West. He became postmaster of Waukesha, member of the Constitutional Convention, judge of the Milwaukee Circuit Court, and finally, at the age of thirty-eight, Governor of Wisconsin. In 1859 he was reëlected, and at the first rumble of the war declared himself and his state for the Union in such ringing tones that the whole country hearkened. In 1861, although he was then forty-two, he wished to have done with politics and to do his part for the Union as a soldier. But Lincoln had other uses for him, and persuaded him to become his Minister to Italy. Remaining there one year he returned, and was later made first assistant to Postmaster Dennison. His appointment, therefore, as head of the Department was a promotion.[23]

In Harlan's place as Secretary of the Interior Johnson selected one of Lincoln's oldest friends, Orville Hickman Browning of Quincy, Illinois. Born one year after Lincoln, in Lincoln's birth state of Kentucky, like Lincoln he went to Illinois and there practiced law. He served with Lincoln in the Black Hawk War of 1832, and four years later became a member of the Illinois State Senate. He assisted Lincoln in forming the Republican party in that state and became a delegate in 1860 to the National Convention in Chicago, where he did much in bringing about Lincoln's nomination. The following year Stephen A. Douglas died, and Browning was chosen to fill his place in the Senate of the United States.[24]

In selecting these new Cabinet members, Johnson once again displayed his predilection for strong and honorable counsel. "It pains me," wrote Seward when he learned of the Cabinet resignations, "that all of my associates have not been able to see it their duty, as I see it mine, to sustain the President."[25] Andrew Johnson had now chosen men who, like Seward, would sustain him

XXXV

MEMPHIS AND NEW ORLEANS

DURING the spring and summer of 1866 there occurred two events, hitherto unnoticed, that were to have not only a large influence on the Congressional elections which soon followed, but upon the success of Johnson's policies.

In Memphis, during April, the third United States colored artillery were quartered. Their mere presence was provocative enough, but when presently their lack of discipline revealed itself in acts of open insolence, the collisions against which Grant had warned [1] were sure to follow. The police of Memphis, as good police should always be, were Irish. The jostling of Irish policemen never has been deemed an act of prudence, yet on the afternoon of April 30th this extra hazardous pastime was engaged in by the black artillerymen. Trouble disproportionate to this origin was not slow in following. It followed on the next day when the municipal officers of the law, with the ready aid of white civilians, made an attack upon the entire negro population of the city. This retaliation resulted in a riot that lasted for two days. When it was over, forty-six negroes had been killed and more were injured. Twelve negro schoolhouses and a third as many churches were put to the torch.[2]

The echoes of this trouble were not slow in reaching Washington, from which sounding-board they reverberated through the land. A golden opportunity was here offered for the enemies of the South to proclaim her "unregeneracy," [3] and for the foes of Johnson mendaciously to declare that he was responsible for this outbreak.

The material for defamation furnished by the Memphis riot, however, was as nothing compared to what transpired at New Orleans on July 30th. The pardoned leaders of the Confederacy

316

in Louisiana had regained control of the state government and occupied every office there, except that of governor. The Radicals of that state, instigated by those at Washington, determined through the medium of negro suffrage, to gain ascendancy.[4]

But the Constitution of 1864, adopted under Lincoln's supervision, had not enfranchised negroes. Nothing could be done unless this Constitution were amended. A new convention would take a long time to procure, and so without authority of law they decided to reconvene the convention that had adjourned two years before. Taking the national leaders as their guide, they determined to work through revolution when they could not otherwise achieve their aims. Accordingly, they sent out an illegal call to the delegates of the old convention, sufficient of whom were known to be now willing for the work in hand.[5] The call set July 30th as the time, and the Mechanics Hall at New Orleans as the place, for the convening of that which in the eyes of the law could be nothing but a mob.

Between July 7th, when the call went out, and the date of the "convention," the opponents of what was nothing short of a conspiracy, determined, if they could, to check it. Sheridan, the military commander, was away, but General Baird was acting in his absence. Mayor Monroe interviewed him on the 25th and again two days later when he told that Federal officer that were the "convention" to assemble, the Grand Jury would indict and the sheriff would arrest the members. Baird agreed to seek instructions from the War Department and suggested that the Mayor and the Lieutenant-Governor should do likewise.[6]

On the very day this conference was going on, the Radicals of Louisiana were inciting the colored population to bloodshed.[7] From the steps of the City Hall, a white scoundrel shouted to a listening black mob: "I want the negroes to have the right of suffrage. We have three hundred thousand black men with white hearts. Also one hundred thousand good and true Union white men who will fight for and beside the black race against the three hundred thousand hell-hound rebels. . . . We cannot only whip but exterminate the other party. . . . If interfered with the streets will run with blood."[8]

All that Johnson knew of what was taking place came to him through telegrams of the Lieutenant-Governor and Attorney-General of Louisiana advising him of the proposed convention, that the matter was before the Grand Jury, but that to execute civil process would result in riot.[9] The question specifically asked him was: "Is the military to interfere to prevent process of court?" [10] Mindful that the civil courts of Louisiana were then open and in the full exercise of their power,[11] on July 28th he sent this telegraphic answer: "The military will be expected to sustain, and not interfere with, the proceedings of the courts." [12] This telegram was, of course, as much intended for the military as for the civil authorities to whom it was sent, but whether it was actually shown to General Baird is not known.[13]

To Stanton, on July 28th, Baird had telegraphed of the proposed arrest of the delegates by the authorities of the city. "I have given no orders on the subject," he wired, "but have warned the parties that I could not countenance or permit such action without instructions to that effect from the President. Please instruct me at once by telegraph." [14] Stanton received this dispatch on the 29th, but it was not until ten days later that the President was told of its existence! [15] If then what subsequently took place was the fault of any man, Stanton and not Johnson was to blame!

On the morning of July 30th a procession of negroes, partly armed, marched through the streets of New Orleans. There was some hooting and jeering from the sidewalks, when suddenly a shot rang out; it had been fired by one of the colored paraders. Other shots soon followed, and the crowd then chased the marchers to the hall of the convention. The police appeared presently on the scene. All the materials for a riot were now present, and a very shocking one ensued. The police rushed into the building firing as they ran. Before it was over nearly two hundred persons had been killed or injured, most of whom were negroes.[16] Soldiers did not reach the scene until the trouble was all over.[17]

Without a shred of proof to substantiate the charge, the Radicals proclaimed that the riot was the result of the President's delinquency, and heralded this accusation in every form of utterance.[18] His exculpation was in the power of Stanton, but Stanton held his peace,[19] except to exclaim against the Attorney-General of Louisiana and the Mayor of New Orleans as "pardoned rebels who had instigated the murder of the people in the streets of the city."[20] The Congressional Committee appointed by Congress would hear nothing from the President, and presently filed their report charging him as an accomplice in the crime,—the possessor in advance of guilty knowledge of the pre-arranged assassination![21]

On the day following the riot, Horace Greeley thundered in the New York *Tribune*: "The hands of the rebels are again red with loyal blood. Rebel armies have once more begun the work of massacre."[22] And presently the Northern Radicals were denouncing the President with every damning word within their large vocabulary of abuse.[23]

No one seems to have mentioned that the combined deaths in Memphis and in New Orleans numbered less than half the negroes who were murdered in the draft riots of New York three years before![24] Such facts would not well have harmonized with the Radical contention that it was only in the South that the race problem gave rise to turbulence!

With the aid of Greeley and other journalist adherents, the followers of Stevens and of Sumner had no difficulty in passing the counterfeit coin of false accusation among most of their contemporaries; but there was one at least who detected its false ring, and who sat from day to day exposing it for posterity. "There is little doubt," wrote Welles four days after the smoke had lifted from Mechanics Hall, "that the New Orleans riots had their origin with the Radical members of Congress in Washington. It is part of a deliberate conspiracy and was to be the commencement of a series of bloody affrays through the states lately in rebellion. Boutwell and others have stated sufficient to show their participation in this matter. There is a determination to involve the country in civil war, if necessary, to secure negro suffrage in the states and Radical ascendancy in the General Government."[25]

XXXVI

THE PHILADELPHIA CONVENTION

FOUR national conventions were held during the summer of 1866.[1] In our entire history there is no other non-presidential year in which this was done. The first was called in furtherance of Johnson's administration to be held in Philadelphia on the 14th of August.[2]

Welles threw himself vigorously into the organization of this demonstration. At a Cabinet meeting on August 7th Stanton remarked that an application had been made to him for bunting with which to decorate the convention hall. He had none for this purpose, he said, and then added, with a sneer, that he would turn this application over to the navy. The retort from the Secretary of that department was like a body blow. "My bunting," said Welles, "has always been promptly shown and it would be well were you now to let us have a sight of yours." Stanton was taken aback, colored, and then repeated that he had no bunting for the Philadelphia gathering. "Oh," said Welles, "show your flag." "You mean the convention," replied Stanton,—"I am against it."[3] "This is wrong," said Welles privately to the President a few hours later. "We cannot get along in this way." "No," answered Johnson, "it will be pretty difficult."[4]

Before the 14th of August, the delegates began to arrive at Philadelphia. From all over the country, North and South, they came. Whether they were Northerners or Southerners, Democrats or Republicans mattered not, so long as they were ready to support Johnson's purpose to preserve the Union from a new destruction. There were not lacking those who felt that a new war was then impending.[5] "I am unwilling to believe," wrote Welles, "that a majority of Congress is preparing for such a step, but the majority is weak in intellect, easily led into rashness and

320

error by the few designing leaders, who move and control the party machinery. There is no individuality and very little statesmanship or wise legislation, and as little in the Senate. The war on the President and on the Constitution as well as on the whole people of the South is revolutionary." [6]

At the corner of Girard Avenue and 20th Street a great building was erected, with a seating capacity for ten thousand persons. Pillars and rafters were draped with bunting even though Stanton had been unwilling to supply it. [7] The national colors and the national flag were everywhere. Above the speakers' platform there rose an arch in thirty-six sections, each bearing the shield of a state and with no state left out, North or South! [8]

To this hall at high noon on August 14th, the appointed day, the delegates had come. And then in the presence of a cheering throng of more than twelve thousand persons, [9]—the men throwing their hats in the air, the ladies waving their handkerchiefs, great bands thundering out "Rally Round the Flag, Boys," the "Star Spangled Banner" and "Dixie" too,—Governor Orr of South Carolina and General Couch of Massachusetts, arm in arm, followed by the other delegates in like posture, marched into the convention hall. Cheer echoed cheer until the rafters rang. [10]

With a gavel fashioned out of an oak timber from the frigate *Constitution,*—"Old Ironsides," whose quarter deck a half a century before had echoed to the tread of Hull and Bainbridge— Senator Doolittle brought the great gathering to order. And then during the ensuing hush, this telegram from President Andrew Johnson was read to the assembled delegates: "The people must be trusted and the country will be restored!" At this there was renewed cheering. [11]

Such formal business as was transacted consisted in the adoption of resolutions declaring that "no state or combination of states has the right to withdraw from the Union, or to exclude, through their action in Congress or otherwise, any other state or states from the Union. The Union of the states is perpetual." [12]

The final paragraph declared that "In Andrew Johnson . . . who . . . has proved steadfast in his devotion to the Constitution, the laws and interests of his country, unmoved by persecution and undeserved reproach, having faith unassailable in the people and in the principles of free government, we recognize a Chief Magistrate worthy of the nation, and equal to the great crisis upon which his lot is cast; and we tender him in the discharge of his high and responsible duties, our profound respect and assurance of our cordial and sincere support." [13]

Finally, on August 16th, the third day of its session, the convention, amid tumultuous cheers for the President of the United States, concluded its labors and adjourned. [14]

The Radicals watched the proceedings with mixed feelings of scorn and of alarm. The sentiments of reunion so eloquently voiced there were endangering their plans of confiscation and military rule. All too plainly these Northern disunionists discerned that the well-considered design of bringing the leading representatives of North and South into a great friendly meeting, where Democrats perhaps prevailed, was making that which was the fact appear all too evident, that the "Democrats were the party of peace and reunion, while the Republicans were in favor of a continuation of the hostile status." [15] With eager satisfaction the Radicals observed the efforts of the notorious Vallandingham and of Fernando Wood to gain seats in the convention, giving scant attention to the fact that neither of these Copperheads were seated. [16]

By ridicule the followers of Stevens and of Sumner sought to reverse all that Johnson's friends had done. The entry of the delegates, each Northerner with his arm thrust through that of an ex-Confederate, was at least a noble gesture, but the Radicals compared the "Wigwam" with "Noah's Ark." They sought their humor from the Book of Genesis, and likened the entry of the delegates, "two and two" with that "of clean beasts, and of beasts that are not clean, and of fowls, and of everything that creepeth upon the Earth." [17]

Having done all within his power to damage the President at home, on the last day of the convention Charles Sumner took up his pen to injure him abroad. To John Bright he wrote: "Our President goes on from bad to worse. He is another James II with Seward for his Sunderland. His apostasy is complete. People now see that I was right at the beginning of the late session when I declared the breach irreparable. I had seen him under such circumstances as to draw him out so that I knew his system. The Philadelphia convention now in session has no constituency behind it except the Democracy. The Republican party stands unmoved, losing very few here and there, but I think not weakened materially." And then returning to his favorite theme that all negroes should immediately be given the same right to vote as white men, Sumner continued: "All this might have been easily established had the President gone with Congress. Now we have before us terrible strife and perhaps war again." [18]

§

The three new members of the Cabinet were earnest participants in the Philadelphia Convention, and wrote frequently to the President portraying the fine spirit that characterized all of its deliberations.[19] They returned to Washington on August 17th with an enthusiastic report. Among other things they told Johnson that "it was the strong and emphatic voice of the convention" that Stanton should leave the Cabinet.[20]

At one o'clock on the following day, in the East Room of the White House, with Ulysses Grant on his right hand, and Gideon Welles on his left, but with Stanton noticeably absent,[21] the President received a committee of one hundred of the delegates. Reverdy Johnson was their spokesman. Looking straight at the President he said: "If you could have seen the men of Massachusetts and South Carolina coming into the convention . . . hand in hand, amid the rapturous applause of the whole body . . . you would have felt as every person present felt, that the time had arrived when all sectional or other perilous dissensions had ceased, and that nothing should be heard in the future but the voice of harmony, proclaiming devotion to a common country, of pride in being bound together by a common Union. . . ."

He spoke of the Convention's commendation of the Presidential course, and continued: "In the measures which you have adopted for the restoration of the Union, the Convention saw only a continuance of the policy which for the same purpose was inaugurated by your immediate predecessor. . . . Being upon the same ticket with that much lamented public servant you would have been false to obvious duty if you had not endeavored to carry out the same policy. . . ." [22]

"Seemingly," replied the President, "I partook of the inspiration that prevailed in the convention when I received a dispatch . . . conveying in terms the scene which has just been described. . . . When I was thus informed that . . . every eye was suffused with tears on beholding the scene, I could not finish reading the dispatch . . . for my own feelings overcame me. . . . The nation is in peril. We have just passed through . . . a bloody . . . ordeal; and yet we do not find ourselves free from the difficulties and dangers that at first surrounded us. While our brave soldiers, both officers and men [turning to General Grant] have by their heroism won laurels imperishable, there are still greater and more important duties to perform, and while we have had their coöperation in the field, now that they have returned to civil pursuits, we need their support in our efforts to restore the government and perpetuate peace. [Applause.] So far as the executive department of the Government is concerned, the effort has been made to restore the Union, to heal the breach, to pour oil into the wounds which were consequent upon the struggle and (to speak in common phrase) to prepare, as the learned and wise physician would, a plaster healing in character and coextensive with the wound. We thought, and we think, that we had partially succeeded; but as the work progressed, as reconstruction seemed to be taking place, and the country was becoming reunited, we found a disturbing and marring element opposing us." [23]

And then he went on: "We have witnessed in one department of the Government every endeavor to prevent the restoration of peace, harmony and union. We have seen hanging upon the verge of the Government, as it were a body called, or which assumes to be, the Congress of the United States, while in fact it is a Congress of only a part of the states. We have seen the Congress pretend to be for the Union, when its every step and act tended to perpetuate disunion and make a disruption of the states inevitable. Instead of promoting reconciliation and harmony its legislation has partaken of the character of penalties, retaliation and revenge. . . . I know it has been said that the executive department . . . has been despotic and tyrannical. . . . So far as charges of this kind are concerned they are simply to delude the public mind. . . . It is done by them for the purpose of covering their own acts. ['That's so' and applause.]" [24]

"Slander upon slander," he went on, "vituperation upon vituperation, of the most virulent character, has made its way through the press. What, gentlemen, has been your and my sin? What has been the cause of our offending? I will tell you, daring to stand by the Constitution of our fathers!" [25]

What was to be done with this man? The truth was in him, and he was not afraid to utter it. Perhaps the whispering of more sinister detractions might terrify him, and so the conspirators began quietly to spread the rumor that could he succeed in procuring the election of sufficient Congressmen from the border and the Northern states to back him, he would then recognize them together with the Southern Senators and Representatives as the true Congress, and would uphold this recognition through his command of the armed forces of the country. [26]

On the alert to damage the President of the United States wherever possible, and especially delighting to prejudice his cause among the more enlightened Englishmen, a few days after Johnson's welcome of the Philadelphia delegates, Charles Sumner penned another missive to John Bright. "Before the adjournment of Congress," he wrote, "many persons were satisfied that the President contemplated a coup d'état. This was discussed in one of our confidential caucuses. Several Senators wished to make some provision against it. I did not see how it could occur without revolution and another civil war, and I did not think the President would dare to commence such proceedings. But there is a painful uncertainty with regard to the future." [27] Not that the President would be unwilling to effect a coup d'état,—merely that he would not dare! Sumner made that point clear and then proceeded: "He is perverse, distempered, ignorant and thoroughly wrong. You may judge him by the terrible massacre at New

Orleans. Stanton confessed to me that he (the President) was its author." [28]

Perhaps this would be as good a place as any in which to examine an honest criticism of the President, formulated by a sincere and honorable Southerner,—Alexander H. Stephens, late Vice-President of the Confederacy. "A negative error of Mr. Johnson," wrote Stephens, "should receive at least a passing notice, and the more so from the fact that I believe his sole object now is to restore the Union and maintain the Federal System established by the Fathers. To this end his every energy seems at this time to be most patriotically directed, and however much I may have disagreed with him in the past, he is in my judgment now entitled to the confidence, support and cordial coöperation of every friend of constitutional liberty throughout the country." [29]

"The error," continued Stephens, "to which I allude was that . . . he did not refuse to recognize as the Congress of the United States any Bodies in which any one of the states of the Union was denied representation in the House and an equal voice in the Senate. Had he thus proclaimed and thus acted, when the policy of the Reconstruction Committee was at first openly declared, he might have sustained his own views and prevented the consummation of that most iniquitous policy. There were then in Congress enough Anti-Centralists in the Senate and House from the Northern states, with the Senators and Representatives returned from the South, to constitute a majority of a legitimate Congress. By such Union, a constitutional Congress could have been organized; and if Mr. Johnson had invited such a Union and recognized such an organization as the only true Congress of the United States, as it would have been, those gross usurpations never would have been perpetrated." [30]

Here is a criticism both sincere and fair. Johnson did indeed have that course open to him, but its inevitable consequence would have been another war. Would he have been justified in plunging the states, bled white already, in still further bloodshed? He thought not; it was the highest form of patriotism that prevented him from following that course.

§

To the strains of martial music Johnson's reception of the committee from the Philadelphia Convention came to an end. In pamphlet form the speeches were preserved and presently were widely circulated by the National Union Executive Committee.[31]

Two days later President Johnson proclaimed: "The insurrection which heretofore existed in the state of Texas is at an end."[32] Five and a half months before he had made a similar proclamation as to all the other Southern states.[33] The war had really ended with the surrender of Lee and Johnston in April of the year before, but now the fact was formally announced "that peace, order and tranquillity and civil authority now exist in and throughout the whole United States of America."[34]

Forty-eight hours later Welles wrote: "The Peace Proclamation takes well with the people. It has the effect which I, and I think Stanton, anticipated. There comes, I see, a strong pressure against Stanton from Philadelphia. Whether it will have an effect upon him or the President is doubtful. The latter cannot need to be undeceived."[35]

Washington was still full of the delegates from Philadelphia,— among these many from the South. "Most of those men," wrote Welles, "have been connected . . . with the Rebellion, but they . . . acquiesce in the result with grace, and I believe with sincerity. But the Radicals are filled with hatred, acrimony and revenge toward them, and would persist in excluding not only them but the whole people of the South from any participation in the government. For four years war was was waged to prevent them from going out; now the Radicals wage as fine a war to shut them out."[36]

The Congressional elections rapidly were drawing nearer, and Johnson resolved to take these issues to the country. He was invited at about this time to be present in Chicago at the laying of the cornerstone of the Douglas monument, and he determined to make this trip an opportunity to address the Northern people face to face.[37] "Now as we swing around the circle of the Union . . . the government must stand unshaken and unmoved on its basis," [38] he had said six months before. And so "Swinging Around the Circle," was the name given to this tour. In verse and prose these words were parodied and ridiculed by the Radicals and their supporters. Before following the President on this journey, however, there are several matters requiring our brief notice.

With the surrender of the Confederates, the Republican party had attained its principal objective; more than its original purpose was secured when, in December, 1865, the Thirteenth Amendment abolishing slavery was adopted. The conduct of the Northern Democrats who had deserved and won the name of Copperhead, had brought their whole party into disrepute among the Unionists. The war had left the Democrats in confusion, and now, a little dazed, they were looking through the lifting smoke of battle, to behold a true champion of the inviolability of the states. Many of them came presently to Johnson's aid, but they did not give him the support that he deserved. They missed a brilliant opportunity. Without waiting eighteen years, they had, if they had been wise enough to see, a Grover Cleveland ready at their hand.

But it was with suspicion that the Democrats recalled that Johnson, although a member of their party, had been elected as the running mate of Lincoln. With a suspicion even greater, the Republican Radicals beheld a President who had been a life-long Democrat. Johnson was now a man without a party, because he had placed his country first. "Party before country," wrote Welles in the early part of 1866, "was inculcated by both Radicals and Democrats. The President had in the past as in the present placed country above party and was consequently not a favorite with either." [39]

But if they were united in their unwillingness to follow Johnson, there was another subject on which the two parties were strongly in accord, and that was upon the desirability of procuring and of holding the patronage of the government. The whole subject of patronage is a festering sore in our Republic, it was cancerous in 1866. Civil service was undreamed of; Job Hedges' aphorism that "government is a thing to live under, not on"

would have struck the "statesmen" of the late sixties as an impertinence.

What hidden chapters of our history lie behind the sullied veil
of patronage! Lincoln, in the darkest days, was harassed by this
problem almost as much as by the task of finding generals who
would fight. Historians have revealed how many measures he
secured from Congress by placating this Senator or that Representative; doubtless other chapters on this subject will yet be
written. They will be creditable to him, because in his case, if
in any, the ends justified the means.

As the contest between Johnson and his Congress became
warmer, the desire of the Radicals to fill all the offices with their
men grew stronger. The two subjects were not unrelated. It
was certainly desirable for the success of the Presidential policy
that the government should not swarm with his enemies. Yet
Johnson was slow to act in this matter.

His unwillingness to use the appointing power for the accomplishment of his ends came from nothing so much as from sheer
honesty. "He was," wrote Hugh McCulloch, "a man of
unblemished personal integrity. He was an honest man, and his
administration was an honest and clean administration. In this
respect it will bear comparison with any that preceded or has followed it. . . . Offices were not merchandise." There were more
offices connected with the Treasury Department than with any
other, and yet "in no instance did he interfere with its management. In his bitter contest with Congress, although most of the
employees of the department were politically opposed to him and
his Reconstruction policy, he never even suggested that changes
be made for that reason. If he did not declare that public offices
were public trusts, his actions proved that he so regarded them." [40]

When the delegates returned from the Philadelphia Convention, they came back filled with plans not only for the removal
of Stanton, the arch Radical of the Cabinet, but for the ejection
of all Radicals from office. Every friend of Johnson felt that this
immediately should be done. "It is to be lamented," wrote one
member of the Cabinet, "that the President permitted the Radicals to remove his friends and substitute their tools; that he had

not drawn the line of demarcation, resented usurpation, and maintained the rights of the Executive six or eight months earlier, before the Radicals had intrenched themselves so strongly. His delay and the activity of the Radicals, who operated through most of the Departments, have weakened his cause and strengthened his opponents, who now bid him defiance. I have little doubt that some contemplate further infringement on Executive rights, provided they can compact their party to that end." [41]

XXXVII

JEFFERSON DAVIS

TWENTY years before Sinclair Lewis began holding up the national mirror to "George Babbitt," Senator Hoar of Massachusetts wrote feelingly of the "standardizing influences of our age." He found his fellow Northern statesmen dull. "You could not," he said, "read the story of their public career without going to sleep." While he expressed respect for them he added: "I would as lief spend my life as an omnibus horse as live theirs." [1] But though he had in Congress many bitter contests with the "Southern brigadiers," he wrote: "It so happens that some of the best and most attractive men I have known were from the South." [2]

Whatever emotions may be stirred by following the annals of the Confederacy, boredom will not be one of them. The charm and courage of her women, the stately poise and valor of her men,—these as in the chivalric chapters of Scott's romances—mark every page of her tragic story. Jefferson Davis had less of personal magnetism than many of his associates in the "Lost Cause," but he was a man of sensitive honor, of complete integrity and unquestionable sincerity. He was loyal to the principles which seemed to him as true as those for which Washington was ready, if need be, to embrace a traitor's fate.

From January 21st, 1861, Davis was something of a problem to Lincoln; he became almost as great a one to Johnson. Now in the late summer of 1866 he was still a prisoner at Fortress Monroe where he had been confined since May of the previous year. What was to be done with him? To the North he was the living embodiment of treason, the target for the accumulated hates of four years of civil strife.

Jefferson Davis had no love for Johnson. When on May 10th, 1865, Davis was captured by James Wilson's cavalry and was informed that he was charged with inciting Lincoln's murder, he quietly replied that Johnson of all men should know the untruth of the accusation, "for he at least knew that I preferred Lincoln to himself." [3]   But Johnson did not then know that the charge was false.   It had originated in the Bureau of Military Justice, —of which Judge-Advocate-General Joseph Holt was head.[4] Johnson did not know Holt then as well as later.   When on May 2nd, 1865, Stanton laid before the Cabinet a paper from Holt to the effect that Davis and others were implicated in Lincoln's murder, Johnson signed the proclamation for their capture.   Welles thought it wise, provided there was proof to support it, "but," he later wrote, "I had no facts," [5]—neither had Holt.

Twelve days after their capture, Jefferson Davis and Clement C. Clay heard the gates of Fortress Monroe clang behind them.[6] They were given inner rooms in a casemate with windows heavily barred.   Elaborate arrangements were made for sentry watch. The outer room of the prisoners' compartments was guarded by two sentries; the key was kept by the general officer of the guard. A strong line of sentries cut off all access, another line was stationed at the top of the parapet overhead, while a third was posted across the moats upon the counterscarp.   In addition to all this, a lamp was kept burning day and night in each of the prisoner's rooms.[7]

As though this were not enough, General Miles at Stanton's instance put Davis in irons and rivetted and padlocked fetters to his legs.[8] It was done, said Miles, to "prevent his running should he endeavor to escape." [9]   When Johnson learned of the treatment that had been accorded the distinguished prisoner, he was outraged.   He later sent Hugh McCulloch in person to the Fortress to investigate.   "Davis," said the President, "was the head devil among the traitors, and he ought to be hung; but he should have a fair trial and not be brutally treated while a prisoner." [10]

On the day of Davis's capture, Atzerodt, Mrs. Surratt and six others had been placed on trial for Lincoln's murder before a military commission, convened especially for that purpose.[11] The charge was that they had conspired with Davis, Clay and Booth to kill not only Lincoln, but Johnson, Grant and Seward also.[12] Holt

Jeff. Davis

was the Judge-Advocate. Each day the prisoners were brought in heavily ironed, nor was any exception made in the case of Mrs. Surratt. The trial dragged on. The accused were allowed counsel and the privilege of summoning witnesses, but they were not allowed much else, and on June 30th they were all found guilty.[13] Herold, Atzerodt, Payne and Mrs. Surratt were hung,[14] O'Laughlin, Arnold and Mudd were sentenced to imprisonment.[15] John H. Surratt, the son of the convicted woman, fled to Canada and thence to England.[16] We shall encounter him again.

Not long after his arrest, Davis was indicted in the District of Columbia for treason,[17] but if he had committed that crime at all, it was not there. Legal problems! Eleven days after the hanging of Mrs. Surratt, Johnson discussed the Davis case with his Cabinet.[18] It was wisely decided that the former President of the Confederacy should be tried before a civil court.[19]

During his incarceration, Davis held many conversations with the kindly physician of the prison, Dr. John J. Craven. One day the former President was asked what he thought of Andrew Johnson. "The position of Mr. Johnson with his associates of the South," replied Davis, "had never been pleasant, not from any fault or superciliousness on their side, but solely due to the intense, almost morbidly sensitive pride of Mr. Johnson. Sitting with associates, many of whom he knew pretended to aristocracy, Mr. Johnson seemed to set before his own mind, and keep ever present with him, his democratic or plebeian origin as a bar to warm social relations. This pride—for it was the pride of having no pride, his associates long struggled to overcome, but without success. They respected Mr. Johnson's abilities, integrity and greatly original force of character; but nothing could make him be, or seem to wish to feel, at home in their society. Some casual word dropped in debate, though uttered without a thought of his existence, would seem to wound him to the quick, and again he would shrink back into the self-imposed isolation of his earlier and humbler life, as if to gain strength from touching his mother earth."[20]

"In a word," continued Davis, "while other members of the Senate were Democrats in theory or as their political faith, Mr.

Johnson was a Democrat of pride, conviction and self assertion—a man of the people, who not only desired no higher grade of classification, but could not be forced into its acceptance or retention when friendly efforts were made to that end. He was an immense worker and student, but always in the practicalities of life; little in the graces of literature. His habits were marked by temperance, industry, courage, and unswerving perseverance; also, by inveterate prejudices or preconceptions on certain points, and these no arguments could shake. His faith in the judgment of the people was unlimited, and to their decision he was always ready to submit. One of the people by birth, he remained so by conviction, continually recurring to his origin, though he was by no means the only Senator of the South in like circumstances." [21]

Continuing with this not unkind and in many ways surprisingly acute analysis, Davis declared that "Of Mr. Johnson's character, justice was an eminent feature, though not uncoupled—as true justice rarely fails to be—with kindliness and generosity. He was eminently faithful to his word, and possessed a courage which took the form of angry resistance if urged to do, or not do, anything which might clash with his convictions of duty. He was indifferent to money and careless of praise or censure, when satisfied of the necessity of any line of action. But for his decided attitude against secession, he would probably have been given the place of Mr. Stephens on the Presidential ticket of the Confederacy. Mr. Stephens, indeed, held the same attitude up to the last moment; but, on the secession of his state, had two alternatives of State or Federal 'treason,' as it was called, presented, and chose the latter." [22]

There is little to be found in Northern literature that can compare for justice with this estimate by one who represented every principle against which Johnson had fought when there was real fighting to be done. The South before the war was as ready as the North to heap its honors on this Tennessee mountaineer. If Johnson was sensitive on the subject of his origin, the Southerners were not. It is from the Northern statesmen that the strictures on this score so largely have come down to us.

XXXVIII

JOHNSON AIDS THE PRISONERS' WIVES

JUDGE-Advocate-General Holt was a Kentuckian. Early in life he had migrated into Mississippi. He announced to Jefferson Davis and to Clement Clay when his adopted state seceded that he would espouse the Southern cause. He became an ardent Union man. "Joseph Holt of Kentucky, did you say, sir? I tell you, by Heaven! there is no such man as Joseph Holt of *Kentucky!*" exclaimed the venerable Crittenden.[1]

Holt was a remorseless prosecutor, the blind patron of notorious informers. His dealings with Sanford Conover make it difficult to believe that Holt was not wilfully blind. Rhodes speaks of him as one "whose credulity for a man of legal training was astonishing," [2]—it was at least that. Anyone who would believe Conover could believe anything. There was no lie so black but that Conover on a moment's notice could produce witnesses to substantiate. Two of Conover's rascals,—Campbell and Snevel—asserted that they were actually present with John A. Surratt in Richmond in the spring of 1865, and personally had heard an interview between Jefferson Davis and Judah Benjamin in which the murder of Lincoln was considered and approved.[3]

Such were the "facts" on which Holt, with Stanton's aid, had induced the President to sign the proclamation of May, 1865, charging Clement Clay and Davis with complicity in Lincoln's murder, and offering a reward for their arrest.[4] Holt and Stanton had been fellow members of Buchanan's Cabinet.[5] They had worked together then,—they were working together now.

Long before Conover's exposure as a suborner of perjury, Johnson had learned to distrust Holt. When on February 1st, 1866, it was suggested that Raphael Semmes should be tried before a military commission, Johnson refused, declaring that he wished

335

to put "no more in Holt's control than was absolutely necessary," that Holt was "cruel and remorseless," and that his tendencies "were very bloody." Pointing to a number of Holt's decisions on his desk, he spoke of them as partaking of the traits of Nero and of Draco.[6]

Mrs. Clement Clay, the lovely lady of the former Senator from Alabama, was in Washington at this time, seeking her husband's release from Fortress Monroe's dark casemates. She had plenty of opportunity for observing Holt, and she has described him as deaf to all appeals of justice and "instinct with the zeal of the fanatic."[7] She called at the White House many times and talked with Andrew Johnson. We catch a glimpse of him there as a man of gentle manners, chivalrous instincts and quiet courtesy. On the last day of January, 1866, she wrote her father: "I send you your long-sued-for pardon. . . . I am pressing my husband's case. . . . I am emboldened to hope the day not far distant when he will be a free man. Great political excitement now reigns. . . . The President is very kind to me always."[8]

One day in February, 1866, after many previous visits, Mrs. Clay entered the parlor of the White House in which the President stood waiting to receive her. She broke into the subject uppermost in her mind, but the President interposed: "Did you meet Stanton as you came in?" "I did," she answered, "and he had the audacity to bow to me." "The scoundrel," ejaculated the President, "he has been here for an hour clamoring for the blood of Davis and Clay!" "But you will release them?" his visitor inquired. "You must be patient," answered Johnson, "I must detain them a little longer to satisfy public clamor!"[9]

The evidence is strong that Holt, knowing how Davis and Clay held the secret of his original espousal of the Southern case, was bent on their "judicial murder."[10] He filed in the War Department his "report on the case of C. C. Clay, Jr."[11] The distracted wife applied there for an opportunity to examine it. It was denied. She wrote to Holt, but received no acknowledgment of her letter. "It was at this juncture," she later wrote, "that Mr. Johnson's friendliness was exhibited toward me; for happening to call upon him while the document was in his hands, I told him of my ill-success and growing despair at the obstacles that were presented to the granting of my every request at the War Department. I begged him to interpose and assist me to an interview with Mr. Clay, but, above all, at this important moment, to aid me in getting a copy of the charges formulated against him. Thereupon exacting from me a promise of complete secrecy, the President delivered his official copy of the 'Report' into my hands, that I might peruse it and make such excerpts as would aid me." [12]

Clay had been Holt's friend, he was a former Senator of the United States, a man of the highest character.[13] Of this former friend, Holt did not scruple to write that his guilt was "relieved of all improbability by his previous history and criminal surroundings." [14]

When Mrs. Clay returned this report to the President, she was keyed to a high pitch of alarm. "It is said, Mr. Johnson," she declared, "that you have refused to allow the military court, composed of Messrs. Holt, Speed and Stanton, to try Mr. Davis and Mr. Clay." The President bowed in affirmation. "Then I pray you," she continued, "to give me your solemn oath in the presence of the living God, that you will *never*, while in the Presidential chair, yield those two innocent men into the hands of that blood-seeking Military Commission!" Johnson answered: "I promise Mrs. Clay; trust me!" "I will; I do!" she cried.[15]

Late in December, 1865, armed with Johnson's permit to visit her incarcerated husband, Mrs. Clay arrived at the Fortress at breakfast time. But it was not until late afternoon that General Miles honored the President's order.[16]

On her return to Washington she called at once on Johnson. "He received me," she has written, "with his usual urbane manner, quite in contrast with my own indignant mood." "Mr. Johnson," she began, "who *is* the President of the United States?" He smiled and shrugged his shoulders. "I am supposed to be!" he said. "But you are not! Your autographed letter was of little more use to me when I reached Fortress Monroe than blank paper would have been! For hours it was not honored, during which time your Secretary of War held the wires and refused to allow me either to see my husband or to communicate with you!" As she continued to narrate what had taken place, Johnson was unable to repress his anger, but he only said: "When you go there again, you'll have no difficulty, I assure you!" "When may I?" she asked eagerly. "When you wish," he answered, and as always he was as good as his word.[17] When in January she again visited the Fortress, she found her way unhindered.[18]

Toward the end of the next month she was still hopefully awaiting her husband's long-deferred release. She understood something both of Johnson's problems and of the man, when she wrote: "The radical pressure on the President is fearful. . . . President Johnson will fall, if fall he must, battling." [19] On April 17th Clay was permitted to return to Alabama.[20] But Jefferson Davis was still in prison.

During this same month, another Southern lady was importuning the President for her husband's liberty. Raphael Semmes, the commander of the *Alabama*, had been in custody since his surrender. He was now released. Johnson admitted that he could no longer withstand the pleas of Mrs. Semmes. "The President," wrote Welles, "has a gentle and kind heart, melted by woman's tears." [21]

It was during that same month that Mrs. Jefferson Davis, who from Canada had written the President her "prayer" to see her husband, penned, she said "with tears enough to float it," was permitted to come on from Montreal to Fortress Monroe and there daily to cheer the prisoner.[22] "Dear wife," he had written her, "this is not the fate to which I invited you when the future was rose-colored for us both . . ." [23] and she had replied: "It is surely not the fate to which you invited me in brighter days, but you must remember that you did not invite me to a great hero's home, but to that of a plain farmer. I have shared all your triumphs, been the only beneficiary of them; now I am but claiming the privilege for the first time of being all to you." [24]

In May, 1866, Boutwell's judiciary committee decided that they would like personally to examine Campbell and Snevel,—Conover's star witnesses. Campbell was found and confessed that his deposition implicating Jefferson Davis was wholly false, that after it had been prepared and written out for him by Conover, he had committed it to memory, and that the other affiants were likewise suborned perjurers. Conover, in whose presence this retraction was made, was then permitted in the custody of the Sergeant-at-Arms to go to New York City in search for his other witnesses. On his arrival at the metropolis he eluded the officer and disappeared! A little later Snevel was found and told the committee that he likewise had been suborned to perjury by Conover. It was rather cheap for perjury,—Campbell had received $625 and Snevel but $475 from the Bureau of Military Justice! [25]

Such little incidents as these, however, had slight effect on Boutwell or his committee, which a few days later reported that Jefferson Davis was guilty not of treason alone, but of complicity in Lincoln's murder also. [26] Nothing further was done, however, toward formally accusing him of the latter crime.

It was at about this time that Secretary McCulloch, at President Johnson's request, paid a visit to the state prisoner at Fortress Monroe. [27] Upon his arrival there, he found Davis pacing one of the ramparts accompanied by two soldiers. McCulloch spent an hour or two conversing with the former President. "There have been few men," McCulloch later wrote, "more gifted than Mr. Davis, and few whose opportunities for intellectual culture have been more improved. . . . He had the bearing of a brave and high-bred gentleman, who, knowing that he would have been highly honored if the Confederate states had achieved their independence, would not and could not demean himself as a criminal because they had not." [28]

Reluctantly and only in response to direct questions, Davis told of the barbarous treatment that had been accorded him. Even then he was allowed no newspapers, and there was but one book in his room, a treatise on military tactics,—"a subject," as McCulloch wrote, "not especially interesting to the prisoner at that time and in that place." [29] Of the better treatment he was then receiving, Davis said: "Now I am permitted to have a daily walk, and my present quarters, as you perceive are such as a prisoner charged with high treason ought not to complain of." [30]

It was for treason that, at the May term of the United States

District Court of Virginia in 1866, Jefferson Davis was indicted. The Department of Justice had finally come to realize that if he were to be tried for treason, it could not be in the District of Columbia, but at the place where the alleged crime had been committed.[31] In his talk with Hugh McCulloch, Davis expressed but one anxiety and that was over the delay in bringing him to trial.[32] The year before, President Johnson had written to Chief Justice Chase to learn whether he would hold a term of the Circuit Court in Virginia during the autumn or early winter.[33] Chase declined.[34] And so Jefferson Davis continued to languish a prisoner of the United States.

XXXIX

SWINGING AROUND THE CIRCLE

SOME time back we were preparing to join Johnson in his "Swing Around the Circle." On the 28th of August, 1866, the Presidential party left the capital. Among the guests were Secretary Seward, Gideon Welles, Postmaster-General Randall, the President's daughter Mrs. Patterson and Senator Patterson of Tennessee, Col. Moore, the President's secretary, Mrs. Welles and her two sons, Edgar and John, Mrs. Farragut and Admiral Farragut, Generals Rousseau, Custer, Stedman, Stoneman, Crook and last, but not least, General Grant.[1] Stanton had advised the trip, but at the last moment declined to come because he said his wife was ill. "I think," wrote Welles, "Mrs. S. may be some but not seriously indisposed." [2]

The route planned and followed was via Baltimore, Philadelphia, New York, West Point, Albany, Auburn, Niagara Falls, Buffalo, Cleveland, Toledo, Detroit, Chicago, Springfield, Alton, St. Louis, Indianapolis, Louisville, Cincinnati, Columbus, Pittsburg, Harrisburg, Baltimore, and so back to Washington.[3]

It was a bold attempt to carry the Congressional elections that had prompted Johnson's purpose to speak face to face with the people of the North. It was by facing hostile as well as friendly crowds that he had risen from obscurity to fame. He was not unaware of his power to sway men, and he had determined to use it in furtherance of the cause of justice. His extemporaneous addresses, however, when reported, especially when badly or dishonestly reported, lack much as polished works of rhetoric. Somehow, nevertheless, in the ashes of the printed page we still can see the embers that once were kindling flames. Down in Tennessee there had been few newspapers, so that one speech could be repeated to many audiences without the danger of any one having heard of it before. How different this was throughout the North he was presently to learn.

The political warfare among the mountains of Tennessee called for quick work, sometimes with the pistol or the bowie knife,— one might be shot, but stabbing in the back was not in vogue; it was not good form down there. Johnson did not fully comprehend how perfectly the Radicals had organized to thwart him or how they would strive to make ridiculous or worse this well-intentioned progress through the cities of the North. They had the organization, they had the newspapers, and especially they had the pencil of Thomas Nast and the pen of Petroleum V. Nasby. They also had within their ranks nearly all the municipal and state officials.

"Along the whole line of travel of over two thousand miles and through perhaps thirty or forty Congressional districts," wrote Welles, "the Radical members absented themselves, evidently by preconcert, and the Radical state and municipal authorities acted in almost every case in concert with them." [4] The President's "speeches though assailed and ridiculed, were sound and patriotic. They were essentially but one speech often repeated. Though poorly reported and often misreported and misrepresented, the speech would do him no discredit as a patriot and a statesman." [5]

The beginning of the journey augured well. Without incident the party arrived at Philadelphia, where the President was escorted to his hotel by a gay procession in which the military was much in evidence. German singing societies sang to him and bands serenaded.[6] At Burlington, Bordentown, Trenton, New Brunswick, and all along, they were met by banners, flags, songs, serenades, girls with flowers and committees with their words of welcome.[7]

New York City then as now, was a gracious and enthusiastic host. At 11.30, on the morning of the 29th, a large and representative committee was in Jersey City awaiting the arrival of the Presidential train. Henry Clews, A. T. Stewart and other leading merchants, public officials, judges, and the members of the Manhattan Club all were there. Amid the white smoke from the fortifications, and the roar of guns that spoke from every warship in the harbor, the party finally landed at the Battery. Then came the march up Broadway to the City Hall.

The parade was headed by the 3rd Hussars, behind them came the 1st and 3rd Regiments of Cavalry. A platoon of mounted police was followed by a "barouche drawn by six black horses neatly caparisoned,"—the equipage of the President.[8] Other carriages followed containing Seward, Welles, Randall, Grant, Farragut and the rest.[9] More than twenty regiments of New York militia were in line. Flags fluttered gaily, while across the way hung banners of welcome. "Thrice welcome Andrew Johnson, the sword and buckler of the Constitution, the Union's hope, the People's Champion" was one. And another: "The Constitution —Washington established it, Lincoln defended it, Johnson preserved it."[10]

From the Battery to the City Hall, so the New York *Herald* tells us, there "was a complete jam from curbstone to doorways. Every window was filled with happy smiling faces, roofs were crowded while every tree and awning post was alive with men and boys. . . . As the cortege drew nearer the vivas grew louder, every window was white with cambric waved by fair hands, flags gracefully dipped and bugles bugled. . . . The windows of the houses surrounding the (City Hall) Park were filled with gaily attired ladies while the roofs were crowded with members of the sterner sex."[11]

When the procession reached the City Hall, the crowds if anything were denser. Mayor Hoffman formally welcomed the President to the city. The Veterans of the War of 1812 were drawn up in his honor. Everyone, declares the New York *Herald,* was "anxious to catch a glimpse of the Chief Magistrate of the country who so well deserved the popular ovation."[12] "Even the old man of the seas, Gideon Welles," this account continues, "unused to and consequently little apt to be moved by popular enthusiasm, was touched by the scene and leaning toward Mr. Johnson asked, 'What do you think of that sir?' 'It's wonderful,' " the President replied.[13] Such were the feelings of the people, before the Radicals had had full opportunity by ridicule and systematic calumny to turn them from approval.

For the evening a great banquet at Delmonico's was planned. William H. Vanderbilt and other leaders in every avenue of endeavor were invited and appeared. There was a sumptuous repast such as only Delmonico's of the old days could provide. Amid tumults of applause Johnson was then introduced. "All that is wanting in the great struggle in which we are engaged," he said, "is simply to develop the popular heart of the nation. It is like latent fire. . . . We have just passed through a bloody perilous conflict . . . we have gentlemen . . . with us . . . who have . . . participated in these struggles for the preservation of the Union. [Great applause.] Here is the army (pointing to the right, where sat General Grant) and here the navy (pointing to the left in the direction of Admiral Farragut) . . . and will it be improper . . . to say that the Secretary of State has done his part? [Cheers.] . . . But though the Government has done its duty . . . there is still a greater and more important task for you and others to perform. [Cheers.]" [14]

Warming to his work, Johnson plunged into the heart of the theme that he was determined to get before the American people. The suppression of the Rebellion, he told them, had established the great fact that no states had the right "by forcible or by peaceable means to separate themselves from the Union. [Cheers. 'Good.'] That having been settled in the field, and in . . . the executive department of the Government . . . there is another department of your Government which has . . . declared . . . that the Government was dissolved and the states were out of the Union. . . . And now when the doctrine is established that they have no right to withdraw . . . and the states again . . . renew their relations, as far as in them lies, with the Federal Government, we find that when they present representatives to the Congress of the United States, in violation of the sacred charter of liberty, which declares that you cannot even by amendment of the Constitution . . . deprive any of them of their representation . . . that these states of the Union have been and still are denied their representation in the Senate and in the House of Representa-

HIS HONOR MAYOR HOFFMAN RECEIVING PRESIDENT JOHNSON AND PARTY AT PIER NO. 1, NORTH RIVER, NEW YORK CITY, AUGUST 29TH.

tives. Will we then in the struggle which is now before us, submit, will the American people submit to this practical dissolution, a doctrine that we have repudiated? . . . The issue is before you, and before the country." [15]

Interrupted with increasing frequency by loud cheering, with a crescendo of rhetorical questioning, Johnson continued to inquire if the country were prepared to permit the states to "remain as they are, in practical dissolution. . . ." Amid cries of "No, no,—never" and renewed cheering he asked: "Are we prepared to renew the scene through which we have passed? . . . Are we again prepared to see . . . this land . . . drenched in a brother's blood? ['Never, never.' Cheers.] Are we not rather prepared to bring from Gilead the balm that has relief in its character and pour it into the wound? [Loud cheering.]" [16]

Comparing his distracted country to a family rent by quarrels, —in language that was now on fire, he thus spoke of his Southern fellow countrymen: "They are our brethren. [Cheers.] They are part of ourselves. ['Hear! Hear!'] They are bone of our bone and flesh of our flesh. [Cheers.] They have lived with us and been part of us from the establishment of the Government to the commencement of the Rebellion. They are identified with its history, with all its prosperity. . . . We have had a hiatus, as it were, but . . . we have come together again; and now after having understood what the feud was, and the great apple of discord removed; having lived under the Constitution of the United States in the past, they ask to live under it in the future." [17]

"Why is a Southern man not to be believed?" he asked. The audience cried out: "They are to be believed!" And Johnson went on: "Thank God, though I say it myself, I feel that I have attained opinions . . . that are coextensive with all these states, with all the people of them." There was great applause and the whole audience rose to its feet waving handkerchiefs, while a voice called out, "That's the best thing tonight!" [18]

As soon as silence was restored, Johnson went on: "While I am a Southern man, I am a Northern man; that is to say I am a citizen of the United States [Cheers], and I am willing to concede to all other citizens what I claim for myself. . . . The

Southern states or their leaders proposed a separation. . . . We said 'You shall not separate, you shall remain with us and the Constitution shall be preserved and enforced.' [Cheers.] The rebellion has ceased and when their arms were put down by the army and navy of the United States they accepted the terms of the Government. We said to them before the termination of the Rebellion, 'Disband your armies, return to your original position in the government and we will receive you with open arms.' . . . They accepted the proposition of the Government and said: 'We have been mistaken, we selected the arbitrament of the sword, and that arbiter has decided against us, and that being so . . . we accept the terms you offer us.' " [19]

"The query comes up," continued Johnson, "will they be accepted? Do we want to humiliate them and degrade them and tread them in the dust? ['No, no.' Cheers.] . . . I do not want them to come back into this Union a degraded and debased people. [Loud cheers.] They are not fit to be a part of this great American family if they are degraded and treated with ignominy and contempt. I want them when they come back to become a part of this great country, an honored portion of the American people. I want them to come back with all their manhood; then they are fit and not without that to be a part of these United States. [Cheers, 'Three cheers for Andrew Johnson.'] . . . Why should we distrust the Southern people?" [20]

"I do not come here tonight to apologize for persons who have tried to destroy this Government; and if every act of my life either in speeches or in practice, does not disprove the charge that I want to apologize for them, there is no use in man's having a public record. [Cheers.] But I am one of those who take the Southern people with all their heresies and errors, admitting that in rebellion they did wrong. . . . We have in the West a game called hammer and anvil, and anvil and hammer, and while Davis and others were talking about separation in the South, there was another class, Phillips, Garrison, and men of that kind who were talking about dissolution in the North; and of these extremes one was the hammer and the other was the anvil; and when the Rebellion broke out one extreme was carrying it out, and now that it is suppressed, the other class are still trying to give it life and effect."

"I fought those in the South who commenced the rebellion, and now I oppose those in the North who are trying to break up the Union. [Cheers.] I am for the Union. I am against all those who are opposed to the Union. [Great applause.] I am for the Union, the whole Union and nothing but the Union. [Renewed applause.]"

Amid increased applause, shouts of approval and loud cheering, Johnson concluded: "The cup of my ambition has been filled to overflowing with the exception of one thing. Will you hear what that is? [Cries of 'Yes' and 'What is it?'] . . . I find the union of these states in peril. If I can now be instrumental in keeping the possession of it in your hands, in the hands of the people; in restoring prosperity and advancement in all that makes a nation great, I will be willing to exclaim as Simeon did of old of Him who had been born in a manger, that I have seen the glory of thy salvation, let thy servant depart in peace. [Applause.] . . . I would rather live in history, in the affection of my countrymen as having consummated this great end, than to be President of the United States forty times." [21]

It was a great occasion, and a great speech. Open-minded, fair, intelligent, New York City heard and approved his denunciation of the Northern disunionists and his fiery determination to defend the Constitution against them. "I am proud," he told them, "to find a liberal and a comprehensive view of this whole question on the part of the people of New York. I am proud to find too that here you don't believe that your existence depends upon aggression and destruction; and while you are willing to live you are willing to let others live." [22]

Later in the evening a great throng marched to his hotel. He appeared upon the balcony and addressed them. Not since the Prince of Wales had thrilled New York six years before, had there been such crowds to welcome any visitor. [23]

Despite his desperately serious resolve to bring his message to the people, he occasionally relaxed. All his cares had not lessened his interest in good horses. He was driven through Central

Park the next day, on his way to board the boat for Albany. But it was no ordinary drive. That evening Joseph Choate wrote to his sister: "The President (Johnson) has gone, and New York has relapsed into its usual repose. There is a very funny story in the evening papers of their departure this morning. They took the boat at Manhattanville, in order to drive through the Park, and General Grant, who was in Mr. Jerome's great 'drag' insisted on taking the reins himself, and four in hand running a race with the President and six, beating him of course." [24]

§

The *River Queen*, whose cabin had furnished a conference room for Lincoln and the Southern commissioners eighteen months before, was the vessel chosen to convey the Presidential party up the Hudson River.[25] As they passed West Point the cadets were drawn up for the President's inspection, while all along the shores, from villages and towns, crowds assembled at the water's edge to cheer. On nearing Albany a reception committee came alongside to welcome the visitors in the name of that historic city.[26] The true feelings of the people were thus reflected, but by no means those of the Radicals, who had been watching with dismay the auspicious beginnings of the tour. "Swinging Around the Circle" was not to be the success it promised, if they could prevent it.

The Radicals had determined to ignore or to insult the President wherever possible, while their newspapers gave caricatured reports of all his speeches.[27] "The reception," wrote Welles, "was everywhere enthusiastic and the demonstrations, especially in the principal cities, were in numbers most extraordinary and overwhelming. In Philadelphia where the Radical authorities would not participate the people filled the streets so that it was difficult to get through them. This proceeding at Philadelphia was the beginning of a series of petty spite on the part of the Radical managers, which was advised and determined upon before we left Washington, and of which I became satisfied Stanton was cognizant." [28]

From Albany the Presidential party hurried on to Auburn, with brief halts at Schenectady, Utica, Rome and Syracuse. When he had not time for more, Johnson would tell his audience: "I leave in your hands the Constitution and the Union, and the glorious flag of your country not with twenty-five but with thirty-six stars." [29]

At Rome the Mayor of the city gave thanks that Andrew Jackson's robes of office had fallen "where they fit so well," to which Johnson replied that if accounts of human affairs could be communicated to the dead, "old Jackson . . . would turn over in his grave, burst open his coffin and leaving the habiliments of the dead would raise his bony arm and extend his long forefinger and say as of old, 'By the Eternal, the Federal Union must and shall be preserved.'" [30]

The party arrived finally at Niagara Falls, where the first Sunday of the tour was passed.[31] With all his great arts of persuasion, Johnson had endeavored to win the people of the Empire State to his support. Those in his party trembled for his health. It seemed to them as if no one could go through such extraordinary labor day after day. They remonstrated with him in vain. He felt, said Welles "that he was performing a service and a duty in his appeals to his countrymen, and desired to address them face to face on the great issues before the country. It was the method to which he had been accustomed in Tennessee and the Southwest, and he believed it would be effective in the North." [32]

§

Johnson and his entourage arrived at Cleveland on September 3rd. On that day there was assembling at Philadelphia another convention,—the handiwork of the Radicals. Its stated purpose was that of "bringing the loyal Unionists of the South into conjunctive action with the true friends of Republican government in the North." [33] Its real design was, if possible, to destroy all the effects achieved by Johnson's convention held in that city twenty days before.[34] Its immediate objective was to furnish a reservoir of abuse, from which might be drawn a propaganda wherewith to counteract the influence of Johnson's speeches in his "Swing Around the Circle."

"The loyal Unionists" of the South were an anomalous body of men. They were those who had not joined their neighbors in 1861 or later, in repelling what the Southerners considered a Northern invasion of their country. There had been, throughout the war, Union men in North Carolina, Eastern Tennessee and Northern Georgia, but in no instance had they maintained a party organization. The landed people, the backbone of the South, had supported the Confederacy.[35] The one influential public character of the South to remain, throughout the conflict loyal to the Union, was Andrew Johnson himself.

The amount of Union sentiment obtaining in the South had, during the war, been overestimated in the North.[36] After the war the Radicals began devoting great attention to the "loyal Unionists" of the South. They well knew that these, both through lack of numbers and of economic and social position, were without influence. The Radical program was to give them power through Northern bayonets and negro suffrage, to continue the Republican party in power in the nation by imposing it upon the South. For purposes both selfish and unworthy, the Radicals were coöperating with the lowest elements of the South. Knowing the South, as no Radical could hope to know it, Johnson was seeking to encourage,—indeed had encouraged—the real South, the leaders of opinion there, to return to their old loyalty to the Union and to reëstablish the United States.

No clearer illustration of these differences could be found than by a comparison of this "loyalist" gathering of September 3rd, with the Johnson convention of twenty days before. To the latter, the leaders of the old South had come seeking peace and concord. To this conclave of September 3rd, in addition to the Radicals who had conceived and planned it, there came a few scattered delegates from the late Confederate states who, as even Rhodes admits, "compared unfavorably in character or ability with those of the earlier convention, and for the most part were soldiers of political fortune." [37]

What a contrast was here presented to the convention that had endorsed Andrew Johnson! Instead of delegates marching arm in arm into the Convention Hall, this gathering immediately split into two unassimilable groups,—one containing the delegates from the South and the other those from the North. Of the former, Durant was chosen temporary chairman, while the permanent chairmanship was given to James Speed.[38] This was the same Speed who had been for fifteen months content to sit in Johnson's Cabinet! He had come now to assail his former chief. For three days the Northern, and for two days longer the Southern half remained in session, rivaling each other in denunciation of Johnson and in praise of Congress. No one was more vitriolic, no one more unfair than Johnson's former Cabinet member.

On taking the chair, Speed let loose a torrent of abuse. Sneering at the former Philadelphia gathering, he declared that it had convened simply to "record in abject submission the commands of one man. That convention did his commands. The loyal Congress of the United States have refused to do his commands; and whenever you have a Congress that does not resolutely and firmly refuse, as the present Congress has done, to merely act as the recording secretary of the tyrant at the White House, American liberty is gone forever." [39]

The strategy of the Radicals was to make it appear that the "loyal men of the South" were crying to the North for aid, and thereby to justify the Fourteenth Amendment and further programs as yet undisclosed that would disfranchise the former adherents of the Confederacy. The Radicals were dreaming, plotting and preparing for the carpet-bag régime.

Before adjournment of the Southern branch of the convention, an appeal "from the loyal men of the South to their fellow citizens of the United States" was prepared. "Having lost our champion" this read, "we return to you who can make Presidents and punish traitors. . . . We cannot better define our wrongs and our wants than by declaring that since Andrew Johnson affiliated with his early slanderers and our constant enemies, his hand has been laid heavily upon every earnest loyalist of the South." [40] As though they were representative of anything, these Southern "loyalists" adopted a long set of resolutions, purporting to speak for the "loyal people of the South." They denounced the "policy pursued by Andrew Johnson" as "oppressive and intolerable." [41]

In language which the ears of all Radicals were attuned to heed, they continued: "The political status of the states lately in rebellion . . . and the rights of the people of such states are political questions, and are therefore already within the control of Congress to the exclusion of the independent action *of any and every other department of the Government*." [42] Here was a plain warning, not to Andrew Johnson only, but to the Supreme Court of the United States as well. Another paragraph of these resolutions declared that "there can be no . . . safety for the country . . . unless the Government by national and appropriate legislation, enforced by national authority, shall confer on every citizen in the states we represent . . . impartial suffrage and equality before the law." [43]

Under the guidance of Speed's legal mind, the draftsmen chose their language carefully. Instead of advocating in plain words the granting to illiterate negroes of the power to vote,—an idea utterly repulsive to the North, except as applied to the South— they prayed for "impartial suffrage." That negro suffrage should be "enforced by national authority" only below the Mason-Dixon line they were careful to make plain by asserting that it should be conferred "in the states we represent."

One would think to read some of the accounts of this Southern half of the convention, that it was a body authorized to declare the sentiments of impressive numbers in the South. How farcical is this view becomes apparent with the realization that it was composed of but seventy-eight "delegates," and that only nine of the Southern states were represented. Two of the nine (Alabama and North Carolina) voted against the resolutions! Three only were represented by as many as ten "delegates"! Georgia had but nine, Alabama five, North Carolina and Florida each three, Arkansas two and Mississippi one! [44]

"The one objective point proclaimed in the address, repeated in the resolutions echoed and reëchoed by every speaker both in the Northern and Southern convention," says Blaine, "was the adoption of the Fourteenth Amendment. It was evidently the unalterable determination of the Republicans to make that the leading feature of the campaign, to enforce it in every party convention, to urge it through the press, to present it on the stump, to proclaim it through every authorized exponent of public opinion. They were determined that the Democratic party of the North should not be allowed to ignore it or in any way to evade it. It was to be the Shibboleth of the Republican canvass. . . ." [45]

§

"At Cleveland there was evidently a concerted plan," wrote Welles, "to prevent the President from speaking or to embarrass him in his remarks. Grant I think had been advised of this, and it affected him unfavorably." [46] Johnson was to be made aware of the conspiracy, when on the evening of September 3rd, from the balcony of one of Cleveland's famous hostelries,—the Kennard House—he stood up to greet a crowd, most of whom had come to welcome and applaud him. [47]

Wherever Johnson had thus far spoken, he had been accorded a respectful audience, in some places, as in New York City, he had encountered wild outbursts of approval. [48] But the gathering of the Radicals in Philadelphia was giving their adherents everywhere new heart, while the Radical press from the beginning of the tour had belched forth every calumny within the range of printer's ink. Johnson had been pilloried as a "renegade," a "traitor," the "great apostate," a "faithless demagogue," the "man made President by John Wilkes Booth," the "great accidental," and the "great pardoner." [49] Six days before his appearance at Cleveland, the Philadelphia press had burst into this rhymed slander:

> Faithful among the faithless once we thought thee,
> Faithless among the faithful now thou art,
> To this sad depth has vain ambition brought thee,
> Man of weak brain and cold ungrateful heart.
> Better for thee, our hope once and our pride,
> If thou hadst fallen when great Lincoln died. [50]

Had Johnson "fallen when great Lincoln died," he would have escaped all that he endured in Lincoln's stead.

Standing there on the balcony of the Kennard House, Johnson

was presently to be aware that he was in Ohio, the state of Benjamin F. Wade. Wade in whose behalf the conspiracy of the Radicals was already well matured,—the conspiracy to make him President of the Senate, and then by impeaching Andrew Johnson, President of the United States! [51] Ben Wade for President! Then could they accord the South the iron terms of the conqueror!

Andrew Johnson was now fighting with his back to the wall. He was fighting one of the brave fights of American history. If he could only win, all of Lincoln's hopes for binding up the nation's wounds might be achieved. But Lincoln's enemies were determined to destroy Lincoln's follower. After all the malice that the Radicals had heaped upon him, is it any wonder that he now struck back, departing perhaps at times, from that abstract standard of dignity that his enemies had erected for him, reserving for themselves, meanwhile, the privilege of bespattering him with the sewage of their malevolence. [52]

Johnson stepped out on the balcony of the Kennard House not to make a speech, but merely to greet the crowd that came to do him honor, little knowing that his enemies had scattered claques and interruptors. [53] He thanked them for their demonstration of approval, adding that he did not consider it personal, but as an indication of the "feeling of the great mass of the people," on the questions then before the country. "I am before you," he said, "as an American citizen simply, and not as Chief Magistrate clothed in the insignia and paraphernalia of state. Being an inhabitant of a state of this Union, I know it has been said that I was an alien [Laughter and cries of 'Shame']. . . . Therefore all that was necessary . . . was to declare the office vacant or, under a pretext to prefer articles of impeachment, and thus the individual who occupies the Chief Magistracy was to be disposed of and driven from power. [Cries of 'Never.'] [54] . . . Notwithstanding a mendacious press, notwithstanding a subsidized gang of hirelings who have not ceased to traduce me, I have discharged all my official duties and fulfilled my pledges. [55] . . . I say here tonight that if my predecessor had lived, the vials of wrath would have been poured out upon him. [Cries 'Never, never,' and three cheers for the Congress of the United States.]" [56]

"Who is he," continued Johnson, "that can come and place his finger upon one pledge I ever violated, or one principle I ever proved false to? [Voice: 'New Orleans.' Another: 'Why don't you hang Jeff Davis.' And still another: 'Hang Thad. Stevens and Wendell Phillips.'] Hang Jeff Davis?" queried Johnson, and then there were cries and shouts of "Down with him." "Why don't you hang him?" Johnson asked. From the crowd came cries: "Give us the opportunity." "Haven't you got the court?" continued Johnson. "Haven't you got the Attorney-General? Who is your Chief Justice who has refused to sit on this trial? [Groans and cheers.] I am not the Chief Justice! I am not the Attorney-General! I am no jury! But I'll tell you what I did do. I called upon your Congress that is trying to break up the Government. [Hisses and cries of 'A lie.'] Great confusion. [Voice: 'Don't get mad.'] I am not mad. [Hisses.]" [57]

The plug-uglies of the Radicals were indeed at work. The scene was fast assuming the dimensions of a riot. Perhaps it would have been wiser for the President to have retired, but he was not accustomed to retiring under fire. It was by conquering such crowds in the mountain towns of Tennessee that he had welded his great strength and had builded a prestige that forced the Unionists in 1864 to make him Lincoln's running mate. Johnson went on. It was rough and tumble repartee. This was no gathering of "cultivated and morally excellent people," it was a fight! "I will tell you," he said, "who is mad. Whom the Gods want to destroy they first make mad." Going back to the former interruption as to the Davis trial, he continued: "Did your Congress order any of them to be tried? [Three cheers for Congress.] . . . My intention was to address myself to your common sense, your judgment and your better feeling, not to the passion and malignancy in your hearts. [Cheers.]" [58]

That was his hope, but he was speaking in the very stronghold of Ben Wade! "In this assembly here tonight," he continued, "the remark has been made traitor! traitor! My countrymen, will you hear me? [Shouts of 'Yes.'] And will you hear me for my cause and for the Constitution of my country? [Applause.] I want to know when or where or under what circumstances

Andrew Johnson, not as Chief Executive, but in any capacity ever deserted any principle or violated the Constitution of his country. [Cries of 'Never.']"

It was evident enough that he had friends as well as enemies in that crowd. Traitor! The Secessionists of Tennessee had called him that, and now that he was seeking to accord the entire South Lincoln's plan of justice, these Northern enemies of reunion were plying him with the same epithet. Traitor! It was to become a watchword with the Radicals! Traitor? But was not William Seward coöperating with him?

"Let me ask . . . this audience," continued Johnson, "if your Secretary of State who served four years under Mr. Lincoln and who was placed upon the butcher's block as it were, and hacked to pieces by the assassin's knife, when he turned traitor? [Cries of 'Never.'] If I were disposed to play the orator and deal in declamation tonight, I would imitate one of the ancient tragedies, and would take William H. Seward and bring him before you and point you to the hacks and scars upon his person. [A voice: 'God bless him.'] I would exhibit the bloody garments saturated with gore from his gushing wounds. Then I would ask you why not hang Thad. Stevens and Wendell Phillips?" [59]

And he continued: "I have been fighting the South and they have been whipped and crushed, and they acknowledge their defeat and accept the terms of the Constitution; and now as I go around the circle, having fought traitors at the South, I am prepared to fight traitors at the North. [Cheers.] God willing, with your help, we will do it. [Cries of 'We won't.'] It will be crushed, North and South, and this glorious Union of ours will be preserved. [Cheers.] . . . Are you for dividing this country? [Cries of 'No.'] Then I am President, and I am President of the whole United States. [Cheers.]" [60]

Blazing away undaunted, he went on: "I understand the discordant notes in this crowd tonight. He who is opposed to the restoration of this Government and the reunion of the states is as great a traitor as Jeff Davis or Wendell Phillips. [Loud cheers.] I am against both. [Cries of 'Give it to them.' Laughter and cheers.] Some of you talk about traitors in the South, who have not courage to get away from your homes to fight them." [61]

Thinking of the grafters, and those who for three hundred dollars had bought their way out of the draft, Johnson continued: "The courageous men, Grant, Sherman, Farragut, and the long list of the distinguished sons of the Union were in the field and led on their gallant hosts to conquest and to victory while you remained cowardly at home. [Applause. 'Bully.'] Now when these brave men have returned . . . they find you at home speculating and committing frauds on the Government. [Laughter and cheers.] [62] . . . You pretend now to have great respect and sympathy for the poor brave fellow who left an arm on the battlefield. [Cries: 'Is this dignified?'] I understand you. You may talk about the dignity of the President. [Cries: 'How was it about his making a speech on the 22nd of February?']" [63]

Realizing full well that his interrupters were the hirelings of the Radicals he continued: "It is time that the great mass of the people should understand what your designs are. [A voice: 'What did General Butler say?'] What did General Butler says? [Hisses.] What did Grant say? [Cheers.] And what does General Grant say about General Butler? [Laughter and cheers.] What does General Sherman say? [A voice: 'What does General Sheridan say? New Orleans? New Orleans?'] General Sheridan says that he is for the restoration of the government that General Sheridan fought for. ['Bully.'] [64]

Dignity! How the historians have assailed him for his supposed lack of it. Hand-to-hand fighting may not be dignified but it is brave, and in a worthy cause admirable. Do you think Roosevelt or Andrew Jackson would have retreated from that crowd? Dignity is an admirable thing in a President, but courage is equally desirable. "I care not for dignity," cried Johnson. "There is a portion of your countrymen who will always respect their fellow-citizens when they are entitled to respect, and there is a portion of them who have no respect for themselves and consequently have no respect for others." [65]

At this point someone called out "Traitor." "I wish I could

see that man," cried Johnson. "I would bet you now that if the light fell on your face cowardice and treachery would be seen in it. Show yourself. Come out here where I can see you. [Shouts of laughter.] If you ever shoot a man you will do it in the dark . . . when no one is by to see you. [Cheers.] I understand traitors. I have been fighting them at the south end of the line, and we are now fighting them in the other direction. [Laughter and cheers.]" [66]

"I come," he continued, "neither to criminate nor recriminate, but when attacked my plan is to defend myself. [Cheers.] When encroached upon, I care not from what quarter it comes, it is entitled to resistance. As Chief Magistrate I felt so after taking the oath to support the Constitution, and when I saw encroachments upon your Constitution . . . I dared to sound the tocsin of alarm. [Three cheers for Andrew Johnson.] Then if this be right, the head and front of my offending is in telling when the Constitution of your country has been trampled upon. . . ." [67]

"I love my country. Every public act of my life testifies that is so. . . . And what is my offending? [A voice: 'Because you are not a Radical,' and cry of 'Veto.'] Somebody says veto. Veto of what? What is called the Freedman's Bureau Bill? I can tell you what it is." And then he launched into a discussion of that measure, and continued: "I tell you, my countrymen, that though the power of hell, death, and Stevens . . . combined, there is no power that can control me save you . . . and the God that spoke me into existence. . . ." [68]

As Johnson himself said: "I have been drawn into this long speech, while I intended simply to make acknowledgments for the cordial welcome. . . ." [69] Trained as he had been in the rough and tumble of Tennessee campaigning, he could not resist the temptation to reply to the premeditatedly insulting interruptions which met him almost as soon as he began to speak. In the midst of a crowd, [70] the large majority of which was orderly, a plainly concerted plan on the part of a few to prevent his speaking was apparent. [71] In Tennessee the episode would have been known only to those who saw and heard, or to the few readers of a small local paper. But this was no longer Tennessee, and when this

Cleveland meeting was broadcast through the nation by an unfriendly press, all that he had thus far accomplished on his tour was endangered, and the future of his policies was put in jeopardy.[72]

But as we turn from the jibes of the historians upon this incident: Rhodes that it was a scene "which seemed to drag the Presidential office to the lowest depth of degradation,"[73] Burgess that it was an "undignified and even vulgar altercation,"[74] and many others,[75] we should not forget that Andrew Johnson was engaged in the most desperate political struggle since secession, that he was carrying on a hand-to-hand combat with Lincoln's enemies, with whom conciliation had proved idle, and soft-spoken words an invitation to new assaults.

§

Lincoln's great Secretary of State, and his trusted former military governor and running mate, were pouring their whole hearts into the fulfillment of Lincoln's hopes. As they went about their work, there sat within his cheerful Elmwood study in literary Cambridge, surrounded by the English poets, detached from all the conflict, the first editor of the *Atlantic Monthly*,—James Russell Lowell. Without personal knowledge of the facts, influenced, of course, by the vituperation which he saw in print, he sat down and wrote in limpid flowing prose, and in the October issue of the *North American Review* published as harsh, as unjust and as untrue reflections upon William Seward and Andrew Johnson as any that could be found within the poisoned columns of the daily press.

Blessed with a large share of "book education," he had also that class consciousness, and lack of broad sympathy so often found in men removed from the hard struggles of real life. At all costs we must be decorous! The voice should never be raised! With blazing eyes and panting breath, back to the wall to fight with all the life force for a principle,—this was unseemly!

Johnson—what could you expect of him, he did not belong to the caste! But Seward, ah, that was different, he was deserting the cause of the well-born! "We pity Mr. Seward in his new office of bear-leader," wrote Lowell. "How he must hate his Bruin when it turns out that his tricks do not even please the crowd." [76]

With unction he spoke of Johnson's "vulgarity" and "catch-rabble devices," [77] and of the "unseemly side of democratic institutions," [78] sneered at New York City's "illustrious guest," and "for so much of Mr. Johnson's harangues as is not positively shocking," expressed derision.[79]

So much for Johnson, but when it came to Seward, a note of hushed regret creeps in, much like the subdued voice of the banker who sadly whispers of some infirmity of a rich depositor. "In speaking," says Lowell, "of the late unhappy exposure . . . we have been far from desirous of insisting on Mr. Seward's share in it. We endeavored to account for it at first by supposing that the Secretary of State seeing into the hands of how vain and weak a man the reins of administration had fallen, was willing by flattering his vanity to control his weakness for the public good. But we are forced against our will to give up any such theory, and to confess that Mr. Seward's nature has been 'subdued to what it works in.' " [80]

"We see it," unctuously continues Lowell, "with sincere sorrow, and are far from adding our voice to the popular outcry against a man the long and honorable services of whose prime we are not willing to forget in the decline of his abilities and that dry-rot of the mind's nobler temper which so often results from the possession of power." He attributed Seward's decline to his "long contact with the meaner qualities of men." [81]

Sorrowfully the strictures upon Seward were put down, but with unmixed glee Lowell wrote that Andrew Johnson "will be indignantly remembered as the first and we trust the last, of our chief magistrates who believed in the brutality of the people and gave to the White House the ill-savor of a corner-grocery. He a tribune of the people? A lord of misrule, an abbot of unreason much rather!" [82]

Disclaiming any bias for Thaddeus Stevens and his "foolish violence," Lowell continued: "Let there be no more foolish talk of impeachment for what is at best a poor infirmity of nature and

THE ARRIVAL OF THE PRESIDENT AND SUITE AT DELMONICO'S, CORNER OF FIFTH AVENUE AND FOURTEENTH STREET, NEW YORK CITY, WHERE THE MILITARY PASSED IN REVIEW.

could only be raised into a harmful importance by being invested with the dignity of a crime against the state. . . ." [83]   How imbued with Radical doctrine this editor of the *Atlantic* was, appeared with this endorsement of the Congressional theory: ". . . the will of the majority, or the national necessity for the time-being has always been constitutional. . . . We have the same right to impose terms and to demand guaranties that Prussia has, that the victor always has." [84]

This was bad enough, but from such a man we should not expect sheer falsehood. Yet Lowell has set down, so all historians might copy, and school boys of future generations read, this mean mendacity; he described Johnson's tour as a "discreditable" and "indecent orgy." [85] Lowell knew that the President was traveling with his daughter and that there were in the party other ladies, among whom were Mrs. Welles and Mrs. Farragut. [86] Had Johnson been the villain that the Radicals depicted, he would never, under these circumstances, have indulged in an "indecent orgy." [87]

To the writings of Lowell, Rhodes would naturally turn. And so we find him soberly declaring, upon the sole authority of Lowell, who knew nothing of the facts, that "part of the journey was 'an indecent orgy.'" As though not content with this, on his own account, without any authority, Rhodes has added: "When Johnson appeared on the balcony of the Kennard House in Cleveland (September 3rd) to speak to the people he was intoxicated. . . ."—"I challenge the proof of these cruel statesments," James Schouler, a careful historian has written, and further: "Not only do I find the evidence for such charges wholly wanting, but not even a responsible charge made by any one who was an eye-witness, nor indeed a clear contemporary charge of the kind at all." [88]

That there was no "responsible" charge "by anyone who was an eye-witness" is true. But when Schouler wrote that there was no "clear contemporary charge of the kind at all," he must have overlooked the speeches of Thaddeus Stevens and the private letters of Edwin Stanton written secretly from Washington, while Johnson and Seward were endeavoring to fulfill Lincoln's aspiration for a "just and lasting peace."

Not only have we the faithful record of Gideon Welles, who was an eye-witness and who fails even to hint at intoxication of the President, but we are furnished with this positive assertion of Benjamin C. Truman who accompanied the Presidential party throughout the entire tour: "As a member of that party I can say," he later wrote, "that there was no drunkenness at all on the trip." [89]

§

On the morning following the Cleveland speech Johnson and his guests pushed on through Ohio to Toledo and Detroit, arriving finally at Chicago. The Radicals had now organized to meet their advance, as though preparing for a hostile army. As the train sped on through Ben Wade's state, the Presidential party was met at Elyria with black flags.[90] At Chicago according to Welles, "the reception was magnificent." [91] But all that it was possible to do the Radicals had done, to dim this welcome. Bands were heard to play the "Dead March." [92] The city of Chicago was the ostensible objective of the whole journey, and it was here amid "imposing ceremonies" that the cornerstone of the Douglas monument was laid.[93] But despite the magnificent reception given Johnson, banners were nevertheless discerned on which the words "No welcome to Traitors" had been written.[94]

From Chicago the party journeyed down to Springfield and thence to Alton, where they were met by thirty-six steamers crowded with people, and were escorted by them to St. Louis.[95] The vessel carrying the President across the Mississippi had been named the *Andy Johnson* in his honor. The thirty-six boats participating were symbolic of the "states within the Union." [96] At St. Louis there was a cordiality and a sincerity elsewhere unsurpassed.[97] And yet it was here that the Radicals had organized their meanest demonstration. Both branches of the "Loyalist Convention" had adjourned, and upwards of a score of the most virulent of the delegates were now following over Johnson's route, seeking to undo all that he had done in furtherance of Lincoln's plan.[98] They had come, these locusts of discord, as their spokesman Parson Brownlow said, "to try to wipe out the moccasin tracks of Andrew Johnson and William H. Seward," and those of the "untamed and unmitigated Copperheads who were sliming and crawling along" in their wake."[99]

Johnson's staunch friend, Senator John R. Doolittle of Wisconsin, had written him ten days before: "I hope you will not allow the excitement of the moment to draw from you any extemporaneous speeches. You are followed by the reporters of a hundred presses who do nothing but misrepresent. I would say nothing which had not been most carefully prepared, beyond a simple acknowledgment for their cordial reception. Our enemies, your enemies, have never been able to get any advantage from anything you ever wrote. But what you have said extemporaneously in answer to some questions has given them a handle to use against us."[100] "I have so expressed myself," wrote Welles, "both to Mr. Lincoln and Mr. Johnson. The former used to say he knew it was 'risky'; that he disliked it, but knew not how he could always escape, and he generally tried to get his thoughts in writing. President Johnson always heard my brief suggestions quietly, but manifestly thought I did not know his power as a speaker."[101] While on the tour, Welles suggested to Seward that Johnson's speaking might be injudicious, but Seward did not think so. He said the President was doing good, and was "the best stump speaker in the country." But, our diarist shrewdly comments: "The President should not be a stump speaker."[102]

On the evening of September 8th the leading citizens of St. Louis, at the Southern Hotel, were tendering the President a great civic banquet. The Presidential party and their hosts were waiting in the hotel parlors for the signal to move out into the banquet room.[103] In the meantime a crowd had been assembling in the street and was now vociferously clamoring for a speech.[104] Some of the citizens even pushed their way into the hotel and asked him to respond to the assembled throng.[105] Mindful of Doolittle's good advice, Johnson declined,[106] but the demands from the outside became louder and more importunate. The members of the reception committee now put their heads together, and as the crowd continued to call, it was finally suggested by members of the committee that Johnson "ought to go out and show himself to the people and say a few words at any rate." [107] Reluctant as he was, he declared finally that he was "in the hands of his friends," and that he would go out and respond to the call. [108] It was an unfortunate decision. He walked out onto the balcony. [109] "I am not here," he said, "for the purpose of making a speech, but after being introduced, I wish to tender my cordial thanks for the welcome. . . . [A voice: 'Ten thousand welcomes.']" [110]

If he had only stopped right there; but he went on: "I wish it was in my power to address you under favorable circumstances upon some of the questions that have . . . grown out of the fiery ordeal that we have passed through. . . ." Here again was a good stopping-place, but the temptation was too great and he continued: "The Rebellion being suppressed . . . it seems that the time has arrived . . . when the bleeding arteries should be tied up." From a voice in the crowd,—a Radical voice—there came the old taunt that had been hurled in Cleveland: "New Orleans!" [111] Johnson was now in for a speech, he could resist no longer.

"Go on," he continued, "perhaps if you had a word on the subject of New Orleans you might understand more about it than you do. [Laughter.] . . . When you design to talk about New Orleans you ought to understand what you are talking about. When you read the speeches that were made and take up the facts on the Friday and Saturday before that convention sat, you will there find that speeches were made . . . exciting . . . the black population to arm themselves, and prepare for the shedding of blood. [A voice: 'That's so' and cheers.] You will find that a convention did assemble in violation of law, and the intention of that convention was to supersede the organized authorities in the state government of Louisiana, which had been recognized by the government of the United States; and every man engaged in that rebellion—in that convention . . . was a traitor to the Constitution of the United States [Cheers] and here you will find that another rebellion was commenced having its origin in the Radical Congress." [112]

Johnson proceeded: "Then when they had established their

government and extended universal and impartial franchise, as they called it, to the colored population, then this radical Congress was to determine that a government established on negro votes was to be the government of Louisiana. [Voices: 'Never!' Cheers and cries of 'Hurrah for Andy!'] . . . And there was the . . . origin of the blood that was shed; and every drop of blood that was shed is upon their skirts and they are responsible for it." [113]

It would have been well if he had found a stopping-place, but he went on: "I know that I have been traduced and abused. I know it has come in advance of me here, as elsewhere,—that I have attempted to exercise an arbitrary power in resisting laws that were intended to be forced upon the government. [Cheers.] That I had exercised that power [Cries 'Bully for you'], that I had abandoned the party that elected me, that I was a traitor because I exercised the veto power in attempting to arrest for a time the . . . Freedman's Bureau Bill. . . . I have been traduced, I have been slandered, I have been maligned, I have been called Judas Iscariot and all that. Now, my countrymen, it is very easy to indulge in epithets; it is easy to call a man Judas, and cry out traitor; but when he is called upon to give arguments and facts, he is very often found wanting." [114]

No American had ever been called upon to suffer a detraction more unjust, and few have been more sensitive to slander. Perhaps it had been better had he always suffered silently, but he was human. "Judas Iscariot,"—he said. "Judas. There was a Judas, and he was one of the twelve apostles. Oh! Yes, the twelve apostles had a Christ. [A voice: 'And a Moses too.' Laughter.]" Undaunted he continued: "The twelve apostles had a Christ, and he never could have had a Judas unless he had had twelve apostles. If I have played the Judas, who has been my Christ that I have played the Judas with? Was it Thad. Stevens? Was it Wendell Phillips? Was it Charles Sumner? [Hisses and cheers.] These are the men that stop and compare themselves with the Saviour; and everybody that differs with them . . . is to be denounced as a Judas. ['Hurrah for Andy' and cheers.]" [115]

To picture adequately the pretended horror which these words evoked among the Radicals and their abettors, would require a full understanding of mid-Victorian hypocrisy, when men went to church three times on Sunday and believed in the twelve-hour day for laborers. And so when Johnson's enemies heard that he had mentioned Christ they shouted blasphemy! There was no blasphemy about it.[116] His speech was a fair argument, and an unanswerable one. He had been compared to the meanest character in history. If Johnson was a Judas whom had he betrayed? Whom indeed! "I simply intended tonight to tender you my sincere thanks," continued Johnson, "but as . . . we are talking about this Congress and these respectable gentlemen who contend that the President is wrong because he vetoed the Freedman's Bureau bill . . . he committed a high offense and therefore ought to be impeached. [Voice: 'Never.'] Yes, yes, they are ready to impeach him. [A voice: 'Let them try it.'] And if they were satisfied they had the next Congress by a decided majority as this, upon some pretext or other . . . they would vacate the executive department of the United States." [117]

In concluding, he declared: "I place myself upon the ramparts of the Constitution and when I see the enemy approaching so long as I have eyes to see, or ears to hear, or a tongue to sound the alarm, so help me God I will do it and call upon the people to be my judges. [Cheers.] It has been my peculiar misfortune to have fierce opposition, because I have always struck my blows direct, and fought with right and the Constitution on my side. [Cheers.] [118] Let us stand by the Union of these states—let us fight the enemies of the government, come from whatever quarter they may. My stand has been taken." [119]

We have quoted from the newspaper accounts of the Cleveland and St. Louis speeches. They were badly and mendaciously reported. Even an honest and intelligent report of an extemporaneous speech will often grossly misrepresent the speaker. We should not have thought those reports worthy to be quoted, were they not later to play so large a part in a great state trial which we shall presently attend. These two speeches were but incidents in a political tour, but his contemporary and historical detractors have seen fit, with great injustice, to judge the whole journey by them. Lest, however, we be accused of partisanship, let us here admit that Johnson was both unwise and mistaken in permitting himself to be drawn into disputation with the hecklers of the crowd. But had he betrayed Lincoln's cause, had he turned Radical, and in pursuance of their policies indulged in equally tempestuous debate, the newspapers would have rung with his praise, his very solecisms would have been hailed as evidence of his stalwart character. These praises would have found their way into the histories.

§

From St. Louis the Presidential party now journeyed on to Indianapolis.[120] The Radicals were becoming better organized, their presses had been working overtime and the whole population was showing increased signs of the infection from their poison. At Indianapolis the crowd shouted when the President appeared: "We want nothing to do with traitors!" "Shut up! We don't want to hear from you."[121] There was here more turbulence and premeditated violence than they had yet encountered. It was here that Welles became convinced of what he "had for some days suspected,—that there was an extreme Radical conspiracy to treat the President with disrespect and indignity."[122]

From Indiana the Presidential party journeyed to Louisville, where a "grand reception" was accorded them;[123] and from thence they pushed on to Cincinnati and Columbus.[124] It was here evident that one of the main lines of Radical strategy was meeting with success,—the defection of Ulysses Grant. The asset of his personal prestige was, as these political schemers so long had clearly seen, at all costs one they must acquire. Grant was a simple man. They knew his hatred for the Copperheads. They knew that many Democrats who, whether justly or unjustly branded with this name, had given their support to Johnson. Hence, the Radicals argued it would not be difficult to persuade so credulous a mind that Johnson in some way shared the taint of Copperhead disloyalty.

"General Grant," wrote Welles, "whom the Radicals have striven to use and to offset against the President, who generally received louder cheers and called out more attention than even the President himself, behaved on the whole discreetly. Of course, he saw as did all others, the partisan designs and schemes of the Radicals, but he did not, so far as I could perceive, permit it to move him from his propriety at least during the first week or ten days. He gave me to understand in one or two conversations that our views corresponded. He agreed with me that he is for reëstablishing the Union at once in all its primitive vigor, is for immediate representation by all the states, etc., but while he would forgive much to the Rebels, he is unsparing toward those whom he denounces as Copperheads. . . . A Rebel he could forgive but not a Copperhead." [125]

Grant was reticent throughout the journey, sometimes stealing off into the baggage coach to find lonely solace with his cigar,[126] smarting perhaps under Horace Greeley's jibe that he and Farragut were "tame lions harnessed to the President's car." [127] "But," says Welles, "first at Detroit, then at Chicago, St. Louis and finally at Cincinnati, it became obvious that he had begun to listen to the seductive appeals of the Radical conspirators. The influence of his father, who was by his special request my companion and associate at Cincinnati in the procession, finally carried him into the Radical ranks." [128] At Columbus, Welles observed what he had not failed to note at other places, "some scheming to antagonize Grant and the President and make it appear that the interest was especially for the former. Great pains have been taken by partisans to misrepresent the President . . . and prejudice the people against him. There is special vindictiveness and disregard of truth by members of Congress everywhere." [129]

The winning of the Congressional elections was the first objective of the Radicals, but they were looking far ahead. Whom could they put forward for the Presidency in 1868? With whom could they combat the claims of Andrew Johnson to renomination and to reëlection? With whom so well as with a popular war hero!

§

William Seward, in the opinion of Lord Charnwood, "was one of the ablest men in America." [130]   He had, says Merriam, "that large wisdom in adapting means to ends which is statesmanship." [131]   He did much for his country, but no part of his long and valuable life is more honorable than the four years following Lincoln's death which he devoted to the furtherance of Andrew Johnson's efforts to fulfill Lincoln's aims.

On the night of Lincoln's murder Seward had indeed, as Johnson later said, been "placed upon the butcher's block" and "hacked by the assassin's knife." [132]   His wife died that June from the shock, and one year later his daughter followed her mother to the grave. [133]   With what a heavy heart, therefore, it must have been that Seward had thrown himself into the solution of the unprecedented problems Lincoln left to his successor.   Nevertheless, he plunged into the work with cheerfulness.   During the "Swing Around the Circle" he had stood by Johnson, caring nothing for the abuse in which he himself was forced to share.   Time and again he addressed the crowds saying: "Here is Grant.   He has done his duty.   Here is Farragut, who has done his duty.   Here is the President, who has done his duty, and now you men who vote,—you are to do yours." [134]

Weakened by all that he had suffered, and depleted by the extraordinary exertions of this extended tour, he was a fit subject for infection.   On the steamer carrying the Presidential party from Louisville, Seward came down with an attack of cholera, and was thereafter detached from his companions, going on by separate train.   When the pilgrims arrived at Harrisburg, and while they were at supper, a whispered message came that Seward was in a car at the depot, unable to be moved, and that Dr. Norris feared he might not last the night.   The President and Gideon Welles quietly withdrew from their table and went to Seward's car.   He was evidently apprehensive that he would not survive.   Welles feared that this was their "last interview." [135]

The invalid reached up his hand and grasped that of Johnson, who leaned over him to catch his every word.   "My mind is clear," whispered Seward, "and I wish at this time to say that your course is right, that I have felt it my duty to sustain you in it, and if my life is spared, I shall continue to do so. Pursue it for the sake of the country, it is correct." [136]

Within a few hours of the utterance of these words Edwin Stanton secretly was writing to his friend, James Ashley of Toledo: "There is indeed 'danger ahead,' the most serious being that Johnson and Grant, as you put it, 'suck through the same quill.' The President has for more than a year put forth persistent efforts to capture Grant for purposes that are unmistakable. He has in a measure succeeded, but I firmly believe that the head of the armies cannot ultimately be corrupted. In fact I may say I know it."

Fully to appraise this letter and to understand why Stanton and his correspondent were so interested in public sentiment would require a little closer view of Ashley and his plans. Presently we shall examine both.

"You say 'with surprise and humiliation,'" he went on, "that Johnson was in such a condition that it would have been better if he had gone into seclusion . . .; when the great concourse of virtuous people behold the head of our nation reeling through the country as set forth daily in the public prints and as described in your letter, I know disrespect and demoralization must follow."

What of this man, Stanton, who could remain in Johnson's Cabinet, giving wider currency to every slander of his chief! "As your letter," he went on, "seems to be somewhat of an appeal to me, I must reply that my hand is not on the tiller, and if it were, the exhibition now going on would do more to bring the General to his senses than anything I could possibly do." "Congress," he wrote, "can so tie the hands of Johnson and Seward that they will not be able to wreck the country and throw us into another revolution, although they have gone so far already that no statutes can prevent their acts from bringing in a reign of chaos and bloodshed in the South that will horrify the civilized world. . . . Come on early, I beg you, for Congress has a heavy task before it." [137]

Something of Andrew Johnson's problem is perceived with the

SCENE AT THE GOVERNOR'S ROOM, CITY HALL, N. Y., HIS HONOR MAYOR HOFFMAN WELCOMING THE PRESIDENT TO THE HOSPITALITIES OF THE CITY, AND PRESENTING THE SERIES OF RESOLUTIONS ADOPTED BY THE COMMON COUNCIL.

recollection that at his council board there sat this double-crossing, underhanded sneak.

§

On Saturday, September 15th, the President and his fellow travelers returned to Washington. In the face of the most sinister opposition that had ever confronted any President he had put his back to the wall and had lashed out with all his strength. He had struck hard blows, but he had told the truth. The Radicals resented both. Perhaps at times under bitter provocation he had departed from so-called "Presidential dignity," but none who heard him failed to sense his deep sincerity.

Johnson came back to Washington with the conviction that his tour would help to turn the tide of opinion in favor of supporting Lincoln's plan. He had employed the methods so familiar to him in Tennessee and the Southwest, and believed they were effective in the North as well. But Welles feared "that the effect would be different, that his much talking would be misapprehended, that the partisan press and partisan leaders would avail themselves of it and decry him. I am still apprehensive that he may have injured his cause by many speeches; but it is undeniably true that his remarks were effective among his hearers and that within that circle he won supporters." [138]

"To a great extent," continued Welles, "the Radicals are opposed to him and his policy, yet when the true issue was stated the people were and are obviously with him. The President himself has sanguine belief that he has so aroused his countrymen that they will sanction his measures for reëstablishing the Union, but the Radicals have the party organizations and have labored to make those organizations effective for almost a year, while the President has done comparatively nothing." [139]

The President had indeed done nothing in party maneuvering. He had believed that the rectitude of his course and the espousal of Lincoln's plan should make their own appeal. Perhaps in our times, with the aid of an enlightened press, Johnson's theory of campaigning might have won. What was he to do? He could not have gained the adherence of the Radicals except by a surrender. The Republicans who were not Radicals were too few and far too weak to count. The Democrats were stigmatized as "Copperheads" throughout the North. The acceptance of their aid was a political liability. But Johnson was appealing to Americans, not to Democrats or Republicans, and he welcomed aid wherever he could find it.

XL

ENDORSEMENTS OF THE PRESIDENT

GENERAL John E. Wool had served with distinction as a major of infantry in the War of 1812, as well as later in the war with Mexico. Although he was already seventy-two when South Carolina fired on Sumter, he volunteered and took an honorable part throughout the war.[1] And now in September, 1866, at the age of seventy-eight, he was still eager "to preserve the Union." Together with other distinguished Union officers, he came forward to rally the disorganized supporters of Andrew Johnson's cause by bringing together a "soldiers and sailors convention." It met on September 17th in Cleveland,—two days after the President's return to Washington.[2]

As delegates there came many who had won imperishable names upon the field of battle.[3] Some were outspoken Democrats, some were Republicans, but into this convention they had come neither as Democrats nor Republicans, but Americans. Among them all there was no more gallant figure than that of General George Custer. Graduating from West Point in 1861, he had joined his regiment on the battlefield of Bull Run. In October, 1863, at the age of twenty-four, his shoulders shone with the two stars of a major-general! At Woodstock and Yellow Tavern, and afterwards at Dinwiddie and Five Forks, he won fame. But it was in the decisive battle of Cedar Creek that his gallantry had been most conspicuous.[4]

Custer was precisely a man after Andrew Johnson's heart, and this singularly gallant young cavalryman found in the President the qualities to rally all of his enthusiasm. He had accompanied the Presidential party on the "Swing Around the Circle." At Louisville, while an old Revolutionary soldier was boarding the train to greet the President, some Radicals standing about, uttered derisive groans. Hearing these, Custer stepped out on the plat-

form to prophesy the Radicals' defeat at the coming elections.
"Wait till next October," he shouted, "and more groans than
these will be heard." [5] Now again he put his back behind the
President as he had done for Sheridan at Cedar Creek. Sitting
Bull and his ferocious Sioux awaited him at Little Big Horn. Perhaps this contest with the Radicals was designed as an initial
training in the art of savage warfare.

Patriarchal General Wool was chosen President of the convention.[6] Discussing how the negro franchise agitation was inextricably bound up with the Radical plan for Southern spoliation,
he declared: "Another civil war is foreshadowed unless the freedmen are placed upon an equality with their previous masters. If
this cannot be accomplished Radical partisans with a raging thirst
for blood and plunder are again ready to invade the Southern
states and lay waste the country not already desolated, with the
sword in one hand and the torch in the other." [7]

Henry Ward Beecher had been invited to invoke the divine
blessing, but he had hay fever, so he wrote a long letter endorsing
the principles of Johnson's Philadelphia convention.[8] How unwelcome to the members of Plymouth Church was this, Beecher was
presently to discover, and to recant his advocacy of so unpopular
a cause with the declaration that he was not " 'a Johnson man,'
in any received meaning of the term." [9]

But it was not from Brooklyn alone that messages of approval
to this convention came. There was assembled at this time in the
city of Memphis a gathering of Confederate officers. A telegram
of sympathy for the proceedings at Cleveland was dispatched.[10]
Nothing could have done the Johnson cause more harm than this
well-intentioned message.[11] The convention, upon receipt of this
Southern message of good will, adopted a resolution thanking the
Confederate soldiers for their words of "magnanimity and kindness." This in the minds of Stevens and his sycophants was proof
of treason. The Forrest telegram furnished Sumner and his followers with new "evidence" that Johnson had gone over to the
Confederacy. "All other circumstances united," wrote Blaine,
"did not condemn the convention in Northern opinion so deeply
as this incident." [12]

Before adjourning, Custer's comrades in arms adopted resolutions approving the work of the National Union Convention held in Philadelphia the month before, and declared that "whenever there shall be any armed resistance to the lawfully constituted authorities of our National Union either in the South or in the North, in the East or in the West . . . we will again pledge to its support our lives, our fortunes, and our sacred honor." [13]

That evening, in New York City, there assembled a great throng in Union Square. All those who approved "the open, manly, and patriotic course of Andrew Johnson in opposition to the illegal assumptions and usurpations of a partisan Congress," were invited to attend. There was a great outpouring. John A. Dix presided, but presently presented the orator of the occasion, Samuel J. Tilden. He spoke of Johnson as the "restorer of the Republic," the same "indomitable man" who alone among the Southern Senators stood by the Union and "never quailed." [14]

"Now I hear it complained," continued Tilden, "that this same Andrew Johnson has the qualities which yesterday we were wont to applaud. I hear it complained of, that his nature is not of the soft and silken texture which drifts along with the current, surrendering convictions, abandoning duty, seeking only ease, and acquiescing in every wrong which it may be inconvenient to resist. . . . I hear it complained of, that this heroic man who has periled more and sacrificed more for the Constitution and the Union than any other man now living, when reviled and traduced, when even denounced as a traitor, feels and expresses something of indignation toward his assailants." [15]

And he concluded: "I thank God that Andrew Johnson is what he is, and not what his assailants wish him to be. Do any, even of them, pretend that he is not a sincere, earnest, truthful, honest man? Does anybody doubt the purity and strength of his convictions? Does anybody doubt his patriotism and his devotion to the country? . . . I say that the doctrine on which Andrew Johnson acted in 1861 in resisting secession, and on which he now acts in insisting that the ten states denied representation in Congress are still in the Union, and are lawfully entitled to representation as states of the Union, is the true constitutional doctrine." [16]

BENJAMIN F. BUTLER

THE Congressional elections were drawing near. The truth so eloquently uttered at the Philadelphia and Cleveland conventions, and the mass meeting at Union Square, could be drowned out by lies, the Radicals believed. But the campaign of detraction must be kept going. They wanted it loud, raucous and offensive. The times were ripe for Benjamin F. Butler. We must know this man if we would understand Johnson's later struggles.

From his retirement in Lowell, where he had remained since January, 1865, when Grant relieved him of command,[1] he now began discerning opportunities in the troubled politics of the hour, and, believing that the Radicals would ultimately triumph, came forward as a candidate for Congress, and as champion of all the enemies of Johnson and of Lincoln.

Butler was then forty-eight years old. In 1840 he was admitted to the bar of Massachusetts.[2] His practice in the beginning was chiefly in the defense of criminals, or in civil cases where persons of that class were parties. "His method of defense," says Senator Hoar, "was frequently almost as objectionable as the crimes he was defending. He attacked the character of honest witnesses, and of respectable persons, victims of his guilty clients, who were seeking the remedy of the law. He had many ingenious fashions of confusing or browbeating witnesses, and sometimes of misleading juries."[3] His reputation at the bar was that of "an unscrupulous practitioner."[4] In July, 1864, Welles wrote: "While Butler has talents and capacity he is not to be trusted. The more I see of him the greater is my distrust of his integrity."[5] And again in March, 1866: "I am told that General Butler has succeeded in inducing the Secretary of the Treasury to interfere in the matter of the *Grey Jacket* condemned as a prize. If so I

Benj. F. Butler

regret it. McCulloch has been imposed upon. Butler is reckless, avaricious, unscrupulous. He knows there is neither law nor justice in his course on this question, but he has the promise of large fees." [6]

Butler began his political life as a Democrat. He was elected to the lower house of Massachusetts in 1853. He was elected to the State Senate in 1859,[7] and in the following year went as a delegate to the Democratic National Convention at Charleston, with instructions to vote for Douglas; he voted thirty-seven times for Jefferson Davis.[8]

At twenty-one he joined the militia of his state, enrolling as a private in the Lowell City Guard,[9] and on the 17th of April, 1861, started gaily for the war in command of a brigade of the militia of Massachusetts.[10] Bullies and braggarts do not make good soldiers. As a commander of troops he became an outstanding failure of the war. With one or two unimportant exceptions, his military career was "disgraceful to himself and unfortunate to the country." [11] Halleck has written eloquently of his "total unfitness to command in the field." Sherman considered him "a mighty man of words but little in deeds of personal valor." [12]

But if our Lowell friend was somewhat deficient as a soldier, his reputation as a spoilsman is unrivaled in the annals of the war between the states. He had been in active service less than nine months when Governor Andrew wrote to the two Senators of Massachusetts "that the course of proceedings under Major-General Butler in this Commonwealth seems to have been designed and adapted simply to afford means to persons of bad character to make money unscrupulously. . . ." [13]

Butler's real opportunity, however, arrived when he assumed command of New Orleans on May 1st, 1862.[14] "We want cotton," the Prime Minister of England had declared in July of the previous year, and Lincoln's government was desirous that both France and England receive it, hoping thereby to minimize the chance of European intervention.[15] Butler had not been in command of New Orleans two months before Washington was reliably informed that he was using his position "to engage in mercantile speculation," and that he had "already made considerable shipments North on private account." [16]   But Butler's reputation for corrupt self-enrichment was not confined to large operations only. The ladies of New Orleans to this day will tell you how he stole the silver spoons from the cupboards of their great-grandmothers.

During his administration in New Orleans, Butler made a requisition on a bank for $80,000.   When the war was over, the bank brought suit to recover its money.   Before the trial, Edward Pierpont called on Butler in the bank's behalf, saying: "Your neighbors in Lowell will not think very well of it when they see you riding in your carriage through the streets and know it was paid for out of money you have taken unlawfully from this bank." Before the case came on for trial Butler paid the money.   "Well, you beat me," he said to Pierpont, "but I want to tell you that you made one mistake.   You said the people of Lowell would not think very highly of me when they saw me riding through the streets in my carriage and knew it was paid for by the money of this bank.   The people would think I was a fool for not having taken twice as much." [17]

Wherever Butler was in command ugly rumors came of jobs and frauds.   "Beyond reasonable doubt," wrote Rhodes, "he was making money out of his country's life-struggle." [18]   "Butler . . . was a spoilsman of the lowest order. . . ." [19]   On June 1st, 1862, our light-fingered commander of New Orleans laid a heavy hand upon a Southern sympathizer who had removed the American flag from the flag-staff of the Mint.   Butler had him shot.[20]   Among certain classes of the North this was a distinct aid to Butlerian prestige.   One enthusiast expressed the wish that Butler "was President, for though he would make millions for himself during the first three months, he would finish the war in three months more." [21]

The study of Butler's face reveals the insolence and the coarseness of the man.   The heavy jowls, the bony forehead, the drooping eyelids and moustache, the rotund clumsy figure,—it is not difficult to associate baseness with the possessor of such features. It is the very model of the shyster lawyer.   As we look into his shifty countenance, we can all but hear him boast: "They say I am sharp.   Of course I am sharp.   It is only when they cannot imitate it that they complain of my sharpness." [22]   But if there are any left who might wish to imitate Ben Butler, they would certainly abandon that desire on an examination of his famous General Order No. 28.

Women are always more intense in war than men, and the ladies of New Orleans, it seems, were pointed in the display of their hostility to the invaders. "I'll put a stop to this," said Butler, handing his chief of staff this order: "As the officers and soldiers of the United States have been subject to repeated insults from the women . . . of New Orleans . . . it is ordered that hereafter when any female shall by word, gesture or movement insult or show contempt for any officer or soldier of the United States, she shall be regarded and held liable to be treated as a woman of the town plying her avocation." [23]

One day as Butler and his aide were walking through the streets of Louisiana's capital, some Southern ladies turned their backs upon them, whirling so fast as to throw out their skirts "in a regular circle like the pirouette of a dancer." Butler, raising his voice so as to be clearly heard by them, called out to his aide: "Those women evidently know which end of them looks the best." [24] We turn from this unspeakable revelation of the cad to a banquet given in his honor by the negroes of New Orleans, with a little keener appreciation of the unconscious truth uttered by the colored toastmaster who proposed this toast: "Here's to General Butler who has a white face but he has a black heart." [25]

Butler's Order No. 28 evoked a storm of criticism in the South, throughout Europe, and especially in England and France. Even in the North it was deplored. [26] It was probably the cause of his removal from New Orleans in December, 1862. [27] But the fact that he had achieved as no other had the hatred of the South, endeared him to many Northerners, among whom were Horace Greeley, Salmon P. Chase, Wendell Phillips, Charles Sumner and William Lloyd Garrison. [28] Of Stanton's relations with Ben Butler, the former's biographer remarks: "The two old Democrats understood each other perfectly." [29] But perhaps the most significant tribute was paid by one who wrote him: "You stand well generally, are well spoken of by the middle class, in the cars, in the barrooms, at the corners, etc., as 'the right man in the right place.' " [30]

In 1864 the Department of Virginia and North Carolina was placed under the command of Butler.[31] Here again trading with the enemy flourished, and here once more, undoubtedly with truth, Butler was believed to be personally profiting from this traffic.[32] It was during this year that his military blunders, if not sheer cowardice, brought his martial career to an inglorious and dishonorable close.

In the final hours of 1864 Wilmington was the last open gateway from the outer world to the Confederacy. Fort Fisher was the key. If this position could be stormed, supplies and ammunition to the Davis government would cease to come. The storming of the fort was entrusted, unhappily, to Butler. He had specific orders from Ulysses Grant, and he had the coöperation of Admiral Porter.

Garrisoned by but four companies of infantry, and one light battery, the Confederates had left Wilmington practically stripped of troops. Butler had under his command the greatest armada ever in American waters. His iron-clads opened fire, throwing a hundred and fifty shells to the minute. The fort answered with all its guns. Those on the northeast ramparts were silenced as soon as the monitors had opened fire, and when all the Union vessels came to anchor and got their batteries in action, they drove the Confederate gunners to the bomb-proofs. After an hour and fifteen minutes every gun within the fort had ceased to speak.[33]

It was at this time that Butler appeared upon the scene. Not a single Union soldier had been scratched. General Curtis was within fifty yards of the fort. General Ames then gave the order for an assault. Curtis and his men rushed forward, they got so near the bastion that a Union soldier snatched a Confederate flag from the parapet, and brought away one of the Confederate horses. At this moment Butler acted! His orders were to cease the charge and reëmbark! "In direct violation of the instructions given," Grant later wrote, "he ordered the reëmbarkation of the troops and the return of the expedition." [34]

Concerning Butler's shameless failure to secure the fort, Porter later wrote: "Had the army made a show of surrounding it, it would have been ours; but nothing of the kind was done. . . . It can be taken at any moment in one hour's time if the right man is sent with the troops." [35] To which on December 30th Grant replied: "Please hold on wherever you are for a few days, and I will endeavor to be back again with an increased force, and *without the former commander*." [36] And the next day the Secretary of the Navy telegraphed to Porter: "Lieutenant-General Grant will send immediately a competent force *properly commanded* to coöperate in the capture of the defenses of Federal Point." [37] Four days later, on January 4th, Grant asked for the removal of Butler for "the good of the service." "In my absence," he wrote, "General Butler necessarily commands, and there is a lack of confidence felt in his military ability, making him an unsafe commander for a large army. His administration of the affairs of his department is also objectionable." [38]

Four days later Butler received his written orders relieving him of command. [39] Thus terminated his activities as a soldier. It was an inglorious termination of an inglorious career, but there was one at least who appraised it highly, and that was Benjamin F. Butler. At the close of his thousand page autobiography, and of his long life, in 1892 he wrote: "If any general officer with the same means did more in the war for the life of the nation, I congratulate him most heartily, but I would like to see his list." [40]

Butler was ordered back to Lowell in disgrace, but the Radicals had use for his peculiar talents, and six days after his dismissal we find him consulting with the troublemakers at the national capital. "The Committee on the Conduct of the War," wrote Welles, "have summoned him to Washington. There was mischief in this. It was well, perhaps, for Butler was off duty. But in Washington he will help the mischief-makers make trouble and stimulate intrigue and faction. Allied with Wade and Chandler and H. Winter Davis he will not only aid but breed mischief. This is intended." [41] While Butler sat glibly testifying before the Congressional Committee that Fort Fisher was impregnable, and that no Union force could take it, a dispatch was received at the committee room that the fort had fallen. [42]

In deliberate violation of his order of dismissal requiring him to "repair to Lowell," Butler spent the winter of 1865 in Washington. Engaged in his favorite occupation of portraiture, the Secretary of the Navy sat watching him. Butler, he declared, "has inordinate and irrepressible ambition and would scruple at nothing to gratify it and his avarice. . . . Butler has the reckless audacity attributed to the worst revolutionists of France, in the worst of times, but is deficient in personal courage. He is a suitable idol for Greeley, a profound philanthropist, being the opposite of G. in almost everything except love of notoriety." [43]

Such a restless soul could not long keep out of politics, but it was not until the summer of 1866 that his opportunity arrived. The rising contest with Andrew Johnson offered a tempting avenue for his powers. [44] Departing from his life-long association with the Democratic party, like many another, he now became a Radical Republican,—opportunity seemed to lie that way. He presided at the Massachusetts State Convention in the summer of 1866, declaring for "impartial suffrage." [45] In a Congressional district in which he did not live, a nomination for Congress was offered to him. "Reflecting upon the matter," he later wrote, "and feeling a little curiosity to know whether I could be elected in a district where I was only a carpet-bagger, I said I would try it." [46] He was nominated. [47] With a "talent for turbulence," if not for fighting, he campaigned both Massachusetts and the country. [48]

He was welcomed by the Radicals with open arms. Whilst in command of Fortress Monroe he had refused to return certain fugitive slaves to their owners calling them "contraband of war." [49] The Abolitionists were delighted with this phrase. There were many in the North for whom this more than compensated for his tarnished military record. And so during all the canvass he was enthusiastically received throughout the North, and the Radicals began to consider him as one of the most valuable spokesmen of their cause. [50]

§

The work of the Cleveland Convention of September 17th, endorsing Johnson's cause, if possible, must be undone, and accordingly, eight days later at Pittsburg the Radicals organized a "Soldiers and Sailors" Convention of their own. There were some regimental and company officers there, and several generals of Volunteers, but the gathering was for the most part an immense outpouring of privates.[51]

The convention divided its attention between attempts to popularize the Fourteenth Amendment and denunciations of Andrew Johnson.[52] Butler was a loud and enthusiastic delegate. It was he who reported the resolutions that were adopted. These declared that the President had "no right to a policy as against the legislative department of the government," and that his plan of reconstruction "if consummated would render the sacrifices of the nation useless." And still further: "That the right of the conqueror to legislate for the conquered has been recognized by the public law of all civilized nations. . . ."[53]

When Butler's convention came to an end on September 26th, it would seem as though the country by this time had heard enough in order to decide. But Thaddeus Stevens and Charles Sumner were yet to have their say. Not long before the election, Stevens thus relieved himself of some part of the pent-up malice accumulating since the adjournment of Congress. "I have amused myself," he said, "with a little light frivolous reading. For instance, there was a serial account from day to day of a very remarkable circus that traveled through the country from Washington to Chicago and St. Louis and from Louisville back to Washington. . . . I expected great wit from the celebrated character of its clowns."[54]

The expected laughter came, and he went on, dividing his insults evenly between Johnson and Seward: "They were well provided with clowns; instead of one there were two. One of these clowns was high in office and somewhat advanced in years; the other was a little less advanced in office, but older in years. They started out with a very respectable stock company. In order to attract attention they took with them for instance a celebrated general; they took with them an eminent naval officer, and they chained him to the rigging so that he could not get away, though he tried to do so once or twice." [55]

It is easy to imagine Thaddeus Stevens there, lurching on his club foot, the malevolent panther-like eyes lighting up his sardonic face as he continued: "But the circus went on all the time,—sometimes one clown performing and sometimes the other. For instance the younger clown told them . . . that he had it in his power, if 'he chose, to be dictator!' The elder clown pointed to the other one and said to the people, 'Will you take him for President or will you take him for King?' [Laughter.] He left you but one alternative. You are obliged to take him for one or the other, either President or King if 'my policy' prevails." [56] This is a fairly good example of Stevens' "wit." And there is a little more: "I am not following them around. I shall not describe to you how sometimes they cut outside the circle, and entered into street broils with common blackguards; how they fought at Cleveland and Indianapolis. . . . They told you that he . . . had been a tailor—I think he did not say drunken tailor—no, he had been a tailor. [Laughter.] He had been city alderman. [Laughter.] He had been in the legislature. God help that legislature! [Great merriment.] He had been in Congress and now he was President. He had been everything but one,—he had never been a hangman, and he asked leave to hang Thad Stevens. [Laughter.]" [57]

This was typical of Stevens. Equally characteristic was Charles Sumner's address which he made to his audience at the Boston Music Hall on October 2nd. "A One Man Power" was the subject of his remarks. They were as vindictive as those of Stevens, albeit cloaked in scholarly and well-rounded periods. "The people wrapt in the great tragedy," he declared, going back to Lincoln's death, "trembled as they beheld a drunken man ascend the heights of power." [58]

Sumner descended to downright mendacity, when a few moments later he declared: "Witness Memphis, witness New Orleans, who can doubt that the President is author of these tragedies. Charles the Ninth of France was not more completely author of the massacre of St. Bartholomew than Andrew Johnson is author of the recent massacre now crying out for judgment." And he went on: "Congress must be sustained in its conflict with the one man power . . . ex-rebels must not be hurried back to power. . . . Of course the Constitutional amendment must be adopted. As far as it goes it is well; but it does not go far enough. More is necessary. Impartial suffrage must be established. . . . If there is added education there will be a new order of things, with liberty of the press, liberty of speech and liberty of travel, so that Wendell Phillips may speak freely in Charleston or Mobile." [59] Whatever else Sumner had in mind for the South, might he not at least have spared them Wendell Phillips? "Senator Sumner has sent me his speech," wrote Welles a few days later,—"he delivers one annually. This one does him no credit. Is not frank and truthful and honest,—traits that I have heretofore awarded him." [60]

§

Never was there a more bitter campaign than that of 1866. At all costs the Radicals must gain their two-thirds control of both the Senate and the House. The "Presidential obstacle,"—they were preparing, if they could, to strike it down! Sumner's impeachment threat made ten months before, like distant thunder, had been rumbling ever since. Johnson had not been deaf to the reverberations. He had watched the heat-lightnings flash their sullen fires,—the heralds of the approaching storm.

Newspapers and orators appealed to all the people of the North, asking them if they would consent that Rebels who had killed their fathers, their brothers and their sons should now be brought back to power. Passion, prejudice and hatred of the South were fanned into a blazing flame while Andrew Johnson was denounced as a traitor "because he does not repel and persecute the beaten Rebels." [61] The real issues were swamped in torrents of abuse. Reason and toleration were discarded. [62]

Andrew Johnson faced the storms alone. He had placed his cause before the country. He had hoped that the rectitude of his course,—Lincoln's course—would make its own appeal. But his hopes were not destined for fulfillment. Vermont spoke on September 4th, and six days later Maine. In both, the Radical majorities were impressive.[63] This was repeated in the October states; Ohio, Pennsylvania, Indiana and Iowa gave the same answer. New York and all the remaining Northern commonwealths joined the others in November. The administration was defeated! The next Senate would contain forty-two Republicans and eleven Democrats, while one hundred forty-three Republicans and forty-nine Democrats would make up the House.[64] The enemies of Johnson had far more than a two-thirds majority in both houses! What would the future now hold for him and for the country? What might the South expect?

XLII

MAXIMILIAN AND CARLOTTA

THE Chateau de Bouchont was silent. All Brussels was silent as the sun rose on the 18th morning of January, 1927,—an Empress was dead. Marie Charlotte Amelia, the daughter of King Leopold the First of Belgium, the wife of Maximilian, "Emperor of Mexico," after eighty-seven years had found rest and peace at last. King Albert, her dutiful nephew, called at the chateau at nine, but it was too late.[1] It was just seventy years before that the young brother of Emperor Francis Joseph had led her to the altar and a tragic fate.[2] She went to live with him at Miramar, but the Hapsburg Court brought her no happiness. She was only seventeen, she was the daughter of a king, she was ambitious,—but how glorious if she could be an Empress. The prospect in Austria did not seem promising.

Her young husband had gracious manners, he cultivated botany, liberal ideas and a profuse blonde beard. When rumors of an empire in Mexico came floating down to him at Miramar,[3] he listened at first without enthusiasm. In Carlotta's active mind, however, gay visions of a trans-Atlantic throne were dancing. The same dreams had animated Louis Napoleon twenty-three years before in his captivity at Ham,—they were enticing him again. As early as 1859 Labastida, one time Archbishop of Mexico, and then a cleric refugee in Paris, had interested both the Empress Eugenie and her husband in the cause of a centralized monarchy and the church. A vision of the Archduke Maximilian as the ruler of the Mexicans danced fitfully before them.[4] But there was the Monroe Doctrine, and the United States were not yet torn by civil strife! The year 1861 seemed more propitious. With the Jecker claims as a pretext, the Emperor of the French prepared to intervene. And he interested others. England

387

and Spain retired in March, 1862, but France pushed on.   In May she landed thirty thousand troops.

They entered Puebla the next spring.   Benito Juarez, the full-blooded Indian President of Mexico, was in flight, and in June, 1863, the city of Mexico was in French hands.[5]   And now it was no rumor, but the crown of Mexico that was offered Maximilian. Again he seemed unwilling to accept, a botanical expedition to the forests of Brazil was calling him, but Carlotta and Napoleon the Third were calling louder, and though it meant the renunciation of the throne of Austria, he yielded.[6]   In the dress of a vice-admiral of the Austrian navy, surrounded by the brilliant uniforms of the chamberlains, the nobles and the aides-de-camp, he gravely listened while Señor Estrada and his attending Mexicans shouted "God save Emperor Maximilian I" and "God save the Empress Carlotta." [7]   Anthony Hope could not have conjured up a picture more vivid, more brilliant or more unreal.

Down the Adriatic a squadron of Austrian warships disappeared and with them the "Emperor and Empress" of Mexico. The French army awaited them, and on June 12th, 1864, while flags and banners waved and bells of the cathedral pealed, "in a clatter of Mexican lancers" they drove into the capital.[8]   With cold disapproval, the people of the United States looked on.   The Monroe Doctrine!   The year before Seward had warned the French against their contemplated course.[9]   But Grant was struggling hard pressed in the wilderness.   McClellan was preparing to become President because the war had been a "failure," and Sumner and his followers were about to turn from Lincoln in the hope of finding "a candidate who would surely win."   Louis Napoleon had selected the right time!

Maximilian drove his cream-colored mules through the countryside and smiled sweetly at the populace.[10]   Juarez and his tattered soldiers were in the North, but "Maximilian's attention wandered easily from politics to botany; and what should have been an Emperor in the saddle was too often an intelligent tourist.   He even ordered nightingales from Styria to moderate to his Austrian ear the song of Mexican birds.   Yet his part in the queer piece was faintly supernumerary.   Cast to play Emperor of Mexico, he could hardly put his name to a decree without French money to finance the policy and French bayonets to enforce the signature." [11]

Americans, pausing now and then in the final hours of their domestic struggle, looked out across the Rio Grande to catch a Meissonier-like glimpse of the Hapsburg Emperor surrounded by the thirty thousand soldiers of Napoleon. But Lincoln's government was not deeply interested in artistic effects for the time being. And so the State Department spoke in guarded tones its messages to France. Seward ground his teeth as he watched this deliberate defiance of the doctrine Mr. Monroe had made so famous, but to the French Ambassador he smiled. [12]

Appomattox came, Lincoln died, and as though there were not enough else to perplex him, the Mexican question fell to Andrew Johnson. Immediately upon the cessation of hostilities, Grant concentrated fifty-two thousand men under Sheridan at the border, [13] and soon was arguing with the Cabinet for "decisive measures." But Seward opposed him,—"the Empire was rapidly perishing," he said, and Maximilian if let alone would leave in less than six months, perhaps in sixty days; interference now would but prolong his stay. [14] Welles listened quietly, and that evening wrote in his diary: "Seward acts from intelligence, Grant from impulse." [15]

The leader of the Union armies was pressing for a war with France. Seward kept his head, he had steered the course thus far,—war could still be avoided! Why bloodshed if diplomacy would serve? Johnson supported him at every step. A week passed and Grant was again urging "the necessity of prompt action." [16] But it was only twenty-two days later that word came to the Cabinet from Bigelow, our Minister to France, that Maximilian was about to leave. From the Prince de Joinville followed a letter of similar import. [17] Seward was making headway.

Grant and Stanton would have plunged us in another conflict. [18] It could easily have been done in the summer of 1865. On the 14th of August of that summer Napoleon was writing to Bazaine that he was not quite ready to relinquish all his trans-Atlantic dreams. He was considering an increase of his force below the

Rio Grande. And at about this time Bazaine began a concentration in anticipation of an American invasion.[19] Eight days later Johnson's Cabinet was receiving melancholy news. Juarez, it seems, was on our borders fleeing thither for protection. "Seward is in trouble," wrote Welles, "all of us are, in fact. Many of the army officers are chafing to make war on the Imperial government and drive the French from that country. They are regardless of the exhausted state of our affairs."[20]

But Andrew Johnson was on the bridge, and with him was his great pilot Seward. Amid the storms they were holding the ship of state steady to her course. Three months later Seward sent August Drouyn de Lhuys this dispatch: "The . . . French army in Mexico . . . is a cause of serious concern to the United States."[21] France said it would be inconvenient to withdraw until we recognized Maximilian. Seward refused.[22] He waited another month, and sent then an even firmer demand for the withdrawal of the French.[23] Napoleon was hearkening now, and as he listened he heard other sounds. There was the heavy rattle of Prince Bismarck's sword. The Rhine was nearer than the Rio Grande. There were the distant rumbles of Sedan.

Napoleon hesitated another thirty days, and then he wrote Bazaine to bring back all his troops "within about a year."[24] And now Seward began to press. In March, 1866, he sent word to de Lhuys that the sympathies of our people with the Mexican Republic were "manifesting themselves more ardently every day."[25] Also quietly he let fall the hint that we might presently accredit an envoy to the Mexican Republic,—to Juarez.[26]

The Johnson-Seward medicine was bitter, but Napoleon was swallowing it, and on April 13th he ordered Bazaine to bring back nine thousand troops that autumn, nine thousand in the spring of 1867, and the rest in October of the same year.[27] Maximilian's reign was drawing to a close. He had little left, but he had Carlotta. Her high courage, her imperious will and her fiery ambition,—these and her love for her ineffectual young Hapsburg, impelled her to save him if she could. Whimsically but with tragic truth he had once said that she was "the better man of the two."[28] She would make a personal appeal to Napo-

leon; he had sent them there, these two helpless children. She would melt him with her tears. He could not desert them! "The crowds were silent at Vera Cruz as she drove down a little wild-eyed to the quay, and she spoke little on the long voyage home." [29]

Twenty-three days before Johnson began his "Swing Around the Circle," Carlotta arrived at Saint-Nazaire; her first news was that of the Emperor of Austria's defeat at Königgrätz. It did not augur well for her interview with Napoleon.[30] He would not help her. He had neither men nor money, and the troops in Mexico would presently be needed,—sorely needed. For there was Prussia! Prussia!! Tragically she made a pilgrimage to Rome. The old Pope heard her through, but she was raving at the end.[31]

The new trans-Atlantic cable brought the news to Maximilian.[32] His Empress was carried under guard to Miramar. To the Tervueren Palace she was presently removed. Flames razed it to the ground. Some thought she fired it in her madness. To the Château de Bouchont she was then taken, and there in the flaming palace of her insanity she dwelt for sixty years.[33] Poor Carlotta!

§

The Radicals were making progress with Ulysses Grant. His defection from the Johnson cause first noted on the western tour was growing. He was watching carefully the progress of events. It is not difficult to imagine him chewing reflectively on his cigar as he pondered the election returns of September and October, 1866. Noticeably his tone began to change.

Less than two months after Seward's hint in March that we might accredit a minister to the Mexican Republic, Lewis D. Campbell was appointed [34] plenipotentiary to the Juarez govern-ment. One of his initial problems was to find it. So great was this that he did not start to look until October. He should have a war vessel with Grant to accompany him.[35] On October 17th Johnson broached the subject to the General, who evinced satis-faction if not pleasure at the arrangement. There was one quali-fication, however; he wished to be in Washington on the return

of Congress. Why? Whatever his reasons were, the President assured him that this could be done. The State Department prepared instructions for his guidance.[36] And then something happened!

At a Cabinet meeting Grant declared that he did not consider it "expedient" for him to leave the country. It was a strange echo of the same idea previously voiced by Stanton! "The President," wrote Welles, "was surprised and a little disconcerted. He could not fail to see that there was an intrigue. I think something more."[37] Grant was near, dangerously near to insubordination!

Many reasons were assigned for his conduct. The rumor ran that Stanton's resignation was impending, that Grant would fill his place, and Sherman that of Grant.[38] During his interview with Grant, Johnson had shown him a letter from Sherman strongly endorsing the Johnson policy. The President suggested publishing it, but Grant expressed disapprobation. It was concluded, therefore, that Grant did not wish to leave the country, lest in his absence Sherman would be exalted to his own position as head of the army, and then elevated to be Secretary of War, and Grant's superior.[39] "He could not be willing," wrote Welles, "to receive orders from his subordinate General Sherman, of whom he is jealous, though intimately friendly."[40]

Grant may have had some jealousy of Sherman, but his growing association with the Radicals is the real explanation of his conduct. That desire to be in Washington when Congress should convene! Was it his, or that of those who were now advising him?

After Grant's curt declination of the appointment, it was offered Sherman. He accepted promptly. "When will you be ready to go?" Johnson asked him. "At once," was the reply.[41]

JOHNSON'S ENEMIES RETURN TO WASHINGTON

THROUGH the chill November days, Gideon Welles sat contemplating the morose political horizon, confiding now and then his dark forebodings to his diary. "The fall elections have passed," on November 17th he wrote, "and the Radicals retain their strength in Congress. False issues have prevailed. . . . President Johnson was and is denounced as a traitor because he does not repel and persecute the beaten Rebels." [1]

And he continued: "The Democrats with equal folly and selfishness strove to install their old party organization in force, regardless of the true interest of the country. . . . The consequence has been that instead of reinstating themselves they have established the Radicals more strongly in power. We have, therefore, had elections without any test, statement or advocacy of principles, except the false one that the Radicals have forced, that the Administration had united with the Rebels." [2]

And still further: "The Radicals have elected General Butler to Congress in a district of which he was not a resident. The Democrats in New York have elected Morrissey, the boxer and gambler, to Congress. It is not creditable that either of these men should have been elected. It shows the depravity of the parties and the times. Two negroes have been elected to the Massachusetts Legislature, not for talents, ability or qualification, but because they are black. Had they been white no one would have thought of either for the position." [3]

November 20th came, as did also the advance guard of Johnson's enemies in Washington. Stevens and his lieutenants were on the ground early to block out work for their followers. [4] There was no doubt that they would press impeachment should occasion offer. "If Thad Stevens can get his caucus machinery at work," our diarist wrote, "he will grind out the refractory and make the timid guilty participants." [5]

§

During Johnson's campaign tour, Charles Sumner had fallen in love. The lady was twenty-eight and she was beautiful. Bancroft sent his congratulations (optimistically as it turned out) "on the impending change which is to make the rest of your life a romance of untold happiness." [6]

To Whittier on October 17th Sumner wrote: "Today at three o'clock I shall be married and at the age of fifty-five begin to live. Your good wishes are precious to me." [7] After the honeymoon Sumner and his bride came on to Washington. A house (No. 322 I Street) was engaged, a pew in the church of the Epiphany was rented, and that nothing might be omitted, a span of horses was duly purchased,—no vulgar beasts it seems, for they had been the property of Lord Lyons. All things seemed auspicious,—but the lady's husband was Charles Sumner.

On December 1st he paid Welles his usual visit preceding the session. "I congratulated him on his marriage," our diarist records. "On politics and public matters we said but little." Sumner was "subdued and almost dejected." He said it was on account of the displacement of his brother-in-law Dr. Hastings as the physician at the Marine Hospital. [8]

The Senators and Representatives had come to town. There were here many men eager for the parts assigned them in the conspiracy now well matured,—a conspiracy to make Ben Wade President of the Senate, to impeach and remove Andrew Johnson and then install Wade in his place; to disrupt the Southern governments, divide the South into military districts, disfranchise the whites and place the negroes over them. It was a pleasing plan.

There was one of Stevens' wharf rats who was particularly fitted for the work at hand. It was James M. Ashley, Stanton's friend, to whom Stanton had just written about "the head of our nation reeling through the country." [9] Ashley represented the Toledo district of Ohio. His early years of altruism were passed on a Mississippi River trading boat. He had engaged there in driving hard bargains with the plantation darkies on the banks. Gradually he had progressed to the dignity of law student, becoming later the editor of a Democratic paper. As an editor, it seemed, neither distinction nor success awaited him, so he became a druggist. He must have learned something about poisons. Presently he joined the Radical party and was sent to Congress. He was a short, fat man, with clean-shaven face. His head was covered with a shock of bushy hair. He wore it in a frousy bang. He was not celebrated for mentality.[10] In short, he was splendid material for Stevens, and presently constituted himself (with Stevens' aid) the "chief impeacher."

§

At the White House a tired man sat waiting. For nineteen months he had been carrying Lincoln's burden. And now, on December 5th, without a trace of bitterness and with a calm that gave no hint of all the storms, he sent his second message to the Congress. The arm that carried Lincoln's torch was not faltering.

He reviewed what he had told them the year before; the appointment of provisional governors, the calling of conventions, the election of governors, the assembling of the state legislatures, the election of United States Senators and Representatives, the opening of the courts, the removal of the blockade, the reëstablishment of custom houses, the enforcement of the laws of internal revenue and the renewal of postal operations. And then to make it doubly plain that the states had again resumed their old position in the Union: "The states themselves had been asked to take part in the high function of amending the Constitution, and of thus sanctioning the extinction of African slavery as one of the legitimate results of our internecine struggle." [11]

He repeated again all that had been done by these commonwealths through the amendment of their state constitutions, the repudiation of Confederate debts and the enactment of laws for the protection of the colored race. And then with great force, but equal calm, he observed: "I deem it a subject of profound regret that Congress has thus far failed to admit to seats loyal senators and representatives from the other states whose inhabitants with those of Tennessee had engaged in the Rebellion. . . .."[12] Their admission, it is believed, would have accomplished much toward the renewal and strengthening of our relations as one people and removed serious cause for discontent on the part of the inhabitants of those states. . . . I do not see that the question will be changed by the efflux of time. Ten years hence . . . the right of representation will be no stronger, the right of exclusion will be no weaker. . . ."[13]

With as much serenity as if the storms had not raged around him, he concluded: "Our government is now undergoing its most trying ordeal, and my earnest prayer is that the peril may be successfully and finally passed without impairing its original strength and symmetry. The interests of the nation are best to be promoted by the revival of fraternal relations, the complete obliteration of our past differences, and the reinauguration of all the pursuits of peace."[14]

§

Johnson's message might as well have been read to the inmates of an insane asylum as to the followers of Thaddeus Stevens. To argue with them was as fruitless as with drunken men; for they were drunk,—drunk with passionate hatred of the South, and of the man who was working for the preservation of the Union. And these followers of Stevens had their friends outside of Congress! With increasing virulence, Horace Greeley was doing all he could through his *Tribune* to poison public opinion against Johnson. Of the Presidential message his *Tribune* editorial announced: "For any living fact or any suggestion, for any helpful thought we might as well turn to the last novel of Mr. Trollope. . . . Andrew Johnson is as much an enemy as when he menaced the nation from the White House steps ten months ago. He does not mean to aid in the work of Reconstruction. . . . We look to Congress with infinite yearning."[15]

What mattered it to the Radicals when such views were penetrating into every Republican home, that the New York *World* on the same day declared: "The President adheres to his former views with resolute indomitable steadiness, but with the calmness of conscious strength. . . . In dignity, decorum and chaste simplicity of language few messages ever sent to Congress have been more creditable." [16]

Despite Greeley's belligerent applause of Congress, there nevertheless seemed few in Washington willing on the opening of the session to join the celebration which the Radicals had planned in their own honor. A parade was organized in which a thousand or more colored persons marched. [17]

Sumner and the negroes were busy in each other's behalf. Sixty minutes of the session had not gone by before Sumner was on his feet with a bill for the enfranchisement of negroes in the District of Columbia. He demanded immediate consideration for his measure. [18] Stevens was ready to assist him. "I was a Conservative in the last session of this Congress," amid laughter he declared, "but I mean to be a Radical henceforth." [19]

Three days after the reading of Johnson's message Welles wrote: "At the Radical, or as they now call it, the Republican caucus,—since the Radicals have absolute control of the organization—last evening, the measures for the session were reported upon and decided, the minority of the caucus surrendering their convictions, their duty, and their oaths to the decision of the party majority. These men have no deference for the Constitution. Parliamentary or Congressional deliberation is trampled under foot. Stevens, Williams, Boutwell, Kelley, others like them do not like the Constitution and are satisfied that they, or either of them, could make a much better instrument." [20]

The language of these men, he continued, and their "abuse of the President are designed to be personally offensive to him, and also to bring him and his office into disrespect. Some of his assailants, and most of them, are intuitively and instinctively blackguards. Stevens has great power of sarcasm. The private character of most of them is better than that of Stevens; but there is something inherently wrong, I apprehend, in each, and with Williams a good deal of whiskey." [21]

In their arsenal of malice there was no weapon too savage for use against the President. Boutwell felt no shame in charging

Johnson with complicity in the escape of John Surratt, the son of one of Lincoln's murderers. Not all of his associates, however, acquiesced in this lie, and some of them condemned it. Later on the floor of the House, Boutwell made a "pitiful half-denial and half-retraction of his caucus tirade." [22]

The Jacobins of ninety-three, under the lash of Mirabeau, Barnave and Robespierre, had set up no more resounding pulpit of defamation, nor pressed forward with more revolutionary purpose than the Radicals of Congress under Thaddeus Stevens. They planned to flaunt the Constitution of their country! They were conspiring the destruction of the Southern states! This they planned and more,—much more, for there was Andrew Johnson standing midway in the path of their criminal designs. "If," wrote Welles, "the Southern states should be put to the ban by Congress and declared territories, the Radicals will not have even then accomplished their purpose. . . . Andrew Johnson must be disposed of and impeachment must be effected. This the less radical partisans are not yet prepared for, but when they have gone so far as to break down the Constitution and the states, they will follow the violent leaders the rest of the way." [23]

Their first objective: the enfranchisement of negroes in the District of Columbia, however base their motives in effecting it, was a lawful one. It was there and there only that Congress had the constitutional power to govern who should vote. But the District of Columbia was an opening wedge. Their real purpose, under the veneer of feigned interest in the black man, presently emerged. They were determined to achieve a new security for the Radical party. With nauseating unction Sumner declared that this negro legislation for the Federal District was to form "an example to the whole country." [24] The Senate listened to these words, and then presently the whole truth was revealed. It would not be enough to bestow the franchise on "those who read and write." If "you give it to those" alone, he blandly said, "you will not secure the new allies which are essential to the national cause!" [25] New allies!

"All these attempts," wrote Welles, "to degrade popular government, to destroy respect for suffrage, have a purpose. It is not to elevate the negro who neither knows nor appreciates the privilege, but it disgraces the white man. The blow is aimed at our system of popular government. In order to prepare the public mind for their work, the President is defamed, traduced, abused, belittled and belied. It is to lessen him in public estimation and reconcile the people to any extreme measure which the conspirators may pursue against him." [26]

Less than two weeks after the reading of Johnson's message, the District of Columbia suffrage bill passed both Houses. [27] "There is not a Senator who votes for this bill," the watchful Secretary of the Navy wrote, "who does not know that it is an abuse and wrong. Most of the negroes of this district are wholly unfit to be electors. . . ." [28]

§

With craft the plot was moving forward. The conspiracy to subvert the Southern governments and trample down the South with negro rule had its ramifications and its subdivisions. One of these was the muzzling of the Supreme Court, should it seek to obstruct them. Each of the principal conspirators was assigned work best suited to his talents. Sumner devoted himself primarily to the enfranchisement of negroes. Wade took up the work of his own elevation. Stevens spread his supervision all along the line, laughing, sneering, and filling the air with defamation of the President. His followers tamely played their parts. Behind Johnson's back, whom he was pretending to serve, Stanton secretly was aiding them.

Early in December, Ben Wade came forward with new bills for the admission of Colorado and Nebraska. It might have been better taste to let some other press these measures, designed as they were to pack a court of whose predetermined verdict he was to be the personal beneficiary. But those engaged in criminal conspiracies are not deterred by such considerations. Wade was not reticent in making his real purpose known. He wanted the votes of the Senators from these territories, should they be granted statehood. "These men," he told the Senate, "believe just as you do; they are ready to . . . assist you in carrying out your great principles. . . . ." [29]   And again: "I want them here because I want this body strengthened immensely by the reinforcement that these gentlemen will bring to bear upon every question you can get up. . . ." [30]   And still further: "When I look to the terrible struggle which is right ahead of us, I feel disposed to arm myself. . . ." [31]

The Radicals, of course, knew what "great principles" they wanted to put through, but remembering their victory at the last election, and that their victorious two-thirds would be in the saddle when the 40th Congress should convene, and considering Wade's methods too transparent, there were some who believed that already they had votes enough for the achievement of their purpose. Admitting that he had once voted for the admission of Nebraska, Senator Howe of Wisconsin declared that there was now no longer a necessity "for reinforcements." [32]

"But," answered Wade, "how he could come to the conclusion, that we shall not want any reinforcements, I am unable to say." Referring to the Supreme Court's decision in the Milligan case handed down eight months before (but in which the opinion had not yet been published), whereby one of the Radicals' favorite devices,—military commissions in peace time—was declared illegal, Wade further answered Howe: "When he gave the vote to which he referred, had the Supreme Court of the United States made a decision which lets loose upon all the Union men of the South the bloodhounds of those rebellious . . . states, and denies the right of the military power to protect them? Did he know that two of the departments of the government . . . were ready now to abet his course? . . . I want to bring you soldiers that will not shirk from any responsibility . . . I want to make sure that if the remedy must be here we shall have force enough to look down all opposition. . . ." [33]

Here again was a warning, not to Andrew Johnson only, but to the Supreme Court as well! Wade and his friends already had their Civil Rights and Freedman's Bureau laws, but they were scheming new measures even more unconstitutional. Would the Supreme Court dare oppose them? They had not frightened

Andrew Johnson! Could they intimidate Chief Justice Chase and his associates?

While Wade was pushing on to pack the high court of impeachment in his own interest, Thaddeus Stevens was gathering his forces to strike the South such a blow as would destroy her states. On the first day of the session, the Joint Committee on Reconstruction was reappointed.[34] Bingham of Ohio, Conkling of New York, Williams of Oregon and Boutwell of Massachusetts were still to serve with Stevens in this council of destruction.[35]

Plans for the destruction of the Southern states went hand in hand with those for the humiliation of their defender. When Boutwell arrived in Washington at the commencement of the session, Stanton sent for him. As he entered the war office, Stanton beckoned him to his private room, where he proceeded to tell how he had been "more disturbed" by the condition of affairs in the preceding weeks and months than at any time throughout the war. Orders, he said, had been issued to the army of which neither he nor Grant had knowledge. He gave Boutwell further to understand that he "apprehended an attempt by the President to reorganize the government by the assembling of Congress in which the members from the seceding states and the Democratic members from the North might attain control through the aid of the Executive." [36]

Having charged Johnson with the preparation of a coup d'état, Stanton proceeded to outline the necessity for a law "by which the power of the President might be limited." With absorbing interest Boutwell listened, and finally under Stanton's dictation drafted an amendment to the appropriation bill for the support of the army.[37]

This measure provided for the headquarters of the General of the army at Washington, where he was to remain unless elsewhere transferred either by his own consent or that of the Senate. Had Grant been personally in conference with the Secretary of War on this plan? Why had he so earnestly desired to be in Washington on the return of Congress? The amendment made it a misdemeanor for the President to transmit orders to any officer, except through the General of the army. Obedience by any officer to any order not issued in this way was likewise to be a misdemeanor. When the bill was written out, Boutwell took it over to the House and handed it to Thaddeus Stevens! [38] It was a direct affront to Johnson! Its purpose was to strike down this constitutional prerogative: "The President shall be the Commander-in-Chief of the Army and Navy of the United States." [39]

With increasing zeal the Radicals were designing bills affecting the powers of the President, and making a violation of their measures misdemeanors. Misdemeanors! Why were they so concerned with them? There was another section of the Constitution they had been reading: "The President . . . shall be removed from office on impeachment for and conviction of Treason, Bribery or *other high crimes and misdemeanors.*" [40] Knowing that they could find neither "treason, bribery or other high crimes," in his career, they were inventing "misdemeanors" in the hope of trapping him into one!

XLIV

THE TENURE-OF-OFFICE BILL

THE warm days of June, 1789, when New York City was still the capital of the United States, witnessed a debate raging on the floor of the first Congress. The giants of the great Constitutional Convention were many of them taking part, but no one spoke oftener or more to the point than James Madison.

The point at issue was whether the Secretary of the new Department of Foreign Affairs could be made removable by the President without the advice and consent of the Senate.[1] Would such a law conflict with the Constitution? Since he wrote much of it, Madison must have known the instrument by heart. Probably he did not have to turn to its pages, but those who did, read this: "The President . . . shall nominate, and by and with the advice and consent of the Senate shall appoint Ambassadors . . . and all other officers of the United States whose appointments are not herein otherwise provided for and which shall be established by law. . . ." [2] But in whom the power of removal rested, whether in the President alone or in the President "by and with the advice and consent of the Senate," the Constitution maintained a sphinx-like silence.

But if the Constitution was silent on this point, those who wrote the instrument were not. Madison contended with impelling logic that the Constitution gave the President the right, without the advice and consent of the Senate, to remove officers whom he had appointed,[3] and that the power of removal was incident to the power of appointment.[4] But perhaps his strongest argument was based upon the constitutional provision requiring the President "to take care that the laws be faithfully executed." [5]

Madison prevailed. He and his associates then sought to make it plain that they were not creating a power, but were merely making a "legislative construction" of the Constitution, by recog-

403

nizing the power as already inherent in that instrument. Their bill, as finally drawn, provided for an officer "to be called the Chief Clerk in the Department of Foreign Affairs, and, who, *whenever the principal officer shall be removed from office by the President* . . . shall during such vacancy have charge" of all records of the department.[6] The work was deftly done. The bill was passed, and on July 27th, 1789, with the signature of President Washington became a law.[7] What interpretation could have been more deserving of respect than this legislative construction made by those who had been the founders of the Constitution? What mattered it to Stevens that this interpretation had been the accepted one for seventy-seven years?

How little he cared appeared on the first Monday of December, 1866, when one of Stevens' Joint Committee, Williams of Oregon, introduced in the Senate a bill declaring that every person, except members of the Cabinet "holding any civil office to which he has been appointed by and with the advice and consent of the Senate . . . shall be entitled to hold such office until a successor shall have been in like manner appointed and duly qualified. . . ."[8] In effect this was a declaration that the President could not remove civil officers whose tenure was not limited by law, without the advice and consent of the Senate. It was a repudiation of Madison and Washington.

Removals from office! On his "Swing Around the Circle," the President had declared that he would make them by the wholesale. Badgered by his assailants he had, during the campaign, removed 1283 postmasters, and had weeded out a few in the internal revenue and the custom houses.[9] And yet, as Oberholtzer says: "Johnson had been far from free and indiscriminate in the removal of office-holders, even when their antagonism to his course was carried to great and offensive lengths. . . ."[10]

Near the end of the campaign Secretary McCulloch wrote to Tilden: "The President desires to make as few changes as possible, and none on political grounds unless it is clear that the interests of the service, or the interests of the administration are to be clearly benefited by them."[11] But the rank and file of Congressmen, pressed as they always are by the home constituency, were bitter even at such removals as were made.[12]

ASHLEY BEGINS WORK ON IMPEACHMENT

IMPEACHMENT! The air resounded with the cry! The Presidential obstacle! Judas! Treason! The follower of Jefferson Davis! The friend of Rebels! The country must be purged! Impeach him now! Impeach him!! The newspapers were filled with the suggestion. The name of Warren Hastings was becoming known to every school child.[1] What mattered it that there was no evidence? What mattered it that there was no treason, bribery or other high crime or misdemeanor? What mattered it that no President had ever been impeached? What mattered anything if Andrew Johnson could be driven out of public life, if he could be disgraced and ruined and Lincoln's libeler lifted to his place!

The Radicals were studying the Constitution. These questions were asked and answered: What is an impeachment? It is a charge or accusation. For what offenses may the charge be made? "Treason, bribery or other high crimes or misdemeanors."[2] Who has the power to make the charge,—that is, to impeach? "The House of Representatives . . . shall have the sole power of impeachment,"—that is, to make the charge. What court tries it? "The Senate shall have the sole power to try all impeachments." Who presides at the trial? "When the President is tried, the Chief Justice shall preside."[3] What is the purpose of the trial? To determine the guilt or innocence of the accused. When must the accused be acquitted? When less than two-thirds of the members of the Senate present do not vote guilty. When must there be a conviction? "No person shall be convicted without the concurrence of two-thirds of the members present."[4] What is the nature of a judgment of conviction? "Judgment in cases of impeachment shall not extend further than to removal

405

from office and disqualification to hold and enjoy any office of honor, trust or profit, under the United States." [5]

The time was ripe, many of the Radicals believed, for action. The House of Representatives (the great Grand Jury) should begin its work, should seek or manufacture some ground for impeachment of the President. James M. Ashley, Stanton's friend, was ready. Exactly two weeks after the beginning of the session, on December 17th, he moved in the House for the appointment of a committee of seven members "to inquire whether any acts have been done by any officer of the United States which in contemplation of the Constitution are high crimes or misdemeanors and whether said acts were designed or calculated to overthrow, subvert or corrupt the Government of the United States." [6]

Ashley approached the work with special pleasure. He had been disappointed in securing an office for a constituent. Lincoln had made a bargain with him to obtain his vote for the Thirteenth Amendment in exchange for a revenue collectorship. Johnson did not like bargains of this kind, and as he had not made it, refused to carry it out. [7] But all the Radicals were not yet ready for impeachment, and Ashley's resolution was not adopted. It was close, five votes only of the necessary two-thirds were lacking. [8]

This was only December! There were nearly three months remaining for the 39th Congress. Perhaps during that time something could be done, if not, the 40th would presently be trooping into Washington and Benjamin F. Butler would be with them! Perhaps, too,—there was just that chance—Johnson would now take note of what his enemies intended, perhaps even now he could be frightened from further obstruction of their aims. They would wait for his action on Sumner's District of Columbia negro franchise bill. Perhaps he would not veto it. And if he did,— well, then there would be time enough to act.

XLVI

THE MILLIGAN CASE

THE childlike pleasure found by so many Americans in secret signs, fantastic pass words, and strange grips was never more manifest than during the middle years of our Civil War. The autumn after Meade had stemmed the tide at Gettysburg, perhaps 175,000 Democrats of Ohio, Illinois and Indiana had organized themselves into the "Knights of the Golden Circle," choosing later as their name the "Order of American Knights." That they were not favoring the Northern cause was sufficiently attested by their pass word: "Nu-oh-lac," which was nothing but Calhoun spelled backward! It was a counter movement to the "Union Leagues," the Republicans had organized.[1]

Between the mutterings of their mysterious oaths and the chanting of their recondite ritual, the "Knights" were fumbling, albeit a little timidly, with dark dreams of a Northwestern Confederacy wherewith they hoped to end the war. Union generals commanding the districts harboring these rather weak-kneed traitors were enormously disturbed.[2] Holt fairly reveled in the reports of his detectives, and discoursed quite eloquently to Stanton, of Judas, Catiline, and other historical characters.[3] But even during the summer of 1864, when McClellan was giving him enough to think about, Lincoln refused to be disturbed by the mummeries of these middle-western "Knights." His attitude towards them, wrote Hay, was one of "good-natured contempt."[4]

There was, however, one member of this brotherhood whose fate concerns this story. He was a citizen of Indiana and his name was Lamdin P. Milligan. He was probably a worthless scamp, yet his name is associated with a principle of liberty. His case is a landmark in our constitutional jurisprudence.

On October 5th, 1864, Major-General Hovey, the military com-

407

mandant of the District of Indiana, found Milligan's activities so distasteful that he charged him with a long list of "disloyal practices," including that of joining the "Order of American Knights" for the overthrow of the government. A military commission before whom he was tried sixteen days later took just twenty-four hours to decide his fate. He was found guilty on all charges and was sentenced to be hung by the neck. His execution was set for May 19th, 1865. Nine days before his appointment with the hangman Milligan obtained from the United States Circuit Court of Indiana a writ of habeas corpus praying either to be turned over to a proper civil tribunal or to be discharged from custody.[5]

Never having been in the military service, and the authority of the general government being unopposed in that state with the courts open and their process unobstructed,[6] he contended that the military commission had no jurisdiction over him, and hence, his conviction was illegal. If he was to be tried at all, he said, it must be before twelve of his peers after an indictment by a Grand Jury, and that as he had not been indicted, he was entitled to his discharge. What happened to Milligan was unimportant. But whether under these circumstances citizens could be tried by military courts was a question lying at the very bottom of the Reconstruction legislation. If such a procedure were unauthorized in Indiana, would it not be equally illegal in Virginia or South Carolina? What would become of the Freedman's Bureau courts and Stevens' further plans to rule the South with bayonets?

During the week of March 6th, 1866, two months after the adoption by Congress of the Fourteenth Amendment, and when the contest between the Executive and the lawmaking branches of the government was already well begun, the Milligan case was argued in the Supreme Court. The accused was represented by an impressive galaxy of legal talent: David Dudley Field, James A. Garfield and Jeremiah Black. Of Black's argument, Levi March later wrote: "He presented an array of law, fact and argument with such remarkable force and eloquence as startled and bewildered those who listened to him. . . . Freedom was his client. The great cause of constitutional liberty hung upon that single life."[7]   James Speed and Benjamin F. Butler argued to sustain the military court.

Here was a signal opportunity for the great tribunal! The balance wheel of the Constitution! Never before or since has the Supreme Court been given larger opportunities for the service it was constructed to perform than during the troubled years of Johnson's administration. Then, as at no other time, was it called upon to stand between the Constitution and the passions of those defying it,—between the rights of states and persons, and a Congress that assailed them!

Chase was the Chief Justice. He had eight associates: Field, Davis, Miller and Swayne appointed by Lincoln, Clifford by Buchanan, Grier by Polk, Nelson by Tyler, and Wayne by Andrew Jackson.[8]   Thus a majority of the nine members came there through Abraham Lincoln. There had been ten judges down to May 30th, 1865, when Catron died. On April 16th of the next year Johnson nominated his Attorney-General Stanbery to fill Catron's place. A Republican paper declared it "a most excellent appointment," but the Radical Senate contemptuously refused a confirmation.[9]   Three months later a law was passed providing that no vacancy should be filled until the number of judges was reduced to seven![10]   It was intended that Johnson should make no appointments to the court. It was already plain that the Radicals would attack the Judicial as well as the Executive department, should the judges dare to thwart them. Would the judiciary display the red badge of courage? Would they, when the test came, stand up to Congress as Johnson had done?

The opinions of the court in the Milligan case were eagerly awaited. Would Johnson find an enemy or an ally in that quarter? Would the five Lincoln appointees prove hostile or sympathetic to Lincoln's great successor? The court was in a strange dilemma. The military commission was an instrument that Lincoln had used during the war, and yet to sustain its use within a state where no war raged, and whose courts were open, would give the Radicals a clear authority for the military tribunals they had planned for the humiliation of the South. What decision would the great umpire of the Constitution give?

On Monday, April 2nd, Johnson had inquired eagerly "whether any facts were yet public in relation to the decision."[11] The next day the decision came. The unanimous holding of the court was that the military commission had condemned Milligan without lawful power![12] But upon what grounds this conclusion had been based were veiled in mystery. It was announced that the opinion of the judges would not be published "until next winter."[13] Why the delay? Nobody knew.

Eight and a half months later the opinions were made public,[14]—the very day that Ashley introduced his resolution looking to the President's impeachment.[15] Judge David Davis delivered the opinion of the court. "During the late wicked Rebellion," he wrote, "the temper of the times did not allow that calmness in deliberation and discussion so necessary to a correct conclusion of a purely judicial question."[16] "Now," continued Davis, "that the public safety is assured, this question as well as all others can be discussed and decided without passion or the admixture of any element not required to form a legal judgment."[17] The question indeed might have been so discussed, not by the court alone, but by the entire country, could Stevens and his fellow revolutionists have been silenced.

"Until recently," continued Davis, "no one ever doubted that the right of trial by jury was fortified in the organic law against the power of attack."[18] Soldiers and sailors might be tried by military courts but "all other persons, citizens of states where the courts were open, if charged with crime, are guaranteed the inestimable privilege of trial by jury. This privilege is a vital principle, underlying the whole administration of criminal justice; it is not held by sufferance, and cannot be frittered away on any plea of state or political necessity.[19] When peace prevails and the authority of the government is undisputed, there is no difficulty of preserving the safeguards of liberty . . . but if society is disturbed by civil commotion—if the passions of men are aroused and the restraints of law weakened, if not disregarded,— these safeguards need and should receive the watchful care of those intrusted with the guardianship of the Constitution and laws. In no other way can we transmit to posterity unimpaired the blessings of liberty, consecrated by the sacrifices of the Revolution." [20]

With great emphasis he went on: "This is not a question of the power to proclaim martial law, when war exists in a community and the courts and the civil authorities are overthrown. . . . If armies were collected in Indiana, they were to be employed in another locality, where the laws were obstructed and the national authority disputed. On her soil there was no hostile foot; if once invaded, that invasion was at an end, and with it all pretext for martial law. Martial law cannot arise from a threatened invasion. The necessity must be actual and present; the invasion real, such as effectually closes the courts and deposes the civil administration. . . . Martial rule can never exist when the courts are open, and in the proper and unobstructed exercises of their jurisdiction. It is also confined to the locality of actual war." [21]

It was a great opinion. It has now long since been justly recognized as "one of the bulwarks of American liberty." [22] It was statesmanship. It was a great pronouncement, but it was not greater or more sound than Andrew Johnson's veto of the Freedman's Bureau bill published ten months before! [23] Both documents excoriated the use of military courts for the trial, in peacetimes, of civilians. Both were founded on the bed rock of the Constitution. Neither could be answered by the Radicals, save through the medium of excoriation. The Supreme Court stood with Andrew Johnson! Its action was a source of great encouragement." [24]

Would the court continue to stand firm? Would it with Johnson's courage, go forward in resistance to the Radical assaults? That they would not hesitate to assail it, as well as Johnson, had long been manifest. Had not the "Southern Loyalist" Convention declared that the "political status" of the Southern states was "clearly within the control of Congress to the exclusion of the independent action *of any and every other department of the government?*" [25] Judges were as liable to impeachment as the Executive. [26] The batteries of the Supreme Court were in action; they were using high percussion, and they had found their target! Would they continue firing until no cannoneer was left to pull the lanyard? Or would the limbers presently be sent for, and the guns driven back along the dusty white roads of surrender?

Some answer to these questions was suggested when Chief Justice Chase, although concurring in the direct holding of the court, filed and secured the concurrence of three of his associates, Wayne, Swayne and Miller in a separate opinion. "There are cases," he said, "in which . . . trial and punishment by military commission, in states where civil courts are open, may be authorized by Congress, as well as arrest and detention." [27] Chase did not seem disposed to place himself against the Revolutionists. The nominations for 1868 were less than two years distant, and he was still bent on the Presidency! His friends already had suggested to him "that the time had come to organize." [28]

§

With storms of denunciation the Milligan decision was greeted by the Radicals. "The Supreme Court, we regret to find," declared the New York *Times,* "throws the weight of its influence into the scale of those who assailed the Union. . . . The whole Copperhead press exults over the decision. . . ." [29] The Indianapolis *Journal* spoke of the decision as one "to create misgivings in the mind of the patriotic people who saved the nation from destruction at the hands of rebels," and declared that it was "intended only to aid the Johnson men, and is so clearly a forerunner of other decisions looking to a defeat of Republican ascendancy and to a restoration of Southern domination that the indignation against the court is just and warranted." [30] *Harper's Weekly* proclaimed that "the Indiana decision operates to deprive the freedmen, in the late rebel states, whose laws grievously outrage them, of the protection of the freedmen's courts." [31]

The *Nation* a few days later said: "Mr. Johnson has at last found what he imagines to be a snug and safe harbor for his 'policy.' The Supreme Court has come to his aid, and has already declared military commissions illegal—thus putting an end to military interference with the action of the local authorities at the South—and it is fully believed will take strong conservative ground in several cases now before it." [32]

Many of the dispatches were distinctly minatory. "Should the Court . . . show that it is irrevocably wedded to pro-slavery ideas, to a sympathy for rebels," wired the Washington correspondent to the Cleveland *Herald*, "then a future Congress will reorganize the court." [33]   And another correspondent wrote: "Thaddeus Stevens today . . . had a long interview with Secretary Stanton. . . . He has a great contempt for the Supreme Court's decision in the Milligan case. He does not favor the project of impeaching several of the Justices, but wants to impeach the President, from whom all the evils flow. . . . A movement that will be started tomorrow for the impeaching of several of the Justices will meet with favor in the House. . . . Mr. Stevens is preparing some stringent measures to protect the country from the evil tendencies of the Supreme Court." [34]   And *Harper's Weekly* suggested that "the Supreme Court be swamped by a thorough reorganization and increased number of Judges. . . ." [35]

There were many to applaud the stand of Chase. "The minority," said the Cleveland *Herald*, "as in the Dred Scott case, will receive the thanks of all loyal men who would seize any means within reach to save a government from the hands of traitors who could subvert it. . . ." ! [36] John Jay wrote to the Chief Justice: "I read your opinion in the Milligan case with warm admiration of its clear statement and sound logic, but with profound regret that you were not speaking for the majority of the Judges. If, as the public begin to fear, their denial in that case of the powers of Congress is any index to the view they are prepared to take of the great questions that will come before them in reference to reconstruction, our situation is certainly a grave one. And it will require more wisdom than the Republican managers have sometimes shown to surmount successfully the formidable opposition no longer of a simply obstinate President's defying the will of the people, but of an Executive furnished with a constitutional standpoint by the Supreme Judiciary, giving validity to his acts and checkmating Congress at the most eventful moment by denying its powers and annulling its legislation." [37]

To find any contemporary estimate of the press in the least suggestive of the views now universally accepted, it is necessary to take up the Democratic papers. "The fact that the Supreme Court has escaped the servile contamination of the times," declared the New York *World*, "and pronounces an independent opinion . . . is full of encouragement." [38] And the *National Intelligencer* proclaimed: "They are disloyal who, under the pretense of preserving the liberties of the citizen, have disregarded the obligations of the organic law. . . . And as in war times, these monopolists of patriotism denounced those who upheld the sacred liberties of the citizen as guaranteed by the Constitution, so now, in the midst of peace, they assail those who maintain the rights of the states as guaranteed by the same instrument. But the Supreme Court has evermore made such an assault upon the rights of citizens impossible; and we doubt not that in due time it will extend its broad aegis over the violated commonwealths of the South. . . . It is not Milligan, the alleged conspirator, who is set free; but Milligan, citizen, tried by an illegal tribunal. . . . It is not the crime of treason which is shielded by this memorable decision, but the sacred rights of the citizen that are vindicated above the arbitrary decisions of military authority. Above the might of the sword, the majesty of the law is thus raised supreme." [39]

But the Radicals were not daunted by the Supreme Court, their revolutionary purpose seemed rather to have hardened to a new resolve. They were determined now to gain their dastard ends, by striking down, if need be, the Judiciary as well as the Executive. Thaddeus Stevens was prepared for any course, his contempt for the court and for the President was equalled only by his disdain of every constitutional restraint. He was old, but his passionate hatred for the South gave him all the energy of youth.

Quietly amid the gathering storms Johnson pursued his way. No American has ever had a lonelier or more treacherous path to tread. Haggard with the cruel load he appeared at times dejected, but when among his friends the subject of impeachment was discussed, it was evident that the matter gave him no concern. [40] For the country's future, however, he was stirred. There was good reason.

Three days before the year was ushered out he alluded at a

Cabinet meeting "to the extraordinary movements in Congress affecting the government, especially the subject of attempting to change the character and status of some of the states." He asked his advisers to consider well the subject, expressing a strong hope for united action. The subject went around the council board and everyone expressed his opposition "to the schemes of territorializing the states,"—until it came to Stanton. They looked at him, waiting to hear him speak, but he "held down his head and said nothing." [41]

The unhappy year was dying. On New Year's eve Johnson and his staunch friend, Gideon Welles, sat talking of the country's troubled hour. Amazing for one who had discerned so much, the President had not yet seen through, or was unwilling to admit, that he had seen through Stanton. Only the day before he had expressed himself as confident that Stanton was his friend. Stanton was playing a double game, he must have been a consummate actor. Welles was fairly trembling with eagerness to discuss the subject with the President, but somehow they did not reach it. "The President," wrote Welles, "must understand my views, must know that Stanton is opposing and betraying him." [42]

It was a gloomy New Year's Eve! Where was there room for hope that 1867 would bring his country greater happiness? If Johnson had failed to see through Stanton, he had not failed to comprehend his other enemies. As he and his faithful Minister of the Navy sat raking up the dying embers of the old year, the sparks seemed fitfully to illuminate the new. Before these two good friends parted, the President declared he had no doubt that the Radicals intended to attack the Executive, the Judiciary, the Constitution and the states. [43]

XLVII

1867 FINDS THE PLOT MATURING

THE Senators and Representatives returned to the capital after their New Year holiday, determined that they would make 1867 memorable. The leading actors in the conspiracy had been well drilled for their parts. The bills intended to consummate the plot had all been introduced; it remained only to lash their program through. Louder and louder they were shouting for impeachment! They hoped the threat alone would frighten Johnson from his course.

As a kind of overture to this symphony of malice, Charles Sumner's District of Columbia negro franchise bill was the first to engage the attention of the President. It entitled the negroes to vote and deprived all those who had "voluntarily given aid and comfort to the rebels in the late rebellion" of this privilege.[1] The bill reached Johnson a few days before the turn of the year, and on January 4th he had his veto message ready, and read it to his Cabinet. All were in agreement with his views, until it came to Stanton! This member now produced a written statement, carefully prepared, declaring that he could perceive no constitutional objections to Sumner's bill, and expressing the hope that "the President would give it his approval." [2] Grant was present by invitation. He expressed his disapproval of what Sumner wanted; he thought it "very contemptible business for members of Congress whose states excluded the negroes to give them suffrage in this district." [3]

On January 7th the veto message reached the Senate.[4] It was as calm as though the relations between him and the Congress were those of perfect amity. The citizens of the District of Columbia at that time possessed the right to vote,[5]—and they had

416

voted on this very question in December, 1865. In Washington 6,556 ballots against, and but 35 in favor of this proposition had been cast, while in Georgetown the votes stood 813 to 1.[6]

Sumner's total indifference to the will of the inhabitants of the district was powerfully presented.[7] Not for one moment gain-saying the unquestioned constitutional right of Congress to legislate for the District, as of course it could not have done for a sovereign state, Johnson placed his main objection on the broad ground of public policy. Interwoven through his argument was the plea for the preservation of that sanctuary of liberty,—the right of local self-government! "The measures suited to one community," he said, "might not be well adapted to the condition of another; and the persons best qualified to determine such questions are those whose interests are to be directly affected by any proposed law." [8]

How about Charles Sumner's state? What could be defter than Johnson's reference to that? "In Massachusetts, for instance," he declared, "male persons are allowed to vote without regard to color, provided they possess a certain degree of intelligence." But there the problem, by reason of the paucity of negroes, was comparatively negligible! But in the District of Columbia the ex-slaves clothed "with the elective franchise, their numbers, already largely in excess of the demand for labor, would be soon increased by an influx from the adjoining states. . . . Hardly yet capable of forming correct judgments upon the important questions that often make the issues of a political contest, they could readily be made subservient to the purposes of designing persons. While in Massachusetts, under the census of 1860, the proportion of white to colored males over 20 years of age was 130 to 1, here the black race numbers nearly one-third of the entire population. . . ." [9]

To force negro suffrage on the District, Johnson said "would be viewed as an arbitrary exercise of power and as an indication by the country of the purpose of Congress to compel the acceptance of negro suffrage by the states. It would engender a feeling of opposition and hatred between the two races, which becoming deep-rooted and ineradicable, would prevent them from living together in a state of mutual friendliness. Carefully avoiding every measure that might tend to produce such a result, and following the clear and well-ascertained popular will, we should assiduously endeavor to promote kindly relations between them, and thus, when that popular will leads the way, prepare for the gradual and harmonious introduction of this new element into the political power of the country." [10]

No publicist has ever written words of greater wisdom or more fundamental truth than these: "The exercise of the elective franchise is the highest attribute of an American citizen, and when guided by virtue, intelligence, patriotism, and a proper appreciation of our institutions, constitutes the true basis of a democratic form of government in which the sovereign power is lodged in the body of the people. Its influence for good necessarily depends upon the elevated character and patriotism of the elector, for if expressed by persons who do not justly estimate its value and who are indifferent as to its results, it will only serve as a measure of placing power in the hands of the unprincipled and ambitious, and must eventuate in the complete destruction of that liberty of which it should be the most powerful conservator." [11]

Like its predecessors, the logic of this message was unanswerable. But revolutionists are not concerned with logic. There were other forms of confutation. There was the argument of force, mob violence, lynch law! They could not answer the President, therefore they would destroy him!

The Senate, on January 7th, listened quietly to the reading of the message, and immediately repassed the vetoed bill by a vote of twenty-nine to ten. [12] The two-thirds were in good working order! Relinquishing no opportunity to insult the President of the United States, before the message even reached the House, Stevens' tools had acted! Springing to his feet, Benjamin F. Loan, of Missouri, offered a resolution declaring that Congress should without delay accomplish the following objects: "1. The impeachment of the officer now exercising the functions pertaining to the office of President of the United States and his removal from said office upon conviction of the high crimes and misdemeanors of which he is manifestly and notoriously guilty. 2. To provide for the faithful and efficient administration of the executive department." [13]

Here was a denial that Johnson was President! He was merely "the officer exercising the functions pertaining" to "that office!" From now on it was to be a leading formula of the Presidential libelers to couple every reference to the President with a denial that he was such.

Through a point of order Loan's resolution was sent to the Joint Committee on Reconstruction. And then like mad dogs, showing their poison fangs, and attacking furtively from every side, and from the rear, others of Stevens' henchmen moved to the affray. From Missouri there was a snarl,—it came from John R. Kelso, who sent to the Speaker's desk another resolution similar to that of Loan. It was put to a vote and lost. [14] And now the opportunity for Stanton's friend and secret correspondent had arrived! Ashley was on his feet crying: "I do impeach Andrew Johnson, *Vice-President and acting President of the United States,* of high crimes and misdemeanors. I charge him with a usurpation of power and violation of law: In that he has corruptly used the appointing power; in that he has corruptly used the pardoning power; in that he has corruptly used the veto power; in that he has corruptly disposed of public property of the United States; in that he has corruptly interfered in elections and committed acts which in contemplation of the Constitution are high crimes and misdemeanors." [15]

The resolution called upon the House Judiciary Committee to inquire and report whether Johnson "had been guilty of acts which are designed or calculated to overthrow, subvert or corrupt the government of the United States or any department or office thereof." [16] By a vote of 108 to 38 it was referred. [17]

The hounds were now in full cry, and Thaddeus Stevens was riding at the head of the pack! Even in that Congress, however, there were some in whom the lust of the chase had failed to work a total corruption of honor. One of these was Senator James W. Grimes of Iowa. With all his strength he declared against this effort "to establish an example which might result in making ours a sort of South American republic where the ruler is deposed the moment popular sentiment sets against him." [18]

"In the House of Representatives," wrote Welles that evening, "fanaticism, prompted by partisanship, ran wild. The reckless leaders were jubilant; the timid followers were abject and obedient." Referring to Ashley's resolution he continued: "It will never result, even under party drill, in an impeachment and conviction, but it is disreputable and demoralizing that a packed party majority should so belittle the government and free institutions as to entertain such a resolution from such a source. But he has not done it without consulting others." [19] And the next day: "Infamous charges, infamous testimony and infamous proceedings will be produced as easily, honestly and legally as Butler could get spoons in New Orleans. . . . Ashley, who introduced the resolution, is a calculating fanatic, weak, designing, fond of notoriety, not of very high-toned moral calibre. I do not think, however, that he is, as some suppose, a tool of others entirely,— certainly not an unwilling tool. He seeks the notoriety and notice, and hounds like Boutwell and Williams of Pittsburg egg him on. Colfax, though feeble-minded, is Speaker, seeks to be foremost, and has been an adviser with Ashley and pioneered the way for him to introduce the resolution. Stevens, much shrewder and abler than either, keeps in the background, though the chief conspirator." [20]

Twenty-four hours later, by a vote of 113 to 38, Sumner's negro suffrage bill passed the House, and so became a law, the President's veto notwithstanding. With such a smooth-working two-thirds in both Houses, were impeachment and conviction an impossibility?

§

The tumult was rising, but Johnson continued on his course unmoved. He was watching the conspirators and quietly preparing for the struggle. The leading measure of the session, of course, was Stevens' Reconstruction bill, whereby he hoped to strip the Southern states of statehood. It had not yet emerged from his Committee, but everyone knew what he was planning. On January 8th the President remarked to his council that "in view of what was taking place around us," he wished to bring forward the subject of throwing the states "into a territorial condition." He considered it important, he said, to "know the opinions and views of each member of the Cabinet. If we are united, that fact would carry weight with it, here and before the country; if we were not united there was weakness." [21] As he spoke, those who watched him noted in his face a look of "firm and fixed resolution. He was pale and calm, but no one could mistake that he was determined in his purpose." [22]

One by one the members of the Cabinet expressed their denunciation of Stevens' revolutionary plans, until it came to Stanton. He had, he declared, communicated his views to no one. He had "assented to and cordially approved of every step" which Johnson had taken to rehabilitate the states, and he saw no reason to change the plan already followed. He said that he had not seen Stevens' proposition "and did not care to, for it was one of those schemes which would end in noise and smoke." He had conversed, he said, a year ago with Sumner, but had "never since conversed with Sumner or anyone else." He did not then nor now concur with Sumner's views, and did not believe that "a state would or could be remanded to a territorial condition." [23] The impression made on his listeners by these pious expressions of loyalty was voiced by McCulloch when four days later he declared that Stanton "whenever it becomes an object" would deny this committal to the administration policy and would "modify and change his views to suit his purposes." In unqualified terms he expressed his belief that the Secretary of War was "false and treacherous," and "a steady spy" upon the other members of that Cabinet. [24]

A half a century later, with the benefit of a calm historical perspective, Professor Dunning, in his essay on the Reconstruction, writes thus of Johnson's Minister of War: "This strange personage, whose amazing record of duplicity strongly suggests the vagaries of an opium eater, assumed now the task of inspiring in Congress the belief that his chief, the President, was a desperate character, bent on overriding the majority by military force." [25]

It undoubtedly was Johnson's cardinal mistake to retain this false and treacherous adviser at his council board. He should long before have thrown him out. It was almost an incredible blunder to keep Stanton on. Utterly lacking even in the faintest trace of duplicity himself, this downright President was slow to credit another with the attributes of a spy, and Stanton's were such as to have required a DeQuincy to unearth and follow.

While Stanton within the Cabinet and Boutwell, his secret confederate in Congress, "exemplifying perfectly the hard merciless type which the Puritan conscience makes of a mediocre man," [26] were doing all within their power to destroy the President, unmoved, the object of all of their conspiracies, was carrying on. But as Boutwell's judiciary committee moved to the attack, scouring the gutters, the sewers and the jails for their ammunition, Welles sat watching, confiding now and then his observations to his diary.

Four days after Ashley had charged the President with high crimes and misdemeanors, Welles recorded: "Although the President has committed no act that can subject him to impeachment, and is in many respects one of the best and most single-minded Executives we have ever had, I have little doubt that the Radical leaders intend to get rid of him. This they feel to be essential to consummate their usurping schemes. There is a conspiracy maturing. How can they reduce the states to the condition of corporations, territorialize them, deprive them of their original reserved and guaranteed constitutional rights without the aid of the Judiciary? How can they get control of the Court except by enlarging its numbers? If the number is to be increased, how can they get Radicals, except by displacing Johnson and getting Wade or one like him in his place." [27]

A few days later Welles noted the beginnings of that propaganda that was yet to grow, wherein it was proclaimed that an impeachment trial was not a judicial proceeding, that no definite charges or proof of guilt were necessary, and that it was a mere form wherewith to do away with a President opposed to the majority in Congress. "I see by the papers this evening," he wrote, "that the Radical legislatures of one or two states are taking the matter in hand, and urging impeachment without any facts or fault, or specified crime, as a mere party measure, but it is all in character—a conspiracy against the Constitution and the President for adhering to it." [28] And then three days later: "The President remains passive and firm, but with no declared policy if the Radicals pursue their design to impeach and suspend him during trial. . . . What General Grant and certain others might do, were Congress to proceed to extremities, neither the President nor any of his true friends are aware. I doubt if Grant himself knows. The Radicals, who distrust him, are nevertheless courting him assiduously." [29]

§

Amid all the distractions of their manifold maneuverings, with angry anxiety, the Radicals were watching the progress of their dear-prized Fourteenth Amendment. It was making progress in the North,—in the South anything but progress. Seward had submitted it to the states on June 16th, 1866, [30] and it will be recalled how Connecticut had ratified it nine days later, New Hampshire on July 6th, and Tennessee (at least so Brownlow claimed) on July 11th. [31]

Before the year was over New Jersey, Oregon and Vermont were added to the list of ratifiers, while in Texas, Virginia, Arkansas, Alabama, Georgia, Florida, Mississippi, North and South Carolina, the amendment was rejected. [32] In January, however, although Kentucky added her rejection, Pennsylvania, New York, Indiana, Maine, Michigan, Illinois, Missouri, West Virginia, Ohio, Minnesota, Kansas, Wisconsin and Nevada voted their acceptance. [33] By the end of January, therefore, although far more than three-fourths of the Northern commonwealths had given their approval, less than that required proportion of all the states within the Union had assented. And with their acquiescence in Seward's submission of the amendment (as well as of its predecessor) to all the states, it was too late for the Radicals to contend that ratification by the "conquered provinces" was unnecessary.

The campaign of 1866 was such as to insure the impossibility of an unbiased consideration of this far-reaching change. In the North the people were indoctrinated with the belief that were the amendment not adopted, "Rebels" would soon control the government at Washington, that there would be a repudiation of the National and an assumption of the "Rebel" debt, that there would be payment for the manumitted slaves, and that loyalty would become the subject of contempt. To these motives manufactured from this propaganda, there was added the cupidity and the fear of Northern bond holders, Northern hatred and misunderstanding of the South, and the desire, by whatever means, to maintain the ascendancy of the Radical party, as well as the sincere wish of many earnest but misguided persons to do what they thought the preservation of the Union needed.[34]

Despite all the agitation, seven months had gone by and the required three-fourths of the states had not yet ratified. The Radicals looked on uneasily as one Southern state after another contemptuously declined to be a party to the humiliation of its leading citizens. They listened with dismay while Governor Walker of Florida told his legislature that the Fourteenth Amendment was "a measure of consolidation entirely changing the form of the government," and that since it would disfranchise the most capable men of his state, to vote in its favor was to work for the destruction of Florida.[35] Angrily they heard Governor Orr say to the legislature of South Carolina: "Let us preserve our own self-respect and the respect of posterity by refusing to be the mean instrument of our own shame."[36]

XLVIII

JOHNSON IS ACCUSED OF LINCOLN'S MURDER

SEVEN days after Ashley introduced his resolution of impeachment, the conspirators were startled as with a thunderclap,—the Supreme Court spoke again! The Cummings and the Garland cases were decided; [1] they came like detonating echoes of the Milligan decision. The great tribunal had not been intimidated. The balance wheel of the Constitution was still in equilibrium!

The question in the Cummings case was: Could a state require a priest or clergyman in order to continue his profession, to take an oath that he had not at any time manifested his desire for the triumph of the South? The Supreme Court thundered no. It was an ex post facto law, and under the Constitution, therefore, void. "We admit," said Mr. Justice Field (a Lincoln appointee) writing for the court, "that the states which existed previous to the adoption of the Federal Constitution possessed originally all the attributes of sovereignty; that they still retain those attributes, except as they have been surrendered by the formation of the Constitution, and the amendments thereto; that the new states upon their admission into the Union became invested with equal rights, and were thereafter subject only to similar restrictions. . . ." [2]

In the Garland case, the act of Congress of January 24th, 1865, imposing a test oath for lawyers practicing in the Supreme Court, was involved. Garland had been admitted in that court before the war. He had been a Representative and then a Senator in the Confederate Congress; he, therefore, could not take the oath. He was pardoned by President Johnson in July, 1865, and afterwards petitioned for leave to practice without being forced to take the oath, claiming that the act of January 24th was ex post facto and unconstitutional,—and further that in any event his pardon

425

had restored his former rights. Were his points well taken? The Supreme Court answered yes. As to ex post facto, the reasoning of the Cummings case was followed. As to the pardon, the court declared that the President's constitutional power was unlimited as to all crimes against the United States, except "in cases of impeachment." "This power of the President is not subject to legislative control. Congress can neither limit the effect of his pardon, nor exclude from its exercise any class of offenders. The benign prerogatives of mercy reposed in him cannot be fettered by any legislative restrictions. . . . When the pardon is full, it releases the punishment and blots out of existence the guilt, so that in the eye of the law the offender is as innocent as if he had never committed the offence." [3]

Here were two further body blows for Stevens and his followers. Not only was Johnson vindicated in his grants of pardon, but a warning to Congress was proclaimed. The Radicals could read that the Constitution was not yet a scrap of paper; that they could not interfere with the President's constitutional prerogatives, they could not pass bills of attainder and ex post facto laws, and last but not least that the states, not some, but all the states, still retained all their attributes of sovereignty not surrendered by them when the Constitution and its amendments were adopted, and that the states, not some, but all the states, when they originally joined the Union, "became invested with equal rights, and were thereafter subject only to *"similar restrictions."* [4]

The Radicals read in these words the ruin of their hopes. How could Stevens' measures survive before such a court? Something must be done! They must strike down the Court as well as the Executive! Unless,—unless they could intimidate the judiciary. After all, four of the nine judges had dissented in each case. One of the dissenters was the Chief-Justice! Apparently Chase was not courting a personal encounter with the enemies of Johnson,— and the elections of 1868 every day were drawing nearer.

The Radicals and their allies in the press began again a campaign of detraction. Their faithful Washington *Chronicle* declared that these two decisions had made "the fortification behind which impertinent rebels may renew or continue their war upon the government," and that "dangerous in the encouragement they have extended to traitors, they have nevertheless produced a reaction, which will not stop until the exact relation of that tribunal to the other departments of the government is absolutely and irrevocably fixed." [5]   The New York *Herald* not only denounced the decisions, but asked for a reconstruction of the court itself,[6] and *Harper's Weekly* spoke of them as "another proof of the disposition of the court to withstand the national will and reverse the results of the war." [7]

Busy with his plots against the President, Boutwell was not too absorbed to turn momentarily his fire upon the court. He introduced a bill that no lawyer who had been engaged in the Rebellion should practice at the Federal bar.[8]   This bill, declared the Springfield *Republican*, "is an attempt to neutralize the decision of the court. It strikes the country as designed to place these two branches of the Government in direct and open antagonism, but that act itself will probably prove a nullity. Congress is not the final judge of the validity of its own acts and cannot make itself so, while there is a Constitution and a Supreme Court." [9]   Boutwell's bill was not passed. But he and his friends had not yet finished with the judiciary. They certainly were not through with the Executive.

On January 24th, the very day the Cummings and Garland decisions were announced, Benjamin Loan, who the week before had offered a resolution to impeach the President, now gained the floor again. Opening all the floodgates of vilification, he let forth at Andrew Johnson such a torrential outburst of defamation as would have shamed the most loutish barroom on the soddenest riverfront of America. "At first," Loan declared, the assassination of Lincoln "was supposed to have been the rash act of a reckless young man rendered desperate by the failure of the cause to which he was devoted. But subsequent developments have shown it to have been the result of deliberate plans adopted in the interests of the rebellion. The appeal to arms on the part of the Rebels had failed. The only alternative left them upon which they could hope for success was fraud and treachery.

Experience had satisfied them that such agencies could not be successfully invoked so long as the incorruptible Lincoln guided the destinies of the Republic. But next to him . . . stood one who by birth, education and association was a Southern man, a life-long pro-slavery Democrat. . . . Powerfully influenced by all the grossest instincts of his nature, without moral culture or moral restraint, with a towering ambition . . . he was peculiarly and preëminently qualified to supply a necessity which the Rebel cause at that time imperatively required for its ultimate success." [10]

And Loan continued: "The leaders of the rebellion, realizing the signal and hopeless appeal to force for the success of their cause, were quick to understand the advantages offered them by such a person occupying the second office in the government. They readily comprehended the means necessary to reach and use such a subject; but one frail life stood between him and the chief magistracy of the Republic. And those who could devise the infernal cruelties of Andersonville . . . would not hesitate to accomplish their purposes by another murder, and hence the assassination of Mr. Lincoln. . . . An assassin's bullet wielded and directed by Rebel hand and paid for by Rebel gold made Andrew Johnson President. . . . *The price that he was to pay for his promotion was treachery to the Republicans and fidelity to the party of treason and rebellion.*" [11]

High crimes and misdemeanors! Here was indeed a charge; conspiracy to murder Lincoln! They had called Andrew Johnson every other name, why not run the whole lying gamut of accusation? Here was an accusation not of treason only, but of murder in the first degree! Andrew Johnson, the murderer of Lincoln!

With complacent pleasure the Radicals drank down the intoxicating dregs of Loan's attack. But there were some respectable characters even in the 39th Congress. Robert S. Hale of New York was one. He had heard all that he could stand,—he had heard more. He broke in now to stem the tide of excrement that flowed from Loan's coarse lips. His point of order was a good one: The House of Representatives could determine whether to prefer charges of impeachment, it had no power to try for murder! Speaker Colfax "with his heartless everlasting smile," [12] declared that he could not restrain the "gentleman from Missouri." Grimly watching the proceedings, Thaddeus Stevens broke in with this comment: "The decision of the chair is all right." His tools were working well! Their master's voice approved!

Encouraged by this approval, Loan went on: "Apostates, renegades, rebel sympathizers and rebel guerillas, bushwackers, and cutthroats, harmonize with the most wonderful unanimity on the President's policy. . . ." Hale again broke in: "The gentleman has upon this floor deliberately charged upon the Chief Executive of the nation complicity in assassination." He demanded proofs. "I propose," answered Loan, "to pursue this matter in my own way . . . the course which this resolution will take will carry it before the proper tribunal to inquire into this matter and there, in a legitimate way, the proofs I presume will be furnished to the gentleman's satisfaction." [13]

Here then was not only a deliberate charge that Andrew Johnson was a murderer, but a definite promise that proof of his guilt would presently be brought forward. No accusation more deliberately concocted or more wantonly false, in all the annals of mankind, is elsewhere recorded!

§

Men who would make a false charge of murder against a President of the United States would not scruple to sustain it by suborned perjury. If, through the medium of this dastard accusation they could further prejudice the President in the eyes of the American people, what mattered it to them how filthy were their lips with lying! Their consciences did not disturb them! What did they care that eighteen months before Mrs. Surratt and seven of her confederates had been tried and convicted, and that four of them were hung for conspiracy to murder Lincoln, Seward, Grant and *Andrew Johnson*? [14] The Radicals were lacking even in a sense of humor. How else could they promulgate a charge that Johnson had joined in a conspiracy, one of whose objects was the murder of himself?

In furtherance of their rascally purpose, Loan, Boutwell and their friends turned naturally to the meanest scoundrel in the country. Conover, who had confessed to the suborning of Campbell and Snevel in February, had been tried and convicted of perjury. He was sentenced to ten years' imprisonment in the Albany Penitentiary. While he awaited transportation thither, he lay temporarily in the District of Columbia jail.[15] His place of incarceration now became a rendezvous for the Radicals, for he had sent forth word that he could furnish damning evidence against the President. Like some loathsome bird of prey, Ashley hovered about this incarcerated scoundrel, hoping to carry back to the Judiciary Committee, in his sharp talons, some further defamation that could be hurled at Andrew Johnson.[16]

Conover had let the word go out that he could lay his hands upon a letter written by Johnson to Jefferson Davis and Booth, implicating Johnson in Lincoln's murder! Ashley pretended to believe him![17] There was just one little favor that Conover desired,—a pardon. Without scruple, and of course with no twinge of a conscience he did not possess, Ashley now set diligently to work to procure for Conover this pardon from the very man they were endeavoring to convict of Lincoln's murder.[18]

§

The 39th Congress was drawing to a close. There would not be time fully to carry out the whole conspiracy before the 4th of March, but all that could be done in the limited hours at their disposal the Radicals were determined to accomplish. Wade pressed on the plot to pack the High Court of Impeachment through the admission of Colorado and Nebraska. Late in January, the bills for the admission of these two territories passed both Houses. On the 29th Johnson vetoed both. These measures differed somewhat from those that had been vetoed at the previous session. But the crafty motives which had the year before resulted in their passage were the same. Knowing full well, of course, the real object of the measures, the President nevertheless directed his fire entirely at the bills themselves. He made it plain enough that there was no need then,—not in Colorado or Nebraska—of making these two territories states.[19]

But on February 8th the Senate, and on the following day the House, repassed the Nebraska bill over the Presidential veto.[20] Two new Senators would presently take their places beside Wade and Sumner,—"soldiers who would not shrink from any responsibility!" [21]   The thirty-seventh star was added to the national emblem.   Would Colorado be the thirty-eighth?   No attempt was made to override the veto at this time.   But if a favorable opportunity arose, would Wade try again?

XLIX

THE TENURE-OF-OFFICE BILL BECOMES A LAW

THERE were only twenty-eight days in February, 1867, but the Radicals had determined that everyone of these should count. While Wade was making every effort to pack the High Court of Impeachment, Williams of Oregon, the sponsor of the Tenure-of-Office Bill, was devising new traps in which he hoped the President would fall. Meanwhile Stevens steadily was driving on his Reconstruction measures for the humiliation of the South. Washington was a seething cauldron!

Retiring as Secretary of the United States legation in Paris, it was during this month that John Hay returned for a brief visit to the national capital. As Lincoln's former private secretary his opportunities for observation were unusual. He saw and talked with everyone. Of Seward he wrote: "He never seemed to me to better advantage. His utter calmness and cheerfulness, whether natural or assumed, is most admirable. . . . He speaks utterly without bitterness of the opposition to him and the President. He thinks the issue before the country was not fairly put, but seems rather to admire the cleverness with which the Radical leaders obscured and misstated the question to carry the election." [1]

One evening Hay attended a reception at the White House. "The President," he wrote, "was very cordial to me; said I must come and see him. Mrs. Johnson received for the first time; a quiet invalid old lady. The crowd not choice, but as good an average as ever; scarcely any distinguished people and none squalid. We used to have plenty of both." [2] And on another occasion: "They took me in the afternoon to the President's to make a bow to Mrs. Patterson and Mrs. Stover. The White House is much more richly and carefully furnished than in my

432

time. But the visitors were not quite up to the old mark, which was not hard to reach." [3]

Hay remained in Washington throughout the month of February, an interested spectator of the hurried scene. He was interested and surprised by many things,—by nothing more than the utter rout of the Conservative Republicans. "The whipped-out stunned way of talking," he wrote, "that I have seen in all the Conservatives is very remarkable. No threats; but a bewildered sort of incapacity to comprehend the earnest deviltry of the other side, characterizes them all,—but Seward, who is the same placid, philosophic optimist that he always was, the truest and most single-hearted Republican alive." [4]

During his stay in Washington John Hay attentively observed the Radicals as they put the finishing touches to their favorite instrument of malice,—the Tenure-of-Office Bill. With a reckless disregard of the early decision of the founders of the nation, as well as the unbroken practice of the government itself for three score and eighteen years, the wild-eyed apostles of vengeance moved forward in their attack on Andrew Johnson, and their determination to strip him of his constitutional power to remove Federal officers! [5]

Early in the debates the question whether the President should not be left, untrammelled by the advice and consent of the Senate, to remove at will the members of his Cabinet, was earnestly discussed. When on January 10th the bill was considered in the Senate for the first time, it was so worded as expressly to exclude Cabinet officers from its operation. Howe of Wisconsin demanded the reasons for this exception, and Edmunds of Vermont replied that not only the precedent of history, but the personal and confidential relations necessarily existing between the President and his constitutional advisers had prompted the exception, and that the Committee had come to their decision "after a great deal of consultation and reflection." [6]

Edmunds' reasons were not satisfactory to Howe. He moved, therefore, to amend the bill so as to make Cabinet officials, like other civil officers, removable by the President, only with the approval of the Senate. Howe could muster but eight votes for his amendment,[7] and now Charles Sumner took a hand. He proposed an additional section, far more drastic, providing that the tenure of office of any head of a department, appointed by the President since July, 1866, and receiving an annual salary of as much as one thousand dollars, should expire on the last day of February, 1867. The suggestion was absurd, but it gave him another opportunity to insult the President of the United States.

"Andrew Johnson," he said, "has become the successor of Jefferson Davis in the spirit by which he is governed and in the mischief he is inflicting on this country. . . . In holding up Andrew Johnson to judgment, I do not dwell on his open exposure of himself in a condition of beastly intoxication while he was taking his oath of office; nor do I dwell on the maudlin speeches by which he has degraded the country as it was never degraded before; nor do I hearken to any reports of pardons sold, or of personal corruption. . . ." Oh, no, far be it from Charles Sumner to "dwell" on that! "The President," he went on, "has usurped the powers of Congress on a colossal scale, and he has employed these usurped powers in fomenting the rebel spirit and awakening anew the dying fires of rebellion. He has become a terror to the good and a support to the wicked." [8]

Sumner's silly slander did not seem to carry the conviction he had hoped, and his amendment was therefore promptly voted down.[9] There was enough of decency even in that Senate not to attempt the shackling of the Chief Executive with a Cabinet officer of whom he wished to be relieved. But when the bill came back to the House, no such attitude was evident, and by a party vote of 111 to 38 there was carried an amendment making the Cabinet, as well as other officers, not removable by the President, save with the approval of the Senate.[10] Would the Upper Chamber now concur?

The House amendment came back to the Senate for its approval or rejection.[11] "It is a question with me," Senator Sherman declared during the debate, "not of constitutional law, but a question of propriety. . . . Suppose that some Cabinet minister under the old administration should hang on to his office. It is hardly a probable supposition, I admit, because I do not see how any gentleman could . . . hold an office of that kind against the will of his chief; yet if we adopt the amendment . . . we compel the President to retain in office . . . any man who has not courtesy enough to retire. . . . I would as soon think of imposing upon the President a private secretary with whom he had no friendly relations, personal and political, as to impose upon him a Cabinet minister with whom his relations were not kind. . . . I cannot imagine a case where a Cabinet officer would hold on to his place in defiance and against the wishes of his chief, and if such a case should occur I certainly would not by any extraordinary legislation protect him in that office." [12]   The Senate at this time refused its concurrence in the House amendment. [13]

That evening John Hay took dinner with Senator and Mrs. Sumner. The latter he described as looking "very sweet and matronly in her *secondes noces.*"   The conversation was all politics. Sumner thought the power of appointing and removing members of the Cabinet "more properly belonged to the Senate as a permanent body than to the President." He said the Senate was "less liable to become depraved and bad than the President." The argument in favor of harmony in the Cabinet he scouted altogether. "It was the duty often of a patriotic minister," he said, "to remain in the counsels of a perverted administration as 'a privileged spy.' " And then in one brief comment he exposed the true inner purpose of the Radicals. Referring specifically to Stanton, he declared that "it should be made impossible for Johnson to remove him." This was the real motive behind the proposed legislation,—the very kernel of the plot!

Had the law which Sumner demanded existed in 1861, responded Hay, "the Rebellion would have had its seat and centre in Washington, and loyalty would have worn the bloody color of revolution." But Sumner could not see it, saying if the South had taken that course they would by that act have "abnegated their rebellion." To his old friend Nicolay, Hay later wrote: "Sumner has blood in his eye. He is splendid in his present temper,—arrogant, insolent, implacable—thoroughly in earnest—honest as the day." [14]   And in his diary he wrote: "Sumner has grown very arrogant with success. He feels very keenly the satisfaction of being able to bind and loose at his full will and pleasure. There is no selfish exultation in it, or too little for him to recognize,—it is rather the fierce joy of a prophet over the destruction of the enemies of his Lord." [15]

What was to be done with the difference between the Senate and the House? The familiar expedient of a conference committee was adopted. Of this body Sherman was the spokesman for the Senate, and Williams for the lower chamber. Finally a compromise was agreed upon. All civil officers in whose appointment the Senate had participated could be removed only with its advice and its consent; but there was a proviso whose meaning and interpretation presently will form the central subject of these pages. The proviso was: "That the Secretaries of State, of the Treasury, of War, of the Navy, and of the Interior, the Postmaster-General, and the Attorney-General, shall *hold their offices respectively for and during the term of the President by whom they may have been appointed*, and for one month thereafter, subject to removal by and with the advice and consent of the Senate." [16]

Had the Radicals blundered in their haste? If their real purpose had been to make it impossible for Johnson to remove Stanton, had they done so? Stanton was appointed by Lincoln during the latter's first Presidential term, he never had received any other appointment.[17] He was, therefore, protected in his office for one month after the first term of Abraham Lincoln,—April 4th, 1865—and for no longer. This is what the plain words meant, but did the Radicals mean that?

What the words meant to the conference committee at least was plain. In his report Sherman said that the proviso had been drawn so that a Cabinet officer would hold "his office during the life or the term of the President who appointed him . . .; if the President dies the Cabinet goes out . . . so that the government will not be embarrassed by any attempt by a Cabinet officer to hold on to his office despite the wish of the President or a change in the Presidency." [18] Williams' report was to the same effect.[19] Whatever the Radicals intended, what they had done was to leave Stanton removable by Johnson without the concurrence of the Senate. Would the time come when this would be denied?

Making every "removal, appointment or employment . . . contrary to the provisions of this act . . . high misdemeanors" punishable by "a fine not exceeding ten thousand dollars or by imprisonment not exceeding five years . . . or both . . ." on February 19th the bill was passed by both Houses and sent on to the President.[20] What would he do with it?

Whatever Johnson's personal feelings may have been, he gave no evidence of them when on February 26th he discussed this measure with his Cabinet. Attorney-General Stanbery, although he had not read it until that day, said that he required no time in order to express his unqualified condemnation. In this expression the whole Cabinet united,—even Stanton.[21] Especially Stanton! He was, wrote Welles, "very emphatic and seemed glad of an opportunity to be in accord with his colleagues."[22]

The bill presented, as Johnson later wrote, "a grave question of constitutional law, in which I would of course rely upon the opinion of the Attorney-General and of Mr. Stanton, who had once been Attorney-General. Every member of my Cabinet advised me that the proposed law was unconstitutional. All spoke without doubt or reservation, but Mr. Stanton's condemnation of the law was the most elaborate and emphatic."[23]

So struck was Johnson with Stanton's full mastery of the question that he requested him to prepare the veto message. Stanton declined on the ground of "physical disability," but expressed his readiness to "furnish what aid might be required in the preparation of materials for the paper."[24] At this the President turned to Welles, and in an undertone "reckoned" that the latter had better prepare something on the subject. Welles assented.[25]

But more than the unconstitutionality of the measure was discussed at that Cabinet meeting. The question of the effect and scope of the bill, assuming it to be constitutional, was explored. It was taken for granted by everyone that Lincoln's appointees could be removed by Johnson without the approval of the Senate.[26] No one was more voluble in denunciation of the bill than Stanton, no one reprobated it more strongly as a "flagrant abuse."

He could not say enough! With ostentatious vehemence he protested that "any man who would retain his seat in the Cabinet when his advice was not wanted was unfit for the place." He would not, he said, under such circumstances "remain a moment." [27]

So emphatic and so unanimous was the opinion of the Cabinet, that, as he later wrote, Johnson "felt no concern so far as the act had reference to the gentlemen then present," that he would "be embarrassed in the future. The bill had not then become a law. The limitation upon the power of removal was not yet imposed, and there was yet time to make any changes. If any of these gentlemen had then said to me that he would avail himself of the bill in case it became a law, I should not have hesitated a moment as to his removal. . . . No pledge was then expressly given or required. But there are circumstances when to give an express pledge is not necessary, and when to require it is an imputation of possible bad faith. I felt that if these gentlemen came within the purview of the bill, it was as to them a dead letter, and that none of them would ever take refuge under its provisions." [28]

On March 2nd, Johnson sent his veto to the Senate. Once more he hurled himself across the path of the on-rushing revolutionists. With uncompromising logic he exposed the unconstitutionality of the measure. His message is a masterpiece of history and law. He quoted from the debates of the first Congress, the words of James Madison showing that from the beginning of the government "legislative construction of the Constitution" had recognized the President's prerogative to make removals from office irrespective of the Senate's consent or its advice. [29]

"The question," he declared, "has often been raised in subsequent times of high excitement, and the practice of the Government has nevertheless conformed in all cases to the decision thus early made. . . ." [30] When the war broke out, rebel enemies . . . and sympathizers were found in every department of the Government. . . . Upon probable suspicion they were promptly displaced by my predecessor. . . . No complaints against that power or doubts of its wisdom were entertained in any quarter. I sincerely trust and believe that no such civil war is likely to occur again. I cannot doubt however, that in whatever form and on whatever occasion sedition can raise an effort to . . . embarrass or defeat the legitimate action of this Government . . . the power of removal from office by the Executive will be found indispensable." [31]

In October, 1926, the Supreme Court of the United States, in passing upon a similar law, sustained Andrew Johnson! An act of Congress declared that postmasters should be appointed by the President for a term of four years, unless sooner removed by the President, "by and with the advice and consent of the Senate." President Wilson in January, 1920, removed Postmaster Meyers of Portland, Oregon, without first obtaining the Senate's advice or its consent. Meyers contended that his removal was illegal, but the Supreme Court, through Chief Justice Taft, treading much of the ground covered by Johnson in his veto message, sustained Wilson and declared the act in question unconstitutional! The Supreme Court sustained Woodrow Wilson, but it sustained Andrew Johnson also! Fifty-nine years is a long time to wait for vindication.

When Johnson's veto message reached the Congress, with a studied disregard of its fundamental truths,—on the very day it reached them—the Tenure-of-Office Bill, by a majority of two-thirds in each House, was repassed and so became a law." [32]

STEVENS' FIRST RECONSTRUCTION ACT

WHILE his fellow conspirators pressed forward to provide the way for Johnson's ruin, Stevens was exerting all his power to bring about the degradation of the South. It would be a beautiful thing, he thought, to watch the white men, especially the white women of the South, writhing under negro domination. And then what a happy harvest for the carpet-baggers!

At the beginning of 1867, in dead earnest, he took up his Reconstruction measures. The plot could never have been carried through but for what Rhodes well calls his "able and despotic parliamentary leadership. The old man's energy was astonishing. Vindictiveness seemed to animate his frame." [1] He denounced the work of Lincoln and of Johnson as a "bastard reconstruction." [2]

With his tongue of vitriol he sought to influence the bewildered minds of his dupes through the venomous propaganda of sheer lying. Southern outrages again! "For two years," he shouted, ten states have endured all the horrors of the worst anarchy of any country. Persecution, exile and murder have been the order of the day. . . ." [3] Through this and long harangues of similar import, he sought to extort from Congress the sharp weapons of vengeance. [4] He was sponsoring his Reconstruction Bill as a war measure! [5] It was twenty months since Lee had made his honorable surrender, it was thirteen since, through the vote of Southern states, the Thirteenth Amendment had been adopted. And yet unblushingly Stevens now declared that the South was in rebellion still! [6] "If this is not so," said Shellabarger, one of Stevens' followers, "then we must abandon the bill." [7]

Stevens called his Reconstruction measure a "police bill." It provided for a military government of the South, authorized the general of the armies (not the President) to appoint an officer of at least the rank of Brigadier-General, to command each of the military districts into which the South was to be divided, and authorized him to compel the trial of civil as well as criminal causes before military commissions.[8]   But the bill contained no method by which the "conquered provinces" could divest themselves of martial rule.   Stevens spoke of his measure as something that "will give protection to the people of the Southern states and prevent murders, robberies and slavery there, until we can have time to frame civil government more in conformity with the genius of our institutions." [9]

It was of course, a thoroughly unconstitutional,—a revolutionary measure.   Its terms, declared LeBlond of Ohio, "strike down every important provision in the Constitution.   You have already inaugurated enough here to destroy any government that was ever founded." [10]   And there were others who dared speak out. Raymond of New York vigorously denounced it.   "Because," he said, "we cannot devise anything of a civil nature adequate to the emergency, it is urged we must fly to the most violent measure the ingenuity of man could devise.   Let me remind you, gentlemen, that this has been the history of popular governments everywhere, the reason of their downfall, their decadence and their death." [11]

Blaine was willing enough to accept Stevens' bill, provided it contained some method by which the people of the Southern states could bring about the reëstablishment of civil government. He implored Stevens to consent to an amendment whereby if the Southern states should assent to the Fourteenth Amendment and other conditions, they might again secure representation in Congress and all the privileges of statehood.[12]   Stevens refused.

Any measure even savoring of justice was unwelcome to the sour-visaged Pennsylvanian.   When the terms by which the South could divest itself of his military yoke were drawn, he wanted the more Radical Congress, which would soon convene, to do it! [13] He did not wish, he said, to see generosity and benevolence "squandered upon vagabonds and thieves."   The forgiveness referred to in the gospel, he declared, had nothing to do with "political sanction of political crimes." [14] With contemptuous insolence he denounced Blaine's proposal as a "step towards universal amnesty and universal Andy Johnsonism,—it lets in a vast number of rebels and shuts out nobody." [15]

In the face of a strong minority of his own party, Stevens lashed his bill through. By "sarcasm, taunts, dragooning and by cracking the party whip," his majority was secured. [16] He sounded all the shrill octaves of partyism. "You must," he said, "divide the South between loyalists, without regard to color, and disloyalists or you will be the perpetual vassals of the free-trade, irritated, revengeful South." [17]

Not if he could help it would the Southern states participate in the Presidential election of 1868. [18] On February 13th, the Blaine amendment was defeated and Stevens' bill, just as he had drawn it, passed the House. [19]

§

Two days later, at a meeting of the Cabinet, there was presented further evidence that not everyone of the conspirators had a seat in Congress. More than five weeks before, Congress had asked the President for facts concerning any failure to enforce the Civil Rights Law. Each Cabinet member had, at the request of Johnson, immediately prepared an answer,—each except Stanton. And now two days after Stevens' bill had passed the House, Stanton brought in his answer.

It was, wrote Welles, "a strange and equivocal document, accompanied by a report which he had called out from General Grant and also one from General Howard." Grant's report was brief, but was accompanied by a singular paper transmitted to him by Howard, being "an omnium-gatherum of newspaper gossip, rumors of negro murders, neighborhood strifes and troubles, amounting to 440 in number,—vague, indefinite party scandal which General Howard and his agents had picked up in newspapers and all other ways during four weeks, under and with the assistance of the War Department, who had aided in the search." [20]

With sensations of evident astonishment and disgust, the other members of the Cabinet listened to this mass of uncertain material relating for the most part to negro quarrels.[21]   Stanton, who was not easily dashed when confident of power, "betrayed guilt." After some discussion it was finally suggested that the President should send in this material to Congress.   Welles, however, dissented and deprecated "communicating this compilation of scandal and inflammable material."[22]   Stanton looked earnestly at the Secretary of the Navy, and then blandly remarked that he was "as desirous to act in unison with the President as any one," but that the material had seemed proper both to him and Grant.   "If others wished to suppress it they could make the attempt," he said, "but there was little doubt that members of Congress had seen this,—likely had copies!"   Stanbery and McCulloch each remarked to Welles before they left "that here was design and intrigue in connection with the Radical conspirators at the Capitol."[23]

The next day Welles talked with his colleague Browning, who declared that having listened to Stanton on the previous day, he "was compelled to believe that there was design and villainy if not absolute treachery at the bottom."[24]   Welles then called upon the President himself and told him that he was convinced "that the details of Stanton's report, the introduction of Grant and Howard with their catalogues of alleged murders and crimes unpunished . . . was part of a conspiracy to overthrow his Administration; that it was intended . . . as a justification for legislative usurpation. . . ."[25]   Radical Congressmen were acting in concert with the Secretary of War. . . .   Grant had been strongly but unmistakably prejudiced,—perhaps seduced, worked over and enlisted— . . . the Administration was coming under the War Department."[26]

Why did not Johnson act?   Welles was becoming increasingly impatient with the President's too long-suffering forbearance. "He still hesitates," wrote Welles.[27]   And the next day: "How long will the President be able to go on with such an opponent at his council board?"[28]   All of Johnson's friends were similarly minded.   At this time, the Tenure-of-Office Bill was still unsigned, and he could without fear of any claimed violation of law, have dismissed the faithless Stanton. It was magnificent restraint, but it was a mistake. No one can thread the troubled story of those times and fail to agree with Hugh McCulloch when he wrote: "The failure of the President to exercise his undoubted right to rid himself of a minister who differed with him upon very important questions, who had become personally obnoxious to him, and whom he regarded as an enemy and a spy, was a blunder for which there was no excuse." [29]

Let us continue on the trail of Stevens' Reconstruction bill. When it reached the Senate, there was one at least to tell the truth about it. "There is," said Senator Saulsbury of Delaware, "not a single provision in the bill that is constitutional or will stand the test in any court of justice." This was none the less true even after Sherman had secured the insertion of an amendment (practically the Blaine proposal) whereby upon certain conditions the South might divest itself of military rule. [30] Being unwilling also to go to the extremes desired by Stevens and his meek followers, the Senate amendment replaced in the President the control over the assignment of army officers. [31]

The subsequent concurrence by the House in the restoration of the President's command of the armed forces was based upon no penitent scruple for the Constitution, but because the representatives held up their sleeves the army appropriation bill into which they were about to slip the Stanton-Boutwell measure requiring the President to transmit all military orders through the "General of the army." [32] Some of the representatives also felt that by leaving the military command in the President, a new trap for him might be sprung. "I want this Congress to give its command to the President of the United States," said Garfield, "and then perhaps some impeachment hunters will have a chance to impeach him." [33]

Realizing that they must get their measure to the President more than ten days before the close of the session if they were to defeat the veto that would surely come, on February 20th the bill, containing the amendment of the Senate, was finally agreed to by both Houses and was forwarded to Johnson. [34] It was an act of revolution! It began with the enunciation of this falsehood: "Whereas no legal state governments or adequate protection for life or property now exists in the rebel states of Virginia, North Carolina, South Carolina, Georgia, Mississippi, Alabama, Louisiana, Florida, Texas and Arkansas; and whereas it is necessary that peace and good order should be enforced in said states until loyal and republican state governments can be legally established: Therefore,"—and then followed the plans and specifications for the carpet-bag régime.[35] Nearly two years after the followers of Lee and Johnston in good faith had laid down their arms, the commonwealths that harbored them were declared "rebel states!"

What followed is such as to explain why historians have been wont with a few stammering embarrassed sentences to pass by the ugly work of Johnson's enemies. "Be it enacted," the bill declared, "that said rebel states shall be divided into military districts and made subject to the military authority of the United States . . . and for that purpose Virginia shall constitute the first district; North Carolina and South Carolina the second district; Georgia, Alabama and Florida the third district; Mississippi and Arkansas the fourth district and Louisiana and Texas the fifth district."[36]

Virginia, whose classic fields had drunk the blood of Revolutionary patriots, Virginia was no longer Virginia but the "first district!" South Carolina, Florida and the rest, these were not states, but conquered provinces where the will of the conqueror was law! It was to prevent such things as these that the armies of the Confederacy, outnumbered three to one, had reeled on from Gettysburg to Appomattox!

The Southern states were gone, and to the command of each of the military districts which supplanted them the President was directed to assign an army officer not below the rank of brigadier-general. Under each of these military satraps he was required to detail a military body sufficient to enable the commander to enforce martial rule.[37] Each of these military rulers was given arbitrary civil and criminal jurisdiction over the civilians! It was made his duty not only to suppress disorder, but actually himself to "punish all disturbers of the public peace and criminals!" He might if he chose,—and he was authorized to choose—"allow local civil tribunals to take jurisdiction of and to try offenders!" He was thus placed as an arbitrary potentate over the civil courts. He could suppress them altogether if he wished! Whenever "in his judgment," it might be "necessary" to try offenders he was vested with "power to organize military commissions or tribunals for that purpose!" Any "interference under color of state authority with the exercise" of the military power was declared "null and void." [38] Sentences of death only were reviewable by the President. [39] With pride in this measure, and in support of it, Garfield said: "It was written with a steel pen made out of a bayonet." [40]

The provisions thus far considered were the product of the brain of Stevens. Those which followed,—added by the Senate— had been opposed by "Thad;" they were not harsh enough for him! These embodied the duress which was to force negro rule upon the South, and place the white man under black control,— the instrument by which they planned to crowd through the Fourteenth Amendment!

From military districts the states were to be again permitted to emerge only after they had complied with these conditions: When any state held a constitutional convention, composed of and elected by male citizens twenty-one years old "of whatever race, color or previous condition," of one year's residence, but not disqualified for felony or participation in the Rebellion; when such a convention adopted a Constitution disfranchising the ex-Confederates and enfranchising the ex-slaves; when such a Constitution had been "submitted to Congress for examination and approval;" when the legislature of any "rebel state" had adopted the Fourteenth Amendment and it had "become a part of the Constitution;"—when all these things were done, then and not till then, were any of these states to be allowed representation in Congress or the rights of statehood! [41]

Finally the bill declared (and here was the final blow to Lincoln's plan) that until these conditions had been met "any civil government which may exist" in any of "said rebel states" was "deemed provisional only and in all respects subject to the paramount authority of the United States at any time to abolish, modify, control or supersede the same." [42]

This bill was a declaration of war against those who had honorably laid down their arms! Every principle of the Constitution, every American conception of fair play was flouted. Less than three years after Lincoln in his last annual message had declared that in stating a condition of peace, he meant "simply to say that the war will cease on the part of the Government whenever it shall have ceased on the part of those who began it;" [43] two years after his second Inaugural expressing his purpose "to bind up the nation's wounds," and "to do all which may achieve and cherish a just and lasting peace;" [44] less than two years after Grant had told Lee that his soldiers would be "allowed to return to their homes not to be disturbed by United States authority so long as they observe their paroles and the laws in force where they may reside,"[45]—with a reckless, wanton and malicious disregard of these solemn pledges the Radicals had perpetrated the most shocking act of bad faith ever witnessed in America!

"There was," Professor Burgess writes, "hardly a line in the entire bill which would stand the test of the Constitution," [46] and further, that to have demanded of the Southern states "as the condition of admission, their acceptance of things not yet in the Constitution of the United States, things not obligatory on the 'states' already in the Union was tantamount to the creation of a new sort of union with another kind of Constitution by an act of Congress." [47]

When South Carolina and her neighbors six years before had attempted to secede, they had at least an arguable claim that no specific section of the Constitution stood in their way, but nearly every line and sentence of that document was violated by the bill which, on February 20th, was forwarded from Congress to the President.[48] Would Johnson once more hurl himself across the path of the onrushing Juggernaut?

§

On Washington's birthday the President laid the Reconstruction bill before his Cabinet. Every member advised the veto,—everyone but Stanton. Stanton urged him to approve! [49]

A few days later Welles called upon the President, who asked whether Stanton supposed that he was not "understood," and as he said it, the sparkle of his eye and his whole manner betokened intense, although suppressed emotion. "Few men," wrote Welles, "have stronger feeling; still fewer have the power of restraining themselves when evidently excited." [50] As they sat there talking of the country, the Secretary of the Navy told the President that Stanton's course in bringing forward the report of the supposed Southern outrages "was but part of the drama which had long been enacting," and asked what "was to be the condition of things if impeachment were pressed and an attempt to arrest him were made." [51] The question was not a new one. At the previous meeting of the Cabinet, thinking it wise "to be prepared for an emergency," Johnson had sought the views of his Cabinet upon this vital matter. [52] While it was a question of law, nevertheless Seward had declared that if the Attorney-General should advise the President to submit to arrest before conviction, he would demand the instant dismissal of that officer. [53] But when Welles asked this question, Johnson did not answer it; he was not ready yet to answer it. If the President were to submit to an illegal arrest, would he not thereby violate his oath to "preserve, protect and defend the Constitution?" Were he to resist arrest, it might bring on another civil war,—and there had been enough bloodshed for one generation!

Two days later, having fortified himself with all the advice that he could get, [54] Johnson sent to the House his veto of the Reconstruction bill. Not one out of a hundred thousand of our contemporaries has ever read that message, historians do not quote it, yet it is one of the great documents of American history. Its breadth and understanding was Lincoln-like, its grasp of the true nature of the Reconstruction problem such as it has taken Americans a half century to comprehend. Had he carried his contentions, there would have been no "Solid South," nor the long decades of misunderstanding,—a misunderstanding that mere bloodshed could never have engendered.

"The bill," declared Johnson, "places all the people of the ten states . . . under the absolute domination of military rulers.

. . .[55] It is not denied that the states in question have each of them an actual government, with all the powers,—executive, judicial and legislative—which properly belong to a free state. . . . To pronounce the supreme law-making power of an established state illegal is to say that law itself is unlawful."[56] He declared that the provisions the Southern governments had made for the suppression of crime and the redress of private injuries were the same as those prevailing in the North. Although admitting that the Southern states had "not succeeded in preventing the commission of all crime," he pointedly continued: "nor has this been accomplished anywhere in the world. . . . All the information I have . . . convinces me that the masses of the Southern people . . . are completely united in the effort to reorganize their society on the basis of peace and to restore their mutual prosperity as rapidly and as completely as their circumstances will permit."[57]

Concerning the bill's requirements for regaining statehood, Johnson declared: "All these conditions must be fulfilled before the people of any of these states can be relieved from the bondage of military domination; but when they are fulfilled, then immediately the pains and penalties are to cease, no matter whether there be peace and order or not, and without any reference to the security of life or property. The excuse given for the bill in the preamble is admitted by the bill itself not to be real. The military rule which it establishes is plainly to be used not for any purpose of order or for the prevention of crime, but solely as a means of coercing the people into the adoption of principles and measures to which it is known they are opposed, and upon which they have an undeniable right to exercise their own judgment."[58]

Referring to the brigadiers, each with his military entourage and his authority "to punish . . . criminals," Johnson went on: "The power thus given to the commanding officers over all the people of each district is that of an absolute monarch. His mere will is to take the place of law. The law of the states . . . is completely displaced. . . . He alone is permitted to determine what are rights of person or property, and he may protect them in such a way as in his discretion may seem proper. It places at his free disposal all the lands and goods in his district, and he may distribute them without let or hindrance to whom he pleases. Being bound by no state law, and there being no other law to regulate the subject, he may make a criminal code of his own; and he can make it as bloody as any in history, or he can reserve the privilege of acting upon the impulse of his private passions in each case that arises. He is bound by no rule of evidence; there is indeed no provision by which he is authorized or required to take any evidence at all. Everything is a crime which he chooses to call so, and all persons are condemned whom he pronounces to be guilty. He is not bound to keep any record or make any report of his proceedings. He may arrest his victims wherever he finds them, without warrant, accusation, or proof of probable cause. If he gives them a trial before he inflicts punishment, he gives it of his grace and mercy, not because he is commanded so to do. . . . He can save his friends from justice and despoil his enemies contrary to justice." [59]

The bill authorized each district commander to "organize military commissions or tribunals when in his judgment it may be necessary for the trial of offenders." Pointing out that this power was merely permissive and not mandatory, Johnson continued: "Even if the sentence of a commission were made a prerequisite to the punishment of a party, it would be scarcely the slightest check upon the officer, who has authority to organize it as he pleases, prescribe its mode of proceeding, appoint its members from his own subordinates and revise all its decisions. Instead of mitigating the harshness of his single rule, such a tribunal would be used much more probably to divide the responsibility of making it more cruel and unjust." [60]

Further, the bill provided that the sentence of a military commission could not be executed, if it affected life or liberty, without the approval of the commander, and that its sentence of death must be approved by the President. "This," declared Johnson, "applies to cases in which there has been a trial and sentence. I take it to be clear, under this bill, that the military commander may condemn to death, without even the form of a trial. . . ." [61]

"It is plain," continued the wielder of these thunderbolts, "that the authority here given to the military officer amounts to absolute despotism. But to make it still more unendurable, the bill provides that it may be delegated to as many subordinates as he chooses to appoint, for it declares that he shall 'punish or cause to be punished.' Such power has not been wielded by any monarch in England for more than five hundred years. In all that time no people who speak the English language have borne such servitude. It reduces the whole population of the ten states,—all persons of every color, sex or condition and every stranger within their limits—to the most abject and degrading slavery. No master ever had a control so absolute over the slaves as this bill gives to the military officers over both white and colored persons." [62]

The contention that an officer of the army would be too humane to trample down a subjugated people Johnson answered thus: "I do not doubt that army officers are as well entitled to this kind of confidence as any other class of men. But the history of the world has been written in vain if it does not teach us that unrestrained authority can never be safely trusted in human hands. It . . . has always resulted in gross tyranny when the rulers who exercise it are strangers to their subjects and come among them as the representatives of a distant power, and more especially when the power that sends them is unfriendly." [63]

And then this analysis of power unrestrained: "The men of our race in every age have struggled to tie up the hands of their governments and keep them within the law, because their own experience of all mankind taught them that rulers could not be relied upon to concede those rights which they were not legally bound to respect. The head of a great empire has sometimes governed it with a mild and paternal sway, but the kindness of an irresponsible deputy never yields what the law does not extort from him. Between such a master and the people subjected to his domination there can be nothing but enmity; he punishes them if they resist his authority, and if they submit to it he hates them for their servility." [64]

Thus did Johnson expose the military oligarchy planned by Stevens for the South. His irrefutable argument, as with the still white radiance of an operating room, penetrated into every gangrenous organ of this Reconstruction measure. He foresaw the carpet-bag régime, and the filthy profits Northern scoundrels were presently to derive from it. He divined all the tragic consequences to the North and to the South.

Every word of that message should be read. You will not find it in the histories. The apologists for Stevens would scarcely dare to print this exposé of his dishonorable work. Johnson picked it up and turned it around, and shook it to the light; he placed it in the scales of the Constitution, and found that it weighed short! He reminded Congress that "no branch of the Federal government has any power save that which it derives through the organic law of the Union. . . . It protects not only the citizens of the states which are within the Union, but it shields every human being who comes or is brought under our jurisdiction. We have no right to do in one place more than in another that which the Constitution says we shall not do at all. If, therefore, the Southern states were in truth out of the Union, we could not treat their people in a way which the fundamental law forbids." [65]

And still further: "Invasion, insurrection, rebellion and domestic violence were anticipated when the Government was framed, and the means of repelling and suppressing them were wisely provided for in the Constitution; but it was not thought necessary to declare that the states in which they might occur should be expelled from the Union. Rebellions which were invariably suppressed occurred prior to that out of which these questions grow; but the states continued to exist and the Union remained unbroken." [66]

Turning once again to history, he recalled how at different periods Massachusetts, Pennsylvania, Rhode Island and New York had each offered armed opposition to the national power. "It is true," he continued, "that in these earlier cases there was no formal expression of a determination to withdraw from the Union, but it is also true that in the Southern states the ordinances of secession were treated by all the friends of the Union as mere nullities and are now acknowledged to be so by the states themselves. If we admit that they had any force or validity, or that they did in fact take the states in which they were passed out of the Union, we sweep from under our feet all the grounds upon which we stand in justifying the use of Federal power to maintain the integrity of the Government." [67]

With force and eloquence Johnson vindicated again the right of trial by jury. "We are," he said, "providing now for a time of profound peace, when there is not an armed soldier within our borders except those who are in the service of the Government. It is in such a condition of things that an act of Congress is proposed which, if carried out, would deny a trial by the lawful courts and juries to 9,000,000 American citizens and to their posterity for an indefinite period. It seems scarcely possible that anyone should seriously believe this consistent with a Constitution which declares . . . that all persons shall have that right and that no person shall ever in any case be deprived of it." [68]

The English Parliament in its early days passed bills of attainder whereby it convicted men of treason and other crimes by legislative enactment. The fathers of our country determined that Congress should never practice such injustice and in the Constitution wrote: "No bill of attainder . . . shall be passed." [69] Referring to this, Johnson said: "Nevertheless here is a bill of attainder against 9,000,000 people at once. It is based upon an accusation so vague as to be scarcely intelligible, and found to be true upon no credible evidence. Not one of the 9,000,000 was heard in his own defense. The representatives of the doomed parties were excluded from all participation in the trial. The conviction is to be followed by the most ignominious punishment ever inflicted on large masses of men. It disfranchises them by hundreds of thousands and degrades them all, even those who are admitted to be guiltless, from the rank of freemen to the condition of slaves." [70]

Exposing Stevens' work, he continued further: "The purpose and object of the bill . . . is to change the entire structure and character of the state governments and to compel them by force to the adoption of organic laws which they are unwilling to accept if left to themselves. The negroes have not asked for the privilege of voting; the vast majority of them have no idea what it means.

This bill not only thrusts it into their hands, but compels them as well as the whites to use it in a particular way."[71]

As to the "policy or impolicy of Africanizing the Southern part of our territory," Johnson did not pause to inquire, deeming it sufficient to point out in minute detail how violative of the Constitution this legislation was. Our Constitution, he declared, provides "the only system of free government which we can hope to have as a nation. When it ceases to be the rule of our conduct, we may perhaps take our choice between complete anarchy, a consolidated despotism, and a total dissolution of the Union; but national liberty regulated by law will have passed beyond our reach."[72] It is the best frame of government the world ever saw. No other is or can be so well adapted to the genius, habits or wants of the American people. Combining the strength of a great empire with unspeakable blessings of local self-government, having a central power to defend the general interests, and recognizing the authority of the states as the guardian of industrial rights, it is 'the sheet anchor of our safety abroad and our peace at home.' . . . It was to punish the gross crime of defying the Constitution and to vindicate its supreme authority that we carried on a bloody war of four years' duration. Shall we now acknowledge that we sacrificed a million of lives and expended billions of treasure to enforce a Constitution which is not worthy of respect and preservation?"[73]

No rhetoric of Hamilton, no eloquence of Webster, or argument of Marshall displayed a finer understanding of our fundamental law, or a more resolute determination to defend it! The Constitution, the whole Constitution and nothing but the Constitution! To preserve it Johnson had suffered everything, dared everything, and now that he was President of the United States his allegiance to that charter of our liberties did not falter.

As though, in full, divining the black decade that was to follow, Johnson's closing paragraph struck again this pure note of justice: "While we are legislating upon subjects which are of great importance to the whole people, and which must affect all parts of the country, not only during the life of the present generation but for ages to come, we should remember that all men are entitled at least to a hearing in the councils which decide upon the destiny of themselves and their children." [74]

But there was to be no hearing either for the South or Andrew Johnson! It was Saturday afternoon, the 2nd of March. The 39th Congress had but two days to live. Action was imperative! The Radicals were equal to the emergency! Stevens lurched to his feet to move the immediate consideration of the question whether the bill should be passed, the President's objections notwithstanding. One minute was allowed the opposition! They used it well. Eldridge excoriated the bill as a "dissolution of the Union." LeBlond called it "the death-knell of republican liberty upon this continent," and Finck denounced it as "a monstrous scheme to subvert constitutional government in this country." [75]

With the light of hatred gleaming in his eyes, his hideous features distorted with a sneer, Stevens was again upon his feet. He did not wish to be discourteous, he mockingly declared, for he was "aware of the melancholy feelings with which they were approaching this funeral of the nation, amid a difference of opinion among the mourners that we cannot expect to harmonize." [76]

But before the funeral came the execution! There was an air of bustle as in the death house on the night of an electrocution. All was in readiness. Quickly Stevens called on Blaine to move for a suspension of the rules; it was done. And then by a vote of 135 to 48 the House repassed the bill! On the same day the Senate by a vote of 38 to 10 concurred in the action of the Lower Chamber. [77] Infamy had been enacted into law! The blackest page that ever disgraced our statute books was written! It was black, but not black enough for Stevens! "It is not improbable that his determined purpose to punish the South," admits his biographer, "would have wrought something worse than this military bill into the legislation of his country could he have had his way." [78]

The dark night of the Reconstruction was now to descend upon the "conquered provinces,"—the suppressed chapter of American history! Where was the Northern sense of justice, honor and fair play? What were our grandfathers doing with the principles of Lincoln?

Revealing in one flash the quiet unconcern with which his contemporaries had trod down the fundamental law, with a naïveté as amusing as it is amazing, Ulysses Grant eighteen years later, in his Memoirs, wrote how it "became necessary to enfranchise the negro in all his ignorance," [79] and still further: "The story of the legislation enacted during the Reconstruction period to stay the hands of the President is too fresh in the minds of the people to be told now. Much of it, no doubt, was unconstitutional; but it was hoped that the laws enacted would serve their purpose before the question of constitutionality could be submitted to the judiciary and a decision obtained." [80]

CLOSING HOURS OF THE 39TH CONGRESS

STANTON'S amendment to the Army Appropriation Bill had passed both Houses by the 20th of February.[1] This, as will be recalled, was the measure which in the early days of the preceding December he had secretly requested Boutwell to push through.[2]

On March 2nd, the day on which he forwarded his veto of the Reconstruction Bill, Johnson sent the House a message on the Stanton-Boutwell measure. But this time it was not a veto. The bill provided that the headquarters of the general of the army should be at Washington, that all orders of the President or Secretary of War should be issued *through* the general of the army, and that all the militia in the ten Southern states should be "forthwith disbanded."[3]

A veto would not only have been useless, it might have been worse than that. With subtle strategy this measure had been tied into the Appropriation Bill as a rider; had Johnson vetoed it, and had it thereafter failed of passage, the army would have been without support, and the time might yet come when Johnson would require the army! And so he signed the bill, but pointed out how it deprived him of his "constitutional function as Commander-in-Chief of the army," and ten states of their "constitutional right to protect themselves in any emergency by means of their own militia."[4] Without the hurdle of a veto, the bill became a law.

Amid all this farrago of lawless laws, there flourished the effort to unearth or to invent some evidence on which to dispossess the tenant of the White House. Ashley paid constant court to Conover in jail; Conover,—the convicted suborner of perjury. Just give him time and he would produce letters from Johnson to Jefferson Davis, establishing the former's connection

457

with Lincoln's murder! Just give him time! All Conover desired was time,—but not time in jail.[5]

When they could not work with convicts they turned to discharged public servants harboring a grievance. LaFayette C. Baker had been the chief of the government's detective bureau. Johnson had dismissed him. Could not Baker furnish something? Yes, indeed! Why, back in 1865 a man from Nashville had showed him a letter written by Johnson, while military governor, to Jefferson Davis! Wonderful! Where was the letter? Well, it seemed that a colored servant of Parson Brownlow's son had stolen it from Johnson's desk before it was sent, and one Adamson had it and would sell it if enough were offered! Marvelous! The letter was not found, but what mattered that,—Baker could remember what was in it! Johnson had agreed in writing upon certain conditions to "turn the whole power he possessed in Tennessee over to the rebel cause." Surely that was probable,— just the kind of thing one would write out in long hand![6]

These and other lies did they search out, publish and pretend to credit. Honorable men, no matter how they yearned for proofs of guilt would, upon finding themselves in such a morass, have promptly exonerated the object of their quest. Not so with the statesmen of 1867!

Four days before Congress adjourned,[7] the majority of Boutwell's committee did not scruple to declare "that sufficient testimony had been brought to its notice to justify and demand the further prosecution of the investigation."[8] The truth was written into the minority report,—the minority consisting of a solitary Democrat! "There is not one particle of evidence to sustain the charges," he declared, and none "upon which impeachment could be founded."[9]

§

Encouraged by the knowledge that the impeachment investigation would go on, knowing that he was presently to be President of the Senate and that the removal of Johnson would make him President of the United States, Wade was stealthily in search of means to make his elevation certain.

Had we not long since grown accustomed to the craft of Andrew Johnson's enemies, we might experience astonishment in watching Wade on the night following the presentation of the report on the impeachment. It is after midnight. The Senate has been in almost continuous session. Suddenly and without warning, Wade is on his feet, moving to postpone all other business. Why? To take up anew the Colorado bill! Three weeks before he had been unable to muster enough votes to pass it over Johnson's veto. What is the reason for his present haste? There is good reason! Excellent reason! It is midnight and Wade finds Grimes, Riddle and Harris absent,—the Senators who had opposed him on the bill before. Hendricks looks at Wade aghast. Surely the Senator will not take advantage of the fact that ill health forbids either Grimes or Riddle to come out at night? Would Wade not wait until to-morrow to give the absent Senators a chance to vote? He would not! Why? "Because I think I am better prepared to-night than I shall be to-morrow to decide this question!" [10]

Wade sees the White House within his grasp. The need of Colorado's two votes in the High Court of Impeachment, as with some strange prescience, he foresees. But Doolittle is on his feet. The request for a delay under such circumstances, he cries, has "never before been declined in the Senate. . . . The people . . . know what is transpiring in this body; and there are peculiar reasons which connect themselves with the Senator from Ohio. . . . We all know . . . that the Senator in pressing the matter of Colorado has said over and over that his purpose was to reinforce a majority in this body, already more than two-thirds, and for what, sir?" [11]

Caught redhanded, Wade capitulates. The vote is deferred until the next day. The question of Colorado is then once more put to a vote, the President's veto is again sustained! Wade had played his trump card, and had lost! [12]

The closing hours of the 39th, and those of the opening of the 40th, were marked by scenes "utterly without a precedent in the annals of the nation." [13] The sittings were continuous. Saturday, March 2nd, by a fiction was extended into Sunday, and on through Sunday night to Monday, the last day. The Radicals had decided that they must stand by to protect the country from the President!

They had passed a law six weeks before providing that the 40th Congress should convene immediately upon the adjournment of the 39th.[14] And so already the new members were at hand. But in addition to the absentees from the ten "erring sisters," Tennessee, Kentucky and five of the Northern states were not at first represented, as no election had as yet been held there. The 40th Congress, therefore, opened with nearly half the states unrepresented.[15] Great crowds filled the galleries, while upon the floor new members stood conversing with the old, until the House resembled a "political exchange."[16]

Throughout the long days of the session Johnson remained quietly at work. Assailed by storms of slander, every form of accusation, from murder down, he had borne without complaint the heavy burdens of his office. As one revolutionary measure was followed by another, he had stood up with his back to the wall, resolved that come what might he would "preserve, protect and defend the Constitution" of his country! He had suffered deeply under the assaults, but with the silence of the mountaineer, even to his close associates he did not complain.

On Sunday, the 3rd of March, five members of the Cabinet were calling at the White House. The President seemed calm, but more dejected than they had ever seen him. The grave questions of the hour were canvassed. While Johnson was absent for a moment in the library, Browning asked: "How is Grant? Does any one know his opinions and what stand he takes?" Seward thought that the President would "have a fast friend in Grant in consequence of the disagreement between him and Butler."[17]

The question, however, principally discussed was that which had long been on the tongue of everyone,—impeachment. Seward felt that "the discontent of the business men would prevent it," perhaps also Congress itself. "But unfortunately," answered Welles, there is "neither good sense, ability nor independence among the Radicals. There is no individuality among the well-meaning members. A few leaders and the Radical cohorts had entire control of the whole mass of Republicans. Stevens, Butler, Boutwell, Schenck, Kelley and a few violent partisans led the positive element, and in revolutionary times such as these, the positive and the violent, always controlled." Such men, he said "would unquestionably impeach, whether they found a reason therefore or not." [18]

Admitting that the positive element invariably holds sway, Seward told how some of the legislators who had recently dined with him had sworn that they would not vote to impeach, and how he had replied that "they would, despite their assertions if Stevens demanded it,—that they were drawn on step by step." [19]

Throughout the day and night great crowds surged in every available space within the capitol. And on Monday they filled not only the galleries but the cloak rooms and corridors as well. One task remained for the Senate to accomplish,—the election of a President pro tem in place of Foster. "You know I am no parliamentarian," said Wade.[20] Yes, they knew. It was not a parliamentarian they were seeking! At half past ten Foster bade farewell to the Senate, and Wade was elected to his place. Between him and the Presidency there remained one obstacle,— Andrew Johnson! [21]

The two Houses were in session until after the meridian. The clock was set back. "It was," wrote Welles, "the only evidence of regard for the Constitution which I witnessed, and this was a fiction." [22]

LII

THE 40TH CONGRESS BEGINS WORK ON
IMPEACHMENT

WADE declared the Senate of the 39th Congress adjourned *sine die,* and without leaving the chair proceeded to organize the Senate of the 40th. Speaker Colfax in the House took up the same work for that body.[1]

Numerous new faces now appeared. In the Senate, Simon Cameron returned from Pennsylvania in place of Cowan. Roscoe Conkling from Utica appeared to represent New York instead of Ira Harris. Oliver P. Morton, the former war governor of Indiana, was there in place of Lane. From Iowa came James Harlan, to renew in the Senate the hostility he had shown Johnson in the Cabinet and at Philadelphia. Drake from Missouri, Cole from California and Corbett from Oregon were the other new members of the upper chamber.

In the House the most conspicuous of the new members was Benjamin F. Butler of Massachusetts. The Radicals were counting strongly upon his peculiar gifts,—not the least of which was his ability to act on any question without restraint of conscientious scruple.[2] In the Senate the Republicans had ten more than a majority of two-thirds and in the House nineteen in excess of that much valued margin.

Welles went over to see the new Senators sworn in. "I could not respect the body or many of its members," he wrote, "they are in their intense faction hate of Southern whites and zeal for the negro determined to pull down the pillars of the Republic."[3]

In the House, the Democrats protested in writing against the election of a Speaker in the absence of the Representatives from seventeen states, seven of which were from the North. Of course, the protest was ignored. Under the rules, clerk Edward McPherson refused even to submit the paper for consideration, and so

462

"Smiler Colfax" was reëlected Speaker. The main business of the session was the enactment of legislation supplementary to the Reconstruction act. In the haste of the former session several things had been forgotten.

Ashley was, of course, on hand to stimulate the movement for impeachment. He moved a resolution to continue the investigation throughout the session and the recess. He declared that Johnson had come "into the Presidency through the door of assassination." He spoke of the "dark suspicion which crept over the minds of men as to his complicity in the assassination plot." He demanded that the American people once and for all declare "that no man hereafter elected President or Vice-President shall present himself at his inauguration drunk; that no President shall be permitted to turn the White House into a den of thieves and pardon brokers; nor shall he be permitted to address, in vulgar seditious language, a drunken howling mob from the steps of the Executive Mansion." He called upon the people to protest against "another drunken election tour such as last year." He declared that the "nation cried out in its agony to Congress to deliver them from the shame and disgrace the acting President has brought upon them." The people were demanding, he said, that the "incubus which has blotted our country's history with the foulest blot should be removed." [4]

This was a little strong even for his Radical allies. One of them branded "the whole scheme of impeachment as one of consummate folly," that "not one act amounting to a crime or misdemeanor has as yet been proved against the Executive," and that many expected that no such proof would be forthcoming. [5]

Ben Butler's first opportunity as a Representative had now arrived and he seized it eagerly. "An absolute majoirty of the whole House," he declared, would "be in favor of the Impeachment of Andrew Johnson," when the final report was made. And here was his chance to adopt the view, previously urged by others, that an impeachment was not a judicial proceeding at all. Even evidence was unnecessary! "Common fame," he cried, "common report of misconduct" is enough. It was a simple matter to depose a President! "If any man stands in the way of the great march of this country to honor, glory, peace, unity, happiness, liberty and law he must be taken out of the way." [6] By an overwhelming vote it was decided that the investigation should go on. [7]

A few hours later when one of his Cabinet made some suggestion to him as to how impeachment might be thwarted, Johnson spoke out: "I will do nothing to check impeachment, if there is any wish to press it. I am tired of hearing allusions to impeachment. God Almighty knows I will not turn aside from my public duties to attend to the contemptible assaults which are got up to embarrass the Administration. Let the House go forward and busy themselves in that matter if they wish." [8]

It was at this time that former Representative Law of Indiana looked in upon the seething cauldron. He called on Andrew Johnson at the White House and reminded him of an incident back in the summer of 1861. Law was at that time at the Burnett House in Cincinnati, on his way to Washington for the extra session called by Lincoln. Finishing his breakfast, he had come out upon the piazza of his hotel, when a troop of horse rode up, riders and animals both jaded. As the column opened, a citizen in citizen's dress, covered with dust, came forward and dismounted. It was Andrew Johnson, Senator from Tennessee, on his way to Washington. So vital was his presence at the capital that the War Department had dispatched the cavalry to escort him through Kentucky.

"I little thought," said Law, as he repeated this narrative to a friend, "that I should ever hear Andrew Johnson denounced as a rebel, or a sympathizer with rebels; that partisan malice would ever accuse him of want of fidelity to the Union; but God only knows what we are coming to in these Radical times. Such a patriot as Johnson,"—and as he spoke the tears were streaming down his cheeks—"a man who has suffered and done so much deserves better treatment from his countrymen." [9]

§

The subject of the hour was the impeachment. If the Radicals succeeded in their intrigue, the first step after the formal accusation, many thought, would be the President's arrest. If he was not ready to submit, was he ready to oppose it? In whom could he confide? It was a time of chaos. There were no precedents to guide. Johnson did not know how to prepare for such a contingency. Not knowing, he delayed action. His hesitation, Welles thought, weakened him in public estimation. He hesitated, as Lincoln many times had done. This hesitation gave perhaps the impression that he was not strong in his opinions. "Yet," wrote Welles, "I know of no man who is more firm when he has once taken a stand." [10]

The President was wise in using caution. For at this time the Radicals were not in entire accord upon the subject of impeachment. "The Senate," wrote Welles on March 7th, "seem determined to adjourn over until the fall, while the extreme Radicals wish to continue in session although there is no business requiring their presence. But they desire to administer the government and impeach the President. Not that he has committed any wrong or that any offense can be stated; but they have a committee searching the country to find, if possible, some mistake, some error, some act which can be construed into a political fault and thus justify his removal, because he is an obstacle in the way of Radicalism." [11]

But if Johnson hesitated on what course to follow in case of his arrest, he did not delay the performance of his official duties. However distasteful were the Reconstruction acts, until the Supreme Court should decide that they were unconstitutional, he determined to obey them. The first duty was the appointment of the brigadiers. "There are rumors," wrote his Secretary of the Navy on March 8th, "as to the persons to be selected as military governors, and I think the President is, unfortunately for himself, consulting with General Grant. How far Grant confers with Stanton, I know not, nor does the President,—if he confers at all. That Grant may be biased by Stanton and Holt, with whom he has constant intimate intercourse, is not improbable. However, my impression has been that Grant is himself rightly disposed, though there are some things which indicate subtlety and duplicity." [12]

Three days later Johnson announced his appointments; for the first district (Virginia) General Schofield, for the second, (North and South Carolina) General Sickles, for the third (Georgia, Florida and Alabama) General Thomas, for the fourth (Mississippi and Arkansas) General Ord, and for the fifth (Louisiana and Texas) General Sheridan.[13]   These appointments, thought one of Johnson's Cabinet, were not in some respects judicious. "That of Sickles," he wrote, "accounts for Stanton's exuberant feelings yesterday, and confirms my impression that he has been instrumental in selections, some of which will be likely to cause difficulty. . . . The War Department has made itself felt in the appointments. 'The slime of the serpent is over them all.' General Grant has apparently borne himself under all influences as well as could be expected, yet I think he is to some extent affected and has been swayed by Radical influence."[14]

It took the Radicals but fifteen days to draft their supplemental Reconstruction bill.   On March 19th it passed both Houses and was forwarded to the President.[15]   It was designed to strengthen the original act of March 2nd.   It was directed principally to the elections for the formation of the State Constitutions.   A registration of voters was provided for, and no one whose name was not admitted to the list could vote.   Negroes could vote, and all white men who had fought for the Confederacy could not.   The commanding general of each district was given full power over both the registration and election.   He was directed to appoint boards of registration and "superintend the elections."[16]

Outside of the administrative details there was nothing much that was new.   It merely gave a new turn to the thumbscrews. Four days later Johnson sent his veto.   With the regularity of a pendulum each bill that was forwarded met with his exposure. So far history has passed them by.   Yet a comparison of them and the measures they laid bare, reveals not only the brilliant picture of a brave man resolved to do his duty come what might, but a study of the negro problem incomparably more illuminating than elsewhere is available.

"When," he said, "I contemplate the millions of our fellow citizens of the South with no alternative left but to impose upon themselves this fearful untried experiment of complete negro enfranchisement—and white disfranchisement, it may be, almost as complete—or submit indefinitely to the rigor of martial law, without a single attribute of freemen, deprived of all the sacred guaranties of our Federal Constitution, and threatened with even worse wrongs if any worse are possible, it seems to me their condition is the most deplorable to which any people can be reduced." [17]

With an optimism, that to our country's shame was not justified, Johnson looked hopefully to the prompt repeal of all this legislation. "When," he said, "this shall have been consummated, I pray God that the errors of the past may be forgotten. . . ." [18] Travel south to-day, and you will find that they are not forgotten yet! But when the great-grandsons of this struggle have forgotten, the "Daughters of the Confederacy" will remember!

After the reading of Johnson's message, the Radicals adopted their usual procedure and repassed the bill, his veto notwithstanding. Negro suffrage and white disenfranchisement were now a veritable reality for the South. The work of Charles Sumner and Thaddeus Stevens was nearing its completion.

Citing the figures as to the relative number of whites and blacks at that time, within the South, Professor Burgess writes: "It will thus be seen that of the ten 'states' to be reconstructed five were to be recreated through an electorate in which the majority would be negroes and mulattoes, about all of whom had been three years before slaves; while in the other five the majority of the constructing electorate would be whites by a comparatively small number. This was a tremendous *bouleversement* of the political society of these sections." [19] And still further: "The imposition of universal negro suffrage upon the Southern communities, in some of which the negroes were in large majority, was one of the 'blunder-crimes' of the century." [20]

§

Sumner looked out upon his work and found it good. He had done everything within his power to ruin Lincoln's plan of justice, yet in December, three and a half months before, to his friend Storey he had written: "I wish you might make a statue of Lincoln. He is an historic character worthy of bronze and marble." Worthy of bronze and marble perhaps, but not worthy to be followed! Erect a statue of him, but tear down the work he had begun! "Congress is doing pretty well," he continued, "every step is forward. The next Congress which will probably meet on the 4th of March will be better inspired. All that is possible will be done to limit the Executive power. It is possible that the President may be impeached." [21]

What Sumner thought of the Southern governments, some of which Lincoln had himself assisted to restore, appeared as he proceeded: "If we go forward and supersede the sham governments set up in the rebel states, we encounter the appointing power of the President, who would put in office men who sympathize with him. It is this consideration which makes ardent representatives say that he must be removed. Should this be attempted a new question will be presented." [22]

What lip service Sumner rendered to the memory of Lincoln appeared from what he wrote of Lincoln's Minister of State: "I sorrow for Seward who seems to be more than usually perverse; but he lost his head when he lost the nomination at Chicago, and has done nothing but blunder since. He never understood our war, and he does not now understand how peace is to be secured."

Congress determined to adjourn on the 30th of March, but there was a difference of opinion as to whether it should reconvene in December or before. December was eight months away and there were those "afraid to trust the President so long." [23] Sumner was the chief spokesman of this group, and the debate on this question furnished him still further opportunity to insult the President of the United States. "You must not forget," he said, "that the President is a bad man, the author of incalculable woe to his country, and especially to that part which, being most tried by war, most needed kindly care. Search history, and I am sure you will find no elected ruler who during the same short time has done so much mischief to his country. He stands alone in bad eminence." [24]

Albeit with misgiving, the Radicals on March 30th decided they would risk the country in Johnson's hands until July 3rd, until which time an adjournment was decided on.[25]

§

George Washington was nine years old when two Russian officers, Chirikov and Captain Vitus Bering, explored Alaska.[26] This vast expanse with its area of more than 590,000 square miles,—[27] a larger territory than the original thirteen states of the Union, or the combined empires of France and Austria,[28] was practically an unknown country to Americans until March, 1867.

There were enough problems confronting the Johnson administration at this time, nevertheless, when on March 19th Seward presented to the Cabinet a treaty for the acquisition of this new section of America, which he had negotiated with Stoeckl, the Russian minister, it found favor with the President and all of his advisers.[29] The Senate met in special session on April 1st to consider this new venture in expansion. To the encyclopedias and the gazetteers men turned in vain for information of this unknown wilderness.[30]

There was opposition, of course. The purchase price, $7,200,000, was said to be too high for this "vast area of rocks and ice;" [31] "Walrussia" others called it.[32] Chandler of Michigan, Roscoe Conkling of New York and others opposed it, but finally, on April 9th, by an overwhelming vote, the Senate ratified the treaty. On April 20th there was an adjournment of the Senate, and Johnson was therefore to rule alone until July 3rd.[33]

Whatever interest the acquisition of Alaska had attracted, it was not to any point so far north that the "conquered provinces" were directing their attention. Immersed in the deluge with which Congress had overwhelmed them, blinded by the black night in which the Reconstruction acts had circled them about, conscious that there was no help for them in Congress, and that the Executive, despite his hammer blows, had not struck down the shameful laws, Governor Humphrey of Mississippi decided to invoke the Supreme Court's intercession.

If it adhered to its convictions expressed in the Milligan,

Cummings and Garland cases, the court, he thought, could not fail to hold that which Johnson had made so manifest: that the Reconstruction acts were unconstitutional and void. And so on April 5th a motion was made in the Supreme Court by Robert Walker, Alexander Garland and William Sharkey for leave to file a bill in equity on behalf of Mississippi to enjoin "Andrew Johnson, a citizen of the State of Tennessee and President of the United States and his officers and agents . . . and especially E. O. C. Ord from . . . carrying out the acts of March 2nd and 25th, 1867." [34]

The whole country was watching when on April 12th the case was argued. The novelty of the issue, the direct and unprecedented attempt of a state to enjoin the President, the vast and far-reaching consequences of the decision, the excitement of the times, and the brilliant array of counsel that appeared, crowded the little courtroom with distinguished officials, great lawyers and curious civilians. It was a striking scene. [35] Yet many felt the court might wilt. "This tribunal," declared the New York *Independent*, "already suspecting that as now constituted, it is regarded as a diseased member of the body politic, will not run the risk of amputation by touching the edged tools of Sharkey and Walker." [36]

The court waited but three days to fulfill the prediction of the *Independent*. It did not intend to run the risk of "amputation"! Avoiding entirely the question of its power in general to control the Executive, it decided that it had no jurisdiction to enjoin him "in the performance of his official duties. . . ." [37] It was a body blow! But such was the need, that the Southerners decided once again to seek the protection of the great guardian of the Constitution. If the court could not enjoin the President, perhaps it could restrain his Minister of War. The state of Georgia, therefore, now came forward seeking to enjoin Stanton from his part in executing the hated acts.

Once more the little courtroom of the great Court was filled. "One-fourth of the spectators were ladies, and some of them well-known secessionists," wrote one correspondent. [38] A few days later the decision came. It was without power, the Court declared, to adjudicate rights not of persons or property, but of a political character.[39] The great tribunal evidently had no wish to become embroiled. "Undoubtedly it is no light matter," declared the *Nation*, "that the highest court in the land should thus disclaim the power of enquiring into the constitutionality of an act of Congress destroying the government of ten states. . . ."[40] Those who were still hoping that here at last Congress would be halted, in despair exclaimed that "no state in the Union could rely upon the protection of the Supreme Court."[41]

Still the Southerners were hoping for relief. The rights of persons or property! Perhaps if the petition were amended so as to disclose the states' property interest in what the Reconstruction Acts affected the court might listen.[42] Accordingly, a motion to amend was made by Mississippi; by a divided court it was denied. "All legal obstacles to reconstruction," wrote the Boston *Daily Advertiser,* "are now removed."[43] Through a technicality the Supreme Court found a way to avoid passing on the great questions that rocked the country. But if the point should some time be so presented that they could not avoid it, would they have courage enough then to act?

§

Congress was not in session, but Boutwell's committeemen determined to press on. On May 4th Washington found them reassembled, pursuing their inquiries. Undismayed by all this, Johnson went forward with his work of justice. There was a May term of the United States Circuit Court in Richmond. As there appeared no likelihood now that Jefferson Davis would be tried, his friends determined, through a writ of habeas corpus, to bring him into court and then apply for his release on bail.[44] Disregarding utterly all possible consequences to himself, but five days after Boutwell's scavengers began their work anew, Johnson issued an order to General Burton,—Fortress Monroe's new commander—to "surrender Jefferson Davis . . . upon any process which may issue from a Federal Court in the state of Virginia."[45] Three days later a steamer left the Fortress. Among its passengers were the former President and First Lady of the

Confederacy. It was nearly sundown when the vessel came along the wharf at Richmond. "I feel," said Mr. Davis, turning to his wife, "like an unhappy ghost visiting this much-beloved city." [46] When the hotel was reached the crowd opened to let the "beloved prisoner" walk through. As he passed, one after another put out a hand and lightly touched his coat. When Mrs. Davis descended from the carriage a low voice said: "Hats off, Virginians," and every head was bared. [47]

Filled with the memories of the war, the Confederate Department Building on Monday, May 13th, was all astir. On the second floor of this structure the United States Circuit Court, with Judge Underwood presiding, was in session. For the accused there was the brilliant Charles O'Conor, while William M. Evarts appeared as special counsel for the government. The door opens and down through the breathless throng, leaning on the arm of General Burton, his jailor, Jefferson Davis,—the prisoner at the bar—walks slowly toward the bench. [48]

The government was not ready to proceed. Must the prisoner return to his dungeon, or would the court order him released on bail? Judge Underwood decided that the case was bailable, and $100,000 was fixed as the amount. [49] Who would furnish it? In the courtroom there were many who were notable, but there was nothing that attracted more attention than the gray head of Horace Greeley, whose excoriating columns for years had branded slavery, secession, the Confederacy and all the "rebels" with every epithet of infamy. Why was he here? He had come to sign the bail bond of Jefferson Davis! He was accepted and so at the head of all the sureties he wrote his name. [50] It was the finest thing he ever did!

"The marshal will discharge the prisoner," declared the Judge, [51] while from the crowd there rose a cheer that told the story of the city's heart. [52] "The ovation given Davis," wrote the Richmond correspondent of the Boston *Advertiser,* "was for intensity and heartiness such as Boston perhaps never gave anybody or any cause." [53] That night the former President and his wife sailed for New York, and presently passed on to Canada to join their children. [54] Upon the return of his strength and the improvement in his eyesight, he embarked upon the principal remaining effort of his life,—the writing of "The Rise and Fall of the Confederate Government." With that encouragement and assistance which only wives can give, Mrs. Davis acted as his amanuensis. Three years after he began,—working one night from eight until four of the next morning—he dictated: "In asserting the right of secession, it has not been my wish to incite to its exercise. I recognize the fact that the war showed it to be impracticable, but this did not prove it to be wrong; and now that it may not be again attempted, and the Union may promote the general welfare it is needful that the truth, the whole truth, should be known, so that crimination and recrimination may forever cease, and then on the basis of fraternity and faithful regard for the rights of the states, there may be written on the arch of the Union 'Esto Perpetua.' " [55]

There was a momentary silence, and Mrs. Davis looked up to remind her husband that he had forgotten to continue. "I think I am done," he answered. He had come back to his old flag,—the flag for which he fought at Monterey and shed his blood at Buena Vista! [56]

§

To Boutwell and the members of his Committee, the release of Davis,—on bail though it was—was like new oil poured out upon a smoldering flame. The New York *Evening Post* declared that it was notice to the world that the "crime of treason" was "as safe to commit" in the United States as peculation in the city of New York.[57] Other leading dailies of the North joined in the denunciation; many placed the blame solely on the President. It was the result, said the Philadelphia *Press,* of his "infirmity of purpose." [58]

Social ostracism awaited Horace Greeley for his bondsmanship. The sale of the first volume of his "American Conflict" had run well towards a quarter of a million, but the new subscriptions to the second were cancelled by the thousand. In the Union League Club there was a movement to expel him, but no action was taken.[59]

The ears of Boutwell and his friends were not attuned to heed the many commendations. The New York *Herald* wrote that the release would give "general satisfaction." Many of the journalists declared that it had done more than all else for "real peace and reconstruction," [60] while from abroad observing statesmen were voicing their approval. Through Bancroft, Thiers sent word that he highly commended the clemency that had been shown to Davis, and that it had won Andrew Johnson the "esteem of the best men in all Europe." [61]

The Radicals had not been very successful thus far in securing proof that Johnson was concerned in Lincoln's murder. Baker, the discharged secret service head, had not proved a complete success. [62] But if Baker had failed, there was always Ashley. Eagerly he now once more stepped forward. There was a Mrs. Harris, he said, who knew about a letter! Perhaps for a consideration she could be coaxed to tell! Wonderful! Baker was dispatched for her at once. She was of course, a myth, but what mattered that? [63] It served to keep alive the tumult through which ultimately they were hoping to depose Johnson and elevate Ben Wade!

When not engaged in charging the President with the murder of his predecessor, there was always the congenial work of proving him a common drunkard. An agent of the Associated Press was eagerly examined. He had "swung around the circle" the preceding autumn. Was the President drunk? He must have been drunk! To their consternation, however, they listened while this witness swore that at no time and at no place on that tour was Johnson ever "drunk" or "excited with liquor." [64] Direct first-hand witnesses were embarrassing to the Committee.

Washington's summer heat was now upon them, and for all their valiant zeal the "statesmen" had thus far failed. So by a vote of five to four [65] on Monday, June 3rd, the Committee with great reluctance voted "that from the testimony before them it did not appear that the President was guilty of such high crimes and misdemeanors as called for the impeaching power of the House." The four dissenting members were all Radicals; one of them of course, was Boutwell. [66]

Horace Greeley

"The Judiciary Committee," our diarist on the following evening wrote, "have by a vote of five to four decided against impeachment, but by a strict party vote passed a resolution of censure against the President. A more shameless and disgraceful proceeding than this whole impeachment conspiracy has never been enacted. For many months a committee, composed mostly of extreme partisans, has been in session, with extraordinary powers to send for persons and papers, and with the public treasury and an army of public scavengers to assist them to find, if possible, some act or transaction or expression which would justify or excuse an arraignment of the Chief Magistrate. His public and his private acts have been scanned, his household affairs, his domestic life, his bank accounts, his social intercourse, as well as all his speeches, conversations and doings as a man and President, have been scrutinized. Failing in their intrigue, scandal and defamation, they have set to work to palliate these outrageous proceedings. Most of the members of the Cabinet and, I believe, all but myself have been summoned before this committee, as well as his private secretaries and members of his family." [67]

Subjected to investigation as no American public man has ever been, Johnson came through all the flames unscathed.

LIII

THE PRESIDENT SUSPENDS STANTON

STRONGLY as Johnson disapproved of the Reconstruction Acts, he nevertheless made it plain that he would see them executed so long as they were laws,[1] never doubting that the Supreme Court would strike these measures down. Until that time should come, he recognized his duty, however distasteful or distressing, as the Chief Executive, to "take care that the laws,"—even these laws— were "faithfully executed."[2]

Immediately upon the passage of the acts, as we have seen, the generals for the command of the military districts had been assigned.[3] Over the fifth,—Louisiana and Texas—Sheridan had been placed with his headquarters at New Orleans.[4] He had been a dashing cavalry commander. He had the qualities that served him well on horseback,—youth, daring, self-assurance and impetuosity. Fine traits for the soldier, but as a civil administrator he was something more than lacking in tact, discretion or restraint. Moreover, like so many of his contemporaries, he harbored Presidential aspirations;[5] the malady of Chief Justice Chase was apparently infectious. New Orleans, with its riot of the year before, would have been a difficult post for the most discreet commander. With Sheridan, trouble began almost at once,—it was the kind of trouble that endeared him to the Radicals.

He had been in office but eight days when his axe began to fall. Summarily he removed Judge Abell of the Criminal Court of New Orleans, as well as Herron, the Attorney-General of Louisiana, and Monroe, the Mayor of the capital. Having thus disposed of these lesser officers he now directed his attention to James Welles, the Governor of the State. The Legislature of Louisiana had appropriated $4,000,000 for repairing the levees. Between the lawmakers and the Governor an argument had ensued as to the expenditure of the money. Sheridan saw here another opportunity for the exercise of arbitrary power, and on June 3rd he dismissed the legislature and removed the Governor! [6] "Little Phil" had indeed become the "little monarch," the viceroy and the "satrap." This, of course, was what Congress had intended the military commanders should become.

Brooding over the South's harsh fate, Andrew Johnson cast about for some alleviation. He besought the services of his Attorney-General. Stanbery set to work. He began the preparation of an opinion whereby through an interpretation of the Revolutionary laws he might hew away some of their most jagged edges. On May 13th he read the first pages of his opinion to Johnson and the Cabinet.[7] On June 12th his work was finished and published to the world.[8] During the course of its preparation the Cabinet discussed little else.[9] Stanton alone opposed this just attempt to ease the friction of the Southern yoke, contending that the Reconstruction acts "invested the commanders with absolute power!" [10] During the discussion which occupied the Cabinet for days, it was obvious, to one who watched him closely, that "Stanton was an original adviser if not the originator of these laws. He may not have drafted them, but he, and propably Holt in consultation with him, devised the plan of military despotic government to rule the South." [11]

Based on the Attorney-General's opinion, on June 20th Johnson issued instructions to the military commanders of the South. He declared that every person offering himself to be registered as a voter must be accepted upon his taking the prescribed oath; that no new oath should be exacted, and that the board of registry could not go behind the oath, and that participation in the rebellion did not work disfranchisement until a law or a judicial sentence of some competent authority declared it; that militia officers were not disfranchised because of their participation in the rebellion; and lastly that no disloyal sentiment or opinion falling short of an incitement to engage in the rebellion should disqualify from voting.[12]

Johnson had for his support the opinion of a great lawyer, and but for Stanton, the unanimous concurrence of his Cabinet.

His plan was at least worth trying,—it was an effort to read into the work of Stevens the justice and mercy which he had intentionally omitted. When Johnson's instructions became public, they were, of course, assailed by every Radical in Congress.[13] Stanbery, they thought, had "driven a coach and six" through their work.[14] Chase, who did not agree with Stanbery's opinion, nevertheless declared: "I see no ground for thinking that the President has not intended to carry out the Reconstruction Acts in good faith or that the Attorney-General has not honestly sought to ascertain and state their true meaning."[15]

This might be the opinion of the Chief Justice of the Supreme Court, but it was not that of "little Phil." "I regret," sententiously he wrote to Grant, "that I should have to differ with the President, but it must be recollected that I have been ordered to execute a law to which the President has been in bitter antagonism."[16] Grant answered: "Enforce your own construction of the military bill until ordered to do otherwise. The opinion of the Attorney-General has not been distributed to the district commanders in language or manner entitling it to the form of an order, nor can I suppose that the President intended it to have such force."[17]

§

Resolved to form such a law as neither Johnson nor his Attorney-General could find mercy in, on July 3rd, the appointed day, Congress reconvened. From the ashes of her ruined homes, stunned and without hope, the South looked on.[18] The House had been in session but five days when Ben Butler returned to the favorite charge of murder. He demanded a special committee to investigate "all the facts and circumstances connected with the assassination of the late lamented President," and offered amnesty to all who would come forward with new proofs. The committee was appointed,—"the Assassination Committee" it was soon appropriately called. Butler, of course, became the chairman.[19]

Deeming any insubordination to the President a badge of merit, and desirous of making friends with all who showed him enmity, the House the day after it convened, by a strict party vote, tendered Sheridan its thanks for the "able and faithful performance of his duties." [20] Having pleasantly dispatched these two items of business, Congress proceeded to the main labor of the session.

A second supplementary Reconstruction Act was ready. [21] The bill authorized the commanders of the military districts to remove or to suspend any person holding office in the "pretended governments" of the "rebel states," and to appoint others in their stead. Such removals or suspensions were made reviewable by the general of the army, not by the President. And it was made the further duty of that general and of the commanders of the districts to remove all "disloyal persons." [22] On the 14th the bill reached the President, and five days later he struck back with his veto.

Referring to the provisions granting unlimited military government over ten states, he declared: "It is impossible to conceive any state of society more intolerable than this; and yet it is to this condition that 12,000,000 American citizens are reduced by the Congress of the United States. . . . Of what avail will it be to any one of these Southern people when seized by a file of soldiers to ask for the cause of arrest or for the production of a warrant?" [23]

Congress had declared the state governments to be illegal and had provided at the same time that they should be carried on by Federal officers, deputed to perform the very duties of the "illegal state authority." "It certainly would be a novel spectacle," said Johnson, "if Congress should attempt to carry on a *legal* state government by the agency of its own officers. It is yet more strange that Congress attempts to sustain and carry on an *illegal* state government by the same Federal agency." [24]

In order to forestall the possibility of another opinion of the Attorney-General or of the President, Congress in this new bill had declared that none of the officers or appointees of the military commanders should "be bound in his action by any opinion of any civil officer of the United States." [25] "But where," asked Johnson, "is the construction to come from? Certainly no one can be more in want of instruction than a soldier or an officer of the Army detailed for a civil service, perhaps the most important in

a state, with the duties of which he is altogether unfamiliar." [26]
The absurdity of such an arrangement was obvious, but Johnson
made it even plainer: "These military appointees . . . might very
well say, even when their action is in conflict with the Supreme
Court of the United States, 'that court is composed of civil officers
of the United States, and we are not bound to conform our action
to any opinion of any such authority.' " [27]

As to the usurpations of his enemies, Johnson thus spoke out:
"Within a period of less than a year the legislation of Congress
has attempted to strip the Executive Department of some of its
essential powers. The Constitution and the oath provided in it
devolve upon the President the power and duty to see that the
laws are faithfully executed. The Constitution, in order to carry
out this power, gives him the choice of agents, and makes them
subject to his control and supervision. But in the execution of
these laws the constitutional obligation upon the President
remains, but the power to exercise that constitutional duty is
effectually taken away. The military commander is as to the
power of appointment made to take the place of the President,
and the general of the army the place of the Senate; and any
attempt on the part of the President to assert his own constitutional powers may, under pretense of law, be met by official
insubordination. It is to be feared that these military officers,
looking to the authority given by these laws, rather than to the
letter of the Constitution, will recognize no authority but the
commander of the district and the general of the army." [28]

Trusting his Northern compatriots, alas, far more than they
deserved, even in this black hour, Johnson had not abandoned
hope. "With abiding confidence in their patriotism, wisdom and
integrity," he said, "I am still hopeful of the future, and that
in the end the rod of despotism will be broken, the armed heel
of power lifted from the necks of the people, and the principles
of a violated Constitution preserved." [29]

There were at least two sentences of that message that attracted
the attention of the Radicals: "Whilst I hold the chief executive
authority of the United States, whilst the obligation rests upon
me to see that all the laws are faithfully executed, I can never

willingly surrender that trust or the powers given for its execution. I can never give my assent to be made responsible for the faithful execution of the laws, and at the same time surrender that trust, and the powers which accompany it to any other officer, high or low, or to any number of executive officers." [30] What did he mean? "I can never willingly surrender that trust or the powers given for its execution!" Would their conspiracy eventually result in bloodshed? Would their aggressions bring on another civil war?

This latest veto message came to the Radicals in the midsummer heat as new evidence that Johnson was an enemy of the Republic. Here, declared Boutwell, was revealed that deadly intent "which provokes and demands the exercise of the highest and gravest duty of the House." [31] Impeachment! With little debate and no endeavor to refute Johnson's truths, both Houses repassed the bill, the veto notwithstanding. [32]

It was the 20th of July and Congress was once more willing to adjourn, but there were certain patriots who were not ready. They demanded a continuous session in order "to keep constant watch of the course of the Administration and be at all times ready to neutralize its evil purposes." [33] "As a Senator I must be plain," said Sumner, "nor can I be constrained by the possibility that hereafter I may be called to judge the President. . . . Now since Andrew Johnson remains President and he is not at your bar, I cannot doubt that we ought to stay in our seats to encounter the evil proceeding from him. There he stands a constant impediment to peace and an ally to the Rebellion. And yet knowing these things it is proposed to go home and leave him undisturbed master till winter." [34]

Senator Sherman could contain himself no longer, and therefore interrupted: "It does seem to me a very strange thing that a judge, by whose vote alone the President can be removed, should declare that he must be removed." [35] But Sumner blandly answered: "The Senator says . . . that this is not the time to discuss the President. He is mistaken; this is the very time. The . . . Senator from Ohio . . . gravely moves that we leave our seats and from this time forward till December abdicate our constitutional guardianship of the public interest. To such a proposition there is but one natural and logical reply. It is that we must not abdicate so long as Andrew Johnson is in the Executive chair. If he continues President we must remain at our posts, precisely as Grant remained before Richmond." [36]

Charles Sumner and his friends were posing as the saviors of the country. "Our President is a public enemy," he sweetly continued, "successor in spirit and opinion of Jefferson Davis, through whom the Rebellion is once more on its legs. . . . Because we have the successor of Jefferson Davis in the Presidential chair, therefore Congress must stay. . . . The President is the Executive; we are the Legislative. His influence is great, ours is greater. If we choose to say so we can be master." [37]

Through no love of Johnson, or dissent from Sumner's slanders, but rather lest a continued session might unfavorably impress the country in the elections which were at hand, Congress adjourned until November 21st. [38]

§

Congress now held the Reconstruction in its power, there was but one remaining barrier,—the Supreme Court. If the opportunity should come, would Chief Justice Chase and his associates display Johnson's courage?

Gloating over their most recent triumph, the Radicals departed from the capital, but not the least member of their inner councils stayed. Stanton was still Secretary of War! During the Cabinet discussions of Stanbery's opinions, however, Johnson had at last come definitely to see that the retention of this hostile and disloyal minister was no longer possible. Even before Congress had convened for its last hectic meeting the President expressed himself to Welles as thoroughly convinced that Stanton had "played a part for himself, had an understanding with the violent Radicals, had embarrassed the Administration and thwarted its policy," and voiced surprise that Stanton should "persist in holding on to his place and mixing with us." [39]

Sheridan's subordination, too, did not increase Johnson's confidence in Stanton; it made him doubtful about Grant. "Do you suppose," the President asked a trusted friend at the time Sheridan's letter became known, "that there has been communication between Grant and Stanton about that letter?" [40]

By every mode short of an express request to resign, the President now gave his faithless minister to understand that his continuance in the Cabinet was unwelcome.[41] Stanton's skin, however, was too leathery to permit the percolation of mere hints. Impatiently Johnson waited for that voluntary withdrawal which under such circumstances must immediately have come from any man of sensitive honor. But there was no manifestation on Stanton's part of any intention to withdraw.[42]

Events, however, which so often shape themselves, at this time conspired to kindle Johnson's desire for Stanton's resignation. Toward the end of July, Sheridan removed Governor Throckmorton of Texas and put E. M. Pease in his place, whom Throckmorton, by a vote of six to one, had defeated for that office twenty months before.[43] Bold and gallant soldier that he was, Sheridan had become unjust and vain, spoiled by partisan flattery and the encouragement of the Radical conspirators.[44]

What course should the troubled President now follow? Should he remove Sheridan? Should he remove Stanton or should he dispense with both at once? Sheridan's most recent act of highhanded power was the subject of excited discussion in the Cabinet two days later. McCulloch thought Sheridan's removal would be "injudicious," and that it "would strengthen the extreme Radicals, who really wanted the President to take this step in order that they might make successful war against him." He feared, too, that Sheridan's popularity was such that his removal would "bring down violence on the administration," and that the Conservatives might be frightened from their opposition to the impeachment.[45]

Browning agreed with McCulloch, but Randall in great excitement advocated turning "the little fellow" out. Welles, who felt that the President had not sufficiently opposed his Radical tormentors, was indignant at the very thought of trying to conciliate them now. What, he said, must we "suppress our convictions, abdicate our duty and in our helplessness trust to division among the Radicals?" Listening to this debate Johnson became thoroughly aroused and his eyes were flashing when he said: "If they would impeach me for ordering away an officer who I believe is doing wrong,—afflicting and oppressing people instead of protecting and sustaining them—if I am to be impeached for this, I am prepared." [46]

And the next day, to Gideon Welles the President declared: "What have I to fear, what to gain or lose by keeping this man who delights in opposing and counteracting my views in this position? It is said that the weak Radicals,—the conservative ones—will join the ultras to impeach me. If Congress can bring themselves to impeach me because in my judgment a turbulent and unfit man should be removed and because I, in the honest discharge of my duty to my country and the Constitution, exercise my judgment and remove him, let them do it. I shall not shun the trial, and if the people can sanction such a proceeding I shall not lament the loss of a position held by such a tenure." [47]

At this point Welles remarked that "Sheridan was really but a secondary personage after all in the business. He would never have pursued the course he has if not prompted and encouraged by others to whom he looked,—from whom he received advice if not orders. Little would be attained if only he were taken in hand." To which the President replied that "there was no doubt of that," and that he was "giving the subject attention." [48]

The subject,—Stanton—was indeed one to which Johnson had been giving his attention. Two days before he had had a long talk with Grant, expressing his intention to remove both Sheridan and Stanton. For some reason Grant seemed determined to make a record of that talk and that evening sent the President a long private letter "on the subject of the conversation we had this morning." Concerning Stanton, Grant declared that "his removal cannot be effected against his will without the consent of the Senate. . . . It certainly was the intention of the legislative branch of the government to place Cabinet ministers beyond the power of Executive removal, and it is pretty well understood that . . . it was intended specially to protect the Secretary of War in whom the country felt great confidence. The meaning of the law may be explained away by an astute lawyer, but common sense and the views of loyal people will give it the effect intended by its framers." [49]

It must indeed have been an "astute lawyer" from whom Grant derived the interesting knowledge that the Tenure-of-Office Bill was "intended specially to protect the Secretary of War." Relying on what the Radicals had told him, Grant had not attentively pursued the report of the Conference Committee of the Congress published before the act became a law. He evidently had failed to read Senator Sherman's statement that the bill as finally passed was drawn "so that the government will not be embarrassed by an attempt by a Cabinet officer to hold on to his office despite the wish of the President," and that it had obviated that "great danger." [50]

Grant argued strongly against the removal of Sheridan. He justly praised his military record and declared that "his civil administration has given equal satisfaction." [51] It had indeed given satisfaction to those with whom Grant evidently was now more and more consorting.

Johnson told Welles of the conference with Grant, and walking over to his desk, handed his faithful Secretary the letter Grant had written. This letter, Welles recorded later, "was not such as I should have at one time expected from Grant,—was not discreet, judicious nor excusable even from his standpoint. If not disingenuous he has, perhaps without being aware of it, had his opinions warped and modified within a year." [52] It was commonly reported that Grant's letter had been inspired by Stanton. [53]

As he finished reading this communication and handed it back to Johnson, Welles remarked. "Grant is going over." "Yes," said Johnson, "I am aware of it. I have no doubt that most of these offensive measures have emanated from the War Department." [54] "Not only that," replied Welles, "but almost all the officers of the army have been insidiously alienated from your support by the same influences. If you had been favored with an earnest and sincere supporter of your measures in the War Department, the condition of affairs in this country would this day have been quite different. It is unfortunate, perhaps, that you did not remove all the Cabinet soon after your administration commenced;

certainly some who have made it a business to thwart and defeat your measures ought to have been changed." [55]   To this, with some emotion, Johnson assented, but expressed doubt as to whether he could rid himself of Stanton. Welles replied that he was unable to believe "Stanton would persist in holding on as an adviser when he understood the President wished him away, or he was requested to relinquish his office, although it was obvious he was very tenacious of his place, and clung to it from personal considerations." [56]

Thrice during this conversation, and at its close, Johnson remarked that he "intended to bring this matter to a conclusion in a few days." [57]

§

More even than Sheridan's removal of Governor Throckmorton, there occurred at this time an incident that revealed the friends and co-workers of Edwin Stanton. One evening toward the end of July, the wife of Sanford Conover, alias Charles A. Dunham, called upon the President to petition for her husband's pardon. This favorite tool of the Radicals, the co-worker of Boutwell, Ashley and Holt, was about to begin his incarceration in the Albany Penitentiary,—a prospect that seemed to Conover increasingly distasteful the more he contemplated it.

At the time of his mother's arrest for Lincoln's murder, John H. Surratt had fled to Canada, whence he escaped to England and then to Rome, where he enlisted in the Papal army. He was finally arrested and brought back to Washington where on June 10th, 1867, his trial for Lincoln's murder was begun before a civil court and jury. [58]   During the trial Conover was literally invaluable in his assistance to the prosecution. Judge Advocate-General Holt and A. G. Riddle of counsel for the United States estimated his services highly,—more highly it appears than did the jury, who after three days and nights of deliberation were discharged because they were unable to agree upon a verdict. [59]

More than ten days before the trial concluded,—the Radicals having done with him—Conover was about to be taken to the Albany Penitentiary. [60]   It was at this time that his wife acted,—

he acted also! The petition Mrs. Conover left with the President contained recommendations for a pardon signed by Holt and Riddle and a letter from Ashley. But Conover, it seems, did not have too much confidence in these friends. His wife told the President when she called that "promises and assurances of pardon had been held out" to her husband "by certain parties on condition he would do certain things," but that they had been "put off and tantalized" until they did not know what to make of it."[1]

With Conover's petition there was inadvertently enclosed another note from Ashley,[62] that led the President to further inquiry. And now Conover saw his chance to act. He determined to expose the scoundrels with whom he had been consorting. He sent his wife back to the President with a long letter denouncing the "nefarious conspiracy" of "Ashley & Co." and other "traitors and conspirators." He charged specifically that Ashley had "thought it would be very plausible to prove" Johnson's participation in the Lincoln murder, and that he (Conover) had assured Ashley that he "should have no difficulty in finding persons of good standing and moral character to prove these matters and it was agreed that he 'should do so as soon as released.' "[63]

At the desire of Ashley and Ben Butler he had sent memoranda of the needed evidence to a "trusty friend" with instructions to procure two others who would commit to memory the statements enclosed, and when sent for would appear in Washington to repeat them. These two willing perjurors were procured and "were inspected by Ashley and Butler, and were found to possess the requisite qualifications as to intelligence and personal appearance." They were "passed" and "introduced to several Radical members of the House." Butler wanted to clinch the matter then and there by taking the depositions of these men, but Conover "would not consent to its being done," until he received his price, —his liberty. With this long letter Conover forwarded a specimen of the memoranda used for the subornation of the witnesses he had secured. He sent also four notes of Ashley concerning this business, in the latest of which Ashley wrote: "If you can put the originals (i.e. letter of A. J. to Davis and Booth) in my hands, I will say that no one shall take or destroy them without your express order in writing except you are released." [64]

The morning following the receipt of these communications Johnson caused his Cabinet to hear them read. "I need say no farther," wrote our diarist that evening, "than that they furnish conclusive evidence of an atrocious conspiracy to impeach the President by manufactured testimony which was to be furnished by this man Conover alias Dunham, who was to be released from prison on condition he procured persons to testify as the parties desired." [65]

On Monday morning, August 5th, the faithful Secretary of the Navy called upon the President and asked him what he intended doing as to Sheridan. Johnson replied that he had "dropped Sheridan for the present and gone to the fountain-head of mischief. . . ." [66] He had done so indeed! On that morning he had sent Stanton this communication:

> "Executive Mansion,
> Washington, August 5, 1867.
>
> Sir:
>   Public considerations of a high character constrain me to say that your resignation as Secretary of War will be accepted.
>   Very respectfully,
>   ANDREW JOHNSON.
> To Hon. Edwin M. Stanton,
>   Secretary of War." [67]

"It is impossible," said Johnson, "to get along with such a man in such a position, and I can stand it no longer." [68]

But having been asked to go, would Stanton go? "What do you think he will do?" the President inquired of Welles. "I think," the latter replied, "he will resign and not intrude himself upon you, and longer embarrass you,—yet his friends are the ones who have tried to tie your hands." "Yes," responded Johnson, "and he instigated it. He has, I am satisfied, been the prolific source of difficulties. You have alluded to this, but I was unwilling to consider it,—to think that the man whom I trusted was plotting and intriguing against me." [69]

But there was the Tenure-of-Office act,—would Stanton seek to barricade himself behind it?

§

Johnson did not have long to wait for Stanton's next move. On the same day he sent the President this letter:

> "War Department
> Washington, August 5, 1867.
>
> Sir:
>   Your note of this day has been received, stating that public consid-erations of a high character constrain you to say that my resignation as Secretary of War will be accepted.
>   In reply I have the honor to say that public considerations of a high character, which alone have induced me to continue at the head of this Department, constrain me not to resign the office of Secretary of War before the next meeting of Congress.
>   Very respectfully yours,
>   EDWIN M. STANTON.
> To the President." [70]

Gradually and by slow stages he had come to this direct and open warfare. By secretly befriending and reporting to the Radicals, he now felt strong enough to take this course. He stood now openly revealed as the friend of the conspirators. Thaddeus Stevens' grim visage was lurking in the background.

Stanton had become the open ally of Ben Butler and Ben Wade. What his convictions were, he expressed two years later when he was about to die. He then declared that he had "never doubted the constitutional right of the President to remove the members of his Cabinet without question from any quarter whatever," and admitted that Johnson had followed Lincoln's recon-struction measures and that "if Mr. Lincoln had lived he would have had a hard time with his party as he would have been at odds with it on Reconstruction." [71]

For seven days after the receipt of Stanton's letter, Johnson waited before making his next move. During this interval two Cabinet meetings were held. Unwilling to push effrontery to such limits, Stanton attended neither. The President as always sought advice and acted carefully. He needed a strong man for his Secretary of War,—if possible, a loyal minister, but above all one whom the Radicals could not cavil at. There was Grant,—

already their candidate for President, clad in the bright glory of his great service in the war. How about Grant? His leanings toward the Radicals were plain enough, but perhaps, so Seward thought at least, the President might find in him a fast friend by reason of the old disagreement between him and Butler.[72] On August 11th Johnson felt him out. As Stanton must leave, would he act as Secretary of War ad interim? If this was decided upon, said Grant, he had "nothing further to say on that point." As for himself,—well he always "obeyed orders." It was evident that he was pleased with the proposed arrangement.[73]

The next day Johnson appointed him, and wrote to Stanton sus· pending him and directing that all records of his department be transferred to Grant. Grant transmitted this letter to the Secretary. "In notifying you of my acceptance," he told Stanton in his letter of transmittal, "I cannot let the opportunity pass without expressing to you my appreciation of the zeal, patriotism, firmness and ability with which you have ever discharged the duties of Secretary of War." [74] Under the circumstances, it was a strange letter for Grant to write. It did not augur well for Grant's relations with the President!

What Grant's real opinion of the Secretary was, he confided to his Memoirs a few weeks before he died. "Mr. Stanton," Grant then wrote, "never questioned his own authority to command unless resisted. He cared nothing for the feelings of others. In fact it seemed to be pleasanter to him to disappoint than to gratify. He felt no hesitation in assuming the functions of the Executive, or in acting without advising him. . . . The Secretary was very timid. . . . The enemy would not have been in danger if Mr. Stanton had been in the field." [75]

On August 12th, the day Stanton received Johnson's order of suspension, he wrote him denying his right "under the Constitution and laws of the United States, without the advice and consent of the Senate and without legal cause to suspend me from office. . . . But inasmuch as the General commanding the armies of the United States has been appointed ad interim, and has notified me that he has accepted the appointment, I have no alternative but to submit under protest to superior force." [76]

LIV

ULYSSES GRANT

JOHNSON now had three and a half months wherein Congress was not present to harass him, but the next hundred days were to bring him anything but peace.

He had had warnings enough that Grant was responding to the Radical advances, and yet wisely, he decided that this appointment, if any, would silence criticism for suspending Stanton. It was good strategy for the President, if possible, to attach Grant to his cause. He did not know how little was the likelihood of this. He did not know that less than six months earlier Grant had written Washburne to denounce Johnson's exposure of the first Reconstruction act as "one of the most ridiculous veto messages that ever emanated from any President." [1] That Grant would receive next year a nomination for the Presidency was more than probable, but whether the Republicans or the Democrats would secure him as their standard bearer was still in doubt. The decision lay with Grant himself; that he could have the support of either party was plain enough. Both were anxious to put forth the popular war hero. [2]

Grant was at this time a pivotal man. His great power of appointment given him as general of the army by the Stanton-Boutwell measure,—unconstitutional though it was—was not lightly to be reckoned with. If he could be won to Johnson's side the Radicals would be indeed discomfited.

Artists, if not historians, must lament that Grant could not have died on the day of Appomattox. His conduct there is a treasured heritage of America. When he stopped his soldiers from firing their salute of joy, saying "The war is over; the rebels are our countrymen again," he reached the zenith of his career. The rest was anti-climax. His career as a "statesman" was anything but statesmanlike. He did not understand civil life, and was a success in it neither before nor after the great conflict. Among politicians he was like one stunned or dazed. "I liked Grant," wrote Lowell when he saw him in Washington in 1870, "and was struck with the pathos of his face; a puzzled pathos as of a man with a problem before him of which he does not understand the terms."[3]

The three coequal powers of the government involved a concept that was beyond Grant,—he thought of Congress as a superior officer to the President.[4] That a law could be so palpably in violation of the Constitution as to require the Executive as a separate and distinct department of the government to decide between his oath to the Constitution and his duty to enforce a law constituting a conspiracy against it, involved a principle beyond Grant's reach.[5] "Was not Congress superior to the President?" he one day inquired of Welles.[6] "It pained me," the latter wrote, "to see how little he understood of the fundamental principles and structure of our government and of the Constitution itself."[7]

To Welles he appeared "somewhat excited and stirred up by appeals of the Radicals and fears that he might lose their good will. None but Radicals, and the most mischievous of them, are hounding and stimulating and cautioning him. Anxious, as I am satisfied he is becoming, for the Presidency, he fears to fall out with them. Hence believing as he does that a majority of the country which is represented is with Congress, he is rather vexed, dissatisfied and somewhat confused, has listened to Radical fallacies and is strangely ignorant of the true character of men as well as the real principles in issue. . . . He is . . . a man of little reading or reflection . . . a political ignoramus. . . . He needs instruction."[8]

This is a harsh judgment, but it is impossible to follow Grant from Appomattox through the two decades to his death, without realizing that the estimate is just.

§

Grant was personally honest, yet his indifference to the corruption that flourished all about him when he became President was such as to cause Americans to blot, if possible, from

their memories all of his career following the collapse of the
Confederacy. We cherish the arresting portrait of a short, somewhat slovenly, yet somehow distinguished officer in "the uniform
of the private with the straps of a lieutenant-general;" [9] and put
away the picture of the commonplace civilian.

No one has made a more penetrating study of Grant the soldier
than Sir Frederick Maurice, the brilliant British military critic.
Speaking of the methods employed by Lee and Grant, Maurice
has written: "On the one side there was the skilled fencer whose
fascinating bladework was marked by perfect timing, the result of
confident interplay of brain and hand; on the other side one, who
disdaining the niceties of fence, took the bludgeon as his weapon,
and relying on his physical strength, careless of pricks, disregarding loss of blood, at length forced his opponent into a corner in
which he had no room to use his skill of fence." [10] There have
been and will continue to be differences of opinion as to Grant's
merits as a soldier. By some he is regarded as one of the world's
great military leaders, by others as destitute of genius though
possessing stubborn courage and unyielding resolution. [11] However his services be characterized, certain it is that for the North
his valorous sword satisfied a great need.

But if there was a difference between Grant and Lee in war,
there was a greater difference in peace. Lee, the descendant of
Alexander Spotswood who had fought with Marlborough at
Blenheim and had become a royal governor of Virginia; Lee, the
son of the famous "Light Horse Harry" of the Revolution, after
the war between the states, put away all thought of politics or personal enrichment. [12] In 1778 his father, as though strangely
prophesying for his son had said: "Virginia is my country. Her
will I obey however lamentable the fate to which it may subject
me." [13]

Lee could no longer speak of Virginia as "my country,"—he
could not speak of her even as "my state!" For she was no longer
a state, but the "first military district,"—a conquered province!
No one had ever fought for her more gallantly, and when he
could no longer fight he bore defeat, like the brave gentleman, the
true Virginian that he was.

The patriarchal simplicity of old Virginia, with her fine old mansions gleaming white amid venerable oaks, was beautiful. There for two hundred years brave, gentle people had lived out their quiet honest lives, untroubled by the mercenary world.[14] And now all this was gone. Slavery was gone, it was true, but much else that was worth preserving.

In the persons of Lee and Grant, the whole difference between North and South dramatically is personified. "One," says Gamaliel Bradford, "was a man of the eighteenth century, the other of the nineteenth, one of the old America, the other of the new. Grant stands for our modern world, with its rough business habits, its practical energy, its desire to do things no matter how, its indifference to the sweet grace of ceremony and dignity and courtesy. Lee had the traditions of an older day, not only its high beliefs, but its grave stateliness, its feeling that the way of doing things was almost as much as the thing done. In short Grant's America was the America of Lincoln, Lee's the America of Washington." Bradford expresses the hope that "without loss of the one we may some day regain something of the other."[15] No one who has ever ridden in a New York subway could entertain a hope of that kind any longer.

But Grant's America was not the America of Lincoln,—it was a new America that Lincoln never saw; it was rather the America of Jim Fisk and Jay Gould, of the Tweed Ring and the Credit Mobilier. Grant, the product of the middlewest,—a middlewest crude beyond anything that Sinclair Lewis could imagine—looked out upon this new post-war world and decided to participate. First, political position and then money,—or if it could honestly be done, and there were not wanting those to assure him that it could, both high office and money at the same time. His early lack of money seemed to foster in him an unbounded esteem for men able to acquire it,—nor did he pause to ask by what means they had gained their riches.[16]

His eight years as President were chiefly marked by maladministration and corruption. "Selfish and ambitious men," says Hoar, "got the ear of that simple and confiding President. They studied Grant, some of them, as the shoemaker measures the foot of his customer." [17]   Men of vulgar tastes and low aspirations were selected by him as friends and confidants.[18]   Such associates made a study of his humors, and if they could not gain their ends by flattery, imposed upon him by the pretense of personal devotion.[19]

Grant liked rich men.[20]   Schemers were not slow to find this out, or to lavish upon him expensive presents in the unblushing expectation of reward.   "Grant openly accepted gifts," says Rhodes, "and sometimes returned favors to the givers, but it is probable that he never consciously connected the two in his mind, for in many worldly matters he was simple as a child.   He undoubtedly looked upon the Presidential office as a present to him for having saved the nation and he hardly deemed it a sufficient reward.   General Richard Taylor, who saw him in 1872, said that he knew 'to the last shilling the various sums voted to the Duke of Wellington.' " [21]

Grant's Presidency reads like the story of a revel; the men whom he appointed and befriended made of it a riot and debauch. Richardson, his Secretary of the Treasury, was a spoilsman.   Bristow, who succeeded Richardson, in 1875 discovered that in St. Louis, McDonald, the supervisor of internal revenue, had aided distillers in that city annually to defraud the government of a million dollars in whiskey taxes.[22]   Much of this went to the raising of Republican campaign funds and especially to secure a second and if possible, a third term for Grant.[23]

Grant knew McDonald well, and when during the previous year he visited St. Louis, McDonald entertained him lavishly. Many presents from this source were forwarded to the White House.[24]   McDonald and other co-conspirators were indicted in 1875, and in September of that year, at the instance of his secretary and confidential friend, Orville E. Babcock, Grant paid a visit to St. Louis.   Babcock conferred with McDonald, and Grant met him also and gave him a pledge of sympathy.[25]   Soon it developed that Babcock was a member of the ring and a sharer in the profits.   He was indicted "for conspiracy to defraud the revenue." [26]   Grant was of great assistance in securing his acquittal, and a little later appointed him to an inspectorship of lighthouses.[27]

Later McDonald wrote a book in which he said that Grant had shared the profits of the ring.[28] Rhodes expresses strongly his disbelief in this accusation.[29] "In money matters," he declares, "Grant was as credulous as a child. He undoubtedly knew of the campaign fund in St. Louis but had not a suspicion of the process through which it was raised."[30] But, says Oberholtzer, "whether the President knew of the existence of a 'Whiskey Ring' or not, the least talent for comprehension must have made it clear to him from the first that the money poured out of McDonald's cornucopia of plenty was procured by some means from the distillers."[31]

During the same year another of Grant's appointees was found out. William Belknap had been appointed to the Cabinet because of some favor he had shown Grant's family.[32] Now it was discovered that for a long time he had been lining his pockets,—as many as he could—with gold. Belknap was impeached, but before he could be tried, sent in his resignation. Grant accepted it,— "with regret!"[33]

Not only was the President complacent in the face of frauds that flourished all about him, but he expressed and displayed vindictive hate toward the exposers of the criminals. He dismissed those who laid bare the culprits in the whiskey ring.[34] Not only was he indifferent to Belknap's crimes, but he evinced a lasting enmity toward those who dared appear against him. Custer had come under orders to give evidence, but the fact that he had come at all "gave offense to Grant whose sympathy with the rascals of his administration made him the spiteful enemy of anyone who was however remotely involved in exposing their iniquities."[35] Not only did Grant refuse to receive Custer when he called upon him at the White House, but later issued orders designed to strip him of his command, and indulged in criticism of him after death.[36]

One of the traits displayed by Grant during the eight years of his Presidency was his predilection for association with low characters.[37] Among the more notorious of these were Jay Gould and Jim Fisk. Fisk was a voluptuary and rake. He was "unscrupulous and cared nothing for the truth nor for decency in living." [38] Gould was the possessor of an amazing talent as a money-maker and was utterly indifferent as to the means employed. He was subtle, untrustworthy and dishonest.[39] These men were the products and the prototypes of the new North.

In July, 1868, control of the Erie Railroad was secured by them. The story of their machinations with this property reads like an unexpurgated page of the Arabian Nights. They were the first to move their business offices uptown. At the corner of 23rd Street and Eighth Avenue they bought a marble palace, which harbored an opera house, as well as the offices of the Erie. At a cost of about $300,000 they furnished this in the most hideous style of the world's worst period in architecture. This place became a kind of mid-Victorian seraglio, combining the qualities of an office and a brothel. "The atmosphere of the Erie offices," wrote Henry Adams, "was not disturbed with moral prejudices; and as the opera supplied Mr. Fisk's mind with amusement, so the opera troupe supplied him with a permanent harem." [40]

In 1869 these two financiers having tired temporarily from toying with the Erie and the opera, evolved the pleasing scheme of cornering the gold market of America. To accomplish this it was essential that the government should not put down the price of gold. If Grant's influence could somehow be enlisted, their conspiracy might succeed. They set to work, and so on June 15th we find Gould and Fisk on the Fall River steamer embarked for Boston, and their guest is none other than Ulysses Grant! The Peace Jubilee was the object of his destination. At supper the conversation was deftly turned toward the governmental policy of selling gold. What Grant said was not encouraging, but Gould and Fisk were not so easily discouraged and they continued their attentions. On the evening of their return the attraction at the Fifth Avenue Theatre was Offenbach's "La Périchole." A box was procured and Gould and Fisk took Grant there as their guest! [41]

Somewhat later Grant wrote the Secretary of the Treasury that "it was undesirable to force down the price of gold lest the West should suffer and the movement of crops be retarded." [42] Grant's brother-in-law, A. R. Corbin, knew that he had written, and told

Gould. Gould began buying gold and kept on until Friday, the 13th of September. The scene among the traders on that day will be remembered as long as Wall Street lasts and probably long after. The shorts were in a panic. Finally when the price reached 162, word came that the Secretary of the Treasury had ordered the sale of gold and the price fell twenty points. Grant had acted at last, but not before the many who had failed were ready to mob both Fisk and Gould. It was "black Friday."

Remembering the hospitality that Gould and Fisk had showered on Grant, there were not wanting those who believed that he and his family were interested in the speculation. "There is, however," said Rhodes, "no ground for the least suspicion," of his or Mrs. Grant's complicity.[43] This undoubtedly is true. The whole affair was but another instance of Grant's political ineptitude.

Instances of his obtuse perceptions might be multiplied without number. Favors were extended to Grant or his needy kindred by Jay Cooke through his bank in Washington, and Cooke's brother was appointed governor of the District of Columbia.[44] But perhaps the least attractive of all the relations he sustained with men of low character were those which, after he became President, sprang up between himself and Benjamin F. Butler.

In June, 1864, Grant was suffering from dejection at the failure of his expectation when he crossed the Rapidan. "It was commonly believed in the army," says Rhodes, "that his misfortunes had driven him again to drink and on this account and others Butler, with crafty method, acquired a hold on him which prevented him from acting for the best interests of the service. It is not a grateful task to relate the story of Butler using Grant as a tool to accomplish his own ends. The picture of such a relation between the two is repulsive, but it may be fraught with instruction, as men of the type of Butler are never absent from our public life."[45]

In the early part of the next month Grant asked Butler's dismissal from active service, and on July 9th Butler paid a visit to him at his headquarters. The next day Grant's request was countermanded. Butler had "some hold on the commander of the armies of the United States, and in that interview of July 9th showed his hand." [46]

We have previously seen how in 1865, to his credit, Grant finally relieved Butler of command.[47] But when Grant became President, Butler regained his old influence. Up in Boston, in 1874, one of Butler's henchmen was a man named William Simmons,—a characteristic product of his times. He was a man "of good private life, a churchgoer, a Methodist class-leader, but a practised adept in manipulating the lowest class of voters and in carrying elections by dubious means." [48] Contrary to the overwhelming sentiment of Massachusetts, Butler was pushing him for the collectorship of the port of Boston. Grant was apprised of the disappointment Simmons' appointment would create, but Butler quietly pursued his way. To Judge Hoar he said: "I have a hold over Grant, and he does not dare withdraw Simmons' name." [49] In a confidential talk with the President, Hoar later observed: "Butler says he has a hold over you." A vigorous denial was expected but none came. "Grant set his teeth, drew down his jaw, and without changing countenance looked Hoar straight in the eye, but said not a word. A long and painful silence ensued." [50] Simmons was appointed!

With this background it is difficult to disagree with George William Curtis when he wrote: "I think the warmest friends of Grant feel that he has failed terribly as President, not from want of honesty or desire but from want of tact and great ignorance." [51] Rhodes summed up the eight years that followed March 4th, 1869, in one unanswerable sentence: "The high-water mark of corruption in national affairs was reached during Grant's two administrations." [52]

§

Heedless of the anachronism, we have made a long digression, —a pardonable one, let us hope, since an understanding of the real Ulysses Grant is necessary to this narrative.

Most of the foregoing events were still within the womb of time, when Gideon Welles in August, 1867, sat confiding to his diary his observations of the new Secretary of War. He read Grant's character and mind and saw in them the things that were to render him the dupe of shady financiers and the cat's-paw of unscrupulous politicians. That he was already in the latter's power was even then apparent.

On August 1st Sheridan removed twenty-two New Orleans aldermen and appointed others in their stead. During the same month he removed the city treasurer, the chief of police and the city attorney and likewise filled their places by appointment. Nor did he confine himself to the city; throughout the parish, justices, sheriffs and other local officers were dismissed.[53] By the 17th the President had had enough of Sheridan, and removed him. He assigned him to the Department of Missouri where his opportunities for arousing discord seemed less promising, and ordered the tried and trusted George H. Thomas to Sheridan's old command.[54]

A correspondence between Grant and Johnson ensued. Grant objected to his friend Sheridan's removal; he thought it "contrary to the wishes of the American people." The President replied, complimenting the soldierly qualities of Sheridan, but declaring that he did not consider him possessed of "the calm judgment, civil qualities and ability of General Thomas." As to the wishes of the people, he was not "aware that they have been expressed."[55]

The Radicals set up a tumult over the removal. "Their editors and speakers," Welles wrote, "have undertaken to control the course of the Government as regards Sheridan, and Grant, if not a participant with, has been led away by them. Undoubtedly many people have read the papers and come to the conclusion that the President could not—dared not—remove Sheridan, and his subordinate, and rash conduct has been commended for its ability. . . . Sickles should also have been cleared out some time ago."[56]

Three days later a dispatch was laid before the Cabinet from General Sickles. It related to his famous Order No. 10 obstructing, by military force, the judgments and processes of all the courts within the Carolinas.[57] He insisted upon this because, he said, if he did not, "the court would soon pass on the Reconstruction acts and pronounce them unconstitutional." [58] He and his Radical advisers knew their favorite measures were in violation of the fundamental law, and they did not propose to give the courts an opportunity to undo their work.

Grant had at first countermanded Sickle's order insofar as it applied to courts of the United States. "But after thinking it over," he explained to the Cabinet, he had "come to the conclusion that General Sickles might have his reasons for what he was doing," and so he had countermanded his order interfering with that general. "Congress," he said, "has put in my hands the execution of this law and I intend to see that it is executed." [59]

"Of course," wrote Welles, "Radical advice and intimacy had overcome his own better judgment. Grant is an insincere man, I fear, very ambitious, has low cunning, and is unreliable, perhaps untruthful. . . . I am not prepared to condemn him as a bad man, but I consider him an insincere one. He has no political experience, has not studied or made himself familiar with our Constitution or the elementary principles of civil government even, but has permitted himself to be flattered, seduced and led away by men who are bad. Unless he can be extricated and that soon, he will, because he has a war record, be made an instrument of evil. The people admire military men and are grateful for military services. Grant has power and position without the knowledge to use them properly." [60]

Then Tenure-of-Office Act was in the minds of everyone. It was as obviously unconstitutional as were the Reconstruction laws. Johnson was eager to have the question tested out; the Radicals planned, if possible, to prevent it. Were the Radicals preparing to defend their work with arms instead of in the courts of justice? August 27th witnessed an important meeting of the Cabinet. The governor of the territory of Idaho, it appeared, was suspected as a swindler and a cheat. Another had been nominated and confirmed at the last session, but the Senate had reconsidered the vote and the subject was still not acted on. Could a successor be appointed or would the Tenure-of-Office Act prevent it? And if a new appointment could be made, suppose the first incumbent would not give up the office? What should then be done? McCulloch had an answer ready. If the governor refused by force —"call on the military!" All looked toward Grant for his answer. Here it was: "In that case the military would not respond. They would sustain the Tenure-of-Office bill, which Congress has enacted, until the judges said it was unconstitutional!" [61] But the Radicals did not intend to give the judges any opportunity to say!

Grant's answer gave food for thought! Suppose, for example, that the Senate should reinstate Edwin Stanton and Johnson should resist, would they enforce their decree by calling in the soldiers or would such a decision lead to an orderly review of their unconstitutional laws in court? The lines were being drawn. Would armed conflict come?

If, before, there could have been any doubt where Grant stood, it was now dispelled at this meeting of the Cabinet. On the day previous, having heard that Thomas was not well enough to serve, Johnson appointed Hancock instead and directed Sheridan to proceed forthwith to Missouri.[62] Grant wished this order countermanded and so stated. He wanted Sheridan to remain in New Orleans until Thomas could relieve him, and when this occurred he thought that Sheridan should have "leave to visit Washington." [63] And as he talked there crept into his tone a bolder note. The law had placed the Reconstruction acts in his hands, he said. And still further: "I have not been consulted when I received orders, and these orders counteracted in their terms some of my orders. While I have no wish to come in conflict with anyone, I have a duty to perform. I must see the Reconstruction law executed." [64] It was the tongue of Grant, but it was the voice of Edwin Stanton!

Here was an impasse! Should Johnson obey the Constitution or the Boutwell-Stanton law? The former made him the commander-and-chief of the army, the latter took that power away. Was it his duty to follow the Constitution or a law that had been passed in wanton disregard of it? He now made his position plain. "General Grant," he said, "will understand it is my duty to see the laws are executed, and also that when I assign officers to their duty my orders must be obeyed. I have made this arrangement and performed this work deliberately, and it will go with as little delay as possible." [65]

There was no doubt whether or not Andrew Johnson was President of the United States. "Grant," wrote Welles, "was humbled by this great rebuke and changed the subject." A little later, "in a subdued manner," he declared that although he performed the duties of Secretary of War ad interim, he was "no politician and preferred not to be mixed up in political questions." He did not wish, he said, "to sit at the Cabinet consultations and pass opinions on the subjects which came up for consideration." [66] Johnson told him that as to that he might do as he chose.

But despite Grant's expressed disinclination for, and his admitted inability to take part in political discussion, there were not wanting those with no aversion to discuss such matters with him. And so after this meeting of the Cabinet the Radicals again took him in hand. [67] As a result he wrote Johnson a letter, almost exclusively devoted to politics. All the Radical doctrines were rehearsed. Congress had superseded the President and conferred on Grant executive authority over the Southern states! The Sheridan order was again attacked. It was Grant and not the President who could make military appointments and originate rules and measures for those states! The Constitution as well as the President were superseded by Congress! Every political fallacy of the time was included. [68] It was, said Johnson, such a letter as he would wish Grant to write "if he was disposed to pursue a course that would embarrass the Administration, for he could be annihilated by a reply." [69]

Instead of writing, however, Johnson sent for Grant. He told him that, while no offense was intended, he would speak without reserve; and he was frank and blunt. He then took up each position of Grant's letter. When he had finished the General said he realized his mistake, and asked for the privilege of withdrawing his communication. The President expressed indifference as to this, and Grant reached out and took it. He said that he would send a note withdrawing it, and he did. [70]

Four days after Grant's expressed desire to absent himself from meetings of the Cabinet, he attended one. An eye witness who observed him noted that he was "communicative, with a mind much softened and more disposed to fellowship than at some recent meetings, particularly at the last." [71]   Grant had now rechanged his mind on Sickles' Order No. 10, and was now once more opposed to it.

On the 31st Welles closed his diary for the month of August with this comment: "Had a pleasant talk with the President this evening. He has great capacity, is conversant with our public affairs beyond most men, has much experience, possesses great firmness, sincere patriotism, a sacred regard for the Constitution, is humane and benevolent. Extreme men and extreme measures he dislikes; secession and exclusion are alike repugnant. The Radicals accuse him of being irritable and obstinate, but the truth is he has been patient and forbearing, almost to an infirmity, under assaults, intrigues and abuse. . . . It is one of his greatest weaknesses that he has no confidants and seeks none. . . . He has wonderful self-reliance and immovable firmness in maintaining what he believes to be right; is disinclined to be familiar with men in prominent positions, or to be intimate with those who fill the public eyes. [72]

Should Johnson have made more confidants? If so who were they? His experience with Stanton, Speed and Grant was not such as to have encouraged confidence. Should he have been warm when he was cool? In his "Swing Around the Circle," when with hot passion he had denounced the enemies of Lincoln's plan, and with equal ardor had championed the cause of justice, he was rewarded with such mountains of abuse as half a century has not melted down. The position of President of the United States is necessarily a lonely one. Washington knew this and so did Lincoln. Johnson, do doubt, had found it out.

Could Lincoln have done better? During his lifetime Lincoln's plan of reconstruction ran a stormy course, although his enemies, diverted as they were by the war, could not devote such concentrated opposition as when war had ceased. They were prepared to stifle a just reconstruction, no matter who its sponsor was. They had assailed Lincoln while he lived, they would have continued to assail him had not death intervened. It is unthinkable that Lincoln would have backed down in the face of opposition. Had Booth's bullet not spared him from a deeper martyrdom, we might even now be plowing through the mountains of detraction that Stevens and his followers would have heaped upon him. It is an interesting conjecture as to the kind of portrait historians would have drawn of Lincoln had he been forced to battle for his plan as Johnson battled for it for him.

§

On November 21st Congress was to reconvene.[73] As the time approached, Grant's adherence to the Radicals was growing more apparent. On September 4th the rumor of sharp differences between him and the President reached the public press, and there became evident something more than a willingness on Grant's part to have this known.[74]

On October 6th Johnson requested General Sherman to come on to Washington. It was hoped that his friendship with Grant might exercise a salutary influence. "There is no doubt," wrote Welles, "that Sherman has more general intelligence and knowledge of the government than Grant, but he is sometimes erratic and uncertain, whilst Grant is prejudiced, aspiring, reticent, cunning and stolidly obstinate in his ignorance. The two men will work well and advantageously together, but when they differ the stubborn will and selfishness of Grant will overpower the yielding genius and generous impulses of Sherman. . . . That Sherman has a mortal antipathy to Stanton and is really in sympathy with the President I can well suppose, but when he associates with Grant, I apprehend from what I have seen and understood he will be powerless. Had he been here for the last fifteen months, his influence upon Grant, who is subordinated by Stanton, whom he dislikes, might have been salutary. He can now do but little." [75]

That Sherman apparently had tried, appears from this letter written by him to his brother a few days later: "I have always talked kindly to the President and advised Grant to do so. I do think that it is best for all hands that his administration be allowed to run out its course without threatened or attempted violence. Whoever begins violent proceedings will lose in the long run. Johnson is not a man of action but of theory, and so long as your party is in doubt as to the true mode of procedure, it would be a great risk that an attempt be made to displace the President by a simple law of Congress." [76]

Welles suggested to the President that Grant though selfish, was "at heart honest, patriotic and desirous of doing right," and that it might be well to have a plain talk with him as to his intentions." [77] Johnson agreed to this and a few days later consulted Grant in a friendly way, telling him that he "could not be ignorant of the schemes and threats that were made," and that it was the President's duty "to be prepared to vindicate the rights of the Executive and maintain the Constitution, and resist invasions and usurpations." He asked Grant what he would do if impeachment really were attempted, and an arrest of the President before trial or conviction were essayed. Would Grant then obey the orders of his Commander-in-Chief? The general answered that he "should expect to obey orders," but he added, if he should change his mind, he "would advise the President in season, that he might have time to make arrangements." [78]

After this conference Johnson told his Secretary of the Navy that he thought that he could rely on Grant. The latter agreed, but urged the President to increase "his intimacy with Grant, who is not intelligent—seems to be patriotic and right-minded, but the Radicals of every description are laboring to mislead him. Defeated in the recent elections and with public opinion setting against the obnoxious measures, the scheming intriguers begin to rally around Grant,—speak of him as their candidate for President—not that they want him, but they are fearful he will be taken up by the Democrats." [79]

A few days later Boutwell began disavowing any intention of arresting the President before impeachment and conviction. He declared that it could not be done, and that he did "not favor the scheme of Stevens to that purpose." It was evident to those who watched that Grant had quietly let Boutwell know that he would not be an instrument in such work. [80]

THE 1867 ELECTIONS GO AGAINST THE RADICALS

WHAT during these times was happening in the North? We have seen something of the politicians and the press,—the Evangelical Church was enlisted with them. With the ineptitude sometimes displayed by clergymen when they depart from spiritual leadership to take the direction of things temporal, the churches had lent themselves, albeit with good motives, to an unjust cause. They sent down their missionaries with the carpet-baggers; both taught much the same doctrine.[1] "Emissaries of Christ and the radical party," an Alabama Leader called them. They taught the negro to regard the Southern whites as "their natural enemies, who, if possible, would put them back in slavery."[2] Other Christian missionaries from the North were said to inculcate the doctrine that "Christ died for negroes and Yankees, not for rebels."[3]

But these were the politicians and the preachers,—what was engaging the attention of the ordinary citizen? The North was busy making money! The hitherto undreamed of natural resources of the country were being now explored and tapped. It was the beginning of the modern industrial America.

"A stranger in traveling through the loyal states in 1864," wrote Hugh McCulloch, "would have seen little to indicate that they were engaged in a civil war of unexampled magnitude. He would have seen men pursuing their usual avocations with ardor; the farmer and mechanic busily employed; new factories being built; the marts crowded with buyers and sellers; and upon inquiry he would have learned that the foreign and domestic trade, and manufacturing in its various branches had never been so prosperous, and that labor had never been so well rewarded."[4]

But if this was true throughout the war, how much more true

was it when peace came! It was at this time that the foundations of great enterprises and great fortunes industriously were laid. It was the beginning of a new age, the age of oil and coal and iron and steel, the age of railroads and expansion,—the "Winning of the West" was under way.

In 1862 John D. Rockefeller was twenty-three years old. He was not in the war; like so many of his contemporaries he was otherwise too busily engaged. That year was not an altogether cheerful one for the Union, but it was quite fruitful for young Rockefeller, for he had invested in an oil refinery. Three years later he bought a larger one. During 1867, when the Northern politicians were busily engaged in the high purpose of absorbing the rights of Southern white men, Rockefeller, with the aid of Andrew and Flagler, bought up the business of his brother William, which three years later became the Standard Oil Company. It prospered. Ida Tarbell has told how this prosperity was brought about.[5]

Young Andrew Carnegie was twenty-eight when the war ended. Before it ended he had earned an honest penny through the introduction of sleeping cars on railroads.[6] May, 1864, was a busy month for General Grant. During that month he crossed the Rapidan, fought the battles of the Wilderness and Spottsylvania and finally was checked by Lee on the North Anna. It was a busy month for young Carnegie also, for it was then, with $8,920, that he bought a one-sixth interest in the Iron City Forge Company and secured Henry Phipps as a stockholder.[7] Henry Clay Frick at that time was a fourteen-year-old errand boy in a village store at Mount Pleasant. His first ventures in iron and coke were not altogether satisfactory, and so in 1873 he became a bookkeeper in his grandfather's distillery. But he did not always stay a bookkeeper.[8]

In 1867 a young man just twenty-one took his degree of LL.B. at the University of Chicago. Four days later he began the practice of his profession there and presently was acquiring quite a name as a corporation lawyer. Another three years and he had organized a bank of which he became the president, later he was a judge, and somewhat later the head of an enterprise of not a little prominence,—the United States Steel Corporation. The town of Gary, Indiana was named after him.[9]

Five years before George Washington departed from the American scene, in a household of extreme obscurity, Cornelius Vanderbilt was born. A year before the Civil War began, he was sixty-six years old. At that not too adolescent age he took up railroading. He bought the Harlem, the Hudson River and finally in the winter of 1866, the New York Central, and consolidated them. It was the beginning of the Vanderbilt system. "He was the Harriman and the Hill of his day." [10] At this time J. Edgar Thomson was the genius of the Pennsylvania,[11] and Daniel Drew the Machiavelli of the Erie.[12]

The marvelous age of invention was beginning. When Elias Howe died in 1867, he was rich from the proceeds of his sewing machine.[13] In that year Thomas Edison was twenty. He had lost his position as a train newsboy a few years before as a result of some phosphorus experiments on a moving train.[14] He was now dreaming dreams such as Aladdin might have dreamt. The telephone and the typewriter were presently to emerge from other minds.

The railroad builders, the inventors, the pioneers of steel and oil, the masters of capital had little time for thought about the problems that the war had left. The war concerned them little while it lasted, and now that it was over it concerned them less. This political indifference on the part of the real leaders of the country consigned the actual leadership to men like Wade and Stevens, who well knew how to secure the backing of the churches and the reformers. In New York, so busy were the capitalists, that they were allowing Tweed to run the city for them.

Despite all the distractions of business, however, so loud was the debate becoming down in Washington in the summer and fall of 1867, that the North looked up from its absorbing interests to take note of what was going on. Johnson's great veto messages were such as even busy men must heed. Then, too, in June he had made a campaign tour through New England where he had been well received. This time no governor ran away, as on the occasion of the "Swing Around the Circle," although Sumner made it his business to be absent.[15]

The Radicals were awaiting with alarm the fall elections of 1867. When the votes were counted they discovered that they had had good cause for fear. Pennsylvania went Democratic in October, and in Ohio Rutherford B. Hayes was elected governor, but by a majority of less than three thousand votes, and with him a Democratic legislature was chosen, while at the same time the negro suffrage amendment to the State Constitution was beaten by 50,000. In November Connecticut went Democratic by nearly a thousand, California by 9,000 and New Jersey by 16,000 votes. The great Empire State swung into the Democratic column with a majority of nearly 48,000. Throughout the entire country Republican majorities were diminishing.[16] "The danger now is," wrote Senator Sherman a little later to his brother, "that the mistakes of the Republicans may drift the Democratic party into power. If so the rebellion is triumphant and no man active in suppressing it will be trusted or honored." [17]

To Ben Wade the election was especially disastrous, the new Democratic legislature of Ohio meant the termination of his Senatorial career after March 4th, 1869. There was a special reason, therefore, that now impelled him to urge on the impeachment. If this were not done, he must needs soon retire from public life.

LVI

IMPEACHMENT IS DEAD! LONG LIVE IMPEACHMENT

WHEN on November 21st the Representatives and Senators returned once more to Washington, Charles Sumner, of course, came with them, but Mrs. Sumner did not accompany him. After a few weeks in their Boston home in Hancock Street she had gone on to Lenox,—not to return. Less than a year of Charles Sumner had been more than adequate.[1] Perhaps she had tired of his bland, complacent smile; perhaps his enthusiastic self-esteem had wearied her; perhaps she grew fatigued from hearing of his early social conquests in England.[2] Or it may be that his "luxuriant platform manner,"[3] his lack of any emotional qualities,[4] and his pedantry had bored her. "These people forget that I am a cistern and require time to fill up,"[5] he once had said,—perhaps she couldn't wait, or it may be that just the continuous observation of that humorless face that had so tempted Preston Brooks, was too much for Mrs. Sumner. Whatever the reasons were, she had had enough. Would that the United States had had a similar discernment!

And so Sumner and his fellow statesmen now returned. Were it not for the harm they wrought, one would be tempted to laugh at their complacent self-esteem and their unfounded pretensions to patriotism, philanthropy and statesmanship. "Great leaders like Sumner and Conkling," however, as Henry Adams has well written, "could not be burlesqued . . . their egotism and factiousness were no laughing matter."[6]

Johnson's enemies had sat all summer to fill twelve hundred octavo pages full of that which they called testimony. With tireless effort to find something with which they could besmirch and then impeach him, ninety-five witnesses had been examined.[7] Once more their dragnets had been spread. Prisons were ransacked, the household of the President was investigated and his

511

bank accounts again were scrutinized! [8]   No rumor too incredible or base but that detained and riveted the eager gaze of the blackmailers and defamers composing the majority of the Judiciary Committee. Their report was submitted on November 25th. [9] Until just before its filing the majority had been against impeachment. At the last moment, however, for reasons that have never been explained, John C. Churchill of New York went over to the impeachers. [10] And so without evidence to support them, Boutwell and his colleagues—Thomas of Maryland, Williams of Pennsylvania, Lawrence of Ohio and Churchill of New York— infamously reported a resolution that "Andrew Johnson, President of the United States be impeached of high crimes and misdemeanors." [11]

The "evidence" on which they acted was the record of failure to find anything. The notorious Baker had been reëxamined, and his testimony established nothing save his failure to produce the mysterious Mrs. Harris who was supposed to possess letters implicating Johnson in his predecessor's murder. [12]

Regretful as they doubtless were that they could not include in their report a charge of murder, the majority consoled themselves with the accusation that Andrew Johnson had been guilty of a "usurpation of power" which he had employed "with the one great overshadowing purpose of reconstructing the shattered governments of the rebel states in accordance with his own will in the interests of the great criminals who carried them into rebellion. . . ." [13] The report of the majority voicing this charge was composed by Williams of Pittsburg.

Two Republican members of the committee,—Woodbridge of Vermont and Wilson of Iowa—submitted a minority report, recommending that the whole impeachment undertaking should be dropped. [14] They analyzed and tore to pieces every charge which the majority had made. [15] But they were Radicals, and so they closed their findings with the observation that although "the case fails upon the law and the testimony, from a political standpoint it is a success," and further charged the President with betraying the confidence of those who had placed him in power, and with having joined "hands with their enemies." [16]

But when the two Democrats of the committee, Eldridge of Wisconsin and Marshall of Illinois, expressed their views they minced no words.[17] "A dragnet," they declared, "has been put out to catch every malicious whisper throughout the land, and all the vile vermin who had gossip or slander to detail, hearsay or otherwise, have been permitted to appear and place it upon record for the delectation of mankind. Spies have been sent all over the land to find something that might blacken the name and character of the Chief Magistrate of our country. Unwhipped knaves have given information of fabulous letters and documents. . . . That most notorious character, General L. C. Baker, chief of the detective police, even had the effrontery to insult the American people by placing spies within the walls of the Executive mansion; the privacy of the President's home, his private life and habits and most secret thoughts have not been deemed sacred or exempt from invasion; the members of his household have been examined; and the chief prosecutor has not hesitated to dive into loathsome dungeons and consort with convicted felons, for the purpose of accomplishing his object of arraigning the President on a charge of infamous crimes."[18]

§

And so on December 3rd, Johnson's third annual message, reasserting the principles of the Constitution for the vindication of which he had borne so much, was forwarded to the Congress. "Candor," he said, "compels me to declare that at this time there is no union as our fathers understood the term, and as they meant it to be understood by us. The Union which they established can exist only where all the states are represented in both Houses of Congress . . . and we must all acknowledge that the restoration of the states to their proper legal relations with the Federal Government and with one another . . . would be the greatest temporal blessing which God, in His kindest providence, could bestow upon this nation. It becomes our duty to consider whether or not it is impossible to effect this most desirable consummation."[19]

Oh, why would not his contemporaries heed! What bitterness

might thus have been avoided! "To me," he said, "the process of restoration seems perfectly plain and simple. It consists merely in a faithful application of the Constitution and laws. The execution of the laws is not now obstructed or opposed by physical force. There is no military or other necessity, real or pretended, which can prevent obedience to the Constitution, either North or South. . . . There is, therefore, no reason why the Constitution should not be obeyed unless those who exercise its powers have determined that it shall be disregarded and violated." [20]

"On this momentous question and some of the measures growing out of it," he continued, "I have had the misfortune to differ with Congress and have expressed my convictions without reserve, though with becoming deference to the opinion of the legislative department. Those convictions are not only unchanged but strengthened by subsequent events and further reflection." [21]

Returning once again to the unanswerable assertion that the states "lately in rebellion are still members of the national union," he continued: "It cannot be that a successful war, waged for the preservation of the Union, had the legal effect of dissolving it. The victory of the nation's arms was not the disgrace of her policy; the defeat of secession on the battlefield was not the triumph of its lawless principle. Nor could Congress with or without the consent of the Executive do anything which would have the effect directly or indirectly of separating the states from each other. To dissolve the Union is to repeal the Constitution which holds it together, and that is a power which does not belong to any department of this Government, or to all of them united." [22]

With the tireless energy of the scientist in a laboratory, Johnson continued his exposure of what the Radicals had done. "The system of measures established by the acts of Congress," he continued, "does totally subvert and destroy the form as well as the substance of republican government in the ten states to which they apply. . . . It denies the habeas corpus and the trial by jury. Personal freedom, property and life if assailed by the passion, the prejudice, or rapacity of the ruler, have no security whatever. . . . These wrongs being expressly forbidden cannot be constitutionally inflicted upon any portion of our people, no matter how they may have come within our jurisdiction, and no matter whether they live in states, territories or districts." [23]

Of course, Thad Stevens and his gang were eager to be rid of one who dared thus expose them. Impeachment! *Impeachment!!* With or without evidence, suborned or unsuborned, by fraud, trick or chicane, everything, anything to be rid of Andrew Johnson! Utterly oblivious to the conspiracy against him now well matured, Johnson invaded once again that Holy of Holies of the Radicals,—negro suffrage. "The blacks in the South," he said, "are entitled to be well and humanely governed and to have the protection of just laws for their rights of person and property. If it were practicable at this time to give them a government exclusively their own, it would become a grave question whether common humanity would not require us to save them from themselves. . . . It is not proposed merely that they shall govern themselves but that they shall rule the white race, make and administer state laws, elect Presidents and members of Congress, and shape to a greater or less extent the future destiny of the whole country. Would such a trust and power be safe in such hands?" [24]

And still further: "Industry must be reorganized, justice reestablished, public credit maintained, and order brought out of confusion. To accomplish these ends would require all the wisdom and virtue of the great men who formed our institutions originally. I confidently believe that their descendants will be equal to the arduous task before them, but it is worse than madness to expect that negroes will perform it for us. Certainly we ought not to ask their assistance till we despair of our own competency." [25]

And then this: "The great difference between the two races in physical, mental and moral characteristics will prevent an amalgamation or fusion of them into one homogeneous mass. If the inferior obtains ascendancy over the other, it will govern with reference only to its own interests—for it will recognize no common interest—and create such a tyranny as this continent has never witnessed. Already the negroes are influenced by promises of confiscation and plunder. They are taught to regard as an enemy every white man who has any respect for the rights of his own race. If this continues it must become worse and worse, until all order will be subverted, all industry cease and the fertile fields of the South grow up a wilderness. Of all the dangers which our nation has yet encountered, none are equal to those which must result from the success of the effort now making to Africanize the half of our country." [26]

With as clear a vision of the future as though he had already seen the day then nearly ten years distant, when the South would rise from its chains to throw off negro rule, Johnson said: "We must not delude ourselves. It will require a strong standing army and propably more than $200,000,000 per annum to maintain the supremacy of negro governments after they are established. . . . It is vain to hope that the negroes will maintain their ascendency themselves. Without military power they are wholly incapable of holding in subjection the white people of the South." [27]

The Credit Mobilier had not yet been exposed, but Johnson knew the low moral tone of the country when he said: "It is well and publicly known that enormous frauds have been perpetrated on the Treasury and that colossal fortunes have been made at the public expense. This species of corruption has increased, is increasing, and if not diminished will soon bring us into total ruin and disgrace. . . . For this discreditable state of things there are several causes. Some of the taxes are so laid as to present an irresistible temptation to evade payment. . . . The system never perfected was much disorganized by the 'tenure-of-office bill' which has almost destroyed official accountability." [28]

And then, not forgetting that Stanton had yielded only to "superior force," and might yet be knocking at the gates of the War Department with Congress at his back, Johnson went on: "The President may be thoroughly convinced that an officer is incapable, dishonest or unfaithful to the Constitution, but under the law which I have named the utmost he can do is to complain to the Senate and ask the privilege of supplying his place with a better man. If the Senate be regarded as personally or politically hostile to the President, it is natural and not altogether unreason-

able for the officer to expect that it will take his part as far as
possible, restore him to his place, and give him a triumph over his
Executive superior." [29] Here again the President had spoken as
though gifted with the tongue of prophecy!

Once more to give the lie to the mendacious Sumner, Johnson
said: "I have no desire to save from the proper and just consequences of their great crimes those who engaged in rebellion
against the Government, but as a mode of punishment the measures under consideration are the most unreasonable that could
be invented. Many of those people are perfectly innocent; many
kept their fidelity to the Union untainted to the last; many were
incapable of any legal offense; a large proportion even of the persons able to bear arms were forced into rebellion against their
will, and of those who are guilty with their own consent the
degrees of guilt are as various as the shades of their character and
temper. But these acts of Congress confound them all together
in one common doom. . . ." [30]

It is not difficult to imagine Stevens listening to this message,
with the sardonic corners of his cruel mouth drawn into a sneer,
or Charles Sumner patiently lifting his eyes to Heaven and holding up his hands in holy horror at its heresies. But all of it was
not lost upon the Radicals; there was one paragraph to which
even they attended. It was this: "How far the duty of the President 'to preserve, protect and defend the Constitution' requires
him to go in opposing an unconstitutional act of Congress is a
very serious question, on which I have deliberated much and felt
extremely anxious to reach a proper conclusion." [31]

Here was something to consider, and especially the sentences
which followed: "Where an act has been passed according to
the forms of the Constitution. . . . Executive resistance to it,
especially in times of high party excitement, would be likely to
produce violent collision between the respective adherents of the
two branches of government. This would be simply civil war,
and civil war must be resorted to only as the last remedy for the
worst evils. Whatever might tend to provoke it should be most
carefully avoided. A faithful and conscientious Magistrate will
concede very much to honest error, and something even to per-

verse malice, before he will endanger the public peace; and he will not adopt forcible measures, or such as might lead to force, as long as those which are peaceable remain open to him or to his constituents." [32]

But, he continued: "It is true that cases may occur in which the Executive would be compelled to stand on its rights, and maintain them regardless of all consequences. If Congress should pass an act which is not only in palpable conflict with the Constitution but will certainly, if carried out, produce immediate and irreparable injury to the organic structure of the Government, and if there be neither judicial remedy for the wrongs it inflicts nor power in the people to protect themselves without the official aid of their elected defender,—if, for instance, the legislative department should pass an act through all the forms of law to abolish a coördinate department of the Government,—in such a case the President must take the high responsibilities of his office and save the life of the nation at all hazards." [33]

Did the Boutwell-Stanton measure fall within this class? Certainly it was perilously close. There could be no doubt among those who heard Andrew Johnson's message that he was not contemplating a surrender.

§

There was a drive, a thrust and an impact in Johnson's message. The Radicals seemed stunned and dazed. Of course, there was the usual abuse. He was called "the nightmare that crouches upon the heaving breast of this nation." Sumner spoke of the message "as an incendiary document calculated to stimulate the rebellion once more and to provoke civil war," and declared that "it is evidence of a direct coalition between the President and the former rebels." [34] These denunciations however, fell short of what their authors hoped for them, and so but four days after the message had been read, by the crushing vote of 108 to 57, the Judiciary Committee's resolution for impeachment was defeated! Forty-two Republicans joined the Democrats to make this great majority! [35]

"I have examined the testimony and reports of the Judiciary

Committee," wrote Garfield two days before the vote was taken, "and have been compelled to conclude that they have not made out a case. I shall therefore vote against the measure. It may and probably will cost me my political life. The greatest prize to which ambition can aspire lies in the grasp of Ben Wade if impeachment carries. His natural fierceness makes him for it on its own merits. His interests multiply his desires by a thousand and his late defeat makes this his only great chance life can offer. For me to vote against the measure is, of course, a heavy blow to him, and will open the way to a campaign in the 19th District, in which he will have all the popular passion added to his own against me." [36] The real reasons which were actuating Garfield appeared a few weeks later when he said: "I voted against it not because I did not believe that his conduct deserved the severest condemnation, but because I did not believe the attempt was likely to be successful. . . ." [37]

While they were still planning for their next step, on December 12th Congress listened to another message from the President.[38] It was a statement of his reasons for suspending Stanton. Large consequences were presently to flow from this. The message told of Stanton's conduct in the Cabinet. It dealt with the "massacre of New Orleans," showed how shiftily Stanton had handled the dispatches,[39] and that he had condemned the Tenure-of-Office bill as unconstitutional.[40] But perhaps the most interesting paragraph related to the day when Johnson became President: "The great duty of the time was to reëstablish government, law, and order in the insurrectionary states. Congress was then in recess and the sudden overthrow of the Rebellion required speedy action. This grave subject had engaged Mr. Lincoln in the last days of his life, and the plan according to which it was to be managed had been prepared and was ready for adoption. . . . The first business transacted in the Cabinet after I became President was this unfinished business of my predecessor. A plan or scheme of reconstruction was produced which had been prepared for Mr. Lincoln by Mr. Stanton, his Secretary of War. It was approved, and at the earliest practicable moment was applied in the form of a proclamation to the state of North Carolina and afterwards became the basis of action in turn for the other states." [41]

And the President then continued: "There is perhaps no act of my Administration for which I have been more denounced than this. It was not originated by me but I shrink from no responsibility on that account, for the plan approved itself to my own judgment and I did not hesitate to carry it into execution." [42] No one more plainly owed the President his support than Stanton, no one gave him less. If ever an Executive was justified in ridding himself of a disloyal minister, Andrew Johnson was. [43]

Stanton wrote out a long reply to Johnson's message, [44] but did not send it to the Senate. [45] The Senate did not require argument from that side of the case; it could formulate its own without assistance. To the Committee on Military Affairs, Johnson's message was referred, where his friends were outnumbered six to one. Senator Howard of Michigan, of this Committee, was chosen as the draftsman of the Senatorial report. [46] Could there be any doubt as to what the contents of his report would be? Impeachment was dead, long live impeachment!

LVII

CREDIT MOBILIER

DECEMBER, 1867, was a month wherein the versatility of our statesmen in both Houses was peculiarly manifest. The "patriots" were deeply engrossed in their plans to subjugate the white South under negro rule. But even amid these grave responsibilities they now found time, opportunity and a strong inclination for a little relaxation,—a moral relaxation.

Out in the west the engineers and the railroad gangs were laying the Union and Central Pacific Railways. The "Iron Horse" was marching steadily across the continent. The hope of linking East and West, the winning of a vast new national domain, the vista of the path of empire,—these dreams and hopes were fascinating the imagination of the people. To some Senators and Representatives they were peculiarly fascinating! A highly respected member of Congress at this time was Oakes Ames of Massachusetts.[1] He was the Union Pacific's leading spirit.[2]

In addition to other aids, Congress had loaned each road $27,000,000 for thirty years without interest. There was then no need for a resort to the customary practice of organizing a construction company whose stockholders, because of the unusual risk, would be tempted to invest in the hope of large returns. But Ames, seeing a chance to make extraordinary profits, formed a subsidiary company. He acquired the charter of an existing Pennsylvania corporation to which was presently awarded the contract for the construction of the Union Pacific. The name of the subsidiary was the "Credit Mobilier." For half a century it has been a synonym for infamy![3]

Before making this contract, Ames and his friends divided the stock of Credit Mobilier among themselves, and then mortgaged the road up to its full value,[4] and presently began dividing the

521

proceeds of the bond issue among the stockholders of Credit Mobilier.[5] The road was not only mortgaged up to its full value, but stripped of the government endowment.[6]

Under such circumstances it was something more than necessary to prevent Congressional interference, and so to keep the statesmen in good humor, a junket was organized in October, 1866. A party of Congressmen headed by Ben Wade was taken as far as Omaha to inspect the progress of construction. No expense was spared. Trains of "palace cars," bearing mottoes and gay flags, were placed at their disposal. Balls were given at the stops, while Pawnee Indians amused the guests with dancing and sham battles.[7] Despite all of these precautions, in December, 1867, Representative Washburne of Wisconsin introduced "a bill to regulate by law the rates of transportation over the Pacific Road," and presently other measures were brought forward threatening the interests of the company.[8] A Congressional investigation seemed imminent. Whatever weapons would allay this threat, Ames was ready to employ; he chose bribery.[9]

Accordingly a quantity of Credit Mobilier stock was given him for distribution at par among the influential members of the Congress. But enormous dividends had been already voted, so that the purchase of one share was "like purchasing for $1000 a bank account which already amounted to, or shortly would amount to, more than double that sum." [10] He took the shares to Washington, from whence he wrote: "I don't fear any investigation here. . . . I have used this where it will produce most good to us, I think. In view of Washburne's move here, I go in for making our bond dividend in full." [11] Washburne's bill died an unnatural death.[12]

The purchase of Senators and Representatives was running hand in hand with the conspiracy against Andrew Johnson and the South. One wonders how much it would have cost to buy them off. Had he possessed the moral obliquity of many of his enemies, it would not have been difficult for him to have purchased peace.

The Poland Committee in 1872 reported "that there has been an attempt to prevent the exercise of the reserved power in Congress by inducing influential members of Congress to become interested in the profits of the transaction." [13] Ames was found guilty of selling the stock to Congressmen at prices far below its true value "to influence the votes and decisions of such members in matters to be brought before Congress for action." His expulsion from the House was recommended. But this was too harsh for mere bribery; it was felt that a vote of censure was enough. [14] Dawes, Scofield, Bingham, Kelley and Garfield were absolved by the Poland Committee "from any corrupt motive or purpose," and from any guilt, impropriety, "or even indelicacy" in becoming purchasers of the stock. [15]

Colfax had agreed to take twenty shares. He later denied this under oath, but Ames' memorandum book showed that $1200 as a dividend on Credit Mobilier had been paid him. In the course of his perjurious endeavor to explain the acceptance of this sum, it soon developed that in addition to the $1200 he had received $4000 from one Nesbitt of New York, as a bribe in securing for him large contracts in government envelopes. [16] Ames swore that Garfield agreed to take ten shares, and his memorandum book corroborated him. Garfield testified that he had never owned any of the stock or received any of its dividends. He had been paid $300 by Ames, he admitted, but this was the repayment of a "loan." The Poland Committee who heard both Ames and Garfield believed the former. [17]

Boutwell, it seems, did not partake. How many others did, no one will ever know. Elihu Root in 1925 referred to the "Credit Mobilier's scandals which embraced a large part of the people concerned in our government." [18] As the impeachers were moving on, those who were not personally concerned in the corruption knew that it was flourishing. Such exposure as was made did not come till three years later, but the "philanthropists" and the lofty guardians of the Constitution were well aware that what General Sherman wrote in 1865, in 1867 and 1868 was even truer: "Washington is as corrupt as Hell." [19]

LVIII

A GLANCE BELOW THE MASON-DIXON LINE

WHILE the statesmen at Washington pushed on their glorious work, their military commanders in the South were attending to the execution of the Reconstruction acts. There was to be no doubt that the "conquered provinces" were conquered! The Northern generals by October 1st, 1867, had completed the registration. In five of the states the whites were outnumbered by the negroes.[1]

The old leaders of the South had been disfranchised. The new electorate consisted of poor white trash, negroes and carpet-baggers.[2] "No such mass of political inexperience, of childish ignorance," says Rhodes,—" 'no such terrible, inert mass of domesticated barbarism' was ever before in our country called upon to exercise the suffrage. . . ."[3]

In the fall elections, by an overwhelming vote, Ohio refused to amend her Constitution so as to enfranchise her few negroes,[4] yet conventions in what had been the Southern states were presently to be convened which were ordered to adopt negro suffrage in their fundamental laws as one of the conditions to regaining statehood.

In Virginia, on December 3rd, the first of these conventions met. Its chaplain came from Illinois, its 105 members from New York, Pennsylvania, Ohio, Maine, Vermont, Connecticut, Maryland, the District of Columbia, Ireland, Scotland, Nova Scotia, Canada, and England. The old Dominion contributed but 35 whites and 24 negroes. The officers of the convention were foreigners and blacks.[5]

The negro delegates were fresh from the tobacco lots and cotton fields; they could neither read nor write, but they wore Prince Albert coats, tall silk hats and flourished their gold-headed canes.

Their knowledge of parliamentary law was not extensive. Before the convention could be organized one exuberant black delegate arose to speak. "No motion is in order until the roll is called," the chairman ruled. The statesman from Africa sank into his seat and in an awed voice whispered to his neighbor: "Whut in de worl' is dat?" [6] When a little later a white member arose to "make an inquiry" a whisper ran around among the blacks: "Whut dat he gwi make?" "Well, it don't make no diffunce," one of the negroes answered, "we ain't gwi let him do it no how case he ain't no Radicule." [7]

White pages and black pages and those of intermediate shades rushed back and forth to wait upon the members. The blacker the statesman the more insistent was he that a white page should attend him, bring him paper, ink and pens, apples, goober-peas and ginger cakes. And it was not long before the darkies began noticing that the white delegates read newspapers. They became imbued with the desire to imitate this intellectual pursuit. They sent out for newspapers on their own account, and presently sat solemnly examining them—upside down. [8]

A debate arose over the employment of a stenographer. "Snographer? What's dat?" "Maybe it's de pusson whut takes down the speeches befo' dee's spoken," another negro obligingly explained. A white man presently advanced towards the desk just vacated by a gentleman of color. "Dar he! dat's him!" "War's good close, anyhow!" were some of the comments. But the negro who had vacated the desk was now attracting the attention of his fellows: "What he done?" "What dee tun him out fuh?" "Ain dee gwi give niggers nothin?" At this point the Honorable Lewis Lindsay who was representing Richmond arose to speak. "Mistah President," he said, "I hopes in dis late hour dat old Fuhginny am imperilated, dat no free-thinkin man kin suppose fuh one minute dat we 'sires tuh misreppersent de idee dat we ain't qualify de sability uh de stenography uh dis convention. I hopes, suh, dat we kin den be able tuh superhen' de principles uh de supposition." [9]

Points of order were continuously made. One darkey advanced the indisputable proposition that it was "not parliamentary" for two persons to occupy the floor at one time.[10]   But never was there forgotten the dependence which they placed upon their fellow delegates from the North.   "Bout dis question uh cyarpet bags," said one, "ef your cyarpet-baggers does go back on us, woes be unto you!"[11]

It was to prevent the enactment of such scenes as these that Andrew Johnson sat in Washington suffering the assaults of those who had conspired to make them possible.   From the national capital the Radicals looked down upon this humiliation of their white fellow countrymen, and enjoyed the spectacle. Charles Sumner's work was moving forward!

§

Congress was now in the saddle, and martial law,—"the rule of the major-generals," was in force.[12]   It was the final chapter in a conflict that had long antedated Sumter,—the war between two civilizations.   It was the lethal blow to the age of chivalry in America, on whose soil the old struggle between the "Round Head" and the "Cavalier" had been once more fought out to the death.   Slavery had furnished the flame but by no means all the fuel for the great conflagration.   The differences between North and South lay far deeper than inability to agree over any single institution.

The two sections had originally invited different kinds of settlers and the different pursuits of these emphasized and stimulated different manners, different customs and institutions, different pursuits and different laws.   There was as much difference between Washington and John Adams as between Robert Lee and Sumner.   The society that Lee knew and fought for was "almost feudal in its splendor, it was almost patriarchal in its simplicity.   Leisure and wealth gave it exquisite culture.   Its wives and mothers, exempt from drudgery and almost from care, gave to their sons, through patient and constant training, something of their own grace and gentleness, and to their homes beauty and light.   Her people, homogeneous by necessity held straight and simple faith and were religious to a marked degree along the old lines of Christian belief.   The same homogeneity bred a hospitality that was as kinsmen to kinsmen, and that wasted at the threshold of every home what the more frugal people of the North conserved and invested in public charities." [13]

Of course, underlying this whole civilization there was slavery. But as Lincoln told the Confederate commissioners on board the *River Queen* two months before he died, "the people of the North were as responsible for slavery as the people of the South." [14] It is not difficult, therefore, to understand why all the objurgations of the Abolitionists upon the slave-holder sounded to the old South like the crackling thorns of sheer hypocrisy,—a new acquired morality that denounced slavery after it had ceased to pay where cotton was not grown.

It is possible without defending slavery to look back upon the old South, regretting that the civilization that there flourished was struck down. Its grace, its hospitality, its chivalry, its inviolable respect for womanhood! [15] The "Fair Maid of Perth," "The Lay of the Last Minstrel," and "The Lady of the Lake" reposed upon the shelves of every Southern planter, and were read and reread until the old ideal of fair lords and fair ladies set a model and standard for all Southerners to imitate. Thomas Carlyle inspired them also. Why talk of abolition? he had asked. "Every man is created to work, some at menial tasks, some at higher callings and others, as God-given heroes, at law making." [16] But whether Scott or Carlyle, or their own native sense of leadership was responsible, there is no gainsaying that the ante-bellum society was powerful and effective. [17]

Slavery is indefensible, and yet one may well inquire whether the great-grandsons of the slaves in America do not owe to slavery the superiority that distinguishes them from their cousins in the jungle of dark Africa where their sires ran naked, and transmitted unchanged to their children the barbarism they inherited. Indefensible as it was, slavery was an education to a backward race. Nor is it possible to peruse any authoritative account of it without reaching the conclusion that the abolition propaganda as to cruel practices was like all propaganda replete with untruths, half-truths and gross exaggerations. [18]

Well knowing the policy of abolitionists to arouse the slaves to insurrection, early in the war a slave police was organized throughout the South. But the absolute faithfulness of the slaves soon showed that such precautions were unnecessary.[19] "If," writes Grady, " 'Uncle Tom's Cabin' had portrayed the rule of slavery rather than the rarest exception, not all the armies that went to the field could have stayed the flood of rapine and arson and pillage that would have started with the first gun of the Civil War. Instead of that witness the miracle of the slave in loyalty to his master . . . maintaining and defending the families of those who fought against his freedom. . . . Often five hundred negroes to a single white man, and yet through these dusky throngs the women and children walked in safety, and the unprotected homes rested in peace. . . . A thousand torches would have disbanded every Southern army, but not one was lighted." [20]

It was not slavery alone that the North determined to strike down, but a civilization which they did not understand, and of which they harbored no little private jealousy. When the war ended the fundamental struggle between North and South did not cease. Stevens, Sumner and their followers determined to humble, humiliate and degrade a civilization they had never understood. When finally at the bar of history these Northerners are arraigned, they cannot plead that they knew not what they did, for there confronting them will be the vetoes and the messages of Andrew Johnson.

§

After the battle of Manassas a fallen Union soldier weltering in his blood exclaimed: "My God, what is all this for?" [21] If he could have but known!

Surely the pledged word of a great people would not be violated,—the South had the Northern pledge and had surrendered on the faith of it.[22] The people of the South, however, especially the women, had attended to the threatening language of the Radicals in Congress and looked forward to the future with but little hope. When the news of Lee's surrender came to Chester, South Carolina, it found Mary Boykin Chestnut, the wife of one of the aides of Jefferson Davis, seated with her friend Mary

Darty, whose husband had been a surgeon in Hood's army. She staggered to a table, sat down and wept aloud. Finally losing all control she shrieked: "Now we belong to negroes and Yankees." [23]

In her diary Mrs. Chestnut on that day thus wrote of North and South: "How different from ours is their estimate of us. How contradictory is their attitude toward us. To keep the despised and iniquitous South within their borders as part of their country, they were willing to enlist millions of men at home and abroad, and to spend billions, and we know they do not love fighting per se, nor spending money." [24] But if the women gave way to the hatred of the North whose armies had not only killed their husbands, but had set the torch to Southern homes,—if the women gave way to these feelings, the returning leaders of the Confederate armies came home counseling forbearance. Great as he was in battle there is no finer picture anywhere than that of the returning Lee. By precept and example he came home teaching peace! His stainless sword had been laid down in good faith, and this was the doctrine that he now advanced: "We have fought a good fight, we have failed, we must accept the inevitable, we must not lose heart, we must work for our country's welfare in peace." [25]

If only the North could have heeded Andrew Johnson's advice to take back the Southerners without humiliating them! There in the South, ready at hand, lay the means for an immediate reunion and reconciliation. They had followed Lee in war, they were ready to follow him in peace. His advice to Captain George Wise tells the whole story. Wise had been hailed before the Provost to take the oath. "Why must I take it? My parole covers the whole ground. I will not," he said. "You fought under General Lee, did you not?" the Northerner inquired. "Yes," said Wise, "and surrendered with him and gave my parole. To require this oath of me is to put an indignity upon me and my general." "Well," said the Northerner, "I will make a bargain with you, Captain. Consult General Lee and abide by his decision." [26]

When Lee was consulted by the young officer he said quietly: "I would advise you to take it. It is absurd that it should be required of my soldiers, for as you say the parole practically covers it. Nevertheless take it I should say." "General," said Wise, "I feel that this is submission to an indignity. If I must continue to swear the same thing at every street corner, I will seek another country, where I can at least preserve my self-respect." For a few moments Lee stood silent, and then with deep sadness in his voice, as quietly as before he said: "Do not leave Virginia. Our country needs her young men now." [27]

When Henry A. Wise heard that his son had taken the oath, he exclaimed: "You have disgraced the family!" "General Lee advised me to do it," said the young man. "Oh," replied the ex-governor, "that alters the case. Whatever General Lee says, is all right, I don't care what it is." [28]

It had been indeed "a long long trail," but the boys,—what were left of them,—were home at last. "It was good to have them home again, our men in gray," a Southern lady wrote, "good though they came gaunt and footsore, ragged and empty-handed. Our men were ready enough for peace,—or what they mistook for peace—when peace came; that is the mass of them were. They had fought and starved their fill. The cries of destitute women and children called them home. They had no time to pause and cavil over lost issues or to forge new occasions for quarrel. All they asked now was a chance to make meat and raiment for themselves and those dependent on them." [29]

Ready for peace indeed they were, but those who controlled the destinies of the nation were not ready. The strife between the two civilizations was not over,—it had just begun. Having abolished slavery, the Northern leaders took up the work of immediately making the ex-slaves the social, economic and political equals of the whites. Not his equal but his superior! The plan to reorganize the South had only started. The puritanical desire to regulate, preach and scold was uncontrollable.

First came the tourists. Their expressed object was to see the battlefields,—their real purpose to disseminate neat homilies, to point out to the erring Southerners the errors of their ways. They journeyed down with the unalterable conviction that all Southerners were negro beaters and cutthroats,—a benighted people needing tutelage in the humanities. "And," wrote Mrs. Avary, "they were not always politic in expressing these opinions." [30]

One day a Northern clergyman called on Mrs. Roger Pryor,— "a smug little man, sleek, unctuous and trim, with Pecksniffian self-esteem oozing out of every pore of his face." "Well, Madam," he began, "I trust I find you lying meekly under the chastening rod of the Lord. I trust you can say 'it is good I was afflicted.'" He paused for an answer, but none came, and he continued: "There are seasons when chastisement must be meted out to the transgressor; but if borne in the right spirit, the rod may blossom with blessings in the end." At this the wife of the former Confederate general looked up and quietly inquired: "Are there none on the other side who need the rod?" [31]

After the tourists, came the school-marms. With true Northern industry it was intended that no time should be lost. And there descended on the South an army of stern-visaged women. They were "educators," "missionaries" and "philanthropists" and they intended that the South should know it. [32] They came spreading their own hatred of the Southern whites and distilling it in the hearts of the negroes where it had never been before. They had the credulity of Sumner. One garrulous old negress was entertaining one of these school teachers with a blood-curdling, but untrue account of what she had suffered as a cook, when the school-marm interrupted: "Why didn't you black people poison all the whites and get your freedom that way." [33] Such advice did not endear these Northern representatives. Nor was it strange that at about this time an unwonted spirit of dislike and opposition to the negroes began to manifest itself in white children. Race antipathy was being sedulously fomented,—fomented by the North, for these teachers came down under the protection of the Freedman's Bureau. [34] Long afterward the founder of the Hampton Institute declared: "The business of educating the negroes was a continuation of hostilities against the vanquished and was so regarded on both sides. And the Yankee schoolma'ams followed in the trail of the Northern armies." [35]

Another and more patent instrument with which the North struck at the South while she was down was the "carpet-bagger."

These adventurers, no one of whom could have been elected a constable in any town or village where he lived, without money or worldly possessions save what they carried with them, pushed south as soon as the fighting was over to marshal the negroes as their followers and thus elect themselves to office.[36] With these came hordes of the worst Northern negroes and mulattoes. Their mission was to steal and plunder what they could, and to assist their white allies in dragooning the ex-slaves. Ready to aid them there were at hand the Southern "scalawags." These had been small slaveholders and secessionists who before the war was over had turned traitor to the South. "The name originated," said General Clanton, "in a fellow being kicked by a sheep so that he died. He said he didn't mind being killed but he hated the idea of being kicked to death by the meanest wether in the whole flock,—the scaly sheep. We mean by scalawag a meaner man than a carpet-bagger." [37]

An effective weapon for achieving the objectives sought by these Northern hosts were the Union Leagues. These Leagues had an honorable origin. In Ohio, in 1862, when the North was deeply afflicted with depression, they had been organized to stimulate and uphold the Union cause.[38] At this time, and as an outgrowth, the Union League Clubs of Philadelphia and New York were formed.[39] When the war ended the Leagues ceased to be important in the North, and the New York and Philadelphia clubs were in no way sympathetic with or concerned in the uses for which the carpet-bagger now employed and debased an honorable name.[40]

Understanding enough of the negro character to appreciate his love of ceremony, mystery and form, and his susceptibility to the influences of superstition inherited from the Voodooism of Africa, these corrupt and unscrupulous adventurers began almost at once to organize the ex-slaves into what they called the "Union Leagues." To this end halls, schoolhouses and churches were employed as headquarters where mystic rites, fires, speeches and military drills, greatly to the delight of the ignorant blacks, were sedulously employed. The professed objects of these, the carpet-baggers said, was "the training of the negro to his duties as a citizen." [41]   The real object was to arouse enmity against the former masters and to weld these new-fledged citizens into a solid phalanx of political support for Northern renegades.

Elaborate and awe-inspiring rituals were used.   The neophytes were led into the Council. Chamber; the marshal sounded the league alarm, and the sentinel cried out: "Who comes under our signal?"   The answer was made, the door opened; the counter-sign was asked and given in the "Four L's—the right hand point-ing upward with the word 'Liberty,' sinking to shoulder level with 'Lincoln,' dropping to the side with 'Loyal,' folding to the breast with 'League.' " [42]   The awe-struck novitiates were then marched in arm in arm singing "John Brown's Body," and were massed about the altar, before which stood the President in full regalia. [43]

The Union flag draped the altar where rested an open Bible, the Declaration of Independence, a sword, a ballot box, a sickle, an anvil and other mysterious and awe-inspiring emblems.   Dark-ness shrouded the room, while groans and clanking chains lent their accompaniment of fear.   Finally the Star Spangled Banner was sung and the initiates were drilled in a catechism inculcating opposition to the Democratic party and fealty to the Republican, with condemnation of Southern whites as traitors. [44]   Frequently the negroes were told that in order to secure the peace and plenty they desired and especially "the forty acres and a mule," the approved method was to "kill some of the leading whites in each community as a warning to others." [45]

About these mysterious meeting places at night armed guards with shot guns and rifles stood to warn away intruders.   The negroes were armed and brought their guns to the League meet-ings.   Here they were drilled and inspired and returned home shouting, firing and indulging in loud boasts and threats.   As time went on military parades of negroes in the daytime were employed; marching up and down those thus engaged amused themselves by pushing Southern whites off the sidewalks or from the roads. [46]

Is it any wonder that race hatred was thus sowed, or that the white man highly resolved that the Anglo-Saxon race should not be defiled, or that crimes against womanhood should receive, and have ever since received, the sternest measures of retaliation? Nor is it strange that black troops were looked on with suspicion. Hoping to prevent these race hatreds and the outrages that were sure to follow, Lincoln had designed his plan of reconstruction and Andrew Johnson had followed it.

As Congress moved on from one aggression to another, the Freedman's Bureau Bill, the Civil Rights Act and finally the Reconstruction Laws, is it strange that the carpet-bagger in the South gained increased confidence in pushing forward his criminal design of stimulating in the black race hatred for the white? Concerning the Northern attitude as reflected in the press and in the pulpit, one Southern woman wrote: "Negroes drew their own conclusions. Violation of a white woman was no harm; indeed as a leveler of social distinction it might almost be construed into an act of grace. The way to become a hero in the eyes of the white North and to win the cross of martyrdom for oneself and new outbursts of sympathy for one's race was to assault a white woman of the South." [47]

It was under these circumstances, with the negroes drilled to a hatred of the native whites, that in the fall of 1867 the military commanders of the Southern district were preparing for the registration which the Reconstruction acts had ordered.

STANTON REINSTATED. GRANT BREAKS HIS PROMISE

STANTON returned to Washington on Christmas eve.[1] But it was no spirit associated with the holiday that had brought him back. He had returned, intending to remain. Not if he could help it would the Senate fail to reinstate him in the War Department. He was now eagerly awaiting his hoped-for triumph over the President of the United States. What mattered it that ten months earlier he had said to Andrew Johnson that any man who would retain his seat in the Cabinet "when his advice was not wanted was unfit for the place," and that under such circumstances he would not "remain a moment?" [2]

While the Radicals of the Senate in executive session were planning how to reintrude their friend into the private councils of the President, there floated up from the South to Washington the stories of distress and the complaints of suffering resulting from the vicious laws that had bound the white man hand and foot. Johnson listened, but he was powerless now to help them.[3]

As 1867 faded out, the purpose of the Radicals to restore their favorite to power became unmistakable. Were this accomplished there would then be for the President but one of two weapons left: an appeal to the courts or an appeal to arms. He was preparing for the former. On January 7th he told his private secretary Colonel Moore to write out an order for Stanton's removal and a brief message to the Senate, advising them of the fact. He wanted these papers, he said, "ready for signature at any moment." [4] But to insure the making of a test case whereby the constitutionality of the Tenure-of-Office Act could be determined Grant's coöperation was indispensable. His refusal to permit Stanton to resume his old office would be necessary. The legality of this refusal, and hence the constitutionality of the law, could then be decided by the Supreme Court. Would Grant coöperate? The subject was not a new one. Not long after Stanton's suspension in the previous summer Johnson had called on Grant at the War Department to find out what the latter would do if Stanton's restoration were attempted. There resulted a distinct understanding that, should Grant prefer not to become a party to the controversy, he would "return the office" to the President "prior to a decision by the Senate," so that the Chief Executive might designate some other for his place.[5]

This promise was subsequently repeated by the General, but at no time in so unequivocal a way as on Saturday, the 11th of January, 1868. It was now well known that the Senate would presently reinstate Stanton. Johnson at this time, therefore, wanted to make doubly sure that Grant would keep his word, and once more the General told the President that he would either remain at the head of the War Department until the court could determine the legality of Stanton's reinstatement, or would vacate the office in time to enable Johnson to fill it before the Senate acted. The conference broke up with Grant's further promise to confer with the President again on Monday, at which time it was agreed the General's final decision would be announced.[6]

Monday came but Grant did not, as he had promised, return to advise the President as to which course he would follow. The Senate's decision hourly was awaited.[7] While Grant throughout that fateful Monday the 13th was scrupulously avoiding contact with the White House, the Senate in executive session sat for six hours debating Stanton's case. But this was not all they were debating, for Senator Edmunds had introduced a resolution inquiring as to the procedural rules in cases of impeachment! What was the relation between these subjects? Had Grant reported to his Radical adherents the private conference he had had with the President two days before?[8]

Finally toward nightfall the Senate adopted this resolution: "Resolved, That having considered the evidence and reasons given by the President in his report of the 12th of December, 1867, for the suspension . . . of Edwin M. Stanton, the Senate do not concur in such suspension."[9] Authenticated copies were directed to be served on Johnson, Grant and Stanton.[10] That evening General and Mrs. Grant attended the President's levee. Before coming he had received notice of the Senate's resolution. There was still opportunity at that time for him to advise the President of his intentions, and thereby belatedly to make good his word, but Grant was silent![11]

At an early hour the next morning, still without communicating with the President, Grant called on General Townsend, the Assistant-Adjutant-General of the army and handed him the key to the War Department, saying: "I am to be found over at my office at army headquarters. I was served with a copy of the Senate resolution last evening." Townsend went upstairs and delivered the key to Stanton, who was there waiting for it.[12] Ulysses Grant had neither refused to surrender the Department, nor had given Johnson opportunity to appoint a man who would!

Grant still absented himself from the White House, but he sent the President a letter notifying him of his receipt the previous evening of the Senate resolution, and concluding his communication with the statement that under the Tenure-of-Office Act his functions "as Secretary of War ad interim ceased from the moment of the receipt of the within notice."[13] General Comstock was the bearer of this letter, and through him Johnson sent back word to Grant that he desired the latter's presence that day at the Cabinet meeting.[14]

When a little later Grant attended, there took place an interview, the details of which have been faithfully preserved by Gideon Welles. Those who were present at this meeting were the President and five members of his Cabinet,—Seward, McCulloch, Randall, Welles and Browning.[15] When Grant appeared, he said that he had come at the President's request though he considered himself relieved of the duties of Secretary. The President asked him if his surrender of the War Department conformed to their "previous understanding." Grant did not give a direct answer, but said that he had promised the President some time ago that he would give him notice before relinquishing the office, but that upon examining the second and fifth sections of the Tenure-of-Office Act, he had found himself "not willing to suffer five years' imprisonment and pay ten thousand dollars fine, but preferred to give up the office." [16]

Johnson heard him through and then asked him why when he had come to this conclusion he had not given notice of his intentions "as agreed," and remarked that he was willing himself to undertake the whole imprisonment or fine which might be adjudged against Grant, and that he had told him so on Saturday when the General's apprehensions were discussed.

Grant's answer was a rambling one. He said that he had not been aware of the penalties until he "saw the discussion in the papers;" that he did not know of these when he had had his first talk with the President; that he had come over on Saturday expressly to take up this subject, had then spoken of these difficulties and had expected to see the President again on Monday, but that he was "busy with General Sherman, and had a good many little matters to attend to," and did not suppose the "Senate intended to act so soon." [17]

Johnson again heard him through and then quietly asked: "Was not our understanding—did you not assure me some time ago and again on Saturday, that if you did not hold on to the office yourself, you would place it in my hands that I might select another?" "That," said Grant, "was my intention. I thought some satisfactory arrangement would be made to dispose of the subject. Mr. Johnson (Reverdy) and General Sherman spent a great deal of time with me on Sunday. Didn't Mr. Johnson come to see you? I sent General Sherman yesterday after talking the matter over. Didn't you see Sherman?" [18]

Johnson listened patiently to this irrelevant digression and then pointedly observed that he had seen each of the persons named, but failed to understand the connection between this and the return of the War Department to the President in accordance with the understanding. "Why did you give up the keys to Mr. Stanton and leave the Department?" he asked. Again Grant fumbled for an answer, replying finally that he had given the key to the Adjutant-General and had sent word to the President by General Comstock. "Yes," said the President, "but that, you know, was not our understanding." [19]

SCENE AT THE OFFICE OF THE SECRETARY OF WAR, ON THE MORNING OF JANUARY 14TH. SECRETARY STANTON RECEIVING THE CONGRATULATIONS OF THE SENATORS AND HIS FRIENDS, UPON HIS REINSTALLATION TO THE OFFICE OF SECRETARY OF WAR.

Grant at this point, says Welles, "attempted some further apologies about being very busy, stammered, hesitated, said Sherman had taken up a great deal of his time, but he had intended to call on the President on Monday; asked to be excused, and left." [20]

The President throughout this interview, the same informant tells us, "was calm and dignified, though manifestly disappointed and displeased. General Grant was humble and hesitating, and he evidently felt that his position was equivocal and not to his credit. There was, I think, an impression on the minds of all present (there certainly was on mine) that a consciousness that he had acted with duplicity,—not been faithful and true to the man who had confided in and trusted him—oppressed General Grant. His manner, never very commanding, was almost abject, and he left the room with less respect, I apprehend, from those present than ever before. The President, though disturbed and not wholly able to conceal his chagrin from those familiar with him, used no harsh expression, nor committed anything approaching incivility, yet Grant felt the few words put to him, and the cold and surprised disdain of the President in all their force." [21]

"There is no doubt," continued Welles, "that Grant has been in secret intrigue in this business, acting in concert with and under the direction of the chief conspirators. He did not put the office in the President's hands on Saturday, because the Senate had not acted, but he anticipated, as I and others did, that they would. If, therefore, the subject was delayed until Monday it would be too late. But the Senate came to no conclusion on Saturday, as he expected; he therefore avoided seeing the President on Monday, as he promised. On Tuesday he yielded to Stanton." [22]

§

On the morning after Stanton's reinstatement there appeared in the Washington *Intelligencer* an article describing Grant's promises and the way in which he had broken them. [23] Upon reading it Grant, in company with General Sherman, called on Johnson at the White House. "Mr. President," he said, "whoever gave the facts for the article of the *Intelligencer* of this morning has made some serious mistakes." "Let me interrupt you just there," replied the President, "I have not seen the *Intelligencer* of this morning, and have no knowledge of the contents of any article therein." Grant then expressed his resentment at the charge of bad faith contained in this newspaper account, but before he finished talking he reaffirmed the fact that he had not been true to his pledged word.[24] He admitted that during the previous summer he had told the President that he had supposed "Mr. Stanton could not regain his office except by a process through the courts," and had promised that if he changed his mind he would notify his superior in sufficient time for him to "put things as they were before" he had taken up the duties of the War Department.[25]

Grant and Johnson then entered into a friendly conversation, and both at least *seemed* satisfied with the interview. The President declared that he had always been most friendly to the General, and the latter insisted that he had temporarily taken the War portfolio "in the general interests of the army."[26] Before they parted Grant volunteered to call on Stanton and urge upon him that "the good of the service required his resignation."[27]

A reconciliation between Grant and Johnson seemed in sight, and as the President's two visitors were taking leave, at the very door Grant turned and said: "Mr. President, you should make some order that we of the army are not bound to obey the orders of Mr. Stanton as Secretary of War." Johnson intimated that he might do so.[28]

That evening General Sherman wrote to his wife: "Today the mutual explanations are full and *partially* satisfactory. I was only a listener. After I got to the War Department Stanton sent for me, and told me how much he respected me and admired me, etc., etc. All very loving, and I told him simply that I should not recall the past, but wanted the army to keep out of politics, etc., etc. I thought he would ask my opinion of his present status, but he did not. I should have advised him to resign. I deem it wrong to hold a Cabinet office, when he knows the President don't want him, and the President will not give any order to the army through him. But as Secretary of War, he has by law power to sign all warrants on the Treasury, to make contracts for supplies, etc., etc., and may embarrass the service. I have done my best to cut the Gordian knot but have failed and shall do no more. . . ." [29]

There was no love lost between Grant and the reinstated Secretary. He had been anything but pleased with Stanton's manner on the morning he resumed his office. No sooner was Stanton back at his old desk than he sent a messenger for Grant with the curt word that "he wanted to see him." Stanton had a habit of issuing orders to his generals as if they had been private soldiers. To Sherman later Grant had bitterly complained of Stanton's conduct,[30] and on January 18th agreed to go with his old comrade in arms and advise Stanton to resign.[31]

"There appears to be a general belief and expectation," wrote Welles that day, "that Stanton will resign. To this I am not a convert, unless he becomes convinced that the Radical Senators will not sustain him. They will come to no such conclusions. Morgan, Fessenden, the Morrills, Patterson and other limber-backed Senators have not the independence to demand such a step. Senator Sherman, whose brother, General Sherman, has been insulted and wronged by Stanton, has not self-reliance, self-respect and strength of mind sufficient to do this duty." [32]

"It is reported," continued Welles, "that Generals Grant and Sherman have said to Stanton that he must resign. They may have done this together, but I doubt if Grant has taken such a stand by himself, for he is cowed and submissive before Stanton. Sherman, if he has had an interview, would be more likely to have expressed himself with some freedom and boldness." [33]

Welles was mistaken in his dates, otherwise how correct his surmise was, will presently appear. On the 18th General Sherman wrote to Johnson that Grant "will call on you tomorrow and offer to go to Mr. Stanton to say for the good of the service and of the country he ought to resign." [34] And a little later Grant wrote the President: "On the 19th I had an interview alone with Mr. Stanton which led me to the conclusion that any advice to him of the kind would be useless, and I so informed General Sherman." [35]

"Our country," wrote Welles the next day, "is in an unhappy condition, and I am not without apprehension of a civil convulsion. There is among the Radicals neither statesmanship, sagacity, nor sense. Hate, revenge, thirst for power govern them. To oppress and persecute the white population of the Southern states is their delight; to place negro governments over them by the aid of the military is their intention." [36]

Two days later Grant made a flying trip to Richmond. Three years before the city had been somewhat less accessible. To General Schofield, on whom he called in the old capital of the Confederacy, he now confided that Stanton's conduct had been "intolerable" to him, and in emphatic terms declared his intention to demand either Stanton's removal, or the acceptance of his own resignation. [37] But Grant was in the hands of the Radicals, and they had no thought of permitting him to spoil the plot. Not if they could help it would he be allowed to vent his personal hatred on the thick-skinned Stanton and thereby destroy their plan to make the hero of Appomattox President of the United States.

The Republican National Convention of 1868 already had been called, and the conspirators had resolved that if Grant was to have any personal altercation it should be with Johnson, not with Stanton. They looked with distaste upon the probable healing of the breach between the President and his former Secretary of War ad interim. They had viewed with strong disfavor Grant's report in 1865 on the condition of the South. They had experienced a profound misgiving when he accompanied the President in 1866 in his "Swing Around the Circle." They had seen how Grant's acceptance of the war portfolio in 1867 had widely been interpreted as a mark of his confidence in the President, and now those who intended to control the coming National Convention bethought themselves how awkward it would be for the draftsmen, and especially the readers of a platform excoriating Johnson, to be reminded that there had once been even seeming friendship between Grant and the Chief Executive. "Such a fact," wrote Blaine, "would embarrass the canvass in many ways, and would dull the edge of partisan weapons already forged for the contest." [38]

During his return from Richmond Grant was given further opportunity for reflection. He must have pondered then his future course. He had come to a final parting of the ways: Johnson or Stanton! Every instinct of personal preference must have repelled him from following the latter. He had had good reason to know that which Don Piatt has since written, that Stanton had "a dislike for Grant," and had "no hesitation in expressing his contempt" for him, and that Stanton was "without exception more subject to personal likes and dislikes, more vindictive in his gratification of the last, than any man ever called to public station." [39]

GRANT ESSAYS THE PEN

GRANT had not been back two days when his determination to make war on Andrew Johnson was revealed. On January 24th he wrote him a peremptory note requesting to "have in writing the order which the President gave me verbally on Sunday the 19th instant to disregard the orders of the Hon. E. M. Stanton, as Secretary of War, until I knew from the President himself that they were his orders." [1] Was Grant working with his friends to help prepare a further trap for Johnson? Was he seeking now to make written evidence on which the conspirators would claim that the President was a law breaker?

Johnson would have had a perfect right to make the order to which Grant referred, but there is no evidence that he had done so, except the word of Grant. To his private secretary, Colonel Moore, Johnson remarked when Grant's letter came, that he did not think he would make the requested order, and "that the General had been very restive under Mr. Stanton, had evidently been very glad to get rid of him, had now put him back in the War Department," and therefore, thought that he would "let them fight it out." [2]

But the more Johnson reflected upon Grant's letter, the plainer must he have seen that the General and Stanton would not "fight it out." Seventeen days before, as will be recalled, the President had prepared an order for the removal of Stanton, [3] and it was now apparent that to test the constitutionality of the Tenure-of-Office Act this order must be used. But this could not be done unless some one were procured to administer the War Department until the legality of the removal could be judicially determined. On the day Grant's letter came, therefore, Johnson sent for General Sherman and offered to appoint him Secretary of War ad interim.⁴ Sherman expressed doubt as to the President's power to remove Stanton, but before giving a definite answer, requested an opportunity to consult his father-in-law Thomas Ewing.⁵ To his wife the next day Sherman wrote: "The President constantly sends for me, and asks opinions and assistance. I have shown him great personal respect. . . . But . . . I don't want to be involved in political combinations. . . . I don't want the place. . . . It is not to my interest to replace Stanton. . . . To remove Stanton by force, or a show of force, would be the very thing the enemies of the President want. . . ." ⁶

We can all but see Sherman standing before us,—the tall, spare wiry frame, the fine-featured yet wrinkled face, and the lock of auburn hair that stuck straight out when he was excited. When he talked, he strode up and down, every fibre was alive and in motion. "He wore his coat unbuttoned and his heart also." ⁷ He had had a versatile career,—banker, farmer, lawyer, president of a railroad, president of a college. And he had marched from Atlanta to the sea! ⁸ At one time he had with difficulty turned a deaf ear to the siren call of art. He wrote from Fort Moultrie, when he was twenty-two: "Not long since I took a notion into my head that I could paint. I went to the city and laid in a full set of artist's equipments, prepared my studio, and without any instructions whatever have finished a couple of landscapes and faces which they tell me are very good. I have a great love for painting and find that sometimes I am so fascinated that it amounts to pain to lay down the brush, placing me in doubt whether I had better stop now before it swallows all my attention, to the neglect of my duties, and discard it altogether, or keep on. What would you advise?" ⁹

Sherman, like many another in our all too practical America, was possessed of temperament. He had his moments of profound depression,¹⁰ but he could be gay as well. One who knew him in his lighter moods has written: "Of a happy nature himself, he strove to make all around him happy." ¹¹ The author of these words was evidently no Georgian. Probably for all time the South will execrate his memory for his dreadful march. War is unpleasant, and Sherman did not mitigate it. And yet even in his official dispatches he revealed anything but indifference to the suffering he caused. "The amount of burning, stealing and plundering done by our armies," he wrote, "makes me ashamed of it. I would quit the service if I could, because I feel that we are drifting to the worst sort of vandalism." [12]

One of Sherman's finest traits was his steadfastness to his friends.[13] His affection for Grant and the fear of being drawn into opposition to him were among the most important reasons for his unwillingness to aid Andrew Johnson, but they were not his only reasons. He hated and mistrusted the press, he despised politicians,[14] he more than once expressed a strong distrust of popular government.[15] He had not changed his views expressed three years before: "Washington is as corrupt as Hell. . . . I will avoid it as a pest house. . . ." [16]

Deep down in his heart the wrinkled old General entertained a kindly feeling for the President. He sympathized with his brave fight, and experienced nothing but contempt for his enemies. In October, 1867, he had a long talk with Johnson's Attorney-General in Washington. "I explained my earnest desire to escape all complications of politics," Sherman later wrote, "that it would do me or the country no good, but on the contrary be an infinite source of trouble to me personally and would impair my military usefulness. He explained to me what I already knew, that the President is peculiarly sensitive to the abuse that pours in on him from all quarters, and that a word of kindness touches him in the tenderest spot. He told me that a letter I wrote him last year of general expression of good will was ever uppermost in his mind. . . . The truth is our press universally is now so harsh and fault-finding that all people, especially the parasites here who look to the press now as the power in the land, are afraid to be even personally kind or respectful to the President, that the simplest expression of that kind comes as a drop of water to the thirsty soul. . . ." [17]

Four days had passed since Grant had written requesting the President in writing to command disobedience to Stanton's orders. But Johnson, as we have seen, was busily engaged in the effort to procure a temporary Minister of War who would not break his word. He had about made up his mind to let Grant and Stanton fight it out, at least until he found someone who would help him test the law. But Grant determined to take up the cudgels against Andrew Johnson now. The weapon which he selected was the pen; for him it was an unfortunate choice. On Tuesday, January 28th, he sat down and wrote the President a long letter. Its tone was provocative and offensive. "To prevent any possible misunderstanding," he wrote, "I renew the request that you will give me written instructions, and till they are received will suspend action on your verbal ones." [18]

This was not only offensive, it was insubordinate. Since when had a general the right to tell the President of the United States that he would disobey his commands unless they were in writing?

"I am compelled to request these instructions," Grant continued, "in consequence of the many and gross misrepresentations affecting my personal honor, circulated through the press for the last fortnight purporting to come from the President, of conversations which occurred either with the President privately in his office or in cabinet meeting. What is written admits of no misunderstanding." [19]

Here was at least an implied charge that misrepresentations had been given to the press by the President himself. There was not then nor has there since been discovered the slightest evidence that Johnson had even an indirect agency in the publication of the accounts with which the newspapers were then teeming. The fact was that certain New York reporters had in some mischievous fashion secured the notes of the Cabinet meeting. [20]

"In view of the misrepresentations referred to," continued Grant, "it will be well to state the facts in the case." [21] He then at great length set forth that he had never agreed either to continue in the War Department until displaced by the courts, or to resign so as to give the President opportunity to fill his place before Stanton could be reinstated. [22] He denied that on Saturday, the 11th, he had agreed to call upon the President on the following Monday, and especially he denied that at the Cabinet meeting of the 14th he had admitted that he had so promised. [23]

Had Johnson been the contentious man his enemies asserted

him to be,—a charge repeated by his historical detractors—he would at this point have handled Grant without gloves. Instead he sat down the next day and quietly wrote out on the back of Grant's letter of January 24th: "As requested in this communication, General Grant is instructed in writing not to obey any order of the War Department, assumed to be issued by the direction of the President, unless such order is known by the General commanding the armies of the United States to have been authorized by the Executive." [24] On the same day Johnson sent again for General Sherman and once more requested him to act as Secretary of War ad interim.[25] He again told Sherman that he was desirous in this way of contesting the constitutionality of the Tenure-of-Office Act, and that if it could be brought before the Supreme Court properly, "it would not stand half an hour." [26] At no time did Johnson suggest that he was contemplating a resort to force for the removal of the trouble-maker, but in the most unmistakable fashion declared that he could have no more intercourse with Stanton "in the relation of President and Secretary of War." [27]

Sherman at first told the President that although it was against his personal and official wishes, he "might be willing to administer the office ad interim." After a brief pause, however, he continued: "Suppose Mr. Stanton do not yield?" "Oh! he will make no objection," Johnson answered, "you present the order and he will retire." Again Sherman voiced his doubts, but the President replied: "I know him better than you do; he is cowardly." Sherman requested a little further time for reflection, and the next day wrote the President declining to accept the proffered office.[28]

On the day following this interview Sherman wrote his wife: "The President yesterday again wanted me to take the office of Secretary of War, but in a letter today I have declined pretty firmly. I have always manifested for him and his office the greatest respect, but he can't vacate Stanton's office without personal violence and that would not do. Stanton's mere sitting in his office don't make him a cabinet officer, but he can do certain parts of the office without the President's consent. I, however, rest my declination on the ground that I do not want to live in Washington. It is full of spies and slanderers who stop at nothing to make game, and I should regret even Grant's elevation, as that might force me to this position. Grant tells me that he will avoid the nomination if he can, but it is doubtful if Chase can get the votes, and Grant don't want to see Pendleton come in because he was an open enemy of the war, which we *must* maintain was right. . . . All sorts of names are bandied about, but Grant's seems to be the favorite. . . ." [29]

Andrew Johnson could fight it out alone! If Grant and Sherman, or either of them, had stood beside the President in this crisis, the assailants of the Constitution never would have had the courage to go on with their conspiracy. But Grant was already blinded with the dust of the political arena, and Sherman had resolved no matter what the merits of the contest were, "to escape all complications of politics." [30]

§

That Grant was determined upon a quarrel with the President appeared on the same day that Sherman sent his declination. The letter that Grant now wrote to his Commander-in-Chief was, if possible, more insubordinate and offensive than his previous communication. He acknowledged the return of his note with the President's "endorsement thereon" and then continued: "I am informed by the Secretary of War that he has not received from the Executive any order or instructions limiting or impairing his authority to issue orders to the army. . . . While this authority to the War Department is not countermanded, it will be satisfactory evidence to me that any orders issued from the War Department, by direction of the President, are authorized by the Executive." [31]

Thus despite the written order from the President, he had himself solicited, that he should not obey the orders of the War Department purporting to have come from the President unless he knew that the President had issued them, Grant now advised his superior that he would obey such orders whether he knew that the President had issued them or not!

The President had restrained himself thus far. He was not seeking for a quarrel. He was not quarrelsome, but he was the last man in the United States to draw back if a fight was thrust upon him. On the day following the receipt of Grant's letter, therefore, he took up his pen, and before he laid it down he had given Grant the lie direct. "In disregard of the understanding between us," wrote Johnson, "you vacated the office without having given me notice of your intention to do so. . . . Had your action been in conformity to the understanding between us, I do not believe that the embarrassment would have attained its present proportions, or that the probability of its repetition would have been so great." [32]

"I know," he continued, "that with a view to an early termination of a state of affairs so detrimental to the public interests, you voluntarily offered, both on Wednesday the 15th instant, and on the succeeding Sunday, to call upon Mr. Stanton and urge upon him that the good of the service required his resignation. I confess that I considered your proposal as a sort of reparation for the failure on your part to act in accordance with an understanding more than once repeated. . . ." [33] Referring to Grant's denial that at the Cabinet meeting of January 14th he had admitted previously promising either to remain in the War Department or to resign in time to permit the appointment of a successor before Stanton could regain it, Johnson continued: "My recollection of what then transpired is diametrically the reverse of your narration." [34]

Johnson then in great detail recited how Grant had at that meeting admitted making such a promise and how he had explained his failure to call upon the President on Monday, the 13th, because he had been in conference with Sherman and was "occupied with many little matters." And then he continued: "Sincerely anxious, however, to be correct in my statements, I have today read this narration of what occurred on the 14th instant to the members of the Cabinet who were then present. They, without exception, agree in its accuracy." [35]

It took Grant and his Radical advisers three days to think up an answer to Johnson's last communication, and it was not until February 3rd that he again wrote the President, once more denying that he had broken any promise. "The performance of the promises alleged by you to have been made by me," he now declared, "would have involved a resistance to law, and an inconsistency with the whole history of my connection with the suspension of Mr. Stanton." And then he advanced to this new ground: as far back as August 1st of the previous year he had feared that the President on the removal of Stanton would appoint someone in his place who would embarrass the army in carrying out the Reconstruction Acts! "It was to prevent such an appointment," he now declared, "that I accepted the office of Secretary of War ad interim, and not for the purpose of enabling you to get rid of Mr. Stanton, by my withholding it from him in opposition to law, or not doing so myself, surrendering it to one who would; as the statements and assumptions in your communication plainly indicate was sought." [36]

Johnson's reply of February 10th must have made Grant and his advisers wish that they had never started on this contest. "You here admit," wrote Johnson, "that from the very beginning of what you term 'the whole history' of your connection with Mr. Stanton's suspension, you intended to circumvent the President. It was to carry out that intent that you accepted the appointment. This was in your mind at the time of your acceptance. It was not then, in obedience to the order of your superior, as has heretofore been supposed, that you assumed the duties of the office. You knew it was the President's purpose to prevent Mr. Stanton from resuming the office of Secretary of War, and you intended to defeat that purpose. You accepted the office not in the interest of the President but of Mr. Stanton. . . . You not only concealed your design from the President, but induced him to suppose that you would carry out his purpose to keep Mr. Stanton out of office, by retaining it yourself after an attempted restoration by the Senate, so as to require Mr. Stanton to establish his right by judicial decision." [37]

Grant answered the next day disavowing insubordination, and

disclaiming any intention then or theretofore of disobeying any legal order of the President distinctly communicated.[38] "I presume," wrote Welles, "he is surprised at his own folly and errors, and will, if he does not already, regret them. But he is now under the control of vicious and very bad men, who are using him for vicious purposes, and he assents with bad intent."[39]

THE McCARDLE CASE

THE seething cauldron of the capital was now boiling over. "The whole Radical nest," wrote Welles, "are hissing and snapping like vipers. . . . Congress is malignantly Radical. The party servers are all-potent. Not a man of the party has sufficient independence to act on his own individual opinions and convictions. Some of them will whisper in confidence their disgust and dissatisfaction, but yet when the test is applied they succumb. . . . I hear that some of them are incensed with Stanton because he does not resign. They expected he would at once leave on being reinstated.[1]

At no time did Grant's bad faith to President Johnson appear more clearly than on the afternoon of February 4th. On that day, about an hour before the General's letter of the 3rd had reached the President,—the letter in which Grant declared that he had originally accepted the war office to thwart the President— a resolution was introduced in the House calling upon Stanton for the Grant-Johnson correspondence. It had not then become public. How did Congress know that Stanton had the letters and could supply them? Representative Chester Hubbard of West Virginia,—a lawyer with whom Stanton had been intimate when both were practicing there—introduced the resolution. "The whole shows an intrigue and conspiracy," our diarist wrote, "on the part of Stanton, Grant and certain Radical leaders. . . . How came Stanton or anyone acquainted with the fact? Grant had intrigued with the Radical members and with Stanton, had tried to entrap the President under their direction, and wrote his insolent letters at their instigation to irritate and provoke, if possible, the President into the commission of some rash or indiscreet act."[2]

Stanton immediately complied with the resolution, and in his letter of transmittal notified the Speaker of the House that he had not had "any personal or written communication with the President since the 12th of August last." [3]   Perhaps this correspondence would furnish that for which the Radicals had so long been seeking,—a basis for impeachment.   If Thaddeus Stevens had previously harbored any reservation as to supporting Grant for the Presidency, all doubts on this score were now abandoned.   He liked Grant's letters.   "He is a bolder man than I thought him," he said, "now we will let him into the church." [4]

"In every point of view," wrote Blaine, "the political situation was satisfactory to the Republicans,—the last possible suggestion of discontent with General Grant's expected nomination for the Presidency having been banished from the ranks of the party." [5]

Stevens, who had for more than two years watched his co-conspirators fumbling with impeachment, while he had busied himself with lashing through his program of malice for the South, now saw his chance to strike down the President of the United States. On February 10th he jammed through a resolution requiring all the evidence that had been taken by the Judiciary Committee to be transferred to his Reconstruction camarilla. [6]   But on the same day that Stevens took command, Johnson wrote Grant his final letter,—the letter which annihilated him.   It not only annihilated Grant, but it destroyed this new impeachment undertaking.   And so on February 13th, despite all of Stevens' efforts, by a vote of six to three of his Committee, the impeachment resolution was laid upon the table. [7]

Here again was an opportunity for the President to draw back! But he was never further from surrender!   Knowing full well what might be the consequences to himself, he determined to press on!   Before the rain and lightnings of the Reconstruction, there he stood, like the hero and the victim of a tragedy from Shakespeare.   General Sherman was back now in St. Louis,—out of range.   He was thinking,—with some twinge of remorse, let us hope—of the President, whose call for help he had not heeded. "He infers," he wrote, "that because I gave him full credit for his first efforts to reconstruct the South, on principles nearer right than have since been attempted, that I will go with him to the death, but I am not bound to do it. He never heeds any advice. He attempts to govern after he has lost the means to govern. He is like a general fighting without an army,—he is like Lear roaring at the wild storm, bareheaded and helpless." [8]

With King Lear, Johnson might have cried: "In such a night to shut me out! Pour on; I will endure. In such a night as this!" [9] King Lear? If that was Andrew Johnson's rôle, to whom had the parts of Goneril and Regan been assigned?

§

On St. Valentine's Day there was a meeting of the Cabinet. One of the members asked: "Who is Secretary of War?" The President looked at him significantly for a moment and then replied: "That matter will be disposed of in one or two days." [10] "I think," wrote Welles that evening, "the President is prepared to take decided action with Stanton, and if he will do it promptly, all may yet be well." [11]

The problem was to find some one who would act as Secretary ad interim so that the constitutionality of the law could be tested out. It was suggested to the President that it would be well to have for this place some gentleman in the Adjutant-General's office who was true to him, and not under the control of Stanton. The name of Assistant Adjutant-General Townsend was brought forward. He was, thought Welles, "a worthy and estimable man, but stands in dread and awe of 'Carnot' who domineers over him. In fact, Stanton has taken all manhood out of Townsend, and I have often been pained to see with what humility the subordinate stood before the imperious tyrant." [12] Other names were considered. How about John Potts, the chief clerk of the War Department? Potts, however, had no stomach for the business. His "relations with Mr. Stanton," he said, "were of a very pleasant nature," and he did "not wish to disturb them." [13]

But Andrew Johnson was not the only one who was considering the constitutionality of the laws. If he was seeking the intervention of the Supreme Court, the Radicals with even greater zeal were determined to prevent any decision from that quarter. [14]

If Johsnon chose to test the Tenure-of-Office Act by removing Stanton, they were prepared. They were ready to impeach, convict and remove him before the Supreme Court could act. But the Reconstruction laws presented greater problems. Through these the white voters of the South must be disfranchised, the negroes placed in power, and the Fourteenth Amendment thus driven through! And all this must be done before the fall elections. To elect Grant President they would need the electoral votes of the "conquered provinces." They must be restored as "states" under black domination!

Eight days before Congress had last reconvened, there occurred in the "fourth district" an incident too common in the "conquered provinces" at that time to have aroused interest in the North. But indifferent as were the Radicals to the injustices which they has fastened on the South, this incident was one that soon was to crowd itself on their attention, like the spark that sputters toward a powder train. It was an incident from which might come explosions that would shatter their unconstitutional and revolutionary laws. On the 13th of November, Colonel McCardle, a Vicksburg editor, found himself within the confines of a military prison. He had dared to criticize General Ord, the commander of the district,—he had dared even to expostulate against that perfect thing, the policy of Congress! [15]

He petitioned the United States Circuit Court of Mississippi for a writ of habeas corpus. It was denied. But as he sat within his cell contemplating his lése majesté, awaiting such a trial as a military commission might accord him, his counsel had a brilliant thought. One of the laws Congress had enacted nine months before, and previous to the passage of their Reconstruction bills, provided for an appeal from the Circuit to the Supreme Court of the United States in "all cases where any person may be restrained of his or her liberty in violation of the Constitution or of any treaty or law of the United States." [16] It had been passed, of course, for the protection of Federal officials and other "loyal persons," against action by the state courts of the South. What perfect irony if this law, enacted as it was to bind the fetters faster, could now be used to strike the fetters off!

If in the McCardle case the Supreme Court should declare the Reconstruction laws unconstitutional, the whole conspiracy might come tumbling to the earth!

Then, too, as the Radicals examined the political barometer, they looked out to see that the horizon was not free from clouds. The elections of 1867 had gone against them, and now and then the faint rumble of thunder could be heard. The North was coming to a better appraisal of the Fourteenth Amendment. On January 11th both Houses of the Ohio legislature adopted a resolution rescinding its assent to this great change. The amendment conferred upon Congress, the resolution said, the power "to legislate on subjects foreign to the original objects of the Federal compact." [17] Three days later a joint resolution of the legislature of New Jersey was reported, withdrawing its assent. The result of the amendment, declared this resolution, would be "the disturbance of the harmony, if not the destruction of our system of government." It would "place new and unheard-of powers in the hands of a faction." [18]

If these sentiments were to grow and spread, the Radicals might be defeated by an aroused conscience of the North! They could not pass laws compelling New Jersey or Ohio to adopt the Fourteenth or any other amendment! They could not control by bayonets the ballots of the North! Their iron grip upon the South, therefore, must not be relinquished. They were watching the McCardle case with deep concern. Attorney-General Stanbery declined to appear for the government against McCardle, as he had previously advised the President that the Reconstruction laws were unconstitutional. [19] Through Grant, Senator Lyman Trumbull was engaged instead. [20] Jeremiah Black was McCardle's lawyer. [21]

On January 17th the Supreme Court set the first Monday of March as the day for argument. [22] The Radicals must act if they were to prevent an adverse decision. In the House of Representatives, therefore, three days after Trumbull was retained, a bill was introduced prohibiting the court from declaring any law unconstitutional, except by a two-thirds vote of the judges. "This measure is hurried through here this morning," declared Representative Samuel S. Marshall of Illinois, "to prevent an adjudication of the validity of their motley Reconstruction Acts. . . . It is a confession of guilt on the part of the majority. It is evident that they feel and know in their hearts that their legislation will not bear investigation by a legal tribunal, made up principally of members of their own party, placed there by their own favored President." [23]

But the Radicals and their adherents were without shame. "There is danger of an adverse decision from the Supreme Court," declared the *Independent*. "Let the bill pass prohibiting a bare majority from declaring any Congressional act void. It is needed now, never more than at this moment; and the fact that it is needed is no argument against the propriety of passing the bill, as some timid people contend. The Supreme Court is at this hour the guilty confederate of Andrew Johnson. The country will rejoice to see it checkmated." [24] The bill passed the House, but not the Senate; [25] other bills of this kind were yet to come.

Trumbull, although a Senator, received a fee of $10,000 in the McCardle case,—a fee for which his own biographer has criticized him. [26] Trumbull determined now to earn it. He was retained to sustain the military sentence of death against McCardle. How could he better earn his fee than by preventing the Supreme Court from passing on the case at all. His position as Senator offered him for this purpose peculiar opportunities. And so on February 18th we find Welles recording: "In their war upon the Court the Radicals, under the lead of Trumbull, have under consideration an act prohibiting the Court from passing judgment on political questions, and they have now a bill declaring what are political questions. These usurpations and intrigues strain our government." [27]

Three days later Andrew Johnson acted.

LXII

JOHNSON REMOVES STANTON

SHERMAN having failed him, Johnson had to find the best substitute he could. Not very happily he now hit on old General
Lorenzo Thomas,—neither a blood nor spiritual relative of the
hero of Nashville. He graduated from West Point in 1819, and
was then nearing seventy. He became Adjutant-General three
days after Lincoln took his first oath of office.[1] His service in the
war had been confined to inspection trips, missions for the
exchange of prisoners and the organization of colored regiments.
His last military duty comprised the examination of soldier ceme-
teries.[2] He was a garrulous old man with an undistinguished
war record. He had never lost his position of Adjutant-General,
but during Stanton's administration had been assigned to duty
far away from Washington. At Welles' suggestion, on February 14th, Johnson directed Grant to restore Thomas to the full
charge of the Adjutant-General's office.

The choice of Thomas was not a fortunate one. He was a
military fuss-budget of the kind not infrequently encountered
among old officers of the regular establishment who have seen
but little active duty. Military men are not often adapted to
civil tasks, and the President had in mind for Thomas such a
service albeit a very temporary one. On February 18th he told
Thomas that he thought of making him his Secretary of War ad
interim.[3] Three days later Thomas was again summoned to the
White House. This time the President handed two letters to
his secretary, Col. Moore, and directed that they be read to
Thomas.[4] This was the first of the two letters to which Thomas
listened:

559

"Executive Mansion
Washington, D. C. Feby. 21, 1868.

Sir:

By virtue of the power and authority vested in me as President by the Constitution and laws of the United States, you are hereby removed from the office as Secretary of the Department of War, and your functions as such will terminate upon receipt of this communication.

You will transfer to Brevet Major General Lorenzo Thomas, Adjutant General of the Army, who has this day been authorized and empowered to act as Secretary of War ad interim all records, books, papers and other public property now in your custody and charge.

Respectfully yours,

ANDREW JOHNSON.

Hon. E. M. Stanton, Washington, D. C.
Official

W. G. Moore, United States Army." [5]

It was the power not only vested in him by "the laws of the United States," but by the Constitution also that the President decided to invoke. The power of removal without the Senate's consent,—a power that had been recognized since the foundation of the government as constitutionally inhering in the Executive, was thus asserted once again. Either Johnson was right in claiming it, or Congress was correct by its Tenure-of-Office Act in denying it. Let the judiciary decide between these rival claims! This was the second letter read to General Thomas:

"Executive Mansion
Washington D. C. Feby. 21, 1868.

Sir:

Hon. Edwin M. Stanton having been this day removed from office as Secretary for the Department of War, you are hereby authorized and empowered to act as Secretary of War ad interim, and will immediately enter upon the discharge of the duties pertaining to that office.

Mr. Stanton has been instructed to transfer to you all the records, books, papers, and other public property now in his custody and charge.

Respectfully yours,

ANDREW JOHNSON.

Brevet Major General Lorenzo Thomas
Adjutant General United States Army
Washington, D. C." [6]

MR. STANTON HOLDING POSSESSION OF THE WAR OFFICE DURING THE NIGHT
OF 21ST ULT.

It was not an appointment to office within the meaning of the constitutional provision granting the President "power to fill up all vacancies that may happen during the recess of the Senate." [7] It was a mere temporary arrangement for the temporary management of a department; [8] it was not the "filling up" of a vacancy. Andrew Johnson knew what he was doing. In 1795 Congress had enacted that in case of a vacancy in the office of Secretary of War, "it shall be lawful for the President . . ., in case he shall think necessary, to authorize any person . . . to perform the duties" of that office "until a successor be appointed." [9] Under this law, time and again Johnson's predecessors, both when the Senate was and when it was not in session, had made such temporary designations. It had become the settled practice of the government. [10]

It was with perfect good faith, therefore, when Johnson handed the two letters to General Thomas, that he declared his determination "to support the Constitution and the laws" and that he expected his temporary Secretary to do the same. [11] Thomas accepted the appointment and proceeded to the War Department to deliver to Stanton in person the order for his removal. [12] Stanton, when he received the letter, put it on the corner of his table and then sat down. Presently he got up, opened and then read the letter. "Do you wish me to vacate the office at once or will you give me time to remove my private property?" he asked. "Act your pleasure," replied Thomas. [13] Stanton did not say how much time he wanted and Thomas did not ask. While they were talking General Grant entered the room and Thomas handed him the order of removal he had shown to Stanton. "Is that for me?" asked Grant. "No," replied Thomas, "merely for your information," and promised him a copy. [14] Thomas then went down to his own room, made a copy, certified it as Secretary of War ad interim, and took it up and handed it to Stanton. [15]

What had Grant said to Stanton during Thomas' absence? We are not told. But when Thomas returned Stanton said to him: "I do not know whether I will obey your instructions or whether I will resist them!" [16] In reporting this interview to the President, Thomas incorrectly led the former to believe that there was no doubt as to Stanton's acquiescence.[17] "Very well," said the President, "go and take charge of the office and perform the duties."[18]

Johnson now notified his Cabinet what had taken place. He had, he said, "perhaps delayed this step too long." At all events it was settled. When asked who was to become Stanton's successor, he replied that Thomas "would officiate ad interim and until a regular Secretary was appointed."[19] The President told his Cabinet further that on the occasion of Thomas' call, "Stanton seemed calm and submissive, . . . and . . . was willing that Thomas should act his pleasure."[20] Secretary Browning remarked that he had been informed that "Stanton intended sending in his resignation today or tomorrow." But Welles expressed strong doubt of this, declaring his belief that Stanton would not resign unless persuaded that he "would not have Radical support." Welles expressed surprise also that Stanton "had quietly surrendered."[21]

§

Wild alarm and rumors filled the capital. Immediately upon receipt of his order of removal, Stanton sent word to the Speaker of the House of Representatives, who forwarded it at once to Thaddeus Stevens' Reconstruction Committee.[22] A few hours later illiterate old John Covode from Thaddeus Stevens' state was on his feet with a resolution that "Andrew Johnson, President of the United States, be impeached of high crimes and misdemeanors."[23]

The Senate was promptly informed by the President of Stanton's removal,[24] and when it heard the news all other business stopped. Far into the night a fierce debate was raging. Finally by a strict party vote, it was resolved: "that under the Constitution and laws of the United States, the President has no power to remove the Secretary of War and to designate any other officer to perform the duties of that office ad interim."[25]

What now had become of Senator Sherman's words? Those words in explanation of the Tenure-of-Office Act uttered ten months before. Had he forgotten how he had then said that through this bill "the government will not be embarrassed by an attempt by a Cabinet officer to hold on to his office despite the wish of the President?"[26]

Not only had Sherman and his colleagues repudiated their own construction of the act, but by their resolution expressed an opinion on the merits of an issue which as a Court of Impeachment they might presently be called upon to try![27] While the Senate was yet in session, a committee of Cameron, Cattell, Conness and Thayer was appointed by a Radical caucus of the House. These men proceeded to the War Department to counsel with Stanton how he might resist the President![28]

During these excitements, Lorenzo Thomas was busy too. He was making preparations to attend a masquerade ball. While thus engaged his friend, Walter Burleigh, called upon him. Seeing that the general was about to leave, Burleigh sought to excuse himself, but Thomas insisted that his friend should hear of his exploits at the War Department. "When are you going to assume the duties of the office?" Burleigh asked, to which Thomas answered that he would "take possession the next morning at ten o'clock." He asked Burleigh to call upon him in the Secretary's office. "Be there punctual at ten o'clock," he said. "You are going to take possession tomorrow?" Burleigh asked. Thomas assured him that he was, and then his friend continued: "Suppose Stanton objects to it,—resists?" "Well," answered Thomas, "I expect to meet force by force." "Suppose he bars the doors," suggested Burleigh. "I will break them down," the doughty General replied.[29]

Like many another arm-chair general, Thomas was bellicose,— in speech. He had had a similar conversation with Samuel Wilkeson a little earlier, declaring that were his demand refused, he would apply to the General-in-Chief for a force sufficient to enable him to take possession. He did not see how the general could refuse his request. And then evidently enjoying the brave sound of his own voice, with mendacious braggadocio he declared that "under the order the President had given," he had "no election to pursue any other course."[30] But Thomas had not yet talked himself out. At Willard's Hotel later in the evening he repeated his bold threats.[31] Under oath a few weeks later he admitted that what he said was "mere boast," and that it had never entered his head "to use force," [32] and that the use of force would not have been in "obedience to the President's orders." [33]

How poor an instrument Lorenzo Thomas was, how inadequately he had reported to the President his previous interview with Stanton, how unjustified his boastings, and how temporary was his status, appeared on the very afternoon of February 21st, when Representative Selye of Rochester and Edwin O. Perrin, who had known Johnson in the old campaigning days of Tennessee, called upon him at the White House. The President told them how Stanton had been removed and Thomas employed to perform the duties ad interim, to which Perrin answered: "Supposing Mr. Stanton should oppose the order?" "There is no danger of that," answered Johnson, "for General Thomas is already in the office," and then he added: "It is only a temporary arrangement; I shall send in to the Senate at once a good name for that office." [34]

At the masked ball Thomas bragged loudly of how presently he would take possession of the War Department and would open all the mails that came to it.[35] The masquerade was held at Mariner's Hall, and thither at 11 o'clock an officer of the Senate came to serve Thomas with the Senate's resolution declaring illegal his appointment. Thomas was masked, but was recognized by his shoulder straps,—apparently they were prominent.[36]

If Washington was seething with excitement on this evening, it seethed with social life as well. The Executive Mansion was resplendent with a state dinner.[37] A little earlier a smart party was in progress at the home of Mrs. Ray. Army officers in large numbers were gracing the occasion and thither also came Edgar T. Welles, the son of the Secretary.[38] While the gaiety was at its height, General Emory, the commander of the Department of Washington, sent an orderly requesting all officers of the Fifth Cavalry to report immediately at headquarters.[39] A little later another orderly appeared requesting all the officers of General Emory's command to report to him.[40] Was Congress preparing for a resort to arms? Young Welles excused himself and hurried home to report the incident to his father.[41] The old Secretary directed his son to go at once to the President with the news. At the White House, however, a Diplomatic dinner prevented him from communicating with the President, and there was no one else to whom the message could be given.[42]

But the activities of this eventful night had not yet concluded. Stanton was busy too. He and his friends were actively engaged in the preparation of an affidavit. When this great document was done, it set forth what had taken place at his office in the morning. It alleged that "your affiant is . . . informed . . . that . . . Lorenzo Thomas . . . threatens that he will forcibly remove your complainant from the building and apartments of the Secretary of War . . . and forcibly take the possession and control thereof under his said pretended appointment. . . ."[43] And that "Thomas by accepting such appointment and . . . attempting to exercise the duties of Secretary of War," had violated the Tenure-of-Office Act, and was therefore, "guilty of a high misdemeanor." This momentous paper was addressed to "Hon. David K. Cartter, Chief Justice of the Supreme Court for the District of Columbia," and its final paragraph demanded "a warrant . . . against Lorenzo Thomas, and that he may be thereupon arrested . . . and . . . dealt with as to the law and justice in such case appertains."[44]

Cartter was a tool of Stanton,[45] and the latter, therefore, had little trouble in routing out this judge that evening and in subscribing to his affidavit before him.[46] Between two and three o'clock in the morning, R. J. Meigs, the clerk of Cartter's court, was aroused from his slumber by Representative Pile of Missouri, who had come posthaste with the Judge's warrant to get the seal affixed.[47] Stanton and his camarilla this time had blundered. They had rushed into a proceeding wherein the constitutionality of the Tenure-of-Office Act might at last be tested. That which above all other things Johnson wished, might thus yet be accomplished!

§

While Lorenzo Thomas was yet dreaming of the masquerade, his legs wearied from dancing and his vocal chords perhaps from talking, at 7 o'clock on the morning of the 22nd, United States

Marshal Gooding, with the warrant in his hand, set out to disturb the slumbers of the masquerader.[48] Before the old General had had his breakfast, the marshal, with his assistant and a constable for his allies, appeared at the Thomas home and there arrested him.

The great culprit requested leave first to call upon the President; it was granted.[49] Flanked by these officers of the law, Thomas visited the White House and told the President what had happened. "Very well," said Johnson quietly, "that is the place I want it in,—the courts."[50] He advised his subordinate to call on Stanbery; this was also permitted by the marshal. Thomas told the Attorney-General of the arrest and asked him what to do.[51] What the reply was we do not know, but from what occurred immediately after, it is apparent that right here perhaps the greatest blunder of Johnson's administration was committed by the legal adviser of the President. For it is obvious from what presently transpired that he did not advise Thomas to refuse bail and apply at once for a writ of *habeas corpus*, whereby the lawfulness of his arrest and necessarily the validity of the law under which it had been made could promptly have been tested out.

From Stanbery's office, accompanied by the two marshals and the constable, Thomas proceeded direct to court. He had no lawyer there, nor was there any friend present to advise him, and there was perhaps no one in Washington more needy of advice. After about an hour's delay Thomas furnished bail, and finally secured Richard T. Merrick, a Washington lawyer of experience, to represent him.[52] The case was continued until the following Wednesday; but, before he left the court, Thomas asked Judge Cartter whether the arrest suspended him from any of his "functions," and was told that "it had nothing to do with them."[53]

Upon his release on bail, Thomas returned to the White House and again reported to the President. "Very well," replied Johnson, "we want it in the courts."[54] From the White House Thomas again proceeded to the War Department. He now found the door of the Adjutant-General's office locked. A messenger told him that the keys had been removed. He went upstairs to Stanton's room and found him closeted with his Congressional advisers.[55] They had been with him throughout the night.[56]

"I do not wish to disturb any of these gentlemen and will wait," said Thomas upon looking around at this Praetorian Guard. "Nothing private here, what do you want, sir?" replied Stanton. Thomas then demanded the surrender of the War Department. Stanton refused and ordered Thomas back to his own office. Thomas declined to go. "I claim the office of Secretary of War and demand it by order of the President," he said, and this dialogue then ensued:

Stanton: "I deny your authority and order you back to your own office."

Thomas: "I will stand here. I want no unpleasantness in the presence of these gentlemen."

Stanton: "You can stand there if you please but you cannot act as Secretary of War. I am Secretary of War. I order you out of this office and to your own."

Thomas: "I refuse to go and will stand here."

Stanton: "How are you to get possession, do you mean to use force?"

Thomas: "I do not care to use force, but my mind is made up as to what I shall do. I want no unpleasantness though. I shall stay here and act as Secretary of War."

Stanton: "You shall not and I order you as your superior back to your own office."

Thomas: "I will not obey you but will stand here and remain here."

Stanton: "You can stand there as you please. I order you out of this office to your own. I am Secretary of War and your superior." [57]

At this point, Thomas went across the hall into General Schriver's room and began issuing orders to him and to General Townsend. Followed by Representatives Moorhead and Ferry, Stanton now entered Schriver's office and directed him and Townsend not to obey Thomas' orders, and denied the latter's authority as Secretary of War ad interim, and the dialogue then continued:

Stanton: "I am Secretary of War, and I now order you, General Thomas, out of this office to your own quarters."

Thomas: "I will not go. I shall discharge the functions of Secretary of War."

Stanton: "You will not."

Thomas: "I shall require the mails of the War Department to be delivered to me and shall transact the business of the office."

Stanton: "You shall not have them and I order you to your own office." [58]

In this bloodless conflict, the honors perhaps were even. But Thomas had not secured possession of the War Department! Having tired of the grand rôle, when Stanton's Congressional advisers presently left the room, Thomas became facetious, and turning to Stanton said: "The next time you have me arrested please do not do it before I get something to eat." [59] Feeling that he had triumphed, Stanton now in his turn abandoned the grand opera manner and, coming over to where Thomas sat, put his arm around his neck and ran his hand through the old general's hair. Then turning to Schriver he said: "You have got a bottle here; bring it out." Schriver unlocked his case and produced a small vial containing about a spoonful of whiskey, remarking as he did so that he occasionally took a little for dyspepsia. Stanton took this and poured it into two glasses, holding them up to the light to see that an equal division had been made. And then the two antagonists drank together.

Presently a messenger entered with a full bottle of whiskey; the cork was drawn and thereupon the two rival secretaries each took another drink. "Now," said Stanton, "this at least is neutral ground." [60] "General Thomas," wrote Welles a few hours later, "proves himself unfit for the place of Secretary of War *ad interim*. He is like a boy, ready to obey orders, but cannot himself act with decision or direct others,—is a mere child or worse in Stanton's presence. Instead of taking upon himself the duties of Secretary of War and commanding Stanton's orders, he is locked out of the Department, laughed at and treated with contempt." [61]

The crisis long deferred was obviously at hand. The contest that raged between Lincoln and the Radicals Johnson had inherited, and it had now reached this pass: that Stevens, Sumner and their friends believed they had it in their power to ruin and disgrace the man who had taken over Lincoln's fight and given all he had to block their revolutionary purpose. Johnson was a courageous statesman, a proven patriot, a profound student of American government, but he was not and did not pretend to be a lawyer. What he needed now was a sound, a daring and a resolute adviser.

"The Attorney-General," wrote Welles, "although a very good

lawyer, is not the best adviser for administrative and executive service in such a time as this. There is a conspiracy against the Executive by Senators who are to adjudge him, and he, the Attorney-General, searches for precedents and authorities when action, decision, and novel questions require a stand to be taken and a path to be stricken out with promptness. In the little conversation we had, and so on some former occasions, he seemed bewildered for precedents and undetermined how to act from the absence of previous authorities." [62]

§

On the morning of the 22nd Welles called on Andrew Johnson to deliver the message that his son had failed to communicate the previous evening. He asked the President whether he had given Emory any orders and was answered in the negative. "Some one has," said Welles. "Who is it and what does it indicate? While you, Mr. President, are resorting to no extreme measures, the conspirators have their spies,—have command of the troops. Either Stanton or Grant or both issued orders which were proclaimed aloud and peremptorily at this large social gathering." [63]

The President was disturbed, but said little. "It is an error with him," Welles later wrote, "that he does not more freely communicate with his Cabinet and friends. This whole movement of changing his Secretary of War has been incautiously and loosely performed without preparation. The Cabinet was not consulted. His friends in the Senate and the House were taken by surprise, and were wholly unaware of the movement." [64] This was probably just criticism. Johnson had overlearned the lesson of keeping his own counsel.

Johnson had ready at this time a document that was confirmatory of his previously expressed purpose to make the duties of Lorenzo Thomas temporary only.[65] This was the document:

"To the Senate of the United States:
I nominate Thomas Ewing, Senior, of Ohio to be Secretary for the Department of War.

ANDREW JOHNSON.

Washington, D. C. Feby. 22, 1868." [66]

If he could not secure General Sherman, he had resolved to appoint Sherman's father-in-law.[67] He directed Col. Moore to take Ewing's nomination over to the Senate, but when he arrived the Senate had adjourned, and so Ewing's nomination was not presented until Monday, the 24th.[68]

The President now sent for General Emory and asked him if there had been any recent troop movements in and about Washington.[69] Carefully suppressing any information as to the import of his orders of the night before, Emory replied that he thought no changes had been made and that "under a recent order issued for the government of the armies of the United States, founded upon a law of Congress, all orders had to be transmitted through General Grant to the army," and that as any such order would come necessarily through him, he would know.[70] It was a long verbose answer, it had the intended effect of deflecting the President from the order of the night before. "What order do you refer to?" the President inquired. "To order No. 17 of the series of 1867," answered Emory. "I would like to see that order," replied Johnson, and a messenger was dispatched for it. The order proved to be a reprint of the Appropriation Act of March 2nd, 1867, declaring that the headquarters of the general of the army should be in Washington, that he should not be removed or assigned to duty elsewhere except with the Senate's consent, and that all military orders should be issued through him. The act had been published as a general order "for the information and government of all concerned." [71]

Upon reading the order the President reflectively remarked to Emory: "This is not in conformity with the Constitution of the United States that makes me Commander-in-Chief, or with the terms of your commission." "That is the order you have approved and issued to the army for our government," replied Emory. Had he known what use the Radicals were presently to make of this colloquy, or soliloquy, for such it really was, Johnson would not have continued. But he went on, half to himself: "Am I to understand that the President of the United States cannot give an order except through the general of the army?" Emory told him that such was his impression, and that of the whole army, and continued: "I think it is fair, Mr. President, to say to you that when this order came out there was considerable discussion as to what were the obligations of an officer under that order and some eminent lawyers were consulted—I myself consulted one—and the opinion was given to me decidedly and unequivocally that we were bound by the order." [72] "The object of the law is evident," replied the President meditatively, and the interview was at an end.[73]

While they were yet talking, lawyer Merrick, who had appeared for Thomas in the morning, called with a copy of the papers in the case. Stanbery had come in. He asked Merrick whether it were possible to get the case to the Supreme Court immediately, and Merrick told him he was not sure. "Look it up," replied Stanbery, and Merrick assented.[74]

Later during the same afternoon the President sent for lawyer Walter S. Cox. The messenger called at the latter's residence in Georgetown and brought him in a carriage immediately to the White House where Johnson and General Thomas were waiting for him. The President told him that he desired the necessary legal proceedings to be instituted without delay to test Thomas' right to the office of the Secretary of War ad interim, and to put him immediately in possession of that office. Cox inquired whether the Attorney-General was to act in the matter, and was informed that Stanbery had been very much occupied in the Supreme Court and had not had time to look into the authorities. The President added, however, that he would be glad to have him confer with the Attorney-General. Cox agreed to do so and withdrew.[75]

LXIII

JOHNSON IS IMPEACHED

IN the general conflagration of February 22nd the House of Representatives was blazing with a white flame. At 12 o'clock a nervous throng was crowding every corner of the galleries, while from without the populace clamored for admission. The lobbies were a seething mass; even the aisles and area opposite the clerk's desk were filled. Near Speaker Colfax a seat had been provided for Ben Wade. There he sat awaiting what he and his co-conspirators believed would lead him to the Presidency of the United States. The very air was vibrant with wild rumor. Men were on the march from Maryland to protect the President, it was whispered.[1] The excited throngs became so out of hand that finally the Speaker called the Capital police to bring the galleries to order.[2] There had not been there such a feverish hour since that March day seven years before, when Senator Andrew Johnson of Tennessee roared his denunciation of secession, and Abraham Lincoln sat in his hotel preparing, none too hopefully, to take his oath of office. But that was all forgotten now.

Impatiently for more than two hours the House gave its indifferent attention to the dispatch of routine business, while behind closed doors Stevens' Reconstruction Committee was preparing its report. Finally at twenty minutes after two, the Committee, with Thaddeus Stevens at its head, made its way into the expectant chamber.[3] Could there be any doubt what the report would be? Was not Andrew Johnson guilty of blood-curdling crime? Had he not sought to rid himself of a disloyal member of his Cabinet? Could such criminality go uncondemned by these highminded patriots? Men who, as Welles declared, were ready to impeach the President "had he been accused of stepping on a dog's tail." [4] The report, of course, recommended an impeachment.[5] Stevens

572

declared that no debate was necessary, Johnson's crime was too plain for argument! His guilt too clear to justify discussion! [6]

But Representative James Brooks of New York, one of the two Democratic members of the Committee, was on his feet "to resist this untoward, this unholy, this unconstitutional proceeding!" "Go on, go on, if you choose," he shouted, ". . . you may strip him of his office, but you will canonize him among those heroic defenders of constitutional law and liberty. . . . Suppose you make the President of the Senate the President of the United States, you settle that hereafter a party having a sufficient majority in the House and the Senate can depose the President of the United States!" [7]

Other Democrats demanded the floor to denounce this effort to "Mexicanize" the American Republic. For what was the President to be impeached? The issue, declared Phelps of Maryland, is "whether white men or negroes shall control ten states and through them the nation." [8] And now young Holman of Indiana is demanding the unwilling attention of the House. "You propose," he said, "to impeach the President upon a mere question of opinion, when in fact no crime or misdemeanor has been committed. . . . It can only be said that the President . . . has assigned a military officer to a given duty, to the same duty to which he recently assigned the General of the Army, and that officer has sought to enter upon the discharge of that duty, but has failed to do so, and the incumbent remains in his office. It cannot be said, no matter what interpretation you place on the tenure-of-office law, that an offense has been in fact committed; for if Edwin M. Stanton was Secretary of War he is still the Secretary of War; he is still in fact as he was in possession of his office; for the Senate has declined to 'confirm' a successor." [9]

"This," declared George Woodward, a Democratic Representative of Pennsylvania, and a former Chief Justice of his state, "is the third attempt to impeach the President. The first, founded on his alleged usurpation of powers which the Constitution had delegated to the legislative department, was crushed to death by a ponderous volume of testimony of more than twelve hundred pages which was brought in with the impeaching resolution. The second attempt, founded on the Johnson-Grant correspondence, was strangled in the birth, and the issue of fact raised between those distinguished correspondents was left to be decided by each man for himself upon evidence that was altogether favorable to the President. Now comes, for the third time during our present session, another resolution . . . founded on the . . . removal of E. M. Stanton from the War Department . . . this resolution is founded in a mistake, and . . . any impeachment of the President on the idea that Secretary Stanton is within the protection of the tenure of office bill is what Fouché, the chief of the . . . French police, would have called worse than a crime—a blunder. . . ." [10]

With logic as clear and passionless as the opinion of a court, Woodward proceeded: "Mr. Stanton was appointed by President Lincoln, and his title to office expired a month after Lincoln's death; from that time . . . he was a mere *locum tenens;* and when Mr. Johnson removed him he acted within the strictest bounds of the Constitution and offended not against the statute. . . ." [11]

He then exposed the favorite Radical delusion that the peculiar enormity of the President lay in his removal of Stanton while the Senate was in session. "The Constitution," he declared, "does not forbid him to do so, but leaves him free at all times to rid himself of an unacceptable Cabinet minister. It is better done when the Senate is in session than when it is in recess, because the new nomination can be immediately considered without prejudice to the public interests from delay of a confirmation; and such has been the practice of the government from its foundation. . . ." [12]

The Representatives and Senators of ten states were absent, he therefore denied the right of the House to impeach or the Senate to try the accusation. "What criminal," he shouted, "was ever before arraigned before a court from which twenty of his legal triers had been excluded?" [13] "Mr. Speaker," he concluded, "so sure am I that the American people will respect this objection that I will say, if I were the President's counselor, which I am not, I would advise him, if you prefer articles of impeachment, to demur both to your jurisdiction and that of the Senate, and to issue a proclamation giving you and all the world notice that while he held himself impeachable for misdemeanors in office before the constitutional tribunal, he never would subject the office he holds in trust for the people to the irregular, unconstitutional, fragmentary bodies who propose to strip him of it. Such a proclamation, with the Army and Navy in hand to sustain it, would meet a popular response that would make an end of impeachment and impeachers." [14]

For answer the accusers of the President again unloosed their musketry of slander. The House of Representatives, under the leering leadership of Thaddeus Stevens, resembled now some barroom brawl. "Mexicanize" the American Republic? Yes, indeed, why not! "I shall, for one, be grievously disappointed," declared Ingersoll of New York, "if, within ten days from this time, honest old Ben Wade is not the President of the United States!" [15] But it was by no means to prophesy alone that these Representatives of a corrupt Congress confined themselves. A Congress in the pockets of many of whose members the gold of Credit Mobilier was jingling! A House of Representatives whose Speaker was a bribe taker! They knew how trivial a thing was the removal of Edwin Stanton. That it was a "relatively small matter," Julian, one of the most obedient of Stevens' followers conceded, expressing his belief that "it would be regarded as scarcely a sufficient ground for this proceeding, if not considered in the light of greater previous offenses." [16] But those "previous offenses" had been previously considered, and by an overwhelming vote had been adjudged insufficient for impeachment!

And so what the charge against the President was lacking in sufficiency, these conscienceless assassins of character determined to make up in sheer vilification. The debate, if such a name may be given to what the Radicals now carried on, resembled the low brawlings of some riverfront resort where argument is given point by flying cuspidors and broken chair rungs. Farnsworth of Illinois was on his feet. The President, he declared, is "an ungrateful, despicable, besotted, traitorous man,—an incubus and a disgrace to this great and glorious nation." [17] Not to be outdone Kelley of New York pronounced the Chief Executive as the "great criminal of our age and country," and charged him with complicity in Lincoln's murder.[18]   Logan of Illinois delighted his appreciative colleagues with the charge that Johnson had dragged his robes of office "in the purlieus and filth of treason." [19]   Julian expressed fervent hope that Johnson would be cast from the White House "once more to the fond embrace of his rebel confederates in the South and their faithful allies in the North." [20] The President, Washburne of Illinois explained, was "surrounded by red-handed rebels," and "was advised and counselled by the worst men that ever crawled like filthy reptiles at the footstool of power." [21]   History, vociferated Newcomb of Missouri, would place Johnson in the company of Torquemada, Nero and George Jeffreys! [22]

And so on and on it went.   No lie was too base, no charge too false to satisfy the meanest partisans America has ever known. Loughbridge of Iowa mendaciously asserted that it was the purpose of the President "at the head of the army" to "take possession of this Capitol, disperse this illegal Congress and consign the people's Representatives here who advocate impeachment to the dungeon or the scaffold." [23]   "Every vile traitor and bloody-handed rebel of the South," shouted Price of Iowa, had crawled into daylight from their hidden dens, and were now "uncoiling themselves" under the warmth of Johnson's smiles.[24]   "For a tithe" of Johnson's "usurpation, lawlessness and tyranny" belched Ben Butler, "our fathers dissolved their connection with the government of King George, for less than this King James lost his throne and King Charles lost his head." [25]

On into the night of February 22nd the tempest raged; it continued through Monday afternoon, the 24th.   With perfidious ingenuity the charges on which they were presently to act were pressed into the background, and general vilification was resorted to instead.   "Apostate," "tyrant," "criminal," "usurper," were accompanied by the old accusation that Johnson had participated in the assassination of his predecessor.[26]

Now and again the real cause of all this hatred emerged from out the storm clouds of vituperation: the fact that Johnson had opposed their Reconstruction schemes!   "His conduct in regard to that transaction," declared Thaddeus Stevens, who closed the disorderly debate, "was a high-handed usurpation of power which ought long ago to have brought him to impeachment and trial, and to have removed him from his position of great mischief. He has been lucky in thus far escaping through false logic and false law." [27]

And now, at 5 o'clock on Monday afternoon, the Representatives prepared to vote. There were some who shuddered at this prostitution of conscience and debauchery of honor, but these soon cowered beneath the sadistic Stevens lash. The more timid among the inmates of this disorderly House, counted as nothing among the brazen political strumpets all about them,—"mere shallow, reckless partisans who would as readily have voted that the President should be hung in front of the White House, as that he should be impeached in the Capitol, provided their leaders— Stevens, Boutwell and others—had presented papers for that purpose." [28] The vote came at last. By 126 to 47 it was decided to impeach the President of the United States for high crimes and misdemeanors! [29] It was the first time in American history!

"The impeachment," wrote Welles that evening, "is a deed of extreme partisanship, a deliberate conspiracy involving all the moral guilt of treason, for which the members if fairly tried would be liable to conviction and condemnation. . . . In this violent and vicious exercise of partyism I see the liberties and happiness of the government imperiled." [30]

Would Lincoln have been impeached? With all his gentleness, there was iron in that great character. He would never have consented to the lawless measures of the Radicals; they would never have agreed to his policy of justice. The victories of Farragut, Sheridan and Sherman alone had saved him from these same Radicals in 1864. They had fought him every inch of the way on Reconstruction. Wade had libeled him because of it. Would they have impeached him had he lived? Did Booth's bullet save him from this less appealing martyrdom? For following the course that Lincoln had marked out, Andrew Johnson was now to be placed on trial. Presently the Senators would resolve themselves into a High Court of Impeachment. Upon the outcome of the trial rested Johnson's right to the continuance of his office. What could he expect from a Senate whose presiding officer had been made such for the very purpose of lifting him to Johnson's place!

§

The House directed its two most vindictive members, Thaddeus Stevens and John Bingham, to go before the upper Chamber, and on Tuesday, the 25th, they appeared at the bar of the Senate.[31] In due time articles of impeachment, they announced, would be presented.[32] Stevens had twisted his hard features into an expression of regret. He looked "as if he were discharging a sad duty."[33] In fact the malevolent heart of the old hypocrite was surging with mean joy. He had come to announce the culmination of his malicious labors. It was with venomous pleasure that he now declared "in the name of the House of Representatives and of all the people of the United States, we do impeach Andrew Johnson, President of the United States of high crimes and misdemeanors in office. . . ." Ben Wade, the President of the Senate, and the expectant beneficiary of that which had thus been finally initiated, was presiding and replied: "The Senate will take order in the premises."[34]

At the White House the President, although keenly sensitive to the outrage of the conspirators, remained serene and offered no complaint.[35]

On the same day John Bigelow, late Minister to France, spent an hour with the Secretary of the Navy. He blamed the President for having permitted himself to be foiled by Stanton. "All this is very true," wrote Welles. "It is easy now that the matter has passed, to say that so great a scoundrel, so treacherous, false and deceitful a man should not have been treated like a gentleman. The President has from the first extended to Stanton a consideration and leniency that has surprised me, for he knew him to be false, remorseless, treacherous and base."[36]

On Wednesday, the 26th, the adjourned day of his case, Lorenzo Thomas again appeared before Judge Cartter. Since his arrest four days before, Cox and Merrick, the old General's

(Sketched by Theodore R. Davis.)

IMPEACHMENT—THADDEUS STEVENS AND JOHN A. BINGHAM BEFORE THE
SENATE.

lawyers, had been considering what procedure most expeditiously would test the constitutionality of the law. They had concluded that a writ of *quo warranto* would not secure a decision of the question for at least a year,[38] and therefore decided to surrender their client to custody, have him committed to prison and then sue out a writ of *habeas corpus*.[38] But if Cox and Merrick had been considering this matter, the Radicals had been reflecting on it also. And so when on the opening of court it was announced on behalf of Thomas that he would surrender himself to custody, Carpenter and Riddle, the lawyers representing Stanton and the prosecution, objected to this course. They did not wish General Thomas to be detained in custody, they said. Judge Cartter, too, despite his midnight issuance of the warrant, had become suddenly solicitous for the accused and declared that he "would not hold him or allow him to be held in custody!"[39] Stanton and his fellow Radicals were emerging from the blunder of the arrest. Under no circumstances would they permit the testing of their unconstitutional laws! And so the case was now dismissed. The Supreme Court could never hear it. "Cartter in this whole proceeding from its inception to its close," wrote Welles, "showed himself a most unfit judge. He has secretly visited Stanton at the War Department, and his associate Fisher has spent much of his time, since Thomas' arrest, with Stanton."[40]

All that he could do to bring the Tenure-of-Office Act to the test, Johnson had now done. The decision Johnson sought was to be deferred for more than half a century. We have previously considered Judge Taft's opinion in the Meyers case handed down in 1926,—a full and sweeping vindication of the views of Andrew Johnson. It was just such a decision as he in 1868 was struggling to secure, it was one the Radicals determined to prevent!

In the meantime Congress was actively engaged in preparation, —the Senate in formulating rules of procedure for the trial, and the House in drawing up their articles of impeachment. But as they went about their work there were not lacking those who felt a sense of shame at their participation in the plot. Woodbridge of Vermont, for example, one of the Judiciary Committee, who until the 24th had steadfastly opposed impeachment, called upon Gideon Welles and spoke deprecatingly of the movement, expressing his regret that he had voted for it under party discipline. He declared that he had voted with reluctance, and against his wishes and convictions. To have voted otherwise would have been political suicide, he said. "It is melancholy to witness such things," recorded Welles. "Woodbridge is but one of many who are guilty of this wrong. A moral infirmity or weakness. They dare not act in accordance with their convictions." [41]

Since his bibulous interview with Thomas, Stanton had beleaguered himself within the War Department surrounded by a company of a hundred men; Representative Logan and Senator Chandler were marshalling them in the basement.[42] The calling out of any troops in Washington was authorized by Grant and he detailed a guard for the War Department building.[43] Stanton's desire for personal protection, no doubt, lingered in Grant's mind when in his Memoirs he spoke of him as a coward.[44] As the Cabinet meeting of February 28th was breaking up, there was considerable laughter among the members at "the fortification and entrenchment of the War Department." [45]

On the same day Kennedy, the Chief of the New York police, threw a new scare into the patriot ranks by writing Colfax that some nitro-glycerine had disappeared from Manhattan Island and that he could not imagine where it was unless in Washington. "The chivalrous and timid Speaker at once laid this tremendous missive before the House, and the consternation of the gallant band of Radicals became excessive," wrote our diarist. "A large additional police force had been placed around the Capitol, but as it was still considered unsafe an immediate adjournment was called for. Stanton, unfortunate man, could not adjourn. There was no refuge for him save in the War Department which is surrounded and filled with soldiers to protect against an inroad from old General Thomas. As Stanton, Grant and the Radical Congress have assumed the active control of the military, to the exclusion of the President, who is Commander-in-Chief, the apprehension seems to be that the Adjutant General and his friends have resorted to nitro-glycerine." [46]

On the last day of this eventful week the House adopted

articles of impeachment. As originally drawn they were based entirely upon the happenings of February 21st and 22nd: the removal of Stanton, the appointment of Thomas and Johnson's interview with General Emory.[47] How flimsy such an accusation was, Thaddeus Stevens was not slow in pointing out. Here was a President, he said, guilty of "monstrous usurpation, worse than sedition and little short of treason," and yet the House had confined its charges to the "most trifling crimes and misdemeanors which they could select from the official life of Andrew Johnson."[48] He proposed an article of his own, declaring "if there be shrewd lawyers, as I know there will be, and cavilling judges, and without this article they do not acquit him, they are greener than I was in any case I ever undertook before the court of quarter sessions."[49]

Ben Butler came forward with a new accusation founded upon the speeches of the President made in his "Swing Around the Circle." Butler's charge was added to the rest,—as Article X becoming famous later. Stevens' proposed charge of treason and sedition was not adopted, so he devised a new one; it was accepted and made Article XI.[50]

When finally complete these were the charges: in the first article, that on February 21st, 1868, Johnson had issued an order for the removal of Stanton with intent to violate the Tenure-of-Office Act and the Constitution. In the second, that he had issued to Thomas the letter of authority of February 21st with like intent. In the third, that he had appointed Thomas with like intent. In the fourth, that he had conspired with Thomas "with intent by intimidation and threats to prevent Stanton from holding his office, all in violation of the Constitution and the Conspiracy Act of July 31, 1861." In the fifth, that he had conspired with Thomas to hinder the execution of the Tenure-of-Office Act and in pursuance of that conspiracy had attempted to prevent Stanton from holding his office. In the sixth, that he had conspired with Thomas to seize government property in the War Department in Stanton's custody with intent to violate both the Conspiracy and the Tenure-of-Office Acts. In the seventh, the same charge as in the sixth, except that the conspiracy was to violate the Tenure-of-Office Act alone.   In the eighth, that he had issued Thomas his letter of authority with intent to control money appropriated for the War Department, in violation both of the Constitution and the Tenure-of-Office Act.   In the ninth, that he had instructed General Emory that the law requiring military orders to be issued through the General of the Army was unconstitutional with intent to induce Emory to disobey the Appropriation Act of 1867, and with the further intent of preventing the execution of the Tenure-of-Office Act.   In the tenth, that with intent to bring disgrace and contempt upon the Congress he had made three public addresses, one at the executive mansion on August 18th, 1866, one at Cleveland on the 3rd of September and one at St. Louis on the 8th of September of the same year, so indecent and unbecoming the Chief Magistrate that they had brought his office into contempt, ridicule and disgrace.   In the eleventh, that in that same speech of August 18th he had declared that the 39th Congress was unauthorized to exercise legislative power, since only part of the states were represented, thereby intending to deny its power to propose constitutional amendments, and that "in pursuance of that declaration," he had afterward unlawfully contrived means to prevent Stanton from resuming his office after the Senate had refused to acquiesce in the first suspension, and that all of this was done to prevent the execution of the military appropriation and the Reconstruction Acts.[51]

This last,—the Stevens' article—was a miserable hodge-podge, the product of diseased malice.   Even Rhodes has called it "a trick to catch wavering Senators."[52]   Of this article Senator Buckalew later wrote: "Its strength consists in its weakness—in the obscurity of its charges and the intricacy of its form.   As an afterthought of the House of Representatives, or rather as a reluctant concession by the House to the pertinacity of its author, it . . . bears upon its face the evidence of its distinct and peculiar origin.   Considered in parts it is nothing—the propositions into which it is divisible cannot stand separately as charges of criminal conduct or intention; and considered as a whole it eludes the understanding and baffles conjecture.   While we cannot suppose it to have been drawn in scorn of the Senate . . . it would be true to the paternity of a scornful spirit and a reckless brain if such paternity were assigned to it." [53]

The substance of the charges was that Johnson had attempted to remove Stanton and appoint Thomas in his stead, had instructed General Emory that the law depriving him of his full command of the army was unconstitutional, and had made three speeches. To give the charges resonance and seeming weight, nine of the articles pronounced the acts set forth as "high misdemeanors," and two as "high crimes in office." [54]

"Traitor," "usurper," "tyrant," "apostate," "drunkard," "murderer," "Nero," "Torquemada!" Where were the allegations to support these tirades? For more than twelve months every power of Congress had been strained to find the basis for a real charge. Having no evidence they had employed abuse instead. And now when they were compelled to put in writing the crimes of this "great criminal,"—what a sorry showing! A shaggy mountain of malice had panted, heaved and labored, and this small and very scaly mouse was the result!

After all their suborned perjurors, their long pages of investigation, after all the dragnets of Ashley, Bingham, Boutwell, Stevens and Ben Butler, the hatred of discharged public servants, the malice of unscrupulous political antagonists, after all the dreary rancorous months of spying,—after all their indefatigable research, it must indeed have been a spotless character against whom the sole accusation could be brought that he had removed a member of his Cabinet, had repeated his opinion that one of their laws was contrary to the Constitution, and exhorted the country against the enemies of Lincoln's hopes!

But what cared Stevens or Ben Butler how poor a showing they had made? Pressing as they were toward a long-considered and a predetermined end! What cared they for the substance of their accusations or the evidence with which to meet them? They had selected impeachment as the cloak under which to disguise their well-matured conspiracy to rid themselves of an antagonist whose character and courage were a constant menace to their machinations!

LXIV

THE VETERANS VOLUNTEER FOR A NEW WAR

AND now above the babel-sounds of Washington, there is a distant rumble as of drum-beats! Like the fitful undefined motif in some great orchestration, there could be now and then discerned the clamor of a new instrument, vague at first and then clear and still more clear, the note is bugle-like. And are those drums or marching feet, or both? Lincoln had found his volunteers, Johnson too, could have them! He did not need to call! From every corner of the United States Union soldiers were offering to defend him. The White House mails were deluged with appeals for this new opportunity to serve!

From New York, John Burleigh wrote: "Being one of those who were first to leave this state in 1861, for the defense of the constitution, and in view of difficulties that may exist, and peril that may environ you; likewise believing that you are the Commander-in-Chief of the army and navy; I beg leave to offer my services toward raising a regiment of infantry to be ready for the field in forty-eight hours after authority to organize the same. . . ." [1]

From far off Omaha, James Hannan sent the President this letter: "I take the liberty to offer you the services of 75 good men as a personal body guard, all of whom are ready to give their lives in the cause of liberty and protection of the respected Chief Magistrate of the nation. . . ." [2] While down from Charlestown, Massachusetts, came this offer from George Walsh: "Old Bunker Hill sends you greeting. I helped to raise one regiment for President Polk against the wishes of Massachusetts and went out with it to Mexico. If necessary I can raise ten regiments for Andrew Johnson, our noble and staunch defender of the Constitution." [3]

584

In the manuscript division of the Congressional Library at Washington you may still read these letters,—these and countless more of similar import. Andrew Johnson read them,—and laid them aside for the historian. Had he placed the bugle to his lips and blown but one blast, regiments and brigades would have answered, and the long faded columns of Union blue would have been upon the march again!

From Pennsylvania came the offer of 2,000 who were "never whipped." From New Jersey, a colonel of cavalry declared that his state was only waiting for the order to "fall in." Indiana tendered 5,000 more. General Harney and General McClernand declared their readiness for the new war! But it was not from the North alone that these volunteers would come. Kentucky proffered if need be, a hundred thousand men. "To preserve the Union and the Constitution," thirty thousand Virginians were clamoring! Nor would his own state desert him in this hour,— "the last drop of blood" that flowed through a hundred thousand Tennesseeans was freely offered him.[4]

Andrew Johnson could have had another civil war! This time no war between the states, but one whose armies would have divided not upon state lines, but upon the great issue of upholding or tearing down the Constitution. Upon the one side would have been ranged the forces of good faith, honor and reverence for the fundamental law, and upon the other the conscripts of dishonor, hypocrisy and confiscation! On the one side, those who would not welch upon the terms of Appomattox, and on the other, the advocates of cowardly assault upon a prostrate foe! The followers of Lincoln and of Johnson, against those of Thaddeus Stevens and Charles Sumner!

No one can read Johnson's story without the temptation to regret that he did not put that bugle to his lips, and fight that war upon hypocrisy with bayonets. Stevens and Sumner had reveled long enough in their sadistic persecution orgies! A fighter every inch, what a temptation for Andrew Johnson to take up arms for the restoration of the white man to his rights and the states to their just representation,—in one red summer to have done with impeachment and impeachers! But one holocaust for a generation was enough! And with a courage that exceeded that of any call to arms, Johnson spurned the proffered wine of **bloody conflict**, accepting, if he must, the bitter hemlock in its place.

LXV

PREPARATIONS FOR THE TRIAL

THE House on Monday, March 2nd, chose seven of its members as a Board of Managers to conduct their case before the Senate. These proven enemies of Johnson were selected: John A. Bingham, George S. Boutwell, James F. Wilson, Benjamin F. Butler, Thomas Williams, Thaddeus Stevens and John A. Logan.[1] They craved the limelight of the country. They planned to dazzle their contemporaries with a radiance that would shine on down to posterity. "They have read," said Welles, "Macaulay's interesting history of the trial of Warren Hastings and flatter themselves they are to be the Burkes and Sheridans of some future historian." [2] With Macaulay they had wandered through the "spacious provinces of Aurungabad and Bejapoor." [3] They had watched the "bands of fierce horsemen of Mysore . . . prowling among the tulip trees," [4] and had seen how "in the bazaars, the muslins of Bengal and sabres of Oude were mingled with the jewels of Golconda and the shawls of Cashmere." [5]

These latter-day Sheridans and Burkes had observed how the greatest orator of the British empire had prepared himself for that prosecution and had stored his mind with knowledge of the "burning sun, the strange vegetation of the palm and cocoa tree . . . the rich tracery of the mosque where the imaum prays with his face to Mecca, the drums and banners and gaudy idols. . . . The black faces, the long beards . . . the turbans and the flowing robes, the spears and the silver maces, the elephants with their canopies of state, the gorgeous palanquin of the prince and the closed litter of the noble lady." They had learned with admiration how Edmund Burke had made these things as familiar to him as his own England,[6] and although they lacked this gorgeous background for their prosecution, they were hoping to achieve a fame that some future chronicler would hold up to the admiration of the world.

Boutwell and his fellow managers had read how the Governor-General of India had treated Rohilcund and Cheyte Sing,[7] and on account of these things and much else, had been arraigned in the great hall of William Rufus for high crimes and misdemeanors. They had visualized the avenues of London lined with grenadiers and the streets kept clear with cavalry. They had watched the gorgeous pageantry of the trial only less brilliant than the dazzling story of India there unfolded. They saw the peers robed in gold and ermine marshaled by the heralds, the judges in their vestments, while the junior barons present led the way and the long procession was closed by the Prince of Wales "conspicuous by his fine person and noble bearing."[8]

Ben Butler and his six associates had looked in upon the hall into which the solemn procession wound its way where the "grey old walls were hung with scarlet" and the "long galleries were crowded by an audience such as has rarely excited the fears or the emulation of an orator." There were gathered from all parts of the empire "grace and female loveliness, wit and learning, the representatives of every science and every art. There were seated round the Queen the fair-haired young daughters of the House of Brunswick. There the ambassadors of great Kings and Commonwealths gazed with admiration on a spectacle which no other country of the world could present. There Siddons, in the prime of her majestic beauty, looked with emotion on a scene surpassing all the imitations of the stage. There the historian of the Roman empire thought of the days when Cicero pleaded the cause of Sicily against Verres, and when before a Senate which still retained some show of freedom, Tacitus thundered against the oppressor of Africa."[9]

Butler and his fellow managers, through Macaulay's eyes, looked in upon that gorgeous scene and determined to make as good an imitation of it as they could. But there were some features of the pageant they were hoping not to copy. The Hastings trial had lasted more than seven years, and had ended in acquittal![10]

However much these American impeachment managers had

been inspired by Macaulay's brilliant pages, to his philosophical reflections they had given but scant heed. Among those was this: "In truth it is impossible to deny that impeachment, though it is a fine ceremony, and though it may have been useful in the seventeenth century, is not a proceeding from which much good can now be expected. Whatever confidence may be placed in the decision of the Peers on an appeal arising out of ordinary litigation, it is certain that no man has the least confidence in their impartiality, when a great public functionary charged with a great state crime is brought to their bar. They are all politicians. There is hardly one among them whose vote on an impeachment may not be confidently predicted before a witness has been examined; and even if it were possible to rely on their justice, they would still be quite unfit to try such a cause as that of Hastings." [11]

If this was true of the House of Lords in 1788, in which whatever else was lacking, an inbred sense of sportsmanship and fair play prevailed, how much more true was it of the American Senate in 1868, where the presiding officer was in the plot to convict and remove, no matter what the facts might be!

Envying as they did the fame that came to Sheridan and Burke, with what poor effect the seven managers had read Macaulay's essay, appeared at their conference the day before the trial began. Wisely enough they decided that one of their members should have charge. Butler was not slow in volunteering. What his conception of the conduct of the trial should be, he has preserved for us in his Memoirs: "I came to the conclusion to try the case as I should try a horse case, and I knew how to do that." [12] And so it was arranged that the President of the United States should be prosecuted as though he were a common horse thief! And thus it now transpired that Ben Butler,—this poltroon, vain braggart, shyster lawyer and corruptionist, this great resounding paunch,— had become for the time being the spokesman of America!

§

While the Radicals were at work, their defamations were echoed and reëchoed by their coadjutors of the Press. With insensate fury the Radical journals bent every feverish effort to contaminate the public mind against the President. The leader of all these journalistic propagandists was Horace Greeley. From day to day his New York *Tribune* spewed forth its poison. He spoke of Johnson's nomination as Vice-President as one of those unhappy freaks of a popular assembly, quite forgetting how he had praised it when it was made. "The apprehension of the Republicans everywhere," he continued, "burst out afresh when the fatal blow fell which ended Mr. Lincoln's life and brought Mr. Johnson reeling into his place under circumstances creating such unbounded disgust and mortification as never before shocked the public mind."

"Impeachment," he went on, "has been since the beginning of the government a power which Congress was more than once tempted to use, but from which it shrank. The thunderbolt was ever within its reach, but was too terrible to lightly grasp. Never was the temptation greater than in the past two years. Twice Congress seized it with fiery indignation; twice it reluctantly relinquished it. The third time it was Johnson who thrust the weapon into the hand of Congress, uplifted its arm and compelled it to strike. . . . He permitted the massacre in New Orleans, and protected the murderers in Texas. Everywhere Andrew Johnson was in the path of the loyal nations resisting its advance. He was multiplied throughout the rebel states; turn where we would there was Andrew Johnson fighting, fighting, fighting against loyalty and order. Peace! There was no hope of peace while he insisted upon war." [13]

The Senate had adopted its rules of procedure, but it had done so as a Senate, not a court, and in the absence of the Chief Justice.[14] Chase was not slow to make the point that what was about to take place was a "trial" before a "court." On March 4th he wrote the Senate that its organization as a court should precede all action on the impeachment.[15] It was no mere technical point; it went straight to the heart of the conspiracy. Knowing the flimsy case they had concocted, the Radicals had sought to free themselves from judicial restraint of every kind. If it were a court, there would be the necessity to prove a case within the principles of justice. If it were merely a branch of Congress, it might hear and condemn, no matter who the proofs revealed.

Chase's letter, recorded Welles, "will be swamped by leading impeachers who are anxious to hurry on their work. Stevens with his arrogance, insolence and vicious despotism, threatens every Senator who shall dare to vote against his party; tells them they are committed by their votes. It must shame and mortify some of the intelligent minds in the Senate to be held in subjection and compelled to receive the excoriations and threatenings of this wicked and bad man, but it is questionable whether they have the moral courage and independence to do right, when the terrors of this party tyrant are before them." [16]

March 4th, the day Chase sent his letter, was the time appointed for the formal presentation of the articles of impeachment. The day was unusually bright for that season. At 12 o'clock the Senate galleries were full. The gentlewomen who composed a majority of the audience, were attired as for a state occasion. [17]

At a little after one, it was whispered that the impeachment managers were on their way, and presently the main doors of the Senate chamber opened, and the managers appeared. They halted a moment at the threshold while the sergeant-at-arms announced: "The managers of the Impeachment on the part of the House of Representatives." Linked arm in arm and walking two by two, they made their entrance. Bingham and Boutwell led the way, then came Butler and Wilson with Logan and Williams following them. Behind these six limped old Thaddeus Stevens. The weight of years and hatreds hung upon him; he could no longer walk alone, and so on either side a friend supported him. Behind the managers came the other members of the House of Representatives who had resolved themselves into a committee of the whole for the purpose of attending at the ceremony. [18]

"The managers of the impeachment will advance within the bar and take the seats provided for them," announced Wade, the presiding officer. [19] In front of the Speaker's desk chairs had been provided for them: Stevens, Bingham, Boutwell and Logan on the left, and Butler, Williams and Wilson on the right. While the interest was at its height, a motion was carried to invite Speaker Colfax to a seat at the right of the presiding officer, and the little smiling grafter was then duly escorted to this post of honor.[20]

Now all were in readiness to hear the great charges read. All eyes were fastened on the seven managers. They were eager to begin their dastard work,—these representatives of malice, these ambassadors of hate, these delegates of a conspiracy! There sat Ben Butler, with his popping eyes and his squat figure, vain, corrupt, and with the instincts of a barroom bully, waiting to strut his brief hour across this stage. There sat George Boutwell of Massachusetts, a narrow-minded and vindictive partisan, a lover of notoriety, a fanatic, an ardent, violent enemy of Johnson,[21] embodying all that is unlovely in the New England character. There was Thomas Williams of Pittsburgh, a remorseless, unscrupulous man, indifferent alike to constitutional obligations and to truth.[22] For these traits he had been selected as a manager,— for these and for one other thing; he had been the law partner of Edwin Stanton.[23] There sat James Wilson of Iowa, who had originally opposed impeachment. As a convert he was welcome, —"a sinner come to repentance."[24] There was John Bingham of Ohio, "a shrewd, sinuous, tricky lawyer," with the face and side whiskers of a church deacon. His proposal after the Milligan case to "sweep away at once"[25] the Supreme Court's appellate jurisdiction in all cases, and his denunciation of the President as a "criminal violator of public trusts,"[26] had endeared him to the Radicals.

There was John Logan of Illinois. He had been one of the valiant hundred that had guarded Stanton from Lorenzo Thomas.[27] His declaration that Johnson had dragged his robes of office in "the purlieus of filth and treason,"[28] was a guarantee that at the trial, so far as he could help it, nothing that was vindictive would be omitted.[29] And there, like some cold-bellied snake with poison-fangs fitfully darting, was old Thaddeus Stevens, with the eyes and visage of Apollyon!

Here they were ready to begin,—these apostles of virtue! They were well fitted for that work! Only four of the seven were later mentioned in the Credit Mobilier investigation! Bingham and

(From a sketch by James E. Taylor.)

J. A. BINGHAM   G. S. BOUTWELL   J. A. LOGAN   B. F. BUTLER

THADDEUS STEVENS   T. WILLIAMS

THE HOUSE COMMITTEE, ELECTED TO MANAGE THE IMPEACHMENT OF THE PRESIDENT, ENTERING THE SENATE
CHAMBER, WASHINGTON, D. C., ON THE 4TH INST., TO PRESENT THE ARTICLES OF IMPEACHMENT.

Wilson admitted that they took the stock, but they escaped censure! [30]   Logan received stock without paying for it, collected one of the dividends, but later returned it to Oakes Ames.[31]   He was pure! It was not proved that Boutwell participated.[32]   Such were the impeachment managers!

"The sergeant-at-arms will make proclamation," announced Wade, and thereupon that dignitary in a clear, round voice proclaimed: "Hear ye! Hear ye! Hear ye! All persons are commanded to keep silence in pain of imprisonment, while the House of Representatives is exhibiting to the Senate of the United States articles of impeachment against Andrew Johnson, President of the United States." [33]   The announcement was unnecessary, for a deathlike silence pervaded the entire chamber.[34]   The managers then arose, and Bingham unfolded two quires of foolscap paper stitched together in book form. From this in slow and measured voice he read the charges. Every word was heard in the remotest corner of the Senate. During the reading all the managers but Stevens remained standing. Old age soon forced him to his seat. But he was an attentive listener, and when Johnson's allusions to him in the St. Louis speech were read, a smile was seen to play upon his hard and cruel face.[35]

§

By nine of the following morning all the avenues leading to the Capitol were thronged, and long before the appointed hour the Senate galleries were filled again. But it was not in the Senate chamber only that the drama was enacting. Argument of the McCardle case was in progress in the Supreme Court! Chief Justice Chase was presiding, when the Committee of the Senate came to escort him to the High Court of Impeachment.[36]   In these two courts the destinies of the South and the destinies of Andrew Johnson were at stake.

Promptly at one o'clock the doors of the Senate chamber were thrown open, and presently the Chief Justice made his entrance, his tall figure clad in black judicial robes, his handsome, well-turned head erect. The galleries were hushed, while the Senators arose, standing silent in their places. Chase was followed by

Nelson, the senior associate Justice of the Supreme Court, walking arm in arm with Senator Wilson.[37] As the Chief Justice entered. Wade rapped his gavel, and then surrendered the chair in obedience to the Constitution, which declares that "when the President of the United States is tried the Chief Justice shall preside." [38]

The Chief Justice took the proffered place, saying: "Senators, I attend the Senate in obedience to your notice for the purpose of joining you in forming a court of impeachment for the trial of the President of the United States, and I am now ready to take the oath." [39] The galleries and the standing Senators then heard, if they did not heed, these words: "I do solemnly swear that in all things appertaining to the trial of the impeachment of Andrew Johnson, President of the United States, I will do impartial justice according to the Constitution and the laws; so help me God." [40] The Senators now took their seats.

The Radicals were wondering about Chase. Would he join them in their plot, or would he, as he had called Almighty God to witness, "do impartial justice?" They had not failed to note his announcement that he had come to form "a *court* of impeachment for the *trial*."

But it was not alone for this that the Radicals mistrusted him. On the previous evening he had held a reception at his residence. Andrew Johnson had been present, and although all that had taken place between them was the merest exchange of formal courtesies, the incident had filled the Radicals with dark suspicions.[41] Nor had they forgotten Chase's insensate craving for the Presidency,— a craving which Lincoln had likened to insanity.[42] They knew that his ambition was not dead, although before the trial began he had become convinced that Grant would be the next nominee of the Republicans.[43] Could it be that thus thwarted, his Presidential aspirations would still live, and seek satisfaction at the hands of Democrats?

After he had himself taken the oath, Chase directed that it be administered to the Senators. Their names were called alphabetically, and to each the same oath was administered by the Chief Justice. After VanWinkle had been sworn, the name of Wade was called. He rose from his seat and advanced toward the chair. But Senator Hendrick was on his feet. "The Senator just called," he said, "is the presiding officer of this body and under the Constitution and laws will become President of the United States should the proceeding now to be tried, be sustained. The Constitution providing that in such a case the possible successor cannot even preside in . . . the trial, I submit . . . the question whether . . . it is competent for him . . . to . . . become . . . a part of the court. I submit . . . that he is interested . . . in the result of the proceedings. . . ." [44]

Senator Sherman now arose. Each state under the Constitution, he said, was entitled to two Senators, Wade was one of the Senators from Ohio, "he is a member of this Senate, and is therefore made one of the tribunal to try all cases of impeachment." The whole matter, he thought, was one of taste, not right. [45]

Through the remainder of that session, the debate ran on. It continued on the following day. Senator Dixon then gained the floor. "Sir, if there is anything desirable in this great trial," he said, "it is, in the first place, that impartial justice should be done; and in the second place that it should appear to be just. . . . If the future historian in recording the fact that the President of the United States had been removed from his office by impeachment should also be compelled to record that his successor was his judge, such a record would violate the sense of justice of the nation and shock the heart of the civilized world." [46]

Finally, upon the theory that the question might be premature and that it could be later raised, Hendrick withdrew his objection, and thereupon the Secretary of the Senate again called Wade's name. Would his conscience deter him from sitting in a case from which he hoped to profit? Wade's conscience? His political fortunes then were almost at as low ebb as his conscience! He had in the preceding autumn failed of reëlection to the Senate. The conviction of Andrew Johnson would make him President,— at least temporarily. It would, no doubt, secure his nomination for Vice-President at the coming Republican convention. If his patronage were shrewdly enough handled it might even enable him to thwart Grant's political ambitions and be nominated for the Presidency himself. What did conscience or sportsmanship weigh when balanced by these considerations? Without shame, the libeler of Lincoln and the arch enemy of Lincoln's follower now advanced to the Speaker's desk and took the oath! [47] Never was blacker perjury committed!

§

On Saturday, March 7th, the Senatorial summons was served upon the President.[48] It did not, nor did any law, require him to appear in person. Should he present himself at the trial? Secretary McCulloch hoped that he would attend on the first day. If he went, thought Seward, the whole Cabinet should accompany him, but Welles registered his strong dissent from either course. To have the President personally appear, he said, "would give dignity and imposing form to the proceedings, which the conspirators wished, but he did not. The managers undoubtedly desired that the President should exhibit himself there, and if surrounded by his advisers it would make the scene more imposing. Men and women, too, would come from a distance and gather at the Capitol to see the victim, if he should consent to gratify them." [49] It was wisely decided that the accused should appear by counsel only.

Who should that counsel be? Many names were canvassed. David Dudley Field was considered, but Seward protested. Field, he said, "was the greatest small man" he had ever known.[50] Charles O'Conor was mentioned, but he had been counsel for Jefferson Davis,—that was enough to exclude him.[51] Johnson as always, wanted about him the best men he could find, and so the galaxy of counsel finally agreed upon were these: Henry Stanbery, the Attorney-General, Jeremiah S. Black, Benjamin R. Curtis, William M. Evarts and Thomas A. R. Nelson of Tennessee.[52] They were all lawyers of the highest standing at the bar and each of them, but Nelson, enjoyed a national reputation. Stanbery was a "chivalric gentleman,"—a man of "surpassing beauty of person and emphasis of presence." [53] At the disposal of his great client, he now placed all of his ability and his character. If for the duration of the trial he could keep well, he told the President, he would be willing to be sick for the remainder of his life.[54]

Curtis was one of the finest representatives of the American bar. Born in the same year as Abraham Lincoln, he was now fifty-nine years old. He was an ornament to the state that Benjamin F. Butler misrepresented. Massachusetts was indeed versatile in her ability to produce two such opposites. He was a man of scrupulous honor. The great talents of this advocate had been refined and strengthened by six years of service on the bench of the United States Supreme Court from which he had resigned eleven years before. As a judge he had followed in the footsteps of John Marshall and Story. He had written one of the great dissents in the Dred Scott case.[55] He brought to the defense of Andrew Johnson all of these unusual professional attainments.

Black we have met before as the Attorney-General and Secretary of State in Buchanan's Cabinet, and the original sponsor there of Edwin Stanton. He was a brilliant master of forensics. His stirring argument in the Milligan case deserves a place second only to the great prevailing opinion which bears the intrinsic evidence of his persuasive power. He had been an intimate of Andrew Johnson, and had counselled with him in the preparation of many of his messages.[56]

But of all the President's counsel, perhaps Evarts was the most sophisticated lawyer. He was a graduate of Yale. He was the acknowledged leader of the New York bar. Fifty years old, in the full prime of life, he was the possessor of iron health and unbounded capacity for hard work.[57] Although no politician, he was not without political experience. It was he who at forty-two had headed the New York delegation in the Republican Convention of 1860; it was his brilliant speech that placed Seward's name in nomination.[58] He looked the lawyer all through,—high forehead, piercing cold eyes, acquiline nose, straight mouth, strong but not too pointed chin. Welles' estimate of him as a "cold, calculating selfish man . . . destitute of enthusiasm or magnetic power," [59] was presently to be disproven. And yet as we study that face, it is possible to discern there a little of what Welles saw. It is a face of the greatest interest to study,—such a one as might have been encountered in the Roman Senate. There is no genial warmth there, but every line betokens the high-bred gentleman, the man of intellectual and moral power, confident, poised, sufficient.

In this brilliant group it was but natural that Johnson should wish included an old friend and fellow townsman,—the kind of a man whom he had known and understood back home. And so he requested Thomas Nelson of Greeneville to join the ranks of his defenders.⁶⁰ Nelson was a typical product of a mountain village. His brief service in Congress had but slightly added to his sophistication. He had been practicing his profession in his native town for thirty years, and as falls to the lot of an able country lawyer, had been engaged in nearly every kind of case from murder down. He was somewhat out of his element in the polished and urbane company of Curtis, Stanbery and Evarts. But he contributed a rough, forensic force lacking in these urbane advocates.⁶¹

While the Capital was filling with expectant throngs awaiting the coming Friday for the real commencement of the trial,⁶² everyone concerned was busy making preparations. Horace Greeley was doing all he could to fan the blaze against the President. On the day of the service of the summons, he wrote in his *Tribune*: "We have yet to find the first square Republican paper that does not justify the impeachment of Andrew Johnson." ⁶³

No doubt as much with the desire to assure a brilliant audience for the spectacle as to relieve congestion, the Senate ordered that with the exception of those having the privileges of the floor, none should be admitted save upon presentation of a ticket to be issued by the sergeant-at-arms. A thousand were printed. The diplomatic gallery was set aside for the diplomatic corps' exclusive use, and forty tickets were delivered to Baron Gerolt for the foreign legations. Four tickets were issued to each Senator, four to the Chief Justice, two to each member of the Cabinet, twenty to the President and sixty to the reporters of the press. The remainder were distributed among the Representatives and other public officers.⁶⁴

The Cabinet was busy in giving aid and comfort to the President, and now the Radicals again attempted to break up this solid phalanx. To Seward they held out the bribe that if he would

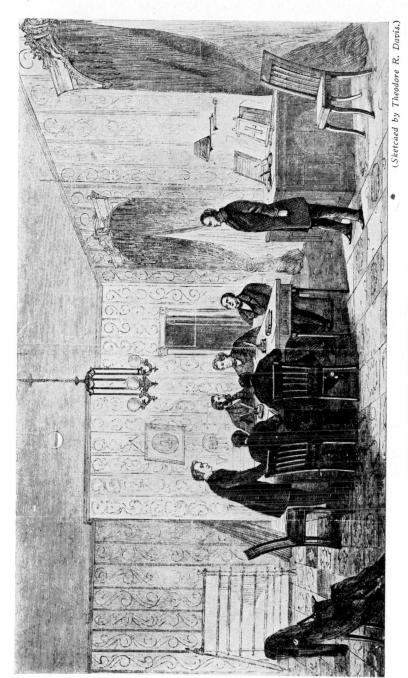

PRESIDENT JOHNSON CONSULTING WITH HIS COUNSEL.

(Sketched by Theodore R. Davis.)

abandon Johnson, they would not disturb his occupancy of the State Department. "I will see you damned first," he told their emissaries, "the impeachment of the President is the impeachment of his Cabinet." [65] Johnson was equally loyal to his Cabinet. If he would make certain changes in his official family, he was assured of his own safety. Concerning those who brought this sinuous suggestion, Johnson privately remarked: "I will have to insult some of these men yet." [66]

In the Cabinet, on March 10th, Stanbery announced his intention to resign as Attorney-General in order to devote his whole

time to the impeachment case. Welles thought that the presence of the Attorney-General as such would lend added weight to the defense. His argument did not prevail and that evening, with some pique, he wrote: "Mr. Stanbery is sensitive and timid. Herein I fear he will fail before the insolent, reckless and audacious Radical Managers and conspiring Senators who are to sit in judgment. Stevens and Butler will take pleasure in bluffing and insulting, and he is too courteous, gentlemanly, and dignified to meet and boldly rebuke them." [67]

"Stanton," he continued, "is still making himself ridiculous by intrenching his person in the War Department, surrounded by a heavy guard. This is for effect. He is, it is true, an arrant coward, but can have no apprehension of personal danger requiring a military force to protect him. Some of his wise Senatorial advisers, doubtless in their conspiracy to defeat executive action, counselled and advised the redoubtable Secretary to hold on to the War Department building, and to fortify himself in it. Thayer, Conness and Cameron would have minds for such work." [68]

Seward was busy searching precedents. He found one of great value. On May 12th, 1800, while the Senate was in session, John Adams had requested Timothy Pickering to resign as Secretary of State. Pickering had refused, Adams had then removed him, and had appointed John Marshall in his stead. [69] Except that there was then no Tenure-of-Office Act, the case was identical with that of Stanton. Johnson was delighted with this precedent. So pleased was he, and so eager that the people should share his knowledge, that although it had been studiously kept secret by his counsel for use upon the trial, he now most indiscreetly revealed it to the press. [70]

On March 12th Stanbery resigned as Attorney-General, and was now acting solely in the capacity of defendant's counsel. As the Cabinet meeting of that day was breaking up and he was about to leave, he stopped, resumed his seat and facing his client, said: "You are now, Mr. President, in the hands of your lawyers, who will speak and act for you, and I must begin by requesting that no further disclosures be made to newspaper correspondents. There was in the papers yesterday, or this morning, what purported to be a conversation between the President and a correspondent, in which the Pickering correspondence was brought out and made public. This is all wrong, and I have to request that these talks or conversations be stopped. They injure your case and embarrass your counsel." [71]

It was a friendly, a merited, although a stern rebuke. It made any further advice of that kind unnecessary.

LXVI

THE SUPREME COURT'S OPPORTUNITY

ON March 9th the Supreme Court took the McCardle case under advisement.[1] Something must be done to forestall the decision! Once more the Radicals were equal to the task! Three days later they rushed through an amendment to a pending measure,[2] whereby they sought to strip the Supreme Court of jurisdiction in the case.[3] On the very day of its introduction it passed both Houses![4] The New York *Herald* satirically observed: "The country is in the hands of Congress. That Congress is the Radical majority, and that Radical majority is old Thad Stevens. Government by the people has its glories."[5] In his unfailing diary Gideon Welles put down: "It is evident that the Radicals in Congress are in a conspiracy to overthrow not only the President but the government. The impeachment is but a single act in the drama. . . . By trick, imposition and breach of courtesy, an act was slipped through both Houses . . . which is designed to prevent a decision in the McCardle case. Should the court in that case, as it is supposed they will, pronounce the Reconstruction laws unconstitutional, the military governments will fall and the whole Radical policy will tumble with it. Only one course can prolong the miserable contrivance, and that is a President like Wade, who will maintain the military governments regardless of courts, or law or right. Hence I have very little expectation that the President will escape conviction. His deposition is a party necessity, and the Senators have not individually the strength, ability nor honesty to resist the Radical caucus decisions which Stevens, Ben Butler and other chief conspirators sent out."[6]

But the Radical press was jubilant. "The passage of that little bill which put a knife to the throat of the McCardle case was a splendid performance," gloated the *Independent*.[7] While the

601

Springfield *Republican* declared: "Congress does not intend to permit the Supreme Court to overthrow it or revive rebellion if it can help it." [8]

Now was the Supreme Court's opportunity. Never before or since has it had a greater one. Here was the chance to show its courage! The "little bill" could not for at least ten days become a law. Here then was time, more than time, in which to act! To write an opinion in the McCardle case would not take long for those who had stood by the Constitution in *Ex parte Milligan.* The country was waiting for the decision. Surely there would be one! It was confidently believed, declared the Boston *Post,* that the great tribunal could not fail to act, if for no other reason than "in defense of its own dignity, and to show that the Court cannot be trifled with by reckless partisans who flippantly speak of 'clipping the wings of the Court.' It is well ascertained that Justices Chase, Nelson, Grier, Clifford, Davis and Field believe the Reconstruction Acts to be unconstitutional. . . . The decision is made up, and they have the power and the right to deliver it. Whether they have the nerve to be an independent Judiciary remains to be seen." [9]

It would take courage to stand up before the Radical conspirators! Andrew Johnson was still standing! Would the judges stand or would they welch? Which should it be, the red badge of courage or the white feather?

LXVII

THE TRIAL BEGINS

FRIDAY, the 13th, the great day, dawned—the real beginning of the trial. Never before had there been such demand for attendance at the Senate. There was everywhere a struggle for the tickets of admission. Ladies of wealth and fashion were importunate in their applications to the Senators and Representatives. At nearly midnight of the previous day one of the Senators was aroused from his bed. A fair visitor had not hesitated to intrude with her demand. Less than half-dressed, he descended from his bed chamber and inquired whether some sudden death in the family was responsible for her late call. No, what she wanted was a ticket for the trial! He had none left, he said. But it was not until he promised somehow to procure one and send it to her residence that she consented finally to take her leave.[1]

The court was not scheduled to sit till one, but by eleven o'clock the galleries began to fill; the ticket system, however, prevented all disorder. There was no queen there, nor were there any "fair-haired young daughters of the House of Brunswick." There was there no historian of the Roman empire thinking of the "days when Cicero pleaded the cause of Sicily against Verres." There were no dukes or duchesses, no Prince of Wales, nor were the "gray old walls hung with scarlet."[2] The pageantry of the Warren Hastings trial was absent, but it was the most brilliant scene that the capital of the new Republic could present.

In the gallery of the diplomats there sat DeBerthemy, Louis Napoleon's ambassador; Baron Gerolt, the Minister from Prussia, dreaming perhaps of that day when King William's soldiers would sweep through Sedan and Metz and the last of the Bonapartes would be humbled. There sat Rangabe, the Minister for Greece, and Blacque-Bey from Turkey. Cerruti, from the land of

603

Garibaldi and Mazzini, was there to interpret the trial to Italy, and Great Britain saw the spectacle through the eyes of Francis Ford, the Secretary of her legation.[3]

The wives and daughters of the Senators were there, with all their spring apparel, to witness the kind of justice the heads of their families were presently to administer. In the foremost seat of the diplomatic gallery sat the wife of Benjamin F. Wade, anxiously to observe a spectacle that was designed to make her the "First Lady of the Land." Near her were the two fair daughters of the Chief Justice; one of these was the wife of Senator Sprague of Rhode Island, one of the judges of the impeachment court. She was a beautiful, a brilliant and an accomplished girl and destined to play a part in furtherance of her father's political ambitions, such as befell no woman of America since Dolly Madison had charmed the friends and foes of Jefferson's successor.

There were then thirty-seven states in the Union, each entitled to two Senators. The Constitution guaranteed it—to Virginia and South Carolina as well as to Ohio, Pennsylvania or Massachusetts. Yet the Senators from ten states had been excluded, and the accused was thus unlawfully deprived of twenty of his legal triers. It was an unconstitutional and irregular court convened and organized in defiance of the fundamental law.

Promptly at one o'clock the Chief Justice entered, and the sergeant-at-arms made proclamation. The Chaplain then prayed "that the proceedings of the high court which is about to meet may be sanctioned by the High Court of Heaven." [4] Apparently he was in agreement with the Chief Justice as to the character of the tribunal! But if the good Chaplain had in mind any method by which an appeal might be taken to that "High Court of Heaven," should this terrestrial tribunal fall a little short of justice, his prayer gave no clew as to the procedure.

The managers were announced by the sergeant-at-arms and were ushered to their places. Tables had been provided for them as well as for the counsel of the accused.[5] The return showing the service of the summons on the President was read and the Chief Justice then announced: "The sergeant-at-arms will call the

THE SENATE AS A COURT OF IMPEACHMEN

(Sketched by Theodore R. Davis.)

THE TRIAL OF ANDREW JOHNSON.

accused." In a loud voice that officer then chanted: "Andrew Johnson, President of the United States; Andrew Johnson, President of the United States: appear and answer the articles of impeachment exhibited against you by the House of Representatives of the United States." [6] But Andrew Johnson did not appear! Presently, however, it was announced that he had retained counsel. They were waiting in the President's room. Thither the sergeant-at-arms disappeared and presently returned with Stanbery, Curtis and Nelson, who were conducted to the seats assigned them.

The sergeant-at-arms now announced the members of the House of Representatives who entered the Senate chamber preceded by Washburne of Illinois, the senior member and the chairman of the Committee of the Whole. He was accompanied by the Speaker and the clerk. [7] They distributed themselves upon the vacant chairs, [8] and the Chief Justice, turning to the counsel for the accused, then said: "Gentlemen, the Senate is now sitting for the trial of articles of impeachment. The President of the United States appears by counsel. The court will now hear you." [9]

"Mr. Chief Justice," responded Stanbery, "my brothers Curtis and Nelson and myself are here this morning as counsel for the President. I have his authority to enter his appearance, which with your leave I will proceed to read." [10] It was a formal paper asking at least forty days for preparation of the answer. [11] The charges against the President, said Stanbery, "involve his acts, declarations and intentions as to all which his counsel must be fully advised upon consultation with him, step by step, in the preparation of his defense. It is seldom that a case requires such constant communication between client and counsel as this, and yet such communication can only be had at such intervals as are allowed to the President from the usual hours that must be devoted to his high official duties. We further . . . suggest . . . that as counsel careful as well of their own reputation as of the interests of their client, in a case of such magnitude as this . . . have a right to ask for themselves such opportunity to discharge their duty as seems to them to be absolutely necessary." [12]

If the fair listeners in the gallery had had any doubt as to what character the trial would take, that doubt was now dispelled. No shrift for Andrew Johnson! No courtesy, not even the common decencies that would be accorded to a pickpocket! Manager Bingham is on his feet. The President's answer should be filed at once! And if this were not done, "the trial should proceed as upon the plea of not guilty!" Manager Wilson spoke to the same effect.[13] "Mr. Chief Justice," answered Stanbery, "the objection taken by the honorable managers is so singular that in the whole course of my practice I have not met with an example like it. A case like this . . . is as to time, to be treated as if it were a case before a police court, to be put through with railroad speed on the first day the criminal appears! . . . We do not wish this case to go by default; we want a reasonable time; nothing more. . . ."[14] Now look back through the whole line of impeachments even to the worst times, go back to English precedents, and English fair play always gave fair time. . . . 'Strike but hear.' . . . Give us time; give us a reasonable time; and then with a fair hearing we shall be prepared for that sentence, whatever it may be, that you shall pronounce."[15]

Manager Bingham again is on his feet, asserting that no time should be given to the President.[16] Finally it was moved that the Senate retire for consultation, and they filed out to their reception room.[17] Any possible illusion of grandeur that might heretofore have elevated the proceedings now disappeared. The galleries thinned out, the Representatives lounged about in the seats of the Senators. Thaddeus Stevens was devouring with great relish a dish of raw oysters which had been brought in to him from the refectory. The managers meanwhile consulted together, or pored over books bound in law calf spread before them on the tables. The Senate chamber resembled now in no way "the great hall of William Rufus," rather did it give the appearance of a county court room when the jury had retired.[18]

After an hour and eleven minutes the Senators returned, and the Chief Justice resumed the chair. The result of their deliberation was announced. Johnson might have until the 23rd of

March to file his answer! He had asked for forty days and they had granted nine! [19]

A debate now ensued as to the precise day when the trial should begin. Ben Butler had thus far been silent. His fellow managers, Bingham and Wilson, had been performing. They were basking in the limelight that he craved for himself alone. A great question was at stake—should the trial begin on April 6th, or three or four days earlier! The great champion of the people's rights is on his feet. [20] He is launching into a great effort. He will let the country know, and incidentally his fellow managers, who it is that was chosen to conduct this prosecution.

"We were told," he declared, "that 'railroad speed' ought not to be used in this trial. Sir, why not? Railroads have affected every other business in the civilized world; telegraphs have brought places together that were thousands of miles apart. . . . We must not shut our eyes that there are railroads and there are telegraphs, as bearing upon this trial. They give the accused the privilege of calling his counsel together instantly, of getting answers from any witness that he may have instantly, of bringing him here in hours where it once, and not long ago, took months. . . ." [21]

Having concluded with this great thought, he pressed on to another: "When ordinary trials are had, there is no danger to the common weal in delay. . . . But here the House of Representatives have presented at the bar of the Senate the Chief Executive officer of the nation. They say . . . that he has usurped power . . . that he is at this very time breaking the laws . . . and that he still proposes so to do. Sir, who is the criminal—I beg pardon for the word—the respondent at the bar? He is the Chief Executive of the nation . . . he is the Commander-in-Chief of your armies; he specially claims that command, not by force and under the limitations of your law, but as a prerogative of his office and subject to his arbitrary will. He controls . . . your treasury. He commands your navy. Thus he has all the elements of power. He controls your foreign relations. In any hour of passion, of prejudice, of revenge for fancied wrong in his own mind, he may complicate your peace with any nation of the earth, even while he is being arraigned as a respondent at your bar. And mark me, sir, . . . the very question here at issue . . . is whether he shall control beyond the reach of your laws . . . the army of the United States . . . and control it if he chooses, at his own good pleasure to your ruin and the ruin of the country." [22]

Butler was indeed determined to conduct the prosecution as though it were a horse case! No shrift for Andrew Johnson! Realizing the flimsiness of the charges, he was painting the portrait of a dangerous enemy of the Republic—a portrait which the House would gladly have placed upon the canvas of its articles—a portrait for which, however, in their depraved studios of malice they had been unable to find either the outlines or the colors. Why should there be a delay of forty days, asked Butler, answering with sarcastic insolence his own question: "In order that five very respectable, highly intelligent, very learned and able lawyers may write an answer to certain articles of impeachment. . . . The great pulse of the state beats perturbedly while this strictly constitutional, but highly and truly anomalous proceeding goes on. It pauses fitfully when we pause, and goes forward when we go forward; and the very question of national prosperity . . . depends upon our actions here and now. . . . We are . . . pressing for trial. . . . Make the days as long as the judges of England made them, when they sat twenty-two hours out of twenty-four in the trial of great criminals, and we the managers . . . God giving us strength, will still attend here at your bar every hour and every moment, your humble servitors, for the purpose of justice." [23]

The President's metropolitan advocates were sitting silent, but the country lawyer, Thomas Nelson of Tennessee, Johnson's old friend, had tired of Butler's tirade and was on his feet to answer it. "I need not tell you," he said, "that in the courts of law the vilest criminal who ever was arraigned in the United States has been given time for preparation, time for a hearing. . . . A large number of these charges—those connected with . . . the Secretary of War . . . involve an inquiry running back to the very foundation of the government. . . . The two last charges . . . open Pandora's box and will cause an investigation as to the great differences of opinion . . . between the President and the House of Representatives . . . which, so far as I can perceive, will be almost interminable. . . . Now what do we ask for the President of the United States? . . . Simply that he shall be allowed time for his defense . . . that same opportunity which you would give to the meanest criminal that ever was arraigned before the bar of justice. . . ." [24]

The ring of sincerity and truth in Nelson's words awakened in that High Court no echo of response. It was decided that after the managers had replied to the President's answer the trial should proceed immediately! [25] "Men who would so limit time in so grave a matter, even under secret caucus stimulant," wrote Welles the following evening, "can scarcely be considered worthy to sit in judgment in such a case. The charges are indeed frivolous, contemptible. . . . But a majority of the Senators have prejudged the case, and are ready to pronounce judgment without testimony." [26]

§

If the Radicals were busy at the trial, to insure that the accused should not receive the common decencies customarily accorded an indicted horse thief, they were busy also out of doors to prevent every possibility of acquittal. They were counting noses in the Senate and canvassing the vote long before the first witness had been sworn. There were but twelve Democrats—these were certain for acquittal. There were forty-four Republicans, but the Radicals well knew that there were in that number a few men of sensitive honor. Thirty-six votes would be required to make the two-thirds necessary to convict. If seven of the forty-four Republicans therefore should refuse to cower beneath the Stevens lash an acquittal would result. Any means were justified to prevent this! Pack the Court?—why not? Suppose the conquered provinces, or some of them, were now restored as states! Senators elected through carpet-bag and negro votes could be counted for conviction! Judges such as these would see to it that the conspiracy did not fail! This plan engaged the active minds of Johnson's enemies! And we shall note now on the part of the Radicals as keen a purpose to readmit the Southern states thus reconstructed as had marked their previous determination to exclude them.[27]

But it was by no means the intention of the Radicals upon the re-admission of the "conquered provinces," to withdraw the armed forces of the North! Well they knew that the corrupt and loathsome negro governments could not last a week were not the Northern bayonets behind them! Through the armed subjugation of the conquered Southern white men alone could be secured the Republican majorities at the next Presidential election and in those that were to follow! Thaddeus Stevens announced that military rule within the Southern states would continue for the next quarter of a century. The *Tribune* applauded loudly. "Surely," wrote Horace Greeley, "there are generals and heroes enough to furnish half a dozen countries with first-class rulers." [28]

The second Reconstruction act declared that no conquered province could again become a state unless a majority of all her registered voters should take part in the election. Hateful as was martial law to Anglo-Saxons, they thought it preferable to the rule of their ex-slaves. The Constitution of Alabama was the first to be completed. It was formulated by a convention in which the negroes had a majority of ten members. "De bottom rail is on de top," declared these descendants of the African jungle, "and wese gwine ter keep it dar." [29]

February 4th, 1868, had been the day set for the election to ratify the Alabama constitution. The white people of the state set a day of fasting and prayer to deliver them "from the horrors of negro domination." [30] They sought not only freedom from the carpet-bag régime, but from the wrongs the "loyal leagues" were stimulating. To Congress they sent this petition: "We are beset by secret oath-bound political societies; our character and conduct are systematically misrepresented to you and in the newspapers of the North . . . industry and enterprise are paralyzed by the fears of the white men and the expectations of the black

that Alabama will soon be delivered over to the rule of the latter.
. . . Continue over us, if you will do so, your own rule by the
sword. . . . But do not, we implore you, abdicate your rule over
us by transferring us to the blighting, brutalizing and unnatural
dominion of an alien and inferior race." [31]

The appeal fell upon deaf ears. But there was one recourse,
albeit a temporary one, to which the white men of Alabama could
resort—an abstention from voting. This plan was followed, and
so the total vote lacked more than 13,000 of the number necessary
to make a majority of all the registered voters. The Radicals
were, however, equal to the emergency. A law was rushed
through Congress on March 11th, providing that "a majority of
the votes actually cast" should be sufficient with which to bring
about the ratification of a state Constitution.[32] But Alabama was
not yet restored to her constitutional relations to the Union.
Could this be done in time to add her two Senators to the conspiracy? The Supreme Court had the McCardle case before it.
Here was the weapon with which the whole putrid plan of reconstruction could be struck down. The Supreme Court was examining this weapon. Would it dare to use it?

LXVIII

ALTA VELA

BETWEEN the 13th and the 23rd of March the President's counsel were busily engaged in the preparation of his answer. But there was one of them who was pressing his enthusiasm and all of his large talents into other channels. He was using these precious days in planning how to take advantage of the embarrassments of his client.

Off the coast of Haiti there lay a guano island, Alta Vela. American citizens in 1859 took possession in the name of the United States. The Dominican Republic later seized it. Two citizens of the United States, Patterson and Murginendo, claimed rights there and had engaged Jeremiah Black to look out for them. He now demanded the dispatch of an armed vessel to safeguard American interests. Seward refused, relying on the precedent established by Black himself, when in 1857 as Buchanan's Attorney-General, he had rejected an American claim to Cayo Verde, an island in the Caribbean.[1]

Black criticized Seward's report with asperity and requested Johnson to review it, and five days after the impeachment articles were filed, began pressing the Alta Vela claim with an unwonted importunity. It was a good time, he thought, to take advantage of the necessities of one client in order to enrich another. What more subtle means of duress could he employ than the enlistment of the managers in furtherance of his demands upon the President! And so, four days before the commencement of the trial, he procured from Butler a written opinion favorable to the claim. But Black went further still, he obtained from Stevens, Logan and Bingham their written concurrence in Butler's opinion, and forwarded this document to the President.[2]

Here was indeed a club! What an opportunity for a trade!

J S Black

In exchange for a little war with Santo Domingo, perhaps all the charges would be dropped. For a part of the fee that Black hoped to win, Butler would have been willing to do anything. Andrew Johnson knew the scoundrel whose opinion Black had forwarded, but Black did not know Andrew Johnson!

On March 18th Black called on Welles and had "a strange talk about Alta Vela"; he reported Seward "as behaving badly." He inquired "in regard to the naval vessels—whether there was not one or more at St. Thomas which could be ordered to protect American interests," which, he said, Seward was abandoning. The blackmailing aspects of the interview made Welles indignant. "You will," remarked Black as he was leaving, "undoubtedly have an interview with the President in the course of the day on the subject," but he was told that nothing could be done in Seward's absence. "This, I saw," recorded Welles, "did not suit Black." [3] In the meantime the press had gotten hold of Black's defection. In his *Tribune* of March 17th, Horace Greeley gave currency to the rumor that there had been an "open rupture." [4]

There was indeed an open rupture. On the day of his interview with Welles, Black called upon the President and told him that all would be well with him in the impeachment trial if he would order a man-of-war to accompany Butler's private vessel to Alta Vela. Johnson told him that he thought he had no right to make such order, but requested Black to call the following day. In the meantime Johnson conferred with Seward. When Black returned he showed the President the written opinion signed by Butler, Logan, Stevens and Bingham. Johnson quietly observed that he had no constitutional right to do as Black desired, and reminded his caller of the opinion he had written as Attorney-General in Buchanan's Cabinet. There was further colloquy, and when the President peremptorily refused, Black indignantly replied: "I have pointed your way to acquittal and advised you to pursue it. You decline to do so. You will be convicted and removed from office. I prefer not to have you convicted on my hands, therefore I resign as one of your counsel from the impeachment case." At this Johnson arose and, looking

Black squarely in the face, answered: "You try to force me to do a dishonorable act contrary to law, as I see it, and against my conscience, and rather than do your bidding I'll suffer my right arm torn from its socket. Yes, quit as you have declared you will do. Just one word more: I regard you as a damned villain, and get out of my office or, damn you, I'll kick you out." On the following day Black wrote the President: "Let bygones be forgotten; I am willing to continue as one of your counsel." But Johnson replied to the bearer of the note: "Tell General Black he is out of the case and will stay out." [5]

Immediately the Radical journals seized on this retirement, and proclaimed that Black, seeing that the President's case was desperate, had withdrawn from it in disgust. [6] No lie was too base for the Radicals or their spokesmen! From day to day Greeley continued pouring in his poison. "It seems to be agreed," he wrote in his editorial of March 20th, "that the President proposes meeting the charges of the Impeachment Committee by procrastination." [7]

Over in the Supreme Court there lay before the judges the undecided record in the McCardle case. Procrastination? Would these guardians of the Constitution postpone their decision until after they were stripped of jurisdiction? They still had the opportunity to strike down the Reconstruction laws—the opportunity and the duty! Would they be equal to them?

LXIX

THE TRIAL PROCEEDS

ON Monday, March 23rd, the trial proceeded. Long before one o'clock, the scheduled hour, the New York *Tribune* was in the hands of the Senators. "The object of impeachment," Horace Greeley wrote that morning, "is not so much the punishment of an individual as the welfare of the country. . . . As a matter of political necessity and statesmanship—for this after all is the highest reason which should influence Congress—the laws relative to Reconstruction and all collateral subjects have got to be fully, faithfully and fearlessly executed, and this cannot be done so long as Congress allows Andrew Johnson to remain in power." [1]

Long before the appointed hour, the Senate galleries were filled. The daughters of Chief Justice Chase again were there, there also were the wives of Benjamin F. Butler, Jeremiah Black and Benjamin F. Wade. Senator Chandler's daughter and his wife sat among the other interested spectators, as did also the wives and daughters of the diplomats. [2] At one o'clock the court came to order with the usual ceremonies. From the counsel table of the President, Black, of course, was absent and in his place sat William S. Groesbeck of Ohio, an able lawyer, a former Representative in Congress and a supporter of the Johnson policies at the Philadelphia Convention. [3] Evarts was also present—for the first time. [4]

The President's answer was read. [5] It recited the entire history of Stanton's suspension and removal. It denied any violation of the Constitution or the laws, or the commission of any high crime or misdemeanor. It cited the Act of 1795 as the authority for Grant's appointment. Upon reinstatement the President was "compelled to take such steps as might . . . be lawful and necessary to raise for a judicial decision the questions affecting

615

the lawful right" of Stanton to resume the office, "and to this end," he had, on February 21st, appointed Thomas.[6]

The President denied that he had told General Emory to disobey any law, and asserted that in his conversation with him he had done no more than to express to Emory "the same opinion which he had expressed to the House of Representatives."[7] As to his speeches, the accounts of them annexed to the articles were not accurate. The speeches which he had delivered were made "in the exercise of that freedom of speech which belongs to him as a citizen of the United States."[8] Furthermore, "in his office of President," he not only had the right but was "held to the high duty of forming and on fit occasions expressing opinions of and concerning the legislation of Congress, proposed or completed in respect of its wisdom, expediency, justice, worthiness, objects, purposes, and public and political motives and tendencies," and he had exercised that right and obeyed that duty, and had done nothing "indecent or unbecoming in the Chief Magistrate or . . . brought the high office of President of the United States into contempt, ridicule or disgrace."[9]

After the reading of the answer ensued another long and spirited debate. Evarts asked for thirty days in which to prepare for trial. The managers bitterly opposed it. "What reasons are given in the application?" Manager Logan inquired, and then mendaciously answered his own question: "None more than that counsel shall have an opportunity to prepare themselves for oratorical displays before this august body."[10] No more consideration should be given this application, with the cheapest of demagogy, he continued, than should be accorded to the "poorest and humblest citizen in the land. . . . It is said that time would be given to an ordinary criminal to prepare his defense. . . . We as the managers . . . consider the President a criminal but not an ordinary one."[11] Logan boasted that the managers' reply would be ready on the following day;[12] why could not the counsel for the President be equally expeditious?

"The honorable managers," replied Evarts, "give us more professional credit than we are entitled to when they assume that our standard of our duty and our means and our needs for properly performing it, are necessarily to be measured by theirs." [13]

The President was asking, retorted Wilson, "for time that he may further imperil the nation, while he endeavors to make good his unlawful assumptions of power. . . ." [14] With dignity Stanbery answered that since March 13th "every moment has been occupied with the pleadings; not an instant lost, not a counsel absent. We have refused all other occupations; we have devoted ourselves exclusively to this day and night, and I am obliged to say two days sacred to other duty. . . . We have been so pressed with this duty that we have not had an opportunity of asking the President 'What witnesses will you have?' " [15]

And he continued: "Now mark, all this time, the advantage that the honorable managers have had over us. . . . Their articles were framed long ago. While we were engaged in preparing our answer, they have been . . . most industriously engaged in preparing the witnesses. Day after day witnesses have been called before them and testimony taken. We have had no such power; we have had no such opportunity . . . we have not had one moment's time to prepare for trial." [16]

At this point Bingham arose to accuse the President of "trifling with the great power which the people, for wise purposes, have placed in the hands of their representatives and their senators in Congress assembled. . . . If it be the judgment of the Senate that he has power thus to lay hands upon the Constitution of the country and rend it to tatters in the presence of its custodians, the sooner that the judgment is pronounced the better." [17]

The court finally adjourned without passing on the President's request. It reconvened the next day. The managers' reply was filed denying "each and every averment" in the President's answer, and realleging the high crimes and misdemeanors asserted in the articles. March 30th was now set as the adjourn day. The President had asked for thirty days and he had been given seven! [18]

"Sumner and certain Senators," wrote Welles, "do not conceal their readiness to proceed at once to judgment and condemnation without proof or testimony. In their unfitness and vindictive partisanship and hate, they would not award the President rights or privileges granted criminals for the court of errors or give him time for preparation. They are really unwilling to allow him to make defense. . . . The Constitution-breakers are trying the Constitution-defender; the law-breakers are passing condemnation on the law-supporter; the conspirators are sitting in judgment on the man who would not enter into their conspiracy, who was and is faithful to his oath, his country, the Union, and the Constitution. What a spectacle! And if successful what a blow to free government! What a commentary on popular intelligence and public virtue." [19]

Three days before the court was to reconvene, every member of the Cabinet considered conviction a foregone conclusion. "The Senate," our diarist recorded, "seems debauched, debased, demoralized, without independence, sense of right or moral courage. It is to all intents and purposes a revolutionary body subject to the dictation of Sumner, who is imperious, and Chandler, who is unprincipled—both are disliked and hated by a considerable portion of the Republicans, who nevertheless bow submissive to the violent extremists.[20]

"I cannot come to the conclusion," he continued, "that the Senate, feeble and timid as it is, will convict the President . . . yet I have no confidence whatever in the fairness or justice of that body. There is a party necessity to obtain possession of the executive in order to put a Radical in the office of President next year. Fraud and force will be resorted to if necessary to accomplish this end. Hence impeachment is a necessity. . . . It is like slaughtering, shooting down, the faithful sentinel because of his fidelity in standing to his post." [21]

LXX

THE SUPREME COURT SURRENDERS

THE Supreme Court had not yet decided the McCardle case! The bill depriving it of jurisdiction would become a law on March 25th unless Johnson vetoed it. If it became a law, the constitutionality of the Reconstruction Acts could not be determined until long after their shameless purposes had been accomplished. Andrew Johnson was on trial. Would he in these circumstances dare to act again? Another veto now would add live fuel to the flames! He was on trial! Could he not now pause in his resistance to the conspirators? How many of our Presidents would thus have reasoned?

But in the midst of his ordeal, assailed by the scoundrel Butler, pilloried by Stevens, defamed by Boutwell, harassed by the most corrupt Congress that ever sat in Washington, slandered by a hostile press, Andrew Johnson did not forget that day at Kirkwood House when he had registered in High Heaven an oath that he would, to the best of his ability, "preserve, protect and defend the Constitution!" The Supreme Court had done nothing; perhaps if Johnson acted now the judges would take courage! And so, encompassed all about by his enemies as he was, he threw his gauntlet in their face! Back to the wall, he was still fighting! He returned their bill to Congress with his veto! What American has shown a finer courage?

On March 25th he sent his message and he minced no words. "The legislation proposed," he said, "establishes a precedent which, if followed, may eventually sweep away every check on arbitrary and unconstitutional legislation. Thus far during the existence of the government the Supreme Court of the United States has been viewed by the people as the true expounder of the Constitution, and in the most violent party conflicts its judg-

619

ments and decrees have always been sought and deferred to with confidence and respect. In public estimation it combines judicial wisdom and impartiality in a greater degree than any other authority known to the Constitution, and any act which may be construed into or mistaken for an attempt to prevent or evade its decision on a question which affects the liberty of the citizens and agitates the country cannot fail to be attended with unpropitious circumstances. It will be justly held by a large portion of the people as an admission of the unconstitutionality of the act on which its judgment may be forbidden or forestalled, and may interfere with that willing acquiescence in its provisions which is necessary for the harmonious and efficient execution of any law." [1]

It was a challenge to Congress to desist from its defiance of the Constitution. It was a challenge to the Supreme Court to stand up as the defender of the Fundamental Law. Johnson had spoken of the court as "the true expounder," he had justly praised its "wisdom and impartiality," he had said nothing of its courage. Was there anything on this score that could be said? It had had sixteen days in which to act and it had not acted. Instead it had sat by—careful to keep out of range—silent and afraid, while the artillery duel between the other two departments of the government was in progress!

Half-stunned by Johnson's bold defiance, Congress hesitated for two days and then repassed the bill, his veto notwithstanding.[2] The McCardle case could not now be decided! The unconstitutional Reconstruction laws were immune from attack until, as Grant later wrote, they could "serve their purpose." [3]

In one of the greatest crises of the country, the Supreme Court of the United States had quavered, faltered and failed! Andrew Johnson could carry on his struggle for the Constitution, unaided and alone!

But there were two judges who were not afraid! They dissented! One of these, Judge Grier, spread upon the records this indictment of his colleagues: "This case," he wrote, "was fully argued in the beginning of this month. It is a case which involves the liberty and rights, not only of the appellant but of millions of our fellow citizens. The country and the parties had a right to expect that it would receive the immediate and solemn attention of the court. By the postponement of this case we shall subject ourselves, whether justly or unjustly, to the imputation that we have evaded the performance of a duty imposed on us by the Constitution, and waited for Legislative interposition to supersede our action, and relieve us from responsibility. I am not willing to be a partaker of the eulogy or opprobrium that may follow. I can only say . . . I am ashamed that such opprobrium should be cast upon the court, and that it cannot be refuted." [4]

Gideon Welles was looking on with sheer disgust. "The Judges of the Supreme Court," he wrote, "have caved in, fallen through, in the McCardle case. Only Grier and Field have held out like men, patriots, judges of nerve and honest independence. These things look ominous and sadden me. I fear for my country when I see such abasement." [5]

LXXI

BUTLER OPENS FOR THE PROSECUTION

HORACE GREELEY in the columns of his *Tribune* was doing all he could to fan the flames. From his cornucopias of vituperation he poured forth an unending stream of low abuse upon the President. The day before the recommencement of the trial he excoriated those who had "seduced Andrew Johnson into treachery and violation of law," and praised with passionate pæans the impeachers. "The Republican party," he wrote in words that he was four years later more than to repudiate, "is to America what the Reformation was to Europe. It is the child of the Revolution of 1776. The pen which wrote the Declaration of Independence unconsciously recorded its triumph." [1] On the following morning the *Tribune* took prominent notice of the fact that Thaddeus Stevens was endorsing Grant for President and had announced Wade as his choice for the Vice-Presidency. [2]

On March the 30th the Senate galleries were crowded with the fashion of the Capital. The diplomats were there, the wives of many of the Senators, and there again, as steady patrons of the drama, were the daughters of the Chief Justice. Carl Schurz had come this day to see and hear. [3]

Long before 12:30, the appointed hour, the Senators were in their seats. The Chief Justice, looking the embodiment of learning, dignity and law, was ushered in. The sergeant-at-arms made proclamation. The President's counsel entered. The sergeant-at-arms announced the presence of the managers. The House of Representatives appear, once more walking two by two, and the court is now prepared to give attention to the opening address of the prosecution. All eyes were riveted on Butler. He was seated at the table facing the Senators and Representatives. The lithe figure of General Stanbery was erect and stiff.

622

(From a sketch by James E. Taylor.)

GEN. BENJAMIN F. BUTLER, DELIVERING THE OPENING SPEECH, AS ONE OF THE
MANAGERS OF IMPEACHMENT, AT THE IMPEACHMENT TRIAL, IN THE SENATE
CHAMBER, WASHINGTON, D. C., ON MONDAY, 30TH ULT.

Evarts was bending over a sheet of paper on which he wrote. Nelson and Curtis were making preparations to take notes, while Groesbeck inquiringly surveyed the scene before him. Manager Bingham ran nervous fingers through his sparse hair, and old Thaddeus Stevens, seemingly a little stronger, clasped his huge walking stick in his skeleton-like, almost transparent, hands. Upon the face of Manager Wilson was the usual air of gravity.[4]

And now Butler advances a few steps from the counsel table, bows first to the Chief Justice and then to the Senate, while in breathless silence the galleries, the Senators and Representatives are leaning forward in their seats. "Now for the first time in the history of the world," he begins, "has a nation brought before the highest tribunal its Chief Executive Magistrate for trial and possible deposition from office. In other times, and in other lands, it has been found that despotisms could only be tempered by assassination, and nations living under constitutional governments even have found no mode by which to rid themselves of a tyrannical, imbecile or faithless ruler, save by overturning the very foundation and framework of the government itself. . . . Our fathers, more wisely founding our government, have provided for such and all similar exigencies, a conservative, effectual and practical remedy by the constitutional provision that the 'President . . . shall be removed from office on impeachment for and conviction of treason, bribery or other high crimes and misdemeanors!' "[5]

Realizing that the articles contained no charge of treason or bribery, that the "high crimes and misdemeanors" charged were based on an erroneous construction of a statute that had been created as a trap—realizing also full well the diminutive stature of the "high crimes" set forth, this shyster lawyer, with the cunning he had learned as a disreputable practitioner of Massachusetts, was ready with expedients to bolster up his case.

There were many judges of the High Court hearing him who were ready to convict regardless of the law or evidence, perhaps there were enough. But Butler knew that there were some who would not violate their oaths to "do impartial justice."[6] If he could convince such men that when the Constitution declared that conviction must be based upon "treason, bribery or other high crimes or misdemeanors," it meant something else—if he could persuade them that the President could be deposed without proof of guilt, the task of destroying Lincoln's follower might be accomplished. With this end in view he set to work. He paraded his English history—learning which had come to him from the brief of his colleague, William Lawrence, [7] and thus fortified quoted copiously from the state trials of England.

"It may not be uninstructive to observe that the framers of the Constitution while engaged in their glorious . . . work," he continued, "had . . . their minds quickened on this very topic. In the previous year, only, Mr. Burke, from his place in the House of Commons in England, had preferred charges for impeachment against Warren Hastings, and three days before our convention sat he was impeached at the bar of the House of Lords for misbehavior in office as the ruler of a people whose numbers were counted by millions. The mails were then bringing across the Atlantic week by week the eloquent accusations of Burke and the gorgeous and burning denunciations of Sheridan, in behalf of the oppressed people of India, against one who had wielded over them more than regal power. May it not have been that the trial then in progress was the determining cause why the framers of the Constitution left the description of offenses, because of which the conduct of an officer might be inquired of, to be defined by the laws and usages of Parliament as found in the precedents of the mother country, with which our fathers were as familiar as we are with our own?" [8]

Even from his vicarious learning Butler must have known that it was exactly because of the founders' knowledge of the injustice that England in her state trials had inflicted, that they wrote into our Constitution a plain definition of impeachable offenses, and had declared that it was only for "treason, bribery or other high crimes or misdemeanors," that a President could be impeached and convicted. But such a definition was too narrow for Butler's purpose. "We define," he declared, ". . . an impeachable high crime or misdemeanor to be one in its nature or consequences subversive of some fundamental or essential principle of government, or highly prejudicial to the public interest, and this may consist of a violation of the Constitution, of law, of an official oath, or of duty by an act committed or omitted, or, without violating a positive law, by the abuse of discretionary powers from improper motives or for any improper purpose." [9]

Having thus to his own satisfaction written and laid down a new rule, a new Constitution, by which he wanted Andrew Johnson tried, he proceeded to the development of his second contention through the adoption of which he hoped to strip the President of his office. "One of the important questions," he exclaimed, "which meets us at the outset is: Is this proceeding a trial, as the term is understood, so far as it relates to the rights and duties of a court and jury upon an indictment for crime? Is it not rather more in the nature of an inquest of office?" [10]

He and his fellow managers since the beginning of the trial had been laying the groundwork for this contention. They had been careful to address the constitutional presiding officer of the court as "Mr. President," while "Mr. Chief Justice" was the form of address adopted by the counsel for the accused. Manager Bingham had thought it his duty to instruct the court, which he called "the Senate," that in this proceeding they were "a rule and a law to themselves." [11] When Butler opposed the President's application for time to prepare, he referred to the Senate as "the court," but asked pardon for thus describing it. [12]

Butler now admitted that "if this body here is a Court . . . many if not all the analogies of the procedures of courts must obtain." [13] It was for the express purpose of avoiding this result that he exclaimed: "We are in the presence of the Senate of the United States. . . . You are a law unto yourselves, bound only by the natural principles of equity and justice, and that *salus populi suprema est lex.*" [14] With such emphasis and gesticulation did he pronounce this that more than ever the attention of his audience was riveted upon him. [15]

Having thus to his own satisfaction established that two-thirds of the Senate could at any time depose a President for the sole reason that they did not want him longer in his office, Butler proceeded with the charges. This was indeed supererogation, if the Senators could remove without the necessity of formal accusation or the need of proof! But Butler wanted two strings to his bow; suppose the doubtful Senators should not be impressed by his contention that the High Court of Impeachment was no court at all! So he launched into a discussion of the articles, and sought to float his water-logged and leaky bark upon an ocean of abuse.

As to the first eight articles—those dealing with the removal of Stanton and appointment of Thomas—he declared that the only question was: "Does the respondent justify himself by the Constitution and laws?" [16] He ridiculed Johnson's contention that he had the power of removal without the acquiescence of the Senate. Has the President, he asked, this "more than kingly prerogative?" [17] If this contention were correct, admitted Butler, "then so far as the first eight articles are concerned—unless such corrupt purposes are shown as will of themselves make the exercise of the legal power a crime—the respondent must go, and ought to go quit and free." [18] "Therefore," he continued, "by these articles . . . the momentous question is raised . . . whether the presidential office itself (if it has the prerogatives and power claimed for it) ought in fact to exist as a part of the constitutional government of a free people, while by the last three articles the simple and less important inquiry is to be determined whether Andrew Johnson has so conducted himself that he ought longer to hold any constitutional office whatever. The latter sinks to merited insignificance compared with the grandeur of the former. If that is sustained, then a right and power hitherto unclaimed and unknown to the people of the country is engrafted on the Constitution . . . most dangerous in its tendencies and most tyrannical in its exercise. Whoever, therefore, votes 'not guilty' on these articles votes to enchain our free institutions and to prostrate them at the feet of any man who being President may choose to control them." [19]

He reviewed the legislative decision of the first Congress declaring that the power of removal was vested in the President alone. He reminded his hearers that in the Senate this result had been attained "by the casting vote of the elder Adams, the Vice-President." And then dramatically exclaimed: "Alas! most of our woes in this government have come from Vice-Presidents." [20]

He touched gingerly upon Senator Sherman's declaration accompanying the passage of the act, that it had been so drawn "that the government will not be embarrassed by an attempt by a Cabinet officer to hold on to his office despite the wish of the President." [21] He knew he was on dangerous ground. "Without stopping to deny the correctness of the general proposition," he declared, "there seems to be at least two patent answers to it. The respondent did not call Mr. Stanton into his council. The blow of the assassin did call the respondent to preside over a cabinet of which Mr. Stanton was then an honored member, beloved of its Chief; and if the respondent deserted the principles under which he was elected, betrayed his trust, and sought to return rebels, whom the valor of our armies had subdued, again into power, are not those reasons, not only why Mr. Stanton should not desert his post, but as a true patriot maintain it all the more firmly against this unlooked-for treachery?" [22]

This method was typical of the trickster. He evaded Sherman's authoritative declaration, and sought to cover the evasion by abuse. Stanton, he said, was not continuing in his position "of his own will alone, but at the behest of a majority of those who represent the people of this country. . . . To desert it now, therefore, would be to imitate the treachery of his accidental chief." [23]

Butler pronounced Johnson's plea that he had removed Stanton for the purpose of testing the constitutionality of the act "a subterfuge." [24] "If," he said, "the President had really desired solely to test the constitutionality of the law, instead of his defiant message to the Senate of the 21st of February, informing them of the removal . . . he would have said in substance: 'Gentlemen of the Senate, in order to test the constitutionality of the law . . . which I believe to be unconstitutional and void I have issued an order for the removal of E. M. Stanton. . . . I felt myself constrained to make this removal lest Mr. Stanton should answer the information in the nature of a *quo warranto,* which I intend the Attorney-General shall file at an early day, by saying that he holds the office of Secretary of War by the appointment and authority of Mr. Lincoln, which has never been revoked. . . .' Had the Senate received such a message, the representatives of the people might never have deemed it necessary to impeach the President. . . ." Of this in his summing up, Evarts later declared: "You as a court upon the honorable manager's own argument are reduced to the necessity of removing the President of the United States, not for the act, but for the form and style in which it was done. . . ." [25]

Butler concluded his discussion of the first eight articles by asking if Johnson's acquittal would not be an invitation "to any bold, bad, aspiring man to seize the liberties of the people which they had shown themselves incapable of maintaining or defending, and playing the rôle of a Cæsar or Napoleon here to establish a despotism, while this the last and greatest experiment of freedom . . . following the long line of buried republics, sinks to its tomb under the blows of usurped power from which free representative government shall arise to the light of a morn of resurrection never more, never more forever!" [26]

By the time he had concluded his discussion of the first eight articles, the Senators were both tired and sleepy,[27] but Butler launched into his elucidation of the three remaining accusations—articles which when contrasted with the first eight, on his admission sank to "merited insignificance." [28] Whatever significance they lacked, however, he determined to make up by calumny.

Upon the tenth and eleventh articles—the products of his own brain and that of Stevens—he bestowed all of his unusual capacity for defamation. "Andrew Johnson," he declared, "the private citizen, as I may reverently hope and trust he soon will be, has the full constitutional right to think and speak what he pleases, provided always he does not bring himself within the purview of the common-law offenses of being a common scold, which he may do (if a male person is ever liable to commit that crime), but the dignity of station, the proprieties of position, the courtesies of office, all of which are a part of the common law of the land, require the President of the United States to observe that gravity of deportment, that fitness of conduct, that appropriateness of demeanor, and those amenities of behavior which are a part of his high official functions.   He stands before the youth of the country the exemplar of all that is of worth in ambition, and all that is to be sought in aspiration . . . and when he disappoints all these . . . expectations and becomes the ribald, scurrilous blasphemer, bandying epithets and taunts with a jeering mob, shall he be heard to say that such conduct is not a high mis-demeanor in office?" [29]

Congress might bandy scurrilous epithets to its heart's content, might call him drunkard, traitor, murderer, and much else, but when Andrew Johnson was opposing the destruction of the Con-stitution and his own good name, he must at all times obey the "courtesies of office" in accordance with the standards his defamers might define!

Knowing full well that all that Johnson uttered in his speeches was the truth, the Radicals had not dared to charge that what he said was false, lest he be given opportunity to prove that every declaration he had made was true.   "The words," declared Butler, "are not alleged to be either false or defamatory, because it is not within the power of any man . . . to slander the Congress of the United States . . . so as to call on Congress to answer the truth of the accusation.   We do not go in, therefore, to any question of truth or falsity.   We rest upon the scandal of the scene.   We would as soon think, in the trial of an indictment against a termagant as a common scold, of summoning witnesses to prove that what she said was not true.   It is the noise and disturbance in the neighborhood that is the offense, and not a question of the provocation or irritation which causes the out-break." [30]

Butler then launched into a description of the scenes at Cleve-land and St. Louis.   He pictured the noisy crowds "of men and boys, washed and unwashed, drunk and sober, black and white," that had assembled in the streets, when the President spoke, but failed to say that the interruptions had been prearranged by the Radicals themselves. [31]   He stripped isolated phrases from their context and lampooned the accused until he tired of his own billingsgate. "I might follow this *ad nauseam*," he said, "I grant the President of the United States further upon this disgraceful scene the mercy of my silence." [32]

But Johnson's denunciations of Congress, declared Butler, "had a deeper meaning than mere expression of opinion." [33] They were the declarations of a usurper intent upon the seizure of the legislative power! Such vituperation was always the prelude to such seizures! "Two memorable examples in modern history," declared Butler, "will spring to the recollection of every man. Before Cromwell drove out by the bayonet the Parliament of England, he and his partisans had denounced it, derided it, decried it, and defamed it, and thus brought it into ridicule and contempt. He vilified it with the same name which it is a significant fact the partisans of Johnson, by a concerted cry, applied to the Congress of the United States when he commenced his memorable pilgrimage and crusade against it. It is a still more significant fact that the justification made by Cromwell and by Johnson, respectively, was precisely the same, to wit: that they were elected by part of the people only. When Cromwell finally entered the hall of Parliament to disperse its members, he attempted to cover the enormity of his usurpation by denouncing this man personally as a libertine, that as a drunkard, another as the betrayer of the liberties of the people. Johnson started out on precisely the same course, but forgetting the parallel, too early he proclaimed this patriot an assassin, that statesman a traitor; threatens to hang that man whom the people delight to honor and breathes out 'threatenings and slaughter' against this man whose services in the cause of freedom has made his name a household word wherever the language is spoken. There is, however, an appreciable difference between Cromwell and Johnson and there is a like difference in the results accomplished by each." [34]

On and on the tirade ran. There was no thrilling tale of India to unfold, no far-away oppressions of Allahabad, no extortions from the Princesses of Oude. The dazzling narrative of burnished gold and ivory was not there to point the declamation of this barroom Burke. But if not as dazzling, were the President's crimes less horrible than those of the Governor of India?

He had been guilty of "an indiscriminate pardon of all who 'came in unto him'!" He had "initiated of his own will a course of reconstruction of the rebel states!" [35]

Butler knew full well that the plan of reconstruction was not "initiated" by Johnson, but by Lincoln. He knew that Johnson had acted exactly as Lincoln would have done had he lived. Nearly a year before Butler had had a long talk with the Secretary of the Navy, who reminded him that Johnson's policy "had commenced with Mr. Lincoln," [36] and that Lincoln "had no intention of calling on Congress to assist in this matter." [37] Butler was not then certain of his position with the Radicals. In fact he was "dissatisfied." [38] He was feeling around to find the highest market for his talents. "These military despotisms over the states, I don't see, General, how you, if a democratic Republican, can sanction such measures," the Secretary had said. "I had nothing to do with them," replied Butler. "They were enacted before I took my seat." "But," said Welles, "you are identified with that party and those acts." "Begging your pardon," retorted Butler, "I do not indorse those acts nor approve them." And then, when he was told that this was welcome news, he asked: "Why does not the President test them? Why does he submit to such laws and attempt to carry them out? He declares them unconstitutional. If so they are no laws. Why does he obey them?" When the Cabinet member answered that the President was required to "see all laws faithfully executed," Butler impatiently interrupted: "But it is no law, the President says it is no law. He is one of the departments of the Government and must decide for himself. If, however, he wants to get a decision from the Court there is no difficulty." [39] He then proceeded to outline a method for the achievement of this end.

This was the same Butler who was now denouncing the President for doing what he had himself advised! But if all the "usurpation," the great wrongs of policy—for the evidence of which Butler said: "We rely upon common fame and current history as sufficient proof"—if all the acts denounced were "high crimes and misdemeanors," how came it that they were not contained with the charges? The great prosecutor saw the need for explanation when he said: "Upon the first reading of the articles of impeachment, the question might have arisen in the mind of some Senator, why are these acts only presented by the House when history informs us that others equally dangerous to the liberties of the people . . . are passed by in silence?" [40] Why, indeed! The true answer was that the House had twice refused to consider them a basis for impeachment. But Butler's answer was that these were "but the culmination of a series of wrongs, malfeasances and usurpations" that "need to be examined in the light of his precedent and concomitant acts to grasp their scope and design." [41]

Finally he brought his long declamation to a close: "The responsibility is with you; the safeguards of the Constitution against usurpation are in your hands; the interests and hopes of free institutions wait upon your verdict. The House of Representatives has done its duty. We have . . . brought the criminal to your bar and demand judgment at your hands for his so great crimes. Never again if Andrew Johnson go quit and free this day, can the people . . . by constitutional checks or guards stay the usurpations of executive power." [42]

Butler at last took his seat eminently satisfied with his effort. "The Managers will proceed with the evidence," declared the Chief Justice. [43] Wilson then arose to present the proofs. Johnson's oath of office, Lincoln's nomination of Stanton, dated January 13th, 1862, and Johnson's message concerning the removal, were all put in evidence. The message was a powerful document. Wilson knew that its reading would not help the prosecution, and so he said: "As this document is somewhat lengthy, I will not read it unless desired." "Read it if you please," said Stanbery quietly. [44] He was in the midst of this when the adjournment came.

LXXII

THE EVIDENCE FOR THE PROSECUTION

THE New York *Tribune* was overjoyed with Butler's opening. It was pleased especially by his assertion that what was taking place was not a trial but a mere inquest of office.[1] Enchanted by this Massachusetts oratory, from his barricaded War Department Stanton wrote the orator: "The world to all time is enriched by it. As an American citizen and as your friend, I rejoice at the mighty blow you struck against the great enemy of the nation."[2] But Gideon Welles recorded: "Though a Radical favorite, he is an unscrupulous and in every respect a bad man. The intelligent Radicals do not seem to be satisfied with his performance, while the Democrats do not feel that Butler has made much headway against the President."[3]

On the reconvening of the trial the following day, it soon developed that despite Butler's pyrotechnics, what the managers had to offer in the way of proof was dull. It consisted of formal documents, and the testimony concerning facts long since of common knowledge.[4]

The first witness was William McDonald. Yes, he had served the Senate resolution on the President,[5] J. W. Jones served it on Thomas at the masquerade ball.[6] Since the Tenure-of-Office Act the form of commission for appointment had omitted the words "during the pleasure of the President of the United States for the time being,"[7] testified Clerk Creecy of the Treasury Department. Next came Representative Van Horn. He narrated what had happened when Thomas demanded possession of the War Department.[8] On cross-examination Stanbery asked him if Thomas at that time was armed. Van Horn had noticed no arms, he said, "except what the Almighty had given him."[9]

Walter Burleigh, a delegate from the territory of Dakota, was the managers' next witness,—called to prove the threats of force employed by General Thomas at the masquerade ball. Stanbery objected. The Chief Justice declared that the evidence was competent. But the Radicals were beginning to entertain serious misgivings as to Chase. They had seen with what an even hand he had been balancing the scales of justice. And it was by no means their intention that justice should be done. And so, although the ruling was favorable to the managers, Senator Drake is on his feet taking "exception to the presiding officer deciding a point of this kind." [10] A long debate ensued. Could the House of Representatives, asked Butler, bring before the Senate a question of law "if the Chief Justice who is presiding chooses to stand between the Senate and the House and its prosecution?" [11]

If it were the right of the Chief Justice even preliminarily to decide the admissibility of evidence, Butler declared that it would be his duty "to ask leave to withdraw and take instruction from the House before we lay the rights of the House bound hand and foot at the feet of any man, however high or good or just he may be. . . . Let us look forward to the time which may come in the history of this nation when we get a Jeffries . . . as Chief Justice. . . . We have had a Johnson in the presidential chair; and we cannot tell who may get into the chair of the Chief Justice in the far future." [12] Manager Bingham observed that in England "the Lord Chancellor presiding is but a ministerial officer to keep order," and that such a rule ought here to apply. [13] A motion to retire for consultation was then put to a vote; it resulted in a tie. This offered the Chief Justice opportunity to assert a further prerogative of his position: the right to vote! "On this question," he said, "the yeas are 25 and the nays are 25. The Chief Justice votes in the affirmative. The Senate will retire for conference." It did retire. Thus far Wade had not voted, and now once more he was recorded as not voting. [14] Would he never cast his vote? Or would he wait until some vital question came,—say the conviction or acquittal of the President?

While the Senate was deliberating behind closed doors, the Representatives gathered upon the floor of the Senate busily discussing what had taken place. But before the expiration of the three hours during which the Senators conferred, the Representatives relapsed into a reading of the newspapers, the telling of stories and the cracking of jokes. The galleries were emptied, and the restaurants and adjoining saloons did a thriving trade.[15]

Finally the Senators filed back to their places. They had decided that the Chief Justice "may rule all questions of evidence and incidental questions, which ruling shall stand as the judgment of the Senate," unless a formal vote upon the question were "submitted to the Senate for decision." The Chief Justice also, if he chose, might "in the first instance" submit any question "to a vote of the members of the Senate." [16] The Radicals had not prevailed in their effort to relegate Chase to the position of mere keeper of good order.

In Washington that night the decision of the High Court was the topic of conversation everywhere. "Very many Congressmen," wrote Greeley, in his *Tribune* of the next day, "are not well satisfied with the result." [17] And Gideon Welles observed: "The extreme Radicals are greatly incensed and have mutterings against Chase. There are growing differences between the Radical and Conservative Senators. The latter lack courage; the former lack sense." [18]

§

On the following day, Sumner took notice of Chase's casting vote, and offered a resolution that "such vote was without authority under the Constitution of the United States." The resolution was not adopted.[19] Sumner's effort to strip the Chief Justice of his right to vote resulted in a confirmation of that privilege.

Burleigh was on the stand again. What Thomas had said to him at the masked ball was still unanswered. Before it could be answered, Senator Frelinghuysen put this pertinent inquiry: "Do the managers intend to connect the conversation between the witness and General Thomas with the respondent?" [20] Another long argument ensued. "We have," declared Stanbery, "at length reached the domain of law; we are no longer to argue questions of mere form or modes of procedure, but have come at last to a distinct legal question, proper to be argued by lawyers and to be considered by lawyers. . . . General Thomas is not on trial; it is

. . . the President alone, and the testimony . . . must be . . . binding upon him. . . . The attempt here is by the declarations of General Thomas, to show with what intent the President issued those orders; not by producing him here to testify what the President told him. . . ." [21]

Butler declared the evidence admissible as the declaration of one co-conspirator against another. "I agree," answered Curtis, "that if they could show a conspiracy between the President and General Thomas to which these declarations relate, then the declarations of one of them would be evidence against the other." [22] But the managers, he said, "have offered no evidence here tending to prove any conspiracy at all." [23]

During the argument, Senator Reverdy Johnson asked the managers whether they intended to prove that before Thomas made his declaration the President had authorized him to use force, and if not, whether the President had knowledge of such declarations and approved them. [24] These questions traveled to the mark like the revolver shots of an expert marksman. The managers knew that the President had never authorized or approved of force, but they were afraid to say so! So Bingham's reply was: "We do not deem it our duty to make answer to so general a question." [25] The admissibility of the evidence was then put to a vote, in which Wade, as on every previous occasion, did not join. The question was, of course, decided against the President. Burleigh then related the silly declarations made by Thomas at the ball.

The trial was dragging. Intensely devoid of thrill the evidence thus far had been. There was little color indeed as yet, with which to paint the portrait of "the great criminal," of "Nero," or "Torquemada!"

The next witness, George Karsner of New Castle, Delaware, aided the managers with that time-honored device known and valued by every lawyer,—the weapon of humor. Many a desperate case has been won through the skillful employment of this instrument. It was unconscious and unintentional humor that Karsner was to furnish,—humor, however, that was to cast ridicule on Lorenzo Thomas and thereby indirectly upon the President who had appointed him.

Stanton had procured this witness for the managers.[26]   Back in Delaware, Karsner had known Thomas as a young West Point graduate.   Prompted by this acquaintance with the great, and by his native curiosity, he had come to Washington to witness the excitement.   On the 9th of March, at his own invitation he attended a levee at the White House.   In the East Room he saw General Thomas, and going up to him gave his name and reminded him that they had been acquainted years before.   The General said that he was "a Delaware boy," and asked Karsner what they "were doing in Delaware."   "General," he replied, fairly bursting with the responsibility of his intimacy with so great a personage, "the eyes of Delaware are on you."   The laughter following his answer was so loud that the Chief Justice was forced to call for order, although he was obliged to join in it himself.[27]

On cross-examination, Stanbery asked Karsner whom he had first favored with the report of this important conference.   After a considerable pause, in which Karsner seemed lost in deep meditation, he answered that his confidant was a man by the name of Smith.   Laughter again followed.   "What was the first name of that Mr. Smith?" was Stanbery's next question.   There was another long wait, and then after what was evidently a titanic cudgeling of memory, came this answer: "It was not John."[28] The court once more rocked with laughter, the galleries participated, and again the dignified Chief Justice was forced to join.[29] Finally Karsner volunteered that Mr. Smith's first name was William.[30]   "What part of Delaware was William Smith from?" inquired Stanbery with mock seriousness.   "He is from the banks of the Brandywine," answered Karsner.   "Which bank of the Brandywine does he live on?" pursued Stanbery, and there was more laughter.[31]   Before he had finished with this witness, Stanbery had turned the laughter upon him, and away from Thomas.

Thursday, April 2nd, the fourth day of the trial, opened under lowering skies.   The rain kept many away, but large numbers of the absentees had lost their taste for the drama. The "high crimes and misdemeanors" were making a pitiable showing. Even the enthusiasm of the Representatives apparently was paling; not more than a third of their number were now at hand.[32] The crowds waiting to hear the crimes of the "great criminal," were rewarded by dull documents and an unexciting narrative. The Barnum of this Greatest Show on Earth had given a feeble one-ring performance instead of what his garish posters had led the populace to expect. "The hollow farce has no friends," Gideon Welles observed.[33]

Karsner was recalled, but furnished no new amusement. Yes, after his interview with Thomas he had called on Stanton. Why? "Well, I had seen all the great men in Washington and I wished to see him." [34]

Representative Ferry followed Karsner to the stand. He had heard Thomas demand the surrender of the War Department. He told what everyone had long since tired of hearing.[35] After Ferry, General Emory was called as the managers' tenth witness. In his opening Butler dramatically had asked: "Is it not a high misdemeanor for the President to assume to instruct the officers of the army that the laws of Congress are not to be obeyed?" [36] Nothing was derived from Emory's testimony to justify the implications of that question. The President had merely repeated to Emory what he had previously said to Congress.[37] He did not tell him that the laws were not to be obeyed.

The managers now offered Johnson's letter of February 10th to Grant. It transmitted copies of the written statements of his Cabinet demonstrating Grant's bad faith.[38] Stanbery objected to the introduction of this letter unless the enclosures referred to in it were likewise put in evidence,[39] and this colloquy between Stanbery and the Chief Justice then ensued: "Mr. Chief Justice, is the question now before your honor or before the court?" The Chief Justice: "Before the body." Mr. Stanbery: "Before the body?" The Chief Justice: "Before the court." [40] Chase was standing firm for the proposition that this was no inquest of office, but a trial before a *court!*

After Stanbery's objection, Chase inquired of Manager Wilson if he would "consider himself entitled to read so much as bore upon his immediate object without reading the whole?" [41]   Yes, the honorable manager would consider himself precisely so entitled!   Upon a vote then taken Stanbery's objection was over-ruled. [42]

Lieutenant-Colonel Wallace was now sworn to contribute his conversation with the President on February 22nd, wherein the latter asked if there had been any recent movement of the troops or changes made within the garrison of Washington. [43]   Surely this did not prove that Johnson was either Nero or Torquemada, or even Cromwell!

Realizing what a trivial showing their evidence was making, the managers now sought to go outside the charges.   They called William Chandler, a former Assistant Secretary of the Treasury, and sought to show by him that the President on November 20th, 1867, had unlawfully appointed his friend and theretofore Private Secretary Edmund Cooper to the position Chandler had formerly held, and that this was done to defeat the Tenure-of-Office Act and other laws of Congress. [44]   But Stanbery objected that the proof should be confined to the articles of impeachment, not to charges which the managers might "choose to manufacture here." [45]   And although Butler bitterly complained that "it is one of the infelicities always of putting in a case that sharp, keen, ingenious counsel can insist at all steps on impaling you upon a point of evidence," [46] the proffered proof was too absurd even for that High Court of Impeachment to consider, and it was not received. [47]

Not discouraged by this rebuff, the managers now offered through Charles Tinker, a telegraph operator, to establish that on January 17th, 1867, Johnson, upon learning from the Governor of Alabama that the legislature there might reconsider its vote on the Fourteenth Amendment, had wired him: "What possible good can be obtained by reconsidering the constitutional amendment? I know of none in the present posture of affairs. . . ." [48]   This was more than three months before the Reconstruction Acts were passed!   Yet Butler contended "that herein we have evidence of the intent of the President to defeat the will of Congress in regard to the enforcement of the Reconstruction laws . . . the offense charged against him in the eleventh article. . . ." [49] The evidence was admitted! [50]

A motion to adjourn was made, and when first put to a vote resulted in a tie. For the second time the Chief Justice exerted his prerogative as a real member of the court and voted in the affirmative. [51] An adjournment was then taken to the next day, April 3rd. [52]

§

As the Radicals throughout the country watched the progress of the trial and noted what shoddy stuff composed the texture of the proof, the fear swept over them that perhaps, after all, an acquittal might result. And so the judges of the High Court began to be bombarded from without. Party assemblages, party conventions and state legislatures where the Radicals controlled, began passing resolutions for conviction and deluging the Senators with these dishonorable persuasions. [53] To attempt such methods on a petty jury sitting at the trial of a common horse thief would be a crime,—such efforts when the President of the United States was the defendant, were evidence of patriotic virtue!

Long before the judges of the High Court were in their seats on Friday, April 3rd, they had read this editorial appearing in the *Tribune* on that morning: "We have assurances from Washington that General Grant finds it not inconsistent with his duty as a soldier to announce it as his opinion that the only hope for the peace of the country is the success of the pending Impeachment trial. He feels that national security demands the removal of the President. . . . The loyal nation demands the President's removal." [54]

The managers now put in evidence Johnson's message of June 22nd, 1866, wherein he suggested "a doubt whether any amendment to the Constitution" ought to be proposed until the South was again represented in both Houses. [55] The Fourteenth Amendment itself was then introduced. [56] That it was for his opposition "to the will of Congress," not for "high crimes and misdemeanors," that the President was on trial, was thus emphasized again.

Stenographer Sheridan was now called. He had taken in shorthand the President's White House speech of August 18th, 1866.[57] Clephane, a stenographer of the Associated Press, followed Sheridan to the stand. He had reported the same speech. And then, crime of crimes,—before it was published the President's secretary, Col. Moore, had corrected a few verbal imperfections! But the Washington *Chronicle*, which under Forney's leadership was one of the bitterest enemies of Johnson, insisted upon printing it "with all its imperfections."[58] The parade of the stenographers continued. Francis Smith, the official stenographer of the House, brought up the rear.

The President's secretary, Col. Moore, was called. Yes, he had made certain verbal corrections of the speech as they appeared in the stenographer's reports.[59] The speech was then put in evidence,—the unrevised and the revised versions.[60]

The Cleveland *Leader* was a paper hostile to the policies of the President.[61] William Hudson, one of its editors, was now placed upon the stand to prove Johnson's Cleveland speech of September 3rd, 1866. He had lost his original notes; they were made in longhand.[62] He could not swear that his paper had reproduced the President's language "with absolute accuracy." He admitted that his article was the joint product of his own and that of another reporter.[63] "Under these circumstances, the Chief Justice thinks that that paper is inadmissible," declared Chase after Evarts had objected.[64] But by an overwhelming vote the Chief Justice was not sustained.

Through McEwen of the New York *World*, and Stark of the Cleveland *Herald*, the accounts of the speech appearing in those papers were put in evidence.[65] Some of Starks' report was "condensed." When Evarts asked him how he could determine what was condensed and what was not, he answered: "I was influenced somewhat by what I considered would be a little more spicy or entertaining to the reader."[66]

The march of the stenographers continued the next day. Walbridge of the Missouri *Democrat*, which despite its name was

Radical Republican, was called to prove his version of Johnson's speech from the Southern Hotel in St. Louis,[67] and Joseph Dear of the Chicago *Republican* gave his version.[68] Robert Chew, the chief clerk of the State Department, was then briefly interrogated, a few more documents were offered, and presently Butler was declaring "that the case on the part of the House of Representatives is substantially closed." [69] With difficulty the President's counsel secured an adjournment until the following Thursday in which to arrange their proofs and enable them to proceed with the defense.[70]

LXXIII

CURTIS OPENS FOR THE DEFENSE

WHEN the court reconvened on Thursday, April 9th, the managers had two more witnesses. Wood of Tuscaloosa, Alabama, made this thrilling contribution: In September, 1866, a few days after the President returned from his "Swing Around the Circle," Wood had called on him to present "testimonials for employment in the government service." [1] The conversation had drifted on to the political sentiments of the applicant. He stated that he was "a Union man, a loyal man, and in favor of the Administration," and that he had "confidence in Congress and the Chief Executive." The President had then asked him whether he "knew of any differences" between that same Chief Executive and Congress. Wood knew, he said, of "some differences on minor points," to which the President replied: "They are not minor points." [2] Surely this was proof that Andrew Johnson was a Nero or at least a Cromwell!

On cross-examination Stanbery brought out that Wood had first confided this great story to a man named Koppel. [3] "Who is Mr. Koppel?" inquired Butler on the re-direct examination. "Mr. Koppel," answered Wood, "is an acquaintance of mine on the avenue—a merchant." "What sort of merchandise, please?" pressed Butler, and Wood answered: "He is a manufacturer of garments,—a tailor." This produced the laughter Butler hoped for. [4]

The managers were about ready to cease firing, but there was still one high percussion shell within their caisson: Foster Blodgett of Georgia. On January 3rd, 1868, the President had suspended him from the postmastership of Augusta! [5] And now Butler is declaring: "We close here." [6]

The prosecution's case had been completed! Twenty-five witnesses had been called. From these the court had learned that Johnson had removed Stanton, appointed Thomas temporarily in his place, had had several conversations with army officers, and had made speeches nearly two years before, the truthfulness of which was not denied. This was the great case!

The galleries on this day again were full. A distinguished audience had come to hear the opening address of the President's counsel. In the diplomatic gallery Mr. Thornton, the British Minister, was noticed among the other plenipotentiaries. Also attracting attention was General Sherman, who had declined the office to which Stanton so assiduously was holding on. Near him sat old Thomas Ewing, his father-in-law, whose nomination for the same office still lay before the Senate.[7]

"Gentlemen of counsel for the President," declared the Chief Justice after the managers had rested, "you will proceed with the defense." [8] Mr. Curtis rose and bowed to the court. Before he even had begun, the contrast between him and Butler rivetted the attention of the audience. Here was a gentleman and a scholar, bred in the earlier traditions of America. A man of gentle courtesy and sensitive honor, calm, fair, judicial, he seemed to have brought into this tribunal some of the dignity of the Supreme Court of which he had been not only a distinguished, but a brave member. All ears were listening now to hear what the celebrated author of the great Dred Scott dissent would have to say in this cause, which like the Dred Scott case, held in it the combustible materials for a civil war. Even in the few seconds during which the Senators and the galleries were settling themselves to listen, his character and personality were making their impression. Clad in simple black that admirably set off his well-proportioned figure, his manner the incarnation of dignity, self-possession and repose, with massive head, eyes steady and serene, lips firm and calm, there he stood! Conscious of his own power, conscious of the justice of his case, conscious of his perfect mastery of the subject, there was withal about him the charm of modesty.[9]

"Mr. Chief Justice," he began, "I am here to speak to the Senate of the United States sitting in its judicial capacity as a court of impeachment, presided over by the Chief Justice . . . for the trial of the President. . . . Here party spirit, political schemes, foregone conclusions, outrageous biases can have no fit operation. The Constitution requires that here should be a 'trial,' and as in that trial the oath which each one of you has taken is to administer 'impartial justice according to the Constitution and the laws,' the only appeal which I can make in behalf of the President is an appeal to the conscience and the reason of each judge who sits before me. Upon the law and the facts, upon the judicial merits of the case, upon the duties incumbent on that high officer by virtue of his office, and his honest endeavor to discharge those duties the President rests his defense." [10]

Curtis then began to rain blow after blow at the very foundation of the prosecution's case. Was Stanton protected by the Tenure-of-Office Act? "Are those words 'during the term of the President' applicable to Mr. Stanton's case?" he asked. "That depends upon whether an expounder of this law judicially, who finds set down in it as a part of the descriptive words 'during the term of the President,' has any right to add 'and any other term for which he may afterward be elected.' " [11]

He launched into a history of the proviso, quoting especially from Senator Sherman, who had declared that the law had been "so framed as not to apply to the present President," [12] and then declared that the real charge against the President was that he had "willfully misconstrued the law." [13] But the fact was that the President had come "to the conclusion that the case of Mr. Stanton was not within this law. He came to that conclusion, not merely by an examination of this law himself, but by resorting to the advice which the Constitution and the laws of the country enable him to call for to assist him in coming to a correct conclusion. Having done so, are the Senate prepared to say that the conclusion he reached must have been a willful misconstruction,—so willful, so wrong that it can justly . . . be termed a high misdemeanor? . . . How is it possible for this body to convict the President . . . for construing a law as those who made it construed it at the time when it was made?" [14]

The President found, continued Curtis, that "it was impossible to allow Mr. Stanton to continue . . . one of his advisers, and to be responsible for his conduct . . . any longer. This was intimated to Mr. Stanton and it did not produce the effect, which according to the general judgment of well-informed men such intimations usually produce. Thereupon the President first suspended Mr. Stanton and reported that to the Senate. Certain proceedings took place which . . . resulted in the return of Mr. Stanton to the occupation by him of this office. Then it became necessary for the President to consider, first whether the Tenure-of-Office law applied to the case of Mr. Stanton; secondly, if it did apply whether the law itself was the law of the land, or was merely inoperative because it exceeded the constitutional power of the legislature." [15]

The assertion that it was the "civil and moral duty of all men to obey" the laws until judicially declared not binding was, declared Curtis, "too broad a statement. . . . If this is the measure of duty there never could be a judicial decision that a law is unconstitutional, inasmuch as it is only by disregarding a law that any question can be raised judicially under it. I submit . . . that not only is there no such rule of civil or moral duty, but that it may be and has been a high patriotic duty of a citizen to raise a question whether a law is within the Constitution of the country. Will any man question the patriotism or the propriety of John Hampden's act when he brought the question whether 'ship money' was within the Constitution of England before the courts of England?" [16]

And then Curtis brought his argument nearer home. "Let me ask any of you," he said, "if you were the trustee for the rights of third persons, and those rights of third persons, which they could not defend themselves by reason of sex or age, should be attacked by an unconstitutional law, should you not deem it your sacred duty to resist it and have the question tried? And if a private trustee may be subject to such a duty . . . how is it possible to maintain that he who is a trustee for the people of powers confided to him for their protection . . . may not . . . defend what has thus been confided to him?" [17]

But Curtis did not wish to be understood as occupying "extreme ground." The President, he said, could not "erect him-

B. R. Curtis

self into a judicial court and decide that the law is unconstitutional. . . . But when . . . a question arises whether a particular law has cut off a power confided to him by the people, through the Constitution . . . and he alone can cause a judicial decision to come between the two branches of the government to say which of them is right, and after due deliberation, with the advice of those who are his proper advisers, he settles down firmly upon the opinion that such is the character of the law, it remains to be decided by you whether there is any violation of his duty when he takes the needful steps to raise that question and have it peacefully decided." [18]

"Where shall the line be drawn?" asked Curtis. "Suppose a law should provide that the President of the United States should not make a treaty with England or with any other country. It would be a plain infraction of his constitutional power, and if an occasion arose when such a treaty was in his judgment expedient and necessary, it would be his duty to make it; and the fact that it should be declared to be a high misdemeanor if he made it would no more relieve him from the responsibility of acting through fear of that law than he would be relieved of that responsibility by a bribe not to act." [19]

With the thoroughness that had marked his opinions as one of the great judges of the Supreme Court, Curtis pressed on. He met, considered and demolished the arguments of the impeachers as a stone crusher grinds a jagged boulder to fine powder. The Radicals could not bear to hear their case destroyed, and so during his address most of the Senators, with a discourtesy which they enjoyed to practice even against the counsel of Andrew Johnson, arose and left their seats. [20] After he had spoken for about three hours, it was evident that he was fatigued. A motion to adjourn was made, but, by a vote of 35 to 2 it was not carried, [21] and so Andrew Johnson's advocate continued.

The President had not wished, if it could be avoided, to bring about a conflict with Congress over their Tenure-of-Office law. Indeed, said Curtis, he had been "anxious to avoid a collision with this law; he has not only on this occasion . . . taken this means to avoid it, but it seems that he has actually in some particulars obeyed the law; he has made changes in the commissions, . . . he has also in several cases—three collectors and one consul—sent into the Senate notice of suspension, notice that he had acted under this law. . . . So long as it is a question of administrative duty merely, he holds that he is bound to obey the law. It is only when the emergency arises, when the question is put to him so that he must answer it 'Can you carry on this department any longer in this way?' 'No.' 'Have you power to carry it on as the public service demands?' 'I believe I have.' Then comes the question how he shall act." [22] It was then that the President had acted as he had a right to act in an effort judicially to test the law. Having established this, Curtis returned to his alternative contention. "The law may be a constitutional law . . . still if Mr. Stanton is not within that law . . . the first article is entirely without foundation." [23]

But the first eight articles were all based upon the supposed illegality of the removal. If the first article must fall the next seven would fall with it!

Curtis was now thoroughly tired. With a courtesy all the more marked because of its notable absence in his adversaries, he presently declared: "I now, Mr. Chief Justice, have arrived at a point in my argument when, if it be within the pleasure of the Senate to allow me to suspend it, it will be a boon to me to do so. I am not accustomed to speak in so large a room and it is fatiguing to me. Still, I would not trespass at all upon the wishes of the Senate if they desire me to proceed further." [24] An adjournment was then taken to the following day.

Refreshed from his night's sleep, Curtis continued in the morning. If there were any in that court worthy of the name of lawyers, they could not have failed to be impressed. He now tore into the second article,—that charging the letter of authority to Lorenzo Thomas as a violation of the Constitution and the laws. He referred to the Act of 1795 empowering the President "in case of vacancy in the office of Secretary of . . . War . . . to authorize any person . . . to perform the duties" of that office "until a successor be appointed." [25] He showed that the Act of 1863 did not, as contended by the managers, work an implied repeal of the former law. "But whether it did or not, is it," he asked, "a crime to be on one side of that question and not on the other?" [26] He demonstrated that the letter of authority did not violate the Constitution, and that "it very early became apparent to those who administered the government that cases must occur to which neither of those modes dictated by the Constitution" (recess commissions and appointments by and with the advice and consent of the Senate), . . . "would be applicable, but which must be provided for. . . . And accordingly, beginning in 1792, there will be found a series of acts on this subject of filling vacancies by temporary or ad interim authority. . . ." [27]

These designations were not "appointments," they were not recess commissions, they provided merely "a mode of designating a particular person to perform temporarily the duties of some particular office, which otherwise, before the office can be filled in accordance with the Constitution, would remain unperformed." [28] Such temporary appointments were authorized either while the Senate was in session or in recess. "In accordance with this view, Senators," he continued, "has been the uniform and settled and frequent practice of the government from its very earliest date. . . ." [29]

Curtis now turned to the fourth, fifth, sixth and seventh articles. The fourth and sixth charged a conspiracy under the Act of July 31st, 1861,—a war measure defining conspiracies "to overthrow . . . by force the government of the United States." [30] The fourth and sixth alleged that the President and Thomas had conspired by force and threats to prevent Stanton from continuing as Secretary of War, and to get control of government property for themselves. [31] "Now it does seem to me," said Curtis, "that the attempt to wrest this law to any bearing whatsoever upon this prosecution is one of the extraordinary things which the case contains." [32]

"The President of the United States," he continued, "is of opinion that Mr. Stanton holds the office of Secretary for the Department of War at his pleasure. He thinks so, first, because he believes the case of Mr. Stanton is not provided for in the Tenure-of-Office Act, and no tenure of office is secured to him. He thinks so secondly, because he believes that it would be judicially decided, if the question could be raised, that a law depriving the President of the power of removing such an officer is not a constitutional law. He is of opinion that in this case, he cannot allow this officer to continue to act as his adviser . . . if he has lawful power to remove him; and under these circumstances he gives this order to General Thomas. . . ." [33] The ninth article accused the President of instructing General Emory to disobey a law in order to prevent Stanton from continuing in his office. Curtis showed that not only had this not been proved, but that it had been "disproved by the witness whom they have introduced to support it." [34]

Johnson's speeches were the basis of article ten. "I do not propose," said Curtis, "to vex the ear of the Senate with any precedents drawn from the middle ages. The framers of our Constitution . . . have drawn from them the lesson which I desire the Senate to receive, that these precedents are not fit to govern their conduct on this trial. . . . I propose, therefore, instead of a search through the precedents which were made in the times of the Plantaganets, the Tudors and the Stuarts . . . to come nearer home and see what provisions of the Constitution of the United States bear on this question and whether they are not sufficient to settle it." [35]

What was meant by the constitutional words "other high crimes and misdemeanors?" Under the rule of "noscitur a sociis," declared Curtis, it meant "High Crimes and Misdemeanors; so high that they belong in this company with treason and bribery." [36] But as there was "no law at all" which declared any speech of any kind a crime, and as there was "no such thing at the common law as an indictment for spoken words," a law could not be made to cover a past transaction, since the making of ex post facto laws was forbidden by the Constitution itself. [37] No Senator, he declared, had the right to say: "if I cannot find a law I will make one. . . . I am a law unto myself, by which law I shall govern this case." [38]

"Well, who are the grand jury in this case?" asked Curtis. "One of the parties spoken against. And who are the triers?

The other party spoken against. . . . The honorable House of Representatives sends its managers here to take notice of what? That the House of Representatives has erected itself into a school of manners, selecting from its ranks those gentlemen whom it deems most competent by precept and example to teach decorum of speech; and they desire the judgment of this body whether the President has . . . spoken improperly. . . ." [39]

And then Johnson's advocate thus closed his opening address: "It must be unnecessary for me to say anything concerning the importance of this case. . . . It must be apparent to every one . . . concerned in this trial, that this is and will be the most conspicuous instance, which ever has been or can ever be expected to be found, of American justice or American injustice, of that justice which Mr. Burke says is the great standing policy of all civilized states, or of that injustice which is sure to be discovered and which makes even the wise man mad, and which, in the fixed and immutable order of God's providence, is certain to return to plague its inventors." [40]

It was a great lawyer's argument, rather it was the argument of an unbiased judge. It was a plea to the mind rather than the emotions,—an effort to persuade the bench rather than the jury. What effect would it have upon the Senators?   In the galleries there was one at least among the women who was deeply moved, and who wrote that afternoon to Mrs. Curtis: "I have just returned from the Senate Chamber, filled with delight and admiration at Mr. Curtis' great argument.   For power and condensation of thought and for dignity and persuasiveness of delivery, it was indeed a glorious effort.   It is so very infrequently that women have such an opportunity that I cannot tell you how we have enjoyed it.   Even political antagonists confess the greatness of the argument; indeed, it seems to bring back the times when there were 'giants on the earth.' " [41]

To his half-uncle, George Ticknor, that evening Curtis himself wrote: "I concluded my argument today. . . . I had an attentive audience from the Senate, and from the crowded galleries and aisles.   How much permanent and useful effect I have produced, I have no means of judging.   Washington is full of rumors, most of which are false, and all of so doubtful authority that nothing can be predicated of them." [42]

What effect the argument had made upon one of the Senators, who was not even present, appeared on the following morning, when a colleague inquired of him if he had heard it. "No," was the reply, "I was absent; but I have read it, and I wish I hadn't." [43]

Curtis told Ticknor that he would come home when the evidence was closed. "The case," he shrewdly added, "will be effectively and actually settled *before* that time. There are from twenty-two to twenty-five Senators who began the trial with a fixed determination to convict. I have no reason to suppose any one of them is shaken or will be. About twelve to fifteen of the dominant party had not abandoned all sense of right, and given themselves over to party at any cost. What will become of them I know not, but the *result* is with them. The President himself preserves his calmness and to a great extent his equanimity. My respect for the moral qualities of the man is greatly enhanced by my knowledge of him. . . ." [44]

LXXIV

THE EVIDENCE FOR THE DEFENSE

AFTER Curtis concluded with his opening, General Thomas was called as the first witness for the defense.[1] The witness-stand is an exposed position always; to Lorenzo Thomas it was denuding. The old arm-chair General was clay in Butler's hands. Garrulous and vain, confused and uncertain, he possessed every qualification to make him one of the poorest witnesses who had ever testified. Despite Butler's interruptions, objections, arguments and comments, under the quiet and skillful handling of Stanbery, Thomas somehow got through the direct examination. He described his instructions from the President and his call on Stanton, the arrest which followed and his second interview in the War Department, the masquerade ball and all that happened there.[2] Somehow he made it plain, too, that at no time had the President authorized him to use force or threats.[3]

Punctuated by the frequent laughter of the Senators, who enjoyed the methods of the chief manager, Butler plunged into the cross-examination, handling Thomas as in former days he had dealt with the good housewives of Lowell. He forced Thomas to admit that when he told Wilkeson that he meant to call on Grant for a military force, it was mere "rhodomontade, boast and brag."[4] Thomas had dropped his voice. "How was that?" shouted Butler. "Speak as loud as you did when you began." "I suppose so," Thomas answered feebly.[5] So confused was Thomas, that on the following day he found it necessary to correct his testimony as to dates. Butler again assailed him. "Did anybody talk with you about your testimony since you left the stand?" he demanded. "Since I left the stand?" rejoined Thomas feebly. "Yes," sneered Butler. "Since yesterday?" "I saw the counsel for the President and told him I wished to make corrections," Thomas finally managed to get out.⁶ Butler used an old trick, the effort to convey that the witness had been improperly approached,—suborned. Shyster lawyers use questions of that kind today.

Finally the ordeal was over. Stanbery announced that he might later recall Thomas. "Call him at any time," observed Butler insolently, "we shall always be glad to see him." Amid the laughter that ensued, Thomas was heard meekly saying, "Thank you, sir." ⁷

And now General Sherman was sworn. Butler would, no doubt, keep a more civil tongue in his head in dealing with this officer. But perhaps he could prevent him from giving any testimony! That this was Butler's plan appeared early in the examination. Sherman had been called by the defense to rebut Butler's opening assertion that the President had attempted "to get control of the military force of the government by the seizing of the Department of War," and that this had been done in "pursuance of his general design, if it were possible, to overthrow the Congress of the United States." ⁸ What could be more proper than to prove by Sherman that in his talks with Johnson the opposite of such intent was demonstrated? Butler clearly saw that such evidence would cut into his case like a bright new axe into a rotten log. He determined therefore, if possible, to keep out this or any other evidence that would demonstrate the true character of what the President had done and said.

Sherman had not been on the stand five minutes when Butler showed his hand. The General was testifying that he had had several interviews with the President, and then Stanbery asked him: "In that interview (February 14th) what conversation took place between the President and you in regard to the removal of Mr. Stanton?" Butler objected, but Chase quietly observed: "The Chief Justice thinks the question admissible . . . but he will put the question to the Senate if any Senator desires it." ⁹ The yeas and nays were asked, but it was to be a long time before the question came finally to a vote.

The Senate now reverberated once again with the quotations from the state trials of England. The words of Erskine, Lord Kenyon and of the Lord Chief Justice of the King's bench, were becoming almost as familiar as the words of Andrew Johnson. Stanbery at last came down to the case in hand, declaring: "Now what we expect to prove is, that, so far from there being any intent on the part of the President to select a tool to take possession of the War Office, he asked first the General of the army, Grant, and when he failed him, who next? The next most honored soldier that we have, Sherman. . . . Now, we want to show his acts and declarations during that time to dissipate this idea that the President had any unlawful intent, to show that he was not seeking after a tool, but seeking for an honest, honorable high-minded soldier to do what? That which was unlawful? No; but to do that which the President thought belonged to him. We will show that . . . the President not only asked General Sherman to take this position, but told him then distinctly what his purpose was, and that was to put that office in such a situation as to drive Mr. Stanton into the courts of law." [10]

At this, with the minatory manners of the cheap police court tout, Butler broke in: "This is wholly unprofessional and improper." "I will judge of that," replied Stanbery quietly, and concluded with his argument. [11] And now Butler is on his feet; his first sentence a direct insult to the Chief Justice. The question put to Sherman was so palpably inadmissible, said Butler, as not to require "a word of argument,"—this despite . Chase's ruling that the question was a proper one. [12] And then with even bolder insolence Butler went on: "I labor, not under any weight of the argument that has just been put forward against me, but labor under the weight of the opinion of the presiding officer. . . ." [13]

Butler had repeatedly interrupted Stanbery during the latter's argument, but when now in the politest manner Stanbery asked "one moment for a correction," Butler replied: "I cannot spare a moment, sir." [14] There is nothing which the unscrupulous practitioner more enjoys than the defamation of an honorable member of the bar, and so frequently throughout his long harangue, Butler mendaciously referred to the "unprofessional act" of his opponent. [15] Evarts now replied: "This is a very peculiar case. Whenever evidence is sought to be made applicable

to it, it is a crime of the narrowest dimensions . . . it exists for
. . . its enormity . . . upon the delivery of a written paper by
the President to General Thomas, to be communicated to the
Secretary of War. . . . But when we come to the magnificence
of the accusation. . . ." Here Evarts reminded the court of
Butler's conveniently elastic definition of impeachable offenses.[16]
On Butler's theory anything was admissible for the prosecution,
while the defense was limited to the bare fact of the delivery of
the order of removal and the appointment of Thomas. "I apprehend," said Evarts, "that this learned court of lawyers and laymen
will not permit this 'fast and loose' game of limited crime for
purposes of proof and unlimited crime for purposes of accusation,
that they will not permit this enlargement and contraction, phrases
sometimes replaced by a more definite and shorter Saxon description." [17]

A twenty minute adjournment was taken. When the court
reconvened, the argument continued. Finally the question on the
admissibility of Sherman's conversations with the President was
put to a vote. By 28 to 23 they were decided inadmissible! No
shrift for Andrew Johnson! Butler had prevailed! Again and
again that afternoon, however, by framing their questions in different ways, the President's counsel sought to elicit from Sherman
that the President had not talked to him of force or the overthrow of Congress, but of the test in the Supreme Court of an
unconstitutional law. But each time on Butler's objection the
court ruled out the evidence. On one occasion Butler objected to
Stanbery's question as "outrageously leading," declaring that the
rule against such questions "has been relaxed in favor of very
young counsel." This cheap thrust at the stately and venerable
Stanbery evoked the laughter of the court.[18] In order to make
it appear that the President's counsel were in some way deliberately violating the rules of evidence, Butler referred to them as
"five gentlemen of the oldest men in the profession, to whom
this rule is well known." [19]

And now Stanbery is on his feet. "Mr. Chief Justice," he
said, "this is quite too serious a business that we are engaged in,
and the responsibility is too great, the issues are too important,

Wm. M. Evarts

to descend to the sort of controversy that would be introduced here. The gentleman says I am an old lawyer, long at the bar. I hope I never have disgraced the position. I hope I am not in the habit of making factious opposition before any court, high or low, especially not before the body that has treated us with so much courtesy." [20]

Again and again the President's counsel sought to get this evidence in, and as often as the attempt was made, they were voted down. Finally the long day ended and an adjournment until Monday, the 13th, was taken.[21]

§

In high crimes and misdemeanors, as in other crimes, criminal intent is the essential element. The importance of establishing the absence of this element was fully appreciated by the counsel for the President. And so when on Monday the 13th the High Court reconvened, they renewed again the struggle to put in Sherman's testimony.

Once more the Senate chamber echoed with the names that both American and British precedents had long made famous. The managers had achieved a rather sorry imitation of the Hastings trial, but the memory of that gorgeous spectacle was still before them. "There is one case in British history," declared Manager Williams, "which is familiar to all of us . . . a case made memorable, I suppose, mainly not by the peculiar interest which it involved, but by the fact that it was illustrated by some of the greatest men that England ever produced. It was not because Warren Hastings was the Governor General of Bengal . . . but because such men as Edmund Burke and Richard Brinsley Sheridan were among the managers." [22]

But what of the American Warren Hastings case? And what especially of the American Burkes and Sheridans? They at least thought well of their own work and they enjoyed the limelight. Williams spoke of the trial as "the drama" in which "the parts" had been distributed.[23] But the American company and the American production were a vast improvement, so he thought, upon the British!

"And now," he exclaimed, "in view of these precedents, I . . . ask how does the present case compare with them? Is it an ordinary one? Why, it dwarfs them all into absolute nothingness. There is nothing in the world's history that compares with this." One hundred per cent Americans were living even then, it seems! "It makes an epoch in history," continued Williams, "and therefore I may well say that you are making history today. . . . Senators, I feel myself the difficulty of realizing its magnitude. I know how hard it is for us, even, who are the actors in this great drama, to rise to the height of this great argument." [24] Yes, it was difficult!

The question now put to General Sherman was: "After the restoration of Mr. Stanton to office did you form an opinion whether the good of the service required a Secretary of War other than Mr. Stanton; and if so did you communicate that opinion to the President?" [25] The managers objected on the ground that it elicited an opinion rather than a fact. [26] But Stanbery replied: "It is not merely what opinion had you, General Sherman; but having formed that opinion, did you communicate it to the President? . . ." [27]

Stanton had had no communication with the President since the previous 12th of August. "How is the army to get along with that sort of thing?" asked Stanbery. "What has the Secretary of War become? One of two things is inevitable; he is running the War Department without any advice or consultation with the President or he is doing nothing. Ought that to be the position of the Secretary of War? The President could not get out of that difficulty. He might have got out of it perhaps by humbling himself before Mr. Stanton, by sending him a note of apology that he had ever suspended him. By humbling himself to his subordinate it might have been that Mr. Stanton would have forgiven him. Would you ask him to do that, Senators?" [28]

Stanbery made it plain that the President had been advised "by General Sherman himself, that the good of the service required that that difficulty should be ended . . . that General Sherman communicated also the opinion of General Grant to the very same point, and . . . we shall follow it up by the agreement of these two distinguished generals to go to Mr. Stanton and to tell him for the good of the service he ought to resign . . .; now when you are trying the President for his intentions . . . will you shut out from him the advice that he received from these two distinguished officers, and will you allow the managers . . . to say . . . that he acted for the very purpose of removing a faithful officer and getting in his place some tool or slave of his?" [29]

Yes, that was exactly what the Senators,—the judges of the High Court—would say! And for good measure they would allow the master scoundrel of the managers to add insult and abuse. "Now," answered Butler, "it is said 'We must show that or we cannot defend the President.' Well, if you cannot defend the President without another breach of the law for his breach of the law, I do not see any necessity for his being defended. You are breaking the law to defend him, because you are putting in testimony that has no relevancy . . . under the law." [30] The question was put to a vote; it was not allowed. The same proof was again elicited in different form and again it was ruled out. No shrift for Andrew Johnson!

§

The defense now called clerk Meigs to tell of the arrest and the discharge of General Thomas. [31] The formal papers in the case were admitted over Butler's violent protest. [32] While Meigs was yet on the stand, Senator Reverdy Johnson of Maryland gained the floor, saying: "Mr. Chief Justice, I desire to put a question to General Sherman. He is in the room, I believe." [33]

Sherman was recalled, and this question was now asked: "When the President tendered to you the office of Secretary of War ad interim on the 27th of January, 1868, and on the 31st of the same month and year, did he, *at the very time of making such tender*, state to you what his purpose in so doing was?" [34]

To the consternation of the managers, by a vote of 26 to 22, the question was allowed, [35] and Sherman then testified that in his interview of the 31st the President had made plain his desire to test the constitutionality of the Tenure-of-Office Act, and that at no time did he convey any suggestion that he contemplated force! [36] But Sherman was not allowed to tell that he had advised the President to remove Stanton, nor of the offer made by him and Grant personally to urge Stanton to resign.

Welles was watching anxiously and that evening wrote: "Butler gives rules to the Senatorial judges and tells them how to vote, and they obey. Unfortunately they are not legally wise, nor honest, nor candid. They are less safe as triers than an ordinary intelligent jury. The latter would give heed to the clear mind of an intelligent and impartial judge. These Senators are judge and jury in a case of their own, prejudiced, self-consequential, and incompetent. Such a tribunal, it appears to me, is to be treated peculiarly, and not upon trust. They must have it made to appear to them that they are in the wrong. Earnest, vigorous, unwearied efforts are wanted. Scholarly, refined legal ability are not alone sufficient with men who were tested before trial was ordered and who meet in secret caucus daily." [37]

On the following day Stanbery was ill and the court, therefore, adjourned till Wednesday. To those who watched, both friend and foe, it seemed that the tide was turning. The tenuous character both of the charges and the evidence offered to support them, was impressing itself upon the public mind. Then too, no doubt, the persistent and usually successful efforts of Butler and his coadjutors to rule out all proof that tended to establish with what good faith the President had acted, was making an unfavorable impression. "Office seekers and politicians," declared the New York *Tribune* on April 14th, "are speculating tonight upon the probabilities of Mr. Johnson's acquittal." [38]

That same evening Welles was writing: "It appears to me impeachment has lost ground in public estimation during the last few days; still I have no confidence in the partisan Senate. There are men there of ability sufficient to know what is right, to act independently, and who should have enough honesty and moral courage to do right. I trust they will, yet I do not rely on them in this excitement. As for the crowd of little creatures who are out of place in the Senate, and who ought never to have been there,—like Chandler, Thayer, Morgan, Nye, Conness, Cameron, and others, who are neither statesmen, enlightened legislators, nor possessed of legal minds—no one expects from them justice or any approach to it. But the question is whether the abler minds will be wholly carried away by chief conspirators who hold in their hands the great amount of partisan small trash." [39]

§

Wednesday's session was largely occupied by the introduction of documentary evidence: Johnson's nomination of Thomas Ewing, the President's message of February 24th in reply to the Senate's resolution declaring that the President had no power to remove Stanton or to appoint anyone ad interim in his place, was also offered.[40]

In this message Johnson had once more argued both that the Tenure-of-Office Act was unconstitutional and that it did not cover Stanton's case. Any doubts upon this score he had said, should be settled by "decision of the Supreme Court. My order of suspension in August last was intended to place the case in such a position as would make a resort to a judicial decision both necessary and proper. My understanding and wishes, however, under that order of suspension were frustrated, and the late order for Mr. Stanton's removal was a further step toward the accomplishment of that purpose. I repeat that my own convictions as to the true construction of the law and as to its constitutionality were well settled and were sustained by every member of my Cabinet, including Mr. Stanton himself." [41]

"Although I have been advised by every member of my Cabinet that the entire Tenure-of-Office Act is unconstitutional and therefore void, and although I have expressly concurred in that opinion in the veto message . . . I have refrained from making any removal of any officer contrary to the provisions of the law, and have only exercised that power in the case of Mr. Stanton, which in my judgment did not come within its provisions. I have endeavored to proceed with the greatest circumspection, and have acted only in an extreme and exceptional case. . . . I have appealed, or sought to appeal, to that final arbiter fixed by the Constitution for the determination of all such questions. To this course I have been impelled by the solemn obligations which rest upon me to sustain inviolate the powers of the high office committed to my hands. . . . ."[42] If . . . I had been fully advised when I removed Mr. Stanton that in thus defending the trust committed to my hands my own removal was sure to follow, I could not have hesitated."[43]

Butler objected to the introduction of this message, declaring that the President's counsel would not "dare" to say that it was admissible. But Evarts replied: "We have not been in the habit of considering the measure for the conduct of forensic disputations to be a question of daring. . . . The measure of duty of counsel to the law and the facts is the measure we shall strive to obey, and not the measure of daring, if for no other reason, for this, that on the rule of law and fact and evidence we might perhaps expect sometimes a superiority, but on the measure of daring, never."[44]

In the course of the argument Butler observed: "If they will fetch the Cabinet here and let us cross-examine them, and find out what they meant when they gave him any advice, and how they came to give it to him, and under what circumstances they gave it to him, we shall have a different reply to make to that."[45] Butler never would have said this had he known that this was precisely what the defense intended doing!

Despite all that the lawyers for the President could do, his message of February 24th was not received in evidence.[46] The remainder of the day was largely occupied with the introduction of statistical matter: charts showing removals made by all the previous Presidents, and the ad interim appointments made both while the Senate was in session and in recess.[47] Even here Butler found opportunity to prove himself a cad. When Buchanan's message showing how he had appointed Holt Secretary of War ad interim in place of Floyd, was offered, Butler objected. "But there is a still further objection," he went on, "and that is, that most of the message is composed of the statements of Mr. J. S. Black—Jeremiah S. Black—who refused to have anything to do with this case anyhow." This sly reference to Black's withdrawal evoked the laughter of the court.[48] None better than Butler knew why Black had ceased to act!

8

On the following day, the lawyers for Lorenzo Thomas,—Cox and Merrick—under Butler's constant protest and objection, told of their attempts to test the law.[49] While Cox was on the stand Butler found another occasion to prove himself a blackguard. Cox was telling of his interview with the President at five o'clock in the afternoon of February 22nd. "Stop a moment," interrupted Butler. "I object to the statement of the President at five o'clock in the afternoon."[50] Once more the High Court was convulsed with laughter.[51] By five o'clock in the afternoon the President, of course, would be too drunk to make any statement! The court enjoyed Butler's innuendo.

Perrin was then called to give his interview with the President on February 21st, in the presence of Representative Selye of New York. The defense offered to establish that Johnson had understood from what Thomas told him on that day, that the latter was then already in possession of the War Department, and that the President had said: "It is only a temporary arrangement; I shall send in to the Senate at once a good name for the office."[52]

Butler objected. "Now I trust," he said, "that is not evidence because it is said to a member of Congress. . . . I do not think it would make it more or less evidence because it should have been made to a woman; I was only foreseeing what might come—quite as probable as this—that some of the lady friends—I beg pardon—the woman friends of the President might have gone to the White House on that day and he might have told them what his purpose was."[53] The evidence was not admitted.[54] The High Court like Butler's humor!

The defense now asked for an adjournment until the next day; they were handicapped by Stanbery's illness. To Butler, this afforded opportunity for another speech. He saw his case was slipping. He could not expect to remove a President on anything he had proved, but another flood of defamation might in the minds of wavering Senators take the place of evidence. Untrammelled by any of the restraints of common decency, he now reached down into the gutter and came up with both hands filled with steaming muck, prepared to hurl it at the President of the United States. "Why should not this President be called upon now to go on?" he shouted. "Now the whole legislation of this country is stopping . . . the whole country waits upon us and our action, and it is not time now for the exhibitions of courtesy . . . this is the closing up of a war wherein three hundred thousand men laid down their lives to save the country . . . and shall the country wait now in its march to safety because of the sickness of one man? More than that, I have here in my hand testimony of what is going on this day and this hour in the South." [55]

Evarts and Curtis had both sprung to their feet objecting. Could it be that in defiance of every known rule Butler would speak of what had not been charged, and therefore could not be proven? That was exactly what this shyster lawyer was about to do. "The relevancy of it is this," Butler insolently replied, "that while we are waiting for the Attorney-General to get well . . . numbers of our fellow citizens are being murdered day by day. There is not a man here who does not know that the moment justice is done on this great criminal these murders will cease." [56]

Curtis rose in his place, but Butler had not yet thought of finishing his tirade. "I cannot be interrupted," he said. "This is the great fact which stands before us and we are asked 'Why stand ye here idle?' by every true man in the country. Mr. Chief Justice, in Alabama your register of bankruptcy, appointed by yourself . . . is driven today from his duties and his home by the Ku-Klux Klan . . . and shall we here delay this trial any longer . . . because of a question of courtesy?" [57] Courtesy? Who would dream of asking it from Butler! "One McGinnis," he went on, "now takes charge of the sale of your gold by order of the Executive as a broker, and we are to wait day by day while he puts into his pocket from the treasury of the country money by the thousands. . . . I say, for the safety of the finances of the people, for the safety of the true and loyal men, black and white, in the South who have perilled their lives for four years; yea five years; yea six years; yea seven years; for the good of the country, for all that is dear to any man and patriot, I pray let this trial proceed. . . . If the President of the United States goes free and acquit then the whole country must deal with that state of facts as it arises; but if he, as the House of Representatives instructs me, and, as I believe, is guilty; if on his head rests the responsibility, if from his policy, from his obstruction of the peace of the country, all this corruption and all these murders come, in the name of Heaven let us have an end of them and see to it that we can sit at least four hours a day to attend to this, the great business of the people." [58]

Heedless of all decency, Butler continued pouring forth his brackish torrent of abuse. "I open no mail that I do not take up the account from the South of some murder, or worse, of some friend of the country. I want these' things to stop. . . . I say nothing of the threats of assassination made every hour and upon every occasion, even when objection to testimony is made by the managers. I say nothing of the threats made against the lives of the great officers of the Senate and against the managers . . . all these threats . . . will go away when this man goes out of the White House." [59]

The harangue was a disgrace to the High Court, it was an insult to the United States, and yet that High Court heard it with complacency! The Senators not only failed to call Butler to order, but listened with satisfaction to his scoundrel attempt to sway them by false and unfounded accusations that the Repre sentatives in the moments of their wildest passion had never dreamed of including in their articles of impeachment. [60]

The President's counsel heard Butler with disgust. But for the great cause they represented, it was debasing to them to be connected with a case in which so low a person was engaged. "I have never heard such a harangue before in a court of justice," said Evarts, "but I cannot say that I may not hear it again in this court." [61] An adjournment until the next day was now finally taken.

On the following day, Friday, April 17th, the defense went forward with its witnesses. Armstrong, one of the editors of the Cleveland *Plaindealer*, told of the interruptions of the crowd that had heard the President at Cleveland in the summer of 1866. [62] Barton Able made it clear how in St. Louis on the same tour, the

President at first declined and then with the greatest reluctance finally consented to appear.[63] George Knapp, a proprietor of the Missouri *Republican*, corroborated Able. He had heard the President. The report of the speech which his paper published he had considered so "imperfect" that he had caused a corrected version to be printed on the following day.[64] The point of all this was that the newspaper accounts of Johnson's speeches had done him anything but justice.

But had Johnson been accurately reported, the printed page would not have revealed the true character of what he said. An intelligent and unbiased listener and observer, who heard many of the President's extemporaneous addresses, later wrote: "Mr. Johnson's manner in delivering public speeches could not be translated into newspaper language. . . . He had a calm, assured way of talking which gave the most startling remarks authority. His bearing was quiet and dignified, his voice low and sympathetic. He had one of the best voices for public speaking that I have ever heard. It was singularly penetrating; he could make it carry to the edge of the largest gathering without effort. Yet it was always a pleasant voice. I have been startled myself to read the same speech in the paper that I had heard the day before. One would think, from what was written, that a violent demagogue was brandishing his arms and shrieking at the top of his lungs. Mr. Johnson was an orator; half of what was said was in the personal relations between the audience and himself; and, being an orator, he was often swayed by the emotion of the crowd. Had he been sympathetically reported, the country would have had a different impression of him." [65]

It was the true impression of the President's addresses that his counsel were now endeavoring to portray. When they had concluded with the newspaper editors and reporters, they called Frederick Seward, the son of the Secretary of State. He presented a long list of consular officers temporarily appointed by other Presidents to fill vacancies even while the Senate was in session.[66] And now Gideon Welles, who had long been waiting for his opportunity, was called. He told briefly of his talk with the President about General Emory,[67] and how at the Cabinet meet-

ing of February 21st the President had evidenced his belief that
Stanton had surrendered when Thomas made his first demand.[68]

Evarts then offered to establish through Welles that before the
Tenure-of-Office Bill became a law and while it was before the
Cabinet, he was assured by them that it was unconstitutional, and
that the duty of preparing a veto message "was devolved on Mr.
Seward and Mr. Stanton."[69] Butler objected, and then obviously
seeking to classify Andrew Johnson with Jefferson Davis, addressing the Chief Justice, he continued: "Let us look at it in the
light of another great criminal, whom you, sir, may be called
upon to try some time or other. I have no doubt he had a cabinet
around him by whose advice he can defend himself from most
of the treasons which he committed."[70] Evarts explained that
the purpose of the proffered proof was to show "what care, what
deliberation, what advice attended the steps of the President in
the stress in which he was placed. . . ."[71] In the midst of the
argument an adjournment was taken to the following day.[72]

On Saturday, April 18th, the trial continued as did the argument on the offer of proof made the day before. Curtis now
explained that this evidence was admissible as showing that the
President "honestly believed that this was an unconstitutional
law" which if he obeyed would force him to surrender "one of
the powers which he believed were conferred upon him by the
Constitution." Further, the evidence would establish, Curtis said,
that the President had "resorted to the best means within his
reach to form a safe opinion upon this subject."[73]

Finally, Chase observed that since from the nature of the
charges the intent with which the removal of Stanton had been
made, was the subject to which much of the evidence on both
sides had been directed, "the Chief Justice conceives that this
testimony is admissible for the purpose of showing the intent
with which the President has acted in this transaction."[74] But
Chase once more was destined to a rebuff. By 20 to 29 the evidence was declared inadmissible![75]

Undaunted, Evarts offered now to establish that while the
Tenure-of-Office Bill was before the President for approval, the
question whether Stanton and the other Secretaries appointed by

Lincoln were covered by the act, was canvassed, and the opinion of the Cabinet was expressed that they were not.[76] Butler again objected,[77] and Evarts declared that "the President had a perfect right to suppose that Mr. Stanton would not attempt to oppose him," that Stanton was not protected by it and had so advised the President, and that, therefore, Johnson had the right to expect that Stanton "would yield to this unimpeded constitutional power."[78] Once more the Chief Justice declared the evidence admissible, and once again he was overruled by the High Court.[79]

But Evarts was still undefeated. He offered now to prove that at various meetings of the Cabinet between the passage of the Tenure-of-Office Bill and until February 21st, 1868, "it was considered by the President and Cabinet that a proper regard for the public service made it desirable that upon some proper case a judicial determination on the constitutionality of the law should be obtained."[80] The High Court rejected this evidence also![81] The defense now made one further attempt. They offered to establish that in all the President's "deliberation for his official conduct force never entered into contemplation." This likewise was rejected![82]

Ready to corroborate the testimony of Welles,—had they been allowed to give it—the defense had in attendance the remaining members of the Cabinet: Seward, McCulloch, Browning and Randall. Stanton, too, they would have called had Welles been allowed to give his evidence.[83]

Malice sometimes defeats itself; conspiracies have been known to fall of their own weight. The Radicals in defying the opinion of the Chief Justice, in thwarting justice itself, thought no doubt that they had made a sharp and clever move. Little did they realize the real effect of their maneuvers. To Gerrit Smith on the day following the rejection of Welles' testimony, the Chief Justice wrote: "I was greatly disappointed and pained . . . when the Senate yesterday excluded the evidence of the members of the Cabinet as to their consultations and decisions (in one of which Mr. Stanton took a concurring part), and the advice given to the President in pursuance thereof. I could conceive of no evidence more proper to be received, or more appropriate to enlighten a court as to the intent with which the act was done; and accordingly ruled that it was admissible." [84]

In the same letter Chase was moved to exclaim: "The trial of the President draws toward its end. . . . To me the whole business seems wrong, and if I had any opinion (option?) under the Constitution, I would not take part in it. . . . Nothing is clearer to my mind than that acts not warranted by the Constitution are not laws. . . . How can the President fulfill his oath to preserve, protect and defend the Constitution if he has no right to defend it against an act of Congress, sincerely believed by him to have been passed in violation of it? To me, therefore, it seems perfectly clear that the President had a perfect right, and, indeed, was under the highest obligation to remove Mr. Stanton, if he made the removal, not in wanton disregard of a constitutional law, but with a sincere belief that the Tenure-of-Office Act was unconstitutional, and for the purpose of bringing the question before the Supreme Court. Plainly it was the proper and peaceful, if not the only proper and peaceful, mode of protecting and defending the Constitution." [85]

It may have been indiscreet for the Chief Justice in the very middle of the trial, even privately thus so frankly to have expressed himself. But it was the honest reaction of an honest man to the dishonesty of time-serving politicians! Despite his personal views as to the conduct of the managers, and of the High Court of Impeachment over which he was presiding, he was, nevertheless, holding the scales of justice with an even hand.

"At the court of impeachment most of the day and for two or three hours on the stand," wrote Welles after his experience, "nearly every question put was objected to and discussed. The Chief Justice presided with fairness, and the Senators, in most cases by a majority, voted against the Managers. About twenty are violent partisans, as much interested in the prosecution as the Managers and some of them taking active part with them. Cameron, Conness, Howard and others manifest this. There is another set of stupid stolid creatures, like Morgan, Chandler, etc. —the latter violent, the former time-serving, who vote uniformly and always to exclude all testimony for the President, and are, and have been, ready from the first to vote to convict. In point of morality, I put these fellows on a par with the thief and the murderer. . . . I perceived that the Radical leaders, as well as Managers were becoming disturbed and discontented by the course things were taking, and, under apprehension that a pending question might go against them, there was a concerted movement to adjourn. A caucus and discipline were necessary. The Managers directed it. I saw it whispered and passed from one to another. Judges! Oh, what judges!" [86]

Welles wrote this after his first day on the stand. "My suspicions," he recorded on the evening of his second, "were at once aroused that there had been caucusing, or both caucusing and drilling, overnight, to exclude, after listening to all hearsay evidence and scandal against him, the President's testimony refuting the lies and manufactured evidence. The suspicion was fully confirmed by the day's action. Nothing from any member of the Cabinet was permitted, from a conviction evidently that it would exculpate and exonerate the President, Sumner therefore, who has to this time voted to admit all testimony, because he was predetermined to convict, absented himself now when votes intended to cut off evidence were to be taken. Morton was not present at all. Sherman, Frelinghuysen, and the equivocal men had been last night whipped in." [87]

Little would the Radicals have cared what Welles thought. Little did they care for the opinion of the Chief Justice,—unless he should perchance seek to cast a deciding vote upon the final question of conviction or acquittal. But what the doubtful Senators were thinking was or should have been a matter of concern to the managers. What two of these Senators were pondering on the rejection of Welles' testimony was revealed later when they filed their written opinions with the High Court. "This evidence," wrote Senator Grimes, "was in my opinion clearly admissible. . . . However widely . . . I may differ with the President respecting his political views and measures . . . I am not able to record my vote that he is guilty of high crimes and misdemeanors." [88]

Concerning this same excluded testimony Senator Henderson

in his opinion said: "I . . . insist that competent evidence such as this, going to explain the character of his intentions, should not have been rejected by the court. . . . A verdict of guilty on these articles, after the exclusion of this testimony would fail to command the respect and approval of any enlightened public judgment. . . . The question is simply one of guilt under the charges presented by the House, and I cannot, in justice to the laws of the land, in justice to the country or to my own sense of right, render any other response to the several articles than a verdict of 'not guilty.' " [89]

Scoundrel lawyers like Ben Butler, political freebooters like the Radicals who applauded and supported him in the Senate and the House, in their lack of conscience and their cynical contempt for it in others, more than once have found to their dismay that there are men whom conscience energizes to resistance, that will not brook defeat. Among those who were presently to pass judgment on the President of the United States there were such men. If there were enough, the lowest conspiracy ever concocted in America might fail!

After Welles was excused, the defense called but two more witnesses, both unimportant, and so by Monday evening of April 20th the evidence on both sides was closed, and there now remained nothing but the closing arguments and then,—the verdict.

LXXV

JOHNSON QUIETLY AWAITS HIS FATE

JOHNSON was bearing his ordeal in silence. Lincoln's plan was gone, the support of the Supreme Court was gone, all of Lincoln's hopes for binding up the nation's wounds and for a speedy reconciliation,—all these were gone! Now in a few days would Lincoln's follower be humbled in the dust? Humbled because he had followed Lincoln! Over the name of the seventeenth President was there presently to be written: "Convicted of high crimes and misdemeanors and removed from office?" After all the gallant years in Tennessee, after all the dauntless days in the Senate of the United States, after all his iron espousal of the cause of justice, was his reward to be conviction and removal?

What must have been Johnson's thoughts as he observed the High Court of Impeachment at its work! The long and sorry farce with its struggling actors clad in the ill-fitting simulacra of judicial fairness! If bitterness and anger seethed within his mind, it was not revealed. His family in the White House saw him go about his daily tasks, as the trial dragged on, serene and apparently oblivious to the infamy that was enacting.[1]

Seldom has the White House been so alive with children as in Johnson's time. He had with him there in addition to his grown son, Col. Robert Johnson, a younger son, Andrew Johnson, Jr., then thirteen, his daughter, Mrs. Daniel Stover, with her two daughters, Sarah and Lillie, and her son, Andrew Johnson Stover. Mrs. Patterson, the President's other daughter, the accomplished mistress of the White House, had with her two children, Mary Belle and Andrew Johnson Patterson.[2] Through all the storms that raged about him, Johnson had the healing solace that flows from children's laughter.[3] He loved children;

672

somehow he always found the time to talk with them. Children loved and trusted him. I have talked with one of those who lived with him at the White House,—Andrew Johnson Patterson. Never, says Mr. Patterson, did the President refuse to talk or listen to his grandchildren. They came to him with their childish problems, and never did he fail to heed their questions or to explain and answer them.[4]

Content to hold his own counsel as few Presidents have been,[5] with the children of the White House he was utterly without reserve. Often he would drive out with them to Pierce's Mill on Rock Creek. A pleasant meadow nestled by the stream where the little Pattersons and Stovers loved to come. There the President would sit watching as they gathered wildflowers or rushed down to the cool brook to wade, or fish, or hunt for water bugs and frogs. Sometimes all would join, the President included, in skipping flat stones on the water.[6] I sat not long ago in Johnson's home in Greeneville and listened to one of these children,—now a man past seventy, as he reminisced of those far-off happy days.

Often the President would drive out alone into the country accompanied only by his faithful bodyguard. He loved to pause within some beautiful and quiet spot, where he would walk in silence by himself. The beauty and the peace of Glenwood Cemetery frequently attracted him. Here for a long time he would wander reading the inscriptions on the stones, and murmuring perhaps Gray's elegy.[7]

Throughout the trial the sturdy resolution of his iron will helped him to maintain his poise. Conviction seemed at times inevitable, and as he had put away all thoughts of force, all that he could do was to await his fate. He was preparing an address to the people which he intended reading after his conviction. He had asked his secretary to investigate the fate of each of the signers of the death warrant of King Charles the First.[8] Some of his time he spent in reading Addison's Cato, in rereading it, and committing many of its passages to memory.[9]

Johnson, unlike many strong men, was on the whole a tractable client, following the advice of his lawyers even when he differed with them. Early in the trial he became firmly imbued with the belief that he should go in person to the Senate chamber, but his counsel tactfully dissuaded him.[10]   On the day that Butler opened for the prosecution, this idea took hold of him once more. After a brief conference with them, once more he was persuaded to follow their advice.[11]   Nothing would have more greatly pleased the Radical conspirators than to have had the chief character in their drama appear in the living flesh upon the stage. But Evarts and his colleagues wisely had determined to deny Ben Butler and his friends this satisfaction.   In doing so the President's defenders well understood that the Producers at the Capitol had been forced to stage a second-rate performance,—Julius Cæsar without Cæsar!

But there was one influence in that White House that more than all else enabled Johnson to go through his great ordeal. His wife, who had weathered with him every storm,—obscurity, illiteracy, poverty, ambition, political strife, war, proscription by the South, proscription by the North, and now this wild hurricane of malice,—was still there comforting him, never doubting that the clouds would lift and that a kindly sun would shine again. She knew Andrew Johnson. "Now, Andrew," she would say, and gently take his arm, and always it quieted and steadied him.[12]

The Tubercle bacilli had her in their dreadful grip,—consumption it was then called—but though they had sharpened the lines of her gentle face, the traces of her early beauty still were there.[13] Most of her days,—such was the treatment then for her malady— were spent within her room.[14]   But always there was in her thought the tired man, whom she had so long loved and cherished.   Tenderly she watched over him, as in the long evenings so many years before she had sat beside him reading while he worked.   She had cheered, advised and comforted him then. Now, after all the years, her judgment, her confidence and her hope were to him as a rod and a staff.   Presently men might come to strip him of his office, but whatever should befall, Eliza McCardle was still with him.

LXXVI

EVARTS' STRATEGY

THE Radicals never forgot that if any seven of the Republican Senators voted for acquittal, this number added to the Democrats would ruin the conspiracy. Wade could not then be President, and what would all the "faithful" do? They especially,—the "faithful"—were surging through the capital shouting that Johnson's conviction was necessary to the country's peace.[1]

The Senators were caucusing, and the managers were threatening that any Senator who dared to vote not guilty would render himself infamous.[2] The managers and the more violent of the Senators were united in this work in an unholy partnership. "When I was coming up H Street this evening between 4 and 5," on April 22nd wrote Welles, "I came upon Conkling and Benjamin F. Butler who were in close conversation on the corner of 15th Street. It was an ominous and discreditable conjunction,— the principal manager, an unscrupulous, corrupt and villainous character, holding concourse with one of the Senatorial triers, a conceited coxcomb of some talents and individual party aspirations. They both were, as Jack Downing says, stumped, and showed in their countenances what they were talking about and their wish that I had been on some other street,—or somewhere else."[3]

No one was more active in furnishing the managers support than Ulysses Grant. Manager Logan later publicly declared that Grant had "stood at the back of the managers in Congress during the whole course of the trial."[4] During the latter part of April Senator Henderson was invited one morning to breakfast with Grant at the home which had recently been given to him. Commodore Porter and other guests were there. On their departure Grant requested Henderson to remain, and upon lighting a cigar proposed a walk. The purpose for this was revealed promptly.

675

There were "personal reasons," he said, why he wanted Henderson's opinion of the probable outcome of the trial. "General Grant," replied Henderson, "you may rest assured the impeachment will fail." "Senator," answered Grant, "I have reason to believe, from good authority, that the managers of impeachment are confident of success." "They have no substantial grounds for such confidence," retorted Henderson. "I may tell you in confidence," the General then replied, "that not only is it expected that Ben Wade will become President, but the members of his Cabinet have already been selected." "Can you tell me, General, who they are to be?" the Senator inquired. "Perhaps I ought not to say," answered Grant, "but I will tell you at least that General Butler has been designated as Secretary of State." [5]

When Henderson reiterated his belief that such a program never would be carried out, Grant retorted: "You know that the people are talking of me for the Presidency at the coming election. I have not had political ambitions, but I begin to think that possibly I might be of great service to the country in bringing peace to the disturbed sections of the Union. These men who are counting on the success of impeachment offer me their influence as the nominee to succeed Wade in case he becomes President by the removal of Johnson." "What are the conditions?" asked Henderson. "That I shall take over Wade's cabinet," answered Grant. "Good God, General," the Senator exclaimed, "you didn't consent to that, did you?" "No," replied Grant, "I did not give them any answer." He then went on to express mistrust of Butler, yet to Henderson it was clear that Grant was leaning toward the bargain. "General Grant," said Henderson finally, "you may feel confident of the nomination whether these men support you or not; and you may rest assured that the succession will not occur as they promise." [6]

About a week later Senator Henderson was riding one day from the Capitol in a street car. General Grant got in, and on seeing him went over, sat down beside him, and asked whether he had changed his mind about the impeachment. "No, General," answered Henderson, "I am of the same mind about it." "Do you think you can defeat it?" asked Grant. "Well, I can't warrant that," answered the Senator, "we have friends enough against it to defeat it, but I cannot give a pledge that we shall actually defeat it." "Well, I hope you won't," said Grant. "Why, General," exclaimed Henderson, "you wouldn't impeach Johnson." "Yes, I would," Grant answered brusquely, "I would impeach him if for nothing else than because he is such an infernal liar." Aroused to indignation by this answer, Henderson looked at the small man beside him and said: "I very much regret to hear you say it, I regret it, because on such terms it would be nearly impossible to find the right sort of man to serve as President." [7] A rapier could not have struck more swiftly or more true.

But if the Radicals, with Grant's coöperation, were preparing thus to parcel out the executive departments,—to divide up the estate before the intestate breathed his last—others among the Republicans were becoming increasingly alarmed the more closely they visualized Ben Wade in the White House. Garfield spoke for the Conservatives when at about this time he wrote to Rhodes: "I have a few words to whisper in your private ear, concerning what Conservative Republicans think. They say that 'conviction means a transfer to the Presidency of Mr. Wade, a man of violent passions, extreme opinions and narrow views; a man who has never studied or thought carefully on any subject except slavery, a grossly profane, coarse nature who is surrounded by the worst and most violent elements in the Republican party; Chandler, the drunken extremist, being his bosom friend in the Senate, and Ben Eggleston, a low, coarse, porthouse politician, being his next friend and champion in the House,—that already the worst class of political cormorants from Ohio and elsewhere are thronging the lobbies and filling the hotels in high hopes of plunder when Wade is sworn in.' " [8]

The Conservatives were Johnson's hope. If they could but be made to see that the country would not be plunged in ruin were the President acquitted,—if seven of the Republicans could be made to see it—perhaps the Radical conspiracy might yet fall! To Senator Reverdy Johnson it was one day suggested that it was unfortunate that there seemed no practicable means whereby the President might now publicly declare that in the event of acquittal he intended no "rash act." This, of course, could not now be done. But Reverdy Johnson did the next best thing; he arranged a meeting between the President and Senator Grimes. There, when the pretended alarms of the alarmists in the Senate were discussed, the President exclaimed: "They have no warrant, whatever, in anything I have said or done for believing that the President intends to do any act which is not in strict conformity with the Constitution and laws." [9]

The evidence was not discussed, nor was any effort made to convince Grimes concerning any issue of the case, only that which was not in the case at all, but which might decide it,—the whispering campaign that the President if acquitted would act recklessly,—was met, and squarely answered. [10]

Evarts also saw the need of reassuring doubtful Senators of the President's intentions. How better could this be done than by nominating for Secretary of War a man who would receive the confidence of everyone, including Grant. Ewing's nomination was still unacted on, why not send in a new name at which even the Radicals could not cavil? On Tuesday, April 21st,—the day before the closing arguments were to begin—General John M. Schofield was in Washington. Why not induce him to accept the office? He had a brilliant military record; he had been with Sherman at Atlanta and with George H. Thomas at Nashville had held Hood at bay. [11] But beyond all other qualifications he possessed Grant's friendship. At two o'clock on the afternoon of the 21st, at the request of Evarts, Schofield called at the former's rooms in the Willard Hotel. Evarts asked him whether, if he were nominated as Secretary of War, he would consent to serve. The question had been scarcely asked when it was announced that General Grant was waiting at the door for Schofield, who thereupon cut short the interview, promising to return at eight. [12]

In discussing Evart's offer with the General, Schofield said he understood that it was made upon the theory that the President would not be convicted. Grant replied that he had not supposed that there was any reasonable doubt of the President's removal, but whether or not this happened, he (Grant) would be glad to see Schofield as Secretary of War during the remainder of the term, as Mr. Wade would have some difficulty in forming a cabinet for so brief a tenure.[13]

At eight, as promised, Schofield again called on Evarts, who declared himself satisfied that were the President removed, it would not be for anything he had done, "but for fear of what he might do." There seemed no way to remove this apprehension, Evarts said, unless the War Department "were placed in a satisfactory condition in advance." A majority of the Republicans, continued Evarts, "now regret the commencement of the impeachment proceedings, since they find how slight is the evidence of guilty intent," but that to such belated penitents the serious question was "how to get out of the scrape?"[14]

A judgment of guilty and removal, continued Evarts, would cause the political death of every Senator who voted for it. The precedent of impeachment for political reasons would "be exceedingly dangerous . . . in short the emergency is one of national peril." Thus felt, he said, the most prominent Republican Senators, and it was they who had suggested that Schofield be nominated in time to enable the Senate to "vote upon the President's case in the light of that nomination."[15]

Schofield listened carefully and said that before he gave his answer he would like to talk again with Grant. Later that evening Schofield made it plain to Grant that the proposed appointment had "originated with Republican Senators." "Under those circumstances," Grant thought that Schofield should accept, but he did "not believe in any compromise of the impeachment question." If the President were acquitted, said Grant, "as soon as Congress adjourned he would trample the laws under foot and do whatever he pleased"; Congress would have to remain in session all summer to protect the country from his lawlessness, and "the only limit to his violation of law had been, and would be, his courage, which had been very slight heretofore, but would be vastly increased by his escape from punishment."[16] "The only safe course," he said, "and the most popular one, would be to remove the President."[17]

LXXVII

THE CLOSING ARGUMENTS

ON the following morning, Wednesday, the 22nd, the High Court was to reconvene. Before going over to the Senate Chamber, Evarts waited at his hotel for Schofield's answer. The General came at ten; he agreed to say nothing as to accepting or declining the appointment, until the Senate acted on the nomination.[1]

At 11 o'clock the gavel of the Chief Justice again brought the court to order. Lest any of the Senators might, since the last session, have grown cold, Horace Greeley had been heaping new fuel on his fiery columns. On Monday he had written: "The Senate cannot vote to loose this mad bull in the national china shop, with full knowledge of his incurably vicious propensities and his furiously savage temper. His acquittal would be a virtual charter of licenses to heap outrage on outrage, evading and defying the laws, and doing his wicked worst to reëstablish a vindictive Rebel domination throughout the South. He is an aching tooth in the national jaw, a screeching infant in a crowded lecture-room; and there can be no peace nor comfort till he is out."[2] And lest this might not be strong enough, his editorial on Tuesday screamed: "He will leave that bar a branded attestation that this is a republic wherein the laws are supreme and the Chief Magistrate is but their honored first servant while he obeys, and their victim when he attempts to subvert them."[3]

As a comfort to any who might be faltering, the headlines of the *Tribune* on Wednesday morning fairly shouted: "CONVICTION ALMOST A CERTAINTY."[4] Whether it was or not, the managers had no intention of neglecting any opportunity to insult the President of the United States. Manager Logan prepared a fifty-two page argument.[5] But instead of reading it he

spared the court and merely filed it with them.[6] Manager Boutwell now addressed the court. "The issues of record," he
admitted, were "technical and limited."[7] But if they were
limited he did not intend to be. "The crime of the President,"
he declared, was not that he had "violated a constitutional law;
but his crime is that he has violated a law, and in his defense no
inquiry can be made whether the law is constitutional. . . ."[8]

Like a vicious wasp enmeshed in tanglefoot, Boutwell beat his
wings in vain against the logic with which Curtis had exposed
the true nature of the prosecution's case. The Tenure-of-Office
Act did not protect Stanton, but if it did, it violated the Constitution as construed since 1789; all that the President had done
was to seek a judicial decision as to the constitutionality of that
law! Boutwell could not answer this, but he could make the air
resound with charges not included in the articles or supported by
the evidence. He exposed both to his listeners and to posterity
the real grievance of his co-conspirators against Johnson: interference with their patronage and disagreement with their Reconstruction laws.

Departing both from the charges and the proof, Boutwell
declared that before the Tenure-of-Office Act Johnson "had
removed hundreds of faithful and patriotic public officers to the
great detriment of the public service. . . . When he removed
faithful public officers, and appointed others whose only claim
to consideration was unswerving devotion to his interest and
unhesitating obedience to his will, they compensated themselves
for this devotion and this obedience by frauds upon the revenues
and by crimes against the laws of the land. Hence it has happened that in the internal revenue service alone—the losses have
amounted to not less than twenty-five and probably to more than
fifty millions of dollars a year during the last two years."[9]

If any of this had been true, why was it not inserted in the
articles and supported by the evidence? Having rung the changes
on this deliberate falsehood, Boutwell continued: "By his acquittal you surrender the government into the hands of an usurping
and unscrupulous man, who will use all the vast power he now
claims for the corruption of every branch of the public service

and the final overthrow of the public liberties." [10]   If ever there had existed the smallest chemical trace of corruption that could even indirectly have been laid at Johnson's door, would the impeachers have failed to unearth it, and then to charge and prove it?

Johnson's defense that at every step he had followed the advice of his Cabinet, Boutwell sought to refute by saying that the President "had no right under the Constitution to the advice of the head of a department except upon subjects relating to the duties of his department." [11]   But in any event, "of what value," asked Boutwell, was the advice of Johnson's Cabinet?   And he answered his own question: "It was the advice of serfs to their lord, of servants to their master, of slaves to their owner. . . . The President is a man of strong will, of violent passions, of unlimited ambition, with capacity to employ and use timid men, adhesive men, subservient men, and corrupt men, as the instruments of his design." [12]

Boutwell was preparing for another sly reference to Jeremiah Black's discontinuance as counsel for the defense. He must have known, as well as Butler, the real reasons underlying this, but what mattered that, so long as it offered opportunity to traduce the President. "He attacks to destroy," said Boutwell, "all who will not become his instruments, and all who become his instruments are destroyed in use. He spares no one. Already this purpose of his life is illustrated in the treatment of a gentleman who was of counsel for the respondent, but who has never appeared in his behalf." [13]

Having thus occupied himself with what was not mentioned in the charges or referred to in the evidence, this slanderous New Englander concluded his argument for the day with this pious hypocritical assertion: "The House of Representatives does not demand the conviction of Andrew Johnson unless he is guilty in the manner charged in the articles of impeachment; nor does the House expect the managers to seek conviction except upon the law and the facts considered with judicial impartiality." [14]

How insincere this declaration was appeared when Boutwell continued the next morning, dwelling on everything but the testimony. He spoke of Johnson's "ambition unlimited and unscrupulous, which dares anything and everything necessary to its gratification." [15] Nor could he get away from his reading of Macaulay. "If the charges against Warren Hastings had been fully sustained by the testimony," he declared, "he would be regarded in history as an unimportant criminal when compared with the respondent." [16] Human annals furnished no record so black as that of Andrew Johnson! "Caius Verres," he continued, "is the greatest political criminal of history. For two years he was praetor and the scourge of Sicily. . . . The respondent at your Bar has been the scourge of a country many times the area of Sicily and containing a population six times as great." [17]

And then, lest his simile should become so absurd as to evoke laughter, he began to qualify. "Verres," he went on, "enriched himself and his friends; he seized the public paintings and statues and carried them to Rome. But at the end . . . of two years he left Sicily as he had found it; in comparative peace. . . . This respondent has not ravaged states nor enriched himself by the plunder of their treasures; but he has inaugurated and adhered to a policy which has deprived the people of the blessings of peace, of the protection of law, of the just rewards of honest industry." [18] Forty millions of people, he declared, were looking "to this tribunal as a sure defense against the encroachments of a criminally minded Chief Magistrate." [19] Was there any punishment enough for such a culprit? No! "Human tribunals are inadequate to punish those criminals, who as rulers or magistrates . . . become the scourge of communities and nations." [20]

§

The President's counsel were now given their brief innings, and from their midst Nelson, the country lawyer, is clambering to his feet,—a striking figure, lean-visaged, clean shaven, firm mouth, strong and aquiline nose, high forehead, piercing, frank and honest eyes. He had been waiting for this opportunity. He would bring to it emotional power that had thus far been lacking in the defense. "An effort has been made," he begins, "to draw a 'picture of the President's mind and heart'; he has been stigmatized as a 'usurper,' as a 'traitor to his party,' as 'disgracing the position held by some of the most illustrious in the land,' as a 'dangerous person, a criminal but not an ordinary one,' as 'encouraging murders, assassinations, and robberies all over the Southern states'; and finally by way of proving that there is one step between the sublime and the ridiculous, he has been charged with being a 'common scold,' and a 'ribald, scurrilous blasphemer, bandying epithets and taunts with a jeering mob,' . . . I am willing to admit that if he is guilty of any of the charges . . . a whip should be put in every honest hand to lash him around the world. . . ." [21]

It was a good beginning. "But," continued Nelson, "who is Andrew Johnson? Who is the man . . . to whom the gaze not of Delaware, but of the whole Union and of the civilized world is directed? . . . Who is Andrew Johnson? Go to the town of Greeneville but a few short years ago . . . and you will see a poor boy entering that village a stranger without friends . . . scarcely able to read, unable to write . . . he enters the state of Tennessee an orphan, poor, penniless, without the favor of the great; but scarce had he set foot upon her generous soil, when he was seized and embraced with parental fondness, caressed as though he had been a favorite child. . . ." [22]

With appealing simplicity Nelson then portrayed the astonishing career of his fellow townsman. And he went on: "Never since the days of Warren Hastings . . . has any man been stigmatized with more severe reprobation. . . . All the powers of invective . . . have been brought into requisition to fire your hearts and to prejudice your minds against him. . . . All the elements have been agitated. . . . The storm is playing around him; the pitiless rain is beating upon him; the lightnings are flashing around him; but . . . in the midst of it all he still stands firm, serene, unbent, unbroken, unsubdued, unawed, unterrified . . . threatening no civil war to deluge his country with blood; but, feeling a proud consciousness of his own integrity, appealing to heaven to witness the purity of his motives . . . and calling upon you, in the name of the living God . . . that you will do equal and impartial justice. . . ." [23]

Nelson's rhetorical questioning continued: "Who is Andrew Johnson? Are there not Senators here who are well acquainted with him? Are there not men here whose minds go back to . . . 1860 and 1861 . . . when men's faces turned pale? . . . Where was Andrew Johnson then? Standing almost within ten feet of the place where I stand now, solitary and alone . . . when 'bloody treason flourished over us,' his voice was heard arousing the nation. Some of you heard it. I only heard the echoes as they rolled along . . . to arouse the patriotism of our common country. . . . The only member of the South who was disposed to battle against treason then . . . now is called a traitor himself!" [24]

Nelson continued to inquire: "Who is Andrew Johnson? . . . When the battle of . . . Bull Run . . . was fought . . ., when men's . . . hearts grew faint where was Andrew Johnson then, this traitor, this usurper, this tyrant? Again he was heard . . . in the Senate . . . undismayed, unfaltering . . . and again the plaudits of hundreds and thousands shook the very walls of this capitol . . . when he . . . vindicated the American Constitution and proclaimed the determination of the government to uphold and to maintain it." [25]

With the true eloquence of sincerity, which sophistication often blunts, Nelson was driving home his arguments as though he stood before a jury, back in some mountain courthouse of Tennessee. He reminded the High Court that when Johnson became President, he "undertook to carry out what he believed to be the policy of his lamented predecessor. He undertook this in good faith. He retained the Cabinet which Mr. Lincoln left. He manifested no desire to segregate himself from the party by whom he had been elected. . . . When he did everything that he thought was necessary to do; when following the example of Mr. Lincoln in regard to Arkansas and Louisiana, and certainly following the spirit of Mr. Lincoln's proclamations and efforts, he sought to restore the Southern States to the relations which they had maintained to our common Union before the civil war commenced, I ask who can say that there was guilt in all this? . . . He was anxious to pour oil upon the troubled waters and heal the wounds of his distracted and divided country. If he erred in this, it was almost a divine error." [26]

In the midst of Nelson's argument, an adjournment until the next day was taken.

§

Nelson proceeded when the High Court reconvened. Feeling that the time had come to answer Boutwell's dishonorable reference to Black's withdrawal, he now stated all the facts of Alta Vela. [27]

The President, he said, "acted like a sentinel upon the watchtower of the Constitution, faithful to the rights of the people who had exalted him. . . . He was determined not to . . . war against a little power . . . that had no capacity of resistance. He was determined not . . . to be used as an instrument in the hands of anybody. . . ." [28]

"They know little of the President of the United States, far less than your humble speaker knows," continued Nelson, "who imagine that they can force or drive or compel him, under any imaginable state of circumstances, to do what he believes to be wrong. He is a man of peculiar temperament and disposition. By careful management and proper manipulation he may, perhaps, be gently led; . . . but . . . no power under the heavens can compel him to go one inch beyond what he believes to be right. . . ." [29]

Nelson's argument was long; it gave evidence of extemporization, but what it lacked in compact form was more than compensated by the downright sincerity of the speaker,—a sincerity that lifted him to moments of dramatic power. He reminded his hearers of the proffered armed support which Johnson spurned. [30] He spoke of Johnson's Cleveland speech where he encountered a mob "prepared to insult and to assail" him. [31] He referred to the familiar Radical charge that because of Johnson's policy the South was given over to assassination. [32] "Why, Senators," he exclaimed, "under whose control is the South? Is not the South under the control of Congress? . . . I live in the South, and . . . my observation ever since the close of the war is, that although there has been a bad state of things in some portions of the Southern states, nine-tenths of the murders and assassinations that have been reported in the newspapers and talked about here in Congress are made to order, got up for political effect, with a view of keeping up agitation and excitement. . . ."[33]

Finally he closed. There was a simplicity, almost a naïveté in what he said. True oratory is in some part made up of such materials. "I have never entered the rotunda of this . . . Capitol," he declared, "when I have not felt as if I were treading upon holy ground." He spoke of the paintings there, "redolent with the history of our beloved country. Columbus studying the unsolved problem of a new world . . ., the embarkation of the Pilgrim Fathers . . . the divine and angelic countenance of Rose Standish. . . . And there is the grand painting that represents Washington, the victor, surrendering his sword after having long before refused a crown. . . ."[34]

The orator was now spellbound by his own words as were those who listened to him. "As I sat . . . gazing upward upon the group (Washington and the sisterhood of early states) who look down from the topmost height of the dome, methought I saw the spirits of departed patriots rallying in misty throngs from their blissful abode and clustering near the wondrous scene that is transpiring now; and as I sat, with face upturned, I seemed to see the shadowy forms descend into the building and arrange themselves with silent but stately preparation in and around this gorgeous apartment."[35]

"There in the galleries, amid those living forms of loveliness and beauty, are Martha Washington and Dolly Madison, and hundreds of the maids and matrons of the Revolution, looking down with intense and anxious expectation, and watching with profoundest solicitude the progress of the grandest trial of the nineteenth century. And there in your very midst and at your sides, are sitting the shades of Sherman and Hamilton, Washington and Madison, Jefferson and Jackson, Clay and Webster, who in years that are past bent every energy and employed every effort to build our own great temple of liberty. . . . Behind the

Chief Justice I see the grave and solemn face of the intrepid Marshall; and above, among, and all around us are the impalpable forms of all the artists of our former grandeur! Mr. Chief Justice and Senators, if you cannot clasp their shadows to your souls, let me entreat you to feel the inspiration of their sacred presence, and . . . determine this great issue in the lofty spirit of impartial justice. . . ." [36]

That night Seward was confidently predicting an acquittal, but Welles was skeptical.[37] Perhaps, however, the optimism of the Secretary of State was gaining ground in other quarters. Greeley now added prussic acid to the daily dose which his *Tribune* was serving. On Saturday morning, April 25th,—the day after Nelson closed—Greeley wrote: "Millions of voices . . . accuse Andrew Johnson of having administered the functions of the Presidency in a way to convict him of hypocrisy and perfidy in every profession and act by which he rose to the Presidency. . . . More impressive than the Senate, more imposing than the Chief Justice in his robes, more irresistible in its logic than any arguments of counsel is the calm judicial voice of the American people in denunciation of the upstart despot. If we are to have a monarch, let him be at least less ugly than Caliban, less cowardly than Falstaff, less treacherous than Andrew Johnson." [38]

This editorial was in the hands of all the judges of the High Court when William Groesbeck rose to make the second closing address for the President. He was a sick man, but the greatness of his cause seemed to give him strength.[39] "You are to try the charges contained in these articles of impeachment," he declared, "and nothing else. . . . Not upon common fame; not upon the price of gold in New York, or upon any question of finance; not upon newspaper rumor; not upon any views of party policy; you are to try them upon the evidence offered here and nothing else, by the obligation of your oaths." [40]

He reminded them again that for seventy-eight years Congress had uniformly upheld the constitutional right of the Executive to make removals without the concurrence of the Senate. And then he asked: "Is this Senate prepared to drag a President in here and convict him of crime because he believed as every other

President believed, as the Supreme Court believed, as thirty-eight of the thirty-nine Congresses believed? . . . I have put the question to myself, putting myself in his place, with the views which I entertain of the President's duty, not to lie down with his hand on his mouth, and his mouth in the dust before Congress, but to stand up as the Chief Magistrate of a nation, whose walls are the shores of a great continent, and maintain the integrity of his department. He shall execute your laws; he shall execute even the doubtful laws; but when you bring to him a question like this, when he has all this precedent behind him and around him, all the voices sounding in his ears, as to what is the right interpretation of the Constitution, and only one the other way, I say you are going too far to undertake to brand him with criminality, because he proposed to go to the Supreme Court. . . . To go there is peaceable, is constitutional, is lawful. What is the tribunal there for? For this very purpose." [41]

He restated the issues of the trial. "It almost shocks me to think," he said, "that the President of the United States is to be dragged out of his office on these miserable little questions . . . that you should . . . empty the office and *fill it with one of your own number*. Not on this case. Surely not on this case, Senators." [42]

"What else did he do? He talked with an officer about the law. That is the Emory article. He made intemperate speeches, though full of honest, patriotic sentiments; when reviled he should not revile again; when smitten upon one cheek he should turn the other. But, says the gentleman who spoke last on behalf of the managers, he tried to defeat pacification and restoration. I deny it. . . . Here too he followed precedent and trod the path on which were the footsteps of Lincoln, and which was bright with the radiance of his divine utterance, 'Charity for all, malice toward none.' He was eager for pacification. He thought the war was ended. It seemed so. The drums were all silent; the arsenals were all shut; the roar of cannon had died away to the last reverberations; the army was disbanded; not a single enemy confronted us on the field. Ah, he was too eager, too forgiving, too kind. The hand of conciliation was stretched out to him and he took it. It may be he should have put it away, but was it a crime to take it? Kindness, forgiveness, a crime? Kindness a crime? Kindness is omnipotent for good, more powerful than gunpowder or cannon. Kindness is statesmanship. Kindness is the high statesmanship of Heaven itself. The thunders of Sinai do but terrify and distract; alone they accomplish little; it is the kindness of Calvary that subdues and pacifies.".[43]

Groesbeck's voice after the first hour had grown so husky as to be almost inaudible. It cleared, however, during the recess, and now with rapt attention, in deathlike stillness the crowded chamber listened. The galleries were silent, no Senator was writing at his desk, no page was summoned, even the cloakrooms were still. With power akin to magnetism, he held his great audience spellbound and subdued. It was such a triumph as only great oratory has achieved upon exceptional occasions. An orator is a conqueror,—his audience is his foe. He must challenge it, defy it, subdue it, and then win it. Groesbeck had done this.[44]

In breathless silence presently they heard him sum up Johnson's case and Johnson's life. He conjured up before them the scenes when Andrew Johnson "alone of twenty-two Senators remained; even his state seceded, but he remained. . . . How his voice rang out in this hall for the good cause, and in denunciation of rebellion. But he . . . was wanted for greater peril, and went into the very furnace of the war. . . . Who of you have done more? Not one." [45]

Faint with illness and worn out by his great effort he sank back into his seat. Men crowded forward to congratulate him, while a wave of admiration swept through the Senate chamber. Comparatively unknown hitherto, the country now became acquainted with the name of William Groesbeck.[46]

§

The rickety case of the prosecution was shaking as with palsy when Groesbeck finished with it. The Radicals were reeling from these assaults, when to their consternation they read that Andrew Johnson, the previous day, had withdrawn Ewing's nomination as Secretary of War, and had sent in that of General Schofield in his stead.[47]   Realizing how this would weaken wavering Senators, Grant immediately wrote to Schofield advising him to decline.   But Schofield answered: "I have already promised not to decline the nomination in advance of any action of the Senate."[48]

Something must be done to counteract the President's latest move!   Butler had a plan.   His dishonorable speech on the supposed frauds of the Treasury, by formal vote had been stricken from the records of the trial.[49]   Perhaps he could bring pressure on the Senators by broadcasting his expunged lies among their constituents.   He caused twenty thousand copies of his speech to be printed for immediate and widespread distribution, making sure that at least one copy was mailed to every newspaper in the United States!   Horace Greeley admiringly proclaimed this fact in the columns of his *Tribune*.[50]

But lest these poisoned entrails should fail to give the witches' brew sufficient savour, Thaddeus Stevens' venom was once more thrown into the seething cauldron.   The diplomats seemed to have had no interest in listening to this atrabilious sansculotte, but in the nearly deserted diplomatic gallery the presence of one notable foreigner was observed.   Anthony Trollope had come to see and hear Stevens sum up for the managers.[51]   He confined himself to the eleventh article,—the child of his own brain.   He began with this false statement: "I desire to discuss the charges . . . in no mean spirit of malignity or vituperation."[52]   How malignant he would presently become, he knew when he disclaimed this spirit, for his was no extemporaneous address, not only was it carefully prepared and written out, but Stevens had himself three times examined all the printed proofs.[53]

Knowing to what low estate the "high crimes and misdemeanors" had now fallen, this malicious master of discord declared that the mere bare removal of Stanton and the appointment of Thomas, irrespective of the motives or intent that prompted them, was sufficient for conviction.[54]   He took up the Grant-Johnson correspondence, declaring it "wholly immaterial" who had told the truth, but asked, "who can hesitate to choose between the words of a gallant soldier and the pettifogging of a political trickster?" [55]

He quoted the Senate resolution of February 21st that the President had no power to remove his Secretary of War. "Yet," he snarled, "Johnson continued him in office. And now this offspring of assassination turns upon the Senate . . . and bids them defiance. How can he escape the just vengeance of the law? Wretched man, standing at bay, surrounded by a cordon of living men each with the axe of an executioner uplifted for his just punishment." No Senator, he declared, would for the "sake of the President . . . suffer himself to be tortured on a gibbet of everlasting obloquy. How long and dark would be the track of infamy which must mark his name and that of his posterity. . . . It requires no gift of prophecy to predict the fate of this unhappy victim." [56]

Exhausted by the passion of hate that had convulsed his old frame, Stevens was no longer able to address the court, and so he handed his prepared speech to Butler, who read the rest of it. [57] There were nineteen pages more of closely packed abuse. "The great crime of Andrew Johnson," this diatribe continued, was not only his violation of his oath, the constitution and the laws, but his "endeavor to set up his own will against that of the law-making power. . . ." [58]

The long address came to a final close with a comparison between the first Congress of 1789 that had construed the right of the President to make removals without recourse to the Senate, and the 39th and 40th Congresses that had denied that right. The comparison was not favorable to James Madison and his contemporaries. He spoke of their "mistakes," of which he said none was greater than "the illusion of supposing that it was impossible for our institutions to throw up to the surface a man like Andrew Johnson. . . ." [59]

§

The managers returned to their work the next day, Tuesday, April 28th. They had enjoyed Stevens' effort to besmirch the President's good name. There was, nevertheless, a growing fear that after all their months of hot-lipped defamation, the plot might yet miscarry. The arguments of the President's counsel had alarmed them as they heard and saw their shabby patch-work torn asunder.[60] Some of the less venturesome rats were preparing to escape the leaky ship, but Horace Greeley was standing to the pumps. Before the reconvening of the court the Senators had read his editorial denouncing Johnson because "instead of obeying the will of those who put him into power," he had "perpetrated a betrayal of the party that had elected him. . . ." [61]

It was now Stanton's former partner's turn to speak. Remorseless, vindictive, unscrupulous,[62] Williams took the floor to arraign the man whom Stanton had betrayed. Have patience, reader; you shall not be forced to bear with much of Williams' ponderosity; you shall be more kindly dealt with than the High Court, that must long ere this have been surfeited with this Gargantuan mass of speaking. Of what moment that Johnson's confidence in Stanton was no longer possible? "His counsel say," declared Williams, "that Mr. Stanton is a thorn in his side. Well, a thorn in the flesh is sometimes good for the spirit." [63] How disastrous to the country if an acquittal were to come! "If you acquit him," shouted Williams, "you affirm all his imperial pretensions. . . . It will be a victory over you and us which will stir the heart of rebeldom to joy, while your dead soldiers will turn uneasily in their graves; a victory to be celebrated by the exultant ascent of Andrew Johnson to the Capitol, like the conqueror in a Roman triumph dragging not captive kings, but a captive Senate at his chariot wheels. . . ." [64]

Williams was done at last. Presently it would be Evarts' turn to speak. The galleries were densely packed to hear him.[65] But Ben Butler had not been heard from in some time! There was present now a large audience,—a further opportunity for the limelight! And then, too, perhaps he could becloud the atmosphere so as to dim the light of the great argument that all were expecting from the New York lawyer! It was four days since Nelson had exposed Butler's tortuous trail that led through Alta Vela.[66] Referring to Nelson as the "veriest tyro in the law in the most benighted portion of the Southern country," [67] he charged him with "deliberate falsehood." [68] But Butler did not deny that he had written the opinion for the Alta Vela claimants.

Nelson was now on his feet to "hurl back with indignation and scorn," the chief manager's "undeserved imputations." [69] "I treated the gentleman on the other side with courtesy and kindness," he said. "He has rewarded me with insult and with outrage in the presence of the American Senate. . . . So far as any question that the gentleman desires to make of a personal character with me is concerned, this is not the place to make it. Let him make it elsewhere if he desires to do it." [70]

Senator Yates now gained the floor to call Nelson to order. [71] In disclaiming the purpose of using any "language improper in this tribunal," Nelson explained that he had referred to the Alta Vela matter only after Boutwell had alluded to Jeremiah Black's withdrawal. "Here is this accusation . . . and here is this astonishing claim . . . signed by four of the managers . . . presented . . . when this impeachment was hanging over him. . . ." [72] Nelson then asked leave to read the documents on the subject, but Butler interrupted with all the insolence of the scoundrel. "I trust not until they are shown not to have been mutilated." [73] At this point the Senators were demanding that the trial proceed. [74]

The well-poised, keen-visaged Evarts now arose to deliver one of the great American orations. As a masterpiece of forensic power it deserves a place alongside Hamilton's great speech at the convention at Poughkeepsie. Unerring comprehension of the issues real and imaginary, wit, eloquence, logic, force, persuasion, and in its highest and best sense oratory, all these and much else were there. He towered above the little snarling figures of the managers, and lifted the debate from the temper of the barroom to the calm intellectual environment of a court of justice. He raised the controversy from the fetid stench of politics to the high domain of statesmanship. "The contrast between the effect of his presence and that of Butler's," says Rhodes, "is a striking illustration of the importance of character when a great case is tried at the bar." [75]

The people, declared Evarts, hearing "this tremendous enginery of impeachment . . ., this power which has lain in the Constitution like a sword in its sheath, is now drawn . . ., wish to know what the crime is that the President is accused of. They understand that treason and bribery are great offenses, and that a ruler guilty of them should be brought into question and deposed. They are ready to believe that . . . there may be other great crimes and misdemeanors touching the conduct of government and the welfare of the state. . . . But they wish to know what the crimes are. They wish to know whether the President has betrayed our liberties of our possessions to a foreign state. They wish to know whether he has delivered up a fortress or surrendered a fleet. They wish to know whether he has made merchandise of public trust and turned authority to private gain. And when informed that none of these things are charged, imputed, or even declaimed about, they yet seek further information and are told that he has removed a member of his cabinet." [76]

" 'Well, but how comes it to be a crime?' they inquire. Why, Congress passed a law for the first time . . . to control by law this matter of removal from office; and they provided that if the President should violate it, it should be a . . . high misdemeanor; and now he has . . . undertaken to remove a member of his Cabinet, and he is to be removed himself for that cause. He undertook to make an *ad interim* Secretary of War, and you are to have made for you an *ad interim* President in consequence!" [77]

And now Evarts moved on to the inquiry: "Is this a court? . . . Nobody is wiser than the intrepid manager who assumed the first assault upon the court, and he knew that the only way he could prevent his cause from being turned out of court was to turn the court out of his case. [Laughter.] . . . The Constitution . . . makes this a court; it makes its proceeding a trial; it assigns a judgment; it accords a power of punishment . . . and it provides that a jury in all judicial proceedings of a criminal character shall be necessary except in this court. . . . We may assume, then, that so far as words go, it is a court and nothing but a court." [78]

Evarts then referred to Butler's English precedents whereby he sought to show that this proceeding was in no wise a judicial one.

"But," continued Evarts, "the learned manager did not tell us what this was if it was not a court. It is not a Senate conducting legislative business; it is not a Senate acting upon executive business; it is not a Senate acting in caucus on political affairs; and the question remains, if it is not a court, what is it? If this is not an altar of justice which we stand about, if we are not all ministers here of justice, to feed its sacred flame, what is the altar, and what do we do here about it? It is an altar of sacrifice if it is not an altar of justice; and to what divinity is this altar erected: What but the divinity of party hate and party rage . . . If this is not a court it is a scaffold. . . ." [79]

§

Before Evarts could continue on the next day, April 29th, the High Court was to hear still more of Alta Vela. Butler at the previous session had asserted that his now famous opinion had been prepared in the early part of February, before the occurrences on which the articles of impeachment had been founded.[80] Nelson had the documents to expose Butler's lie, but before he could do so, Sumner was on his feet with a resolution that "Mr. Nelson . . . has justly deserved the disapprobation of the Senate." [81] The resolution was not immediately acted on, and so Nelson offered for the inspection of the Court the original manuscript of Butler's opinion in which three of the managers had joined. It was dated March 9th, 1868! [82]

And now Evarts went forward with his argument. It was brilliant, complete, fascinating. He pierced through the managers' equivocation, casuistry and chicane, and evoked to their chagrin the constant, if unwilling, laughter of the Court at their expense. If, he said, "the President is here no longer exposed to attacks upon the same principle on which men claim to hunt the lion and harpoon the whale, then indeed, much that has been said by the honorable managers . . . falls harmless in your midst." [83]

The pharisaical insincerity, the cant, the humbug and the hypocrisy of the accusations and of the accusers were laid bare as with a surgeon's knife. He spoke of the managers' contention that the court need not worry over a conviction, because the punishment did not touch life, limb or property. "It is gravely proposed to you," he said, "that it is a little thing to take a President from his public station and strike him to the ground, branded with high crime and misdemeanor, to be a byword and reproach through the long gauntlet of history forever and forever. . . . If these are the estimates of public character, of public fame, and of public disgrace by which you . . . are to record your estimate of the public spirit and of the public virtue of the American state, you have indeed written for the youth of this country the solemn lesson that it is dust and ashes." [84]

Before he finished on that day, Evarts paid his compliments to the Press. "The idea that a President," he said, "is to be brought into . . . this court by a limited accusation, found 'not guilty' under that, and convicted on an indictment that the House refused to sustain, or upon the wider indictment of the newspaper press, and without any opportunity to bring proof or to make arguments on the subject, seems to us too monstrous for any intelligence . . . to maintain. . . ." [85] When the session ended, Evarts had not yet finished.

On the following day, April 30th, before he could proceed, Charles Sumner demanded action on his resolution to discipline Nelson for his "willingness to fight a duel" with Butler.[86] Senator Anthony asked Nelson if it had been his intention to challenge the manager to a mortal combat.[87] "I cannot say," replied the Tennesseean, "I had particularly the idea of a duel in my mind, as I am not a duellist by profession; but, nevertheless, my idea was that I would answer the gentleman in any way he chose to call upon me for it. I did not intend to claim any exemption on account of age or any exemption on account of other things that are apparent to the Senate. That was all I meant to signify, and I hope the Senate will recollect the circumstances under which this thing was done." [88] Apparently the Senate did, for Sumner's resolution was promptly laid upon the table,[89] and Evarts now proceeded.

He took up the President's speeches. "My first difficulty about them," he said, "is that they were made in 1866 and related to a Congress that has passed out of existence, and were a subject in the report to the . . . House upon which the House voted that they would not impeach." [90]   And he continued: "I find that the . . . charge against the President is that he has been 'unmindful of the harmony and courtesies which ought to exist and be maintained between the executive and legislative branches of the government.' If it prevails from the executive toward the legislative, it should prevail from the legislative toward the executive, unless I am to be met with . . . a most novel view presented by Mr. Manager Williams . . . that . . . it is a rule that does not work both ways." [91]   [Laughter.]

"I find," Evarts went on, "a direct determination of the Senate itself passing upon . . . what . . . freedom of speech as between the two departments of the government permitted." He then reminded them how Sumner had called the President of the United States "the enemy of his country" and how, when called to order, the presiding officer of the Senate had declared: "It is the impression of the chair that these words do not exceed the usual latitude of debate which has been permitted here," and how Senator Sherman had then said: "I think the words objected to are clearly in order. I have heard similar remarks fifty times without any question of order being raised." [92]

The day's session came to a close, but still Evarts was not done. In the morning he concluded, exhorting the High Court to ignore politics and to vote guilty only if upon the same proofs they would render judgment "against President Lincoln with his good politics and General Washington with his majestic character. . . ." [93]

But who could say that any case had been established against Andrew Johnson? "And," he continued, "how much is there in his conduct . . . that up to this period of division commends itself not only to your but to the approval and applause of his countrymen? . . . Bred in a school of Tennessee democratic politics, he had always learned to believe that the Constitution must and should be preserved; and I ask you to recognize that when it was in peril, and all men south of a certain line took up arms against it, and all men north ought to have taken up arms in politics or in war for it, he loved the Constitution more than he loved his section and the glories that were promised by the evil spirits of the rebellion." [94]

"He is no rhetorician and no theorist, no sophist and no philosopher. The Constitution is to him the only political book that he reads. The Constitution is to him the only great authority which he obeys. His mind may not expand; his views may not be so plastic as those of many of his countrymen; he may not think we have outlived the Constitution, and may not be able to embrace the Declaration of Independence as superior and predominant to it. But to the Constitution he adheres. For it and under it he has served the state from boyhood up,—labored for, loved it. For it he has stood in arms against the frowns of a Senate; for it he has stood in arms against the rebellious forces of the enemy; and to it he has bowed three times a day with a more than eastern devotion. . . . We could summon from the people a million of men and inexhaustible treasure to help the Constitution in its time of need. Can we summon now resources enough of civil prudence and of restraint of passion to carry us through this trial, so that whatever result may follow, in whatever form, the people may feel that the Constitution has received no wound!" [95]

Evarts' speech had lasted fourteen hours and consumed parts of four days for its delivery. He had examined and destroyed the prosecution's case. Not often in this country has hypocrisy found such an airing. Men of all parties, and women too, had been fascinated as through the long hours they watched Evarts at his work of vivisection. The enemies of justice were dismayed, alarm filled the heart of every Radical. The conspiracy was tottering, the bigots and the charlatans were in fear lest in the general debâcle they themselves might be engulfed. [96]

§

As Evarts was concluding the stately Stanbery was seen entering the Senate chamber. Sickness for the past two weeks had confined him to his bed, and though even now he ought not to have come, he came. The weight of five and three score years hung heavily upon him, but he was there to lend a hand in the closing battle of the defense.[97] "It may seem an act of indiscretion," he began, "that in my present state of health I should attempt the great labor of this case. . . . My watchful physician has yielded a half-reluctant consent to my request. . . . But, Senators, an irresistible impulse hurries me forward. . . . Unseen and friendly hands seem to support me. Voices inaudible to all others, I hear, or seem to hear. They whisper words of consolation, of hope, of confidence. They say or seem to say to me: 'Feeble champion of the right, hold not back; remember that the race is not always to the swift nor the battle to the strong; remember in a just cause a single pebble from the brook was enough in the sling of the young shepherd!' "[98]

Stanbery's opinions on the Reconstruction laws had made him an object of execration among the Radicals, yet his dignity, his logic, and especially his insistence upon coming, sick man that he was, commanded the respectful, almost the sympathetic, attention of his enemies. "Senators," he concluded, "I have done with the law and the facts. . . . Now, listen for a moment to one who perhaps understands Andrew Johnson better than most of you; for his opportunities have been greater. When nearly two years ago he called me from the pursuits of professional life to take a seat in his Cabinet, I answered the call under a sense of public duty. I came here almost a stranger to him and to every member of his Cabinet except Mr. Stanton. We had been friends for many years. . . . From the moment I was honored with a seat in the Cabinet of Mr. Johnson not a step was taken that did not come under my observation, not a word was said that escaped my attention. I regarded him closely in Cabinet, and in still more private and confidential conversation. . . . I knew that evil counsellors were more than once around him. I observed him with the most intense anxiety. But never, in word, in deed, in thought, in action, did I discover in that man anything but loyalty to the Constitution and the laws. He stood firm as a rock against all temptation to abuse his own powers or to exercise those which were not conferred upon him."[99]

Stanbery's strength was failing, but he still pressed on: "Yes,

Senators, I have seen that man tried as few have been tried. I have seen his confidence abused. I have seen him endure day after day provocations such as few men have ever been called upon to meet. No man could have met them with more sublime patience. Sooner or later, however, I knew the explosion must come. And when it did come my only wonder was that it had been so long delayed. . . . Fear not . . . to acquit him. The Constitution is as safe in his hands from violence as it was in the hands of Washington. But if, Senators, you condemn him, if you strip him of the robes of his office . . . mark the prophecy: The strong arms of the people will be about him. They will find a way to raise him from any depths to which you may consign him, and we shall live to see him redeemed, and to hear the majestic voice of the people, 'Well done, faithful servant; you shall have your reward!' " [100]

And now Stanbery uttered a bolder challenge than any of the President's counsel had yet spoken: "But if, Senators, as I cannot believe, but as has been boldly said with almost official sanction, your votes have been canvassed and the doom of the President is sealed, then let that judgment not be pronounced in this Senate chamber; not here where our Camillus in the hour of our greatest peril, single-handed, met and baffled the enemies of the republic; not here where he stood faithful among the faithless, not here where he fought the good fight for the Union and the Constitution. . . . No, not here, seek out rather the darkest and gloomiest chamber in the subterranean recesses of this Capitol, where the cheerful light of day never enters. There erect the altar and immolate the victim." [101]

§

The President's counsel had exposed the work of the conspirators. Johnson was watching with the faith that right would triumph. But some of his best friends were desponding. "With the party appeals and party demands throughout the country," wrote Welles a few hours after Stanbery closed, "I have but slight expectation of an acquittal." [102]

Sunday intervened between Stanbery's closing and the reconvening of the High Court on Monday, May the 4th. Not since the beginning of the trial had so many persons sought admission. They had come to hear Bingham's final argument for the prosecution. Welles' characterization of him as a "shrewd, sinuous, tricky lawyer,"[103] was presently to be more than justified. The claques of the conspirators were there to cheer and to applaud. Every seat was filled, the aisles were filled, doorways, passages and stairways all were filled. The Senate chamber was jammed to suffocation.[104] All was in readiness for a prepared demonstration. The crowded scene was the culmination of many weeks of poisoned propaganda. No weapon was too dishonorable for use against the wavering Senators. Under the Radical whip two months before the State Convention of Ohio had adopted resolutions in support of the impeachment. A few days later the Pennsylvania Convention did likewise, as did also Massachusetts, Michigan, New Jersey and Vermont. More than half the Northern states, through Radical legislatures or conventions, recorded themselves for conviction and removal.[105]

Despicable enough were these means, but incomparably more dishonorable was the personal pressure brought with increasing force to bear on every doubtful Senator. Letters were poured in upon them—letters with promises, letters with intimidations, signed letters, anonymous letters, forged letters hinting that should the recipients fail to vote for conviction their private lives would be exposed. The wives of the Senators were importuned for their influence; their "women friends" were diligently sought out and enlisted in the low plot of dishonorable persuasion. And all of these counsellors of dishonor were carrying on their criminal approaches with the protestations of high virtue.

Even during the sessions of the court, the pages flitted through the doorways bringing cards and missives, and now and again one of the Senators,—one of the judges—would slink into the corridor to be told what to do. And after the adjournments of the court at night secret conclaves hummed with the conspiracy. The gambling saloons and retreats of lower moral worth were populous with politicians all intent upon this subtle and corrupt diplomacy.[106]

In that High Court, all of whose members had sworn to do "impartial justice," John Bingham, the last of the managers, arose to gratify the claques who crowded in to hear him.[107] He had a loud voice and a confident bearing. "But his law was partisanship, his logic unbridled political passion and his history came from the grammar school."[108] His address was the least intellectually honest of any to which the Court was forced to listen. He met no question fairly, and resorted to the shyster tricks of misstating issues, and of personal abuse of his opponents. With nauseous hypocrisy he spoke of the "strange great sorrow" occasioned by Lincoln's death,—a sorrow so great, he said, that the people "forgot for the moment the disgraceful part which Andrew Johnson had played upon the tribune of the Senate on the 4th day of March, 1865. . . ."[109]

Mendaciously he asserted that the issue was whether the President could judicially construe the Constitution and determine whether the laws were "not to be executed because it suits the pleasure of his highness Andrew Johnson, first king of the people of the United States, in imitation of George III to suspend their execution."[110]

Washburne and Ben Butler were thrilled by Bingham's oratory. The Republican Convention of New Hampshire was in session on that day to choose its delegates to the National Convention. "Bingham is making a splendid speech," Washburne telegraphed them, "all looks well, the Constitution will be vindicated and the recreant put out of the White House before the end of the week." And these glad tidings were forwarded by Butler: "The removal of the great obstruction is certain. Wade and prosperity are sure to come with the apple-blossoms."[111]

On through Monday and Tuesday Bingham continued hurling his abuse at the President of the United States and his distinguished counsel. The most significant thing to be learned from Evarts' address, he said, was that the "way by which a man may make his speech immortal is to make it eternal." This evoked loud laughter; the claques liked that.[112] Bingham spoke of what had been advanced in the President's behalf as a "monstrous proposition."[113] "When that day comes," he went on, "that the Constitution . . . rests exclusively upon the fidelity and patriotism and integrity of Andrew Johnson, may God save the Constitution and save the republic from its defender." [114] Sometimes he spoke of the respondent as "your recusant President," [115] sometimes he referred to him as "this accused and guilty culprit." [116]

Finally on Wednesday, Bingham was bringing his misrepresentations to a close. The claques were waiting for these final words: "We stand this day pleading for the violated majesty of the law, by the graves of a half million of martyred hero-patriots who made death beautiful by the sacrifice of themselves for their country. . . ." [117] When Bingham finished, the claques were ready for their work, and from the galleries there now burst forth a torrent of applause and cheers, swelling presently into a veritable tumult. [118] "Order! Order!" shouted the Chief Justice. "If this be repeated the sergeant-at-arms will clear the galleries." The announcement was received with hisses and with laughter, and there was more clapping of hands and renewed cheering. The Chief Justice now directed the Sergeant-at-arms to clear the galleries and to arrest offenders. [119] How prearranged this outburst was and how little the conspirators desired it quelled, became presently apparent. Senator Cameron was on his feet shouting: "I hope the galleries will not be cleared. . . ." [120] Order was restored at last, and with it came the announcement that the case was closed. [121]

THE HIGH COURT DELIBERATES

The following Monday was devoted to deliberation and debate among the Senators. Many spoke, but what they said was not reported. The session lasted until nearly midnight.[1] From the written opinions, however, which thirty of the Senators later filed, the nature of the debate may be reconstructed.

"This is one of the last great battles with slavery," Sumner wrote in his opinion. "Driven from these legislative chambers, driven from the field of war, this monstrous power has found a refuge in the Executive Mansion where, in utter disregard of the Constitution and laws, it seeks to exercise its ancient and far reaching sway. . . . Andrew Johnson is the impersonation of the tyrannical slave power. In him it lives again. He is the lineal successor of John C. Calhoun and Jefferson Davis; and he gathers about him the same supporters. Original partisans of slavery North and South; habitual compromisers of great principles; maligners of the Declaration of Independence; politicians without heart; lawyers for whom a technicality is everything, and a promiscuous company who at every stage of the battle have set their faces against equal rights; these are his allies. It is the old troop of slavery, with a few recruits, ready as of old for violence —cunning in device, and heartless in quibble. With the President at their head, they are now entrenched in the Executive Mansion. Not to dislodge them is to leave the country a prey to one of the most hateful tyrannies of history. Especially is it to surrender the Unionists of the rebel states to violence and bloodshed. Not a month, not a week, not a day should be lost. *The safety of the Republic demands action at once.* The lives of innocent men must be rescued from sacrifice."[2]

Nearly sixty years have yellowed the printed page on which

these insane words of bigotry and folly lie wallowing in their shame. In that paragraph Charles Sumner's autobiography was published. A narrow, bigoted, opinionated, smug, complacent, muddle-headed man! To read it is to wonder why in his long life he encountered but one Preston Brooks! Perhaps it was because, unlike the lying hypocrites with whom he consorted, his pretensions to virtue were sincere. He believed that he was not as other men. His fellow impeachers deserve to be despised. Sumner should have pity; he was a mental case—an egomaniac needing treatment. But his dementia was dangerous to the Republic.

"Slavery," said Sumner, no doubt without the realization of how black a lie he uttered, "now rears its crest anew with Andrew Johnson as its representative. . . . It is very wrong to try this impeachment merely on those articles. It is unpardonable to higgle over words and phrases when, for more than two years the tyrannical pretensions of this offender . . . have been manifest in their terrible, heart-rending consequences." [3]

John Sherman's opinion is even more damaging to his reputation than Sumner's was to his. Sherman knew better. He admitted that he and his colleagues had solemnly declared that the Tenure-of-Office Act did not prevent Stanton's removal.[4] "A Roman emperor," he said, "attained immortal infamy by posting his laws above the reach of the people and then punishing their violation as a crime. An American Senator would excel this refinement of tyranny if, when passing a law, he declared an act to be innocent, and then as a judge punished the same act as a crime." [5] This was both fine and true, but it did not prevent Sherman from finding guilt in the ad interim appointment of Lorenzo Thomas! [6] These sentiments were uttered by Sherman before the Senate in its debate of May 11th, and that evening Welles observed: "Sherman declared himself opposed to the first article, but would vote for the second. In other words the President had the right to remove Stanton, but no right to order another to discharge the duties. Poor Sherman! He thinks the people fools; they know him better than he does them." [7]

No one can lay claim even to have begun the study of American history who has not perused the four hundred and one pages of the Senatorial opinions in this case. Judge Taft and his associates, we are told, pondered them well, when in 1926 they vindicated Andrew Johnson's conception of his constitutional powers. Some of the opinions, such as those of Cattell, Pomeroy and Stewart, are almost as bigoted as that of Sumner. Some, such as those of Reverdy Johnson, Grimes and Buckalew, constitute a permanent and dispassionate analysis of the conspiracy.

"If," wrote Reverdy Johnson, "members of Congress in debate assail the President in disparaging and vituperative language,—if they charge him with treason—a violation of every duty—a want of every virtue and with every vice; if they even charge him with having been an accessory to the murder of his lamented predecessor—charges calculated to bring him 'into disgrace,' 'hatred,' 'contempt and reproach'—they are exempt from responsibility by any legal proceeding, because 'freedom of speech" is their right,—how can it be that the President is responsible for the speeches alleged to have been made by him at the places and times referred to in the tenth and eleventh articles, when freedom of speech is equally secured to him?" [8]

"It has been said," he concluded, "that our judgment should be influenced by party consideration. We have been told . . . that party necessity requires a conviction; and the same is invoked to avoid what it is madly said will be the result of acquittal—civil commotion and bloodshed. Miserable insanity; a degrading dereliction of patriotism! These appeals are made evidently from the apprehension that Senators may conscientiously be convinced that the President is innocent of each of the crimes and misdemeanors alleged in the several articles, and are intended to force him to a judgment of guilt. No more dishonoring efforts were ever made to corrupt a judicial tribunal." [9]

Grimes of Iowa, Trumbull of Illinois and Fessenden of Maine were all Republicans, but they had not abandoned conscience or forgotten their oaths as judges. In his opinion, Fessenden later wrote: "To the suggestion that popular opinion demands the conviction of the President on these charges, I reply that he is not now on trial before the people, but before the Senate. In the words of Lord Eldon, upon the trial of the Queen, 'I take no notice of what is passing out of doors, because I am supposed constitutionally not to be acquainted with it.' And again, 'it is the duty of those on whom a judicial task is imposed to meet reproach and not court popularity.' The people have not heard the evidence as we have heard it. The responsibility is not upon them but upon us. They have not taken an oath to 'do impartial justice according to the Constitution and the laws,' I have taken that oath. I cannot render judgment upon their convictions, nor can they transfer to themselves my punishment if I violate my own. And I should consider myself undeserving of the confidence of that just and intelligent people who imposed upon me this great responsibility, and unworthy a place among honorable men, if for any fear of public reprobation, and for the sake of securing popular favor, I should disregard the convictions of my judgment and my conscience." [10]

These sentiments were voiced by Fessenden in the Senatorial debate of May 11th. Grimes boldly denounced all the articles and the whole proceeding. Trumbull joined them. Here were three Republicans who dared bid the conspirators defiance. If four more could be found, the impeaching hypocrites would yet fail. For their courage in following their consciences these three Republican Senators were rewarded with the violent denunciation of the conspirators. [11]

LXXIX

THE CONSPIRACY ASSUMES ITS MOST DISGRACEFUL PHASE

THE hopes of the President's supporters were now rising. The defeat of the conspiracy in many quarters was openly predicted.[1] Six days before, Seward had wagered a basket of champagne on an acquittal,[2]—but Secretary Browning declined the wager.[3]

As the judgment day approached, with a frenzy of dishonor the scoundrels who had brought their country to this pass, joined now in one last demoniacal attempt to corrupt the High Court of Impeachment. In aid of his political confederates, Horace Greeley opened every stop in his siren-voiced steam piano of abuse. "To remand the American Republic to the custody of Andrew Johnson," shrieked the New York *Tribune* on May 6th, "and to give him, in addition to the impulses of his own disloyal nature, the triumph of an acquittal would be to commit an act of treason only equalled by that of Benedict Arnold. We have no fear that this will be done. We shall do no Senator, in whom we have confidence, the injustice to believe that he is base enough to court dishonor, or stolid enough to feel that he can make himself the defender and apologist of Andrew Johnson, without standing in history as the partner of his crimes." [4]

And in his editorial of the next day, Greeley declared: "A verdict may be rendered at any hour, although it is not expected for a few days. . . . The Republican party has taken the responsibility of Impeachment. . . . To presume that any Republican will deliberately vote to acquit Mr. Johnson is to assume that his course hitherto has been a fraud. . . . If it were wise to assail Mr. Johnson for his policy, it is just to punish him. His impeachment is the logical consequence of Republicanism, and no Republican can vote against it without making himself infamous. The only

709

alternative is Impeachment or Infamy. If Johnson is acquitted, then the whole course of these men is a lie, and their deception is infamous. They led the party to this issue. They educated it to the work. They echoed every denunciation and emphasized every criticism of the President's policies. If they have been honest in this, then . . . we rest assured of a favorable verdict. American history has had one Benedict Arnold. Money is precious and sweet is the revenge of disappointed ambition. We are certain that neither money nor revenge will seduce any Senator into an infamous association with America's most degraded son." [5]

To whom were these fanfaronades primarily addressed? To the wavering Senators! Trumbull, Fessenden and Grimes had boldly announced that they would not soil their hands with the conspiracy,[6] and the conspirators well knew that there were others who might join this incorruptible triumvirate. Wiley and Van Winkle of West Virginia, Fowler and Henderson of Missouri, Anthony of Rhode Island and Ross of Kansas, these were the men on whom the conspirators were now employing every weapon of persuasion. If four of these six stood up, Abraham Lincoln's follower would still be President! Every intimidation must be employed!

But suppose this number could not be intimidated or polluted? Thaddeus Stevens was ready for just such a contingency! Pack the High Court! Arkansas was under carpet-bag, bayonet and negro rule, her Senators could be counted on! They had heard none of the evidence, they had not been present at the trial, but what mattered that? Why should a juror need to hear the case against Andrew Johnson? He was too black a criminal to merit such consideration! Pack the High Court? It had been tried before and failed, but why not try again? *Pack the High Court!!* Thaddeus Stevens was more than ready for such work. On May 8th he reported a bill for the admission of Arkansas as a state.[7] "There are reasons which I do not think it proper or necessary to mention now," he said, "why this bill should be considered, passed and sent to the Senate before next Monday!" [8] No, it was not necessary to enumerate the reasons!

"Impeachment is statesmanship—justice—peace," shouted

Horace Greeley in his *Tribune* the next morning. "The logic of the Republican party brings it directly to this issue. . . . If war was statesmanship, what is impeachment? In what essential do the issues between Bingham and Evarts differ from those between Grant and Lee?" [9]

On the evening of May 11th, the day when the High Court met behind closed doors, three of the Senators, Reverdy Johnson, Sprague and Henderson, dined at the house of the Chief Justice. What meant this? There was an evening session of the House of Representatives as well as of the High Court. "We are sold out!" shouted Butler as he came storming into the House when he learned the news. But Stevens wastes no time in exclamation, he is on his feet with a bill for the admission of the Africanized governments of Louisiana, Georgia, Alabama and the Carolinas. Ten more Senators such as carpet-bag legislatures would select, would aid the cause indeed! [10] Impeachment statesmanship? So was this!

But what if the Senate lacked the daring for the consummation of this sinister design? Pressure on the doubtful Senators must not be relaxed! Pressure! *Pressure!!* Press on then, Thaddeus Stevens, for you have but little time! Throw new fagots underneath your steaming putrid cauldron! Cast new entrails in! For you cannot long hobble through your witches' dance! Soon all your dancing on this earth will halt!

On Tuesday, May 12th, the great decision was to come. "Another day and we shall have the verdict," proclaimed the New York *Tribune* of the previous morning. "In the minds of the American people the President stands condemned. . . . We recall no time when the popular anxiety has been so intense. . . . The removal of Mr. Johnson will be an event as important in its consequences as the execution of Louis. . . . Therefore we await the verdict with hope and confidence. Every business and national interest waits. The feeling that removal could not be avoided has given the nation comfort and we see no danger but that of acquittal. . . . The issue is plainly this: Andrew Johnson is either a Criminal or he is a King." [11]

But what of the doubtful Senators? What, for example, of

John B. Henderson of Missouri? Under Stevens' lash, the majority of Missouri's representatives in Congress criminally concerned themselves in an endeavor to intimidate this Senator. No jury-fixer within or without the penitentiary ever entered upon his work with more felonious intent. On the very morning scheduled for balloting on the verdict, these shameless Representatives called on Senator Henderson at his home. A vote against impeachment, they told him, would defy the all but unanimous desires of the "Union party" of his state.

Importunate and peremptory, they bore down upon him with their arguments. Bloodshed, they said, would follow an acquittal! Their manner and their speech were having their effect. Presently Henderson was offering to resign as Senator,—yes, he would wire the Governor of Missouri so that his successor could immediately take his place in the High Court. But it was not Henderson's resignation that was wished; what they wanted was his vote! The Missouri Representatives withdrew, but a little later on the same day, they put their demands in black and white; they wrote Henderson requesting him to withhold his vote on any article upon which he could not vote "affirmatively." "This request," they wrote, "is made because we believe the safety of the loyal people of the United States demands the immediate removal of Andrew Johnson from the office of President of the United States." [12] Would Henderson find his manhood, or would he quail beneath the lash?

§

At half past eleven on the morning the Missouri Representatives were practising their blackmail, the High Court was called to order.

The New York *World* of that day contained an interview with Andrew Johnson. "What news today, how stands the impeachment?" with calm imperturbability the President inquired of the journalist. "Mr. Johnson," wrote the correspondent, "never looked better than he does today, and his fine flow of good humor indicates anything but a troubled mind." In response to an inquiry as to his views of the situation, the President exclaimed:

"Oh I have never allowed myself to believe or feel that the American Senate would prostitute its great power of impeachment to base party purposes, and I shall not believe it until I know the vote for conviction has been recorded." [13]

In the Senate chamber all is in readiness, the final scene of the drama is about to be enacted. But Senator Chandler is on his feet with the announcement that his colleague, Jacob Howard, had been taken suddenly ill and for twenty-four hours had been delirious.[14] The great hour must be postponed! An adjournment until May 16th was presently agreed upon.[15] Is Howard's health the sole cause for the postponement? Four days will give added time to the criminal importuning of the doubtful Senators! "The Radicals, fearful of the result of the vote," wrote Welles that evening, "have postponed the question until next Saturday. The excuse for this is the illness of Howard, one of their members, who is said to be delirious,—the brain fever—some say delirium tremens. I suppose he is really ill, though many think not. Had it been one of the Senators friendly to the President, there would have been no four days' postponement. . . . When Attorney-General Stanbery was taken ill, the leading Radicals would not consent to delay a day, although he was the principal counsel of the President. . . . Very likely a still further postponement will take place, if the Senatorial conspirators have not sufficient force to convict. There is little honor, justice or truth with the impeaching judges. If by any trick or subterfuge they can succeed, the Radicals will resort to it, however unprincipled. The President was, I think, more disturbed by the postponement than I have ever seen him, but he soon rallied." [16]

Now, Thad Stevens, is your chance! You and your dupes have four days in which to work! Push on then with your embracery! Ninety-six hours are now vouchsafed you to debauch the judgment of those whose oaths have bound them to administer impartial justice! And you will not cry in vain for help! There are many to assist you! There is the "Union Congressional Committee," with its Senators and Representatives already long concerned in your conspiracy. Robert Schenck of Ohio is the chairman of this camarilla! He will apply the party lash until the blood flows. On this very day he is sending out a hundred telegrams to the Loyal Leagues to influence the judges of the High Court.[17] To every state whose Senator is wavering against conviction, this electric message storms its way along the wires: "Great danger to the peace of the country and the Republican cause if impeachment fails. Send to your Senators public opinion by resolutions, letters and delegations."[18] Never was Morse's marvelous invention put to baser use!

Answers came pouring in the next day! To Senator Henderson, E. W. Fox, one of St. Louis' important men, dispatched this telegram: "There is intense excitement here. Meeting called for tomorrow night. Can your friends hope that you will vote for the eleventh article? If so all will be well."[19]

Well then, John Henderson, how say you? What shall your answer be? You have wavered somewhat before these disorderly demands of the Republicans from your state. Your time to play the man or the poltroon has come! Henderson decides! "Say to my friends," he wires Fox, "that I am sworn to do impartial justice according to law and evidence, and I will try to do it like an honest man."[20]

And now what of Lyman Trumbull? The eleven Republican Representatives of Illinois are conferring with a view to influencing him for conviction.[21] But five of the eleven sway their colleagues against this course. Too well they knew the man who had defeated Lincoln for the Senatorship in 1859.[22] There are some men whom it is unwise even to attempt to blackmail!

Senator Waitman Willey of West Virginia was a Methodist. By a coincidence fortunate for the conspirators, the General Conference of the Methodist Episcopal Church was at this time in session at Chicago.[23] Bishop Simpson, a sectarian politician of great ability and shrewdness, conceived the pleasing plan of bringing all his clerical and church influence to bear upon the Senator from West Virginia.[24] There was then no other "reform" to deflect his spiritual exertions. To what better purpose could they be employed than in the holy effort to dissuade one of the judges of the High Court from his obedience to an oath to do impartial justice? With all the effervescent energy so characteristic of his kind, he now set to work.

On the 13th of May a motion was made at the General Conference for an hour of prayer in aid of the impeachment. But there was one old delegate whose conscience was not dead. He moved to lay the proposal on the table. "My understanding is," he said, "that impeachment is a judicial proceeding and that Senators are acting under an oath. Are we to pray to the Almighty that they may violate their oaths?" That was precisely what the smug and sinuous Bishop Simpson wanted them to do! But this effort to enlist God himself in the conspiracy,—at least through so frank an overture—was not destined to success. The motion for the hour of prayer was laid upon the table.[25]

The next day, however, Simpson offered a new resolution. Its preamble omitted the direct statement that Johnson's judges should vote for a conviction, but it recited that "painful rumors" were in circulation that "corrupt influences" had been brought to bear upon the Senators to prevent them from the performance of their "high duty." It was resolved, therefore, that upon the following day an hour for prayer be set aside in which to beseech God to "save our Senators from *error*."[26] This hypocritical circumlocution, they thought, while relieving them of earthly criticism, would be perfectly clear to the Almighty. Their relations with Him were so intimate, that they felt sure He would not misunderstand them. The negro Methodists, in conference at the same time in Washington, either through greater honesty, or from the fear that there might be some divine mistake,—some heavenly crossing of the wires—employed no pious ambiguity, but prayed directly for the President's conviction, and directed their petition not to God, but to the Senate![27]

But it was not only Thaddeus Stevens' followers and the negroes who made the air of the National Capitol vibrant with the conspiracy to obstruct justice. Grant was putting all his influence behind the managers.[28] Scores of lesser army officers took their cue from him. Aides-de-camp rushed back and forth, as though in battle.[29] In the War Department there was neither sleep nor rest. Day and night Stanton was at work. Lists of doubtful

Senators were checked and checked again. Generals were summoned and instructed, discarded generals who had been stripped of their command, and generals who were manoeuvering to stand right with the administration that was presently to take charge.[30]

Fessenden, Fowler, Willey, Grimes, Sprague, Van Winkle, Trumbull, Henderson and Ross! These were the nine on whom the hottest political fire of American history unceasingly was turned. Any seven of the nine could ruin the conspiracy. Four of them, Grimes, Fessenden, Henderson and Trumbull, already were despaired of by the Radicals.[31] Letters, dispatches, telegrams and resolutions of excited mass meetings unceasingly were hurled upon them.

On May 13th, at Steinway Hall in New York City, the thirty-fifth annual meeting of the American Anti-Slavery Society was held. Slavery was dead, but not so Wendell Phillips! The great "treason" of the President, declared Phillips to his idolators, lay in the fact that he had attempted in the South to "save their pet white man's government,—the aristocratic indolence—this idea of a gentleman." [32]

And then with incomparable insolence, not to say contempt of court, and with a square-toed humor not infrequently encountered among professional reformers, Phillips continued: "The Republican party is breaking, and behind those factions in the Senate which are hiding Andrew Johnson from justice sits the Chief Justice with 'Presidency' on the brain. The plot which saves Andrew Johnson is a plot hatched under the ermine of the Supreme Court. Whatever Chase does he does deliberately. But I am not so sure of Fessenden. I think we ought to be very patient with him. My own opinion is that if impeachment had lasted six months Mr. Fessenden would have seen things in their right light. It takes six months for a statesmanlike idea to find its way into Mr. Fessenden's head. . . . He is very slow. I don't think he is lacking; he is only slow." [33]

On the same day Horace Greeley centered his fire on the Senator from Iowa. "Those who know Mr. Grimes' temper," he wrote, "can easily understand how he has become the Timon of the Senate. A Republican raised to eminence by Republicans,—

trusted, honored, promoted and cherished—now that he retires from public life, the necessity of his nature seems to compel him to turn and send a Parthian arrow at the party life. It is not too much to expect these secessions. The history of this day merely repeats the history of other days. It seems as if no generation could pass without giving us one man to live among the Warnings of history. We have had Benedict Arnold, Aaron Burr, Jefferson Davis, and now we have James W. Grimes." [34] Grimes that afternoon suffered a stroke of paralysis. [35] If Greeley could not deter him from following his conscience, his abuse had so broken him as to render him perhaps incapable of voting!

The more the list-makers pondered names of doubtful Senators, the clearer it appeared that the verdict might depend upon one vote,— that of Edward Ross of Kansas. Sumner did not think that "a Kansas man could quibble against his country," but the conspirators were unwilling to take chances. [36] He was watched and spied upon. Eager informers recorded all his minutest goings out and comings in. Every domestic and political affiliation of his life was probed. Vinnie Ream, the young sculptress commissioned to create a statue of Lincoln, was sought out. She was the daughter of Perry Fuller, with whom Ross had his lodgings. At the studio where the young girl was busily at work Ross, it was said, went frequently to call. There, it was believed, more than one effort had been made to mould the Senator's opinion in favor of acquittal. [37] Representative George Julian was sent by his colleagues to warn the girl. He called upon her. That he threatened her was later charged upon the floor of the House, but he denied it. [38]

And now Samuel C. Pomeroy, the other Senator from Kansas, attempted to take Ross personally in hand. How little loath was Pomeroy to embark upon intrigue is suggested by the sobriquet "Subsidy Pom" which, by reason of his intimate relations with Credit Mobilier he subsequently won. [39] Pomeroy entered upon his work with vigor, albeit with slight finesse. On Wednesday, the 13th, he found Ross in the room of the sergeant-at-arms and asked him bluntly what his vote would be. Effrontery so brazen might well have justified a physical rejoinder, but so common had

the efforts to seduce the judges grown that Ross, instead of insulting his crude interlocutor, replied merely that his decision was
uncertain, that he probably would vote guilty on some articles
and not guilty on the others.[40]

The next day Pomeroy sought out Ross again, finding him
this time in the company of Willey, Henderson, Trumbull and
Van Winkle in the latter's room. His presence there with these
doubtful Senators was not auspicious, but Pomeroy without ado
plunged into the work once more. Conviction on the eleventh
article was certain, he declared; it would be carried by one vote!
One of the necessary votes would come from Ross, he casually
remarked. But Ross answered: "Do not count on my vote for
conviction under any circumstances." On the following morning
he received this telegram from Leavenworth:

> Kansas has heard the evidence and demands the conviction of
> the President.
>
> D. R. ANTHONY AND 1000 OTHERS.[41]

On the same morning Horace Greeley's editorial was boasting:
"Altogether the prospect brightens, and there is every reason to
suppose that the would-be usurper will be driven from the White
House before another week shall have passed."[42] But some of
the more conservative journals such as the Chicago *Tribune* and
the New York *Evening Post* were rebuking the conspirators.[43]

As the day of the verdict approached, however, the conspirators
with feverish zeal redoubled their dishonorable efforts. More
letters and more telegrams, at the instance of the "whippers-in,"
poured down upon the doubtful Senators. Members of the House
continued calling on them, seeking to extort a decision adverse to
the President. Never in the whole history of shame was a more
discreditable object sought or were more dishonorable means
employed. At nearly midnight of the 14th Pomeroy again sought
out Ross. He went to the latter's lodgings and waited there until
four of the next morning, but Ross did not return.[44]

All of this hectoring met with Greeley's enthusiastic approbation. So many persons were influenced, his editorial of the next
morning bemoaned, by the "erroneous views of those who insist

upon regarding the impeachment as a judicial proceeding held to ascertain and punish guilt." But, continued Greeley, "the guilt is merely an incident. The proceeding is purely political; its object is not necessarily to punish guilt but to exchange a bad officer for a good one. . . . Impeachment is provided by the Constitution as a political remedy for political evils. . . . General Grant . . . declares that the acquittal of Johnson would threaten the country and especially the South with revolution and bloodshed." [45]

LXXX

ACQUITTED ON THE ELEVENTH ARTICLE

SATURDAY, the 16th of May came at last,—Johnson's judgment day. In front of the City Hall the day before, the Capital's first Lincoln monument was dedicated. Andrew Johnson presided at the exercise, but neither House of Congress paid the least attention, or adjourned in honor of the dead President's memory.[1]

Down to the last hour the impeachers like patients in a psychopathic ward, with all of their unnatural ingenuity, were planning and employing every means wherewith to ruin and strike down the follower of Lincoln. One of the questions before them was: Upon which article could the most votes be surely counted for conviction? At the home of "Subsidy Pom," two caucuses of Radical Senators had been held the previous day to decide this vital matter. Theodore Tilton, "a flaming sword and a crusader,"—a sword whose cutting edge Henry Ward Beecher was later to encounter—had come to this conference to lend strength to the impeachers.[2] If the eleventh article were first voted on, he assured them, a conviction would ensue.[3] This might be true, but surely the making of one further effort to intimidate Senator Ross could do no harm! But this was not the only subject under consideration at that caucus. Mr. Wade's cabinet was there finally agreed upon![4]

The court was scheduled to reconvene at noon. Ten minutes before the appointed hour "Subsidy Pom" found Ross in the lobby of the Senate. Thaddeus Stevens was there listening with grim approval while Pomeroy told his colleague that his political death would surely follow if he voted to acquit, and that he might also find himself entangled in a charge of bribery. But Pomeroy was wasting breath, for earlier that morning Ross had sent to Anthony and the "1000 others" this telegram: "I do not recognize your

720

right to demand that I shall vote either for or against conviction. I have taken an oath to do impartial justice . . . and I trust I shall have the courage and honesty to vote according to the dictates of my judgment and for the good of my country." [5]   Later on that day Anthony and his thousand replied to Ross: "Your vote is dictated by Tom Ewing, not by your oath.   Your motives are Indian contracts and greenbacks.   Kansas repudiates you as she does all perjurers and skunks." [6]   With this urbanity the correspondence between Ross and Anthony came now to a close.

But we must have done with all these preludes, for the Senate chamber is now filling up.   Citizens from all parts of the Republic are wedging themselves into the galleries.   The diplomats and foreign ministers all are present eager to observe the novel spectacle of a "peaceful deposition of a sovereign ruler." [7]   Both the friends and enemies of Andrew Johnson wait with hushed intensity. [8]

Promptly at 12 o'clock the Chief Justice, in his black robes enters, and the sergeant-at-arms brings the court to order.   The managers are in their seats, as are all of the President's counsel, except Curtis.   "Subsidy Pom's" conference of the night before has borne its fruit, for Senator Williams is on his feet with a motion that the vote should be first taken on the eleventh article. Here was the charge which no one understood, designed by Thaddeus Stevens not to be understood, a hodge-podge catch-all, a trap for wavering and doubtful Senators.   The yeas and nays were called, 34 yeas and 19 nays.   Of the doubtful Senators all had voted in the negative, all but Grimes who was not present. And now for the first time a new voice is heard in the calling of the roll, Ben Wade had voted with the majority! [9]   It was his first vote.   His ostentatious silence on all previous roll calls was revealed now as a sham.

And where is Senator Grimes this morning?   After his stroke of paralysis three days before, could he attend?   Fessenden is requesting a half hour's delay.   Grimes had assured him that he would come, but Reverdy Johnson interrupts: "I have sent for him.   He is downstairs.   He will be in the chamber in a moment. Here he is!" [10]   And as he spoke the doors opened and Grimes was borne through the struggling crowds and lifted to his seat. Faint and pale, he had brushed aside the apprehensions of his friends, and shattered and disabled as he was, had nerved himself for the occasion.[11]   His coming on that day is one of America's unsung acts of heroism!

And now the great hour is at hand.   The Chief Justice is admonishing the "citizens and strangers in the galleries that absolute silence and perfect order are required."[12]   The order was unnecessary, for there was everywhere a death-like stillness.   The very breathing in the galleries could be heard.[13]   The faces of the President's friends and of his foes were haggard with anxiety.[14] "Some of the members of the House near me," wrote Julian, "grew pale and sick under the burden of suspense."[15]   But the suspense so evident in the Senate chamber was not confined to the actors or the witnesses of the drama.   In a little upper chamber at the White House, Eliza McCardle was waiting for the verdict. Would it never come?[16]

At the direction of the chair the secretary reads the eleventh article.   The droning of this unintelligible jumble ends at last, and the voice of the Chief Justice sounds: "Call the roll."[17]   The secretary drones: "Senator Anthony."   Senator Anthony rises in his place.   "Mr. Senator Anthony," interrupts the Chief Justice, "how say you?   Is the respondent Andrew Johnson, President of the United States, guilty or not guilty of high misdemeanors as charged in this article?"   Hundreds of pencils on the floor and in the galleries are suspended over tally papers.[18]   Anthony's answer came: "Guilty!"   "Not guilty," answered Bayard and Buckalew, the next two called.   Then Cameron: "Guilty," followed immediately by seven more votes for conviction, and then three for acquittal.[19]   And now the first of the seven doubtful is called out: "Mr. Senator Fessenden, how say you?"   In deathlike stillness, clear and strong, Fessenden's answer came: "Not guilty."   Relief spread through the ranks of Johnson's friends.[20] Fowler of Tennessee came next; he seemed to answer: "Guilty." But he had not spoken clearly and the Chief Justice again asked him: "How say you?"   This time Fowler found his voice and answered as he had intended: "Not guilty."[21]   The followers of

(*From a sketch by James E. Taylor.*)

TAKING THE VOTE ON THE IMPEACHMENT OF PRESIDENT JOHNSON, SENATE CHAMBER, WASHINGTON, D. C., MAY 16, 1868. SENATOR ROSS, OF KANSAS, VOTING "NOT GUILTY."

Johnson breathed again. And now it was Grimes' turn to speak. The Chief Justice tells him that he need not rise. But with the aid of friends, Grimes clambers to his feet, and with what remaining strength he has, answers: "Not guilty." Harlan is recorded for conviction, but immediately is followed by Henderson who votes not guilty, the black looks from the Representatives of Missouri notwithstanding. Four of the doubtful Senators have been heard from, all in favor of acquittal! Fifteen more votes follow, ten of them for conviction. And now, "Mr. Senator Ross, how say you?" "Not guilty," comes the quiet answer. The conspiracy was tottering! Fifteen votes had been thus far recorded for acquittal, four more would achieve it. One of these came at once from Saulsbury, then followed Sumner and five others for conviction.[22]

Forty-six votes so far; thirty for, and sixteen against conviction. But there were eight votes yet to come! Trumbull and Van Winkle now promptly voted for acquittal, as did Vickers of Maryland. And now is called the name of the intended beneficiary of the conspiracy,—"Mr. Senator Wade, how say you, is the respondent Andrew Johnson guilty or not guilty of the high misdemeanors as charged in this article?" drones the Chief Justice. Can it be that disregarding every principle of honor he will cast his own vote to remove the only obstacle that lay between him and the Presidency? Throughout the long trial he had sat silent. Would he now speak? Yes! "Guilty!" he answers. In all the shady story of the conspiracy there is no more dishonorable act than this.

Willey follows Wade, voting for conviction,—and the Methodists. Williams, Wilson and Yates are recorded to the same effect, and it is over! "Upon this article," announces the Chief Justice, "35 Senators vote 'guilty' and 19 Senators vote 'not guilty.' Two-thirds not having pronounced guilty, the President is therefore acquitted on this article."[23] One vote had saved him!

Col. Crook, the President's bodyguard, sprang down the steps of the Capitol and ran the entire length of Pennsylvania Avenue to the White House. He pushed his way into the library where sat the President surrounded by his friends. He responded calmly to their congratulations, but the tears were rolling down his face.[24] Hurrying from the library, Crook sped upstairs to the little bedroom in the northeast corner of the Executive Mansion. His first knock admitted him. There sat Eliza McCardle in her rocking chair,—sewing. "He's acquitted," he cried. "The President is acquitted." The frail little lady rising from her chair, clasped his right hand with her emaciated fingers. "Crook," she said, "I knew he would be acquitted; I knew it." [25]

LXXXI

THE REPUBLICAN NATIONAL CONVENTION

BUT impeachment was not over. The hard-bitted enemies of Lincoln and of Lincoln's follower had still ten articles to vote upon. What they wanted now, however, was more time. Time and further opportunity to dragoon the seven Senators! Chase ruled that the balloting must continue, but he was overruled and an adjournment was taken until Tuesday, the 26th.[1] The Republican National Convention was to meet in Chicago on the 20th. There, it was hoped, such enthusiasm could be engendered as to stimulate the judges of the High Court when next they met! New pressure could thus be brought to bear! Therefore, on to Chicago!

"Well!" wrote Greeley two days after the adjournment, "Mr. Johnson remains in the White House. The 11th was deliberately, and we doubt not judiciously, selected as the article that would command the most votes. This failing, all fails."[2] He was voicing the disappointment of the partisans over their defeat. But hope lingered still. Through group malice, perhaps the inflamed delegates might heap such contumely on the name of Andrew Johnson that when the adjourn day came, one or more of the seven Republican Senators would no longer dare to play the man.

The nomination of Ulysses Grant was a foregone conclusion. The Convention lasted but two days. Conspicuous among the delegates were Joseph Hawley of Connecticut, General Sickles, Lyman Tremaine and Chauncey M. Depew of New York, John Bingham of Ohio, ex-Attorney-General Speed of Kentucky, Carl Schurz of Missouri and John Logan of Illinois.[3]

Hawley was made President of the Convention, and then the platform makers went to work. On the second day the result

725

of their deliberations was reported. If there is one thing more than another in which Americans can take no pride, it is their party platforms. The one approved by this convention was a model of chicane. It was founded upon mean hatred of the man who had given all he had to champion the cause of Lincoln. The praise of Lincoln in that platform was hypocrisy. "We profoundly deplore," it declared, "the untimely and tragic death of Abraham Lincoln and regret the accession to the Presidency of Andrew Johnson, who has acted treacherously to the people who elected him and the cause he was pledged to support; who has usurped high legislative and judicial functions; who has refused to execute the laws. . . ." [4] And so on and on the tirade ran. Nearly all of the old charges, except that he had killed his predecessor, were here repeated. [5]

And then lastly, with a duplicity worthy of the conspiracy of which their platform was a part, by a trickster's use of words, the result of the balloting on the eleventh article was wilfully misrepresented. Upon this the only article so far voted on Andrew Johnson had been acquitted, yet the platform makers declared that he had been "justly impeached for high crimes and misdemeanors, *and properly pronounced guilty thereof by the vote of thirty-five Senators.*" [6]

Never was more brazen effort made to make white seem black, to distort acquittal into a conviction! One more plank and then we shall pass on to the nominations. The second paragraph declared: "The guarantee by Congress of equal suffrage to all loyal men at the South was demanded by every consideration of public safety, of gratitude, and of justice, and must be maintained; *while the question of suffrage in all the loyal states properly belongs to the people* of those states." [7] The age-old story of sauce for the goose, but for the gander something else! Professor Burgess has well called this plank "a mean, shuffling bit of partisan politics." [8] But no one has condemned it more wholeheartedly than Blaine when eighteen years later he pronounced it "unworthy of the Republican party . . ., a mere stroke of expediency to escape the prejudices which negro suffrage would encounter in a majority of the loyal states, and especially in Indiana and

California where a close vote was anticipated. The position carried with it an element of deception, because every intelligent man knew that it would be impossible to force negro suffrage on the Southern states by national authority, and leave the Northern states free to exclude it from their own domain. It was an extraordinary proposition that the South, after all the demoralization wrought by the war should be called upon to exhibit a higher degree of political justice than the North was willing to practice." [9]

Not forgetting to endorse "bounties and pensions," or to speak highly of the Declaration of Independence, the platform came at last to a close. The nominations were now in order. By acclamation the 650 delegates unanimously nominated Grant for President.[10] A great demonstration followed.[11] But everyone knew that Grant's choice came because of fear that if he were not chosen by the Republicans the Democrats would take him. "His nomination," says Julian, "was only secured by cautious and timely diplomacy, and potent appeals to his sordidness, in the shape of assurances that he should have the office for a second term." [12]

And now the scuffle for the Vice-Presidency began. If Wade's co-conspirators could only have succeeded in convicting Johnson, Wade's prestige would, no doubt, have been irresistible. But even as it was, his "bluff address," so much admired by his contemporaries, might bring him the nomination for the Vice-Presidency. Governor Fenton of New York, however, who had superseded Thurlow Weed as party boss, was eager for the place.[13] So also were Hannibal Hamlin, James Speed, "Subsidy Pom," "Smiler Colfax" and several others.[14] There were five ballots, Wade leading on the first four, followed closely by Fenton and Colfax. But on the fifth, the "available candidate" as always, was successful. Colfax was then in the third term of his speakership. "Genial and cordial with unfailing tact and aptitude, skillful in cultivating friendships, and never provoking enmities, he had in a rare degree the elements that insure popularity." [15] And so he was nominated for Vice-President. It had not yet come out,—in print— that he was one of the cheapest grafters in the most corrupt decade of our history.[16]

Grant and Colfax! This ticket would surely sweep the country, and perhaps Johnson from the White House, when four days hence the High Court would be returning to its work! In the meantime Welles was writing: "Grant . . . is the designated candidate if not the choice of the Radicals for the office of Chief Magistrate. A feeling of gratitude for military service, without one thought of his . . . experience in civil affairs, has enlisted popular favor for him, and the conspirators have availed themselves of it, though the knowing ones are aware of his unfitness for administrative duties. They expect to use him; he intends to use them. . . . There was an attempt to make him Commander-in-Chief over the President, to which Grant was nothing loath, and finally, uniting with the Radicals, he entered into the conspiracy to impeach the President and was slyly active in that intrigue. I have little doubt that the Radicals intend to make him President the next four years by fraud and force if necessary. Their moral sense is blunted and politically they are unprincipled. They have Congress which opens and declares the vote; they have the general of the army who is their candidate; and if they can by any means secure the President before the vote is counted next February, they will not hesitate to override the popular verdict, should it be against them." [17]

In Washington a procession headed by the Marine band marched to Grant's home on the evening of the day following his nomination. Grant, with Manager Boutwell at his side, came to the door and made a speech, as did Colfax when later the serenaders reached his home. [18]

LXXXII

FULL ACQUITTAL AT LAST. THE CONSPIRACY IS BROKEN

BUTLER did not attend the National Convention; he had work to do in Washington. Immediately after the vote on the eleventh article he began again his efforts to intimidate the Senators, and a veritable inquisition into their private affairs was instituted. But Ross was the centre of attack. It was claimed that he had been "pledged" to vote for a conviction, but that he had broken his promise. "The managers," our diarist wrote on May 19th, "are sitting as a committee to investigate the Senators under the authority of the House, and Butler, vile and unscrupulous, is calling men before him and compelling them to disclose their private affairs. Last night he spent several hours at Jay Cooke's bank, overhauling private accounts. These outrages are tamely submitted to, and are justified and upheld by Radical *legislators*, *patriots* and *statesmen*. Heaven save the mark!" [1]

Butler's tools pushed their researches everywhere. They raided the telegraph offices of Baltimore and Washington. All dispatches to or from these cities during the four days before May 16th were confiscated! [2] The headquarters of the inquisition were in the basement of the Capitol. Characteristic of all revolutions, there was a tame submission to outrage, an indifference to villainy. [3]

The Senate, too, was aflame with zeal. The Chamber was scarcely cleared after the vote upon the eleventh article before a legislative session had begun. The House bill to admit the Carolinas, Alabama, Georgia and Louisiana must be passed "within the next three or four days," declared Senator Wilson. [4] Let it be "before the sun goes down," responded Nye. [5] Some one raised the question whether the Senators from these states who had neither participated in the trial nor heard the evidence

729

could at this late hour become members of the High Court. "Of course they can be," answered Sumner.[6] But Sumner's theories of justice this time did not prevail.[7]

Twenty-four hours before the reconvening of the High Court Butler presented a misleading report of the testimony he had taken. The lobbyists, the claim agents, the gold gamblers and the whiskey ring who hovered about Congress "like buzzards around carrion," had wagered heavily on the outcome of the trial. "Into the nests of these unclean birds," the managers had thrust their noses, but nothing was established even faintly discreditable to the acquitting Senators.[8] Yet Butler's report was artfully and unscrupulously designed to make innocent men appear guilty.[9] *"The Impeachment Managers' Report—Conclusive Evidence of Corruption,"* ran Greeley's headline.[10]

Tuesday, May the 26th, the adjourn day of the trial, came at last. An acquittal on the remaining articles was anything but certain. Perhaps all that had taken place since the last session of the court might change the vote! "Intrigues pervade the whole atmosphere," wrote Welles. "I hear of no one but the seven 'recreants' who can be relied upon, and it is not certain that Ross will vote for acquittal on every article."[11]

At 12 o'clock the High Court once more came to order. Stimulated by the proceedings at Chicago, could the managers this time muster enough votes? Could the infamy that Wade and his confederates so long had planned be pressed this time to consummation? Was the blackest page of American history presently to be written? What of the seven Senators? What especially of Ross? Had the conspirators frightened him enough? It was whispered everywhere that a further adjournment would be taken! More time was needed![12] More opportunity for coercion of the judges!

The galleries once more were crowded. The diplomats in full force again were there. The Chief Justice enters, the chaplain prays, the sergeant-at-arms proclaims, the House of Representatives two by two make their silent entrance. The managers are there. Stanbery, Evarts and Nelson of the President's counsel are in their places.[13]

Senator Morrill now presses forward with a motion to adjourn until the 23rd of June. And now what is this? Has Ross at last been captured? He asks that the adjourn day be September first! Ross was voting with the Radicals! When this news was flashed to the White House, it threw a damper over the President and his confidants.[14] But the amendment and the motion are both voted down.[15] From the private caucusing it was believed that the second and the third articles could now muster enough votes, and so a motion by Senator Edmunds "that the Senate proceed to vote upon the second article" is carried.[16]

And now once more the roll is called. "Senator Anthony," booms the voice of the Chief Justice, "how say you, is the respondent, Andrew Johnson, President of the United States, guilty or not guilty of a high misdemeanor, as charged in this article of impeachment?" Anthony again votes guilty.[17] In breathless silence the fifty-four names are called, and each Senator responds exactly as he had done on the eleventh article.[18] "Thirty-five Senators," announces the Chief Justice, "have pronounced the respondent Andrew Johnson, President of the United States, guilty; nineteen have pronounced him not guilty. Two-thirds not having pronounced him guilty he stands acquitted upon this article." And now upon the third article the roll is called; the responses are the same, and Chase announces the acquittal on this article as well.[19] On each of the roll calls Wade had again registered his vote for conviction!

The conspiracy had failed! "If there be no objection," the Chief Justice is declaring, "the judgment will be entered by the clerk," and presently a "judgment of acquittal" was recorded.[20] It was all over! "I move," said Senator Williams, "that the Senate sitting as a Court of Impeachment do now adjourn *sine die*."[21] The motion was agreed to; the High Court had finished with its labors! Eight of the articles had not been voted on and they never would be. The first and thus far the last impeachment trial of an American President was over. In some hot partisan day, some red hour of revolution, when some future American executive stands Johnson-like refusing to defy the Constitution, will that High Court meet again?

§

Seven Republican Senators with consciences had saved America's good name. "No intelligent, honest, candid man who regarded his oath would have voted otherwise than these seven Senators," wrote Welles, with all too little an appreciation of what these men had endured, and would surely yet be called upon to suffer because they had done right.[22]

The readers of Macaulay's gorgeous history of England will remember how the Archbishop and six of his Suffragans refused to read King James' Declaration of Indulgence in their pulpits, how they protested in writing to the King and because of this were prosecuted on a criminal charge of libel.[23] They bade defiance to the last of English tyrants amidst the turbulent acclaim of his liberty-loving subjects. Bishop Trelawney of Bristol was one of those seven gallant churchmen. For him the bold and fierce people of Cornwall expressed their fighting sympathy in this ballad that swept all England:

> And shall Trelawney die, and shall Trelawney die?
> Then thirty thousand Cornish boys will know the reason why.

While from their caverns the miners varying the refrain re-echoed it:

> Then twenty thousand underground will know the reason why.[24]

When the verdict of acquittal came the King's soldiers and his subjects mingled their shouts of joy, whilst the bells of all the parishes of London rang. And when finally the seven Bishops emerged from Westminster Hall, the cries of the people greeted them: "God bless you! God prosper your families! You have saved us all today."[25]

Fessenden of Maine, Fowler of Tennessee, Henderson of Missouri, Trumbull of Illinois, Van Winkle of West Virginia, Grimes of Iowa and Ross of Kansas, these seven Senators who dared to defy the Congressional tyranny of 1868 are well deserving of a place of honor alongside the seven English Bishops.[26] But it was proscription rather than acclaim that greeted them. The Radical

journals had long denounced them as "Judases," "recreants,"
"apostates," [27] and now new defamations were sedulously heralded
abroad. Those of Forney's Philadelphia press were typical.
According to this spokesman for the Radicals, Trumbull's "statesmanship" had dwindled into selfishness, Fessenden's "conservatism" had "turned to cowardice," "treachery" was the crime of
Henderson, "impotence and idiocy" had marked the course of
Grimes, "treason" that of Fowler, and Van Winkle's "cloak of
fair protestation" had been "dyed in infamy," while in Ross "lit-
tleness" had "simply borne its legitimate fruit." [28]

But it was not to printer's ink alone that their proscription was
confined. Trumbull was warned not to show himself on the
streets of Chicago lest the nearest lamp post be chosen as his
gallows. [29] The statesmen in the halls of Congress passed by
Ross as though he were a leper. To associate with him was
deemed "disreputable and scandalous." [30] When finally he left
the Senate, desperately poor, he eked out for a time his scanty
livelihood from a starving country newspaper. But even the elements seemed leagued with the Radicals, when a cyclone burst
upon the town of Coffeyville and scattered his newspaper office
and all its contents over the surrounding prairie. Forty years
later in New Mexico, old and poor, he died. [31]

In 1884 Henderson was made chairman of the convention that
nominated Blaine; he alone of the seven was forgiven by his
party. [32] But if the lot of these gallant seven was a hard one,
unlike their colleagues who had cowered beneath the Stevens'
lash, they could enjoy such peace as a clear conscience brings.
"Perhaps I did wrong not to commit perjury by order of a party,"
declared Grimes to an old friend, "but I cannot see it that way." [33]
Paralysis, calumny and vituperation had not broken him. While
the objurgations of the conspirators were at their height, the
Chief Justice one day called upon him. "I would rather be in
your place, Mr. Grimes," he said, "than to receive any honor in
the gift of our people." [34]

To less credit than the seven, but no doubt to some, were
Sprague of Rhode Island, Willey of West Virginia and Morgan
of New York entitled. Should their votes be needed, they had

given the President's friends to understand, that they would cast them for acquittal.[35] Their votes were not needed, and so rather than incur the wrath of party tyrants, they chose to write their names upon the scroll of the conspiracy.

To those who joyously had voted for conviction or had advocated it, only a few lived who dared express repentance for their wrong. "It is impossible now to realize," wrote George Julian sixteen years later, "how perfectly overmastering was the excitement of those days. The exercise of calm judgment was simply out of the question. . . . Patriotism and party animosity were so inextricably mingled and confounded that the real merits of the controversy could only be seen after the heat and turmoil of the strife had passed away. Time has made this manifest. Andrew Johnson was not the Devil-incarnate he was then painted, nor did he monopolize the 'wrong-headedness' of the times. No one will dispute that the popular estimate of his character did him very great injustice. It is equally certain that great injustice was done to Trumbull, Fessenden, Grimes and other Senators who voted to acquit the President and gave proof of their honesty and independence by facing the wrath and scorn of the party with which they had so long been identified. The idea of making the question of impeachment a matter of party discipline was utterly indefensible and preposterous."[36]

In the same year these words were penned Blaine wrote: "The sober reflection of later years has persuaded many who favored impeachment that it was not justifiable on the charges made, and that its success would have resulted in greater injury to free institutions than Andrew Johnson in his utmost endeavor was able to inflict. No impartial reader can examine the record of the pleadings and arguments of the managers . . . without feeling that the President was impeached for one series of misdemeanors and tried for another series."[37]

But after thirty-four years had passed, George Boutwell was still without contrition. "It is not improbable," in 1902 he wrote, "that a majority of the people now entertain the opinion that the action of the House of Representatives in the attempt that was made to impeach President Johnson was an error."[38]

But in the next paragraph he declares that this effort was "a gain to the public," and that the "proceedings against Mr. Johnson were free from any element or quality of injustice." [39]

With greater wisdom, Grant, when he came to write his Memoirs refrained from all discussion of the impeachment or his participation in it.[40] His choice of silence on this subject was a wise one. John Sherman, who had solemnly declared, when he Tenure-of-Office Act was passed, that it was not intended to cover Stanton's case, in 1895 wrote in his autobiography: "I felt bound with much regret, to vote 'guilty' in response to my name, but I was entirely satisfied with the result of the vote, brought about by the action of several Republican Senators." [41]

Sumner before he died eschewed such shuffling and manfully confessed his wrong. To Senator Henderson one night in Washington, in the early seventies, he said: "I don't want to die without making this confession, that in the matter of impeachment you were right and I was wrong." [42]

§

At the conclusion of the trial Stanton surrendered.[43] Schofield's nomination, which came before the Senate on April 24th, was now confirmed.[44] The resolution confirming it declared that although Stanton had "not been legally removed," as he had "relinquished his place as Secretary of War for causes stated in his note to the President," Schofield's appointment was approved.[45] A resolution later was adopted thanking Stanton for the discharge of his duties "as well amid the open dangers of a great rebellion as at a later period when assailed by the opposition, inspired by hostility to the measures of justice and pacification provided by Congress for the restoration of a real and permanent peace." [46]

The Senate derived from this a petty satisfaction, but even more did it enjoy rejecting the name of Stanbery when Johnson sought to reappoint him as his Attorney-General.[47]

Upon this rejection the President sent in the name of another of his counsel, Benjamin R. Curtis. Curtis had no desire for public life whilst the Radicals were in control. Though he had

had, he wrote the President, "very slight connection with the politics of this country, and they are now in a condition when one would not willingly plunge into them," he assured his former client that there was nothing in his "general course of political action" of which he did not approve, and that his declination was "not in the least degree influenced" by any apprehension as to the future measures of his administration.[48]

Johnson now turned to still another of his defenders, and sent in the name of Evarts. Despite his merciless destruction of the prosecution's case, his nomination was confirmed, and he now, at past fifty, began a public life as brilliant as it was useful.[49]

Let us here turn aside for a moment to observe the Democrats in action, for their National Convention is presently to meet in New York City. What use would they make of their great opportunity?

LXXXIII

THE DEMOCRATIC NATIONAL CONVENTION

THE opportunity presented to the Democrats of 1868 was an unusual one. They had that rare combination of resources which statesmen seek but politicians overlook,—an issue and a man. The issue was the Constitution, and the man Andrew Johnson. But political parties in America are none too eager to accept real issues, or candidates with courage to espouse them.

Andrew Johnson was a lifelong Democrat. Neither Jefferson nor Jackson was more loyal to the principles of his party. His struggle culminating finally in his acquittal had every element of drama, every ingredient of popular appeal. It would enlist the sympathies of Democrats, and the approbation of all Republicans capable of seeing that he was the bold disciple of his predecessor. He had every claim to the Democratic nomination and he had strong hopes of receiving it.[1] But he was not the only prominent figure of the impeachment trial who harbored this ambition. The old Presidential fever had taken hold of Chase again! The trial was little more than well begun when the malady once more held him in its grip.[2]

Chase's conduct throughout the trial afforded one of the strangest contrasts. In the daytime he presided at the sessions of the High Court with dignity, impartiality and great skill, while at night he plied his pen in writing letters unworthy of a college sophomore. His clumsy angling for the Democratic nomination was such an act of folly as to render him ludicrous and his judicial robes less than immaculate.

Coyness is not appealing in a man over six feet tall,[3] and Chase was coy. On March 2nd to W. S. Hatch he wrote: "I rather think you give me credit for more political ambition than I have. . . . I have never had any sanguine expectation that the people would call me to the Presidency. There have been now

737

and then some indications of that sort but none so marked as to raise in me very troublesome thoughts." [4] Seven days later Chase again took up his pen. This time he declared to Francis Tucker that he was not "an aspirant for any political position," and did not want his name "connected with the Presidential nomination in any way." [5] And he continued to discuss his great unwillingness three days later when he wrote: "I seek no political office. I am neither candidate nor aspirant." [6]

Chase now waited for ten days and then he wrote to Gerrit Smith: "The subject of the presidency has become distasteful to me. Some will say 'sour grapes'; and there may be some ground for the application of the proverb. But I really think that I am not half so ambitious of place as I am represented to be." [7] But to Alexander Long, less than three weeks later, he composed a letter in the nature of a party platform. If the Democratic party, he said, would come out against military governments and commissions and in favor of the restoration of the states on the basis of universal suffrage and amnesty, he would wish for its success. If this were done he would not be at liberty, he declared, "to refuse the use" of his name.[8] With increasing frequency down to the conclusion of the impeachment trial he kept declaring to his numerous correspondents that he was not a "candidate." But after the first vote of acquittal, his craving for the Presidential office was finally admitted. "If I know my own heart," he wrote John Gilmer the day after the vote on the eleventh article, "I desire much more to merit than to receive the approval of my fellow citizens." [9]

Four days after the final acquittal was pronounced Chase wrote to August Belmont that he did not know whether he was "a suitable candidate of any party," but that if his fellow countrymen thought fit "to require such services as I can render, they are without doubt entitled to them." [10] The "Chase movement" was under way at last! Is it any wonder that since Chase's day the American people have insisted that their Chief Justice shall hold himself aloof from politics?

Chase was not lacking in integrity, but he was wanting in good sense and a sense of humor.[11] With his strong features and high forehead, his face seemed cast in the Websterian mold, yet somehow it was anything but Websterian. He lacked both inspiration and a sense of proportion.[12]   As we study his somewhat self-satisfied expression it is easy to understand why during his whole stay in Washington his only intimate was Sumner.[13]   Nor is it difficult to see why he was so incapable of appreciating Lincoln.   When after his fourth or fifth resignation from the Treasury Lincoln accepted it on the ground that the differences between them had created embarrassment, Chase was surprised, angry and disappointed.   "I had found," he wrote in his diary, "a good deal of embarrassment from him; but what he had found from me I could not imagine, unless it has been caused by my unwillingness to have offices distributed as spoils or benefits, with more regard to the claims of divisions, factions, cliques and individuals than to fitness of selection."[14]   The real reason for his resignation, he afterwards told Whitelaw Reid, was that he had "never been able to make a joke out of this war."[15]

When Lord Charnwood called Chase "unhappily a sneak,"[16] he did him less than justice, but it is not difficult to see how he arrived at that conclusion.   And yet Lincoln said: "Chase is about one and a half times bigger than any other man that I ever knew,"[17] and when Taney died, appointed him to the Supreme Court, although he struggled for some time with the doubt whether, beset as he was by his craving for the Presidency, Chase could ever become a great Chief Justice.[18]   And now in 1868 on the eve of the Democratic Convention we find him dissatisfied with the judicial post and moving, albeit clumsily, to gratify his festering ambition.   His indiscretion in the choice of his supporters was amazing.   No public man of his time numbered a cheaper set of correspondents or fraternized more willingly with worthless characters.   Don Piatt, who knew Lincoln's cabinet well, has told us that Chase was the only member of it "who was shocked at the coarse humor of his Chief," and yet when Chase chose his adherents, he "had around him from first to last about the worst set of men that ever environed a leader."[19]   But he had one ally of whom he justly could be proud, his remarkably accomplished daughter Kate.[20]

Not since the days of Dolly Madison was there in Washington a woman of such compelling charm or marked political acumen. Of her Mrs. Lincoln had complained that while coming to the White House as a guest she had held court there on her own account.[21] She had stimulated her father's Presidential aspirations in 1864, and now in 1868 she became virtually his manager.[22]

But Andrew Johnson and the Chief Justice were not the only contenders for the nomination. George H. Pendleton of Ohio had come forward with a slogan with which he hoped to stampede the convention: "The same currency for the bond holder and the plow holder!" He was sponsoring a plan whereby the depreciated wartime legal notes instead of gold were to be used in payment of the national debt. "The Ohio idea," it was called.[23] The West was infatuated with it. Chivalrous in bearing, fastidious in dress, Pendleton was a popular contender.[24] By his three hundred partisans who had come on from the West in linen caps and linen dusters he was hailed as "Young Greenback" and "Gentleman George."[25]

There were still other names. There was Winfield S. Hancock who in the first day's fighting at Gettysburg had inspired confidence and restored order among the Union troops on Cemetery Hill, and whose coolness and magnificent presence on the third day of that battle had fired his soldiers to hurl back Pickett's charge.[26]

There was James R. Doolittle of Wisconsin who had supported Johnson's vetoes and had been permanent chairman of the Philadelphia National Union Convention in 1866.[27] There was Thomas A. Hendricks of Indiana, who had done all within his power to prevent Wade from sitting as member of the High Court of Impeachment.[28] There was Joel Parker of New Jersey, Asa Packer of Pennsylvania, Sanford E. Church of New York, and many others with lightning rods erected.[29]

But what everyone was wondering was where the crafty politicians of New York would throw their influence. Church was their "favorite son," or if they could not have him (and they never imagined that they could) they modestly suggested Hendricks of Indiana, the co-laborer of Pendleton.[30] Back of all this, however, the New York leaders were quietly pushing Chase, planning a platform that would omit all reference to issues he opposed.[31] Underneath, had the New Yorkers still a better plan concealed? Horatio Seymour had been permanent chairman in 1864, he was again to be thus honored. Worn down by the city's summer heat, when the delegates were tired from many futile ballots, would New York's real hand then be shown? What of Horatio Seymour?

§

Mr. William Tweed, although eminently satisfied with Tammany, had been feeling for a long time that the old Tammany Hall building was inadequate.[32] A site on Fourteenth Street was secured and presently a new structure had arisen. By feverish energy it was completed just in time for the Democratic National Convention of 1868.[33] Madison Square Garden had not yet come.

The "Wigwam" inside and out was gayly decorated on the morning of July 4th. One hour before the convention came to order, the Tammany Society, headed by Mayor Hoffman, marched in to take possession and to dedicate their new headquarters. Judge Albert Cardozo read the Declaration of Independence and all joined in the singing of "America."[34] The Tammany Society retired, and now presently the delegates of the National Convention were assembling. There was Judge Woodward of Pennsylvania, who had denounced the impeachment of Andrew Johnson, James A. Bayard of Delaware, John G. Carlisle of Kentucky, Daniel W. Voorhees of Indiana, Francis Kernan, Samuel J. Tilden, and especially Horatio Seymour of New York. From Maryland Montgomery Blair had come, having readopted the party to which his family naturally belonged. And there, to the pretended horror, but the real delight of the Republicans, were many of the former leaders of the Confederacy with their slouch hats, long hair and gray clothing.[35] Among these were A. H. Garland of Arkansas, Benjamin H. Hill of Georgia, Zebulon B. Vance and R. Barnwell Rhett from the Carolinas, North and South.[36]

By no means the least inconspicuous among the delegates was

Vallandigham of Ohio, the best known and the most poisonous of the Copperheads.[37]   Because of his disloyalty he had been excluded from the National Union Convention at Philadelphia two years before;[38] he should have been denied admission here, yet he was received if not welcomed.[39]   The Democrats well knew how effectively their political opponents would make capital of his unwelcome presence.   But Vallandigham was too thick-skinned to mind; he had come to the convention for a purpose. His object was the nomination of Chief Justice Chase.   Chase appreciated this support, Copperhead though it was, and wrote to one of his friends: "The assurance you give me of the friend-ship of Mr. V. affords me real satisfaction.   He is a man of whose friendship one may well be proud."[40]

On the morning the convention opened, a military pageant lent color to the day.   The city took on a holiday appearance, nor was the pleasure marred by what appeared that morning in the newspapers.[41]   Andrew Johnson had issued to all who had par-ticipated "in the late insurrection," except those under indict-ment, a full pardon "for the offense of treason against the United States."[42]   There was but one man whom this pardon did not cover,—Jefferson Davis.[43]

Little was accomplished on the first day and it was not until the third that the platform was finally approved.[44]   The "Radical party" was arraigned for "the unparalleled oppression and tyr-anny which had marked its career. . . . Instead of restoring the Union it has, so far as in its power, dissolved it, and subjected ten states, in the time of profound peace, to military despotism and negro supremacy."[45]

The Radicals, this document continued, had "established a sys-tem of spies and official espionage to which no constitutional monarchy would now dare to resort; it has abolished the right of appeal on important constitutional questions to the supreme judicial tribunals, and threatened to curtail or destroy its original jurisdiction, which is irrevocably vested by the Constitution; while the learned Chief Justice has been subjected to the most atrocious calumnies, merely because he would not prostitute his high office to the support of the false and partisan charges preferred against the President. . . . It has stripped the President of his constitutional power of appointment even of his own cabinet. Under its repeated assaults the pillars of government are rocking on their base, and should it succeed in November next and inaugurate its President, we will meet as a subjected and conquered people, amid the ruins of liberty and the scattered fragments of the Constitution." [46]

Here was a platform broad enough to support both Johnson and the judge who had presided at his trial. Johnson's friends were given even greater ground for hope when in a further plank it was resolved: "that we regard the Reconstruction Acts (so called) of Congress as . . . usurpations, and unconstitutional, revolutionary and void. . . . That the President of the United States, Andrew Johnson, in exercising the powers of his high office in resisting the aggressions of Congress upon the constitutional rights of the states and the people, is entitled to the gratitude of the whole American people, and in behalf of the Democratic party we tender him our thanks for his patriotic efforts in that regard." [47]

Had the Democratic party been content to go before the country with these issues, it might have triumphed,[48] but the "Ohio idea" was too strongly sponsored and in the west too popular to be ignored, and so before they finished with their platform they had written into it the greenback heresy.[49]

These declarations of principles were not adopted until Tuesday, July 7th, and it was not till then that the convention proceeded to the nominations. Chase remained in Washington, but his daughter Kate was in New York pulling all the wires she could. "Oh, if the convention would only have the courage to do right," she wrote her father on that day.[50]

Johnson too, of course, was at the national capital, but friends of his were on the ground sponsoring his claims and sending him dispatches filled with optimism.[51] His own attitude he expressed by the assertion that he was "in the hands of the people and at their disposal." [52] He did not lack for practical suggestions, many advised him to remove McCulloch; there must be a Democrat in the Cabinet.[53] The retention of Seward also was a "stumbling block," [54] but Johnson refused even to consider the elimination of these loyal friends. [55]

Fresh from his laurels won in the impeachment trial, Tom Nelson journeyed to New York to make the nominating speech for Andrew Johnson. He spoke of him as one who was "in favor of the Union in times that tried men's souls," one who as President had been "maligned, calumniated, traduced, vilified and persecuted by the Radical party," but who had "stood up for the Constitution" against the efforts of those who attempted to destroy it. Great applause and cheers rewarded Nelson's effort. [56]

Presently all the other candidates were placed in nomination and the balloting began. Pendleton led on the first with 105 votes, Johnson came next with 65, Hancock followed them with $33\frac{1}{2}$, Church with 33, while $79\frac{1}{2}$ were scattered among the many other aspirants. Chase did not receive a single vote on the first ballot. [57] It was evident to those of his Cabinet who were with the President in Washington that night that his vote and the cheers with which it was announced had gratified him. [58] But if this had made him sanguine, his Secretary of the Navy was something more than skeptical, when he recorded: "Pendleton leads as was expected, and the President was next which was not expected. Most of his votes must have been from the South." The New York vote for Church, Welles thought, was a mere "blind," and meant that "the New Yorkers intended Seymour should be the candidate, and Seymour also intended it, provided he became satisfied he could secure the nomination; but unless certain, he would persist in declining." [59]

The balloting continued for three days. As one result after another was announced, it became increasingly apparent that the delegates were falling away both from Pendleton and Johnson, while the votes for Hendricks and Hancock were constantly on the increase. It was not until the twelfth ballot that Chase's name was even mentioned; he then received half of one vote from California amid prolonged outbursts of cheering. [60]

The sphinx-like Horatio Seymour presided as the balloting continued. On the fourth, North Carolina gave him her nine votes, but he declared: "I must not be nominated by this convention. I could not accept the nomination if tendered which I do not expect." [61] Was it a final declination?

As one ballot after another revealed no candidate who could muster the required two-thirds, the excitement grew. When the eighteenth had been counted, Johnson had dwindled to ten votes.[62] It was plain now that he could not secure the prize. The platform was based upon his stalwart fight with Congress. The Democrats generally would have welcomed him as their standard bearer, but Tammany was in control of the convention, and she was not eager for a candidate strong enough to discipline the tiger. The blunders of the Radicals, they felt, were such as to secure a Democratic victory regardless of the candidate. Why not then choose one of their own? [63]

Horatio Seymour had been governor of New York from 1862 to 1864. In the midst of the draft riots in 1863, from the steps of City Hall in New York City, he had truckled to the rioters and had addressed them as "my friends." [64] "Governor Seymour," recorded Welles at that time, "whose partisans constituted the rioters, and whose partisanship encouraged them, has been in New York talking namby-pamby. This Sir Forcible Feeble is himself chiefly responsible for the outrage." [65] But Seymour's connection with the draft did not stop there. Throughout the remainder of his term as governor he had harassed Lincoln with complaints as to the unfairness of the quotas, and while not thus engaged, had badgered the war President with his demands for a suspension of the draft law until the courts had passed upon it. "It seems that Governor Seymour," Lord Charnwood has written, "was very decidedly in the common acceptance of the term, a gentleman. This has been counted unto him for righteousness. It should rather be treated as an aggravation of his very unmeritable conduct." [66]

This was the Seymour who was now presiding at the convention. Finally the twenty-first ballot came and still there was no choice. Hancock and Hendricks were in the lead, but neither was acceptable to New York. And now the twenty-second roll-call has begun. Ohio's delegates are called, but General McCook is on his feet proposing the name of Horatio Seymour with a stirring speech. Cheers of the delegates are reëchoed by the cheers from the galleries, nor would the demonstration cease until Seymour rose and waved his hand for order. "Gentlemen," he said, "I thank you and may God bless you for your kindness to me, but your candidate I cannot be." [67]   In a moment it was all over. One state after another fell into line, and presently his nomination was made unanimous. [68]

Just before the convention came together, Frank Blair had written General Broadhead of Missouri on the Reconstruction laws: "There is but one way to restore the government and the Constitution; and that is for the President to declare these acts null and void, compel the army to undo its usurpations at the South, dispossess the carpet-bag state governments, allow the white people to reorganize their own governments and elect Senators and Representatives." [69]   These ideas were somewhat, but not too far, in advance of those in the party platform. Blair was "available." And now General Preston of Kentucky, formerly of the Confederate army, was nominating him for Vice-President. The nomination came by acclamation. [70]

At the Manhattan Club, Seymour and Blair were found and were there notified of their nomination, while at Tammany Hall, on the following evening, Seymour explained that under so great a pressure he had found himself "unable to resist." [71]

News of the nomination came to Chase on the croquet field. He read the telegram, handed it to his opponent who read it, too, and then continued with the game. [72]   His Presidential aspirations had gone glimmering,—but he liked croquet. Johnson received the word calmly. [73]   It was not the first time he had known disappointment. The man who had made the issue, and the judge who had presided at his trial, were both tasting the bitterness of defeat. Chase, however, might take such comfort as he could from a resolution added to the platform, giving him the thanks of the convention "for the justice, dignity, and impartiality with which he presided over the court of impeachment on the trial of President Andrew Johnson." [74]   Cold comfort!

Wild enthusiasm filled the convention hall when the nominations finally were made, while in the street a band was playing

"The Battle Cry of Freedom." [75]   But that night in Washington, Gideon Welles was writing: "I do not consider the nomination a fortunate one for success or for results.   Seymour has intellect but not courage.   His partyism predominates over patriotism. His nomination has been effected by duplicity, deceit, cunning management, and sharp scheming." [76]

THE GRANT-SEYMOUR CAMPAIGN

Just two years before the Democratic National Convention Robert E. Lee had written: "Everyone approves of the policy of President Johnson, gives him his cordial support and would I believe confer on him the presidency for another term if it was in his power." [1]   The Democratic party, however, though praising all that Johnson had attempted, chose another as its standard bearer.   Their candidate was a veritable foil for Grant.   They might have had the champion of Lincoln's cause, instead they singled out one of his most bickering critics.   They might have presented the staunchest living defender of the Union, but they preferred the New York governor who had so embarrassed the National administration in the war as to raise the question of his personal disloyalty. [2]

The Radicals had not foreseen how weak a contender the Democrats would put forth, but they had resolved to take no chances.   The fraudulent carpet-bag governments of the South were looked to earnestly for aid.   As many of the Southern states as could be "reconstructed" under negro rule must be promptly "readmitted" to the Union,—their electoral votes might make the difference between electing or defeating Grant.   "I have little doubt," wrote Welles, "that the Radicals intend to make him President the next four years by fraud and force if necessary. . . . The bogus Senators and Representatives from the States which have bogus constitutions, will, in the meantime, be admitted to seats, and how is the country to rid itself of the imposition?" [3]

Stevens' attempt to pack the High Court of Impeachment had met with failure.   But if the "bogus senators" could not be employed to thwart justice, the Radicals were determined that the electors from their "states" should be available for Grant.   Before

748

the conclusion of the impeachment trial seven of the ten conquered provinces had held their "carpet-bag, scalawag, negro con-
ventions," had adopted state constitutions in conformity with the
National Reconstruction Acts and had elected "state" officers
and legislators. The seven conquered provinces thus acting were
Georgia, Florida, Alabama, Louisiana, Arkansas and the two
Carolinas. Of these, Arkansas had gone so far as to adopt the
Fourteenth Amendment, she was ready, therefore, for "readmission," [4] and on June 20th Stevens' bill was rushed through both
Houses to "readmit Arkansas into the Union." [5] Five days later
a bill was passed for the "readmission" of the other six. [6] The
purpose of these measures was made plain enough by their chief
sponsor. "I trust," said Thaddeus Stevens, "the Almighty ruler
of nations will never again permit this land to be made slave;
or in other words that he will never permit the Democratic party
to gain the ascendancy." [7]

Johnson vetoed both of Stevens' measures. "I could not consent," he wrote, "to . . . the assumption . . . that Congress may
at its pleasure expel or exclude a state from the Union. . . ." [8]
Of the act admitting the Carolinas and their four neighbors he
said: "It assumes authority over six states of the Union which
has never been delegated to Congress, or is even warranted by
previous unconstitutional legislation upon the subject of restoration. It imposes conditions which are in derogation of the equal
rights of the states, and is founded upon a theory which is subversive of the fundamental principles of the government." [9] Even
an impeachment trial had not taught Andrew Johnson to coöperate
with the Radicals in their defiance of the Constitution.

They had failed to strip the President of his office and to seat
Wade in his place, but they had no intention of weathering defeat
at the polls. These laws, they knew, would render this unlikely.
Mockingly, therefore, they marshaled once again the necessary
two-thirds, and repassed both bills, the vetoes notwithstanding. [10]

Arkansas had ratified the Fourteenth Amendment in the spring,
Florida on June 8th, the other five were yet to act, but action
on their part was not long deferred. By July 13th all of the
seven had ratified save Georgia, and she followed eight days

later.[11] On July 20th Secretary Seward issued his proclamation plainly enough setting forth his doubts as to whether the Fourteenth Amendment had lawfully become part of the Constitution. It recited the ratification by the twenty-three Northern states, and that the amendment "has also been ratified by newly constituted and newly established bodies avowing themselves to be and acting as the legislatures of . . . the states of Arkansas, Florida, North Carolina, Louisiana, South Carolina and Alabama." [12]

It was a polite but effective description of assemblies unconstitutionally ordained by Congress. If the ratification by these bodies were accepted, and the attempt of New Jersey and Ohio to take back their previous approval were ineffective, then twenty-nine states,—the necessary three-fourths—had ratified, and the amendment had become "a part of the Constitution." [13] It was an accurate state paper, but it was far from satisfactory to Congress, which resolved the next day that the amendment had been legally adopted, and must be "duly promulgated by the Secretary of State." [14] Seward complied on July 28th; the Fourteenth Amendment became an accomplished fact.[15]

The assent of the Southern states was no assent at all; it was an acquiescence resulting from duress. Congress was without constitutional power to make the adoption of the amendment a condition precedent to the right of representation of the states. It was without power to prescribe the voting qualifications for the members of the several constitutional conventions, it was without power to disfranchise whites and enfranchise blacks. The Fourteenth Amendment was made a part of our fundamental law by an act of bad faith. It was a repudiation of the terms on which the Southern armies had surrendered. Their artillery had been parked and their arms stacked and turned over to the North, on the faith of Grant's word that "this done, each officer and man will be allowed to return to their homes, *not to be disturbed by United States authority* so long as they observe their paroles and *the laws in force where they may reside.*" [16]

The forcing of the amendment on the unwilling South by means of negroes, scalawags, bayonets and carpet-baggers was a deliberate and cowardly violation of a solemn treaty! No one can defend this act of pure brute force except upon the theory of revolution. "It will not be profitable at this time," says William D. Guthrie in his authoritative work, "to discuss at length whether the conditions exacted upon recognition or readmission into the Union were or were not technically constitutional. . . . The statesmen of the North would have been perfectly justified in compelling the adoption of the Fourteenth Amendment by force of arms or revolutionary methods." [17]   But force of arms in times of profound peace can have but a temporary and a dear-bought success. American history is the record of notable achievements and great failures. None of its failures is more marked than this crude attempt to introduce negro suffrage with a bludgeon.

But if so able a constitutional lawyer as Mr. Guthrie has been forced, inferentially at least, to justify the adoption of the Fourteenth Amendment as a permissible act of revolution, listen to one of the ablest historians of the period. "This amendment," writes Samuel S. Cox, "introduced into the organic law a principle so abhorrent to liberty and justice that from time immemorial it had been regarded by the American people and their ancestors as one of the vilest which could be resorted to, under the worst forms of tyranny. It was thought that no free people could submit to it, under any circumstances. But there it stands. It is to day a monument to the satanic malice of the Radical party. It is a warning to succeeding generations of the excesses of partisan lust." [18]

Texas, Virginia and Mississippi had not yet complied with the Congressional terms; they were still unreconstructed,—conquered provinces under martial law! [19] To insure their elimination from the work of making a new President, a joint resolution of the Congress was now passed "excluding from the electoral college the votes of states lately in rebellion which shall not have been reorganized." [20] Andrew Johnson's vetoes would have now no effect on his contemporaries, but he could at least write for the historian, and so he forwarded his veto of this resolution.

The resolution, in harmony with all the Reconstruction laws, assumed that through the insurrectionary acts of some of the inhabitants of the Southern commonwealths their rights as states were forfeited until Congress should again readmit them. "If," said Johnson, "this position be correct, it follows that they were taken out of the Union by virtue of the acts of secession and hence that the war waged against them was illegal and unconstitutional." [21]

Congress had no power under the Constitution to reject the electoral vote of any state, its function in relation to the count was purely ministerial. But the 40th Congress cared as little for the Constitution as it did for Johnson's vetoes, and so the joint resolution was immediately repassed despite all his objections. [22] And now presently the Senators and Representatives of the seven "reconstructed" states came trooping into Washington. They were without social or political influence in their own communities. They were mere creatures of the carpet-bag régime. Ten of the Senators and sixteen of the Representatives were Northern men, some were foreigners by birth, at least one of them had served in the Union army. [23] The Carolinas and their five neighbors were now "states" again, but the Federal troops were still stationed there. Five of these "states" were organized into the "Department of the South." [24] The Radicals intended to take no chances with the election fast approaching. Bayonets!

§

While the impeachment trial was still in progress the President held one day a reception at the White House. Without shame fifteen of the Radicals accepted of his hospitality. After paying their "respects" to the man whom they were struggling to destroy, fifteen or more of these had gathered in the East Room to compare notes. "What are you here for?" one asked of his colleague. "Why, I want to see how Andy takes it," was the answer. [25] But the wish of those who longed to see him wince was never gratified, for Johnson bore his burdens with the stark silence of a stoic. "Never but once in more than two years," one of his private secretaries has written, "did I see him unbend from his grim rigidity, to the flexibility of form and feature which belongs to ordinary humanity." [26]

Johnson was too intellectually keen to be lacking in a sense of humor, and yet he was a humorless man. His hard life, his unrelenting struggle with poverty had suppressed if not destroyed his lighter moods. To him life had been no laughing matter. To those about the White House who saw him every day he always seemed "the grimly stern great man." [27] One who was with him constantly at this time later wrote: "I pondered over the chilling manner, and scrutinized his every expression of face and gesture and motion of body, to reconcile it with . . . his kindly tones to all about him. . . . It is true I have seen him greet friends with pleasure portrayed in his countenance, and have seen him with a grim cast-iron wrinkle on the nether half of his face at public receptions; but his eye lacked the luster of a light heart. . . ." [28]

Johnson cracked no jokes and told no stories; his fame had flourished better with posterity if he had. In his face, his body-guard has written, there were none of the lines "with which Mr. Lincoln showed just how many times he had laughed and how many times he had grieved." [29] America, however, has furnished but one Lincoln. Then, too, hard as were Lincoln's four years in Washington, they were less cruel than those which fell to Johnson; great as was the load of Civil War, it was less than that of Reconstruction. But heavy as the Reconstruction was, it was not the only cross which Johnson bore. He was never free from physical pain. Always in discomfort from a deep organic disorder, he suffered at times excruciating torture. [30]

More, however, than his own physical pain was his distress over the mortal illness of his wife. Eliza McCardle lay a constant invalid in a room across the hall from his library, where through doors ajar, her cough, her sobs and sometimes her moans of anguish summoned him to her bedside. [31] "When I learned all this," Frank Cowan, one of Johnson's secretaries, wrote, "it was not a feeling akin to dread I had for the harrowed President, but reverence and awe, at the might of the heart and will within him to be—to act as I saw him, and to work, work, work, with a sullen fixedness of purpose as the sole means of rendering tolerable his existence." [32]

As the summer wore on, Johnson took longer drives into the country. Returning to the Capital one afternoon from one of these, he said to his bodyguard: "Everybody misunderstands me. I am not trying to introduce anything new. I am only trying to carry out the measures toward the South that Mr. Lincoln would have done had he lived." [33]

Congress did not adjourn until the 27th of July.[34] Like the sullen thunders of a departing storm there rumbled through the session's closing days new outbursts against the President. Thaddeus Stevens' colleague, Thomas Williams of Pennsylvania, offered fourteen new articles of impeachment, and Representative Charles Hamilton elect, a creature of the carpet-bag régime in Florida, seized his first opportunity of currying favor with his patrons by denouncing Andrew Johnson.[35]

Thaddeus Stevens' hour had nearly struck. He was seventy-six years old, thin, pale and haggard. Each morning now he was carried up the steps of the Capitol to his seat. He seemed to keep himself alive by brandy.[36] But on the 7th of July the old fires of malice, like the bright flame that bursts out from a smoldering log, illuminated and distorted his old and cruel face once more. He offered three additional articles of impeachment.[37] "The block must be brought out," he said, "and the axe sharpened; the only other recourse from intolerable tyranny is Brutus' dagger." [38] He hoped there would be no necessity for this!

The work of Thaddeus Stevens and his fellow apostles of discord this time came to nothing; Congress adjourned without acting on it. Stevens stayed on in Washington. He was not strong enough to make the trip to Lancaster, but in the second week of August he performed an act of real and lasting service to the Republic; on the eleventh of that month he died. Mrs. Smith, his colored housekeeper, was with him at the end.[39]

Charles Sumner was a pallbearer. On the floor of the Senate three months later he gave utterance to this eulogy: "I see him now as I have so often seen him during life. His venerable form moves slowly and with uncertain steps; but the gathered strength of years is in his countenance and the light of victory on his path.

Politician, calculator, time server, stand aside! A hero statesman passes to his reward." [40]

Through the simple alchemy of death more than one time-serving politician has been transformed into a statesman!

§

Meanwhile the Presidential campaign was getting under way. The Democrats had chosen Andrew Johnson's program as their platform, but when they failed to cast him for the leading rôle they did not even seek an understudy. Throughout the four years of Johnson's struggle Seymour had not once lifted a finger to sustain him. [41] In putting Seymour forward the Tammany politicians probably entertained no hopes of victory, but through his candidacy thought to strengthen their organization in the state. [42] As the contest opened up, it became increasingly apparent that the Democratic nominees were not making headway. "There is, apparently," wrote Welles on July 17th, "unappeasable discontent with the New York nominations." [43] And again one week later: "The public do not get reconciled to the nomination of Seymour and Blair." [44]

Seymour's letter of acceptance was moderate and conservative. "I have been caught up by the whelming tide that is bearing us on to a great political change," he wrote. [45] That tide, however, was to prove less sustaining than he expected. But Blair's acceptance was in the spirit of his previous letter to General Broadhead, and furnished a pretext for the assertion of his opponents that democracy was synonymous with secession and rebellion. "What civilized people on earth," he wrote, "would refuse to associate with themselves in all the rights and honors and dignity of the country, such men as Lee and Johnston? What civilized country on earth would fail to do honor to those who fighting for an erroneous cause, yet distinguished themselves by gallantry in that service?" [46]

Everything contributed to aid the Radicals' contention that the rebellion through the aid of Democrats was seeking resurrection. Seymour's war record, and Blair's speeches lent color to the picture of the Gorgon's head, but firebrands of the South did most of all, although unwittingly, to aid Grant's cause. Howell Cobb and Benjamin A. Hill both made incendiary speeches. They proclaimed their confidence in the practical victory of those who had fought for the Confederacy. Governor Vance of North Carolina also boasted that what the South had lost through Grant would be triumphantly regained with Seymour.[47]

Then, too, there were not lacking in the South occurrences that gave the Radicals a chance to talk of "outrages" again. What occurred was the result of provocation furnished by the negroes who had been stimulated by the scalawags and carpet-baggers. The Freedman's Bureau had gone heavily into politics. Many of its agents had become aspirants for office.[48] To combat this alien power, as well as the debased Loyal League, the Ku Klux Klan had been organized two years before, and now numbered more than half a million members.[49] The manhood of the South had rallied to the defense of wives and daughters.[50]

It was not strange that clashes now and then occurred; one happened at Camilla, Georgia, destined to play a large part in the Presidential canvass. Three hundred negroes, more than half of whom were armed, marching behind bands and banners, had come to hold a mass meeting. Realizing the provocative character of their demonstration, the sheriff met them three miles out from town, and endeavored to dissuade them from their purpose, or at least to lay aside their arms. But the negroes would not heed. When they arrived, a riot followed in which one white man and eight or nine negroes died. Their deaths furnished great campaign material for the Radicals.[51]

Seymour made no speeches until October. But the managers of Grant's campaign never permitted the country to forget his speech five years before to the Draft Rioters of New York. The pencil of Thomas Nast was again requisitioned. His cartoon entitled "Matched" depicted on the one side Grant demanding Vicksburg's "Unconditional Surrender" in July, 1863, while on the other Seymour was portrayed addressing in the same month the Draft Rioters as "My friends." [52]

Grant in the meantime was conducting a well-planned campaign,—by doing nothing.[53] He spent most of his time on his farm near St. Louis. His old friend General Sherman drove out one evening to find the Grants "comfortably settled for the summer almost as plainly as before the war. He has a horse and borrowed buggy, a pair of mules and ambulance borrowed of the quartermaster, and I have loaned Buck, the horse I brought for Minnie which he likes very much." [54]

Grant and Sherman visited Sheridan at Fort Leavenworth, and Grant alone made a few casual trips about the country. He called on his parents in Covington, Kentucky; he visited his birthplace at Point Pleasant, and stopped at Galena, Illinois, the scene of his endeavors in the leather store. But the conduct of the campaign was in other hands. [55] He made no addresses, he spoke but seldom and then awkwardly and briefly, but this enhanced rather than impaired his popularity. The picture of the grim, silent fighting man stood out more clear.

But if Grant's participation in the campaign was slight, his followers were working up enthusiasm. In every town and village "Boys in Blue" with oilskin capes and torches, and "Tanners" carrying lighted flambeaux, marched and countermarched. [56] Grant's services in the leather store were receiving a belated recompense.

What with Grant's war record and Seymour's lack of one, with distorted propaganda as to Southern "outrages," and with a solid South,—solid under Northern bayonets for the Republican party —the outcome from the outset was easy to predict. It was, therefore, with no great political acumen that Sumner on July 28th wrote the Duchess of Argyll: "You approach your election as we approach ours. With you it is Gladstone; with us it is Grant,— two G's. I do not doubt the success of each." [57]

§

Johnson was accorded no part in the campaign and he assumed none. He had given the Democrats their issue, they had deprived him of the post of honor, yet he was harboring no bitterness. As Hugh McCulloch wrote: "He never cherished animosity after a contest was over." [58] In the very middle of the campaign he left a record of his magnanimity. With his acquittal less than three months old, and his defeat at the New York Convention fresh and poignant, the harried President on August 3rd wrote his old friend Benjamin Truman a letter filled with charity and no malice.

"You allude," he wrote, "to the vote on impeachment as a 'close shave.' It was not so close as most people think; for Senator Morgan of New York would have cast his vote against impeachment rather than to have seen Ben Wade succeed to the Presidential chair. Now I have been true to the Union and to my friends, and have been generally temperate in all things. I may have erred in not carrying out Mr. Blair's request in putting into my Cabinet Morton, Andrew and Greeley. I do not say I should have done so had I my career to go over again, for it would have been hard to have to put out Seward and Welles who had served satisfactorily under the greatest man of all. Morton would have been a tower of strength, however, and so would Andrew. No Senator would have dared to vote for my impeachment with those two men in the Cabinet." [59]

"I told Mr. Blair," continued Johnson, "that I wouldn't have Greeley on any account. I always considered Greeley a good enough editor before the war, although I never agreed with him, but in all other matters he seemed to me like a whale ashore. He nearly bothered Mr. Lincoln's life out of him, and it was difficult to tell whether he wanted Union or separation, war or peace. Greeley is all heart and no head. He is the most vacillating man in the country or was during the war. He runs to goodness of heart so much as to produce infirmity of mind. Blair reasoned with me as a friend. But I could not see the point. I told him that Greeley was a sublime old child and would be of no service to me. The others I thought well of at the time." [60]

It was the middle of the campaign. Johnson was forced to sit by idle, when every instinct of his nature craved the center of the contest. He suffered not only an enforced idleness, but was compelled to witness the inept Seymour fumbling with his issues, and Grant racing on to victory. Of all his enemies none had played a less estimable part than Grant, and yet Johnson could thus write of him: "Grant was untrue," he began, but he continued, "he meant well for the first two years, and much that I did that was denounced was through his advice. He was the strongest man of all in the support of my policy for a long while, and did the best he could for nearly two years in strengthening my hands against the adversaries of constitutional government. But Grant saw the Radical handwriting on the wall, and heeded it. I did not see it or if seeing it did not heed it. Grant did the proper thing to save Grant, but it pretty nearly ruined me. I might have done the same thing under the same circumstances. At any rate most men would." [61]

But this was not all. He continued with his appraisal: "Grant had come out of the war the greatest of all. It is true that the rebels were on their last legs, and that the Southern ports were pretty effectually blockaded and that Grant was furnished with all the men that were needed or could be spared after he took command of the army of the Potomac. But Grant helped more than any one else to bring about this condition. His great victories at Donelson, Vicksburg, and Missionary Ridge all contributed to Appomattox." [62]

Johnson then referred to his old friend General George H. Thomas as in many respects "the greatest general the war produced, and the only one who annihilated an army. Yet Thomas would not have done as well as Grant under the circumstances. Grant has treated me badly; but he was the right man in the right place during the war, and no matter what his faults were or are, the whole world can never write him down,—remember that. I have always liked Sherman. He is our greatest military genius. He is erratic and stubborn, but he don't know how to lie. The time will come when Sheridan will be looked upon by many distinguished military men as greater than Grant. But Sheridan would not have had his great opportunity had it not been for Grant. . . . Mr. Lincoln is the greatest American that has ever lived. I do not mean by this to detract from the name of Washington; but Washington was an Englishman, you know, after all. I doubt whether there will ever be another Washington or another Lincoln." [63]

Before he closed this interesting letter, Johnson revealed how free from prejudice had been his Presidential course. The man whom Sumner had called the successor of Jefferson Davis was still burning with his old hatred of secession and rebellion. He had suffered everything in his effort to do justice to the South despite his unquenched wrath against those who led the war for Southern independence. "I shall go down to my grave," he wrote, "with the firm belief that Davis, Cobb, Toombs, and a few others of the arch conspirators should have been tried, convicted, and hanged for treason. There was too much precious blood spilled on both sides not to have held the leading traitors responsible."

"If it was the last act of my life," he continued, "I'd hang Jeff Davis as an example. I'd show coming generations that, while the rebellion was too popular a revolt to punish many who participated in it, treason should be made odious and arch traitors should be punished. But I might lose my head, for Horace Greeley, who made haste to bail out Jeff Davis, declares that I am a traitor. Just think of it!" [64]

§

The President sometimes varied his simple recreations. The Thursday before Labor Day he went with one of the members of his Cabinet to a German "Schützenfest." The managers of the affair received him with enthusiasm and escorted him about the grounds. He tried a shot, and was made a member of the association. [65]

As the campaign wore on, Welles was watching it with infinite disgust. "There is no love for Grant," he wrote on September 21st, "there is positive dislike of Seymour." [66] And twelve days later: "The country is absorbed with politics and parties. More of the latter than the former. Speakers are overrunning the country with their hateful harangues and excitable trash. . . . Those of the Radicals are manufactured . . . of the same material. Hatred of the rebels, revenge, the evils of reconciliation, the dangers to be apprehended if the whites of the South are not kept under, the certainty that they will, if permitted to enjoy their legitimate

constitutional rights, control the government,—the Radicals will
be deprived of power—this is the stuff of which every Radical
oration is made, interlarded sometimes with anecdotes. No allu-
sion to the really great questions before the country,—the rights
of man, the rights of states, the grants and limitations of the
Constitution." [67]

Both parties, as always, were prophesying victory, but to the
shrewd observers it was every day more plain that Seymour was
marching to defeat. "It was not a time," said Welles, "to nominate a Copperhead." [68] A sure forecast of the result would come
when the October states had spoken. Three days before these
elections, the Secretary of the Navy once more soliloquized: "I
have had no heart in this campaign since the nominations were
made. This Saturday night, alone by myself, I make this jotting,
not to prophesy but to write down frankly my opinions. The
elections will, I think, be adverse to the Democrats next Tuesday
and also in November. If so, a sad fate, I fear, awaits our
country. Sectional hate will be established." [69]

Both forecasts proved correct. On October 13th Pennsylvania,
Ohio, Indiana and Nebraska were carried by the Radicals for
Grant. [70] In a frenzy of printer's ink, the New York *World* burst
forth with the demand that Seymour and Blair should both retire
and other candidates be chosen in their stead. [71] Some talked of
Chase, some talked even at this late hour of nominating Andrew
Johnson. [72] Could the inarticulate electorate have spoken, it
might yet have been accomplished, but the so-called leaders of
the Democratic party preferred defeat to the selection of a man
they could not dominate. [73] The President listened not without
hope to those coming with assurances that the people wanted
him. But it was not to be. [74]

The Democratic National Committee held out against all
changes in the ticket, [75] and now for the first time Seymour took
an active part in the campaign, to rally if he could his wavering
party ranks. He campaigned through New York and pressed
out as far as Illinois. He was versatile and brilliant, and his
addresses riveted the attention of the country. "No man," says

Blaine, "was more seductive in appeal or more impressive in sedate and stately eloquence. With his art of persuasion he combined rare skill in evading difficult questions while preserving an appearance of candor. His speeches were as elusive and illusive as they were smooth and graceful." [76]

He spoke of the taxes, the currency and the cost of government, and assured the country that the Democrats, if successful, would still be "practically powerless." [77]   But even a strong and trusted candidate could not at this late hour have changed the tide. There had been no zeal for Grant at first; his popularity began with Seymour's nomination, and it had been growing ever since. [78] His letter of acceptance had concluded with the words "Let us have peace," [79]—reminiscent of his terms at Appomattox, they were noble words, albeit the platform and principles of his party had belied them. "Let us have peace," despite the falsity of the slogan, became the shibboleth of the campaign. These words, and the blunders of the Democrats, greatly aided the Radicals' contention that the issue lay between "Grant and Peace," and "Blair and Revolution." [80]

But Grant's mentors never forgot that the South's vote might be needed, and as election time approached, the carpet-bag governors called loudly to the Federal government for arms and troops to aid them at the polls. [81]   Finally November 3rd arrived, and when the casting of the vote was over, Grant and Colfax were elected. New Jersey and New York went Democratic! South Carolina and all of her six neighbors, except Georgia, were recorded in the Republican column. [82]   The negro scalawag and carpet-bag régime had done its work.

Without the enforced aid of the bayonet-ridden South and the exclusion of Texas, Mississippi and Virginia from the right to vote, Grant would have been defeated. [83]   Even with this aid his popular majority was less than 310,000 in the entire country. [84]

Under the heel of the conqueror there had been a nearly solid South in favor of the Republican party. Measures of duress, force and repression breed hatred and retaliation. Is it any wonder, therefore, that since 1877, when the last Northern bayonet was withdrawn, the South (until 1928) regardless of the issue or the candidate, with an enthusiasm amounting almost to religious frenzy, has recorded itself against the party that sponsored its oppression? Why the Solid South? Why indeed!

LXXXV

CLOSING DAYS OF JOHNSON'S PRESIDENCY

Two days after Congress reconvened, on Monday the 7th of December, Andrew Johnson sent in his last annual message as President of the United States. The winds had come and the tempests blown, but like a mighty oak whose deep roots hold fast to the firm earth, Johnson stood unshaken and unscathed. He had not budged one inch from the Constitution of his fathers or from his support of what his predecessor had striven to accomplish. The serene and passionless paragraphs of this great state paper gave no hint of all the storms of passion that had played about him since his annual message of the year before. He wrote in the spirit of reasonable conciliation, as though there were the hope that Congress would give heed. Jubilant with Grant's election, and now more than ever domineering, there was, of course, no chance that these sectional partisans would concern themselves with anything except the spoils traditionally belonging to the victor. Johnson was writing for the historian.

"It may be safely assumed as an axiom in the government of states," he wrote, "that the greatest wrongs inflicted on a people are caused by unjust and arbitrary legislation, or by the unrelenting decrees of despotic rulers, and that timely revocation of injurious and oppressive measures is the greatest good that can be conferred upon a nation. The legislator or ruler who has the wisdom and the magnanimity to retrace his step when convinced of error will sooner or later be rewarded with the respect and gratitude of an intelligent and patriotic people." [1]

He referred to the exclusion of Texas, Mississippi and Virginia from participation in the recent elections as a denial of their constitutional rights. And he continued: "The attempt to place the white population under the domination of persons of color

764

in the South has impaired, if not destroyed, the kindly relations that had previously existed between them; and mutual distrust has engendered a feeling of animosity which, leading in some instances to collision and bloodshed, has prevented that coöperation between the two races so essential to the success of industrial enterprise in the Southern states." [2]

Johnson's message covered the whole domain of national endeavor. It gave an interesting review of our relations with South America. It predicted that ere long it would become necessary for our government "to lend some effective aid to the solution of the political and social problems . . . in Cuba." [3] It suggested a reciprocity treaty with Hawaii as a "guaranty of the good will and forbearance of all nations until the people of the islands shall of themselves at no distant day, voluntarily apply for admission into the Union." [4]

His reference to the West Indies contained a vigorous assertion of the Monroe Doctrine. He emphasized that the United States would not permit any part of this continent or of its adjacent islands to be made "a theater for a new establishment of monarchical power." [5] All too little had been done by us, he said, "to attach the communities by which we are surrounded to our country, or to lend even a moral support to the efforts they are so resolutely and so constantly making to secure republican institutions for themselves." [6]

Then with telling force he continued: "It is indeed a question of grave consideration whether our recent and present example is not calculated to check the growth and expression of free principles, and make those communities distrust, if not dread, a government which at will consigns to military domination states that are integral parts of our Federal Union, and while ready to resist any attempts by other nations to extend to this hemisphere the monarchical institutions of Europe, assumes to establish over a large portion of its people a rule more absolute, harsh, and tyrannical than any known to civilized powers." [7]

The arraignment of Congress was complete and crushing. It had, however, no effect on the conspirators, save to increase their hatred of the man who had exposed them. As we read this message, we can all but see its author standing like a giant rock that rears its crest above the angry waves. The study of all his messages is rewarding; but Americans thus far have ignored them. One, however, who was competent to judge, has left us his appraisal. Major Richardson of Tennessee some thirty years ago was authorized by Congress to compile the state papers of all our Chief Executives. Ten massive volumes are the monument of his research. To his friend Archelaus Hughes, Richardson one day remarked that he was probably the only man who had ever read all the messages of all the Presidents. Next to those of Jefferson and Lincoln, Johnson's, he declared, were the greatest.[8]

We should like to have looked in on Johnson as he was writing that last message. One who saw him a few weeks earlier has left a record of his call. Young Henry Adams, in pursuit of that education of which he was to make a lifetime's work, came to Washington in the late fall of 1868. Evarts took him to call upon the President at the White House. "Musing over the interview as a matter of education long years afterwards," Adams wrote that he "could not help recalling the President's figure with a distinctness that surprised him. The old-fashioned Southern Senator and statesman sat in his chair at his desk with a look of self-esteem that had its value. None doubted. All were great men; some, no doubt, were greater than others; but all were statesmen, and all were supported, lifted, inspired by the moral certainty of rightness. . . . The Southerner could not doubt; and this self-assurance not only gave Andrew Johnson the look of a true President, but actually made him one. When Adams came to look back on it afterwards, he was surprised to realize how strong the Executive was in 1868,—perhaps the strongest he was ever to see. Certainly he never found himself so well satisfied, or so much at home."[9]

§

Smarting from the new rebukes, Congress was enraged at the President's message. The House permitted it to be read and then denounced it as "infamous, abominable, wicked."[10] In the Senate an adjournment was taken before the reading was half done, but the next day they heard it through.[11]   The New York *Tribune* spoke of it as Johnson's "worst and fortunately his last insult to the American people."[12]   But this vented spleen insured the message a more general reading than it might otherwise have had.[13]

Congress, however, did not pause long with this; it had other work in hand.   After much debate a new amendment to the Constitution,—the Fifteenth—was proposed,[14] declaring that "The rights of citizens of the United States to vote shall not be denied or abridged by the United States or by any state on account of race, color or previous condition of servitude."[15]   This was necessary, the Radicals declared, in order to make "permanent the results of the Union victory in the Civil War."[16]   No one of the reformers seemed to understand that law, whether constitutional or statutory, to enlist the respect and obedience of the people, must be expressive of the will of the great mass whom it affects.   Mandates lacking this are a mere waste of printer's ink.   By the end of February, 1869, the new amendment was ready for submission to the states, both those that were free and those ruled by negroes, carpet-baggers, scalawags and martial law.

Only a little interval yet remained of Andrew Johnson's tenure, but he resolved to use it well.   On Christmas day he issued his last proclamation,—it was one befitting the occasion.   To all who had participated in the late insurrection he granted a "full pardon and amnesty for the offense of treason against the United States," together with a restoration of all rights under the Constitution.[17]   It was the end of the Jefferson Davis case!   "By what authority of law" was this proclamation made? the Senate asked him.   "The second section of article second" of the Constitution, answered Johnson.[18]   It was a good answer.

Grant was back in town, but on December 28th he left Washington with his wife to spend New Year's day in Philadelphia in order to avoid attendance at the President's reception.   He had not visited the White House since his exposure there.[19]

On December 30th Johnson celebrated his sixtieth birthday with a party for his grandchildren.   Three hundred of their young friends were decorously invited to a "Juvenile soirée given by the children of the President's family,"[20] and were informed that dancing would be conducted "under the direction of L. G. Marini." [21] At the appointed hour the great chandeliers in the East Room were ablaze with light, and every space was redolent with flowers. [22] The President received with Mrs. Patterson, the little Pattersons and Stovers. Mrs. Johnson appeared for a brief glimpse of the gay scene. It was her second public appearance since entering the White House. [23] It would have been interesting to have seen Andrew Johnson's face as he watched his little guests, while to the accompaniment of gay music they went through the Polka, the Lancers, the Schottische, the Galop, the Waltz, the Esmeralda and Quadrille. [24] Grant's children were invited, but he forbade them to attend. [25]

The next day was the last of the tempestuous 1868. "The closing hours of the year are stormy," Gideon Welles recorded. "The year has been eventful and there is much that is painful in the recollection. I speak of political and public affairs. There has been much to impair confidence in the intelligence and integrity of the mass of the people to govern themselves. Under the influence of passion and led on by bad men, they plunge into war. . . . The Radical Congress in the excess of party have trampled the organic law under foot when party ends were to be subserved. . . . In all this reckless wickedness they have been under party discipline, sustained by the people, and a majority of the next Congress is elected to support their vicious revolutionary proceedings. An amicable, forbearing, and honest President, striving to uphold the government, has been impeached in party hate, and barely escaped conviction. Representatives and Senators readily forswore themselves, became persecutors of the Chief Magistrate, conspired against him, and committed perjury in obedience to the dictates of party leaders who found him an obstruction to their revolutionary schemes." [26]

Sixty-four days of the Johnson administration now remained! The long agony was nearly over.

§

New Year's day dawned bleak and gloomy. There was a disagreeable rain, and dismal patches of disappearing snow made the soggy earth uninviting. The weather seemed in keeping with the times. On this day the President held his last New Year's reception. The diplomatic corps headed by Baron Gerolt came to pay their last official call, and there also, as always on such days, a miscellaneous crowd appeared.[27] But there was one who came who might have had the decency to stay away. With an impudence that would have been surprising if manifested by any other, Ben Butler pushed his way into this New Year's throng. The vulgar vilifier who had slandered and abused the Chief Executive now came to shake his hand. Butler explained that he was discriminating "between the President and the man"; he had had, he said, "no controversy or differences with Andrew Johnson."[28] It was an explanation worthy of the cad of New Orleans.

Grant was not present at the reception.[29] He could not forget how Johnson had exposed him in their famous correspondence. His absence was an intentional affront. "If he had any cause to be offended with either the President or the gentlemen of the Cabinet," wrote Welles, "it was because they had not remained silent and suppressed the truth when he had equivocated and falsified what had taken place. It is the consciousness of unsuccessful guilt and detected error as much, perhaps, as weak and unhappy traits of character, which excites his animosity. He is deficient in some of the nobler qualities of mind. . . . Ten years ago he was a porter . . . in a leather store; but for the war he would be there still."[30]

Washington, always a whispering gallery, fairly buzzed with rumors at this time. What policy would the President-elect follow? Who would compose his Cabinet? "As regards policy and measures," our faithful diarist wrote, "he has none. . . . Yet he has shrewdness and a certain amount of common sense, with avarice, selfishness, and ambition. Of the structure of the government, and a proper administration of its affairs, he is singularly and wonderfully ignorant. . . . Horse flesh has more charm for him than brains or intellect. . . . The race course has more attractions for him than the Senate or the council room. He loves money, admires wealth, is fond of power and ready to use it remorselessly."[31]

Everyone was wondering what Grant would do as President. The thoughts then widely current were later voiced by Julian when he wrote: "The idea of his nomination was exceedingly distasteful to me. I personally knew him to be intemperate. In politics he was a Democrat. He did not profess to be a Republican, and the only vote he had ever given was cast for James Buchanan in 1856, when the Republican party made its first grand struggle to rescue the government from the clutches of slavery. Moreover, he had no training whatever in civil administration, and no one thought of him as a statesman." [32]

There was not much further opportunity for Congress to insult Andrew Johnson, but even the little time at their disposal was employed diligently for this purpose. They sought to make it clear that the Tenure-of-Office Act had been a personal affront to him. On January 11th, Butler carried a repeal through the House," [33] but the Senate failed to act before adjournment. [34]

The 4th of March was fast approaching now; Grant and his partisans presently would take control. As his Inauguration day drew nearer, one of the questions agitating Johnson's Cabinet was the part that he would play in the inauguration of his successor. A few days before the great event, the Committee on Ceremonies was informed by Grant that he would not ride in the same carriage with the President, nor speak to him. [35] The Committee was perplexed, but presently evolved a plan whereby the President and President-elect were to proceed up Pennsylvania Avenue in separate carriages, the former on the right, the latter on the left. [36]

This plan evoked new Cabinet discussions. The President's self-respect, said one of his advisers, demanded that he take no part in the parade; Seward, Schofield and Evarts, however, were insistent that he should. The President hesitated and seemed to yield, but said that they should assemble at the White House at nine o'clock on March the fourth, when the matter would finally be decided. "So," with sheer disgust, wrote Welles, "we are likely to form part of the pageant,—be a tail to the Grant kite." [37]

Congress prepared wildly for the Inaugural. It offered new opportunities, they thought, for demonstrating once again their deep affection for the negro. Negro vagabonds were present at the Capital in force, and so a Congressional resolution was adopted authorizing muskets to be placed in their hands. The last official act of Andrew Johnson was his veto of that resolution.[38]

On the evening of the 3rd of March, Johnson held his last reception at the White House. The city was populous with hungry office-seekers, and sight-seeing strangers.[39] These added to the "jam." The approaches to the Executive Mansion were crowded with a pushing, jostling crowd. From idle curiosity they forced their way into the lighted chambers,—many with their overcoats, their hats and bonnets unremoved. Hundreds of friends and officials who sought this final opportunity of paying their respects, came and drove away, unable to pass through the throng.[40]

At nine in the morning of the following day the Cabinet assembled by appointment at the White House. Most of them were eager to attend the ceremonies at the other end of Pennsylvania Avenue. Evarts displayed his anxiety to be off, by refusing to remove his overcoat. Seward came in last, smoking his cigar, and asked if all were ready. But the President continued silently at his desk. "Will we not be late? Ought we not to start immediately?" Seward presently inquired. "I am inclined to think," replied Johnson quietly, "that we will finish up our work here by ourselves."[41]

Down Pennsylvania Avenue the Inaugural Procession passed. Two-thirds or more of those in line were negroes who had come from Baltimore and the surrounding country. But thanks to Andrew Johnson they were not armed. Grant drove up to the Capitol in a dog cart, with Rawlins, his old chief of staff.[42] His Inaugural Address was short, flat and trite. His platitudes gave no real clew to his policy, but they did reveal how slight was his appreciation of the task before him, and of his own limitations to perform it. "The responsibilities of the position," he said, "I feel but accept them without fear."[43] One of the ablest of the Republican Senators met the retiring Secretary of the Treasury the next morning. "Have you read Grant's inaugural?" he asked, and was answered in the affirmative. "You know, McCulloch, that I am not a religious man," the Senator then said, "but if I had been elected President, I should not have accepted the responsibilities without fear. I should on my knees have asked God to help me." **

While Grant was delivering his Inaugural, there sped along the wires the farewell address of Andrew Johnson. "My thoughts," he said, "have been those of peace, and my effort has ever been to allay contention among my countrymen. Forgetting the past let us return to the first principles of the government, and, unfurling the banner of our country, inscribe upon it in ineffaceable characters 'the Constitution and the Union, one and inseparable.' " **

With eyes front, head erect and his strong shoulders squared, Andrew Johnson had remained to the last hour faithful to the cause of Lincoln. To those who watched and saw, moreover, it was plain that he would continue in the struggle for that "just and lasting peace," for which his predecessor prayed and worked. He had turned sixty, he had endured much physical pain, he had borne such assaults from his political opponents as no American had yet endured, but there was still fight left in Lincoln's former running mate!

At a little after twelve o'clock, Johnson arose and, remarking to his Cabinet that the time of parting had arrived, shook hands with each of them. At the portico of the White House the carriage of the President and those of the ex-ministers were waiting. They entered and were driven quietly away.** A few minutes later the President and Mrs. Grant drove down Pennsylvania Avenue to their new home. In the Blue Room, the Red Room and the Green Room, an eager throng awaited them.**

LXXXVI

JOHNSON RETURNS TO TENNESSEE

JOHN COYLE, one of the editors of the *National Intelligencer*, extended the hospitality of his home to Johnson and his family, and there for twelve days they stayed, while purchases were made for the old home in Greeneville, which he had not seen since 1861.[1] For the first time in thirty years Johnson was a private citizen again. He faced the future quietly but with resolute determination. During his final days at the White House, and especially during those last trying hours, no word of complaint escaped him. His vindication would yet come![2] What would the immediate future hold? Some thought that he would make a European trip. English, French and German steamship companies tendered free passage for his family and himself.[3] But Johnson took no gifts.

The city of Baltimore sought an opportunity to do him honor before he should return to Tennessee. Johnson accepted. And so, on the 12th of March, business was forgotten in that city. At the rotunda of the Post Office he stood from one till three, while men, women and children passed by to shake his hand.[4] At Barnum's Hotel that night a banquet was given in his honor. This was one of the toasts: "Our guest,—the patriot statesman, Andrew Johnson, as President of the United States, the bulwark of equal rights, the champion of the only true and permanent Union of the United States, and the defender and martyr of the Constitution. History will vindicate his fame, and record an impeachment of his impeachers. . . . Baltimore . . . bids him welcome to a place in the hearts of a great people, for whose protection and happiness he bared his breast to the shafts of calumny, and for their sakes hazarded all that was dear to the man and the citizen. In his retirement . . . in the full vigor of his manly faculties stimulated by the applause of all good citizens, we look with great assurance to his future efforts and influence for the liberation of the captive states of the Union and the rescue of their now true and faithful citizens from political slavery. . . ." [5]

Meanwhile the Grant administration was beginning; it started with a blunder. He designated as one of his Cabinet a man ineligible for the appointment. A. T. Stewart was then America's most successful storekeeper, and possessed one of the largest fortunes in the country. Grant owed him much for his aid, his hospitality and his gifts. A few days before taking office, Grant's $30,000 home, which had been bought for him by public subscription, was repurchased by a group of friends at more than twice its cost. Stewart handed him a check for $65,000. He and other rich men had made up the purse.[6] Grant nominated him for Secretary of the Treasury!

The nomination promptly was confirmed, but presently it was discovered that a law passed in Hamilton's time forbade the appointment of any one concerned in "trade or commerce." [7] Grant immediately requested Congress to exempt Stewart from the law.[8] Congress refused. Stewart's name was withdrawn and Boutwell, one of the impeachment managers, was substituted in his stead.[9] Welles had characterized him as "a fanatic, impulsive, narrow-minded partisan," [10] while Henry Adams wrote that the name of George S. Boutwell as Secretary of the Treasury suggested only a "somewhat lugubrious joke." [11]

For his Secretary of State Grant selected his fellow townsman from Galena, Representative Elihu B. Washburne. Of foreign affairs he knew nothing. He was without the least qualification for the office.[12] He was impulsive, headstrong, combative and unbalanced.[13] There was, however, one qualification he possessed; he had sponsored Grant's cause when, after the Battle of Shiloh, the latter had fallen in disfavor.[14] And there was still another: he was a violent enemy of Andrew Johnson. It was he who, when the question of impeachment was debated, had described Johnson as "the opprobrium of both hemispheres." [15]

But Washburne's appointment, it seems, was intended as a

temporary one. It had been given him, so Grant told Admiral Farragut, merely as "a compliment." [16] This established a new standard for the public service! Washburne was to initiate no policies and to make no appointments. He did both. Grant thereupon suggested that he leave the office. He did so with alacrity; his real ambition was to become our Minister to London. For this post, however, his want of knowledge of the English language was so insurmountable that his assignment there was deemed inadvisable, so he was made Minister to France. [17]

Despite the fact that he had been Governor of New York, a Representative in Congress and a United States Senator, Hamilton Fish was a colorless figure. [18] For the past decade he had played no part in public affairs. "He seemed," wrote Hugh McCulloch, "to belong to a past generation, to be politically superannuated." [19] But in his New York City mansion and in his home upon the Hudson, Grant had been his guest, and he now made him Secretary of State. It was one of his best appointments." [20]

For his Secretary of War, the President-elect chose another fellow townsman from Galena, John A. Rawlins. [21] He had been Grant's adjutant general, his friend and mentor. [22] He was a lawyer with a limited education, but with a clear, strong mind. At Grant's headquarters he had "bossed everything," using, when the need arose, a profanity more picturesque than most men could command. [23] It was to Rawlins that Grant, at the beginning of the war, had pledged himself to refrain from liquor while the conflict lasted, and Rawlins had never hesitated to remind Grant of his pledge when he broke it. [24]

E. Rockwood Hoar became Attorney-General; he had been a judge of the Supreme Court of Massachusetts and was a lawyer of high ability and character. It was in every way a fine appointment,—Grant's best. [25] But when the name of Creswell of Maryland was announced for Postmaster-General, it was recalled that though his Radicalism had long been unexceptionable, he had at the outbreak of the war been a Secessionist, and had raised a company for the Confederacy. [26]

Adolph E. Borie was a rich resident of Philadelphia. He had recently been connected with a scheme to present Grant with a home there. He was appointed Secretary of the Navy. Farragut had never heard of him. He was unknown outside of Philadelphia. Indeed, when his appointment was announced everyone was asking: "Who is Adolph E. Borie?" [27] Borie did not get on with Admiral Porter, and resigned three months later.[28] Grant's administration was under way.

On the evening of March 17th Welles bade good-bye to Johnson and his family. "No better persons have occupied the Executive Mansion," he wrote, "and I part from them, socially and politically, with regret." [29] When the ex-President and his party boarded the train for Tennessee the following day, a small group came to witness his departure. As the train moved out, they stood respectful, silent and uncovered.[30]

§

Andrew Johnson was coming home at last. Unchanged, the old lion was returning! All along the route the people came to do him honor. As he neared home, the enthusiasm of the populace increased. At Bristol, on the boundary of Tennessee, a committee of old friends from Greeneville appeared in a private car to escort him. He came at last to his native village, while crowds from all around had gathered to express the enthusiasm of their welcome.[31]

To the very spot where eight years before he had last championed the Union cause in East Tennessee, the Reception Committee led him. Eight years before the Confederates were in control, and across the street the word "Traitor" had been written. Now a banner spanned the way with "Welcome Home." [32] On behalf of the people of Greeneville, James Britton delivered the address of welcome: "You are welcome, thrice welcome, to . . . spend the evening of your life after your laborious . . . duties in the highest . . . trust within the gift of the American people. . . . It is our most sincere desire that you may live to enjoy the reward of your labor, until your motives will be correctly interpreted and your struggle for constitutional liberty will be better understood, and when you come to die . . . may your mortal remains be left as a heritage to the people of your adopted home!" [33]

It was old-fashioned Southern oratory, but it was spoken with utter and profound sincerity. "When affection," the orator concluded, "shall have reared a monument to your memory, and the curious of future generations come to visit the tomb of the illustrious dead, they will find at Mount Vernon the remains of Washington . . . at Monticello they will find the remains of Jefferson . . . at Montpelier . . . the remains of Madison . . . at the Hermitage . . . all that was mortal of Jackson . . . and when they come to linger about . . . the last resting place of Andrew Johnson, they will say, 'There lie the remains of a man who had the patriotism of George Washington, the political sagacity of Thomas Jefferson, the prudence and caution of James Madison, and the physical and moral courage of Andrew Jackson.' " [34]

It was a welcome home, but it was more than that. Before he had had time to catch his breath, Tennessee's old spokesman was in politics again. Other cities were clamoring to hear him. He was granted but a few days rest before the citizens of Knoxville demanded an opportunity to see him. Presently it was being whispered that if he again desired the suffrages of Tennessee, the people would once more rally to his cause. From Knoxville he journeyed on to Chattanooga, Mulfreesboro, Memphis and finally to Nashville. There, where he had twice presided as the elected governor, and later as the military appointee of Lincoln, his reception was particularly brilliant. [35]

From the balcony of the St. Cloud Hotel, from which he spoke six years before when he assumed the trying rôle of military governor, Johnson once again addressed the people. His old fire had not been dimmed. "When I was inaugurated President," he said, "I felt that if the destruction of the government could be arrested . . . until the whole American people could be aroused, that they . . . would . . . come to the rescue and save the Constitution and the country. . . . I ask nothing at your hands. . . . I feel prouder today, standing in your midst, privileged and authorized to advocate those great principles of free government, than I would of being President on the ruins of the

Constitution of my country; . . . I intend to appropriate the remainder of my life, short as it may be, in the vindication of my character and that of the state. . . ." [36]

But he had not yet finished. "It is my own choice," he said, "to come to my own adopted state and lay my weary bones down in peace; and, if I can do nothing more, I will adopt the language of Cato . . . when Caesar was making his inroads upon him. . . . Cato said to his son, 'Retire to the Sabine fields, and there with a pure and sincere heart, if you can do nothing more, pray for Rome.' If I can do nothing more, I can retire to my humble home, and with a good conscience I can pray for my country. I feel prouder in my retirement than imperial Caesar . . . for, my countrymen . . . in these corrupt times . . . when 'vice prevails and impious men bear sway, the post of honor is a private station.' " [37]

His old power had not deserted him. Was it likely that he would long be permitted to continue as a private citizen? "I accepted the Presidency," he went on, "as a high trust . . . not . . . as a horn of plenty; with sugar plums to be handed out here and there to that individual that had presented the greatest gift." [38]

Johnson finally concluded: "I stand before you unscathed, and put the whole pack at defiance. Thank God, I can stand before the people of my state, and lift up both my hands, and say, in the language of Samuel, 'Whose ox have I taken, or whose ass have I taken? At whose hands have I ever received bribes, and had my eyes blinded?' If there is any, let them answer and I will return it. Thus I return to you, feeling in my own conscience that I have discharged my duty as a faithful man." [39]

Those who saw him noted that, while there were a few more grey hairs and the face perhaps a little paler, he seemed as vigorous, as well poised and as self-reliant as when a quarter of a century before they first had heard him.[40] Had he the strength to find, or make new opportunities in public life?

From the moment he left Washington, Johnson began planning his return. There was enough there that would need denouncing! If only once more in the Senate he could expose what Lincoln's enemies and his, had wrought! But the way did not seem promising. Brownlow was still in control of Tennessee. He had been reëlected governor in 1867,[41] and his hatred for his old political opponent had not cooled. The State Convention that nominated Brownlow had declared itself "ashamed of the unprincipled adopted son of Tennessee, now President of the United States, for his deception and degeneracy, and will endorse any action of Congress that will legitimately deprive him of continued power."[42]

During the session of the next legislature, Brownlow was elected United States Senator in place of Johnson's son-in-law, David Patterson. Brownlow's term began the day that Johnson left the White House. The "Fighting Parson" was therefore absent from the state on the ex-President's return, but his Radical adherents, stimulated by his policies and protected by his "County Guards" were in control. Twelve companies of these made up a state-wide military organization, with officers and non-commissioned officers, mounted scouts and what not. In reality they were a mere adjunct of Brownlow's political machine. Their sole duty was to appear at public meetings in order to "protect" Republicans in their rights of free speech and to repel "rebel assaults."[43] Outstanding among their military triumphs was the riding of a too free-spoken citizen on a rail.[44]

At Nashville, since 1867, a particularly enterprising thief by the name of Alden had been doing a large business, first as Commissioner of Registration and latterly as Mayor,—elected by the aid of Brownlow's guards. Carpet-baggers came with him to fill the minor offices, and through their frauds upon the public treasury were able to maintain themselves in ostentatious grandeur. The total sum of all their larcenies was never known, but twenty-three years later it was computed that there was still unpaid $700,000 of state debts attributable to "Alden's Ring."[45]

Nearly all the whites of west and central Tennessee,—"rebels and rebel sympathizers," of course, had been disfranchised, and their places at the ballot box had been taken by the negroes.[46] Now and then the Ku Klux Klan rode, but for the most part the persecuted whites quietly went their law-abiding way. But as the months rolled by, their political condition grew no better, and their taxes became heavier,—taxes in the voting, levying and collection of which they had no voice.[47] Would the time ever come when the white men of the state would take hold of their government again?

Johnson looked out upon the troubled scene, but his gaze did not linger at the boundaries of Tennessee; he saw the whole South in sackcloth and ashes writhing in her chains. Could anything be done to help her? Would he ever have the chance?

From afar men watched his homecoming, and wondered if his part in national affairs were over. "He has been an effective speaker in Tennessee in former years and may succeed again," Welles confided to the last pages of his diary at this time, "but ten years have changed the character of the people, nor is it likely that he remains unchanged. I shall not be surprised, therefore, if he is not as successful as in former years, and, under the sweeping proscription by which Brownlow and his faction have aimed to disfranchise all who are opposed to them, the ex-President may find it more difficult than he apprehends to serve the state." [48]

LXXXVII

JOHNSON LOOKS OUT UPON THE RECONSTRUCTION

ELBERT CLAY REEVES was a soldier of the Confederacy. Reeves had been reared on a farm in the County of Washington adjoining that where Johnson lived. He had nevertheless, at the very outbreak of the war between the states, cast in his lot upon the side of Southern independence. Major General Cheatham, the "Bull-Dog Fighter" of Bragg's army, had been the commander of his division. But when finally the tattered followers of the Stars and Bars came trooping home, Col. Reeves selected Greeneville as the point from which to embark upon the practice of the law. His diminutive law library contained the Code of Tennessee and the law course of Cumberland University, and such hopes and fears as young and impecunious lawyers traditionally have known. Here in April, 1869, amid the fresh hot memories of the war, surrounded by more ardent and aggressive Union sympathizers than Massachusetts could have boasted, this youthful Confederate veteran, having abandoned arms, took up his new profession.[1]

It was at about this time that Greeneville's most distinguished citizen came home. With such prejudice against the great Union leader as would be natural in a young Confederate soldier, Col. Reeves had had Andrew Johnson pointed out to him, but he had never met him. He was able then to recognize by sight the caller who entered his small office not more than three days after it was opened. "Mr. Reeves, I suppose," his visitor observed, "my name is Andrew Johnson. I was informed that you had come to our town and had opened a law office. Pardon me; I have called to meet you and to give you a welcome."

The ex-President declined a seat, but pacing the floor continued: "I beg pardon for volunteering a few remarks; a young attorney must build up a practice; fees come slowly at first, and

781

often he becomes disheartened, but pluck and energy will win. Our people were impoverished by the war. I have traveled the road of poverty, and have felt its pinch. Pardon my seeming impertinence, but I make no inquiry into your financial matters, yet will add: By living economically I have laid up a small sum, and, if at any time you shall be in need of some financial help, just call on me and it will be my pleasure to aid you. Good day." [2] How many young lawyers choosing to espouse the cause of justice, and who have selected New York or Boston as the place in which to do it, have been thus welcomed by a leading citizen?

A man of warm and generous instincts, it was but natural that Col. Reeves should appreciate the kindliness of Johnson's call, nor was it strange that he immediately attached himself to Johnson's cause. Ten days later the owner of the *National Union,*— Greeneville's weekly paper, and Andrew Johnson's organ—put Reeves in charge of its editorial policy. And now the visits of the former President to the small law office grew frequent, Reeves became his private secretary, and thence on an intimacy and friendship sprang up between the one-time military governor of Tennessee and the soldier of Bragg's army that lasted and increased as long as Johnson lived.

Fifty-eight years after Col. Reeves began the practice of his profession, he was still engaged in it, and in September 1927, I called upon him at his law office in Johnson City, Tennessee. The six and four score years had not dimmed the lustre of his eye or bent the tall spare frame. With tears in his voice he told me of his old friend, whom he had not seen for more than half a century, and as I listened, it seemed as if he stood before us in the living flesh. Poignant and real, the political struggles and the colorful campaigns, the hopes and the disappointments, all the aftermath of Johnson's Presidency stood out before me,—the impenetrable veil of time momentarily was lifted.

Finally when he had finished with the narrative of his friend, as he had known him, he spoke of the long misunderstanding with which history has surrounded Johnson's memory, and of his hope that some day America would come to know and love him as he had. He told me of his interview with Woodrow Wilson when

Mr. Tumulty introduced him to the President as Johnson's friend. Johnson's was a "wonderful life," said Wilson, "his name and fame will grow with the years,—one of the most wonderful men in history." [3]

But it was of the calumnies against the old Tennessean of which Col. Reeves spoke to me with the most feeling, and when he came to the recent strictures of George Creel, his eyes flashed and his old hands that more than sixty years before had primed and loaded muskets of the Confederacy, were doubled into clenched fists. It was fortunate for Creel that he was not there.

As I was leaving, I said: "Col. Reeves, are you sorry that the Southern cause did not triumph?" "No," he said, "it is better as it is,—the Union and one flag." "Yes," I answered, "but with the exception of slavery, have we not lost many of the fine things for which the Confederacy stood?" He looked out of his office window and smiled,—a little wistfully.

§

Upon Brownlow's departure for Washington, DeWitt C. Senter, who had been Speaker of the Tennessee Senate, became acting Governor. [4] The state elections were at hand. He was a candidate to succeed himself. [5] The Republican State Convention came to order on the 20th of May; Senter there found himself opposed by Col. William Stokes. [6] The former declared for immediate restoration of the franchise to the submerged whites; Stokes took the Radical position. [7] The negroes attended the convention in large and strident numbers. The contest between the candidates waxed so warm that presently the convention split in two, each division nominating its own favorite. There was that year no Democratic nomination for the governorship. [8] Johnson threw himself into the contest on Senter's side. He stumped the state, and on August 5th his candidate was elected by a majority of more than 50,000 votes, together with a Democratic legislature. [9] Andrew Johnson had returned to Tennessee!

Everyone was now predicting that this legislature would make him United States Senator when Fowler's term expired on March 4th, 1871. [10]

Edmond Cooper had been one of Johnson's secretaries in Washington, and later his Assistant Secretary of the Treasury.[11] Cooper was a member of this legislature, and when finally it met to choose a Senator, Cooper became a Johnson leader there. The contest for the Senatorship was a long one. After many ballots Johnson still lacked two votes of election. It was at this time that a former president of the N. & C. Railroad entered Johnson's room with welcome news.

"Mr. President," he said, "you will be elected tomorrow." "Why do you think so?" Johnson asked. "Because," his caller answered, "I have secured the necessary two votes." When he was asked how this had been accomplished, he told how he had promised to pay a $1000 for each vote. "You will do no such thing," thundered Johnson, "go tell those rascals the deal is off." "I can't do that," his friend replied, "I am honor-bound. It is not your money to be used." "No," retorted Johnson, "but it is my honor that is involved. If I am elected by those purchased votes, as sure as the Lord lets me live, I will go before the Legislature and expose the fraud and refuse to accept the election." And so that deal was not put through.[12]

Johnson's enemies were resourceful and presently they evolved a plan for securing the two needed votes for themselves. Edmund Cooper, the supposed leader of the Johnson forces, had a brother in the legislature by the name of Henry. They were both supporters of the former President. What if their influence could be weaned away? How could this be better done than by giving one the nomination, securing thereby the other's vote? The plan was well conceived,—it worked. Henry Cooper was now placed in nomination, Edmond deserted Johnson to support him. Cooper was elected by one vote.[13] Johnson's hour had not yet come!

Johnson could accept defeat after a fair fight as gamely as the finest sportsman, but he had the sportsman's hatred and contempt for bad faith and betrayal. Edmond Cooper, who had betrayed him, now sought him out to "explain" what he had done. He found Johnson in the Governor's reception room. It was filled with people at the time. As Cooper approached, Johnson's eyes blazed as he exclaimed: "Caesar had his Brutus, Jesus Christ his

Judas, and I've had my Ed. Cooper.   Get thee behind me, Satan." [14]   Like Satan, Cooper fled.   He never emerged from his retirement, his political career was over. [15]

Johnson returned to Greeneville without bitterness, and with no trace of his sudden storm of anger.   He was the tender nurse of his invalid wife.   His plans, if any, for the future were locked within his own heart.   Even to his friend, Col. Reeves, who came daily to his residence, and to whom he talked much of the past, no inkling of his future course was given. [16]

§

Johnson knew how to bide his time.   In his dignified and unpretentious home he awaited what the future might unfold, dividing his time between ministrations to his wife and a close watch on the political horizon.   His only visits were those made to the small law office of his private secretary.   "Mr. Johnson was a very serious man," Col. Reeves has written me.   "Affable in his home, I never knew him to visit a neighbor nor anyone." [17] Yet in his retirement he did not lose his fellow townsmen's sympathy, affection and respect.

I have talked with old residents of Greeneville who well remember him.   Absorbed as he was, as he passed to and fro upon the village streets, he met them always with his kindly smile and with a pleasant word of greeting.   His perfect courtesy and gentle manners seemed somehow to enhance his indefinable distinction.   Faultlessly neat always, he never showed himself in public except in clothes of finest texture.   He was too good a politician not to know that "people are never flattered by having a favorite appear before them in mean garb." [18]

Col. Reeves came frequently to his home and would write down what Johnson dictated for editorial publication in friendly newspapers.   Johnson did not write out these articles himself.   The physical act of writing for him was a painful one, owing to an injury suffered in a railroad accident years earlier. [19]   This, no doubt, accounts for the paucity of letters written in his own hand, as well as for the fact that the drafts of so many of his messages are not in his handwriting,—a circumstance his critics erroneously have relied upon as showing that his great state papers were composed by others.

Sometimes, as Reeves and Johnson sat together, the former President would reminisce, expressing his opinion of both friends and enemies. He spoke of Lincoln always with the deepest admiration and affection. He had, said Johnson, "a strength of intellect much greater than that usually conceded to him by the public." He talked of his attempt to carry out Lincoln's "wise restoration policy." [20] He referred to the impartiality with which Chase presided at the trial, and discoursed upon the loyalty of Welles, Seward and McCulloch. He thought that Thaddeus Stevens was "honest" and "open" despite his insanity on the negro question, and that while there was "method" in Sumner's "madness," that he had acted from "no sordid motives." But when it came to Butler, Johnson would lash out,—a man "whose ideal was to ruin by vilification and abuse." Grant, he thought, was at his best "when behind two bob-tailed ponies with whip in hand saying: 'Git up and along.'" He considered him a "dullard whose brain could have been compressed within the periphery of a nut shell,"—"untruthful," one who would "betray a friend for selfish ends." [21]

But Johnson was not living in the past, he looked out upon the red horizon of a new day. He was not watching Tennessee alone, but the American scene in its entirety, the statesmen at the National Capitol, the fruits of their endeavors, as well as the results that flowed from a refusal to abide by Lincoln's plan and his. It was the very middle of the Reconstruction, "The suppressed chapter of American history,"—the chapter which we Northerners should read with penitential and bowed heads.

In Washington, Ulysses Grant, confused and dazed, was fumbling with his office. Ben Butler had become his champion in the House and his mentor in the Executive Mansion. Grant had accepted cheap and low associates as his advisers. [22] Less than fifteen months after the beginning of his administration, without reason or explanation, he sent a curt note to Attorney-General Hoar, the outstanding character of his Cabinet, demanding his immediate resignation. He appointed in his stead one Akerman, a "Southern Republican" from Georgia,—a native of New Hampshire. Grant thought this appointment would assist in winning carpet-bag support within the Senate for the achievement of his ambition to annex San Domingo.[23]

Black Friday and the Gold Conspiracy had come and gone.[24] The Whiskey Ring contributions and the Belknap's bribe-taking were presently to be unearthed.[25]   Grant's own acceptance of gifts and his return of favors to the givers had become a national scandal.[26] It was "the high-water-mark of corruption in national affairs."[27]

Grant had been in office but five days when at Butler's instigation the Tenure-of-Office Act was repealed by the House of Representatives.[28] To force action by the Senate, Grant announced that as long as that law was on the books he would make neither suspensions nor appointments. The Republicans were anxious to be rid of Johnson's appointees and to fill the vacancies with their henchmen.[29] "The Augean Stable" must be cleaned, they said.[30] But the Senate, as always, jealous of its prerogatives, proposed an amendment merely suspending the act until the next session.[31] This plan, however, to suspend the act just long enough to permit Grant to remove Johnson's appointees, was "so baldly and shamelessly partisan. . . . that the common instincts of justice, even of public decency, revolted."[32]

A compromise therefore, was resorted to. The law finally adopted permitted the President, during any recess of the Senate, to suspend civil officers until the end of the next session, but if in the meanwhile the Senate were to refuse its consent to such suspension or to the appointment of a successor, the suspended officer was to be restored.[33] "Casting off all political disguises and personal pretenses," the Speaker of the House admitted later, "the simple truth remains that the Tenure-of-Office Law was enacted lest President Johnson should remove Republican officeholders too rapidly, and it was practically repealed lest President Grant should not remove Democratic office-holders rapidly enough."[34]

The law was practically repealed, but not sufficiently to satisfy Ulysses Grant. He saw less merit in this curb now that he was

President than at the time when he was advocating the conviction and removal of his predecessor. "It may be well," he wrote in his first annual message a few months later, "to mention the embarrassment possible to arise from leaving on the statute books the so-called 'Tenure-of-Office Acts,' and to earnestly recommend their total repeal." [35]

Grant, it seems, was making a belated study of the Fundamental Law, for he continued: "It could not have been the intention of the framers of the Constitution, when providing that appointments made by the President should receive the consent of the Senate, that the latter should have the power to retain in office persons placed there by Federal appointment against the will of the President. The law is inconsistent with a faithful administration of the government. What faith can an Executive put in officials forced upon him, and those, too, whom he has suspended for reason? How will such officials be likely to serve an administration which they know does not trust them?" [36]

These were the questions Johnson had asked,—questions for the asking of which Grant had urged his conviction and removal! But this Congress was as ill-disposed to listen now as it had been twenty-two months earlier. Other than his protest, however, the new President made no attempt to vindicate his prerogative. He remembered Johnson's effort. "I feel for Grant in his sad position," wrote General Sherman in 1872. "When he entered his present office, I believe he intended what he said,—to administer his office according to his own best judgment—but he soon found that he reckoned without his host, that Congress and individual senators controlled all the details of government, and that if he did not concede to senators and representatives the appointing power, they would Johnsonize him." [37]

§

In his quiet home in Greeneville, Andrew Johnson was watching,—and waiting. He looked out upon the dreadful Reconstruction, and longed for one more chance to help undo the awful work his enemies had wrought.

With blind indifference to the facts of race, the sentiments of human nature and the future of their country, the Radicals pressed on. Their purpose was so to organize the negroes as to maintain the Republican party permanently in power.[38] In early April, 1869, Congress enacted that Mississippi, Texas and Virginia should hold elections for the ratification of state constitutions drawn in accordance with the Reconstruction acts. But the adoption of these constitutions was not enough to secure for them the right of representation. A new condition was imposed! They must adopt the Fifteenth Amendment also![39] This, like its predecessor, was to become an amendment by duress.

Under the heel of Southern negroes, carpet-baggers and Northern arms, these three states complied, and by March, 1870, were all "readmitted" to the Union.[40] In the same month the Fifteenth Amendment was proclaimed part of the Constitution.[41] Negro suffrage full and complete had come at last,—on paper. Throughout the North the negroes celebrated. In Washington Sumner and Grant were both serenaded.[42]

The Southern states were all "back in the Union," but their Senators and Representatives for the most part were aliens. From North Carolina came Senator Abbot of New Hampshire; from Florida, Osborn and Gilbert, natives of New Jersey and New York; from South Carolina, Sawyer of Massachusetts; from Alabama, Warner and Spencer of Ohio and New York; from Louisiana, Harris and Kellogg of New York and Vermont. Many of these "Southern" Senators had been officers in the Union army.[43]

This alien representation, the product of the Reconstruction policy, was pleasing to the Radicals, but what pleased them most was the appearance of Hiram R. Revels as a Senator from Mississippi,—he was a negro. He occupied the seat of Jefferson Davis. "Poetic justice, historic revenge!"[44] Senator Wilson conducted him to his seat with an air that said: "Massachusetts has done it all." Colfax administered the oath with unction and then shook Revel's hand with great warmth. The Radical Senators fairly scrambled for an opportunity to offer personal congratulation.[45] Sumner was almost beside himself with joy.[46] Presently other black legislators came, Bruce to the Senate, and Rapier, Lynch and Rainey to the House.[47]

How false and how temporary was this truckling to the blacks the more intelligent of the negroes easily discerned. Booker Washington, himself destined to become a leader of his race, was one of these. "Though I was but little more than a youth during the period of Reconstruction," he wrote in 1901, "I had the feeling that mistakes were being made, and that things could not remain in the condition that they were in then very long. I felt that the Reconstruction policy, so far as it related to my race, was in a large measure on a false foundation, was artificial and forced. In many cases it seemed to me that the ignorance of my race was being used as a tool with which to help white men into office, and that there was an element in the North which wanted to punish the Southern white men by forcing the negro into positions over the heads of the Southern whites. I felt that the negro would be the one to suffer for this in the end. Besides, the general political agitation drew the attention of our people away from the more fundamental matters of perfecting themselves in the industries at their doors and in securing property." [48]

The seeds of race hatred, like dragon's teeth, were being sown. A proud, high-spirited, self-governing people after they had surrendered in good faith were trampled under foot by their ex-slaves stimulated, encouraged and protected by Northern arms and Northern laws. History reveals no episode more tragic. Unprincipled adventurers from the North held sway, plundering a disarmed and defenseless people. The dregs from the Federal army, the meanest of her camp followers, the fugitives from Northern justice, combined for any safe and profitable deed of shame. Marshaling the negroes and joining with the Southern renegades, backed and encouraged by the authorities at Washington, these thieves and gangsters bore down upon the ruins of the Confederacy, like the robber bands that swept through Germany after the Thirty Years' war. From the Potomac to the Gulf, and back again they swarmed, feeding on the substance of a conquered people. By fraud and by force these brigands from the North gathered into their hands all the reins of power,—all public offices, the courts, the legislatures and the churches. [49]

To help maintain themselves in power, they divided up the lesser spoils with the ex-slaves and organized and drilled negro constabularies. In Mississippi, Louisiana and the Carolinas they armed the black militia. In North Carolina alone, 96,000 of these were enrolled, and 20,000 were armed and trained. The Governor of Louisiana held at his call a black standing army,—the Metropolitan Guard. Whites were everywhere disarmed,— white companies were disbanded.[50]

What the inevitable result of placing the "bottom rail upon the top" would be, was pointedly revealed one day in South Carolina not long after the war ended. In September, 1865, Calvin Crozier of Mississippi, a veteran of the Confederate army and a former prisoner of war, upon his release from a Federal jail, was making his way home. At Orangeburg a gentleman journeying in the same direction placed two young ladies in his charge. At Newberry, negro soldiers derailed the train. Crozier got out to investigate. On his return he found two half-drunk, cursing privates in his coach. One attempted gross familiarities with one of Crozier's charges. He ejected him; the second negro joined the fray. There was a scuffle; one of the blacks ran toward the camp screaming: "I am cut by a damned rebel."[51]

A mob of black soldiers now appeared intent upon revenge. In the nighttime Crozier was marched to the bivouac of the regiment, and was condemned to death without a trial. In the morning he was made to kneel at the brink of his own grave. As the smoke of the firing party lifted, his lifeless body lurched forward. The black troops filled in the earth and jumped upon it, laughing, dancing and stamping.[52]

Now and then the Ku Klux Klan rode, but for the most part, under all but incredible indignities and wrongs, the Caucasians of the South suffered through the dreadful Reconstruction years with prudence and with patience. "No brave people, accustomed to be free, ever endured oppression so peacefully or so wisely."[53] At Lexington, as the President of Washington College, Robert Lee was setting an example: "I have a self-imposed task," he said, "which I must accomplish. I have led the young men of the South in battle. I have seen many of them fall under my standard. I shall devote my life now to training young men to do their duty in life." [54]

Winnie Davis, the child of the ex-President,—"the daughter of the Confederacy"—many years after the war, was studying in Carlsruhe. "Miss Em," she said one day to Emily Mason, a Southern lady who had called upon her, "what did Papa do just after the war,—just after Richmond fell?" Her caller would not answer. When a little later Miss Mason met the former President in Paris, she spoke of his daughter's ignorance of his prison life, and expressed surprise that he had not claimed the sympathy of his child. "I was unwilling to prejudice her," said Davis, "against the country to which she is now returning and which must be hers. I thought that but justice to the child. I want her to love her country." [55]

§

South Carolina had been the first state to secede. Upon South Carolina the worst punishments of the Reconstruction were inflicted. The history of civilization affords no blacker picture. Bribery, corruption, embezzlement, fraud, infamy, demoralization, flourished like poisonous weeds within some pestilential swamp. The dregs of society were in control. It was the prostitution of government, the nadir of democracy. "The civilization of the Puritan and the Cavalier, of the Roundhead and the Huguenot is in peril," wrote one competent observer. [56] Through the desolate and charred streets of Charleston defiant bands of roistering negroes roamed shouting: "De bottom rail's on de top and we's gwine to keep it dar." [57]

In 1872 a black Lieutenant-Governor was chosen. [58] In the hands of the ignorant ex-slaves and their Northern white allies South Carolina entered upon an era of darkness and despair. Every plan for pilfering the public treasury was resorted to. Fraudulent guarantees of railroad bonds, the special frauds of the printing ring, and every devious device in which rascals are adept, drained dry the mounting taxes wrung from an impoverished people. [59]

The state capitol was refurnished with barbaric splendor. For two hundred imported china cuspidors sixteen hundred dollars were expended.   Six-hundred-dollar clocks, sixty-dollar plush gothic chairs, two-hundred-dollar crimson sofas, six-hundred-dollar mirrors were soon installed.[60]   Kept open day and night, a bar was added to the furnishings of the State House.   For the more important members whiskey and cigars, brandy and champagne were added to the appropriation bills. In the city of Columbia a brothel maintained by a colored woman was furnished at the state's expense.[61]   Moses, the Speaker of the lower House, and a former resident of Brooklyn, was voted a "gratuity of $1000" to reimburse him for a lost bet on a horse race.[62]   To the public debt of seven millions in 1868, twenty-two millions were added in two years.[63]

The worst criminals were turned loose from the jails by Governor Moses, who sold his pardons by the wholesale.[64]   The first district sent Whittemore as its representative to Congress.   His specialty was the sale of cadetships to Annapolis and West Point. He resigned and was "censured."[65]   Criminality, ignorance and depravity were everywhere.   During the administration of one governor, two hundred trial justices who could neither read nor write held office by executive appointment.[66]

Society itself seemed to have broken down.   Drunkenness and crimes of violence increased.   White women no longer ventured out of doors unattended, even in the daytime.   White girls were assaulted and defiled under circumstances too horrible to recount. Frightened and dismayed, the old residents of South Carolina looked out upon this scene of horror.[67]

James S. Pike, a staunch Republican from Maine, visited this conquered province in the early seventies, and wrote a book describing what he saw.   It was well named "The Prostrate State."   "Fancy," he said, "the moral condition of a state in which a large majority of all its voting citizens are habitually guilty of thieving and concubinage.   Yet such is the condition of South Carolina.   Are we to be told that the civilization of the nineteenth century has nothing better to propose than this for the government of one of the oldest and proudest states of the American Union?   As it is morally, so it is intellectually.   These same rulers of a great state, speaking of them as a whole, neither read nor write. They are as ignorant and as irresponsible in the exercise of their political functions as would be the Bedouin Arab of the desert, or the roving Comanches of the plains, if called upon to choose the rulers of New York or Massachusetts." [68]

Here is the testimony of no Southern partisan, but the word of a Northern anti-slavery Republican. "The changes here experienced," he continued, "have been accomplished by outside forces. . . . It is not the rule of intrinsic strength; it is the compulsive power of the Federal authority at Washington. But for that, the forces of civilization would readjust themselves and overturn the present artificial arrangement." [69]

At the State House, one day, Pike looked in to watch the legislators at their work. His description of the "Black Parliament" deserves a high place in American letters. "A white community," he wrote, "that had gradually risen from small beginnings till it grew into wealth, culture and refinement, and became accomplished in all the arts of civilization; that successfully asserted its resistance to a foreign tyranny by deeds of conspicuous valor, which achieved liberty and independence through the fire and tempest of civil war, and illustrated itself in the councils of the nation by orators and statesmen worthy of any age or nation— such a community is then reduced to this. It lies prostrate in the dust, ruled over by this strange conglomerate gathered from the ranks of its own servile population. It is the spectacle of a society suddenly turned bottom-side up. The wealth, the intelligence, the culture, the wisdom of the state, have broken through the crust of that social volcano on which they were contentedly reposing, and have sunk out of sight, consumed by the subterranean fires they had with such temerity braved and defied." [70]

In the place of this old aristocratic society stands the rude form of the most ignorant democracy that mankind ever saw, invested with the formation of government. It is the dregs of the population habilitated in the robes of their intelligent predecessors, and asserting over them the rule of ignorance and corruption, through the inexorable machinery of a majority of numbers. It is barbarism overwhelming civilization by physical force. It is the slave rioting in the halls of his master, and putting that master under his feet." [71]

Against this, by his vetoes and his messages, Andrew Johnson had warned his fellow countrymen. To prevent this prostitution of free government, he had carried on perhaps the bravest struggle in American history, suffering calumny, impeachment and almost conviction, as well as slander and misunderstanding from half a century of historians.

But let us continue with Mr. Pike's description of the South Carolina House of Representatives. "Here sit one hundred and twenty-four members," he wrote. "Of these, twenty-three are white men, representing the remains of the old civilization. These are good-looking substantial citizens. They are men of weight and standing in the communities they represent. They are all from the hill country. The frosts of sixty and seventy winters whiten the heads of some among them. There they sit grim and silent. They feel themselves to be but loose stones, thrown in to partially obstruct a current they are powerless to resist. They say little and do little as the days go by. They simply watch the rising tide and mark the progressive steps of the inundation. They feel themselves to be in some sort martyrs, bound stoically to suffer in behalf of that still great element in the state whose prostrate fortunes are becoming the sport of an unpitying fate. Grouped in a corner of the commodious and well-furnished chamber, they stolidly survey the noisy riot that goes on in the great black Left and Centre, where the business and debates of the House are conducted, and where sit the strange and extraordinary guides of the fortunes of a once proud and haughty state." [72]

Of the one hundred and twenty-four members of the legislature, ninety-four were black; these, together with their seven white allies, outnumbered the thirty-three representatives of the old civilization more than three to one. It was, said Pike, "almost literally a Black Parliament, and it is the only one on the face of the earth which is the representative of a white constituency and the professed exponent of an advanced type of modern civilization. . . . The Speaker is black, the clerk is black, the doorkeepers are black, the little pages are black, the chairman of the

Ways and Means is black, and the chaplain is coal-black. At some of the desks sit colored men whose types it would be hard to find outside of Congo; whose costumes, visages, attitudes and expression only befit the forecastle of a buccaneer." [73]

And now the legislature is proceeding with its work. "No one is allowed to talk five minutes without interruption, and one interruption is the signal for another and another, until the original speaker is smothered under an avalanche of them. . . . The inefficient colored friend who sits in the Speaker's chair cannot suppress this extraordinary element of the debate. Some of the blackest members exhibit a pertinacity of intrusion in raising these points of order and questions of privilege that few white men can equal. Their struggles to get the floor, their bellowings and physical contortions, baffle description. . . . The Speaker orders a member whom he has discovered to be particularly unruly to take his seat. The member obeys, and with the same motion that he sits down throws his feet onto his desk hiding himself from the Speaker by the soles of his boots." [74]

In a moment the same member appears again upon the floor. After several experiences of this kind, "the Speaker threatens, in a laugh, to call 'the gemman' to order. This is considered a capital joke and a guffaw follows. The laugh goes round, and then the peanuts are cracked and munched faster than ever; one hand being employed in fortifying the inner man with this nutriment of universal use, while the other enforces the views of the orator. This laughing propensity of the sable crowd is a great cause of disorder. They laugh as hens cackle—one begins and all follow." [75]

"My God," exclaimed a low-country planter as he leaned over the rail of the House to survey the scene, "this is the first time I have been here. I thought I knew what we were doing when we consented to emancipation. I knew the negro, and I predicted much that has happened, but I never thought it would come to this. Let me go." [76]

For a perfect grasp of all that Andrew Johnson struggled to prevent, for a complete understanding of his warnings, there should be presented the entire story of the Reconstruction, not in

South Carolina only, but in Virginia, Georgia, Mississippi, Louisiana and the rest.   This chapter of our criminal annals has never yet been written.   Historians have touched it lightly and passed on, yet there it lies, the damning proof of what Thad Stevens, Sumner and their followers had wrought.

Tourgée's interesting, but old-fashioned novels, "The Fool's Errand," "Hot Plowshares," "An Appeal to Caesar," "Bricks With Straw," and "The Invisible Empire" throw light upon this epoch.   In later years Thomas Nelson Page's "Red Rock" and Owen Wister's "Lady Baltimore," have contributed to an understanding of the black régime.   But a full and complete portrayal of the "blunder-crime" of Reconstruction [77] awaits the master hand of some Macaulay, Victor Hugo, Zola or Carlyle.   Some day he will come to paint the dreadful picture of the aftermath of Appomattox,—the crimes against the state, the crimes against the home, the larcenies, the robberies, and the rapes, political and domestic, the prostitution of public virtue, the domination of the negro and the adventurer.   And when the awful masterpiece is done, there, against a flaming background of desolation, the hopes, the aspirations, the struggles, the character and the life of Andrew Johnson will stand forth like an unscathed cross upon a smoking battlefield.

§

Johnson looked out upon this Southern desolation.   He watched the poisonous work that was to alienate the two sections of the United States as no war could have done.   He saw the President in the hands of his old enemies, confused and dazed, pliant and yielding, credulous of "Southern outrages," the steady patron of Northern intervention and of every measure of oppression.[78]   The Grant of Appomattox was no more,—the magnanimous conciliation there begun had long since been forgotten; he had accepted the Radicals and had assented to their Southern policy.[79]

But in the North there were growing signs of discontent with what her statesmen had achieved.   Perhaps the fairminded could yet be aroused to the need for treatment of the festering sore of

Reconstruction. The Senate of the United States had once echoed with the patriot voice of Andrew Johnson,—why not again? There, if anywhere, the blundering malice of Grant's followers and advisers could be exposed. Johnson resolved that he would go back to the Senate![80]

In 1870, in Missouri, the Republican party was divided on the question of removing the political disabilities of those who had aided the Confederacy. Carl Schurz was the leader of the Liberal wing of the Republicans. B. Gratz Brown was nominated for governor by this faction, was endorsed by the Democrats and was elected. It was the beginning of the Liberal Republican movement.[81] In Jefferson City in January, 1872, the "Liberal Republicans" invited all those who were opposed to the national administration to meet in Cincinnati on the first Wednesday of the following May.[82]

Horace Greeley in New York was dissatisfied with Roscoe Conkling's leadership of that state; he was disgusted with the national administration, and he threw the whole weight of his *Tribune* behind the "Liberal Republicans." The Cincinnati *Commercial* and the Chicago *Tribune* joined him. In May the convention met as scheduled, in Cincinnati. A large and an enthusiastic gathering set to work with Carl Schurz as the leading spirit.[83]

The platform declared that "The President of the United States has openly used the powers and opportunities of his high office for the promotion of personal ends. He has kept notoriously corrupt and unworthy men in places of power and responsibility, to the detriment of the public interest. He has used the public service of the government as a machinery of corruption and personal influence and has interfered with tyrannical arrogance in the political affairs of states and municipalities. He has rewarded with influential and lucrative offices men who had acquired his favor by valuable presents, thus stimulating the demoralization of our political life by his conspicuous example."[84]

No platform ever made used plainer speech or greater truth. It continued: "The partisans of the administration, assuming to be the Republican party and controlling its organization, have

attempted to justify such wrongs and palliate such abuses to the
end of maintaining partisan ascendency. . . . They have kept
alive the passions and resentments of the late war, to use them
for their own advantage; they have resorted to arbitrary measures
in direct conflict with the organic law, instead of appealing to the
better instincts and latent patriotism of the Southern people by
restoring to them those rights the enjoyment of which is indispensable to a successful administration of their local affairs. . . .
We demand the immediate and absolute removal of all disabilities
imposed on account of the rebellion, which was finally subdued
seven years ago, believing that universal amnesty will result in a
complete pacification of the country." [85]

Charles Francis Adams, Lyman Trumbull, Horace Greeley, B.
Gratz Brown and many others, among whom, of course, was
Salmon P. Chase, were contenders for the nomination. [86] Chase
like Barkis in Dickens' novel, was still "willin'." He had continued his letter writing with obscure correspondents. He used
his old formula when he confided to one of these: "If those who
agree with me in principles think that my nomination will promote
the interests of the country, I shall not refuse the use of my
name." [87]

Horace Greeley was nominated on the sixth ballot. Brown
was named for the Vice-Presidency. [88] The leaders of this movement were painfully disappointed because Adams was not nominated. The choice of Greeley was a "wet blanket" on their
nomination. [89] *The Nation* and the *Evening Post* withheld their
support. Carl Schurz at first declined to help, but later gave his
reluctant support to the convention's choice. [90]

The Springfield *Republican* too, under the leadership of Samuel
Bowles, took up the cudgels in favor of the Cincinnati nominees.
The "risk is worth taking" this influential organ stated, "in
view of the great good to be secured,—the final pacification and
genuine reunion of these states. . . ." Grant, it continued, "has
affiliated as President with politicians of a very bad sort. He
surrendered to them long ago and has ever since allowed himself
to be 'run' by the Mortons and Tom Murphys. He lives and
moves and has his being in an atmosphere of materialism; and

has neither the power nor the wish to rise above it. He does not even seem to understand that there is anything higher and better; he acts as though he held it the whole duty of an American President to enjoy himself in his office, punish his enemies, and make the 'patronage' go as far as possible in national and local politics." [91]

The regular Republicans met that year in Philadelphia on June 5th. Their platform endorsed Grant's "practical wisdom," and declared that the recent amendments to the national Constitution should be "cordially" sustained. [92] Grant was renominated on the first ballot, and Henry Wilson of Massachusetts was selected as his running mate. "Smiler Colfax" was quietly discarded, despite the fact that his participation in the Credit Mobilier was not yet public property. [93]

Thirty-four days later the Democratic National Convention convened at Baltimore. [94] "Anybody to beat Grant," was the cry. [95] To accomplish this the followers of Thomas Jefferson were willing to endure humiliation, even that of accepting as their standard bearer the old arch enemy of democracy, Horace Greeley. Thomas Jefferson Randolph of Virginia was temporary chairman, and James R. Doolittle of Wisconsin was made permanent president of the convention. Under their leadership, Greeley's platform was adopted without change, and Greeley and Brown were made the Democratic nominees. Many of the delegates complained, some later bolted, but the bitter dose was grimly swallowed. [96]

Never did our politics present a stranger spectacle than this acceptance by the Democrats of one who had been their bitterest antagonist. Anticipating Dr. Burchard by more than twenty-three years, in 1861 Greeley had declared: "The essential articles of the Democratic creed are 'love rum and hate niggers.'" [97] And further: "I do not say that all Democrats are rascals but it is undeniably true that all rascals are Democrats." [98] Nor could the Southern Democrats forget how in the month following Sumter Greeley's *Tribune* had thundered: "When the rebellious traitors are overwhelmed in the field, and scattered like leaves before an angry wind, it must not be to return to peaceful and contented

homes. They must find poverty at their firesides. and see priva-
tion in the anxious eyes of mothers and the rags of children." [99]

But Greeley had had a change of heart, and there was the Cincinnati platform! The sole chance for the South lay in the acceptance of this strange candidate. Andrew Johnson looked on in
Tennessee, and joined the Greeley movement, "on the principle of
universal pressure of circumstances beyond human control." [100]
Politics, that whimsical hotel-keeper, was indeed to make strange
bed-fellows during that campaign,—Sumner came out for Greeley
also! [101] There was little else that he could do after the wild
philippic against Grant he had delivered a few weeks earlier in
the Senate.[102] But early in September Sumner sailed for
Europe.[103]

Greeley plunged into the campaign, speaking in Pennsylvania,
Ohio and Indiana to great crowds. He struck at Pittsburg the
keynote of his canvass. "I ask you," he there said, "to take the
hand held out to you by your Southern brethren in the adoption
of the Cincinnati platform, by those who were our enemies, but
are again our fellow countrymen. I ask you to grasp that hand
and say—'Brothers, we differed, we fought. The war is ended;
let us again be fellow countrymen and forget that we have been
enemies.'" [104]

Everywhere great audiences came to hear and see him. His
countenance and his grotesque figure became even more familiar
to his fellow countrymen,—his spectacled blue eyes, his farmer-like
fringe of white whiskers, his white coat worn and wrinkled with
pockets stuffed with newspapers, and his baggy trousers thrust
into his boot tops.[105] But he spoke with ability and what he said
was well thought out. "His name had been honored for so many
years in every Republican household," wrote Blaine, "that the
desire to see and hear him was universal, and secured to him the
majesty of numbers at every meeting. So great indeed was the
general demonstration of interest, that a degree of uneasiness was
created at Republican headquarters as to the ultimate effect of
his tour." [106]

But Grant's Republicans were equal to the task at hand, and
they fell upon their adversary with unbridled fierceness. Their

attacks, says Julian, "were unrelieved by a single element of honor or fair play." [107] The pencil with which Thomas Nast had just driven Tweed from power, once again was called into play by *Harper's Weekly*. His cartoons pilloried Greeley as the associate of "rebels." [108] The strange costume and eccentric dress of the old editor were tempting material for the cartoonist, and Nast used these with savagery. [109]

Greeley made a brave and an effective canvass, but the time of liberalism had not yet come; his campaign was foredoomed to failure. [110] His personal peculiarities, the unceasing war which he had waged upon the "evils of intemperance," his previous denunciation of Southerners and of Democrats, and his present communion with them, the omission from his platform of any stand upon the tariff, the smoldering embers of the war and the zeal of the Radicals in fanning them into a flame, the failure of the North fully to comprehend the dreadful consequences of the Reconstruction laws,—these things combined to render Liberal success impossible.

Then too, there was the great weight of conservative inertia. "Money bags are always and everywhere conservative," wrote Samuel Bowles in his Springfield *Republican*. "When you have proved to the busy wealth-seekers that the President has shown an indecent fondness for gifts, that he has appointed rascally or incapable kinsmen to office, that he has cracked if not broken the laws, what have you accomplished by your denunciation? They will reply to you 'General Grant is a safe man. The country has prospered and its credit improved under his administration. We know him and know that he can be trusted not to smash things. It would be folly for us to take the risk of a change. Let well enough alone." [111]

During the last days of the canvass Greeley was called home to the bedside of his dying wife. He buried her before election. Election day brought him new disasters. No candidate for President had ever been defeated so decisively. He was successful nowhere in the North, and in six only of the Southern states. One of these was Tennessee. [112] Broken in body and in spirit, he died within the month. Clergymen who had stood by silent while he was pelted by the demagogues and mercenaries, at his grave were eloquent in their eulogies.[113]

§

During the Greeley campaign, Johnson again became an active participant in the politics of Tennessee. At Nashville early in the fall of that year there was a Democratic State Convention to nominate a candidate for Congress from the state at large. Johnson arrived early. On leaving Greeneville he asked Col. Reeves to meet him at Room 5 of the Maxwell House on the day preceding the convention.[114] When Reeves entered Johnson's room at the appointed time, the latter closed the door, locked it, and turning to his secretary said: "There is much pressure for me to become a candidate before the convention tomorrow." He did not want this done because he feared it might decrease his chances for the Senate three years later. He had the program of his campaign well matured. He outlined it, and then moving his chair a little closer to his friend, for the first time, the pent-up emotion of three years was released. With all the fervor of his soul he said: "I was impeached, and while legally vindicated, yet by a minority vote. I would rather have the vindication of my state by electing me to my old seat in the Senate of the United States than to be monarch of the grandest empire on earth, God being my judge! For this I live and will never die content without it! Go to the Convention tomorrow and if my name is put in nomination, promptly withdraw it on my authority." [115]

Col. Reeves followed his instructions, and the Convention nominated his old division commander General Cheatham. There was nothing further for Johnson's secretary then to do, and he went home. On his return journey, the news reached him at Chattanooga, to his surprise, that Johnson in the public square at Nashville had announced himself as an independent candidate. He had yielded to his friends' solicitations.[116]

A stirring contest now ensued,—a three-cornered fight with Cheatham as the Democratic nominee, Horace Maynard that of the Republicans, and Johnson as an independent candidate.[117] In his whole career he had never weathered a more strenuous campaign. He stumped the state. He never dreamed that he could win, but he seized this opportunity of vindicating once again his policy as President. And he had another object: the election of a legislature that would favor his return to the Senate.[118] What success attended him in this, we shall presently discover, but he lost his fight for Congress. Maynard was elected.[119]

Johnson had, however, gained a new hold on the affections of his old state. "A more striking illustration of one man's power," declared one newspaper, "was never before given in this country than in Mr. Johnson's canvass of the state; and though not elected, he is more firmly intrenched in the hearts of the people, and more conscious of his hold upon their confidence than at any time since 1860." [120] Those who came within the spell of those black eyes, seemed transformed, electrified,—ready to follow where he led. I have talked with men who knew him. As they told me of their recollections, the old magic of his personality,—even after half a century—seemed to animate them once again.

David Rankin Barbee, the distinguished editor of the Asheville *Citizen*, recalls how when a lad in Nashville he used to go to market with his mother. Stall No. 1 was maintained by a "large overflowing Dutchman" named Chris. He had had the same stall for more than fifty years. Young Barbee had noticed how his mother always beamed upon the stallkeeper. One day he asked her why. "My son," she answered, "that man was Andrew Johnson's friend." [121]

After his unsuccessful campaign Johnson returned once more to Greeneville. He spoke neither of his defeat nor of his future plans, but his keen eyes were watching the political horizon.[122]

LXXXVIII

VINDICATION

It was a strange and altered country on which Johnson looked. The corruption of the carpet-bag negro governments in the South had their counterparts in the North. The war seemed to have polluted every channel of the nation's life. Demoralization was everywhere. Crude new rich men appeared upon the scene. Tweed finally went to jail, but Grant's friends, Jim Fisk and Jay Gould, were flourishing. The bench and the bar were both debased. The Credit Mobilier revealed corruptions such as to make the whole government seem scandalous. Ill-gotten luxury, gambling, bribery, embezzlement and depravity made the lovers of their country tremble for the Republic.[1]

The year 1873, with its financial panic, came and went. With increasing restlessness the American people were watching Grant and his henchmen in Washington and elsewhere. In the fall of 1874 a resolute electorate came to the polls, and chose a Democratic House of Representatives,—the first in fourteen years. The friends of decency were refreshed to learn that, in Massachusetts, Ben Butler had been defeated in his effort to return to Congress.[2] In New York, Samuel J. Tilden was elected governor by 50,000 votes.[3] The conscience of the country was awakening from its long sleep. There seemed hope even for the South. Now if ever was the time for Andrew Johnson!

In the early winter of 1875 a successor to Senator Brownlow was to be chosen by the legislature of Tennessee. In what seemed a desperate endeavor, Johnson determined that this time he would not fail. With all of his old fire, he entered the campaign and once more canvassed the entire state. Campaigning then seemed no less fraught with danger than in those days, when he had courted death to stand up for a principle. Especially was this true when his travels led him to Columbia, the home town of Col. Cooper, whose brother Edmond had betrayed Johnson four years earlier.

He arrived to find that Col. Savage, a bitter political opponent, had taken possession of the Court House. He had been warned that if in Columbia he were to attack Edmond Cooper he would be assassinated. On learning that others held possession of the court room, Johnson said to his young followers, Captain Irvine and Archelaus Hughes: "You boys go and get some good boxes and put them on the outside of the Court House and I will speak outdoors." [4] A temporary platform was thus constructed underneath the very window of Col. Cooper's office.

Johnson presently appeared and to the audience that gathered said: "Fellow citizens, I have been told that if I repeated here what I have said on former occasions, perhaps I would be assassinated. But these two eyes have never yet beheld the man that this heart feared. I have said . . . and I repeat it now, Jesus Christ had his Judas, Cæsar had his Brutus, Charles I had his Cromwell, Washington had his Benedict Arnold, and I have had my Edmond and Henry Cooper." [5] The cocking of pistols all around was heard. The crowd expected Col. Cooper to commence firing. Johnson waited, but nothing happened, and he finished with his speech. [6]

The legislature met in January to choose its Senator from among the many aspirants. Among these were Governor Brown, just closing then his second term, Bate and Quarles, all three ex-Confederate major generals and able lawyers. There also was Col. Savage, Key, who was later Postmaster-General in Hayes' cabinet, and there too was Gustavus A. Henry, whom Johnson had defeated for the governorship in 1853. [7]

A desperate contest, with such candidacies, was inevitable. For more than a week the balloting continued. No one except Johnson believed that he could win, yet day after day he directed his small forces with a master hand. Thirty-five legislators never wavered in their support, but they were less than a majority. [8] "Never," says Judge Temple, "did the invincible will of Mr. Johnson to control men appear to more conspicuous advantage than

during this memorable contest. All the opposition to him in the
state, which had been gathering for forty years, was concentrated
in an unrelenting, determined effort to overthrow him." [9]

Ballot after ballot came, but still no choice. Once General
Bate was within one vote of victory, but it did not come. Finally
on the fifty-fifth ballot, on January 26th, a majority for Johnson
was revealed. His long awaited triumph was at hand. He had
never known a prouder day. [10]

Col. Reeves hurried from the Capitol to the Maxwell House to
congratulate his friend, but others were before him. "Mr. Johnson, you are elected," panted A. A. Taylor, a member from Carter
County, who had run all the way, and as he spoke he fell in a
dead faint. The Senator-elect was dashing water in his face when
Reeves arrived. Others soon appeared, wild with enthusiasm
and excitement. A sturdy representative from Marion County
seized Johnson, flung his feet toward the ceiling and his head
downward, and thus holding him, trotted around the room in
ecstasy. [11]

Johnson was a favorite of Nashville; men rushed from their
stores and offices to take part in a public demonstration. [12] The
great throng that packed the State House when the decisive vote
was taken pushed out into the street cheering as they came, and
marched on to the Maxwell House to congratulate the Senator-
elect in person. In the evening ten thousand Tennesseans assembled in the public square to see the old lion flushed with victory,
and to hear him speak. [13] No oration in his whole career was comparable with this, [14] and at no time did he seem greater. [15]

The champion of justice for the South assured his hearers that
he would return to Washington with no personal hostility toward
anyone. He would advocate, he said, a union of all men who
loved their country, against aggression on the Constitution, and
would devote his few remaining years to that country which from
childhood up he had loved more than life itself. [16] Others spoke;
two of them put forth the suggestion that in 1876 the Senator-
elect should be nominated for President!

The state of Tennessee received the news of Johnson's triumph
with keen satisfaction. Even in the North his dramatic victory

was hailed in many quarters with approval.[17] The temper of the public mind was changing. The country had been through six years with Grant; it was tiring of his policies and of his followers. Johnson's downright honesty and independence were needed at this time. "We shall not be sorry to see him again in public life," declared the New York *Times*. "Whatever his faults as President may have been, at any rate he went out of the White House as poor as he entered it and that is something to say in these times. The public generally take a more favorable view of Mr. Johnson's character now."[18]

The New York *World* voiced its sincere pleasure at "the return of so experienced and upright a man as Mr. Johnson to the Senate. . . . His election to succeed that very disreputable person Brownlow is a public boon. Mr. Johnson's past proves that his future course . . . will be unselfish, honest and very courageous."[19] He had, declared the New York *Herald*, "fortunately lived to see his vindication. . . . Because the American people know him so well, because he was impeached and hounded as a traitor and chained and handcuffed by Congress, the contest in the Tennessee legislature possessed a national interest and is really a national victory. He is the best man Tennessee could have chosen, not merely for herself but for democracy of North and South. . . . The Senate needs men who have the courage to speak the truth, and besides Mr. Johnson has probably profited by time and experience. . . . It is now generally conceded that the imaginary misdemeanors of 1868 . . . were in fact official merits. . . ."[20]

From all over the United States telegrams and letters of congratulation came pouring in upon him. "There is great rejoicing everywhere over your election. It is a great triumph," wrote William Groesbeck from Cincinnati.[21] While from Hartford, Gideon Welles sent this word to his old chief: "The indications are that the 'gospel of hate' is drawing to a close, and that we may now hope for peace and reconciliation and a return to the true principles of the Constitution,—a restoration of the states to their rights."[22]

Presently Johnson would be journeying to Washington. With

increasing zeal his many friends were planning how they might send him back next year as President.[23] Seymour had failed, Greeley had failed, but Johnson would not fail!

§

In the normal course of events Johnson would not have entered upon his Senatorial duties until December. But President Grant on March 4th had convened the Senate in executive session to act upon a treaty with King Kalakaua of the Sandwich Islands.[24] Before the upper chamber came to order for this purpose, Senator Andrew Johnson arrived in Washington. The Senators who had taken part in his impeachment were anything but cheerful over his return. "It is acknowledged by both parties," said the New York *Herald*, "that he will be a free lance and likely to do as much harm to one side as the other. It is felt . . . by the best men that Mr. Johnson very probably will become a power in the Senate. . . . It is thought that he will not fail to make it uncomfortable in the Senate for gentlemen who leave their Constitution of the United States at home."[25] Even Johnson's bitterest enemies, declared the New York *Tribune*, were "compelled to admit his sterling honesty and unswerving rectitude. In these days of moral and official delinquency, it is no ordinary gratification for the people at large to have their national councils honored by the presence of such a man."[26]

A little before noon of March 6th Johnson appeared within the Senate chamber to take his oath of office. It snowed that morning, but this did not deter a great crowd from packing all the galleries to see the old lion returning to the fray.[27] He was an object of intense interest to everyone. "Physically," wrote the New York *Herald* correspondent, he had "undergone less change than almost any other Senator on the floor. His hair may be a shade lighter as it is undoubtedly somewhat thinned, but there is no evidence of baldness. There are neither hard lines nor deep wrinkles in his face, but his expression is a mixture of sadness and earnestness,—an expression which has been habitual with him during the past ten years."[28]

There were three new Senators to be sworn in that day: General

Burnside of Rhode Island,—and alas, of Fredericksburg—Hannibal Hamlin of Maine, whom Johnson had superseded as Vice-President ten years before, and Andrew Johnson of Tennessee. They stood before the presiding officer of the Senate, Henry Wilson of Massachustts, Vice-President-elect of the United States, —the same Henry Wilson who as a member of the High Court of Impeachment had voted not only for Johnson's conviction, but "for his disqualification from hereafter holding any office under the Constitution he has violated and the government he has dishonored." [29]

There were many familiar faces in that Senate. There was John A. Logan, now a Senator from Illinois, who as one of the impeachment managers had done all he could to ruin Johnson. There was Boutwell, one of the most virulent of that band of prosecutors. There were Senator Frelinghuysen of New Jersey, Anthony of Rhode Island, Sherman of Ohio, Cameron of Pennsylvania, Howe of Wisconsin, Morrill of Maine and Roscoe Conkling of New York, to whose "majestic supereminent, overpowering, turkey-gobbler strut," Blaine had once so tellingly referred.[30] The Senators who had voted for Johnson's conviction and removal, were now watching his return to office. Would he give vent to the malice they expected him to harbor? Without hesitation or embarrassment, Johnson shook hands with Hamlin and then with Wilson, and as he did so there burst forth from the floor a tumult of applause and cheers.[31] Both Wilson and Hamlin were tall men, and Andrew Johnson was short, one observer later wrote, "but to everyone present in the Senate there was no taller man in the Senate that day." [32]

As he returned to his seat he found his desk heaped high with flowers from his admiring friends.[33] A little page stepped up at the same time and handed him a bouquet.[34] "Personally," said the New York Tribune, "Mr. Johnson has always been popular in Washington, where he is regarded as a dignified, considerate and large-hearted gentleman. He bore himself with great self composure." [35] To avoid a further demonstration, he retired to the cloak room, but was soon surrounded there by Senators all eager now to shake his hand.[36] And,—such is fame—to many of the new members already prominent, both Johnson's form and face were utterly unknown.[37]

Sumner was dead,[38] Wade had eschewed politics to become counsel for the Northern Pacific Railway.[39] Of the stalwart seven Republicans who had voted to acquit, Grimes was dead,[40] and the other six politically were numbered with the dead.

Upon returning from the capitol to his hotel, Johnson was welcomed by a steady stream of callers who came to offer their felicitations. Old friends and old enemies were both there to extend their personal congratulations.[41]

There also came a reporter from the New York *Tribune* to interview him. "Will you not in your new position have an opportunity to pay off some old scores? You must have a mass of facts against many of the leaders of the parties of today," his interviewer said.[42] "Whatever I may have, I do not say, but I shall use nothing," replied Johnson. "I have no enemies to punish nor friends to reward." [43] The whole nation was again watching Andrew Johnson. "He gives signs of understanding the real temper of the times," declared a *Tribune* editorial two days later.[44]

His simple quarters consisted of two rooms on the second floor of the old Willard on Pennsylvania Avenue.[45] One visitor who glanced about, remarked to the ex-President that his present lodgings were hardly as commodious as those which he had once occupied further up the avenue. "No," said Johnson with a twinkle in his eye, "but they are more comfortable." [46]

§

The North was preparing for the Centennial Exposition to be held in Philadelphia the next year, and George F. Hoar was presently to write: "I have heard the taunt from the friendliest lips that when the United States presented herself in the East to take part with the civilized world in generous competition in the arts of life, the only product of her institutions in which she surpassed all others beyond question was her corruption." [47]

In Brooklyn the first of our judicial three-ring circuses was in progress,—the case of Tilton against Beecher. Had Henry Ward

Beecher's relations with Mrs. Tilton been more than friendly,—and if so how much more? This was the question that had rocked the newspaper-reading public for many months. The Brooklyn courtroom day after day was jammed with the parishioners of Plymouth Church. Holding a bunch of white violets and sniffing fitfully at these, Beecher took the stand tearfully to deny the charges of wrongdoing, but to admit that he had made a practice of going, during Tilton's absence, to Tilton's home, and there kissing Tilton's wife,—"very much." [48] Marse Henry Watterson called Beecher "a dunghill covered with flowers." [49]

The times were thick with insincerity, dissimulation, pietism, sanctimoniousness and sham. Organized corruption put forth the false pretense of moral excellence. Rascals were in the saddle, while honest men despaired. It was the era of the Tweed Ring, Jay Gould, Jim Fisk, Credit Mobilier and the Reconstruction. It was the day of shoddy affectation in matters of taste, intellect, government, morals and religion,—in architecture, painting, books and education. [50] American hypocrisy was blossoming in full flower. The simple honest standards of an earlier day had disappeared in public life, as well as in public buildings and in other forms of life and art.

New Yorks charming city hall park was desecrated by that hideous architectural abortion, the monstrous Mullet Court House at the south, and by the Tweed corrupt monstrosity, the County Court House, at the north. It was the day of brownstone fronts. The lovely Georgian models were forgotten and in many instances destroyed. Indoors a vandal taste held sway. Mahogany was abandoned. Heppelwhite and Chippendales were all discarded or hidden under ugly coats of paint. Fireplaces were bricked up, and beautiful mantels hacked apart. Tables of golden oak and chairs and sideboards of incredible design were eagerly sought out. The pleasant inns of former years were replaced by garish new hotels in cheap imitation of the palaces of Europe. "Bedchamber, drawing room, hotel rotunda, Pullman car, steamboat,—all were parts of a great vulgar spectacle prepared to open the eyes of our insolent new democracy." [51]

Against a background of such public taste and public morals

the nightmare of the Reconstruction, like some primeval, baggy-eyed and scaly shape, reared its hideous and shocking form. No wonder that historians have sought to lock its monstrous and mis-shapen skeleton within the closet of our country's annals!

It was with no mere skeleton, however, but with a living monster that our St. George from Tennessee had come to Washington to fight. No knight was ever readier for the fray. "The only way to fight error," he had once said, "is to strike it a direct blow. Hit it between the eyes, and drop it to its knees. If it trembling rise again, strike it and continue to strike, till it shall rise no more. Live or die, that is the way I shall conduct this campaign." [52]

§

The proud and happy people of Louisiana had known the governments of Spain, of France and, through Jefferson, that of the United States, but never until 1868 had they experienced a rule like that of their own negroes and the carpet-baggers whom the Northern bayonets protected and encouraged.

Louisiana, as will be recalled, was one of the four states where Lincoln had begun the operation of his plan of Reconstruction. His letter to Governor Hahn in 1864 proved that he held no illusions as to the elective franchise in the hands of ignorant negroes. [53] Four years later, however, through the Federal Reconstruction acts, the work of Lincoln and of Johnson was undone and a state constitution was adopted giving universal negro suffrage and disfranchising practically all whites who by sword, pen, word or vote had aided the Confederate cause. [54] The whites were outnumbered in the state by negroes. [55] Under the negro carpet-bag régime, a veritable anarchy ensued. The agriculture of Louisiana and the commerce of New Orleans were both in ruins. Both were plundered by gangs of alien thieves abetted by the blacks, and protected by the government in Washington. [56]

The notorious Henry Warmoth, who had come to Louisiana with the Federal army and from which, it was reliably reported, he had been dishonorably discharged, had made himself the governor and the terror of the state. [57] "Corruption is the fashion," he declared, "I do not pretend to be honest, but only as honest as anybody in politics." [58] Beginning with nothing, at the end of his reign in 1872, he was the proud possessor of a princely fortune. [59]

Fraud and embezzlement were universal. [60] So little did the law-makers think of bribery that they refused to consider it a crime. [61] In the legislature of 1870, Warmoth said, there was "but one honest man." [62] Bribery in Louisiana had ceased to be a crime,—rather was it regarded as a public virtue. Among the railroad lobbyists, who had come to New Orleans, this was the inquiry heard frequently in the rotunda of the St. Charles Hotel: "How are negro votes selling today!" [63] Corruption everywhere raised its miscegenetic and unblushing face. Men and laws were both for sale. There was unrestricted prostitution of legislators and of legislation. "What was the price of a senator?" a member of a Congressional Investigating Committee asked. "I think six hundred dollars," was the answer. [64]

As usually happens among thieves, the time came when they fell out, yet the proverbial dues for honest men had not yet come. By 1872 the Republicans were divided into two factions. On the one hand there was Warmoth, and on the other the "custom house ring" led by Casey, the brother-in-law of President Grant. Casey was the Collector of the Port of New Orleans. He and his adherents, among whom was Packard, the United States Marshal and a resident of Maine, had involved themselves in a dispute with Warmoth over a division of the spoils. Warmoth was accused by Casey's ring of every crime, and he retaliated in like vein. Both sides of this pot-and-kettle controversy for once told the truth. To make the confusion worse, Pinchback, the mulatto Lieutenant-Governor, who usually had abetted Warmouth, now headed a third faction. [65]

In the fall of 1872, Warmoth and his adherents went over to the Democrats and supported John McEnery, a native of Louisiana and a veteran of the Confederate army, as their candidate for governor. Pinchback united with Grant's brother-in-law in furthering the candidacy of William Kellogg, a carpet-bagger from Vermont. [66] When the votes were counted, each side claimed the victory; each side determined at all hazards to secure the fruits of victory.[67] Warmoth set his "Returning Board" to work,—an instrumentality of which the country was to hear more four years later, when through this means more than thirteen thousand Democratic votes in Louisiana were thrown out, and Hayes was declared President instead of Tilden.[68]

Warmouth's "Returning Board" consisted of himself, the Lieutenant-Governor, the Secretary of State and two others. It had power to reject returns from any voting places, if in its sole judgment bribery or other corrupt influences had been employed. This machine, as Americans learned later, was an extraordinary institution.[69] Under Warmoth's guidance it promptly decided that McEnery had been elected governor.[70] The negro carpet-bag Republicans, through a returning board of their own manufacture, declared that Kellogg was entitled to the office. At midnight on December 5th they obtained from Judge Durell of the United States District Court an order directing the marshal and the commander of the United States troops to take possession of the State House and to hold it for Kellogg against McEnery and all comers.[71]

The order was a palpable outrage, an illegal and an indecent abuse of process.[72] It was said that when he signed it Durell was drunk. As a defense this will not hold, for when he became sober he did not revoke it.[73] Marshal Packard, with the aid of United State troops, now seized and held the State House. Kellogg and his legislature were installed, but all knew that their possession could not last an hour if the support of Federal soldiers were withdrawn.[74]

The inevitable result of this Federal intermeddling was further bloodshed. In anger and despair the white men of Louisiana had read Grant's message of February, 1873, in which he said that if Congress did not interfere to support the Kellogg government, he would.[75] A few days later, in his second inaugural, Grant was complacently declaring: "The states lately at war with the General Government are now happily rehabilitated."[76] It was, however, but a few days later that at Colfax, in Grant Parish, a clash occurred between those who recognized the authority of a judge and sheriff whom Kellogg had appointed, and those who did not recognize that authority. A battle followed in which fifty-nine negroes and two whites were killed.[77]

The Radicals, of course, proclaimed this as a "horrible massacre," "but," said Godkin in *The Nation*, "there was no outcry . . . over the disgraceful connivance at Washington at the state of things which has converted Louisiana into a South American republic. . . ." [78] In May Grant again interfered in behalf of the Kellogg government. Referring to McEnery and his followers as "turbulent and disorderly persons," he ordered them to retire peacefully to their respective abodes "and within twenty days to submit themselves to the 'constituted authorities of said state.'" [79]

Kellogg was now governor of Louisiana by the grace of Federal soldiers, and Casey's powerful brother-in-law in Washington. Grant was maintaining him in office despite the fact, which he was later to admit, that the legality of Kellogg's election was "not altogether certain." [80] McEnery did not give up his claim, but counseled against resistance that would be futile.[81]

This dominion of an alien power was provocative,—further trouble was inevitable. In the late summer of 1874 Louisiana was absorbed in another state campaign. An outbreak occurred in Coushatta in Red River Parish, and Grant again intervened. The forced continuance of Kellogg was infuriating to the native whites. Finally, on September 14th, at New Orleans, a mass meeting assembled in Canal Street to denounce Kellogg as a "usurper." [82] Words led to deeds, and presently the "battle of Canal Street" was in progress. Barricades were thrown up, and in a bloody struggle causing many casualties, the black Metropolitan police were finally subdued. The native whites then marched to the State Capitol,—and Kellogg fled for shelter to the Custom House. The rule of the carpet-bagger had been put down! [83]

There is in New Orleans today a granite shaft that marks the place where brave men fell. September 14th is still celebrated in Louisiana as a second Independence Day.[84] Wearied of "bloodyshirt" orators, and of Grant's régime, intelligent Northerners looked on not without approval. Godkin in *The Nation* spoke for these, when on September 24th he wrote: "We know of no case of armed resistance to an established government in modern times in which the insurgents had more plainly the right on their side." [85]

But Grant had no intention of abandoning his policy of interference and on the day following the Canal Street outbreak he issued another proclamation commanding "turbulent and disorderly persons to disperse." [86] He followed this by the dispatch of three warships and more troops to New Orleans. On September 17th the native whites surrendered, and Kellogg was reinstalled as "governor." Through Federal force the rule of the carpet-bagger was reinstated! [87] But the trouble was not over. When the state legislature met on January 4th, 1875, the question arose as to whether the carpet-baggers or the native whites were in control. The question was decided by the bayonets of Federal soldiers. General de Trobriard was summoned. Clad in uniform and with his sword at his side, accompanied by two members of his staff, he presently appeared. He called five of his soldiers from the hall. With fixed bayonets they appeared, and advancing upon five members of the legislature, drove them from the State House. [88]

"If this can be done in Louisiana, and if such things be sustained in Congress, how long will it be before it can be done in Massachusetts and Ohio?" asked Carl Schurz on the floor of the United States Senate seven days later. "How long before the constitutional rights of all the states and the self-government of all the people may be trampled under foot? How long before the general of the army may sit in the chair you occupy, sir, to decide contested election cases for the purpose of manufacturing a majority in the Senate? How long before a soldier may stalk into the national House of Representatives and pointing to the Speaker's mace say 'take away that bauble!' " [89]

But Grant, not done with his bungling in Louisiana, now perpetrated a new blunder, he put General Sheridan in charge! [90] To accomplish this, he went over Sherman's head,—"the general of the army." It was, said Godkin, "a direct insult to

Sherman." [91] Perhaps one motive for Grant's action lay in his recollection of how Johnson had dismissed Sheridan eight years earlier.

Among all the officers from whom he might have chosen, he could have made no worse selection. Sheridan was a brave cavalry commander, but of civil government he knew nothing. "No one," Godkin later wrote, had thought of him "as a person of sound political judgment. Indeed the selection of him for such an office as he has been filling in Louisiana without the knowledge of his superior officer, General Sherman, was one of the strangest acts of the Administration." [92]

Sheridan marked the beginning of his duties by an act arousing indignation in the North as well as in the South. On the day following the expulsion of the five members he sent Grant a dispatch in which he spoke of Louisiana's native white men as "banditti." He asked Congress to enact a law declaring them "banditti," and providing for a military commission in which to try them. "It is possible," he said, "that if the President would issue a proclamation declaring them banditti, no further action need be taken except that which would devolve upon me." [93] Belknap had not yet been detected in his bribe-taking,—he was still Secretary of War. He wired Sheridan that the President had confidence in his "wisdom," and was sure that all his acts would be "judicious." [94]

A wave of indignation swept the North when Sheridan's message became public. "If General Grant," declared the New York *Tribune* on January 7th, "had the ordinary common sense or humanity which belong to most men of our race, General Sheridan could not have held his place an hour after that crazy and brutal dispatch. He is a fire-brand in a powder magazine." [95]

Two of Grant's Cabinet denounced what Sheridan had done, and one threatened to resign. [96] Indignant mass meetings were held in Cooper Institute in New York City, and Faneuil Hall in Boston. Other cities in the North were aflame with wrath. [97] The crowds that came laid party predilections to one side. William Cullen Bryant, then past eighty, but seemingly with the fire of youth, denounced the Federal rule of Louisiana. [98]

§

The elections of 1874 had warned the professional Republicans that the temper of the times was changing. The better sentiment of the party was swinging rapidly away from the policy of Southern interference. But Grant was in the hands of a designing camarilla whose scheme was so to administer the Southern states that their electoral votes in 1876 could all be counted for the party.[99]

The government of Arkansas in 1875 had experienced several years of profound peace, yet on the 8th of February the President sent a message asking for its overthrow by Congress.[100] The reason for this was plain. The state officials recently elected were politically opposed to Dorsey and Clayton, the Senators, both of whom were members of the Grant faction.[101] The "English" of Grant's message, declared the Springfield *Republican,* was: "Authorize me to make war upon the government and people of Arkansas in the interest of my third term." [102]

During the same month Grant placed all his influence behind the passage of a second "Force Bill." Its purpose was to give the Federal courts jurisdiction over every conceivable injury to the blacks, real or threatened; to bring all elections under Federal supervision and to enlarge the President's authority to suspend the writ of habeas corpus.[103] "The reason why we desire to have this bill passed," unblushingly declared Ben Butler, "is the fact which has so often been put before us, that we are about passing from power." [104] Its passage was required, declared the administration organ in Washington, "to preserve to the Republican party the electoral vote of the Southern states." [105] But a filibuster of the Democrats defeated it.[106]

Having failed in this project, denounced by the Springfield *Republican* as "a treason to the cause of civil liberty and self-government," [107] Grant's partisans employed the month of February in one further effort to curry favor with the former slaves. They pushed through an amendment to the Civil Rights Law giving to the negroes equality in theatres, public conveyances and inns.[108] It was one of Sumner's favorite projects.[109] "Civil rights prodded in with bayonets," observed one Northern paper.[110] The only result of this amendment was, of course, to inflame race hatred and to accentuate sectional prejudice.[111]

Johnson observed these things, but especially he had attended to Grant's outrages on Louisiana. The New York *Tribune* was giving some attention to this also. "The stubborn silent man in the White House sets his teeth and announces his purpose to sustain his military favorite," one of its editorials declared. "The country waits, the masses of the Republican party wait for a man, for some one . . . to say in clear ringing phrases: 'This is not Republicanism but Grantism. The President is not the party!' and no one stirs. James G. Blaine from the Speaker's chair looks only through the avenue to the mansion at the end . . . and he says not a word. . . . Sitting there in front of him are Garfield and Hawley and a dozen more who know . . . that a great crime against a state, against the Constitution and against liberty has been committed by the President, and not a mother's son of them dares open his mouth except to tell some inquisitive correspondent that he is 'waiting to hear both sides.' "[112]

Johnson understood this crime, and he was not afraid to speak. There was pending before the Senate at this time a resolution to approve Grant's conduct in Louisiana. On March 22nd Johnson stood up to oppose it. There in that chamber that fourteen years ago had echoed with his orations for the Union,—the same chamber that seven years later had resounded with the slanders of Thad Stevens and Ben Butler—the Senator from Tennessee again arose to champion the Constitution. Despite his nearly sixty-seven years he pressed into his sentences the fire that in his country's darkest hour had made him one of her most sturdy patriots. "The President of the United States," he said, "assumes to take command of the state and assign these people a governor. What does he say himself on this point?" Johnson then read from Grant's message: "It has been bitterly alleged that Kellogg was not elected. Whether he was or not is not altogether certain, nor is it any more certain that his competitor McEnery was chosen. The election was a gigantic fraud and there are no reliable returns of its result."[113] If there had been a "gigantic fraud," both con-

testants, declared Johnson, were disqualified, "but the President
finds a usurper in power, and he takes it upon himself to make
the government of the United States a party to his usurpation.
. . . Is not this monstrous in a free government?" [114]

It was a long time since anyone had come to champion the Constitution in that Senate. "We have been in a great war," he continued. "The public mind has been agitated, the Constitution
has been violated . . . and trampled under foot . . . so often,
that the public mind at this day scarcely has any firm mooring to
which it can anchor. . . . Where are we going, Mr. President?
Is Louisiana a commonwealth as it now stands? Or is her government maintained by military power, and that through the
President of the United States? Is it his government? . . . What
does he do in regard to Arkansas? Sends a message to Congress
with a threat, 'If you do not do something I will.' It is not his
place to interfere with either of the contending parties." [115]

Instead of passing the proposed resolution, Johnson declared
that he would go to the "emperor of the empire," and in the
language of Cato's reply when Cæsar's ambassador demanded his
capitulation, would "Bid him disband his legions; return the
commonwealth to liberty." [116]

Why had Kellegg been installed in opposition to the wishes of
Louisiana? Was it, asked Johnson "for the purpose of irritation
. . . for the purpose of getting up insurrection . . . so as to
raise the cry 'these Southern people are in revolt'? The people
of Louisiana were anxious for full restoration to the Union, but
what is that to those acting behind the curtain and who are aspiring to retain power, and if it cannot be had by popular contest
. . . would inaugurate a system of terrorism, and . . . in the
midst of the war-cry triumphantly ride into the Presidency for a
third Presidential term. And when this is done, farewell to the
liberties of the country!" [117] The galleries burst forth into
applause at this.

It was high time that some one should speak out. Grant's
craving for a third term had become a national scandal. His lust
for office was to receive its full revelation five years later. But
what was indeed a scandal was Grant's gift-taking and his rewards

to the designing givers.[118] "There is a provision in the Constitution," continued Johnson, "which declares that: 'No title of nobility shall be granted by the United States, and no person holding an office . . . under them . . . shall accept any present . . . from any king, prince, or foreign state.' The minds of those who made the Constitution were directed to the other side of the water, they thought temptation was most likely to come from that direction. If in the last line of this clause . . . they had added 'or any citizen of the United States,' what a fortunate thing it would have been!" [119] There was laughter in the galleries at this well-aimed thrust.

Grant's pitiable administration, its monstrous abuse of power, cried out for denunciation. The great voice of Andrew Johnson spoke not for the distracted South alone, but for the conscience of the North as well. "I have shown you," he continued, "in reference to the Kellogg government, General Grant said it was a 'gigantic fraud,' and that neither Kellogg nor his opponent was entitled to the office, but having a usurper in he takes him by the hand and sustains him. . . . How far off is empire? How far off is military despotism?"

Finally he concluded: "Sheridan says the people are all banditti, and if he had a military commission the President need not disturb himself any further, for he would manage all the rest! . . . Give me the Constitution of my country unimpaired. . . . Give me back the Constitution of my country! . . . In the language of Webster, let this Union be preserved 'now and forever, one and inseparable.' Let us stand equals in the Union, all upon equality. Let peace and union be restored to the land. May God bless this people and God save the Constitution!" [120]

Like thunder's deep voice upon a torrid afternoon, Johnson shook the sleeping conscience of the North. The South took hope like a desponding army that hears the rumble of its artillery supports, long, long awaited!

LXXXIX

PEACE AT LAST

Two days after his denunciation of the Grant administration, the executive session of the Senate ended, and Johnson returned to Greeneville. The consciousness of personal power, and the exhilaration of his opportunity to use it, seemed to give him a new strength.[1] The chance to lead in the Senate of the United States the lost cause of justice, the chance, perhaps, once more to vindicate his own and Lincoln's cause, had fired his spirit. He was the first ex-President to come back to the Senate, perhaps his full vindication would lead him to the White House once again!

He rested quietly in his home until the summer came. Some forty miles from Greeneville, in the mountains of Carter County, on the lovely banks of the Watauga River, his daughter Mary Stover lived. In the torrid last days of July Johnson went to visit her. He seemed in splendid health and walked the half-mile to the station with elastic step. Those who saw him on that journey spoke later of his high spirits.[2]

Peace settled upon him, as he sat with his granddaughter and looked out on the smooth waters of the Watauga, discoursing happily of her approaching marriage. The whole world seemed at peace, and then like a blow struck from behind,—apoplexy! Physicians came, but he had gone beyond their power. For thirty-six hours he lay unconscious; on July 31st his lion heart had ceased to beat.[3]

"All seems gloom and despair," two years earlier in what seemed a mortal illness he had written, "I have performed my duty to my God, my country and my family. I have nothing to fear. Approaching death to me is the mere shadow of God's protecting wing."

"When I die," in one of his great speeches he had declared,

823

"I desire no better winding sheet than the Stars and Stripes, and no softer pillow than the Constitution of my country." [4] Remembering these words, loving hands now granted him his wish. Wrapped in the flag he had so well defended, and pillowed on the Constitution in whose defense he had endured so much, they brought the old warrior back to Greeneville on his shield. [5]

Until August 3rd the Executive Mansion and the several departments of the government in Washington were draped in black, and on that day the troops at every army post throughout the Union were paraded, with the colors of their several regiments in mourning. At each naval station, and on board every battleship, the solemn tribute of the guns was paid. [6]

But in Greeneville on that day it was with no mere formal ceremony that the people from the hills and from the valleys, and from near and far, had come to make the last journey with their great neighbor. To the top of a windswept knoll not far from town they bore him. He himself long before had chosen it as his final resting place. In the distance, the glorious Unaka mountains watched, standing there like Sentinels of Time, while in the Stars and Stripes he loved so well, the old patriot sank gently to his rest.

APPENDIX

APPENDIX

THE REAL ANDREW JOHNSON *

BY

E. C. REEVES

The lion is dead. It is the time when the prowling jackals creep from their slimy lairs to nose among the tombs for putrid flesh with which to appease their carnivorous appetites.

In an article written by one Mr. George Creel, published in *Collier's Weekly* of November 27th, 1926, under the caption, "The Tailor's Vengeance," is a mendacious attack on the character of Andrew Johnson, and is so malignant and untruthful as to provoke contempt and the feeling of resentment of all who knew the character of Tennessee's favorite son. Strange indeed that any one possessing the instincts of a man should hurl a bomb, surcharged with poison gas, into the tomb of one whose voice is hushed by death; whose tongue is ashes, and whose lips are dust. Hand to hand, arm to arm, ego to ego, there is something chivalrous and ennobling in a contest of equal chance; but he who makes ruthless war on the dead is held by all the honorable of mankind as barren of the elements that constitute a manly man.

Andrew Johnson was my friend, and though I carry the weight of eighty-seven years, and am way-worn, I would be craven not to resent the calumnies heaped upon my voiceless friend.

During almost all of the last seven years of Mr. Johnson's life I knew him more intimately than did any other, and because the political incidents of my own life were, during those years, so interwoven with the activities of Mr. Johnson, I cannot detail one without giving the other; and further, giving the actions of both actors showing the opportunities I had for personal knowledge of the real character of the man.

I was reared on a farm in the county of Washington, adjoining

* Col. Reeves, who was Johnson's private secretary from 1869 to 1875, has greatly aided me with facts and suggestions. The foregoing article, "The Real Andrew Johnson," I have at his request placed here as an appendix. It has never before been printed. It is a reply to George Creel's "The Tailor's Vengeance" appearing in the November 27th, 1926, issue of *Collier's National Weekly*. Col. Reeves' article is a valuable first-hand historical document. It has given me great assistance in understanding the years between Johnson's Presidency and his return to the Senate.—L. P. S.

Mr. Johnson's county of Greene. In April, 1869, I opened a law office in Greeneville, Tennessee. My law library consisted of the law course of Cumberland University and the Code of Tennessee.

I had never met Mr. Johnson; had seen him only once when a day or two before opening my office he was pointed out to me as ex-President Johnson. Having been a Confederate soldier I held prejudice against the great Union leader and supposed he would have no liking for a "rebel" who was politically below the most ignorant negro at the ballot-box.

Some two or three days after opening my office a gentleman entered and said: "Mr. Reeves, I suppose; my name in Andrew Johnson." He declined to be seated, but paced my office floor, and said much, but only in part as follows: "I was informed that you had come to our town and had opened a law office. Pardon me; I have called to meet you and to give you a welcome. I beg pardon for volunteering a few remarks: A young attorney must build up a practice; fees come slowly at first, and often he becomes disheartened, but pluck and energy will win. Our people were impoverished by the war. I have traveled the road of poverty, and have felt its pinch. Pardon my seeming impertinence, but I make no inquiry into your financial matters, yet will add: By living economically I have laid up a small sum, and, if at any time you shall be in need of some financial help, just call on me and it will be my pleasure to aid you. Good day."

Such was the character exemplified of the man portrayed by George Creel as a beast in human form. I was surprised beyond expression over the visit of Mr. Johnson, and especially over his fatherly advice and his unselfish and kind offer to aid me in case of need. Is it any wonder I became the friend of Andrew Johnson?

Within ten days from that meeting the owner of the *National Union,* a weekly paper in Greeneville, Tennessee, put me in editorial charge of what was called Andrew Johnson's organ because it supported him loyally in his later political career; and I occupied that position for several years. Mr. Johnson's visits to my office then became frequent, and soon I became his private secretary, and on one night every week I called at his residence to read to him articles marked by him in his many newspapers; and when through reading I would be entertained by his rehearsal of many incidents in his political life, especially those that occurred in the impeachment trial, that were never published. I wrote for him, on his dictation, articles for other papers, even editorials. He explained: "My thoughts, your language." I accompanied him to joint debates and reported his speeches for publication in the public press; represented him in state political conventions; was one of the two marshals appointed to handle the immense throng at his burial, and, finally, as Clerk of the Supreme Court of Tennessee, in a report made by me as clerk, and confirmed by the Court, as to the division of the estate (the largest of any in Greeneville) settled the question of the divisions and partition between the heirs of Mr. Johnson.

As to the character of the real Andrew Johnson, I do not have to speak from stolid ignorance, nor even from idle rumors. Mr. Creel says: "Unhappy, lonely man, walking the world from birth to death with only his hates to keep him company; born sordidly; sitting cross-legged as he cut and sewed, he flamed with rage against the slim, graceful patricians that passed his shop, cursing them as 'aristocrats,' blaming them for his misery, and aching for the day when he might drag them down and make them suffer what he had suffered."

Now, Mr. Creel, you must admit that Andrew Johnson, if a howling "demagogue" as you portray, was not an idiot to curse the "patricians" of Greeneville for the lack of "a single day's schooling during the whole of his youth," spent in North Carolina.

This tissue of false fabrication, made to order, carries its own contradiction, but is furthermore repelled by Jacob and John Naff, and by Louis Self, late a State Senator, all of whom worked the tailor's trade beside Mr. Johnson, and all of whom, especially two of them, frequently gave incidents to this writer, portraying Mr. Johnson's early character, but neither ever hinted the libelous rot promulgated by Mr. Creel.

It is passing strange that the "savage demagogue walked the world from birth to death" a "lonely man with only his hates to keep him company," for he was elected to more offices than any living man, and in his entire life, from early manhood to his death, he had more "company" following him as a statesman, patting him on the back, as it were, and bidding him God-speed, than had any other man of his day. This statement of Mr. Creel's has no more basis in fact than a midnight dream of a frenzied mind.

"Indecently, dishonestly, he tried to prove that Jefferson Davis had 'incited, concerted and procured' the assassination of Lincoln; offered $100,000 reward for his capture, and had him treated as a common criminal."

All of the foregoing, except the offer of the reward, is a libelous misrepresentation, as everyone knows who has read the history of the war between the States, and of the Johnson Administration. There was no excuse for Mr. Creel to either fabricate or to quote as true a deliberate falsehood, the vicious purpose of which was manifest.

Mr. Johnson did offer the $100,000 reward for the capture of Mr. Davis, as in duty he was bound to do, especially after his Secretary of War had assured the President and his cabinet that positive proof had been secured showing that Mr. Davis conspired with John H. Surratt, the son of Mrs. Surratt (who was judicially murdered for no greater offense than having had as boarders some of the assassins of Mr. Lincoln). Mr. Davis was captured, and under an order of Sec. Stanton, incarcerated in irons in a gloomy cell in Fortress Monroe, which fact, when learned by the President, he ordered kind treatment of the distinguished prisoner, and later sent Secretary McCulloch to Fortress Monroe to see that his humane order was being executed, as it was.

The alleged conspiracy proof against Mr. Davis was made by two witnesses before a military committee; their names were Campbell and Snevel, whose depositions were furnished by one Sanford Conover, and both witnesses later confessed that their testimony was entirely false; that Conover wrote their depositions and they memorized them, and Conover was arrested for perjury and for subornation of perjury; tried, convicted and sentenced for ten years in the penitentiary.

If Mr. Creel aimed at truth he missed the mark a thousand leagues. A more reckless perversion of the truth, either ignorantly or wilfully, was never forged in the farthest reach by human language.

Later, Mr. Johnson pardoned Mr. Davis, a fact suppressed by Mr. Creel.

As to the impeachment trial of Mr. Johnson, the real crux in the case was a constitutional question of the right of the President to suspend or remove a cabinet member. Mr. Stanton, the Secretary of War, a hold-over from the Lincoln cabinet, a man whose ability almost equalled his boundless ambition, was a spy in the cabinet of the President. Congress passed the Tenure-of-Office Act to prevent Stanton's removal by President Johnson, who ignored the act as unconstitutional, and suspended Stanton. That drove Sumner, Stevens, Butler and other radicals to madness, and impeachment followed, and for once Mr. Creel told the truth when he said: "And from the very start there was plain evidence that neither decency nor fairness was to be considered by the prosecution."

It is doubtful if any trial of national import was ever staged and pushed with as much venom as was the impeachment trial of Andrew Johnson. Relying on the Constitution of his country, unawed by force, he stood as firmly as Gibraltar's Rock, oppened to compromise; as placid, and yet as determined, as if the word surrender had never been written in the lexicon of his life. The major question in the impeachment trial was not the vindication of Mr. Johnson, but the integrity of the government, for if impeachment had been sustained it meant the practical elimination of the executive as a co-ordinate branch of the government, and the elevation of the legislative branch to supreme power, as Mr. Creel admits. So, Mr. Johnson, in securing his acquittal, not only saved himself but the integrity of the government, and kept it saved by persuasive authority for nearly a half-century, when in October, 1926, in the case of Myers vs. United States, the Supreme Court of the United States authoritatively affirmed the constitutional holding of Mr. Johnson. Andrew Johnson, although not a licensed lawyer, was withal a great constitutional lawyer, and gained not only a wonderful victory for himself, but also for his government; and yet Mr. Creel insanely asserts that Mr. Johnson "left the White House as much discredited as though the High Court of Impeachment had found him guilty."

Will Mr. Creel explain why it was, for he so states, that "Sumner and Wade felt the acquittal as a mortal blow, and crippled Thaddeus Stevens, carried away on the shoulders of his henchmen, suffered agonies." Why, indeed, did these malignant haters and persecutors of the President become so distressed over the acquittal of an alleged crime, if acquittal and conviction meant the same? Mr. Creel avers too much; so much so that pro and con he reduces the whole to senseless gabble!

There is a feature of the impeachment trial full of meaning, related by Mr. Johnson, that was given to the public, that illustrates the moral fiber of the man During the dark days of the preparation of the impeachment trial, Mr. Johnson's most eminent counsel, Jeremiah S. Black, called on Mr. Johnson and reported that the outlook was very disheartening and that it looked like conviction would follow, and that he saw but one avenue for escape. "And what is that way?" inquired Mr. Johnson. Judge Black said that General B. F. Butler, one of the chief managers of the impeachment trial, had been gathering guano from a small island called Alta Vela, which Santa Domingo claimed to own, and which had objected to any more forceful taking of fertilizer, and General Butler had assured Mr. Black that if the President would order a man of war to accompany Butler's private vessel it would go well with the President in the impeachment trial. Mr. Johnson said he did not believe he had the right to make such an order, but for General Black to call the following day. In the meantime he conferred with Secretary Seward, and reached his conclusion. General Black reported the following day and showed a paper signed by four of the managers, including Butler and Stevens, holding the claim valid and that it should be enforced, and General Black insisted that the President sign the order at once. The President urged that he had not the constitutional right to do so, and showed General Black that while he was Attorney-General in Buchanan's cabinet he had held unconstitutional such a claim, and declared that his judgment and conscience forbade his signing such an order, and peremptorily refused, over the urgent request of General Black (who seems to have been counsel for Butler, et al) to do so. General Black then indignantly remarked: "I have pointed your way to acquittal and advised you to pursue it. You decline to do so. You will be convicted and removed from office. I prefer not to have you convicted on my hands, therefore, I resign as one of your counsel, from the impeachment case."

Mr. Johnson arose and looking General Black in the face, said: "I regard your demand as dishonorable and insulting. Resign and quit. Before I will sign an order contrary to law, as I believe, and against my conscience, and be driven by coercion to that end, I'll suffer my right arm torn from its socket. I denounce the course you advise me to pursue and will not adopt it, for I will not purchase my acquittal at the cost of my integrity. You have announced your resignation as one of my counsel. It is my pleasure to accept your resignation." And thus General Black got out as counsel for Johnson.

Mr. Johnson was the great leader against secession, ranking with Stephen A. Douglas, the lion of the tribe of Union Democrats of the West, in the United States Senate. Mr. Johnson's masterful orations in the Senate against secession were fully equal to those against nullification delivered by Mr. Webster, which have made him immortal. Because of this, the Confederates did, for a time, despise Mr. Johnson, but having steadily maintained that a state could not secede from the Union as did Sumner, Stevens and the Radicals generally, Mr. Johnson consistently, as President, declared that the Southern states were in the Union and should be reorganized by the intelligent whites, which meant as a rule, the ex-Confederates; while the Radicals, reversing themselves, declared the Southern states were out of the Union, and could return only by a majority vote of loyal persons, which consisted mostly of ignorant negroes and carpet-baggers.

The wise and just policy of President Johnson not to treat the Southern states as conquered provinces endeared him to the ex-Confederates generally. Another act of Mr. Johnson's that won the admiration of many thousands of former political enemies in the South, seemingly insignificant, but in fact far reaching in its influence was: Mr. Stanton, Secretary of War, in his bitterness against Southern Methodists who, as a rule, were either in the Confederate army or were in sympathy with the cause, issued an order to dispossess the Southern Methodists of their property, and they were ousted from their leading church building— McKendree College—in Nashville, Tennessee, the hub of the M. E. Church, South. Mr. Johnson, learning the fact, promptly revoked the Stanton order, and the owners of McKendree had their property speedily restored to their possession. This act of justice made Mr. Johnson friends by the million. It made him the most popular politician in the State, especially in Nashville where the Southern Methodists predominated, and was a potent factor in his last and triumphant contest for the United States Senate, and as I do know from my connection with it as a helper for Mr. Johnson.

Mr. Creel says that the "President left the White House with not a single voice raised to wish him well," but that rash statement is belied by the history following his reconstruction policy and supplemented by the revocation of the infamous Stanton order, which made Mr. Johnson the most popular citizen in all of the South.

Having returned from the White House in 1869, Mr. Johnson in 1871 stood for an election to the United States Senate before a Democratic Legislature. He had no party behind him; he had no platform, only the Constitution, the Union and the enforcement of the laws. Edmond Cooper, Mr. Johnson's private secretary, while in Washington, was a member of the State Legislature and the Johnson leader. The contest was long drawn out. Mr. Johnson lacked two votes of an election. Thus stood the repeated ballots when an ex-President of the Nashville & Chattanooga Railroad entered Mr. Johnson's room and said: "Mr. President, you will be elected to-morrow." "Why do you think so?" "Because I have secured the necessary two votes." "How?" "I have to pay $1000 for each vote." "You will do no such thing. Go tell those rascals the deal is off." "I can't do that. I am honor-bound. It is not your money to be used." Mr. Johnson replied: "But it is my honor that is involved. If I am elected by those purchase votes, as sure as the Lord lets me live, I will go before the Legislature and expose the fraud and refuse to accept the election."

The deal was not consummated. The following day Judge Henry Cooper, my law professor in Cumberland University, was put in nomination and Edmond deserted his chief and voted for his brother and secured his election, while Johnson was defeated for lack of two additional votes.

Will Mr. Creel with all his rashness contend that this crucial test of high integrity was simply "following his hates with the tenacity of a hound?"

After Mr. Johnson's defeat, through the treachery of Edmond Cooper, he returned to his home where he was the tender nurse of his invalid wife, to my personal knowledge. If he had any political plan formulated for the future he kept it secret; however, secretiveness was one of his winning cards he always played.

A Democratic State Convention to nominate a candidate for Congress for the state at large was called to meet at Nashville in the fall of 1872. Major General Cheatham, called the "Bull-Dog Fighter" of the Johnson Bragg army, not highly equipped to discharge the duties of a Congressman but very popular, was a candidate. Mr. Johnson left for Nashville with a request for this writer to meet him in Room No. 5, Maxwell House, on the evening preceding the day the Convention was to meet. And we so met. Johnson locked his door and said: "There is much pressure for me to become a candidate before the Convention tomorrow. I cannot for the following reasons." He then gave his plan in detail for his expected contest for election to the United States Senate in 1875. Then, moving his chair to the front of mine, with all the fervor of his soul cried out: "I was impeached, and while legally vindicated, by a minority vote, yet I would rather have the vindication of my state by electing me to any old seat in the Senate of the United States than to be monarch of the grandest empire on earth, God being my judge. For this I live, and will never die content without." "Go to the Convention tomorrow and if my name is put in nomination, promptly withdraw it on my authority." All of which was done, and General Cheatham, my old division commander, was nominated by acclamation, much to my liking, for he was grave and much beloved, and though short in education, he was a man of good common sense.

Now commenced the siege of Mr. Johnson by unwise friends to proclaim himself an independent candidate for Congressman at large. The alleged lack of Congressional qualifications of General Cheatham was the stock-in-trade against him. The pressure surpassed anything of the kind I had ever known. But, knowing the tenacity of Mr. Johnson in holding to the uttermost a plan matured, and not believing he would cast to the winds his matured plan, as detailed in confidence to me, and thus commit political suicide, I left for my home, but in passing through Chattanooga, learned to my amazement that Mr. Johnson, on the public square in Nashville, had announced himself an independent candidate. What it meant and why I have never known, only surmised. The Republicans, seeing their opportunity, nominated Horace Maynard, their strongest debater in the State, if not in all the states, and it was a royal combat between Mr. Johnson and the Honorable Mr. Maynard, on the stump. At the request of Mr. Johnson I attended the joint canvass over East Tennessee, to report his speeches for publication. General Cheatham read his speech at each joint meeting.

The joint discussion having ended, Mr. Johnson then commenced the most strenuous campaign of his life, making from two to three speeches daily and often in the open air. But, his cause as well as that of Gen. Cheatham's, was fore-doomed to failure. Cheatham's alleged lack of qualifications was largely compensated by being the Democratic nominee, while Mr. Johnson's ability was discounted by being a bolter. The Democratic party was divided, and Mr. Maynard had a walk-over to Congress and thus a Democratic State was turned over to the Republican party by the unfortunate candidacy of Mr. Johnson, which ended his political career as seemed to all—Johnson, perhaps, excepted.

The oft-repeated statement, even by misinformed biographers, that Mr. Johnson, when he quit the White House even in the sharp decline of life, was emphasized into a "mortal malady" by Mr. Creel, is unsupported by fact, for during the six years I knew him intimately, except when he had a violent attack of cholera in 1873, I never knew him to be sick or ailing. During his campaign of 1872, having spoken in Sequatchie Valley, he crossed the country, by private conveyance, to the Tennessee River opposite Shellmound, where he wished to take the train for Chattanooga, to meet an appointment there. The ferry was kept by an Irishman, who took Mr. Johnson into his yawl and began to row him across the river. The yawl ran aground, the train was seen approaching, Mr. Johnson leaped into the river and commenced to wade to the bank while Pat screamed unceasingly: "Mr. Conductor, hold your train, the President must get to Chattanooga to speak tonight." Mr. Johnson made his speech that night and suffered not a bit from his bath.

The canvass of 1872 and the fateful election of 1873 having gone into history, Mr. Johnson remained in his quiet home, as secretive as to what his political purpose was, as was his habit, concerning such matters. I read to him regularly his papers, listened to his interesting talks, but as to the reason why he made his disastrous independent campaign he was as silent as a mummy.

Governor Brown was closing his second administration in 1874. He was a candidate to succeed W. G. Brownlow in the United States Senate. So was Bate and Quarles, all three ex-Confederate Major-Generals, and able lawyers, as was Colonel Savage, a prominent lawyer and brave soldier, and W. B. Stevens, a fine lawyer and able citizen. Such an array of legal talent and Confederate officers had never before been engaged in a senatorial struggle. Mr. Johnson was considered a back number on account of his blunder in wrecking the Democratic party.

In the fall of 1874 he asked me to go with him to Knoxville, Tennessee. There he made a speech in which he attacked the administration of Governor Brown without mercy. And he kept up the attack from time to time, never uttering a harsh word about either of the other four candidates. Brown grew desperate. Johnson was in fact a candidate, but no one living believed he could win unless it was Johnson himself. The Shelby delegation was instructed at the ballot box for Johnson and the members pledged their honor to abide instructions. This writer was asked to see every member elect to the legislature, except the Shelby Delegation, ascertain his choice for Senator, and report to Mr. Johnson, which was done. Bate led Brown by a small majority. "All right," Mr. Johnson said, "Brown can't be elected, but he is desperate—says I have attacked the Democratic party of which he is the head, and the party must be endorsed by my election. So Brown will not let Bate be elected; and Bate being the stronger of the two will not let Brown be elected, therefore the two will fight each other instead of fighting me; my plan is working just as I have contrived." And work it did most successfully. For more than a week the legislature in convention assembled and balloted for senator. The fight between Brown and Bate grew more bitter daily. Savage became disgusted over the fight between Brown and Bate, and withdrew, and Stevens followed and Quarles' vote was reduced to a minimum. Another ballot was taken and Bate's vote dropped by two and adjournment followed to the next day.

Bate had almost crossed the line, and would have done so but a couple of Brown's men refused to vote for Bate, wishing to give their chief another chance on the following day; but on the morrow Brown seeing he would be slaughtered, was dropped, and on the 55th ballot Mr. Johnson crossed the line. We had no telephone then. I was hurrying from the capital to Mr. Johnson's room to give him the news of his election, but A. A. Taylor, member from Carter County, then a Conservative, later, twice a Republican congressman and later still a Republican Governor of Tennessee, passed me on the run, and reaching Mr. Johnson first, exclaimed: "Mr. Johnson, you are elected!" and fell into a dead faint, and water was being dashed into his face by Mr. Johnson when I entered the room. Next entered N. B. Spears, member from Marion County who grabbed Mr. Johnson, flung high his feet toward the ceiling; his head downward toward the floor, and trotted around the room with his burden, all forgetful of the dignity of the Senator-elect. The news spread rapidly over Nashville, where Mr. Johnson was a prime favorite. Business men rushed into the streets and joined in the volume of the grand triumphal shouts, and Edgefield took up the wild acclaim of joy and Mr. Johnson received the grandest ovation of his life, even where a reckless writer falsely alleged that the military governor "filled the jails" with Confederates.

The historian DeWitt says of this last triumph: "A harder won, better deserved, and more signal triumph does not adorn the annals of time."

The only occasion I ever met Woodrow Wilson, on being introduced by Mr. Tumulty as having known Mr. Johnson intimately, Mr. Wilson said: "And you knew Andrew Johnson well. His was a most wonderful life. I read it with great pleasure. It is a study. His name and fame grow with the years. Yes, one of the most wonderful men in history."

The great Secretary of the Navy, under the administrations of Lincoln and Johnson, Welles, in giving his estimate of President Johnson, says in his private diary: "He has great capacity; possesses great firmness; sincere patriotism; a sacred regard for the Constitution; is humane and benevolent—is as pure, as honest, as patriotic a chief magistrate as we have ever had."

His triumph, the greatest of his life, the triumph of his reconstruction policy of the Southern states, the greatest victory ever accomplished by any chief executive in civil government, though delayed by frenzied partisanship, gave way to Mr. Johnson's reconstruction policy, and within six years the Democrats predominated in both branches of Congress. A more notable achievement is not recorded in all civil government.

When Mr. Johnson, on March 3rd, 1875, reappeared on the floor of the Senate he was greeted by a spontaneous outburst of applause from the crowd assembled in gallery and corridor to do him honor. As he marched down the aisle to take the oath, on his return to his desk he found it covered with flowers which his admiring friends had furnished, and his colleagues flocked around him with congratulations, even Senators who had found him guilty; and he wore his hard-earned laurels with the utmost modesty.

Notwithstanding all of the foregoing from friends and foes in flat contradiction of all contained in almost every paragraph of the screed of Mr. Creel, he heaps calumnies upon the character of Mr. Johnson. Mr. Creel is like the man of Gadara who also dwelt among the tombs and cried night and day, and no man could tame him for he had an unclean spirit!

Mr. Creel has made the farthest reach in human language to vilify and blacken the character of one who never fought the dead, but in his life never feared to meet the loftiest son of Adam's race.

Mr. Johnson, after securing his coveted prize, made his last trip to Washington early in March, 1875, to attend a special session of the Senate and be sworn in as the successor of his implacable enemy, Senator Brownlow. On the following day, in one of the most elaborate speeches of his life, boldly, but not bitterly, he criticized the administration of President Grant, the weakest and the worst-laden with scandal of any predecessor.

He returned home to enjoy a surcease from politics. For more than a third of a century he had known no rest. He was to the depth of his soul a Democrat in the broadest sense. In a party sense he was its leader in Tennessee, and in fact an autocratic one. Prominent Democrats like Isham G. Harris, W. B. Bate, Atkins and Peter Turney, hated Johnson and envied his personal rise, but admired his leadership that brought victories to their party.

He delivered mortal blows to the Whig Know-Nothing and American parties. Personally, he won victories always or else achieved splendid defeats; one time, however, excepted, and that was when he "swung around the circle." Combative by nature under great provocation by the organized mobs whose insults were heaped upon Mr. Johnson, he retaliated with anger and thus cast reproach upon his own dignity as well as upon that of the chief executive office.

Andrew Johnson was as pure a Caucasian as was ever cast in human mold. His face indicated culture and refinement, as well as strength of character. His body in perfect proportion in all its parts, showed a build for strength and long endurance. His presence was commanding. Always neat in person and attire, alike on the street or occasions of state, his well-fitting apparel was as appropriate as a lady well-dressed, fresh from her boudoir.

Poor indeed was the boy when first he plied the needle to support himself and his widowed mother, but he never felt the "pinch" of poverty from a lack of the necessaries of life. He was independent, and from his own labor always paid for all received; and from habits of economy, not penuriousness, he became a man of considerable property, including slaves, and at his death was the wealthiest person in Greeneville. Mr. Johnson possessed great dignity that repelled undue familiarity. He held his friends at arm's length and some thought him haughty and unappreciative, yes,

> "Lofty and sour to those who knew him not;
> To those who knew him, sweet as summer."

He spoke in the kindliest terms of Abraham Lincoln; he admired the character of Stephen A. Douglas, but Andrew Jackson was his model, whom he regarded as the greatest statesman of his day.

The hot summer days of July induced Mr. Johnson to seek the home of his daughter, Mrs. Stover, on the banks of the beautiful Watauga River, in the mountains of Carter County, where cooling breezes fan the brow unceasingly. He left Greeneville full of cheer and walked half a mile with elastic step to the station and took the train for Mrs. Stover's home, where for several days he enjoyed rest free from care. Sitting beside his granddaughter, Miss Lillie Stover, overlooking the glassy waters of the Watauga, and happily discoursing about her near-approaching nuptials, like a lightning bolt from a cloudless sky, an apoplectic stroke shot through the brain and hurled the victim into a state of unconsciousness from which he was not released for two days later when summoned to appear before the only power that controlled him while he lived—Andrew Johnson was dead! The body was placed in its coffin-home and its pillow was a copy of the Constitution of his country, and its flag its winding sheet. The body was carried back to its Greeneville home to be buried under the auspices of the Knight Templars 'mid his surviving friends.

On the day of the burial the people came from the hills and valleys; from everywhere near and far, until Greeneville was filled as never before, and the cortège was so dense the marshals were unable to control the human masses and make a passage for the hearse carrying the coffined body to its sepulchral home on the way to the apex of the knoll which was to be the final sleeping place of the deceased, pointed out by negro Sam, a former slave, as having been so designated by his master; and the way had to be opened by the body of Knight Templars with fixed bayonets. It was the largest burial attendance, probably, ever known in the state, indicating the passing of her most illustrious son.

And there the sacred dust sleeps under a marble shaft guarded by his government, and the unpretentious tailor shop, wherein his towering ambition was first to bud and bloom, has been inclosed by his state, within a more pretentious building to preserve it in all its pristine simplicity in tender memory of the early days of her beloved son.

My work is done; I would that it were better done; I close my article on this 88th anniversary of my birthday.

Johnson City, Tennessee,
March 2nd, 1927.

AUTHORITIES AND ABBREVIATIONS USED

Abbreviations

Charles Francis Adams, An Autobiography (1835-1915)..Adams
The Education of Henry Adams, An Autobiography
(Houghton Mifflin Co. 1918).......................Adams (Henry)
Notes of Col. W. G. Moore, Private Secretary to President
Johnson, with introduction by Prof. St. George L. Sioussat
(American Historical Review vol. xix, No. 1, Oct. 1913)..Am. Hist. Rev.
The Life of John A. Andrew, Governor of Massachusetts
1861-1865, by Henry Greenleaf Pearson (Houghton
Mifflin Co. 1904)..................................Andrew
Dixie After the War, by Myrta Lockett Avary (Double-
day Page & Co. 1906)..............................Avary
Life and Letters of George Bancroft, by M. A. DeWolfe
Howe, 2 vols. (Scribner 1908).....................Bancroft
Review of Winston's "Andrew Johnson" by David Rankin
Barbee in the Asheville (N. C.) Sunday Citizen,
May 13, 1928......................................Barbee
A Short History of the United States (1492-1920) John
Spencer Bassett (Macmillan 1924)..................Bassett
The Constitution of the United States, by James M. Beck
(George H. Doran Co. 1924)........................Beck
The Writings and Speeches of Samuel J. Tilden, edited by
John Bigelow (Harper & Sons 1885)................Bigelow
Twenty Years in Congress 1861-1881, by James G. Blaine,
2 vols. (Henry Bill Publishing Co. 1884)..........Blaine
Reminiscences of Sixty Years in Public Affairs, by George
S. Boutwell (McClure Phillips & Co. 1902)..........Boutwell
Confederate Portraits, by Gamaliel Bradford (Houghton
Mifflin Co. 1912)..................................Bradford-C. P.
Damaged Souls, by Gamaliel Bradford (Houghton Mifflin
Co. 1922)...Bradford-D. S.
Lee, the American, by Gamaliel Bradford (Houghton Mifflin
Co. 1912) ....Bradford-Lee
Union Portraits, by Gamaliel Bradford (Houghton
Mifflin Co. 1916).................................Bradford-U. P.
Wives, by Gamaliel Bradford (Harper & Bros. 1925)....Bradford-Wives
Thirty Years of New York Politics, by Matthew P. Breen
(New York 1899)...................................Breen
Washington on Lincoln's Time, by Noah Brooks (The
Century Co. 1895).................................Brooks
Sketches of the Rise, Progress and Decline of Secession
with a Narrative of Personal Adventures Among the
Rebels, by W. G. Brownlow, editor of Knoxville Whig
(Applegate & Co. 1862)............................Brownlow
The American Commonwealth, by James Bryce, 2 vols.
new ed. (Macmillan Co. 1924)......................Bryce
Life of James Buchanan, by George Ticknor Curtis, 2 vols.
(Harper & Bros. 1883).............................Buchanan
The Law of the American Constitution, by Charles K.
Burdick (C. P. Putnam's Sons 1922)................Burdick

Abbreviations

Reconstruction and the Constitution, by John W. Burgess
(Charles Scribner's Sons 1902) . . . . Burgess
Autobiography and Personal Reminiscences by Major Gen-
eral Benjamin F. Butler, "Butler's Book" (A. M. Thayer
& Co. Boston 1892) . . . . Butler
Vol. 7 of the Cambridge Modern History . . . . Cambridge
The Struggle Between President Johnson and Congress
Over Reconstruction, by Charles Ernest Chadsey, Ph. D.
(Studies In History, Economics and Public Law, edited
by the Faculty of Political Science of Columbia Uni-
versity) vol. 8, No. 1, 1896 . . . . Chadsey
Abraham Lincoln, by Lord Charnwood (Henry Holt & Co.
1917) . . . . Charnwood
Diary and Correspondence of Salmon P. Chase in annual
report of the American Historical Association (vol. II
for year 1902) . . . . Chase
A Diary from Dixie, as written by Mary Boykin Chesnut
(D. Appleton & Co. 1905) . . . . Chesnut
The Chronicles of America Series (50 vols.), Allan Johnson
(Yale University Press 1921) . . . . C. of A.
"Belle of the Sixties"— The Memoirs of Mrs. Clement C.
Clay of Alabama (Doubleday Page & Co. 1905) . . . . Clay
Congressional Globe, being the official minutes of the
Records and Debates in Congress . . . . Cong. Globe
"The President's Defense" by Moncure Conway in Fort-
nightly Review 1866 . . . . Conway
Andrew Johnson, President of the United States, Reminis-
cences of his Private Life and Character by one of his
secretaries (Frank Cowan) (The Oliver Publishing
House, Greenesburgh, Pa. 1894; See E. 667 C. 87
Toner Collection, Library of Congress) . . . . Cowan
Three Decades of Federal Legislation, by Samuel S. Cox
(J. A. & R. H. Reid, Providence 1885) . . . . Cox
Prison Life of Jefferson Davis by Bat. Lieut.-Col. John J.
Craven, M.D. (Carleton Pub. Co. 413 Broadway) . . . . . . Craven
Memoirs of the White House—The Home Life of Our
Presidents from Lincoln to Roosevelt, being personal
collections of Col. W. H. Crook, sometime bodyguard
to Lincoln, since then disbursing officer of the Execu-
tives; compiled and edited by Henry Rood (Little,
Brown & Co. 1911) . . . . Crook Memories
Andrew Johnson in the White House, being the Reminis-
cences of William H. Crook, written by Margarita
Spalding Gerry (Century Magazine Part I in Sept. 1908)
vol. 76, No. 5, Part II in October 1908, vol. 76,
No. 6 . . . . Crook Reminiscences
Fifty Years of Public Service, by Shelby M. Collum (A. C.
McClurg & Co. Chicago 1911) . . . . Cullom
A Memoir of Benjamin Robbin Curtis, L.L.D., with some
of his professional and miscellaneous writings, edited
by his son, Benjamin R. Curtis, 2 vols. . . . . Curtis
Recollections of the Civil War, by Charles A. Dana,
Assistant Secretary of War 1863-1865 (D. Appleton
& Co. 1899) . . . . Dana
Jefferson Davis, a memoir by his wife, 2 vols. (Belford
& Co. 1890) . . . . Mrs. Davis
Chauncey M. Depew, My Memories of Eighty Years (New
York 1922) . . . . Depew

Abbreviations

The Impeachment and Trial of Andrew Johnson, by David
Miller Dewitt (The MacMillan Co. 1902) .... Dewitt

Reconstruction; Political and Economic 1865-1877, by
William Archibald Dunning (vol. 22 of "The American
Nation") a History edited by A. B. Hart (Harper
& Bros.) .... Dunning

Works of Ralph Waldo Emerson, 12 vols. (Houghton
Mifflin & Co. 1875) .... Emerson

Encyclopedia Britannica (11th ed.) .... Encyc.

History of the United States, by John Fiske .... Fiske

The Adoption of the Fourteenth Amendment, by Horace
Edgar Flack (The Johns Hopkins Press 1908) .... Flack

Edwin McMasters Stanton, The Autocrat of Rebellion,
Emancipation and Reconstruction, by Frank Abial Flower
(Salfield Pub. Co. 1905) .... Flower

A Fool's Errand, by Albion W. Tourgée (Fords, Howard
& Hulbert 1880) .... Fool's Errand

James A. Garfield, Life and Letters, by Theodore Clarke
Smith (Yale University Press 1925) .... Garfield

History of Tennessee, by Goodspeed .... Goodspeed

Life and Public Services of Edwin M. Stanton, by George
C. Gorham, 2 vols. (Houghton Mifflin & Co. 1899) .... Gorham

The New South, by Henry W. Grady (Robert Bonner's
Sons 1890) .... Grady

Personal Memoirs of Ulysses S. Grant, 2 vols. (Charles L.
Webster & Co. 1885) .... Grant

The Second Empire, by Philip Guedalla (Putnam & Sons
1922) .... Guedalla

The Fourteenth Amendment of the Constitution of the
United States, by William D. Guthrie (Little, Brown
& Co. 1898) .... Guthrie

Andrew Johnson, Military Governor of Tennessee, by Clifton
R. Hall, Ph.D. (Assistant Professor of History and
Politics in Princeton University) (Princeton University
Press 1916) .... Hall

Life and Times of Hannibal Hamlin, by his grandson
Charles Eugene Hamlin (Printed at the Riverside Press,
Cambridge 1899) .... Hamlin

Recollections Grave and Gay, by Mrs. Burton Harrison
(Smith, Elder & Co. 1912) .... Harrison

Salmon Portland Chase, by Albert Bushnell Hart (American Statesmen Series) .... Hart

"Emancipation and Impeachment" by Gen. John B. Henderson (The Century Magazine Dec. 1922, vol. LXXXV,
No. 2) .... Henderson

Abraham Lincoln, by William H. Herndon and Jesse W.
Weil, 2 vols. (D. A. Appleton & Co. 1896) .... Herndon

Henry Ward Beecher, by Paxton Hibben (George H.
Doran Company 1927) .... Hibben

Lincoln, The Lawyer, by Frederick Trevor Hill (The
Century Company 1906) .... Hill

Autobiography of Seventy Years, by George F. Hoar,
2 vols. (Scribner's sons 1903) .... Hoar

Julia Ward Howe 1819-1910, Reminiscences by L. L.
Richards and M. H. Elliott, 2 vols. (Houghton Mifflin
& Co. Boston 1915) .... Howe

Remarkable Career of Andrew Johnson, Depicted by
Archelaus N. Hughes (Nashville Banner, Dec. 18, 1927) .. Hughes

Abbreviations

The President's Defense, by Gaillard Hunt (The Century Magazine, January 1913, vol. LXXXV, No. 3)........Hunt

Memorial Addresses, January 1876, published by order of Congress ....Johnson Memorial

Johnson's Papers in the Congressional Library at Washington ....J. P.

Life of Andrew Johnson, by Rev. James S. Jones (Greeneville Pub. Co. 1901)................................Jones

Political Recollections 1840-1872, by George W. Julian (Jansen McClurg & Co., Chicago 1884)..............Julian

History of the City of New York, by Martha J. Lamb, 3 vols. ....Lamb

Personal Reminiscences, Anecdotes and Letters of Gen. Robert E. Lee, by Rev. J. William Jones, D.D. (D. Appleton & Co. 1875)..............................Lee Reminiscences

Complete Works of Abraham Lincoln, 2 vols. (The Century Company 1894) ....Lincoln

The Works of Alexander Hamilton, edited by Henry Cabot Lodge (Constitutional edition)..................Lodge

William Henry Seward, by Thornton Kirkland Lothrop (American Statesmen Series 1896)....................Lothrop

Works of James Russell Lowell, 10 vols. (Houghton Mifflin & Co.).......................................Lowell

Miscellaneous Works of Lord Macaulay, edited by his sister, Lady Trevelyan, 5 vols. (Harper & Bros. 1880)....Macaulay

History of England, by Lord Macaulay, 5 vols. (Harper & Bros. 1879).......................................Macaulay's England

Life of Joseph Hodges Choate, by Edward Sanford Martin, 2 vols. (1920)..Martin

Robert E. Lee, the Soldier, by Major General Sir Frederick Maurice (Houghton Mifflin & Co. 1925)..............Maurice

Thaddeus Stevens, by Samuel W. McCall (American Statesmen Series 1900)..............................McCall

Lincoln's Plan of Reconstruction, by Charles H. McCarthy (McClure, Phillips & Co.)..........................McCarthy

Men and Measures of Half a Century, by Hugh McCulloch (Charles Scribner's Sons 1899)....................McCulloch

McCulloch's Preface to his "Men and Measures",.........McCulloch Preface

Grover Cleveland, the Man and the Statesman, by Robert McElroy (Harper & Bros. 1923) with preface by Elihu Root ....McElroy-Root

The Political History of the United States of America During the Period of Reconstruction (James J. Chapman, Chicago 1880) ....McPherson

A Compilation of the Messages and Papers of the Presidents 1789-1897, by James D. Richardson, 10 vols. (unless otherwise mentioned vol. 6 will be referred to)..M. & P.

A Compilation of the Messages and Papers of the Confederacy, 2 vols. (published by James D. Richardson, Nashville 1906) ....M. & P. Conf.

The Life and Times of Samuel Bowles, by George S. Merriam (The Century Co. 1885) ....Merriam

Biographical Introduction to Speeches of Andrew Johnson, by Frank Moore (Little Brown & Co. 1866)...........Moore

The Life of William Ewart Gladstone, by John Morley, 2 vols. (Macmillan & Co. 1905)...................Morley

More Light on Andrew Johnson, by William A. Dunning (American Historical Review, vol. xi, No. 3, April 1906)..M. L. on A. J.

Abbreviations

Abraham Lincoln, by John T. Morse, Jr. 2 vols. (American Statesmen Series 1893)..........................Morse
Introduction to Welles' Diary, by John T. Morse, Jr., 1911 (See Welles) ....Morse-Welles
The History of Tammany Hall, by Gustavus Myers (New York 1901) ....Myers
National Cyclopedia of American Biography (James T. White & Co., New York 1895).....................Natl. Cyc.
Abraham Lincoln, a History, by John G. Nicolay and John Hay, 12 vols. (The Century Co. 1894-1905)..........N. & H.
Files of the New York Herald........................N. Y. Her.
Files of the New York Evening Post....................N. Y. Evening Post
The Nation ....Nation
Files of the New York Times..........................N. Y. Times
Files of the New York Tribune........................N. Y. Trib.
Files of the New York World..........................N. Y. Wor.
A History of the United States Since the Civil War, 3 vols. by Ellis Paxson Oberholtzer (Macmillan Co. 1922).....Oberholtzer
Official Records of the Union and Confederate Armies......O. R. Series
The Causes of Impeachment, by Harrison Gray Otis (The Century Magazine, Dec. 1912, vol. LXXXV, No. 2)....Otis
General Jackson, by James Parton (D. Appleton & Co. 1897) ....Parton
Author's Conversations and Correspondence with Andrew Johnson Patterson of Greeneville, Tennessee (Johnson's Grandson) ....Patterson
Perley's Reminiscences of Sixty Years in the National Metropolis (Hubbard Bros. Publishers, 1886).........Perley
Speeches, Lectures and Letters, by Wendell Phillips (James Redpath 1867)...................................Phillips
Memories of the Men Who Saved the Union, by Don Piatt (Bedford Clarke & Co. 1887).......................Piatt
The Heart of a Soldier, as Revealed in the Intimate Letters of General George E. Pickett, C.S.A. (Seth Moyle & Co.)..Pickett
Memoir and Letters of Charles Sumner, by Edward L. Pierce, 4 vols. (Roberts Bros. 1893)..................Pierce
The Prostrate State—South Carolina Under Negro Government, by James S. Pike (D. Appleton & Co. 1874)....Pike
Poore's Political Register and Congressional Directory (Boston 1877)...................................Poore
Reminiscences of Peace and War, by Mrs. Roger A. Pryor (The Macmillan Co. 1904).........................Pryor
The Real Andrew Johnson (see appendix) Conversations and Correspondence with Col. Elbert C. Reeves, who was Andrew Johnson's Private Secretary from 1869-1895..Reeves
History of the United States from the Compromise of 1850, 7 vols. by James Ford Rhodes (The Macmillan Co.)....Rhodes
Biographical Note on Andrew Johnson (pp. 301-5 in vol. 6 of the Messages and Papers on the Presidents (compiled by James D. Richardson).........................Richardson
Stenographic Report of Speech Made by Elihu Root at The Union League Club, Feb. 13, 1925..................Root
Trumpets of Jubilee, by Constance Mayfield Rourke (Harcourt Brace & Co. 1927).........................Rourke
Men and Things I saw in War Days, by James F. Rusling (The Methodist Book Concern 1914)................Rusling
The Life of James W. Grimes, by William Salter (D. Appleton & Co. 1876)............................Salter

Abbreviations

Life of Andrew Johnson, by John Savage (Derby & Miller Publishers 1866)................................ Savage

Forty Years in the Army, by Lieut. Gen. John M. Schofield (The Century Co. 1897).......................... Schofield

History of the United States Under the Constitution, by James Schouler, 7 vols. (Dodd, Mead & Co.)......... Schouler

The Life and Public Services of Salmon Portland Chase, by J. W. Schuckers (D. Appleton & Co. 1874)......... Schuckers

The Reminiscences, by Carl Schurz, 3 vols. (Doubleday Page & Co. 1909)................................ Schurz

Seward at Washington as Senator and Secretary of State, a Memoir of His Life with Selections from his Letters, by Frederick W. Seward (1891).................... Seward

Correspondence between General and Senator Sherman from 1837 to 1891 (Charles Scribner's Sons 1894)......... Sherman Corres.

Home Letters of General Sherman, edited by M. A. De-Wolfe Howe (Charles Scribner's Sons 1909)......... Sherman Home Letters

John Sherman's Recollections of Forty Years in The House, Senate and Cabinet (Werner Company 1895)......... Sherman (John)

Memoirs of General William Tecumseh Sherman, 2 vols. (D. Appleton & Co. 1904)........................ Sherman Memoirs

Why the Solid South? or Reconstruction and Its Results, by Hilary A. Herbert and others (R. H. Woodward & Co. Baltimore 1890)................................ Solid South

Speeches of Andrew Johnson, compiled by Frank Moore (Little Brown & Co. 1866)....................... Speeches

A History of the Presidency from 1788 to 1897, by Edward Stanwood, 2 vols. (Houghton Mifflin & Co.).......... Stanwood

The War Between the States, by Alexander H. Stephens, 2 vols. (Zeigler, McCurdy & Co. 1867)............. Stephens

Charles Sumner, by Moorfield Storey (American Statesmen Series)..................................... Storey

The Works of Charles Sumner, 15 vols. (Boston 1883).. Sumner

The Life of Abraham Lincoln, by Ida Tarbell, 2 vols. (The Macmillan Co. 1917)........................... Tarbell

Notable Men of Tennessee, from 1833-1875, by Oliver P. Temple (The Cosmopolitan Press, New York 1912).... Temple

The Life and Letters of John Hay, by William Roscoe Thayer, 2 vols. (Houghton Mifflin Co 1908)......... Thayer

The Life of John Bright, by George Macaulay Trevelyan (Boston 1913)................................ Trevelyan

Trial of Andrew Johnson, President of the United States, before the Senate of the United States on Impeachment by the House of Representatives for High Crimes and Misdeameanors, 3 vols. (Government Printing Office 1868) .... Trial

Anecdotes of Andrew Johnson, by Major Benjamin C. Truman, Secretary to Andrew Johnson as Military Governor and as President (The Century Magazine, Jan. 1913).... Truman

An Account of the Private Life and Public Services of Salmon Portland Chase, by Robert B. Warden (Wilstach, Baldwin & Co. 1874)........................... Warden

The Supreme Court in United States History, by Charles Warren, 3 vols. (Little Brown & Co. 1922)......... Warren

Up From Slavery, an Autobiography, by Booker T. Washington (Doubleday Page & Co. 1901)............... Washington

The Life of Thurlow Weed, 2 vols. (Houghton Mifflin & Co. 1883)................................... Weed

Abbreviations

Diary of Gideon Welles, 3 vols. (Houghton Mifflin & Co.
1911) ....Welles
The Life of Lyman Trumbull, by Horace White (Hough-
ton Mifflin & Co. 1913)............................White
Division and Reunion, by Woodrow Wilson (Longmans
Green & Co. 1925 edition).........................Wilson
The President of the United States, by Woodrow Wilson
(Harper & Sons 1908)............................Wilson (Pres.)
Lady Baltimore, by Owen Wister (The Macmillan Co.
1906) ....Wister
The Life of Thaddeus Stevens, by James Albert Woodburn
(Professor of American History and Politics in Indiana
United States Constitution...........................Woodburn
University (Bobbs-Merrill Co.)....................U. S. Con.
United States Supreme Court Reports.................U. S.

REFERENCES

INTRODUCTION

(1) Burgess p. 246; (2) Rhodes vol. v, p. 517.

CHAPTER I

(1) Savage p. 13; (2) Jones p. 14; (3) Jones p. 13; (4) Jones p. 11; (5) Jones p. 14; (6) Savage p. 13; (7) Savage p. 13; (8) Savage p. 318; (9) Savage p. 14; (10) Savage p. 14; (11) Savage p. 14; (12) Savage p. 15; (13) Savage p. 23; (14) Savage p. 15; (15) Savage p. 16; (16) Savage p. 17; (17) Savage p. 17; (18) Johnson Memorial p. 49, (19) Jones p. 17; (20) Jones p. 17; (21) Jones p. 18; (22) Jones p. 17; (23) Moore p. vi; Richardson p. 301; (24) Jones p. 393; (25) Savage p. 19; (26) Jones p. 19; (27) Parton pp. 273-6; (28) Savage p. 20; (29) Savage p. 20; (30) Savage pp. 20-21; (31) Savage p. 22; (32) Savage p. 22; (33) Natl. Cyc. vol. 3, p. 300; (34) Savage p. 23, (35) Moore p. viii; (36) Jones pp. 398-9; (37) Savage p. 26; (38) Jones p. 21; (39) Jones p. 22; (40) Jones p. 22; (41) Encyc. vol. 26, p. 619; (42) Hall p. 4; (43) Hall p. 4; (44) Hall p. 4; (45) C. of A. vol. 28, p. 33; (46) Jones p. 11; (47) Jones pp. 28-9; (48) Jones p. 30; (49) Jones p. 30; (50) Hall p. 182; (51) Savage p. 27; (52) Jones p. 22; (53) Dana p. 105; (54) Johnson Memorial p. 18; (55) Jones p. 22; (56) Savage p. 28; (57) Savage p. 29; (58) Fiske p. 331; (59) Jones p. 25; (60) Savage p. 29; (61) Jones p. 24; (62) Savage p. 29; (63) Richardson p. 302; (64) Encyc. vol. 26, p. 624; (65) Jones p. 32; (66) Jones p. 32; (67) Jones p. 32.

CHAPTER II

(1) Charnwood p. 63; (2) Charnwood pp. 62-7; (3) Charnwood p. 7; (4) Natl. Cyc. vol. 3, p. 300; (5) Bradford U. P. p. 247; (6) Bradford U. P. p. 248; (7) Natl. Cyc. vol. 2, p. 94; (8) Natl. Cyc. vol. 4, p. 30; (9) Natl. Cyc. vol. 4, p. 30; (10) Natl. Cyc. vol. 4, p. 30; (11) Natl. Cyc. vol. 4, p. 30; (12) McCall p. 31; (13) McCall p. 32; (14) Natl. Cyc. vol. 4, p. 30; (15) McCall p. 61; (16) Globe Feb. 20, 1850, Append. vol. 22, Part 1, pp. 141-143; (17) Globe Mar. 11, 1850; (18) Woodburn p. 112.

CHAPTER III

(1) Poore p. 469; (2) Savage p. 30; (3) Savage pp. 26-36; (4) Jones p. 37; (5) Moore pp. 91-2; (6) U. S. Con.; (7) Savage p. 35; (8) Savage p. 35; (9) Savage p. 35; (10) Fiske p. 337; (11) C. of A. vol. 28, p. 33; (12) C. of A. vol. 28, p. 86; (13) C. of A. vol. 28, p. 88; (14) Savage p. 31; (15) Savage p. 32; (16) Savage p. 32; (17) C. of A. vol. 28, p. 20; (18) Charnwood p. 76; (19) Brownlow pp. 63-4; (20) Jones p. 39; (21) Jones p. 40; (22) Poore p. 469; (23) Poore p. 469; (24) Poore p. 469; (25) Tarbell vol. 1, p. 208; (26) Speeches p. 67; (27) Savage p. 32; (28) Charnwood p. 94; (29) Savage p. 143; (30) Morse vol. 2, p. 108; (31) Charnwood p. 93; (32) Savage p. 41; (33) Charnwood p. 94; (34) Speeches pp. 1-11; (35) Speeches p. 10; (36) Savage p. 43; (37) Speeches p. 14; (38) Speeches p. 12; (39) Jones p. 41; (40) Jones p. 46; (41) Richardson p. 302; (42) Jones p. 47; (43) Jones p. 48; (44) Jones p. 48; (45) Jones p. 47; (46) Jones p. 47; (47) Jones p. 51; (48) Jones p. 53; (49) Jones p. 53; (50) Jones p. 53; (51) Richardson p. 302; (52) Jones p. 56;

845

(53) Fiske p. 362; (54) Jones p. 54; (55) Fiske p. 362; (56) Jones pp. 54-5; (57) Jones p. 47; (58) Richardson p. 302; (59) Jones p. 56; (60) Speeches p. 253; (61) Savage p. 46; (62) Rhodes vol. I, pp. 439, 475; (63) Fiske p. 359; (64) Speeches p. 63; (65) Speeches p. 48; (66) Speeches p. 289; (67) Jones p. 56; (68) Jones p. 56; (69) Savage p. 48; (70) Savage p. 49; (71) Savage p. 49; (72) Jones p. 59; (73) Jones p. 60; (74) Speeches p. 66.

CHAPTER IV

(1) Savage p. 51; (2) Savage p. 150; (3) Speeches p. 28; (4) Speeches p. 34; (5) Speeches p. 16; (6) Speeches p. 44; (7) Savage pp. 56-7; (8) Speeches p. 52; (9) Speeches pp. 54-6; (10) Speeches pp. 56-7; (11) Speeches p. 54; (12) Speeches pp. 65-6; (13) Speeches pp. 66-7; (14) Speeches p. 68; (15) Speeches p. 76.

CHAPTER V

(1) Speeches pp. 56-7; (2) C. of A. vol. 28, p. 7; (3) Fiske pp. 43, 67; (4) Fiske p. 313; (5) Bassett pp. 144-5; (6) Beck pp. 135, 147; (7) C. of A. vol. 13, p. 130, Beck pp. 337-8; (8) C. of A. vol. 13, p. 130; (9) U. S. Con. Art. I, Sec. 2, Art. I, Sec. 9, C. of A. vol. 28, p. 12, U. S. Con. Art. 4, Sec. 2, C. of A. vol. 28, p. 8; (10) C. of A. vol. 28, pp. 11-12; (11) C. of A. vol. 28, p. 12; (12) Morse vol. 2, p. 108; (13) Bradford D. S. p. 163; (14) Bradford D. S. p. 164; (15) Welles vol. I, p. 502; (16) Howe vol. 1, p. 205; (17) Rhodes vol. vi, p. 24, note 2; (18) Rhodes vol. vi. p. 24, note 2; (19) Welles vol. 1, p. 502; (20) McCulloch p. 234; (21) Bradford U. P. p. 256; (22) McCulloch pp. 233-4; (23) Bradford U. P. p. 254; (24) Bradford U. P. p. 239; (25) Bradford U. P. p. 235; (26) Bradford U. P. p. 235; (27) Bradford U. P. p. 245; (28) Bradford U. P. p. 245; (29) C. of A. vol. 28, p. 167; (30) Natl. Cyc. vol. 3, p. 300; (31) Natl. Cyc. vol. 2, p. 314; (32) Natl. Cyc. vol. 2, p. 314; (33) Natl. Cyc. vol. 2, p. 314; (34) Natl. Cyc. vol. 2, p. 314; (35) C. of A. vol. 28, p. 56; (36) Natl. Cyc. vol. 2, p. 314; (37) Natl. Cyc. vol. 2, p. 314; (38) Natl. Cyc. vol. 2, p. 314; (39) Natl. Cyc. vol. 2, p. 314; (40) C. of A. vol. 28, p. 25; (41) Rhodes vol. I, p. 74; (42) Welles vol. II, p. 383; (43) C. of A. vol. 28, p. 55; (44) C. of A. vol. 28, p. 55; (45) C. of A. vol. 28, p. 54; (46) C. of A. vol. 28, pp. 11, 62; (47) C. of A. vol. 28, p. 63; (48) C. of A. vol. 28, pp. 63-4; (49) C. of A. vol. 28, p. 66; (50) C. of A. vol. 28, p. 34; (51) C. of A. vol. 28, p. 54; (52) C. of A. vol. 28, p. 40; (53) Encyc. vol. 25, p. 222; (54) Wilson p. 130; (55) Natl. Cyc. vol. 2, p. 314; (56) C. of A. vol. 28, p. 32; (57) C. of A. vol. 28, p. 33; (58) Fiske p. 313; (59) Rhodes vol. v, p. 71; (60) Welles vol. II, p. 313; (61) Bradford-Lee p. 42; (62) C. of A. vol. 28, p. 56; (63) C. of A. vol. 28, p. 57; (64) C. of A. vol. 28, p. 31; (65) Wilson p. 244; (66) Guthrie p. 6; (67) N. & H. vol. 1, p. 613; (68) Messages p. 136; (69) Messages p. 136; (70) C. of A. vol. 28, p. 58; (71) C. of A. vol. 28, p. 60; (72) C. of A. vol. 28, p. 60; (73) Wilson p. 130; (74) C. of A. vol. 28, p. 59; (75) C. of A. vol. 28, p. 57; (76) C. of A. vol. 28, p. 65; (77) C. of A. vol. 28, p. 65; (78) C. of A. vol. 28, p. 175; (79) C. of A. vol. 28, p. 176; (80) C. of A. vol. 28, p. 177; (81) Bradford U. P. p. 255; (82) Speeches p. 259; (83) Speeches p. 260; (84) Speeches p. 260; (85) Speeches p. 261; (86) Speeches p. 261; (87) Speeches p. 262; (88) Speeches pp. 262-3.

CHAPTER VI

(1) Charnwood p. 166; (2) Wilson p. 207; (3) Wilson p. 205; (4) Wilson p. 205; (5) Jones p. 64; (6) Savage p. 148; (7) Jones p. 65; (8) Jones p. 68, Savage p. 212; (9) Wilson p. 206; (10) Speeches p. 171; (11) Wilson p. 209; (12) Wilson p. 204; (13) N. & H. vol. 1, p. 609; (14) C. of A. vol. 29, p. 64; (15) Stanwood vol. I, p. 292; (16) M. & P. p. 5; (17) Wilson p. 210; (18) Pickett p. 25; (19) Pickett p. 37; (20) Pickett pp. 34-5; (21) Speeches pp. 79-80; (22) Speeches pp. 91-2; (23) Speeches pp. 102-3; (24) Speeches p. 106; (25)

Speeches p. 88; (26) Speeches p. 150; (27) Speeches p. 146; (28) Speeches p. 145; (29) Speeches pp. 147-151; (30) Speeches p. 152; (31) Speeches pp. 153-4; (32) Speeches p. 437; (33) Speeches p. 420.

CHAPTER VII

(1) C. of A. vol. 29, p. 85; (2) C. of A. vol. 29, p. 88; (3) Moore pp. 275-6; (4) Encyc. vol. 25, p. 783; (5) Dewitt pp. 246-7; (6) Dewitt p. 247; (7) Dewitt p. 247; (8) Dewitt p. 248; (9) Bradford U.P. p. 177; (10) Morse-Welles p. xxxi; (11) Dewitt p. 240; (12) Dewitt p. 251; (13) Buchanan vol. 2, p. 55; (14) Wilson p. 211; (15) C. of A. vol. 31, pp. 3-6; (16) Dewitt p. 252-3; (17) Rhodes vol. 2, p. 246; (18) Rhodes vol. 2, p. 246; (19) Encyc. vol. 10, pp. 573, 574; (20) Rhodes vol. 2, p. 246; (21) Rhodes vol. v, p. 22; (22) Sherman Memoirs, vol. 2, p. 185; (23) Dewitt p. 253; (24) Dewitt p. 254; (25) Dewitt p. 252.

CHAPTER VIII

(1) Speeches p. 178; (2) Speeches p. 189; (3) Speeches p. 283; (4) Speeches pp. 203-4; (5) Speeches p. 205; (6) Speeches pp. 263-4; (7) Speeches p. 214; (8) Speeches pp. 310-11; (9) Speeches p. 248; (10) Speeches p. 249; (11) Speeches p. 256; (12) Speeches pp. 285-6; (13) Blaine vol. 1, p. 522; (14) Hall p. 3; (15) Speeches pp. 283-4; (16) Hall p. 4; (17) Hall p. 5; (18) Charnwood p. 203; (19) Globe, Part 1, 2nd Session, 36th Cong. p. 857; (20) Charnwood pp. 205-6; (21) N. & H. vol. iii, pp. 319-23, 327-43; (22) Speeches p. 290; (23) Speeches pp. 311-3, (24) Speeches p. 169; (25) M. & P. p. 5; (26) M. & P. p. 11; (27) M. & P. p. 7; (28) Speeches p. 112; (29) M. & P. p. 7; (30) Speeches p. 153; (31) M. & P. pp. 11-12; (32) M. & P. p. 11; (33) C. of A. vol. 31, p. 13; (34) C. of A. vol. 31, pp. 13-16; (35) Speeches p. 374; (36) M. & P. p. 13; (37) Goodspeed's History of Tennessee, pp. 513-19; quoted Hall p. 5; (38) Hall p. 7; (39) Hall p. 7; (40) "The President's Defense" by Moncure Conway in Fortnightly Review 1866, vol. 5, p. 99; (41) Savage p. 236; (42) Hall p. 7; (43) O. R. Series 1, vol. lii, Part II, p. 96, quoted Hall p. 8; (44) Acts 33rd Tenn. General Assembly, Second Extra Session 1861, p. 21, quoted Hall pp. 8-9; (45) Acts 33rd Tennessee General Assembly, Second Extra Session 1861, p. 19, quoted Hall p. 9; (46) Jones p. 72; (47) Jones pp. 72-3; (48) Jones p. 72; (49) Speeches p. 395; (50) Hall p. 10; (51) Hall p. 10; (52) Wilson p. 219; (53) Speeches p. 316; (54) Speeches p. 319; (55) Jones p. 73; (56) Speeches p. 326; (57) Speeches pp. 325-7; (58) M. & P. p. 29; (59) M. & P. p. 30; (60) M. & P. p. 30; (61) M. & P. p. 26; (62) C. of A. vol. 31, p. 34; (63) C. of A. vol. 31, p. 40; (64) Cox p. 137, (65) C. of A vol. 31, pp. 52-3; (66) C. of A. vol. 31, p. 53; (67) Cox p. 158; (68) Buchanan vol. 2, p. 559; (69) Speeches pp. 403-4; (70) Speeches p. 330; (71) Speeches p. 331; (72) Speeches p. 340; (73) Speeches pp. 341-2; (74) Speeches p. 350; (75) Speeches p. 363; (76) Speeches pp. 354-5; (77) Speeches pp. 367-8; (78) Speeches p. 386; (79) Speeches p. 383; (80) Speeches p. 385; (81) Speeches pp. 396-7; (82) Speeches pp. 398-9; (83) Bradford C. P. pp. 153-181; (84) Hall pp. 29-30; (85) C. of A. vol. 29, p. 142; (86) Tarbell vol. 2, pp. 76-8; (87) C. of A. vol. 29, p. 135; (88) Tarbell vol. 2, pp. 76-8; (89) Buchanan vol. 2, p. 545; (90) Buchanan vol. 2, pp. 524-5; (91) Buchanan vol. 2, p. 538; (92) Buchanan vol. 2, pp. 538-9; (93) Buchanan vol. 2, pp. 538-9; (94) C. of A. vol. 31, p. 13, Fiske p. 376; (95) Buchanan vol. 2, p. 540; (96) Buchanan vol. 2, p. 545; (97) Buchanan vol. 2, p. 518; (98) Buchanan vol. 2, pp. 519-20; (99) Buchanan vol. 2, p. 521; (100) Welles vol. i, pp. 128-9; (101) Lincoln-Morse vol. i, p. 328; (102) Morse-Welles, p. xxxi.

CHAPTER IX

(1) Encyc. vol. 26, p. 624; (2) Hall pp. 14-16; (3) Goodspeed's History of Tennessee, p. 486; (4) Speeches pp. 428-30; (5) Moore pp. 444-7; (6) Hall

p. 17; (7) Fiske pp. 338-90; C. of A. vol. 31, pp. 124-42; (8) Hall p. 19; (9) Jones p. 76; (10) Hall p. 19; (11) O. R. Series 1, vol. IX, p. 396, vol. xvl, 3688 Stanton Papers March 4, 1862, Library of Congress, quoted Hall p. 32; (12) O. R. Series I, vol. ix, p. 396, quoted Hall pp. 32-3; (13) Hall p. 40, note 13; (14) Hall p. 34; (15) Hall p. 38; (16) Jones p. 77; (17) Jones pp. 77-8; (18) Jones p. 76; (19) Speeches p. 451; (20) Speeches p. 453; (21) Speeches p. 453; (22) Speeches pp. 451-7; (23) Speeches p. 455; (24) Speeches pp. 455-6; (25) Speeches p. 456; (26) Speeches p. 456; (27) Brownlow pp. 381-2; (28) Brownlow p. 400; (29) Brownlow pp. 409-10; (30) Hall p. 42; (31) Speeches p. 455; (32) Annual Cyc. 1862, p. 766, quoted Hall p. 43; (33) N. Y. Tribune July 4, quoted Hall p. 44; (34) J. P. vol. xxiv, 5281, vol. xxvi, 5705 et passim, quoted Hall p. 44; (35) Hall pp. 67-8; (36) C. of A. vol. 31, p. 154; (37) Hall p. 51; (38) Hall p. 52; (39) Hall pp. 52-3; (40) Hall p. 55; (41) Hall p. 64; (42) Savage pp. 273-4; (43) O. R. Series 1, vol. xvi, Part II, p. 122, quoted Hall p. 57; (44) N. Y. Tribune Nov. 18, 1862, Hall p. 62; (45) O. R. Series 1, vol. xvi, Part II, p. 490, Part I, Hall p. 64; (46) Rhodes vol. iv. pp. 183-4; (47) Jones p. 80; (48) Hall p. 78; (49) Hall p. 80; (50) Hall p. 81; (51) Hall p. 81; (52) Hall p. 81; (53) M. & P. pp. 96-8; (54) M. & P. pp. 96-8; (55) M. & P. pp. 96-8; (56) M. & P. pp. 96-8, Blaine vol. 1, p. 446; (57) Blaine vol. 1, p. 446; (58) Hall p. 92; (59) Savage p. 270; (60) O. R. Series III, vol. II, p. 675, quoted Hall p. 88; (61) Hall p. 89; (62) Hall p. 90; (63) Hall p. 93; (64) Hall p. 94; (65) Hall pp. 94-95; (66) Hall p. 95; (67) Hall pp. 96-9; (68) Hall p. 106; (69) Hall p. 101; (70) Hall p. 101; (71) Lincoln's Complete Works, vol. ix, p. 116, quoted Hall p. 106; (72) Moore p. xxix; (73) Bassett pp. 532-5; (74) Bassett pp. 532-5.

CHAPTER X

(1) N. & H. vol. 6, p. 348; (2) McCarthy p. 39; (3) McCarthy p. 39; (4) McCarthy p. 45; (5) Letters and State Papers of Lincoln, vol. 2, p. 247, quoted McCarthy p. 44; (6) McCarthy p. 46; (7) McCarthy p. 46; (8) Wilson p. 219; (9) McCarthy p. 83; (10) McCarthy pp. 81-2; (11) McCarthy p. 78; (12) McCarthy p. 82; (13) McCarthy p. 82; (14) N. & H. vol. 6, p. 346, quoted McCarthy p. 82; (15) McCarthy p. 83; (16) McCarthy p. 83; (17) McCarthy p. 95; (18) Encyc. vol. 28, p. 563; (19) McCarthy pp. 95-6; (20) McCarthy pp. 95-6; (21) McCarthy pp. 100-1; (22) Encyc. vol. 28, p. 563; (23) McCarthy p. 103; (24) McCarthy pp. 102-5; (25) Encyc. vol. 28, p. 563; (26) McCarthy p. 117; (27) McCarthy pp. 117-8; (28) Why the Solid South, p. 219; (29) McCarthy pp. 119-24; (30) Letters & State Papers of Lincoln, vol. II, pp. 285-7, quoted McCarthy p. 125; (31) McCarthy p. 129; (32) Letters and State Papers of Lincoln, vol. II, pp. 619-21, quoted McCarthy p. 136; (33) M. & P. p. 7; (34) M. & P. p. 213; (35) M. & P. pp. 213-4; (36) M. & P. p. 214; (37) Curtis p. 13; (38) M. & P. p. 214; (39) M. & P. p. 215; (40) M. & P. p. 190; (41) M. & P. p. 190; (42) M. & P. p. 7; (43) M. & P. p. 27; (44) M. & P. p. 68; (45) Lincoln's Complete Works vol. II, p. 156, Rhodes vol. iv, pp. 65-6; (46) M. & P. p. 142; (47) McCarthy pp. 196-7; (48) Globe, 1st Session, Part I, 37th Cong. pp. 239-43, McCarthy p. 215; (49) Globe, 1st Session, Part I, 37th Cong. pp. 239-43, McCarthy p. 216; (50) Globe, Part I, 38th Cong. p. 317, McCarthy p. 217; (51) Hall p. 198; (52) Hall p. 198, J. P. vol. xli, 9062; (53) Hall pp. 205-6; (54) Hall p. 112; (55) N. & H. vol. viii, p. 443.

CHAPTER XI

(1) Nashville Union June 4, quoted Hall p. 128; (2) Hall pp. 128-9; (3) Rhodes vol. iv, p. 456; (4) Rhodes vol. iv. pp. 457-9; (5) Rhodes vol. iv, p. 457; (6) N. & H. vol. viii, p. 316; (7) Charnwood p. 329; (8) Rhodes vol. v. p. 46; (9) Rhodes vol. iv, p. 462; (10) Rhodes vol. iv, p. 462; (11) Rhodes vol. iv, p. 468; (12) Rhodes vol. iv, p. 463; (13) Blaine vol. 1, p. 517; (14) Memphis Bulletin June 11, 1864, Hall p. 128; (15) Blaine vol. 1, p. 519; (16) Blaine

vol. 1, p. 520, Rhodes vol. iv, p. 468; (17) Encyc. vol. 12, p. 896; (18) Rhodes vol. iv, p. 470; (19) Jones pp. 118-9; (20) Blaine vol. 1, p. 522; (21) Stanwood vol. 1, pp. 303-4; (22) Stanwood vol. 1, p. 299; (23) Morse vol. ii, p. 264; (24) Hamlin pp. 460-489; (25) Hamlin p. 473; (26) Hamlin p. 472; (27) Hamlin p. 472; (28) Hamlin p. 483; (29) Depew p. 60; (30) Welles vol. ii, p. 47; (31) Rhodes vol. v, p. 543; (32) C. of A. vol. 29, p. 234; (33) Stanwood vol. 1, p. 301; (34) C. of A. vol. 29, p. 234; (35) Stanwood vol. 1, p. 301; (36) Blaine vol. 1, p. 522.

CHAPTER XII

(1) N. Y. World June 9, 1864; (2) N. Y. Trib. June 9, 1864; (3) Morse vol. 2, p. 198, Encyc. vol. 19, p. 623; (4) Encyc. vol. 19, p. 623; (5) Martin vol. 1, pp. 255-6; (6) Wilson p. 244; (7) Martin vol. 1, p. 132; (8) Martin vol. 1, p. 31; (9) Martin vol. 1, p. 220; (10) Martin vol. 1, p. 242.

CHAPTER XIII

(1) Savage p. 291; (2) Savage pp. 293-7; (3) Savage pp. 293-7; (4) Savage pp. 293-7; (5) Savage p. 291; (6) Stanwood vol. 1, p. 302; (7) Savage pp. 293-7; (8) Savage p. 296; (9) Savage p. 295; (10) M. & P. p. 132; (11) Stanwood vol. 1, p. 303; (12) Savage p. 297; (13) Savage pp. 293-7; (14) Savage p. 298; (15) Savage p. 299; (16) Savage p. 300.

CHAPTER XIV

(1) Herndon vol. II, p. 227; (2) McCarthy p. 224; (3) Encyc. vol. vii, p. 866; (4) McCarthy p. 226; (5) Bassett p. 598, Curtis pp. 16-7; (6) McCarthy pp. 226-36; (7) Globe Part III, 1st Sess. 38th Cong. pp. 2039-41; (8) McCarthy p. 248; (9) Globe Part III, 1st Sess. 38th Cong. pp. 2039-41; (10) McCarthy p. 275; (11) McCarthy p. 256; (12) Globe Part III, 1st Sess. 38th Cong. p. 2108, McCarthy pp. 260-1; (13) Storey p. 271; (14) McCarthy p. 265; (15) Rhodes vol. iv, p. 485; (16) N. & H. vol. ix, pp. 120-22; (17) N. & H. vol. ix, pp. 120-22, McCarthy pp. 273-4; (18) N. & H. vol. ix, pp. 120-22; (19) M. & P. pp. 222-3; (20) Storey p. 271, Morse vol II, pp. 235-6; (21) N. Y. Trib. Aug. 5, 1864; (22) Morse p. 236; (23) Welles vol. ii, p. 95; (24) Welles vol. ii, pp. 95-6; (25) Welles vol. ii, p. 96; (26) Blaine vol. ii, p. 44.

CHAPTER XV

(1) Encyc. vol. 12, pp. 531-3; (2) Encyc. vol. 12, pp. 531-3; (3) N. & H. vol. ix, pp. 196-7; (4) Rhodes vol. iv, p. 461; (5) Rhodes vol. iv, p. 518; (6) Rhodes vol. iv, p. 518; (7) Andrew vol. II, p. 159; (8) Andrew vol. II, p. 159; (9) Andrew vol. II, p. 159; (10) Andrew vol. II, p. 159; (11) Andrew vol. II, p. 159; (12) Andrew vol. II, p. 159; (13) Stanwood vol. I, p. 304; (14) Stanwood vol. I, p. 301; (15) Rhodes vol. iv, p. 519; (16) N. & H. vol. ix, p. 218; (17) Rhodes vol. iv. p. 523; (18) Andrew vol. II, p. 159; (19) Rhodes vol. iv, p. 524; (20) Andrew vol. II, p. 161; (21) Rhodes vol. iv, p. 523; (22) Rhodes vol. iv, p. 527; (23) Rhodes vol. iv, p. 526; (24) N. Y. World Sept. 22, 23, Oct. 1, 1864, quoted Rhodes vol. iv, p. 531; (25) Rhodes vol. iv, p. 531; (26) Rhodes vol. iv, p. 536; (27) Rhodes vol. iv, p. 527; (28) Rhodes vol. iv, p. 528; (29) Rhodes vol. iv, p. 528; (30) Stanwood vol. I, p. 308; (31) Stanwood vol. I, p. 308.

CHAPTER XVI

(1) Encyc. vol. 26, p. 396; (2) Welles vol. II, p. 181; (3) Rhodes vol. v, p. 45; (4) Rhodes vol. iv, p. 478; (5) Rhodes vol. v, p. 46; (6) Rhodes vol. v p. 46; (7) Rhodes vol. v, p. 46; (8) Rhodes vol. v, p. 46; (9) Welles vol. ii, pp. 192-3.

850   REFERENCES

CHAPTER XVII

(1) Lincoln vol. I, Intro. iii; (2) M. & P. p. 254; (3) McCarthy p. 90; (4) McCarthy p. 75; (5) McCarthy pp. 75, 88; (6) M. & P. pp. 251-2; (7) McCarthy p. 289; (8) McCarthy p. 297; (9) McCarthy p. 303; (10) McCarthy p. 303; (11) McCarthy pp. 303-4; (12) Globe, Part II, 2nd Sess. 38th Cong. pp. 969-70; (13) Cox Rem. vol. II, p. 396, quoted Rhodes vol. v, pp. 51-2; (14) Globe, Part II, 2nd Sess. 38th Cong. pp. 969-70; (15) McCarthy p. 313; (16) Globe, Part II, 2nd Sess. 38th Cong. p. 1002; (17) Encyc. vol. 7, p. 866.

CHAPTER XVIII

(1) M. & P. p. 254; (2) Stephens vol. ii, pp. 599-601; (3) Rhodes vol. v, p. 69; (4) Stephens vol. II, p. 600; (5) Stephens vol. II, p. 613; (6) Stephens vol. II, p. 614; (7) Stephens vol. II, p. 616; (8) Stephens vol. II, p. 617; (9) N. & H. vol. x, p. 133 et seq.; (10) Blaine vol. I, p. 542; (11) M. & P. Conf. vol. I, p. 530; (12) Pickett pp. 167-8; (13) M. & P. Conf. vol. I, p. 519; (14) Rhodes vol. v, p. 72; (15) Stephens vol. II, p. 623; (16) Rhodes vol. v, p. 73; (17) Rhodes vol. v, p. 73, note 5; (18) Rhodes vol. v. p. 73; (19) O. R. vol. xlvi, Part II, pp. 1209-10, quoted Rhodes vol. v, p. 74; (20) Bible, Book of Daniel, Chap. 5, Verse 5; (21) Bible, Book of Daniel, Chap. 5, Verse 25; (22) M. & P. Conf. vol. I, p. 533; (23) M. & P. Conf. vol. II, p. 694; (24) Rhodes vol. v, p. 81; (25) Blaine vol. ii, p. 25; (26) Globe, Part I, 1st Sess. 37th Cong. pp. 239-43; (27) Globe, Part II, 2nd Sess, 38th Cong. pp. 969-970; (28) Blaine vol. II, p. 26.

CHAPTER XIX

(1) McCarthy p. 46; (2) Rhodes vol. v, p. 52; (3) McCarthy p. 70; (4) Stanwood vol. I, p. 279; (5) Rhodes vol. v, p. 52; (6) Lincoln vol. ii, p. 496; (7) Rhodes vol. v, p. 53; (8) Lincoln vol. ii, pp. 597-9; McCarthy pp. 401-2; (9) Rhodes vol. v, p. 53; (10) Globe, Part II, 2nd Sess. 38th Cong. p. 1129; (11) Rhodes vol. v, p. 54, note 3; (12) Globe, Part II, 2nd Sess. 38th Cong. p. 1128; (13) Rhodes vol. v, p. 55; (14) McCarthy p. 92; (15) M. & P. p. 252; (16) McCarthy p. 92; (17) McCarthy pp. 129, 195; (18) U. S. Con. 12th Amendment; (19) Rhodes vol. v, p. 51; (20) Globe, Part I, 2nd Sess. 38th Cong. p. 556; (21) McCarthy p. 338; (22) Burgess p. 23.

CHAPTER XX

(1) Hall p. 157; (2) Bassett pp. 537-8; (3) Bradford U. P. p. 100 et seq.; (4) Bassett p. 538; (5) Rhodes vol. v, p. 42; (6) Hall pp. 159-60; (7) Hall p. 167; (8) Hall p. 167; (9) Hall pp. 165, 170; (10) O. R. Series iii, vol. iv, p. 1050, quoted Hall pp. 172-3; (11) Lincoln vol. ii, p. 628; (12) Hall p. 173; (13) Jones p. 89; (14) Lincoln vol. ii, p. 631; (15) Hall p. 173; (16) J. P. vol. lvii, 2426, quoted Hall pp. 222-3.

CHAPTER XXI

(1) M. & P. p. 276; (2) M. & P. p. 277; (3) N. Y. Tri. Mar. 6, 1865; (4) N. Y. Tri. Mar. 6, 1865; (5) Welles vol. ii, p. 252, McCulloch p. 373; (6) Hamlin p. 497; (7) N. Y. Her. Mar. 5, 1865, Welles vol. ii, p. 253, Rhodes vol. v, p. 147, Hamlin p. 498, Charnwood p. 411; (8) Hamlin p. 498; (9) N. Y. Wor. Mar. 7, 1865; (10) Hamlin p. 504; (11) Hamlin pp. 497-8; (12) Hamlin p. 497; (13) Hamlin p. 497; (14) McCulloch p. 373; (15) Andrew vol. ii, p. 262.

CHAPTER XXII

(1) M. & P. Conf. vol. I, p. 544; (2) M. & P. Conf. vol. I, p. 544; (3) Rhodes vol. v, p. 109; (4) M. & P. Conf. vol. I, p. 551; (5) Welles vol. ii, p. 264; (6) Welles vol. ii, p. 269; (7) Rhodes vol. v, p. 113; (8) Pickett pp.

174-5; (9) Rhodes vol. v, p. 114; (10) Rhodes vol. v, p. 118; (11) Grant's Memoirs, vol. ii, p. 458; (12) Rhodes vol. v, p. 119; (13) Savage p. 322; (14) Rhodes vol. v, p. 120; (15) Pickett p. 17; (16) Pickett p. 42; (17) Pickett p. 133; (18) Pickett p. 58; (19) Pickett pp. 167-8; (20) Pickett pp. 16-7; (21) Rhodes vol. v, p. 133; (22) C. of A. vol. 32, p. 67; (23) Welles vol. ii, pp. 279-80; (24) Morse vol. ii, p. 345; (25) Grant vol. ii, p. 489; (26) Grant vol. ii, p. 490; (27) Grant vol. ii, pp. 490-1; (28) Grant vol. ii, pp. 491-2; (29) Grant vol. ii, p. 492; (30) Grant vol. ii, p. 493; (31) Grant vol. ii, p. 493; (32) Grant vol. ii, p. 496; (33) Rhodes vol. v, p. 129; (34) Pickett p. 179; (35) Grant vol. ii, p. 498; (36) Grant vol. ii, p. 498; (37) Pierce vol. iv, pp. 235-9; (38) Rhodes vol. v, p. 134; (39) Welles vol. ii, p. 278; (40) Perley vol. ii, p. 168; (41) N. & H. vol. ix, p. 457; (42) N. & H. vol. ix, p. 459 et seq.; (43) N. & H. vol. ix, p. 459 et seq.; (44) Perley vol. ii, p. 168; (45) Pierce vol. iv, p. 236; (46) Welles vol. ii, p. 280; (47) Rhodes vol. v, p. 138; (48) Welles vol. ii, p. 282; (49) N. & H. vol. x, p. 282, Rhodes vol. v, p. 138; (50) Rhodes vol. v, p. 138.

CHAPTER XXIII

(1) Welles vol. ii, p. 275; (2) Encyc. vol. xxiv, p. 733; (3) Weed vol. I, p. 423; (4) Encyc. vol. xxiv, p. 733; (5) Lothrop p. 149; (6) Encyc. vol. xxiv, p. 734; (7) Lothrop p. 203; (8) Savage p. 222; (9) Encyc. vol. xxiv, p. 734; (10) Rhodes vol. ii, p. 467; (11) Encyc. vol. xxiv, p. 734; (12) Lothrop p. 150; (13) Weed vol. ii, p. 277; (14) Lothrop p. 155; (15) Lothrop p. 171; (16) Lothrop pp. 185-6; (17) Lothrop p. 194; (18) Lothrop p. 194; (19) Lothrop p. 191; (20) Lothrop pp. 211-12; (21) Morse vol. I, p. 161; (22) Rhodes vol. ii, p. 468; (23) Rhodes vol. ii, p. 460; (24) Lothrop p. 215; (25) Stanwood vol. I, p. 294; (26) Rhodes vol. ii, p. 471; (27) Morse vol. I, p. 172; (28) Morse vol. I, p. 171; (29) Lothrop p. 219; (30) Lothrop p. 219; (31) Morse vol. I, pp. 237-8; (32) Morse vol. I, pp. 237 8; (33) Rhodes vol. iii, p. 320, note 3; (34) Morse vol. I, p. 276; (35) Morse vol. I, p. 278; (36) N. & H. vol. iii, p. 448; (37) Morse vol. I, p. 279; (38) Rhodes vol. iv, p. 207; (39) Lothrop p. 361; (40) Rhodes vol. iv, p. 211; (41) Lothrop pp. 322-3; (42) Lothrop pp. 327-47, Morse vol. I, pp. 381-2, Rhodes vol. iii, pp. 537-8; (43) Morse-Welles p. xli; (44) Rhodes vol. iv, p. 204; (45) Rhodes vol. iv, p. 203; (46) Welles vol. I, p. 203; (47) Charnwood p. 329, Welles vol. I, p. 203, N. & H. vol. vi, p. 268; (48) Lothrop p. 363; (49) C. of A. vol. 29, p. 103; (50) Welles-Morse Intro. lii; (51) Rhodes vol. iv, p. 211; (52) Rhodes vol. iv, p. 212; (53) Rhodes vol. iii, p. 336; (54) Rhodes vol. iii, p. 341; (55) Welles vol. I, p. 24; (56) Bradford U. P. p. 228; (57) Bradford U. P. pp. 200-1; p. 229; (58) Bradford U. P. p. 203; (59) Bradford U. P. p. 199; (60) Bradford U. P. pp. 200-1; (61) Seward pp. 271-2; (62) Encyc. vol. xxv, p. 783; (63) Welles vol. I, p. 203; (64) Welles vol. ii, p. 17; (65) Encyc. vol. xxviii, p. 506; (66) Welles-Morse Intro. lii; (67) Blaine vol. I, p. 552; (68) Blaine vol. I, pp. 552-3; (69) Blaine vol. I, p. 553; (70) Welles-Morse Intro. xxxviii; (71) Welles-Morse Intro. xxxviii; (72) Welles-Morse Intro. xxxix; (73) Welles-Morse Intro. xlii; (74) Rhodes vol. v. p. 221; (75) Rhodes vol. v, p. 138, note 1; (76) Welles-Morse Intro. xlvii; (77) Bradford U. P. p. 173; (78) Welles-Morse Intro. xxxvi; (79) Natl. Encyc. vol. iv, p. 249, Encyc. vol. 10, p. 293; (80) Bassett p. 660; (81) Welles vol. ii, pp. 576-7; (82) Encyc. vol. xii, p. 954; (83) Blaine vol. ii, p. 61; (84) Rhodes vol. iv. p. 529; (85) Rhodes vol. iv, p. 529; (86) Encyc. vol. iv, p. 33, Blaine vol. II, p. 61; (87) Herndon vol. I, p. 175; (88) Herndon vol. I, p. 195; (89) Herndon vol. I, pp. 200-2; (90) Blaine vol. ii, p. 62; (91) Charnwood p. 405; (92) Rhodes vol. iii, p. 596.

CHAPTER XXIV

(1) Tarbell vol. ii, p. 235; (2) Herndon vol. II, p. 275; (3) Rhodes vol. v, p. 140; (4) Tarbell vol. ii, p. 239; (5) Herndon vol. ii, p. 278; (6) McPherson p. 7; (7) M. & P. pp. 342-8; (8) Rhodes vol. v, pp. 145-6; (9) McCulloch

p. 223; (10) Rhodes vol. v, p. 150; (11) Savage p. 327, Welles vol. ii, p. 288; (12) Savage p. 328, Blaine vol. ii, pp. 1-2; (13) Schuckers p. 519; (14) U. S. Con. Art. II, Sec. I, Rhodes vol. v, p. 150; (15) Schuckers p. 519; (16) Adams p. 79; (17) Adams p. 92; (18) M. & P. p. 58; (19) M. & P. pp. 305-6; (20) McCulloch p. 376; (21) Welles vol. ii, pp. 289-90; (22) Welles vol. ii, p. 290; (23) Grant vol. ii, p. 509; (24) Welles vol. ii, p. 290; (25) Rhodes vol. v, p. 146; (26) Trevelyan p. 326; (27) Welles vol. ii, p. 292; (28) Rhodes vol. v, pp. 152-3; (29) Speeches p. 205; (30) Speeches p. 294; (31) Speeches p. 456; (32) Julian p. 255; (33) Julian pp. 255-6; (34) Rhodes vol. v, p. 154, note 1; (35) Rhodes vol. v, pp. 154-5, note 1; (36) Rhodes vol. v, p. 154, note 1; (37) N. Y. Trib. Apr. 17, 1865; (38) Rhodes vol. v, p. 153; (39) Rhodes vol. v, p. 159.

CHAPTER XXV

(1) Rhodes vol. v, pp. 172-3; (2) Sherman's Home Letters, pp. 349-50; (3) Rhodes vol. v, pp. 168-9; (4) Sherman Home Letters pp. 351-2; (5) Cambridge vol. vii, p. 622; (6) Sherman Home Letters p. 353; (7) Rhodes vol. v, pp. 186-7; (8) Rhodes vol. v, p. 188, note 3; (9) Rhodes vol. v, p. 189; (10) Rhodes vol v, p. 154, note 1; (11) Emerson vol. xi, pp. 313-4; (12) Julian pp. 258-9; (13) Julian p. 257; (14) Julian p. 257; (15) Julian, p. 257; (16) Welles vol. ii, p. 291; (17) Speeches pp. 469-70; (18) Speeches p. 470; (19) Speeches pp. 471-3; (20) Speeches p. 473; (21) Speeches p. 475; (22) Speeches p. 478; (23) Speeches p. 479; (24) Speeches pp. 479-80; (25) Speeches p. 480; (26) Speeches p. 481; (27) Speeches pp. 483-4; (28) Perley vol. ii, p. 181; (29) Perley vol. ii, p. 181; (30) McCulloch p. 374; (31) McCulloch p. 374; (32) Welles vol. ii, p. 300; (33) Rhodes vol. vi, p. 34; (34) Rhodes vol. v, pp. 527-8; (35) Rhodes vol. v, p. 525; (36) Welles vol. ii, p. 302; (37) Welles vol. ii, pp. 302-3; (38) Welles vol. ii, p. 303; (39) Sherman vol. ii, p. 376, Perley vol. ii, p. 187; (40) Perley vol. ii, p. 187; (41) Perley vol. ii, p. 186; (42) Sherman vol. ii, p. 376; (43) Stephens vol. ii, p. 766; (44) Rhodes vol. v, p. 101; (45) Rhodes vol. v, p. 103.

CHAPTER XXVI

(1) M. & P. p. 310; (2) M. & P. p. 311; (3) M. & P. pp. 213-5; (4) M. &. P. p. 312; (5) Rhodes vol. v, p. 535; (6) U. S. Con. Art. II, Sec. II; (7) Blaine vol. ii, p. 68; (8) Blaine vol. ii, p. 68; (9) Rhodes vol. v, p. 587; (10) Lothrop p. 415; (11) Blaine vol. ii, p. 67; (12) M. & P. pp. 312-3; (13) M. & P. p. 313; (14) M. & P. p. 313; (15) M. & P. p. 313; (16) Perley vol. II, p. 181; (17) N. Y. Trib. June 10, 1865; (18) Perley vol. II, p. 204; (19) Natl. Encyc. vol. 2, p. 457; (20) Natl. Encyc. vol. 2, p. 457; (21) Perley vol. II, p. 193; (22) Rhodes vol. v, p. 137; (23) Rhodes vol. v, p. 137; (24) M. & P. p. 315; (25) M. & P. pp. 320, 323; (26) M. & P. p. 325; (27) M. & P. p. 327; (28) M. & P. p. 331; (29) McPherson p. 8; (30) Blaine vol. ii, p. 79; (31) M. & P. p. 318; (32) Blaine vol. ii, p. 79; (33) Rhodes vol. v, p. 527, Cambridge p. 625, Chadsey p. 39, Wilson p. 257, Schouler vol. vii, p. 143, Bassett p. 600; (34) Dunning p. 35; (35) Burgess pp. 36-7; (36) McPherson pp. 18-28; (37) McPherson p. 19; (38) McPherson pp. 19-20; (39) McPherson pp. 20-1; (40) McPherson p. 21; (41) McPherson pp. 18-28; (42) Blaine vol. ii, p. 76; (43) McPherson p. 49; (44) N. Y. Herald May 10, 1865; (45) N. Y. Herald May 13, 1865; (46) N. Y. Herald May 31; (47) McCulloch p. 378; (48) Impeachment Inv. p. 40, Rhodes vol. v, p. 528; (49) Rhodes vol. v, p. 534, note 4; (50) Rhodes vol. v, p. 533; (51) Julian p. 264; (52) Rhodes vol. v, p. 534, Welles vol. ii, p. 363; (53) Rhodes vol. v, p. 534; (54) Rhodes vol. v, p. 534, note 4; (55) Rhodes vol. v, p. 535; (56) Welles vol, ii, p. 363; (57) Welles vol. ii, p. 363; (58) Welles vol. ii, pp. 355-6; (59) Welles vol, ii, pp. 355-6; (60) Welles vol. ii, p. 364; (61) Welles vol. ii, p. 364; (62) Welles vol. ii, p. 369; (63) Welles vol. ii. pp. 372-3; (64) N. Y. Herald June 2; (65) N. Y. World Oct. 19, 1865; (66) Rhodes vol. ii, p. 473; (67) Phillips pp. 359, 362, 370; (68) Phillips pp. 390, 392; (69) Phillips pp. 448, 450, 454, 457; (70) Rhodes vol. v, p. 577, note 2;

(71) Rhodes vol. v, p. 534, note 2; (72) Rhodes vol. v, p. 533; (73) Rhodes vol. v, p. 533; (74) Sherman Corres. p. 257.

CHAPTER XXVII

(1) McPherson p. 107; (2) McPherson p. 108; (3) McPherson p. 107; (4) McPherson p. 109; (5) Welles vol. ii, p. 385; (6) Rhodes vol. v, p. 544; (7) Welles vol. ii, p. 387; (8) McPherson p. 108; (9) Chadsey p. 51; (10) Welles vol. ii, p. 388; (11) Blaine vol. ii, pp. 112-3; (12) Blaine vol. ii, p. 113; (13) Blaine vol. ii, p. 113; (14) Chadsey p. 51; (15) McCall p. 257; (16) McCall p. 257; (17) McCall p. 258; (18) McCall p. 258; (19) McCall pp. 308-22; (20) McCall p. 257; (21) McCall p. 258; (22) McCall p. 258; (23) McCall pp. 258-9; (24) McCall pp. 258-9; (25) Blaine vol. ii, p. 113; (26) Storey p. 298; (27) Storey pp. 299-300; (28) Blaine vol. ii, p. 114; (29) Blaine vol. ii, p. 114; (30) Blaine pp. 113-4; (31) Jones p. 173; (32) Jones pp. 173-4; (33) Andrew vol. ii, p. 280; (34) Andrew vol. ii, p. 284; (35) M. & P. p. 353; (36) M. & P. p. 353; (37) M. & P. pp. 355-6; (38) M. & P. p. 356; (39) M. & P. p. 356; (40) M. & P. pp. 356-7; (41) M. & P. p. 357; (42) M. & P. p. 357; (43) M. & P. pp. 357-8; (44) M. & P. p. 358; (45) M. & P. p. 358; (46) McPherson p. 21; (47) McPherson pp. 18-28; (48) M. & P. p. 359; (49) M. & P. p. 360; (50) M. & P. p. 360; (51) Rhodes vol. v, pp. 562-3; (52) Rhodes vol. v, p. 563; (53) M. & P. p. 360; (54) Rhodes vol. v, p. 548; (55) M. L. on A. J. p. 575; (56) M. L. on A. J. p. 575; (57) Rhodes vol. v, p. 548; (58) Rhodes vol. v, p. 546; (59) Rhodes vol. v, p. 546; (60) Rhodes vol. v, p. 548; (61) Rhodes vol. v, p. 548; (62) Rhodes vol. v, p. 546; (63) M. L. on A. J. p. 578; (64) M. L. on A. J. p. 578, (65) Blaine vol. ii, p. 115; (66) Welles vol. ii, p. 392.

CHAPTER XXVIII

(1) Pickett pp. 48-9; (2) Pickett p. 81; (3) Pickett pp. 82-3; (4) Pickett p. 151; (5) Pickett p. 152; (6) Pickett p. 19; (7) Pickett p. 16; (8) McCall p. 321; (9) Rhodes vol. v, p. 542; (10) Blaine vol. I, 325; (11) Woodburn p. 601; (12) Woodburn pp. 601-2; (13) Woodburn p. 603; (14) Dewitt p. 24, McCall p. 318; (15) Schurz vol. iii, pp. 212-7; (16) Chadsey p. 57, note 2, quoting from Taylor's Destruction and Reconstruction; (17) Bradford U. P. p. 182.

CHAPTER XXIX

(1) M. & P. p. 214; (2) Rhodes vol. v, p. 559; (3) Blaine vol. ii, p. 163; (4) Rhodes vol. v, p. 557; (5) Rhodes vol. v, p. 558; (6) Rhodes vol. v, p. 558; (7) McPherson pp. 28-32; (8) McPherson p. 29; (9) McPherson p. 29; (10) McPherson pp. 28-44, Burgess pp. 46-53, Wilson pp. 259-61; (11) Rhodes vol. v, p. 527; (12) Dunning p. 57; (13) Chadsey p. 47, Solid South p. 35; (14) McPherson p. 24; (15) McPherson p. 24; (16) Charnwood pp. 381-5, C. of A. vol. 29, pp. 166-7, 160, 239-40; (17) Blaine vol. ii, pp. 118-121; (18) Storey pp. 302-3; (19) Welles vol. ii, pp. 393-5; (20) Welles vol. ii, p. 394; (21) Welles vol. ii, p. 394; (22) Welles vol. ii, p. 395; (23) Welles vol. ii, p. 395; (24) Welles vol. ii, p. 395; (25) Welles vol. ii, p. 399; (26) Blaine vol. ii, pp. 112-6; (27) Blaine vol. ii, p. 127; (28) Blaine vol. ii, p. 127; (29) Blaine vol. ii, p. 127; (30) Welles vol. ii, p. 396; (31) Welles vol. ii, p. 397; (32) Welles vol. ii, p. 397; (33) Blaine vol. ii, p. 152; (34) Blaine vol. ii, p. 147; (35) M. & P. p. 372; (36) M. & P. pp. 372-3; (37) Blaine vol. ii, p. 153; (38) McPherson pp. 67-8; (39) Rhodes vol. v, p. 552; (40) Rhodes vol. v, pp. 552-3; (41) Storey p. 305; (42) Storey p. 306; (43) Storey p. 307; (44) Blaine vol. ii, p. 144; (45) Sumner vol. xi, p. 25; (46) Cong. Globe 1st Sess. 30th Cong. Part I, 1865, p. 72 et seq.; (47) Blaine vol. ii, p. 130; (48) McCall p. 263; (49) McCall p. 263; (50) McPherson p. 6; (51) McPherson p. 6; (52) Blaine vol. ii, p. 137; (53) Blaine vol. ii, pp. 136-7; (54) Blaine vol. ii, p. 137; (55) Welles vol. ii, pp. 412-3.

CHAPTER XXX

(1) Oberholtzer vol. I, p. 161; (2) Burgess pp. 44-5, Blaine vol. ii, pp. 163-5; (3) McPherson p. 68; (4) McPherson p. 73; (5) McPherson p. 74; (6) McPherson p. 74; (7) Burgess p. 65; (8) Welles vol. ii, p. 414; (9) Welles vol. ii, p. 415; (10) Welles vol. ii, p. 416; (11) Welles vol. ii, p. 417; (12) Welles vol. ii, p. 417; (13) Welles vol. ii, p. 414; (14) McPherson p. 74; (15) Welles vol. ii, p. 419; (16) Welles vol. ii, p. 421; (17) Welles vol. ii, p. 421; (18) Welles vol. ii, p. 424; (19) Welles vol. ii, p. 425; (20) McPherson p. 74, Burgess p. 66; (21) Welles vol. ii, pp. 430-1; (22) Welles vol. ii, p. 431; (23) Welles vol. ii, p. 431; (24) Welles vol. ii, p. 431; (25) Welles vol. ii, p. 431; (26) Sherman Corres. p. 262; (27) Welles vol. ii, p. 432; (28) Welles vol. ii, pp. 432-3; (29) Welles vol. ii, p. 433; (30) Welles vol. ii, p. 434; (31) Welles vol. ii, p. 435; (32) Welles vol. ii, p. 435; (33) Welles vol. ii, p. 435; (34) M. & P. p. 398; (35) M. & P. p. 398; (36) M. & P. p. 399; (37) M. & P. p. 399; (38) M. & P. p. 399; (39) M. & P. pp. 399-400; (40) M. & P. p. 400; (41) M. & P. p. 400; (42) M. & P. p. 402; (43) M. & P. pp. 402-3; (44) M. & P. p. 403; (45) M. & P. pp. 403-4; (46) M. & P. p. 404; (47) M. & P. p. 405; (48) M. & P. p. 404; (49) Rhodes vol. v, p. 574; (50) N. Y. Trib. May 16, 1926; (51) Dewitt p. 49; (52) McPherson p. 74; (53) McPherson p. 74; (54) Welles vol. ii, pp. 435-6; (55) Welles vol. ii, p. 436; (56) Rhodes vol. v, p. 577, note 2; (57) Cong. Globe 1st Sess. 39th Cong. App. p. 124 et seq.; (58) Storey p. 303; (59) Dewitt p. 55; (60) McPherson p. 51; (61) Cong. Globe 39th Cong. 1st Sess. p. 536; (62) Welles vol. ii, p. 409; (63) Welles vol. ii, p. 431; (64) Welles vol. ii, p. 438.

CHAPTER XXXI

(1) Blaine vol. ii, p. 181; (2) McPherson pp. 58-59; (3) McPherson p. 58; (4) McPherson p. 59; (5) McPherson p. 59; (6) McPherson pp. 59-60; Blaine vol. 2, p. 181; (7) McPherson p. 61; (8) McPherson p. 61; (9) McPherson p. 61; (10) McPherson p. 62; (11) McPherson p. 62; (12) Sherman Corres. p. 263; (13) Sherman Corres. pp. 263-4; (14) Sherman Corres. pp. 263-4; (15) Rhodes vol. v, p. 578, see note; (16) Globe 1st Sess. 39th Cong. App. p. 124 et seq.; (17) Blaine vol. ii, p. 182, Rhodes vol. v, p. 577; (18) N. Y. Herald Feb. 24, 1866; (19) N. Y. Times Feb. 24, 1866; (20) Oberholtzer vol. I, p. 171; (21) Oberholtzer vol. I, p. 168; (22) N. Y. Herald Feb. 28, 1866; (23) Welles vol. ii, pp. 439-40; (24) Globe 1st Sess. 39th Cong. p. 124 et seq.; (25) Globe 1st Sess. 39th Cong. App. p. 124 et seq.; (26) Globe 1st Sess. 39th Cong. App. p. 124 et seq.; (27) Globe 1st Sess. 39th Cong. App. pp. 140, 142.

CHAPTER XXXII

(1) Blaine vol. ii, p. 172; (2) Burgess p. 72; (3) McPherson p. 81; (4) Globe 1st Sess. 39th Cong. pp. 1307-8; (5) Welles vol. ii, pp. 451-2; (6) Blaine vol. ii, p. 175; (7) McPherson p. 74, Blaine vol. ii, p. 155; (8) Blaine vol. ii, pp. 155-9; (9) Blaine vol. ii, pp. 155-9; (10) M. & P. p. 406; (11) M. & P. pp. 406-7; (12) McPherson p. 79; (13) M. & P. pp. 408-9; (14) M. & P. p. 411; (15) M. & P. p. 411; (16) M. & P. p. 412; (17) M. & P. p. 413; (18) M. & P. p. 413; (19) Dewitt pp. 77-83; (20) Blaine vol. ii, p. 178; (21) Welles vol. ii, p. 475; (22) McPherson p. 82; (23) Welles vol. ii, p. 477; (24) McPherson p. 82; (25) Blaine vol. ii, p. 179; (26) Blaine vol. ii, p. 179; (27) Encyc. vol. 6, p. 723; (28) McPherson p. 81; (29) Welles vol. ii, p. 395; (30) U. S. Con. Art. I, Sec. 3; (31) M. & P. p. 413; (32) M. & P. p. 414; (33) M. & P. p. 415; (34) M. & P. p. 414; (35) M. & P. p. 416; (36) Encyc. vol. 6, p. 723.

CHAPTER XXXIII

(1) Rhodes vol. vi, pp. 37-8; (2) Charnwood p. 124; (3) Avary p. 37; (4) McPherson p. 55; (5) Bryce vol. ii, p. 516; (6) Bryce vol. ii, pp. 523-4; (7)

Bryce vol. ii, pp. 524-5; (8) Morse-Welles xlix; (9) McElroy-Root vol. I, p. viii; (10) Beck p. 163; (11) Blaine vol. ii, p. 193; (12) Blaine vol. ii, p. 194; (13) Blaine vol. ii, pp. 198-9; (14) Blaine vol. ii, p. 205; (15) Welles vol. ii, p. 494; (16) Burdick p. 640, note 1, p. 641, note 2; (17) McPherson p. 51; (18) McPherson p. 51; (19) Blaine vol. ii, p. 205; (20) Blaine vol. ii, p. 214; (21) Blaine vol. ii, p. 211; (22) Blaine vol. ii, p. 214; (23) Blaine vol. ii, p. 210; (24) Merriam vol. ii, p. 27; (25) Blaine vol. ii, p. 215; (26) Burgess p. 81; (27) McPherson p. 87; (28) McPherson p. 93; (29) McPherson p. 93; (30) McPherson p. 91; (31) McPherson p. 92; (32) McPherson p. 93; (33) Burgess p. 85; (34) McPherson p. 93; (35) McPherson p. 87; (36) McPherson p. 94; (37) McPherson pp. 94-5; (38) McPherson p. 99; (39) McPherson p. 101; (40) McPherson p. 101; (41) McPherson p. 84; (42) Burgess p. 80; (43) U. S. Con. Art. V; (44) McPherson p. 83; (45) McPherson p. 83; (46) Schuckers p. 527; (47) Gorham vol. ii, p. 309; (48) Pierce vol. iv, pp. 288-9; (49) Blaine vol. ii, p. 213; (50) Solid South p. 184; (51) Solid South p. 185; (52) Solid South p. 186; (53) Solid South p. 186; (54) McPherson p. 89; (55) Solid South pp. 186-7; (56) Welles vol. ii, pp. 554-5; (57) Welles vol. ii, p. 555; (58) Solid South p. 187; (59) Welles vol. ii, p. 557; (60) Welles vol. ii, p. 557; (61) Solid South p. 187; (62) Solid South p. 188; (63) Solid South p. 187; (64) Dewitt p. 100; (65) Solid South p. 187; (66) Solid South p. 188; (67) Welles vol. ii, p. 558; (68) McPherson p. 152; (69) Welles vol. ii, p. 559; (70) M. & P. p. 396; (71) Blaine vol. ii, p. 216; (72) Oberholtzer vol. I, p. 187; (73) M. & P. p. 397; (74) M. & P. p. 397; (75) M. & P. p. 397; (76) Rhodes vol. v, p. 598, note 3; (77) Rhodes vol. v, p. 598, note 3; (78) Dewitt p. 106; (79) Cong. Globe 39th Cong. 1st Sess. p. 4113.

CHAPTER XXXIV

(1) Blaine vol. ii, p. 217; (2) McPherson pp. 149-151; (3) M. & P. p. 424; (4) Burgess p. 89; (5) McPherson p. 151; (6) Burgess p. 90; (7) McPherson p. 151; (8) Burgess p. 89; (9) Dewitt p. 105; (10) Encyc. vol. 19, p. 330; (11) Pierce vol. iv, p. 286; (12) Pierce vol. iv, p. 286; (13) Cong. Globe 39th Cong. 1st Sess. p. 4276; (14) Welles vol. ii, p. 563; (15) Welles vol. ii, p. 537, Welles vol. ii, pp. 537-8, 551-2, 553, Rhodes vol. v, p. 611; (16) Welles vol. ii, p. 552; (17) Rhodes vol. vi, p. 48; (18) Burgess p. 91; (19) Welles vol. ii. p. 558; (20) Welles vol. ii, p. 403, note 1; (21) 2 Natl. Encyc. p. 458; (22) Blaine vol. ii, p. 219; (23) 2 Natl. Encyc. p. 458; (24) 2 Natl. Encyc. p. 457; (25) Rhodes vol. v, p. 611, note 2.

CHAPTER XXXV

(1) McPherson pp. 67-8; (2) Oberholtzer vol. I, p. 379; (3) Oberholtzer vol. I, p. 380; (4) Welles vol. ii, p. 570; (5) Burgess p. 93; (6) Burgess pp. 92-5; (7) Rhodes vol. v, p. 612; (8) Rhodes vol. v, p. 612; (9) M. & P. p. 590; (10) M. & P. p. 590; (11) M. & P. p. 590; (12) M. & P. p. 590; (13) Burgess p. 96; (14) M. & P. p. 590; (15) M. & P. p. 590; (16) Burgess p. 97; (17) Burgess p. 97; (18) M. & P. p. 591; (19) M. & P. p. 591; (20) Welles vol. ii, p. 570; (21) Blaine vol. ii, p. 237; (22) N. Y. Trib. July 31, 1866; (23) Blaine vol. ii, p. 237; (24) Lamb, vol. iii, p. 775; (25) Welles vol. ii, pp. 569-70.

CHAPTER XXXVI

(1) Rhodes vol. v, p. 614; (2) Rhodes vol. v, p. 614; (3) Welles vol. ii, p. 573; (4) Welles vol. ii, p. 574; (5) Welles vol. ii, p. 555; (6) Welles vol. ii, pp. 555-6; (7) Oberholtzer vol. I, p. 386; (8) Oberholtzer vol. I, p. 386; (9) Rhodes vol. v, p. 614; (10) Oberholtzer vol. I, p. 388; (11) Oberholtzer vol. I, p. 388; (12) McPherson p. 251; (13) McPherson p. 241; (14) Oberholtzer vol. I, p. 389; (15) Burgess pp. 99-100; (16) Blaine vol. ii, p. 221; (17) Blaine vol. ii, p. 223; (18) Pierce vol. iv, p. 297; (19) Oberholtzer vol. I, p. 389; (20) Welles

vol. ii, p. 581; (21) Welles vol. ii, p. 582; (22) Trial vol. I, pp. 66-7; (23)
McPherson p. 127, Trial vol. I, p. 9; (24) McPherson pp. 127-8; (25) McPherson
p. 128; (26) Rhodes vol. v, p. 617; (27) Pierce vol. iv, p. 298; (28) Pierce vol.
iv, p. 298; (29) Stephens vol. ii, p. 649; (30) Stephens vol. ii, p. 649; (31)
Oberholtzer vol. I, p. 391; (32) M. & P. p. 438; (33) M. & P. p. 432; (34)
M. & P. p. 438; (35) Welles vol. ii, p. 583; (36) Welles vol. ii, p. 583; (37)
Rhodes vol. v, p. 617; (38) McPherson p. 58; (39) Welles vol. ii, p. 425, note 1;
(40) McCulloch p. 377; (41) Welles vol. ii, p. 587.

CHAPTER XXXVII

(1) Hoar vol. ii, pp. 174-5; (2) Hoar vol. ii, pp. 175-7; (3) Rhodes vol. v,
p. 522; (4) Rhodes vol. v, p. 521; (5) Welles vol. ii, p. 300; (6) Dana p. 284;
(7) Dana pp. 284-6; (8) Mrs. Davis vol. ii, p. 657; (9) Rhodes vol. vi, p. 51;
(10) McCulloch p. 410; (11) M. & P. p. 342; (12) M. & P. p. 343; (13)
M. & P. p. 345; (14) M. & P. pp. 347-8; (15) M. & P. 345-6; (16) Rhodes
vol. v, p. 158, note 1; (17) Schuckers p. 534; (18) Welles vol. ii, p. 335; (19)
Welles vol. ii, pp. 335, 337, 339; (20) Craven pp. 299-300; (21) Craven
pp. 300-1; (22) Craven pp. 301-2.

CHAPTER XXXVIII

(1) Clay p. 338, note; (2) Rhodes vol. v, p. 521; (3) Dewitt p. 138; (4)
Welles vol. ii, p. 300; (5) Rhodes vol. iii, p. 183, note 1; (6) Welles vol. ii,
p. 423; (7) Clay p. 288; (8) Clay p. 354; (9) Clay p. 364; (10) Clay p. 337,
note; (11) Clay p. 320; (12) Clay p. 321; (13) Clay p. 322; (14) Clay p. 324;
(15) Clay pp. 328-9; (16) Clay pp. 334, 335, 336; (17) Clay pp. 340-1; (18)
Clay p. 345; (19) Clay p. 371; (20) Clay p. 374; (21) Welles vol. ii, p. 474;
(22) Oberholtzer vol. I, p. 446; (23) Bradford-Wives p. 182; (24) Bradford-
Wives p. 196; (25) Dewitt p. 139; (26) Dewitt p. 140; (27) Rhodes vol. vi,
p. 55; (28) McCulloch pp. 410-11; (29) McCulloch p. 410; (30) McCulloch
p. 410; (31) Schuckers p. 534; (32) McCulloch p. 411; (33) Schuckers p. 535;
(34) Warren vol. iii, p. 143, note 2.

CHAPTER XXXIX

(1) Welles vol. ii, pp. 588-9; (2) Welles vol. ii, p. 587; (3) Welles vol. ii,
p. 588; (4) Welles vol. ii, p. 589; (5) Welles vol. ii, p. 647; (6) Oberholtzer
vol. I, pp. 396-7; (7) Oberholtzer vol. I, p. 397; (8) N. Y. Herald Aug. 30, 1866;
(9) N. Y. Herald Aug. 30, 1866; (10) Oberholtzer vol. I, p. 397; (11) N. Y.
Herald Aug. 30, 1866; (12) N. Y. Herald Aug. 30, 1866; (13) N. Y. Herald
Aug. 30, 1866; (14) McPherson pp. 129-130; (15) McPherson p. 130; (16)
McPherson p. 130; (17) McPherson p. 130; (18) McPherson p. 131; (19)
McPherson p. 131; (20) McPherson pp. 131-2; (21) McPherson pp. 133-4; (22)
McPherson p. 133; (23) Oberholtzer vol. I, p. 398; (24) Martin vol. I, p. 272;
(25) Oberholtzer vol. I, p. 398; (26) Oberholtzer vol. I, p. 398; (27) Welles vol.
ii, p. 588; (28) Welles vol. ii, p. 592; (29) Oberholtzer vol. I, p. 401; (30) N. Y.
Herald Sept. 1. 1866; (31) Welles vol. ii, p. 588; (32) Welles vol. ii, pp. 589-90;
(33) McPherson p. 124; (34) Rhodes vol. v, p. 621; (35) Rhodes vol. v, p. 449;
(36) Rhodes vol. v, p. 449; (37) Rhodes vol. v, p. 621; (38) Blaine vol. ii,
p. 225; (39) Blaine vol. ii, p. 226; (40) Blaine vol. ii, p. 227; (41) McPherson
p. 241; (42) McPherson p. 242; (43) McPherson p. 242; (44) McPherson p. 242;
(45) Blaine vol. ii, p. 228; (46) Welles vol. ii, p. 593; (47) Rhodes vol. v,
p. 618; (48) Welles vol. ii, p. 592; (49) Oberholtzer vol. I, p. 404; (50) Oberholtzer vol. I, p. 404, note 2; (51) Welles vol. ii, p. 552; (52) Welles vol. ii,
p. 594; (53) McPherson p. 134, Trial I, p. 328; (54) Trial I, p. 326; (55)
Trial I, p. 326; (56) Trial I, p. 326, McPherson p. 135; (57) McPherson p. 135;
(58) McPherson p. 135; (59) McPherson p. 135; (60) McPherson p. 135; (61)
McPherson p. 135; (62) McPherson p. 135; (63) Trial I, p. 327; (64) McPher-

REFERENCES 857

son p. 135; (65) McPherson pp. 135-6; (66) McPherson p. 136; (67) McPherson p. 136; (68) Trial I, p. 335; (69) McPherson p. 136; (70) Welles vol. ii, p. 593; (71) Welles vol. ii, p. 593; (72) Rhodes vol. v, p. 618; (73) Rhodes vol. v, p. 618; (74) Burgess p. 102; (75) N. Y. Evening Post Sept. 11, 1866, N. Y. Trib. and other Radical newspapers, Blaine vol. ii, p. 238, Oberholtzer vol. I, pp. 400-1, Bassett p. 611; (76) Lowell vol. v, p. 292; (77) Lowell vol. v, p. 294; (78) Lowell vol. v, p. 292; (79) Lowell vol. v, p. 289; (80) Lowell vol. v, p. 292; (81) Lowell vol. v, p. 292; (82) Lowell vol. v, p. 297; (83) Lowell vol. v, p. 326; (84) Lowell vol. v, pp. 298, 317; (85) Rhodes vol. v, p. 618; (86) Welles vol. ii, p. 589; (87) Schouler vol. vii, p. 73; (88) Century Jan. 1913, p. 438; (89) N. Y. Herald Sept. 7, 1866; (90) Oberholtzer vol. I, p. 405; (91) Welles vol. ii, p. 594; (92) Oberholtzer vol. I, p. 405; (93) Jones p. 220; (94) Oberholtzer vol. I, p. 405; (95) Oberholtzer vol. I, p. 399; (96) Oberholtzer vol. I, p. 399; (97) Welles vol. II, p. 594; (98) N. Y. Herald Sept. 12, 1866; (99) Oberholtzer vol. I, p. 409, note 2; (100) Welles vol. ii, p. 648; (101) Welles vol. ii, p. 648; (102) Welles Vol. ii, p. 594; (103) Trial I, p. 640; (104) Trial I, p. 637; (105) Trial I, p. 637; (106) Trial I, p. 637; (107) Trial I, p. 640; (108) Trial I, p. 638; (109) Trial I, p. 639; (110) Trial I, p. 639; (111) McPherson pp. 136-7, Trial I, p. 9; (112) McPherson p. 137, Trial I, pp. 9, 341; (113) McPherson p. 137, Trial I, pp. 9, 341; (114) McPherson p. 137, Trial I, p. 9; (115) McPherson p. 137; (116) Rhodes vol. v, p. 619; (117) McPherson p. 138; (118) Trial I, p. 344, McPherson p. 140; (119) McPherson p. 140; (120) N. Y. Herald Sept. 12, 1866, Oberholtzer vol. I, p. 407; (121) Welles vol. ii, p. 594; (122) Welles vol. ii, p. 594; (123) Welles vol. ii, p. 588; (124) Welles vol. ii, p. 588; (125) Welles vol. ii, pp. 591-2; (126) Oberholtzer p. 407; (127) N. Y. Trib. Sept. 8, 1866; (128) Welles vol. ii, p. 592; (129) Welles vol. ii, p. 595; (130) Charnwood p. 211; (131) Merriam vol. I, pp. 190-1; (132) McPherson p. 135; (133) Lothrop p. 397; (134) Oberholtzer vol. I, p. 407; (135) Welles vol. ii, pp. 594-5; (136) Welles vol. ii, p. 595; (137) Flower pp. 310-12; (138) Welles vol. ii, p. 590; (139) Welles vol. ii, p. 590.

CHAPTER XL

(1) Rhodes vol. iii, p. 182, vol. iv, p. 146; (2) Oberholtzer vol. I, p. 395; (3) Blaine vol. ii, p. 229, Grant vol. I, pp. 288-298; Rhodes vol. iv, p. 398; (4) Encyc. vol. 7, p. 668; (5) N. Y. Trib. Sept. 13, 1866; (6) Blaine vol. ii, p. 229; (7) Blaine vol. ii, p. 229; (8) Hibben p. 201; (9) Hibben p. 202; (10) Blaine vol. ii, pp. 229-30; (11) Blaine vol. ii, p. 230; (12) Blaine vol. ii, p. 230; (13) McPherson p. 243; (14) Bigelow vol. I, p. 343; (15) Bigelow vol. I, pp. 343-4; (16) Bigelow vol. I, p. 344.

CHAPTER XLI

(1) Butler pp. 827-8; (2) Natl. Cyc. vol. I, pp. 119-22; (3) Hoar vol. I, p. 330; (4) Rhodes vol. v, p. 312; (5) Welles vol. ii, p. 81; (6) Welles vol. ii, pp. 469-70; (7) Natl. Cyc. vol. I, pp. 119-22; (8) Hoar vol. I, p. 332; (9) Butler p. 123; (10) Butler p. 173; (11) Hoar vol. I, p. 335; (12) Bradford-D. S. pp. 227-8; (13) Hoar vol. I, p. 335; (14) Rhodes vol. v, p. 303; (15) Rhodes vol. I, p. 275; (16) Rhodes vol. v, p. 303; (17) Hoar vol. I, pp. 343-4; (18) Rhodes vol. v, p. 313; (19) Rhodes vol. vi, p. 389; (20) Encyc. vol. iv, p. 881; (21) Rhodes vol. v, p. 310; (22) Bradford D. S. pp. 251-2; (23) Butler p. 418; (24) Butler p. 416; (25) Cox p. 425; (26) Encyc. vol. iv, p. 881; (27) Encyc. vol. iv, p. 881; (28) Bradford D. S. p. 238; (29) Gorham vol. I, pp. 314-5; (30) Bradford D. S. p. 238; (31) Rhodes vol. v, p. 310; (32) Rhodes vol. v, pp. 310-11; (33) Hoar vol. I, pp. 336-7; (34) Grant vol. ii, p. 605; (35) Hoar vol. I, p. 339; (36) Hoar vol. I, p. 339; (37) Hoar vol. I, p. 339; (38) Hoar vol. I, p. 340; (39) Butler pp. 827-8; (40) Butler p. 1036; (41) Welles vol. ii, p. 224; (42) Hoar vol. I, p. 341; (43) Welles vol. II, pp. 223-4; (44) Merriam vol. ii, p. 26; (45) Merriam vol. ii, p. 26; (46) Butler p. 919; (47) Butler p. 919; (48) Blaine vol. ii, p. 289; (49) Encyc. vol. iv, p. 881; (50) Blaine vol. ii, p. 289;

(51) Blaine vol. ii, p. 230; (52) Blaine vol. ii, p. 233; (53) McPherson p. 243; (54) McCall pp. 282-3; (55) McCall pp. 282-3; (56) McCall pp. 282-3; (57) McCall pp. 283-4; (58) Sumner vol. xi, p. 19; (59) Sumner vol. xi, p. 19; (60) Welles vol. ii, p. 616; (61) Welles vol. ii, p. 617; (62) Welles vol. ii, pp. 616-7; (63) Oberholtzer vol. I, p. 419; (64) Rhodes vol. v, p. 625.

CHAPTER XLII

(1) N. Y. Trib. Jan. 30, 1927; (2) Encyc. vol. 17, p. 924; (3) Guedalla pp. 322-7; (4) Encyc. vol. 18, p. 341; (5) Encyc. vol. 18, p. 341; (6) Encyc. vol. 17, p. 925; (7) Oberholtzer vol. I, pp. 505-6; (8) Guedalla p. 327; (9) Lothrop p. 391; (10) Oberholtzer vol. I, p. 523; (11) Guedalla p. 328; (12) Lothrop p. 392; (13) Rhodes vol. vi, p. 206; (14) Welles vol. ii, p. 317; (15) Welles vol. ii, p. 317; (16) Welles vol. ii, p. 322; (17) Welles vol. ii, p. 322; (18) Welles vol. ii, p. 348; (19) Rhodes vol. vi, p. 206; (20) Welles vol. ii, p. 367; (21) Rhodes vol. vi, p. 207; (22) Rhodes vol. vi, pp. 207-8; (23) Rhodes vol. vi, p. 208; (24) Rhodes vol. vi, p. 208; (25) Rhodes vol. vi, p. 208; (26) Rhodes vol. vi, p. 208; (27) Rhodes vol. vi, p. 208; (28) Encyc. vol. 18, p. 342; (29) Guedalla p. 330; (30) Guedalla p. 330; (31) Guedalla p. 331; (32) Guedalla p. 331; (33) N. Y. Trib. Jan. 20, 1927; (34) Welles vol. ii, p. 501; (35) Am. Hist. Rev. p. 99; (36) Am. Hist. Rev. p. 99; (37) Welles vol. ii, p. 621; (38) Am. Hist. Rev. p. 101; (39) Am. Hist. Rev. pp. 101-2; (40) Welles vol. ii, p. 621; (41) Am. Hist. Rev. p. 102.

CHAPTER XLIII

(1) Welles vol. ii, pp. 616-7; (2) Welles vol. ii, pp. 617-9; (3) Welles vol. ii, pp. 619-20; (4) Welles vol. ii, p. 626; (5) Welles vol. ii, p. 627; (6) Pierce vol. iv, p. 303; (7) Pierce vol. iv, p. 304; (8) Welles vol. ii, p. 629; (9) Flower p. 311; (10) Perley vol. ii, pp. 201-2; (11) M. & P. p. 445; (12) M. & P. p. 446; (13) M. & P. pp. 446, 448; (14) M. & P. p. 459; (15) N. Y. Trib. Dec. 4, 1866; (16) N. Y. World Dec. 4, 1866; (17) Welles vol. ii, p. 631; (18) Cong. Globe 39th Cong. 2nd Sess. p. 2; (19) Oberholtzer vol. I, p. 422; (20) Welles vol. ii, pp. 633-4; (21) Welles vol. ii, p. 634; (22) Welles vol. ii, p. 634; (23) Welles vol. ii, p. 636; (24) Globe 2nd Sess. 39th Cong. p. 107; (25) Globe 2nd Sess. 39th Cong. p. 107; (26) Welles vol. ii, p. 636; (27) McPherson p. 160; (28) Welles vol. ii, p. 640; (29) Globe 2nd Sess. 39th Cong. p. 127; (30) Globe 2nd Sess. 39th Cong. pp. 147-163; (31) Globe 2nd Sess. 39th Cong. pp. 335-6; (32) Globe 2nd Sess. 39th Cong. pp. 335-6; (33) Globe 2nd Sess. 39th Cong. pp. 335-6; (34) Chadsey p. 109; (35) Chadsey p. 54, note 2; (36) Boutwell vol. ii, pp. 107-8; (37) Boutwell vol. ii, pp. 107-8; (38) Boutwell vol. ii, p. 108; (39) U. S. Con. Art. 2, Sec. 2; (40) U. S. Con. Art. 2, Sec. 4.

CHAPTER XLIV

(1) Myers v. U. S. Sup. Ct. Oct. Term 1926, p. 7; (2) U. S. Con. Art. 2, Sec. 2; (3) Myers v. U. S. Sup. Ct. pp. 5-20; (4) Myers v. U. S. p. 11; (5) Myers v. U. S. p. 9; (6) Myers v. U. S. pp. 6-7; (7) Myers v. U. S. p. 8; (8) Blaine vol. ii, p. 270; (9) Rhodes vol. v, p. 621; (10) Oberholtzer vol. I, p. 438; McCulloch p. 377; (11) Bigelow vol. I, p. 270; (12) Chadsey p. 128.

CHAPTER XLV

(1) Oberholtzer vol. I, p. 440; (2) U. S. Cons. Art. II, Sec. 4; (3) U. S. Cons. Art. I, Sec. 3; (4) U. S. Cons. Art. I, Sec. 3; (5) U. S. Cons. Art. I, Sec. 3; (6) McPherson p. 187; (7) Oberholtzer vol. I, p. 440, note 2; (8) McPherson p. 187.

CHAPTER XLVI

(1) Rhodes vol. v, pp. 317-8; (2) Rhodes vol. v, p. 327; (3) Rhodes vol. v, p. 327; (4) N. & H. vol. viii, p. 8, Rhodes vol. v, p. 328; (5) Ex Parte Milligan

4 Wall. pp. 5-8; (6) Ex Parte Milligan 4 Wall. p. 123; (7) Warren vol. iii, p. 147, note 2; (8) 4 Wall. p. v; (9) Warren vol. iii, p. 144; (10) Bryce vol. I, p. 276; (11) Welles vol. ii, p. 471; (12) Warren vol. ii, p. 148; (13) Welles vol. ii, p. 476; (14) Warren vol. iii, p. 146; (15) McPherson p. 187; (16) 4 Wall. p. 109; (17) 4 Wall. p. 109; (18) 4 Wall. pp. 121-3; (19) 4 Wall. pp. 121-3; (20) 4 Wall. p. 124; (21) 4 Wall. pp. 126-7; (22) Warren vol. iii, p. 149; (23) M. & P. pp. 398-405; (24) Welles vol. ii, p. 644; (25) McPherson p. 242; (26) U. S. Cons. Art. I, Sec. 3; (27) 4 Wall. p. 137; (28) Hart p. 363; (29) quoted Warren vol. iii, p. 151; (30) quoted Warren vol. iii, pp. 151-2; (31) quoted Warren vol. iii, p. 154; (32) quoted Warren vol. iii, p. 165, note 1; (33) quoted Warren vol. iii, p. 167; (34) quoted Warren vol. iii, pp. 167-8; (35) Warren vol. iii, p. 169; (36) Warren vol. iii, p. 152; (37) Chase pp. 518-9; (38) Warren vol. iii, p. 160; (39) quoted Warren vol. iii, p. 157; (40) Welles vol. ii, pp. 646-7; (41) Welles vol. ii, p. 650; (42) Welles vol. ii, pp. 652-3; (43) Welles vol. ii, p. 653.

CHAPTER XLVII

(1) McPherson p. 159; (2) Welles vol. iii, p. 4; (3) Welles vol. iii, p. 5; (4) McPherson p. 160; (5) 28 Encyc. p. 351; (6) M. & P. p. 473; (7) M. & P. p. 474; (8) M. & P. p. 476; (9) M. & P. pp. 476-7; (10) M. & P. p. 477; (11) M. & P. p. 478; (12) McPherson p. 160; (13) Cong. Globe 39th Cong. 2nd Sess. pp. 319-21; (14) Cong. Globe 39th Cong. 2nd Sess. p. 320; (15) Cong. Globe 39th Cong. 2nd Sess. pp. 319-21; (16) Cong. Globe 39th Cong. 2nd Sess. pp. 320-21; (17) Cong. Globe 39th Cong. 2nd Sess. pp. 320-1; (18) Salter p. 323; (19) Welles vol. iii, p. 8; (20) Welles vol. iii, p. 12; (21) Welles vol. iii, p. 10; (22) Welles vol. iii, p. 10; (23) Welles vol. iii, p. 11; (24) Welles vol. iii, p. 17; (25) Dunning p. 91; (26) Dunning p. 87; (27) Welles vol. iii, p. 17; (28) Welles vol. iii, p. 20; (29) Welles vol. iii, p. 27; (30) Burgess p. 80; (31) McPherson p. 194; (32) McPherson p. 194; (33) McPherson p. 194; (34) Flack p. 208; (35) Flack p. 193; (36) Rhodes vol. vi, p. 6.

CHAPTER XLVIII

(1) 4 Wall. pp. 277, 333; (2) 4 Wall. pp. 318-9; (3) Ex Parte Garland, 4 Wall. pp. 333, 380; (4) 4 Wall. p. 319; (5) quoted in Warren vol. iii, p. 173; (6) quoted in Warren vol. iii, p. 173; (7) quoted in Warren vol. iii, p. 174; (8) quoted in Warren vol. iii, p. 175; (9) quoted in Warren vol. iii, p. 176; (10) Cong. Globe 39th Cong. 2nd Sess. pp. 443-6; (11) Cong. Globe 39th Cong 2nd Sess. pp. 443-6; (12) Welles vol. iii, p. 24; (13) Cong. Globe 39th Cong 2nd Sess. pp. 443-6; (14) M. & P. pp. 343, 345-7; (15) Dewitt p. 142; (16) Dewitt p. 154; (17) Dewitt p. 155; (18) Dewitt p. 155; (19) M. & P. p. 485 Dewitt pp. 172-3; (20) McPherson p. 166; (21) Cong. Globe 39th Cong. 2nd Sess. pp. 335-6.

CHAPTER XLIX

(1) Thayer vol. I, p. 250; (2) Thayer vol. I, p. 263; (3) Thayer vol. I, p. 257; (4) Thayer vol. I, p. 255; (5) Blaine vol. ii, p. 270; (6) Blaine vol. ii, p. 271; (7) Blaine vol. ii, p. 271; (8) Cong. Globe 39th Cong. 2nd Sess. pp. 542-4; (9) Cong. Globe 39th Cong. 2nd Sess. pp. 542-4; (10) Blaine vol. ii, p. 272; (11) Blaine vol. ii, p. 272; (12) Cong. Globe 39th Cong. 2nd Sess. pp. 1039-40, 1043, 1046; (13) Blaine vol. ii, p. 272; (14) Thayer vol. I, p. 270; (15) Thayer vol. I, p. 267; (16) McPherson p. 176, Blaine vol. ii, p. 272; (17) Trial III, p. 52; (18) Trial III, p. 53; (19) Trial III, p. 53; (20) McPherson p. 177; (21) Welles vol. iii, p. 50; (22) Welles vol. iii, pp. 50-51; (23) M. & P. p. 587; (24) M. & P. p. 587; (25) Welles vol. iii, p. 51; (26) M. & P. p. 587; (27) Welles vol. iii, p. 158; (28) M. & P. p. 588; (29) M. & P. pp. 494-5; (30) M. & P. p. 495; (31) M. & P. p. 497; (32) McPherson p. 177.

860 REFERENCES

CHAPTER L

(1) Rhodes vol. vi, pp. 14-15; (2) Woodburn p. 456; (3) Cong. Globe 39th Cong. 2nd Sess. p. 1076; (4) Rhodes vol. vi, p. 24; (5) Woodburn p. 461; (6) Woodburn p. 461; (7) Cong. Globe 39th Cong. 2nd Sess. p. 1099; (8) Blaine vol. ii, p. 251; (9) Cong. Globe 39th Cong. 2nd Sess. p. 1177; (10) Blaine vol. ii, p. 252; (11) Blaine vol. ii, p. 254; (12) Blaine vol. ii, p. 256; (13) Woodburn p. 477; McCall p. 288; (14) Woodburn p. 471; (15) Woodburn p. 470; (16) Rhodes vol. vi, p. 17; (17) Woodburn p. 448; (18) Woodburn p. 477; (19) Blaine vol. ii, p. 257; (20) Welles vol. iii, p. 42; (21) Welles vol. iii, pp. 42-3; (22) Welles vol. iii, p. 43; (23) Welles vol. iii, p. 44; (24) Welles vol. iii, p. 45; (25) Welles vol. iii, pp. 45-6; (26) Welles vol. iii, p. 46; (27) Welles vol. iii, p. 46; (28) Welles vol. iii, p. 49; (29) McCulloch p. 391; (30) Blaine vol. ii, p. 258; (31) Blaine vol. ii, p. 258; (32) McPherson p. 157, Woodburn p. 480; (33) Blaine vol. ii, p. 259; (34) Blaine vol. ii, p. 261; (35) McPherson p. 191; (36) McPherson p. 191; (37) McPherson p. 191; (38) McPherson p. 191; (39) McPherson p. 192; (40) McCall p. 289; (41) McPherson p. 192; (42) McPherson p. 192; (43) M. & P. p. 255; (44) M. & P. p. 277; (45) Grant vol. ii, p. 492; (46) Burgess p. 113; (47) Burgess p. 116; (48) McPherson p. 173; (49) Welles vol. iii, p. 49; (50) Welles vol. iii, p. 49; (51) Welles vol. iii, p. 50; (52) Welles vol. iii, p. 50; (53) Welles vol. iii, p. 50; (54) Welles vol. iii, p. 54; (55) M. & P. p. 498; (56) M. & P. p. 499; (57) M. & P. p. 499; (58) M. & P. p. 500; (59) M. & P. pp. 500-1; (60) M. & P. p. 501; (61) M. & P. p. 502; (62) M. & P. p. 502; (63) M. & P. p. 502; (64) M. & P. pp. 502-3; (65) M. & P. p. 503; (66) M. & P. pp. 503-4; (67) M. & P. p. 504; (68) M. & P. p. 506; (69) U. S. Con. Art. I, Sec. 9; (70) M. & P. p. 507; (71) M. & P. p. 507; (72) M. & P. p. 508; (73) M. & P. pp. 508-9; (74) M. & P. p. 510; (75) Woodburn pp. 481-2; (76) Woodburn p. 482; (77) Blaine vol. ii, p. 262; (78) Woodburn pp. 482-3; (79) Grant vol. ii, p. 512; (80) Grant vol. ii, p. 523.

CHAPTER LI

(1) McPherson p. 178; (2) Boutwell vol. ii, p. 108; (3) McPherson p. 178; (4) M. & P. p. 472; (5) Dewitt pp. 154-5; (6) Dewitt p. 155; (7) Chadsey p. 131; (8) Dewitt p. 157; (9) Dewitt p. 157; (10) Dewitt pp. 177-8; (11) Dewitt p. 178; (12) Dewitt p. 179; (13) Oberholtzer vol. I, p. 451; (14) Chadsey p. 117, note 1; (15) Oberholtzer vol. I, p. 451; (16) Oberholtzer vol. I, p. 451; (17) Welles vol. iii, p. 56; (18) Welles vol. iii, p. 57; (19) Welles vol. iii, p. 57; (20) Globe 2nd Sess. 39th Cong. p. 2003; (21) Dewitt p. 179; (22) Welles vol. iii, p. 58.

CHAPTER LII

(1) Oberholtzer vol. I, p. 452; (2) Blaine vol. ii, pp. 284-9; (3) Welles vol. iii, p. 58; (4) Globe 1st Sess. 40th Cong. pp. 18-25; (5) Globe 1st Sess. 40th Cong. pp. 18-25; (6) Globe 1st Sess. 40th Cong. pp. 18-25; (7) Globe 1st Sess. 40th Cong. pp. 18-25; (8) Welles vol. iii, p. 62; (9) Welles vol. iii, pp. 62-3; (10) Welles vol. iii, p. 61; (11) Welles vol. iii, p. 61; (12) Welles vol. iii, p. 62; (13) M. & P. p. 551; (14) Welles vol. iii, p. 65; (15) McPherson p. 180; (16) McPherson pp. 192-4; (17) M. & P. p. 534; (18) M. & P. p. 535; (19) Burgess p. 147; (20) Burgess p. 245; (21) Pierce vol. iv, p. 307; (22) Pierce vol. iv, pp. 307-8; (23) Storey p. 337; (24) Storey p. 337; (25) M. & P. p. 517; (26) 1 Encyc. p. 477; (27) 1 Bryce p. 585; (28) Oberholtzer vol. I, p. 542; (29) Welles vol. iii, p. 68; (30) Oberholtzer vol. I, p. 540; (31) Rhodes vol. vi, p. 212; (32) Oberholtzer vol. I, p. 549; (33) M. & P. p. 517; (34) Warren vol. iii, pp. 177-8; (35) Warren vol. iii, pp. 177-9; (36) quoted Warren vol. iii, p. 181; (37) Mississippi v. Johnson, 4 Wall. p. 475; (38) quoted Warren vol. iii, p. 183; (39) Georgia v. Stanton, 6 Wall. p. 50; (40) quoted Warren vol. iii, pp. 183-4; (41) Warren vol. iii, p. 184; (42) Warren vol. iii, p. 185;

(43) quoted Warren vol. iii, p. 186, note 1; (44) Mrs. Davis, vol. ii, p. 777; (45) Mrs. Davis vol. ii, p. 790; (46) Mrs. Davis vol. ii, p. 794; (47) Mrs. Davis vol. ii, pp. 794-5; (48) Oberholtzer vol. I, p. 448; (49) Rhodes vol. vi, pp. 56-7; (50) Oberholtzer vol. I, pp. 448-9; (51) Oberholtzer vol. I, p. 449; (52) Rhodes vol. vi, p. 57; (53) Rhodes vol. vi, p. 57; (54) Mrs. Davis vol. ii, pp. 795-7; (55) Mrs. Davis vol. ii, pp. 829-30; (56) Mrs. Davis vol. I, pp. 303, 316; (57) quoted Oberholtzer vol. I, p. 450; (58) quoted Oberholtzer vol. I, p. 450; (59) Rourke p. 335; (60) quoted Oberholtzer vol. I, p. 449; (61) Bancroft vol. 2, pp. 167-8; (62) Dewitt pp. 156, 234; (63) Dewitt p. 234; (64) Dewitt p. 235; (65) Welles vol. iii, p. 102; (66) Dewitt p. 235; (67) Welles vol. iii, p. 102.

CHAPTER LIII

(1) 4 Wall. 492; (2) U. S. Cons. Art. II, Sec. 3; (3) M. & P. p. 551; (4) M. & P. p. 551; (5) Rhodes vol. vi, p. 78; (6) Cox pp. 544-5; (7) Welles vol. iii, pp. 93-4; (8) Oberholtzer vol. I, p. 458, note 2; (9) Welles vol. iii, pp. 93-117; (10) Welles vol. iii, p. 111; (11) Welles vol. iii, p. 110; (12) M. & P. pp. 552-6; (13) Welles vol. iii, p. 117; (14) Rhodes vol. vi, p. 63; (15) Rhodes vol. vi, p. 63; (16) Cox p. 546; (17) Cox p. 546; (18) Oberholtzer vol. I, p. 459; (19) Dewitt p. 237; (20) Globe 30th Cong. 1st Sess. p. 500; (21) Blaine vol. ii, p. 294; (22) Burgess pp. 138-9; (23) M. & P. p. 537; (24) M. & P. p. 539; (25) M. & P. p. 539; (26) M. & P. p. 539; (27) M. & P. pp. 539-40; (28) M. & P. pp. 543-4; (29) M. & P. pp. 544-5; (30) M. & P. p. 544; (31) Blaine vol. ii, p. 295; (32) Blaine vol. ii, p. 296; (33) Blaine vol. ii, p. 296; (34) Sumner vol. xi, pp. 421-2; (35) Sumner vol. xi, p. 422; (36) Sumner vol. xi, p. 424; (37) Sumner vol. xi, p. 424; (38) Blaine vol. ii, p. 296; (39) Welles vol. iii, p. 123; (40) Welles vol. iii, p. 127; (41) M. & P. p. 584; (42) M. & P. p. 584; (43) Welles vol. iii, p. 146; (44) Welles vol. iii, p. 150; (45) Welles vol. iii, pp. 150-2; (46) Welles vol. iii, p. 151; (47) Welles vol. iii, p. 154; (48) Welles vol. iii, p. 154; (49) McPherson p. 307; (50) Trial III, p. 53; (51) McPherson p. 307; (52) Welles vol. iii, p. 155; (53) Welles vol. iii, p. 240; (54) Welles vol. iii, p. 155; (55) Welles vol. iii, p. 155; (56) Welles vol. iii, pp. 155-6; (57) Welles vol. iii, p. 156; (58) Rhodes vol. v, p. 159; (59) Dewitt pp. 279, 281; (60) Dewitt p. 279; (61) Welles vol. iii, p. 143; (62) Welles vol. iii, p. 144; (63) Dewitt p. 280; (64) Dewitt pp. 280-1; (65) Welles vol. iii, p. 144; (66) Welles vol. iii, p. 157; (67) McPherson p. 261; (68) Welles vol. iii, p. 157; (69) Welles vol. iii, p. 157; (70) McPherson p. 261; (71) McCulloch pp. 401-2; (72) Welles vol. iii, p. 156; (73) Welles vol. iii, p. 167; (74) McPherson p. 261; (75) Grant vol. ii, pp. 536-7; (76) McPherson pp. 261-2.

CHAPTER LIV

(1) Oberholtzer vol. I, p. 475, note 2; (2) Rhodes vol. vi, p. 66; (3) Rhodes vol. vi, p. 384; (4) Welles vol. iii, p. 177; (5) Welles vol. iii, p. 177; (6) Welles vol. iii, p. 177; (7) Welles vol. iii, p. 169; (8) Welles vol. iii, pp. 180-1; (9) Grant vol. ii, p. 490; (10) Maurice p. 260; (11) McCulloch p. 341; (12) Bradford-Lee pp. 26, 249; (13) Maurice pp. 4-5; (14) Piatt p. 175; (15) Bradford-Lee p. 169; (16) Rhodes vol. vi, pp. 383-4; (17) Hoar vol. I, p. 197; (18) Rhodes vol. vi, p. 377; (19) Hoar vol. I, p. 304; (20) McCulloch p. 360; (21) Rhodes vol. vi, p. 383; (22) Bassett p. 651; (23) Rhodes vol. vii, p. 183; (24) Oberholtzer vol. iii, p. 148, Rhodes vol. vii, p. 184; (25) Oberholtzer vol. iii, p. 151; (26) Rhodes vol. vii, p. 185; (27) Bassett p. 651, Oberholtzer vol. iii, p. 155; (28) Bassett p. 651; (29) Rhodes vol. vii, p. 188; (30) Rhodes vol. vii, p. 188; (31) Oberholtzer vol. iii, p. 148; (32) Oberholtzer vol. iii, p. 160; (33) Rhodes vol. vii, pp. 190-1; (34) Oberholtzer vol. iii, p. 277; (35) Oberholtzer vol. iii, p. 410; (36) Oberholtzer vol. iii, pp. 410, 417, note 1; (37) Rhodes vol. vi, p. 377; (38) Rhodes vol. vi, pp. 247-9; (39) Rhodes vol. vi, p. 247; (40) quoted Rhodes vol. vi, p. 248; (41) Rhodes vol. vi, p. 250; (42) Rhodes

vol. vi, p. 251; (43) Rhodes vol. vi, p. 256; (44) Oberholtzer vol. ii, p. 78; (45) Rhodes vol. iv, p. 493; (46) Rhodes vol. iv, pp. 494-5; (47) Rhodes vol. v, p. 311; (48) Merriam vol. ii, p. 266; (49) Rhodes vol. vii, p. 24; (50) Rhodes vol. vii, p. 24; (51) Rhodes vol. vi, p. 377, note 1; (52) Rhodes vol. vii, p. 191; (53) Cox p. 547; (54) M. & P. p. 556; (55) Welles vol. iii, p. 174; (56) Welles vol. iii, pp. 174, 176; (57) Welles vol. iii, p. 185; (58) Welles vol. iii, p. 182; (59) Welles vol. iii, p. 182 (I have changed the third person to the first); (60) Welles vol. iii, p. 185; (61) Welles vol. iii, p. 186; (62) M. & P. p. 557; (63) Welles vol. iii, p. 186; (64) Welles vol. iii, p. 187 (I have changed the third person to the first); (65) Welles vol. iii, p. 187; (66) Welles vol. iii, pp. 187-8; (67) Welles vol. iii, p. 187; (68) Welles vol. iii, p. 189; (69) Welles vol. iii, p. 188; (70) Welles vol. iii, p. 189; (71) Welles vol. iii, p. 190; (72) Welles vol. iii, p. 190; (73) M. & P. p. 517; (74) Welles vol. iii, p. 196; (75) Welles vol. iii, pp. 221-2; (76) Sherman Corres. p. 297; (77) Welles vol. iii, p. 234; (78) Welles vol. iii, p. 234; (79) Welles vol. iii, pp. 234-5; (80) Welles vol. iii, p. 235.

CHAPTER LV

(1) C. of A. vol. 32, p. 206; (2) C. of A. vol. 32, p. 205; (3) C. of A. vol. 32, p. 205; (4) McCulloch pp. 336-7; (5) Encyc. vol. 23, p. 433; (6) Encyc. vol. 5, p. 364; (7) C. of A. vol. 41, pp. 42-3; (8) C. of A. vol. 41, pp. 46-7; (9) Encyc. vol. 31, p. 182; (10) C. of A. vol. 38, pp. 29-33; (11) C. of A. vol. 38, p. 50; (12) C. of A. vol. 38, pp. 70-94; (13) C. of A. vol. 37, p. 104; (14) C. of A. vol. 37, p. 205; (15) Welles vol. iii, p. 119; (16) McPherson p. 373, Rhodes vol. vi, p. 93, Burgess p. 148; (17) Sherman Corres. p. 299.

CHAPTER LVI

(1) Pierce vol. iv, pp. 304-5; (2) Adams p. 30; (3) Bradford U. P. p. 245; (4) Bradford U. P. pp. 236-40; (5) Bradford U. P. p. 236; (6) Adams p. 261; (7) Blaine vol. ii, p. 343; (8) Welles vol. iii, p. 238; (9) Blaine vol. ii, p. 343; (10) Welles vol. iii, p. 239; (11) Blaine vol. ii, p. 345; (12) Dewitt pp. 290-1; (13) Dewitt p. 298; (14) Blaine vol. ii, p. 345; (15) Dewitt pp. 303-6; (16) Dewitt p. 308; (17) Blaine vol. ii, p. 345; (18) Dewitt p. 294; (19) M. & P. p. 559; (20) M. & P. pp. 559-60; (21) M. & P. p. 560; (22) M. & P. p. 560; (23) M. & P. p. 563; (24) M. & P. p. 564; (25) M. & P. p. 566; (26) M. & P. p. 566; (27) M. & P. p. 567; (28) M. & P. p. 569; (29) M. & P. p. 569; (30) M. & P. p. 563; (31) M. & P. p. 568; (32) M. & P. p. 568; (33) M. & P. pp. 568-9; (34) Dewitt pp. 311-2; (35) Blaine vol. ii, p. 346; (36) Garfield vol. I, p. 423; (37) Cong. Globe 2nd Sess. 40th Cong. p. 1560; (38) Blaine vol. ii, p. 349; (39) M. & P. p. 591; (40) M. & P. p. 587; (41) M. & P. p. 588; (42) M. & P. pp. 588-9; (43) Blaine vol. ii, p. 349; (44) Gorham vol. ii, pp. 412-26; (45) Rhodes vol. vi, p. 99, note 3; (46) Dewitt p. 315.

CHAPTER LVII

(1) Hoar vol. I, p. 316; (2) Rhodes vol. vii, p. 1; (3) Rhodes vol. vii, pp. 2-3; Hoar vol. I, pp. 314-5; (4) Hoar vol. I, p. 315; (5) Hoar vol. I, p. 323; (6) Hoar vol. I, p. 315; (7) Oberholtzer vol. I, p. 326; (8) Rhodes vol. vii, p. 6; (9) Hoar vol. I, p. 320; (10) Hoar vol. I, p. 317; (11) Rhodes vol. vii, p. 7; (12) Rhodes vol. vii, pp. 9-10; (13) Hoar vol. I, p. 323; (14) Rhodes vol. vii, p. 10; (15) Rhodes vol. vii, p. 9; (16) Rhodes vol. vii, p. 14; (17) Rhodes vol. vii, p. 17; (18) Sherman Home Letters p. 352; (19) Steno Rep. Speech by Elihu Root at The Union League Club, Feb. 13, 1925, p. 19.

CHAPTER LVIII

(1) Rhodes vol. vi, p. 82; (2) Burgess p. 147; (3) Rhodes vol. vi, p. 82; (4) Burgess p. 148; (5) Avary pp. 253, 255; (6) Avary pp. 253-4; (7) Avary

p. 254; (8) Avary p. 254; (9) Avary pp. 255-6; (10) Avary p. 257; (11) Avary p. 256; (12) C. of A. vol. 32, p. 140; (13) Grady p. 154; (14) Stephens vol. ii, p. 617; (15) Grady p. 159; (16) C. of A. vol. 27, pp. 62-3; (17) Grady pp. 156-7; (18) Rhodes vol. I, Chap. 1-3; (19) C. of A. vol. 30, p. 102; (20) Grady pp. 149-151; (21) Stephens vol. ii, p. 493; (22) M. & P. p. 255, Stephens vol. ii, appendix S. pp. 805-8; (23) Chesnut p. 378; (24) Chesnut pp. 378-9; (25) Avary p. 67; (26) Avary p. 70; (27) Avary pp. 70-1; (28) Avary pp. 70-1; (29) Avary p. 68; (30) Avary p. 114; (31) Pryor p. 393; (32) Avary p. 311; (33) Avary p. 314; (34) C. of A. vol. 32, pp. 209-210; (35) C. of A. vol. 32, pp. 211-12; (36) Rhodes vol. vi, p. 90; (37) Rhodes vol. vi, p. 91; (38) Encyc. vol. 27, p. 593; (39) Rhodes vol. iv, pp. 241-2; (40) C. of A. vol. 32, pp. 178-9; (41) Avary p. 263; (42) Avary p. 264; (43) Avary p. 264; (44) Avary p. 264; (45) C. of A. vol. 32, p. 184; (46) C. of A. vol. 32, p. 187; (47) Avary p. 384.

CHAPTER LIX

(1) Welles vol. iii, p. 246; (2) Welles vol. iii, p. 158; (3) Welles vol. iii, p. 248; (4) Am. Hist. Rev. p. 115; (5) McPherson p. 284; (6) McPherson p. 285, Am. Hist. Rev. p. 115; (7) Welles vol. iii, p. 258; (8) Dewitt p. 321; (9) Trial I, p. 155; (10) Trial I, p. 155; (11) Am. Hist. Rev. p. 115; (12) Sherman Memoirs vol. ii, p. 420; (13) McPherson p. 262; (14) McPherson p. 283; (15) McPherson pp. 289-291; (16) Welles vol. iii, p. 259; (17) Welles vol. iii, p. 259-60; (18) Welles vol. iii, p. 260; (19) Welles vol. iii, p. 260; (20) Welles vol. iii, p. 260; (21) Welles vol. iii, p. 261; (22) Welles vol. iii, p. 261; (23) J. P. vol. 129; (24) Sherman Memoirs vol. ii, p 420; (25) Sherman Memoirs, vol. ii, p. 420; (26) Sherman Memoirs vol. ii, p. 420; (27) McPherson p. 285, but see p. 286; (28) Sherman Memoirs vol. ii, p. 420; (29) Sherman Home Letters pp. 365-6; (30) Sherman Memoirs vol. ii, p. 420; (31) McPherson p. 286; (32) Welles vol. iii, p. 263; (33) Welles vol. iii, p. 263; (34) Am. Hist. Rev. p. 117; (35) McPherson p. 286; (36) Welles vol. iii, p. 264; (37) Schofield p. 413; (38) Blaine vol. ii, pp. 351-2; (39) Piatt pp. 78, 83, 85.

CHAPTER LX

(1) J. P. vol. 130; (2) Am. Hist. Rev. p. 117; (3) Am. Hist. Rev. p. 114; (4) Sherman Home Letters p. 368; (5) Sherman Home Letters p. 369; (6) Sherman Home Letters p. 368; (7) Bradford U. P. pp. 133-4; (8) Bradford U. P. p. 136; (9) Sherman Home Letters p. 24; (10) Bradford U. P. p. 157; (11) Bradford U. P. p. 158; (12) Bradford U. P. p. 154; (13) Sherman Home Letters pp. 278, 392-3; (14) Sherman Home Letters pp. 238, 240, 241, 246, 353; (15) Bradford U. P. pp. 146-7; (16) Sherman Home Letters p. 352; (17) Sherman Home Letters p. 361; (18) McPherson p. 283; (19) McPherson p. 283; (20) Sherman Home Letters p. 371; (21) McPherson p. 283; (22) McPherson pp. 283-4; (23) McPherson pp. 283-4; (24) J. P. vol. 130; (25) Trial I, p. 529 (date of this interview was testified to by Sherman as the 30th, but in his contemporary letter to his wife he fixed it as January 29th), Sherman Home Letters p. 369; (26) Trial I, p. 529; (27) Trial I, p. 529; (28) Trial I, p. 529; (29) Sherman Home Letters pp. 369-70; (30) Sherman Home Letters p. 361; (31) McPherson p. 284; (32) McPherson p. 285; (33) McPherson p. 285; (34) McPherson p. 285; (35) McPherson pp. 285-6; (36) McPherson p. 286; (37) McPherson p. 287; (38) McPherson p. 292; (39) Welles vol. iii, pp. 276-7.

CHAPTER LXI

(1) Welles vol. iii, p. 267; (2) Welles vol. iii, pp. 269, 274, McPherson p. 282; (3) McPherson p. 282; (4) Oberholtzer vol. I, p. 489; (5) Blaine vol. ii, p. 352; (6) Woodburn p. 498; (7) Woodburn p. 498; (8) Sherman Home

Letters p. 373; (9) Lear, Act III, Scene 4; (10) Welles vol. iii, p. 280; (11) Welles vol. iii, p. 280; (12) Welles vol. iii, p. 279; (13) Am. Hist. Rev. p. 119; (14) Grant vol. ii, p. 523; (15) Rhodes vol. vi, p. 96; (16) Warren vol. iii, p. 187; (17) Flack p. 170; (18) Flack pp. 165-6; (19) Warren vol. iii, p. 187; (20) White p. 327; (21) White p. 327; (22) Warren vol. iii, p. 187; (23) Warren vol. iii, p. 189; (24) Warren vol. iii, pp. 189-90; (25) White p. 328; (26) White pp. 330-32; (27) Welles vol. iii, p. 282.

CHAPTER LXII

(1) Trial I, p. 415; (2) Trial I, p. 416; (3) Trial I, p. 435; (4) Trial I, p. 435; (5) Trial I, p. 248; (6) Trial I, p. 248; (7) U. S. Con. Art. II, Sec. 2; (8) Trial II, p. 334; (9) Trial II, p. 337; (10) Trial I, pp. 401, 403, 574-6; (11) Trial I, p. 437; (12) Trial I, p. 418; (13) Trial I, pp. 418-19; (14) Trial I, p. 419; (15) Trial I, p. 419; (16) Trial I, p. 419; (17) Trial I, p. 675; (18) Trial I, p. 675; (19) Welles vol. iii, p. 284; (20) Welles vol. iii, p. 284; (21) Welles vol. iii, p. 284; (22) Welles vol. iii, p. 285; (23) Globe 40th Cong. 2nd Sess. pp. 1329-30; (24) Welles vol. iii, p. 285; Trial I, p. 156; (25) Trial I, pp. 156-7; (26) Trial III, p. 53; (27) Welles vol. iii, p. 285; (28) Welles vol. iii, p. 285; (29) Trial I, p. 210; (30) Trial I, p. 221; (31) Trial I, p. 221; (32) Trial I, p. 439; (33) Trial I, p. 443; (34) Trial I, p. 625; (35) Welles vol. iii, p. 290; (36) Trial I, p. 159; (37) Trial I, p. 706; (38) Trial I, pp. 704-5; Welles vol. iii, p. 289; (39) Welles vol. iii, p. 289; (40) Welles vol. iii, p. 289; (41) Trial I, p. 706; (42) Trial I, pp. 706, 663; (43) Trial I, pp. 515-16; (44) Trial I, p. 516; (45) Welles vol. iii, p. 286; (46) Trial I, p. 516; (47) Trial I, p. 509; (48) Trial I, p. 516; (49) Trial I, p. 427; (50) Trial I, p. 427; (51) Trial I, p. 427; (52) Trial I, p. 617; (53) Trial I, p. 428; (54) Trial I, p. 428; (55) Trial I, p. 428; (56) Rhodes vol. vi, p. 112; (57) Trial I, pp. 232-3; (58) Trial I, p. 233; (59) Trial I, p. 429; (60) Trial I, p. 429; (61) Welles vol. iii, p. 289; (62) Welles vol. iii, p. 287; (63) Welles vol. iii, p. 289; (64) Welles vol. iii, p. 289; (65) Trial I, p. 625; (66) Trial I, pp. 537, 675; (67) Welles vol. iii, p. 286, note I; (68) Trial I, pp. 556-7; (69) Trial I, p. 234; (70) Trial I, p. 235; (71) Trial I, pp. 235, 249-252; (72) Trial I, p. 236; (73) Trial I, p. 236; (74) Trial I, pp. 236, 619-20; (75) Trial I, p. 605.

CHAPTER LXIII

(1) Dewitt p. 358; (2) Oberholtzer vol. ii, p. 72; (3) Dewitt p. 359; (4) Welles vol. iii, p. 299; (5) Globe 40th Cong. 2nd Sess. Part 2, p. 1336; (6) Globe 40th Cong. 2nd Sess. p. 1336; (7) Globe 40th Cong. 2nd Sess. pp. 1336-9; (8) Globe 40th Cong. 2nd Sess. Appendix p. 247; (9) Globe 40th Cong. 2nd Sess. p. 1354; (10) Globe 40th Cong. 2nd Sess. p. 1382-83; (11) Globe 40th Cong. 2nd Sess. p. 1384; (12) Globe 40th Cong. 2nd Sess. p. 1384; (13) Globe 40th Cong. 2nd Sess. p. 1385; (14) Globe 40th Cong. 2nd Sess. p. 1385; (15) Globe 40th Cong. 2nd Sess. p. 1385, Part 2; (16) Globe 40th Cong. 2nd Sess. p. 1386; (17) Globe 40th Cong. 2nd Sess. pp. 1344-7; (18) Globe 40th Cong. 2nd Sess. p. 1347; (19) Globe 40th Cong. 2nd Sess. p. 1353; (20) Globe 40th Cong. 2nd Sess. p. 1386; (21) Globe 40th Cong. 2nd Sess. p. 1369; (22) Globe 40th Cong. 2nd Sess. Appendix p. 191; (23) Cong. Globe 40th Cong. 2nd Sess. Appendix p. 207; (24) Cong. Globe 40th Cong. 2nd Sess. Appendix p. 223; (25) Oberholtzer vol. ii, p. 77; (26) Oberholtzer vol. ii, p. 77; (27) Dewitt pp. 372-3, Cong. Globe 40th Cong. 2nd Sess. p. 1400; (28) Welles vol. iii, p. 300; (29) Cong. Globe 40th Cong. 2nd Sess. p. 1400, Welles vol. iii, p. 292; (30) Welles vol. iii, p. 292; (31) Trial I, pp. 2, 3, 5; (32) Trial I, p. 5; (33) Storey p. 347; (34) Trial I, p. 5; (35) Welles vol. iii, p. 292; (36) Welles vol. iii, p. 293; (37) Trial I, p. 606; (38) Trial I, p. 609; (39) Trial I, p. 609; (40) Welles vol. iii, p. 294; (41) Welles vol. iii, p. 296; (42) Rhodes vol. vi, p. 113, Gorham vol. ii, pp. 442-4; (43) Rhodes vol. vi,

p. 113, Gorham vol. ii, pp. 442-4; (44) Grant Memoirs vol. ii, p. 537; (45) Welles vol. iii, p. 297; (46) Welles vol. iii, p. 297; (47) Dewitt pp. 379-80; (48) Dewitt p. 381; (49) Dewitt p. 382; (50) Dewitt p. 386; (51) Trial II, pp. 362-3, Trial I, pp. 6-10; (52) Rhodes vol. vi, p. 116; (53) Trial III, p. 228; (54) Trial II, p. 362.

CHAPTER LXIV

(1) J. P. vol. 133; (2) J. P. vol. 133; (3) J. P. vol. 133; (4) J. P. vol. 133, Oberholtzer vol. I, pp. 491-2.

CHAPTER LXV

(1) Trial I, p. 4; (2) Welles vol. iii, p. 300; (3) Macaulay vol. iii, p. 198; (4) Macaulay vol. iii, p. 208; (5) Macaulay vol. iii, p. 211; (6) Macaulay vol. iii, p. 240; (7) Macaulay vol. iii, p. 245; (8) Macaulay vol. iii, pp. 251, 634; (9) Macaulay vol. iii, p. 251; (10) Macaulay vol. iii, p. 260; (11) Macaulay vol. iii, p. 257; (12) Butler p. 929; (13) N. Y. Trib. Mar. 2, 1868; (14) Trial I, p. 6; (15) N. Y. Trib. Mar. 5, 1868; (16) Welles vol. iii, p. 301; (17) N. Y. Trib. Mar. 5, 1868; (18) Trial I, p. 6, N. Y. Trib. Mar. 5, 1868; (19) Trial I, p. 6; (20) N. Y. Trib. Mar. 6, 1868; (21) Welles vol. iii, p. 239; (22) Welles vol. iii, p. 239; (23) Welles vol. iii, p. 239; (24) Oberholtzer vol. ii, pp. 92-3; (25) Warren pp. 170-1; (26) Cong. Globe 40th Cong. 2nd Sess. p. 1387; (27) Rhodes vol. vi, p. 113; (28) Cong. Globe 40th Cong. 2nd Sess. p. 1353; (29) Cox p. 586; (30) Oberholtzer vol. ii, p. 605; (31) Oberholtzer vol. ii, p. 603; (32) Oberholtzer vol. ii, p. 602; (33) Trial I, p. 6, N. Y. Trib. Mar. 5, 1868; (34) N. Y. Trib. Mar. 5, 1868; (35) N. Y. Trib. Mar. 5, 1868; (36) Warren vol. iii, p. 195; (37) N. Y. Trib. Mar. 6, 1868; (38) U. S. Con. Art. I, Sec. 3, Clause 6; (39) Trial I, p. 11; (40) Trial I, p. 11; (41) Dewitt p. 389; (42) Rhodes vol. vi. p. 168; (43) Rhodes vol. vi. pp. 162-3; (44) Trial III, p. 360; (45) Trial III, pp. 360-1; (46) Trial III, p. 399; (47) Trial III, p. 401; (48) Welles vol. iii, p. 303; (49) Welles vol. iii, p. 302; (50) Welles vol. iii, p. 303; (51) Welles vol. iii, p. 298; (52) Welles vol. iii, p. 308; (53) Cox p. 587; (54) Am. Hist. Rev. p. 124; (55) Curtis vol. I, pp. 106-264; (56) Welles vol. iii, pp. 51, 205; (57) Rhodes vol. vi, p. 135; (58) Oberholtzer vol. ii, pp. 90-1; (59) Welles vol. iii, p. 307; (60) Oberholtzer vol. ii, p. 90; (61) Oberholtzer vol. ii, p. 90; (62) N. Y. Trib. Mar. 7, 1868; (63) N. Y. Trib. Mar. 7, 1868; (64) Trial I, p. 10; (65) Am. Hist. Rev. p. 123; (66) Am. Hist. Rev. pp. 125-6; (67) Welles vol. iii, pp. 308-9; (68) Welles vol. iii, p. 309; (69) Trial I, pp. 363, 555; (70) Welles vol. iii, p. 311; (71) Welles vol. iii, p. 311.

CHAPTER LXVI

(1) Warren vol. iii, p. 195; (2) Welles vol. iii, p. 314, McPherson p. 351; (3) McPherson p. 351; (4) McPherson p. 351; (5) N. Y. Herald Mar. 14, 1868; (6) Welles vol. iii, p. 314; (7) Warren vol. iii, pp. 198-9; (8) Warren vol. iii, p. 199; (9) Warren vol. iii, p. 202, note 2.

CHAPTER LXVII

(1) N. Y. Trib. Mar. 14, 1868; (2) Macaulay p. 634; (3) N. Y. Trib. Mar. 14, 1868; (4) N. Y. Trib. Mar. 14, 1868; (5) N. Y. Trib. Mar. 14, 1868; (6) Trial I, p. 18; (7) Trial I, pp. 4, 18; (8) N. Y. Trib. Mar. 14, 1868; (9) Trial I, p. 18; (10) Trial I, pp. 18-19; (11) Trial I, p. 19; (12) Trial I, p. 20; (13) Trial I, p. 20; (14) Trial I, p. 21; (15) Trial I, p. 22; (16) Trial I, p. 23; (17) Trial I, p. 24; (18) N. Y. Trib. Mar. 14, 1868; (19) Trial I, p. 24; (20) Trial I, p. 25; (21) Trial I, p. 25; (22) Trial I, p. 26; (23) Trial I, p. 27; (24) Trial I, pp. 30-1; (25) Trial I, p. 34; (26) Welles vol. iii, pp. 313-14; (27) Rhodes vol. vi, pp. 93-4; (28) N. Y. Trib. Mar. 14, 1868;

(29) Oberholtzer vol. ii, p. 39, note 3; (30) Rhodes vol. vi, p. 95; (31) Rhodes vol. vi, p. 95; (32) Rhodes vol. vi, p. 96.

CHAPTER LXVIII

(1) Welles vol. iii, p. 305, note 1, Trial II, pp. 144-5; (2) Trial II, p. 145; (3) Welles vol. iii, p. 316; (4) N. Y. Trib. Mar. 17, 1868; (5) Reeves' "The Real Andrew Johnson" pp. 829-30 and letter to the author; (6) Trial II, p. 266; (7) N. Y. Trib. Mar. 20, 1868.

CHAPTER LXIX

(1) N. Y. Trib. Mar. 23, 1868; (2) N. Y. Trib. Mar. 24, 1868; (3) Welles vol. iii, p. 302, note 1, Oberholtzer vol. ii, p. 96; (4) Trial I, p. 34; (5) Trial I, p. 37; (6) Trial I, p. 42; (7) Trial I, p. 48; (8) Trial I, p. 50; (9) Trial I, p. 51; (10) Trial I, p. 69; (11) Trial I, pp. 70-1; (12) Trial I, p. 71; (13) Trial I, p. 72; (14) Trial I, p. 74; (15) Trial I, pp. 75-6; (16) Trial I, pp. 76-7; (17) Trial I, pp. 79-80; (18) Trial I, pp. 83-6; (19) Welles vol. iii, p. 321; (20) Welles vol. iii, p. 324; (21) Welles vol. iii, p. 324.

CHAPTER LXX

(1) M. & P. pp. 647-8; (2) McPherson p. 351; (3) Grant vol. ii, p. 523; (4) 7 Wall. p. 506; (5) Welles vol. iii, p. 320.

CHAPTER LXXI

(1) N. Y. Trib. Mar. 28, 1868; (2) N. Y. Trib. Mar. 30, 1868; (3) N. Y. Trib. Mar. 31, 1868; (4) N. Y. Trib. Mar. 31, 1868; (5) Trial I, pp. 87-8; (6) Trial I, p. 15; (7) Trial I, pp. 88, 123-147; (8) Trial I, p. 88; (9) Trial I, p. 88; (10) Trial I, p. 89; (11) Trial I, p. 23; (12) Trial I, p. 81; (13) Trial I, p. 89; (14) Trial I, p. 90; (15) N. Y. Trib. Mar. 31, 1868; (16) Trial I, p. 96; (17) Trial I, p. 96; (18) Trial I, p. 96; (19) Trial I, pp. 96-7; (20) Trial I, p. 99; (21) Trial III, p. 53, I, p. 103; (22) Trial I, p. 103; (23) Trial I, p. 103; (24) Trial I, p. 110; (25) Trial I, pp. 110-11, Trial II, p. 346; (26) Trial I, pp. 111-12; (27) Dewitt pp. 414-15; (28) Trial I, p. 96; (29) Trial I, pp. 116-17; (30) Trial I, p. 117; (31) Trial I, p. 117; (32) Trial I, p. 119; (33) Trial I, p. 115; (34) Trial I, p. 115; (35) Trial I, p. 121; (36) Welles vol. iii, p. 81; (37) Welles vol. iii, p. 82; (38) Welles vol. iii, p. 82; (39) Welles vol. iii, p. 82; (40) Trial I, p. 121; (41) Trial I, p. 121; (42) Trial I, p. 122; (43) Trial I, p. 147; (44) Trial I, p. 148.

CHAPTER LXXII

(1) N. Y. Trib. Mar. 31, 1868; (2) Oberholtzer vol. ii, p. 98, note 2; (3) Welles vol. iii, p. 326; (4) Trial I, pp. 155-7; (5) Trial I, p. 158; (6) Trial I, p. 159; (7) Trial I, pp. 160-1; (8) Trial I, pp. 164-72; (9) Trial I, p. 172; (10) Trial I, p. 175; (11) Trial I, p. 178; (12) Trial I, p. 179; (13) Trial I, pp. 180-1; (14) Trial I, p. 185; (15) N. Y. Trib. Apr. 1, 1868; (16) Trial I, p. 186; (17) N. Y. Trib. Apr. 1, 1868; (18) Welles vol. iii, p. 327; (19) Trial I, p. 187; (20) Trial I, p. 188; (21) Trial I, pp. 189-90; (22) Trial I, p. 200; (23) Trial I, p. 201; (24) Trial I, p. 206; (25) Trial I, p. 206; (26) Dewitt p. 394; (27) Trial I, p. 223, N. Y. Trib. Apr. 2, 1868; (28) Trial I, p. 228; (29) N. Y. Trib. Apr. 2, 1868; (30) Trial I, p. 228; (31) Trial I, p. 229; (32) N. Y. Trib. Apr. 3, 1868; (33) Welles vol. iii, p. 312; (34) Trial I, p. 232; (35) Trial I, pp. 232-3; (36) Trial I, p. 114; (37) Trial I, pp. 235-6; (38) Trial I, p. 241; (39) Trial I, p. 245; (40) Trial I, p. 245; (41) Trial I, p. 246; (42) Trial I, p. 247; (43) Trial I, pp. 253-54; (44) Trial I, p. 263; (45) Trial I, p. 261; (46) Trial I, p. 259; (47) Trial I, p. 268; (48) Trial I, pp. 271-72; (49) Trial I, p. 275; (50) Trial I, p. 276; (51)

Trial I, p. 276; (52) Trial I, p. 276; (53) Welles vol. iii, p. 320; (54) N. Y. Trib. Apr. 3, 1868; (55) Trial I, p. 278; (56) Trial I, p. 279; (57) Trial I, pp. 280-3; (58) Trial I, p. 284; (59) Trial I, pp. 294-7; (60) Trial I, pp. 298-304; (61) Trial I, p. 305; (62) Trial I, p. 307; (63) Trial I, p. 309; (64) Trial I, p. 325; (65) Trial I, pp. 328-36; (66) Trial I, p. 321; (67) Trial I, pp. 337-45; (68) Trial I, pp. 345-6; (69) Trial I, p. 369; (70) Trial I, p. 371.

CHAPTER LXXIII

(1) Trial I, p. 372; (2) Trial I, p. 373; (3) Trial I, p. 373; (4) Trial I, p. 374; (5) Trial I, p. 375; (6) Trial I, p. 376; (7) N. Y. Trib. Apr. 10, 1868; (8) Trial I, p. 377; (9) Curtis vol. I, p. 413; (10) Trial I, p. 379; (11) Trial I, p. 379; (12) Trial I, p. 382; (13) Trial I, p. 383; (14) Trial I, p. 384; (15) Trial I, p. 386; (16) Trial I, pp. 386-7; (17) Trial I, p. 387; (18) Trial I, p. 387; (19) Trial I, p. 387; (20) Trial I, p. 390; (21) Trial I, p. 390; (22) Trial I, p. 396; (23) Trial I, p. 397; (24) Trial I, p. 397; (25) Trial I, p. 401; (26) Trial I, p. 402; (27) Trial I, p. 402; (28) Trial I, p. 402; (29) Trial I, p. 403; (30) Trial I, p. 405; (31) Trial I, p. 405; (32) Trial I, p. 406; (33) Trial I, p. 406; (34) Trial I, pp. 407-8; (35) Trial I, p. 408; (36) Trial I, p. 409; (37) Trial I, pp. 411-13; (38) Trial I, p. 410; (39) Trial I, p. 411; (40) Trial I, p. 414; (41) Curtis vol. I, p. 415; (42) Curtis vol. I, p. 416; (43) Curtis vol. I, p. 417; note 1; (44) Curtis vol. I, pp. 416-17.

CHAPTER LXXIV

(1) Trial I, pp. 414-15; (2) Trial I, pp. 415-453; (3) Trial I, p. 430; (4) Trial I, p. 439; (5) Trial I, p. 439; (6) Trial I, p. 456; (7) Trial I, p. 460, (8) Trial I, p. 463; (9) Trial I, p. 462; (10) Trial I, pp. 467-9; (11) Trial I, p. 469; (12) Trial I, p. 469; (13) Trial I, p. 469; (14) Trial I, p. 472; (15) Trial I, p. 471; (16) Trial I, pp. 475-6; (17) Trial I, p. 477; (18) Trial I, p. 487; (19) Trial I, p. 487; (20) Trial I, p. 488; (21) Trial I, pp. 488-90; (22) Trial I, p. 493; (23) Trial I, p. 492; (24) Trial I, p. 493; (25) Trial I, p. 498; (26) Trial I, p. 499; (27) Trial I, p. 499; (28) Trial I, p. 500; (29) Trial I, p. 500; (30) Trial I, p. 501; (31) Trial I, p. 510; (32) Trial I, pp. 510-16; (33) Trial I, p. 517; (34) Trial I, p. 517; (35) Trial I, p. 518; (36) Trial I, p. 529; (37) Welles vol. iii, p. 331; (38) N. Y. Trib. Apr. 15, 1868; (39) Welles vol. iii, pp. 332-3; (40) Trial I, p. 537; (41) M. & P. p. 625; (42) M. & P. p. 627; (43) M. & P. p. 627; (44) Trial I, p. 538; (45) Trial I, pp. 542-3; (46) Trial I, p. 545; (47) Trial I, pp. 548-89; (48) Trial I, p. 582; (49) Trial I, pp. 595-623; (50) Trial I, p. 597; (51) Trial I, p. 597; (52) Trial I, p. 625; (53) Trial I, p. 627; (54) Trial I, p. 628; (55) Trial I, pp. 628-9; (56) Trial I, p. 629; (57) Trial I, p. 629; (58) Trial I, pp. 629-30; (59) Trial I, p. 631; (60) Welles vol. iii, p. 333; (61) Trial I, pp. 631-4; (62) Trial I, pp. 634-5; (63) Trial I, pp. 537-40; (64) Trial I, pp. 640-3; (65) Crooks Rem. First Paper p. 665; (66) Trial I, pp. 660-3; (67) Trial I, pp. 663-6; (68) Trial I, pp. 667, 675; (69) Trial I, p. 676; (70) Trial I, p. 677; (71) Trial I, p. 679; (72) Trial I, p. 679; (73) Trial I, p. 691; (74) Trial I, p. 693; (75) Trial I, p. 693; (76) Trial I, p. 694; (77) Trial I, p. 694; (78) Trial I, p. 696; (79) Trial I, pp. 696-7; (80) Trial I, p. 698; (81) Trial I, p. 700; (82) Trial I, p. 701; (83) Rhodes vol. vi, p. 125; (84) Warden p. 685; (85) Warden pp. 684-5; (86) Welles vol. iii, pp. 333-4; (87) Welles vol. iii, pp. 334-5; (88) Trial III, pp. 336, 340; (89) Trial III, pp. 304, 309.

CHAPTER LXXV

(1) Patterson to Author; (2) Crooks Memories p. 45; (3) Crooks Memories p. 48; (4) Patterson to Author; (5) Crooks Rem. Part I, p. 659; (6) Crooks Rem. pp. 665, 669, Crooks Memories p. 61; (7) Crooks Rem. p. 665; (8) Cowan p. 13; (9) Cowan p. 11; (10) Am. Hist. Rev. p. 127; (11) Am. Hist. Rev.

p. 130; (12) Crooks Rem. p. 655; (13) Crooks Rem. p. 655; (14) Crooks Mem. p. 49.

CHAPTER LXXVI

(1) Rhodes vol. vi, p. 145; (2) Cox p. 592; (3) Welles vol. iii, pp. 336-7; (4) Dewitt p. 572; (5) Henderson p. 205; (6) Henderson p. 205; (7) Henderson p. 207; (8) Garfield vol. I, p. 425; (9) Cox pp. 592-3; (10) Cox pp. 592-3; (11) Rhodes vol. iv, p. 448, vol. v, p. 13; (12) Schofield pp. 413-4; (13) Schofield p. 414; (14) Schofield p. 415; (15) Schofield p. 415; (16) Schofield p. 416; (17) Schofield pp. 416-7.

CHAPTER LXXVII

(1) Schofield pp. 417-8; (2) N. Y. Trib. Apr. 20, 1868; (3) N. Y. Trib. Apr. 21, 1868; (4) N. Y. Trib. Apr. 22, 1868; (5) Trial II, pp. 14-66; (6) Trial II, p. 14; (7) Trial II, p. 67; (8) Trial II, p. 72; (9) Trial II, p. 81; (10) Trial II, p. 81; (11) Trial II, p. 81; (12) Trial II, p. 82; (13) Trial II, p. 82; (14) Trial II, p. 98; (15) Trial II, p. 113; (16) Trial II, p. 115; (17) Trial II, p. 116; (18) Trial II, p. 116; (19) Trial II, p. 116; (20) Trial II, p. 116; (21) Trial II, p. 119; (22) Trial II, pp. 119-120; (23) Trial II, p. 120; (24) Trial II, pp. 120-1; (25) Trial II, p. 121; (26) Trial II, pp. 124-7; (27) Trial II, pp. 144-6; (28) Trial II, p. 146; (29) Trial II, p. 146; (30) Trial II, p. 178; (31) Trial II, p. 182; (32) Trial II, p. 184; (33) Trial II, p. 184; (34) Trial II, p. 186; (35) Trial II, p. 186; (36) Trial II, p. 187; (37) Welles vol. iii, p. 337; (38) N. Y. Trib. Apr. 25, 1868; (39) Trial II, p. 189; (40) Trial II, p. 192; (41) Trial II, pp. 206-7; (42) Trial II, p. 215; (43) Trial II, p. 216; (44) Storey p. 349; (45) Trial II, pp. 216-17; (46) Oberholtzer vol. ii, pp. 111-12, Dewitt pp. 480-1, Welles vol. iii, p. 338; (47) N. Y. Trib. Apr. 25, 1868; (48) Schofield p. 418; (49) Trial I, p. 634; (50) N. Y. Trib. Apr. 25, 1868; (51) N. Y. Trib. Apr. 28, 1868; (52) Trial II, p. 219; (53) Welles vol. iii, pp. 340-1; (54) Trial II, p. 223; (55) Trial II, p. 225; (56) Trial II, p. 227; (57) Trial II, p. 230; (58) Trial II, p. 234; (59) Trial II, p. 246; (60) Welles vol. iii, p. 342; (61) N. Y. Trib. Apr. 28, 1868; (62) Welles vol. iii, p. 239; (63) Trial II, p. 252; (64) Trial II, p. 261; (65) N. Y. Trib. Apr. 30, 1868; (66) Trial II, pp. 144-5; (67) Trial II, p. 263; (68) Trial II, pp. 264-5; (69) Trial II, p. 266; (70) Trial II, p. 266; (71) Trial II, p. 266; (72) Trial II, p. 267; (73) Trial II, p. 268; (74) Trial II, p. 268; (75) Rhodes vol. vi, p. 135; (76) Trial II, p. 273; (77) Trial II, p. 274; (78) Trial II, p. 276; (79) Trial II, pp. 277-8; (80) Trial II, p. 264; (81) Trial II, p. 280; (82) Trial II, p. 283; (83) Trial II, p. 284; (84) Trial II, p. 288; (85) Trial II, p. 304; (86) Trial II, p. 306; (87) Trial II, p. 307; (88) Trial II, p. 307; (89) Trial II, p. 307; (90) Trial II, p. 326; (91) Trial II, p. 327; (92) Trial II, p. 327; (93) Trial II, p. 355; (94) Trial II, p. 356; (95) Trial II, pp. 356-9; (96) Welles vol. iii, p. 342; (97) Dewitt p. 502; (98) Trial I, p. 359; (99) Trial II, p. 388; (100) Trial II, p. 388; (101) Trial II, pp. 388-9; (102) Welles vol. iii, p. 344; (103) Welles vol. iii, p. 274; (104) N. Y. Trib. May 5, 1868; (105) N. Y. Trib. May 5, 1868; (106) N. Y. World May 4, 1868; (107) Oberholtzer vol. ii, p. 121; (108) Oberholtzer vol. ii, p. 120; (109) Trial II, p. 390; (110) Trial II, p. 391; (111) Rhodes vol. vi, p. 139; (112) Trial II, p. 394; (113) Trial II, p. 403; (114) Trial II, p. 415; (115) Trial II, p. 435; (116) Trial II, p. 440; (117) Trial II, p. 468; (118) N. Y. Trib. May 7, 1868; (119) Trial II, p. 469; (120) Trial II, p. 469; (121) Trial II, p. 473.

CHAPTER LXXVIII

(1) Dewitt p. 482; (2) Trial III, p. 247; (3) Trial III, p. 248; (4) Trial III, p. 11; (5) Trial III, p. 12; (6) Trial III, pp. 1-16; (7) Welles vol. iii, p. 351; (8) Trial III, pp. 50-51; (9) Trial III, p. 58; (10) Trial III, pp. 30-31; (11) Welles vol. iii, p. 351.

CHAPTER LXXIX

(1) Welles vol. iii, p. 351; (2) Welles vol. iii, p. 345; (3) Welles vol. iii, p. 345; (4) N. Y. Trib. May 6, 1868; (5) N. Y. Trib. May 7, 1868; (6) Welles vol. iii, p. 350; (7) Rhodes vol. vi, p. 174; (8) Dewitt p. 518; (9) N. Y. Trib. May 9, 1868; (10) Dewitt p. 521; (11) N. Y. Trib. May 11, 1868; (12) Dewitt pp. 525-6; (13) N. Y. Wor. May 12, 1868; (14) Trial II, p. 482; (15) Trial II, p. 484; (16) Welles vol. iii, pp. 352-3; (17) Welles vol. iii, p. 357; (18) Dewitt p. 530; (19) Dewitt p. 528; (20) Dewitt p. 528; (21) Dewitt p. 529; (22) White pp. 44-6, Dewitt p. 529; (23) White p. 317; (24) Welles vol. iii, p. 358; (25) White p. 317; (26) White p. 317; (27) Dewitt p. 531; (28) McCulloch p. 403; (29) Dewitt pp. 532-3; (30) Dewitt p. 531; (31) Dewitt p. 536; (32) N. Y. Wor. May 14, 1868; (33) N. Y. Wor. May 14, 1868; (34) N. Y. Trib. May 13, 1868; (35) Welles vol. iii, p. 353; (36) Dewitt p. 537; (37) Dewitt pp. 539-40; (38) Dewitt p. 540; (39) Dewitt p. 541; (40) Dewitt p. 541; (41) Dewitt p. 543; (42) N. Y. Trib. May 14, 1868; (43) Welles vol. iii, p. 355; (44) Dewitt p. 544; (45) N. Y. Trib. May 15, 1868.

CHAPTER LXXX

(1) Crooks Rem. Part II, p. 867; (2) Hibben p. 203, Welles vol. iii, p. 357; (3) Welles vol. iii, p. 357; (4) Schuckers p. 559, note 1; (5) Dewitt p. 544; (6) Dewitt p. 545; (7) Blaine vol. ii, p. 374; (8) Blaine vol. ii, p. 374, Julian, p. 316; (9) Trial II, pp. 484-5; (10) Trial II, p. 485; (11) Salter p. 357, Oberholtzer vol. ii, p. 131; (12) Trial II, p. 486; (13) Julian p. 316; (14) Julian p. 316; (15) Julian p. 316; (16) Crooks Mem. p. 67; (17) Trial II, p. 486; (18) Blaine vol. ii, p. 374; (19) Trial II, pp. 486-7; (20) Dewitt p. 331; (21) Julian p. 317; (22) Trial II, pp. 486-7; (23) Trial II, p. 487; (24) Crooks Rem. Part II, p. 870; (25) Crooks Mem. pp. 66-7.

CHAPTER LXXXI

(1) Trial II, p. 489; (2) N. Y. Trib. May 18, 1868; (3) Blaine vol. ii, p. 386; (4) Stanwood vol. I, p. 319; (5) Stanwood vol. I, p. 319; (6) Stanwood vol. I, p. 319; (7) Stanwood vol. I, pp. 318-9; (8) Burgess p. 207; (9) Blaine vol. ii, p. 388; (10) N. Y. Trib. May 22, 1868, Stanwood vol. I, p. 320, Blaine vol. ii, p. 389; (11) Oberholtzer vol. ii, p. 156; (12) Julian p. 320; (13) Blaine vol. ii, pp. 389-90; (14) Stanwood vol. I, p. 321; (15) Blaine vol. ii, p. 390; (16) Rhodes vol. vii, pp. 13-15, Oberholtzer vol. ii, pp. 602-5; (17) Welles vol. iii, pp. 363-4; (18) Oberholtzer vol. ii, pp. 156-8.

CHAPTER LXXXII

(1) Welles vol. iii, p. 362; (2) Dewitt p. 567; (3) Welles vol. iii, p. 366; (4) Dewitt p. 560; (5) Dewitt p. 561; (6) Dewitt p. 562; (7) Dewitt p. 569; (8) Welles vol. iii, p. 369, Dewitt p. 571; (9) Welles vol. iii, pp. 368-9; (10) N. Y. Trib. May 25, 1868; (11) Welles vol. iii, p. 367; (12) N. Y. Trib. May 27, 1868; (13) N. Y. Trib. May 27, 1868; (14) Welles vol. iii, p. 368; (15) Trial II, p. 495; (16) Trial II, p. 491; (17) Trial II, p. 496; (18) Trial II, p. 496; (19) Trial II, p. 497; (20) Trial II, p. 497; (21) Trial II, p. 497; (22) Welles vol. iii, p. 369; (23) Macaulay's England vol. II, pp. 320-358; (24) Macaulay's England vol. II, p. 344; (25) Macaulay's England vol. II, p. 358; (26) Rhodes vol. vi, p. 156; (27) Welles vol. iii, p. 353; (28) Oberholtzer vol. ii, p. 136; (29) White p. 315; (30) Oberholtzer vol. ii, p. 133; (31) White p. 322; (32) White p. 326; (33) Salter p. 358; (34) Salter p. 358; (35) White p. 321; (36) Julian pp. 317-8; (37) Blaine vol. ii, p. 376; (38) Boutwell vol. ii, p. 122; (39) Boutwell vol. ii, p. 122; (40) Grant vol. ii, pp. 508-34; (41) Sherman (John) vol. I, p. 432; (42) Henderson p. 209; (43) Gorham vol. ii, p. 456; (44) Schofield p. 418; (45) Gorham vol. ii, pp. 456-7; (46) McPherson p. 350; (47) Blaine vol. ii, p. 384; (48) Curtis vol. I, p. 419; (49) Blaine vol. ii, p. 384.

CHAPTER LXXXIII

(1) Welles vol. iii, p. 394; (2) Rhodes vol. vi, pp. 162-3; (3) Hart p. 415; (4) Warden pp. 677-8; (5) Warden p. 578; (6) Warden p. 683; (7) Warden p. 683; (8) Schuckers p. 586; (9) Warden p. 695; (10) Schuckers p. 586; (11) Hart pp. 424, 428; (12) Hart p. 431; (13) Hart p. 422; (14) Hart pp. 317-18; (15) Hart p. 318; (16) Charnwood p. 329; (17) Hart p. 435; (18) Charnwood p. 430; (19) Piatt pp. 117, 98; (20) Hart p. 420; (21) Hart p. 420; (22) Hart p. 420; (23) Blaine vol. ii, p. 392; (24) Oberholtzer vol. ii, p. 165; (25) Rhodes vol. vi, p. 164, Oberholtzer vol. ii, p. 165; (26) Rhodes vol. iv, p. 283; (27) Rhodes vol. v, pp. 571, 585, 616; (28) Trial III, pp. 361-401; (29) Stanwood vol. I, p. 325; (30) Blaine vol. ii, p. 392; (31) Blaine vol. ii, p. 392; (32) Myers pp. 257-8; (33) Breen p. 167; (34) Breen p. 167; (35) Blaine vol. ii, p. 397; (36) Blaine vol. ii, p. 397; (37) Rhodes vol. iv, pp. 226-7, 245-6, 247-55, 412-15; (38) Rhodes vol. v, p. 615; (39) Blaine vol. ii, p. 395; (40) Blaine vol. ii, p. 395; (41) Breen pp. 167-8; (42) M. & P. pp. 655-6, Breen p. 167; (43) Welles vol. iii, p. 395; (44) Rhodes vol. vi, p. 164, Breen p. 169; (45) Stanwood vol. I, p. 323; (46) Stanwood vol. I, p. 324; (47) Stanwood vol. I, pp. 324-5; (48) Burgess p. 213; (49) Stanwood vol. I, p. 322; (50) Oberholtzer vol. ii, p. 173, note 1; (51) Oberholtzer vol. ii, pp. 174-5; (52) Oberholtzer vol. ii, p. 166; (53) Oberholtzer vol. ii, p. 175; (54) Welles vol. iii, p. 397; (55) Oberholtzer vol. ii, p. 175; (56) N. Y. Trib. July 8, 1868; (57) Stanwood vol. I, p. 325; (58) Welles vol. iii, p. 397; (59) Welles vol. iii, p. 396; (60) Blaine vol. ii, p. 402; (61) Rhodes vol. vi, p. 167; (62) Stanwood vol. I, p. 325; (63) Welles vol. iii, p. 400; (64) Rhodes vol. iv, p. 325; (65) Welles vol. I, pp. 372-3; (66) Charnwood pp. 385-6; (67) Oberholtzer vol. ii, p. 179, Rhodes vol. vi, p. 167; (68) Oberholtzer vol. ii, p. 179; (69) Blaine vol. ii, p. 404; (70) Blaine vol. ii, p. 404; (71) Oberholtzer vol. ii, p. 180; (72) Schuckers p. 566; (73) Welles vol. iii, p. 398; (74) Stanwood vol. I, p. 325; (75) Oberholtzer vol. ii, p. 179; (76) Welles vol. iii, p. 398.

CHAPTER LXXXIV

(1) Lee Rem. p. 218; (2) Blaine vol. ii, p. 406; (3) Welles vol iii, p. 364; (4) Burgess p. 197; (5) Rhodes vol. vi, p. 175; (6) Rhodes vol. vi, pp. 175-7; (7) Rhodes vol. vi, p. 176; (8) M. & P. p. 648; (9) M. & P. p. 651; (10) Burgess p. 202; (11) Flack pp. 190-1; (12) McPherson p. 380; (13) McPherson p. 380; (14) McPherson p. 380; (15) Burgess p. 202; (16) Grant vol. ii, pp. 491-2; (17) Guthrie pp. 10-11; (18) Cox p. 257; (19) Burgess p. 202; (20) M. & P. p. 651; (21) M. & P. p. 652; (22) McPherson p. 379; (23) Rhodes vol. vi, pp. 178-9; (24) Rhodes vol. vi, p. 178; (25) Crooks Rem. Part II, p. 867; (26) Cowan p. 6; (27) Cowan p. 6; (28) Cowan p. 6; (29) Crooks Rem. Part I, p. 653; (30) Cowan p. 7, Welles vol. ii, pp. 468, 472, 479; (31) Cowan p. 7; (32) Cowan p. 7; (33) Crooks Rem. Part II, p. 871; (34) Pierce vol. iv, p. 360; (35) Cong. Globe 40th Cong. 2nd Sess. pp. 4473-4; (36) Julian pp. 313-14; (37) Cong. Globe 40th Cong. 2nd Sess, p. 3786; (38) Crooks Rem. Part II, p. 871; (39) Woodburn p. 586; McCall p. 352; (40) Pierce vol. iv, p. 361, McCall p. 336, note 1; (41) Welles vol. iii, p. 403; (42) Schouler vol. vii, pp. 125-6; (43) Welles vol. iii, p. 405; (44) Welles vol. iii, p. 411; (45) McPherson p. 381; (46) McPherson p. 382; (47) Blaine vol. ii, p. 404; (48) Rhodes vol. vi, p. 185; (49) Rhodes vol. vi, p. 180; (50) Rhodes vol. vi, p. 181; (51) Rhodes vol. vi, pp. 190-2; (52) Rhodes vol. vi, p. 194; (53) Oberholtzer vol. ii, pp. 184-5; (54) Sherman Home Letters p. 377; (55) Oberholtzer vol. ii, pp. 184-5; (56) Rhodes vol. vi, p. 194, Oberholtzer vol. ii, p. 187; (57) Pierce vol. iv, p. 359; (58) McCulloch p. 405; (59) Truman pp. 438-9; (60) Truman p. 439; (61) Truman p. 439; (62) Truman p. 439; (63) Truman pp. 439-40; (64) Truman p. 440; (65) Welles vol. iii, p. 426; (66) Welles vol. iii, p. 440; (67) Welles vol. iii, p. 445; (68) Welles vol. iii, p. 450; (69) Welles vol. iii, p. 451; (70) Oberholtzer vol. ii, pp. 191-192; (71) N. Y. Wor. Oct. 15, 1868, Blaine vol. ii, p. 405; (72) Welles vol. iii,

p. 455; (73) Welles vol. iii, pp. 455, 457; (74) Welles vol. iii, p. 459; (75) Welles vol. iii, p. 459; (76) Blaine vol. ii, p. 406; (77) Blaine vol. ii, p. 406; (78) Welles vol. iii, p. 464; (79) Oberholtzer vol. ii, p. 159; (80) Rhodes vol. vi, p. 93; (81) Welles vol. iii, p. 462; (82) Stanwood vol. ii, p. 328; (83) Burgess p. 212; (84) Stanwood vol. ii, p. 328.

CHAPTER LXXXV

(1) M. & P. p. 672; (2) M. & P. pp. 672-3; (3) M. & P. p. 689; (4) M. & P. p. 689; (5) M. & P. p. 688; (6) M. & P. p. 688; (7) M. & P. p. 688; (8) Hughes p. 13; (9) Adams (Henry) pp. 245-6; (10) Welles vol. iii, p. 479; (11) Oberholtzer vol. ii, p. 200; (12) N. Y. Trib. Dec. 10, 1868; (13) Welles vol. iii, p. 480; (14) Pierce vol. iv, p. 365; (15) U. S. Con. 15th Amendment; (16) Rhodes vol. vi, p. 202; (17) M. & P. 708; (18) McPherson p. 420; (19) Welles vol. iii, p. 491; (20) Crooks Mem. pp. 70-1; (21) Crooks Mem. pp. 70-1; (22) Crooks Mem. pp. 70-1; (23) Crooks Rem. p. 873; (24) Crooks Mem. pp. 70-1; (25) Welles vol. iii, p. 494; (26) Welles vol. iii, p. 495; (27) Welles vol. iii, p. 496; (28) Welles vol. iii, p. 497; (29) Welles vol. iii, p. 497; (30) Welles vol. iii, p. 498; (31) Welles vol. iii, p. 483; (32) Julian p. 319; (33) Welles vol. iii, pp. 503-4; (34) Oberholtzer vol. ii, p. 204; (35) Welles vol. iii, p. 536; (36) Burgess p. 218; (37) Welles vol. iii, p. 538; (38) Welles vol. iii, p. 542; (39) Welles vol. iii, p. 542; (40) Welles vol. iii, pp. 537, 557; (41) Welles vol. iii, p. 539; (42) Welles vol. iii, p. 542; (43) Welles vol. iii, p. 542; (44) M. & P. vol. vii, p. 6, Welles vol. iii, p. 544; (45) McCulloch p. 346; (46) Oberholtzer vol. ii, p. 209; (47) Welles vol. iii, p. 542.

CHAPTER LXXXVI

(1) Truman p. 440, Crooks Mem. p. 73, Jones p. 335; (2) Truman p. 440; (3) Oberholtzer vol. ii, p. 210; (4) Jones p. 334; (5) Jones pp. 334-5; (6) Oberholtzer vol. ii, pp. 215-6; (7) M. & P. vol. vii, p. 8; (8) M. & P. vol. vii, p. 8; (9) Blaine vol. ii, p. 426; (10) Welles vol. iii, p. 239; (11) Adams (Henry) p. 263; (12) Rhodes vol. vi, p. 237; (13) White p. 333, Welles vol. iii, p. 543; (14) White p. 333; (15) Dewitt p. 364; (16) Welles vol. iii, p. 546; (17) Oberholtzer vol. ii, p. 217; (18) McCulloch p. 351, Oberholtzer vol. ii, pp. 217-18; (19) McCulloch p. 351; (20) McCulloch p. 351; Oberholtzer vol. ii, p. 218; (21) Rhodes vol. vi, p. 240; (22) Rhodes vol. iv, p. 302; (23) Dana p. 62; (24) Dana pp. 72-3; (25) McCulloch p. 349; (26) Welles vol. iii, p. 543; (27) McCulloch p. 350, Oberholtzer vol. ii, p. 216; (28) Welles vol. iii, pp. 549, 556, 568, 587-8, McCulloch p. 350; (29) Welles vol. iii, p. 556; (30) Truman p. 440; (31) Jones p. 335; (32) Jones p. 336; (33) Jones pp. 336-8; (34) Jones p. 338-9; (35) Jones p. 340; (36) Jones pp. 340-44; (37) Jones p. 344; (38) Jones p. 344; (39) Jones pp. 344-5; (40) Jones pp. 345-6; (41) Solid South p. 198; (42) Solid South p. 193; (43) Solid South p. 196; (44) Solid South p. 197; (45) Solid South p. 199; (46) Solid South p. 190; (47) Solid South p. 195; (48) Welles vol. iii, p. 565-6.

CHAPTER LXXXVII

(1) Reeves Appendix p. 826; (2) Reeves Appendix p. 826; (3) Reeves Appendix p. 834; (4) Temple p. 183; (5) Temple p. 183; (6) Solid South p. 214; (7) Solid South pp. 214-15; (8) Solid South pp. 214-15; (9) Temple pp. 441-2, Dewitt p. 616; (10) Dewitt p. 617; (11) Reeves Appendix p. 831; (12) Reeves Appendix p. 831; (13) Hughes p. 13; (14) Barbee p. 4; (15) Barbee p. 4; (16) Reeves Appendix p. 831; (17) Reeves to Author; (18) Temple p. 461; (19) Reeves to Author; (20) Reeves to Author; (21) Reeves to Author; (22) Rhodes vol. vi, pp. 377, 383, vol. vii, pp. 20, 23-4, Oberholtzer vol. ii, p. 314, Hoar vol. I, pp. 361-2; (23) Oberholtzer vol. ii, p. 311, Rhodes vol. vi, pp. 379-381; (24) Rhodes vol. vi, pp. 249-56; (25) Rhodes vol. vii, pp. 183-191; (26) Rhodes vol. vi, p. 383, Stanwood vol. I, p. 342, McCulloch p. 357, Oberholtzer

vol. ii, pp. 543-4; (27) Rhodes vol. vii, p. 191; Piatt p. 85; (28) Hoar vol. ii, pp. 137-8; (29) Blaine vol. ii, p. 449; (30) Blaine vol. ii, p. 451; (31) Blaine vol. ii, p. 450; (32) Blaine vol. ii, p. 452; (33) Blaine Appendix B, Hoar vol. ii, p. 138; (34) Blaine vol. ii, p. 455; (35) M. & P. vol. vii, p. 38; (36) M. & P. vol. vii, p. 38; (37) Sherman Home Letters p. 381; (38) Cambridge p. 632; (39) McPherson pp. 408-9; (40) Rhodes vol. vi, p. 286; (41) M. & P. vol. vii, p. 55; (42) Oberholtzer vol. ii, p. 267; (43) Blaine vol. ii, pp. 447-8; (44) Blaine vol. ii, p. 448; (45) Avary pp. 243-4; (46) Storey p. 375; (47) Blaine vol. ii, pp. 304, 515; (48) Washington p. 84; (49) Cox p. 625; (50) C. of A. vol. 32, pp. 236-7; (51) Avary p. 141; (52) Avary pp. 141-2; (53) Cox p. 625; (54) Avary pp. 159-60; (55) Avary p. 416; (56) Rhodes vol. vii, p. 167; (57) Rhodes vol. vii, p. 156; (58) Rhodes vol. vii, p. 142; (59) Solid South pp. 95-7; (60) Solid South p. 89; (61) Rhodes vol. vii, pp. 145-6; (62) Pike pp. 199-200; (63) Pike Chap. xviii; (64) Rhodes vol. vii, p. 150; (65) Rhodes vol. vii, p. 149; (66) Solid South p. 104; (67) Oberholtzer vol. ii, p. 339; (68) Pike p. 70; (69) Pike p. 83; (70) Pike pp. 11-12; (71) Pike p. 12; (72) Pike p. 13; (73) Pike p. 15; (74) Pike pp. 19-20; (75) Pike p. 20; (76) Pike p. 11; (77) Burgess pp. 297, 246; (78) C. of A. vol. 32, p. 240; (79) Rhodes vol. vi, p. 390; (80) Reeves Appendix p. 831; (81) Rhodes vol. vi, p. 412; (82) Rhodes vol. vi, p. 412; (83) Blaine vol. ii, pp. 520-1; (84) Stanwood vol. I, pp. 341-2; (85) Stanwood vol. I, pp. 342-3; (86) Stanwood vol. I, p. 344; (87) Hart p. 413; (88) Stanwood vol. I, p. 344; (89) Julian p. 340; (90) Merriam vol. ii, p. 189; (91) Merriam vol. ii, pp. 193-4; (92) Stanwood vol. I, pp. 346-8; (93) Stanwood vol. I, p. 345; (94) Blaine vol. ii, p. 528; (95) Stanwood vol. I, p. 345; (96) Stanwood vol. I, p. 349; (97) Oberholtzer vol. iii, p. 55; (98) Rhodes vol. vi, p. 430; (99) Oberholtzer vol. iii, p. 55; (100) Oberholtzer vol. iii, p. 51; (101) Pierce vol. iv, p. 530; (102) Pierce vol. iv, p. 523; (103) Blaine vol. ii, p. 533, note 1; (104) N. Y. Trib. Sept. 20, 1872; (105) Merriam vol. ii, p. 181, Oberholtzer vol. iii, p. 31; (106) Blaine vol. ii, p. 534; (107) Julian p. 343; (108) Oberholtzer vol. iii, p. 57; (109) Rhodes vol. vi, p. 435; (110) Burgess p. 266; (111) Merriam vol. ii, pp. 195-6; (112) Blaine vol. ii, p. 535; (113) Julian p. 352; (114) Reeves Appendix p. 831; (115) Reeves Appendix p. 832; (116) Reeves Appendix p. 832; (117) Reeves Appendix p. 832; (118) Jones p. 348; (119) Reeves Appendix p. 832; (120) Jones p. 348; (121) Barbee p. 4; (122) Reeves Appendix p. 833.

CHAPTER LXXXVIII

(1) Oberholtzer vol. ii, pp. 538-614, Rhodes vol. vii, pp. 185-206; (2) Rhodes vol. vii, p. 68; (3) Rhodes vol. vii, p. 67; (4) Hughes p. 13; (5) Hughes p. 13; (6) Hughes, p. 13; (7) Reeves Appendix p. 833; Temple pp. 440-1, Jones pp. 47-9, 349; (8) Reeves Appendix p. 833; Jones p. 349; (9) Temple pp. 441-2; (10) Temple p. 442; (11) Reeves Appendix p. 834; (12) Reeves Appendix p. 834; (13) Jones pp. 349-50; (14) Reeves Appendix p. 834; (15) Temple p. 442; (16) Jones p. 350; (17) Jones p. 350; (18) N. Y. Times Jan 27, 1875; (19) N. Y. World Jan. 27, 1875; (20) N. Y. Her. Jan. 27, 1875; (21) Jones p. 352; (22) Jones p. 353; (23) Jones p. 353; (24) Temple p. 442; (25) N. Y. Her. Jan. 27, 1875; (26) quoted Truman p. 440; (27) N. Y. Her. Mar. 6, 1875; (28) N. Y. Her. Mar. 8, 1875; (29) Trial III, p. 218, N. Y. Her. Mar. 8, 1875; (30) Cong. Globe 39th Cong. 1st Sess. p. 2299; (31) N. Y. Her. Mar. 8, 1875; (32) Crooks Rem. vol. ii, p. 877; (33) Reeves Appendix p. 835; (34) N. Y. Her. Mar. 8, 1875; (35) N. Y. Trib. Mar. 8, 1875; (36) Crooks Rem. vol. ii, p. 877; (37) N. Y. Her. Mar. 8, 1875; (38) Storey p. 430; (39) Encyc. vol. 28, p. 227; (40) Salter p. 387; (41) N. Y. Trib. Mar. 8, 1875; (42) N. Y. Trib. Mar. 8, 1875; (43) N. Y. Trib. Mar. 8, 1875; (44) N. Y. Trib. Mar. 8, 1875; (45) Crooks Rem. vol. ii, p. 877; (46) N. Y. Trib. Mar. 8, 1875; (47) Hoar vol. I, p. 308; (48) Hibben p. 315; (49) Hibben p. 319; (50) Oberholtzer vol. iii, pp. 443-99; (51) Oberholtzer vol. iii, p. 445; (52) Barbee p. 4; (53) Lincoln L. & S. P. vol. ii, p. 496; (54) Encyc. vol. 17, p. 60; (55) Rhodes

vol. vii, p. 104; (56) Rhodes vol. vii, p. 107; (57) Solid South p. 397; (58) Solid South p. 429; (59) Oberholtzer vol. iii, p. 230; (60) Rhodes vol. vii, p. 106; (61) Solid South p. 401; (62) Solid South p. 429; (63) Rhodes vol. vii, p. 105; (64) Rhodes vol. vii, p. 105; (65) Oberholtzer vol. iii, p. 230; (66) Burgess pp. 269-70, Oberholtzer vol. iii, p. 231; (67) Rhodes vol. vii, p. 109; (68) Rhodes vol. vii, pp. 232-3; (69) Rhodes vol. vii, p. 109; (70) Rhodes vol. vii, p. 110; (71) Burgess pp. 270-1, Solid South p. 414; (72) Oberholtzer vol. iii, p. 233, note 2; (73) Burgess p. 271; (74) Rhodes vol. vii, pp. 110-11; (75) M. & P. vol. vii, p. 212; (76) M. & P. vol. vii, p. 221; (77) Rhodes vol. vii, pp. 112-13; (78) quoted Rhodes vol. vii, p. 113; (79) M. & P. vol. vii, p. 224; (80) M. & P. vol. vii, p. 307; (81) Oberholtzer vol. iii, p. 235; (82) Oberholtzer vol. iii, p. 236; (83) Oberholtzer vol. iii, p. 237; (84) Encyc. vol. 17, p. 60; (85) The Nation, Sept. 24, 1874; (86) M. & P. vol. vii, p. 276; (87) M. & P. vol. vii, p. 309, Oberholtzer vol. ii, pp. 237-8; (88) Rhodes vol. vii, pp. 117-19; (89) Cong. Globe 43rd Cong. 2nd Sess. p. 367; (90) Rhodes vol. vii, pp. 119-22; (91) The Nation, Jan. 28, 1875; (92) The Nation, Feb. 4, 1875; (93) Rhodes vol. vii, pp. 119-20; (94) Rhodes vol. vii, p. 120; (95) N. Y. Trib. Jan. 7, 1875 (96) Oberholtzer vol. iii, p. 240; (97) Oberholtzer vol. iii, p. 240; (98) Rhodes vol. vii, p. 122; (99) Merriam vol. ii, p. 237; (100) M. & P. vol. vii, p. 319; (101) Merriam vol. ii, p. 238; (102) Merriam vol. ii, p. 238; (103) Merriam vol. ii, pp. 238-9; (104) N. Y. Trib. Feb. 9, 1875; (105) Merriam vol. ii, p. 239; (106) Oberholtzer vol. iii, pp. 195-6; (107) Merriam vol. ii, p. 238; (108) Oberholtzer vol. vii, p. 196; (109) Pierce vol. iv, p. 598; (110) Merriam vol. ii, p. 240; (111) Oberholtzer vol. iii, p. 196; (112) N. Y. Trib. Jan. 13, 1875; (113) M. & P. vol. vii, p. 307, Cong. Record 44th Cong. 1st Sess. pp. 121-7; (114) Cong. Record 44th Cong. 1st Sess. pp. 121-7; (115) Cong. Record 44th Cong. 1st Sess. pp. 121-7; (116) Cong. Record 44th Cong. 1st Sess. pp. 121-7; (117) Cong. Record 44th Cong. 1st Sess pp. 121-7; (118) Rhodes vol. vi, p. 383; (119) Cong. Record 44th Cong. 1st Sess. pp. 121-7; (120) Cong. Record 44th Cong. 1st Sess. pp. 121-7.

CHAPTER LXXXIX

(1) Dewitt p. 628; (2) Reeves Appendix p. 836, Jones p. 371; (3) Reeves Appendix p. 836; (4) Jones p. 371, Reeves Appendix p. 836; (5) Reeves Appendix p. 836; (6) M. & P. vol. vii, pp. 330-1.

INDEX

Adams, C. F., on Johnson, 195.

Agassiz, Louis, quoted, on negro suffrage, 293-294.

Alaska, 469.

Alta Vela, 612-614.

American Knights, 407.

American Party, 26.

"American Speaker," read aloud to Johnson, 2-3.

Anderson, Robert, occupies Fort Sumter, 66; surrenders, 77.

Andrew, J. A., quoted on South, 236.

Arkansas, late in joining Confederacy, 108; 8 regiments enlisted in Union Army, 1863, 108; abolishes slavery, 150.

Ashley, J. M., presents bill, 151; quoted, 151-152; sketch of, 394-395; moves appointment of committee of seven, 406; moves impeachment, 419; quoted, 463.

Bancroft, G., credited with writing Johnson's message, 243.

Beecher, H. W., 374; trial of, 811-812.

Bingham, J., 702; quoted, 703-704.

Birney, James, advocates gradual emancipation, 46.

Black, Jeremiah S., 65; quoted, 91.

Blaine, J. G., on Johnson, 123, 215, quoted, 232, 234, 256, 308.

Blair, Frank, nominated, 746.

Blockade of Southern ports, 87.

Booth, John Wilkes, shoots President Lincoln, 193.

Bowles, S., quoted, 802.

Bradford, Gamaliel, on Sumner, 51.

Breckenridge, John C., nominated for President, 1860, 56; quoted, 85.

Brooks, J., 233, 573.

Brooks, Preston, attacks Sumner, 51.

Brown, Albert, Jr., quoted on Johnson, 168.

Brown, John, 39-40, Lincoln on, quoted, 57.

Browning, O. H., 315.

Brownlow, William, "Fighting Parson," 21; at Cincinnati, 98; delegate, 118; quoted, 120; elected

Governor of Tennessee, 164; forces legislation, 304-306; elected U. S. Senator, 779.

Bryant, W. C., opposes Lincoln's renomination, 119.

Buchanan, James, 63-64, 69.

Buell, Don Carlos, 100, 101.

Buell, Sir F., quoted, 206.

Bull Run, First Battle, 83-84.

Butler, B. F., sketch of, 376-383; quoted 463-464, 607-608, 623-624, 625, 626-632, 653-654, 664-665; 819.

Cameron, Simon, 88; appointed Secretary of War, 89.

Camilla, Ga., riot, 756.

Campbell, L. D., 391-392.

Cartter, D. K., 565.

Catholics, attacked by Clingman, 17; defended by Johnson, 18, 19, 27-28.

Charnwood, Life of Lincoln, quoted, 55; on Chase, 119.

Chase, Salmon P., 64; on Lincoln, 118; possible candidate, 144; speaks in Boston, 147; quoted, 303, 669, 737-739.

Choate, Joseph H., quoted, 127-128; character, 128.

Cincinnati, Johnson denounces secession, 80.

Cincinnati *Gazette*, quoted, 145.

City life, 33.

Civil Rights Bill, 286-291.

Clay, Clement, 33, 338.

Clay, Mrs. Clement, 336-338.

Clingman, Thomas L., attacks Catholics, 17.

Colfax, Schuyler, nominated, 727.

Colorado seeks admission, 291; bill vetoed, 292; new bill, 399.

Confederate Congress, quoted, 157-158.

Confederate States of America, 66; organized February, 1861; eleven states, 80.

Congress, 39th, 1865, 229.

Conover, Sanford, 335, 339, 486-488.